ADVANCE PRAISE FOR THE BOOK

Representation, Delimitation by Ravi K. Mishra is a deeply d thought-provoking exploration of India's demographic trends act on governance and representation. Drawing on over a century ook offers a nuanced perspective on regional population shifts, ds, and their implications for policy and democracy.

eful and analytical approach, the author presents a comprehensive challenges conventional understandings of demographic change shaping political representation. A significant focus is placed on the 42nd Amendment, enacted during the Emergency, which atorium on the reallocation of parliamentary seats based on he book critically examines how this decision, later extended by endment, altered the balance of representation and continues to a's democratic framework today.

k is an essential read for scholars, policymakers, and anyone the complex interplay between population dynamics and

d Ravi K. Mishra for this insightful contribution to the discourse lving demographic landscape and its significance in shaping the e.'

— Shivraj Patil, Former Speaker Lok Sabha

ud to be the largest democracy as well as the most populous it has achieved. From thirty-five crore at Independence, India is a billion and more. No longer poor nor in any way troubled in its ourney. But could it all be at risk?

masterly, exhaustive treatment of this big challenge facing Indian Ravi Mishra has put together a thorough description of how the verpopulation in India was manufactured by international opinion, om developed country agencies and how shallow it was. He then crucial regional difference between the Hindi belt in the north and in Tamil Nadu where population trends have been in a different e then traces out the problem it will raise for the future of Indian f the south is to lose MPs to the north just because it achieved better pulation control when delimitation occurs.

k will inform students and teachers of demography and politics but be read by political decision-makers and concerned citizens as it is a

DEMOG
REPRESE
DELIMIT

'*Demography*
researched a
and their im
of data, the
historical tre

With a ca
narrative tha
and its role i
the impact
placed a m
population.
the 84th An
influence In

This wo
interested i
governance.

I comme
on India's e
nation's futu

'India is pr
nation statu
now beyon
democratic

Here is
democracy.
scare about
especially f
explores th
the situatio
direction. I
democracy
results of p

This bo
should also

warning to heed a train crash which could hit India in much the same way as the national language issue did in the 1960s. Read it and react.'

— Lord Meghnad Desai

'Dr Ravi K. Mishra has done academic analysis of India's demographic history over the last 150 years. Based on statistics drawn from all the decennial censuses of India from 1872 to 2011, district gazetteers, boundary commission reports, states reorganisation commission reports and various surveys, the study shows that over the long term, all states and geographical regions of India have enjoyed rapid population growth during their demographic transition. Providing a fresh, evidence-based perspective on the subject of demography and delimitation, the book is a valuable addition to the current debates in India.'

— Nripendra Misra, Chairman, Executive Council,
Prime Ministers Museum and Library (PMML)

'Dr Ravi Mishra has produced a sensational study that is certain to change many misconceptions shaping the debate on delimitation of parliamentary constituencies. His book should warn both political activists and policymakers of the grave dangers of being swayed by bazaar wisdom. It is a must-read.'

— Swapan Dasgupta, Former MP (Rajya Sabha)

'Ravi Mishra's *Demography, Representation, Delimitation* is a seminal work, meticulously crafted from 150 years of Census data, offering a ground-breaking re-evaluation of India's demographic and political landscape. In many respects, I believe, this is a uniquely conceived research-based work.

Through a data-driven, compelling account, the book challenges long-held assumptions about the so-called north–south divide. The launch of this book is very timely as it tries to demolish some presumptions on the basis of which some people play politics.

A critical aspect of this book is its deep exploration of the 42nd Amendment, enacted during the Emergency, which froze parliamentary seat allocation, altering the trajectory of political representation in India. Ravi Mishra also sheds light on the Emergency-era excesses, particularly the coercive population control measures, including forced sterilisations, which disproportionately affected certain regions and social groups. These policies not only shaped India's demographic trajectory but also had long-term socio-political consequences, reinforcing regional disparities in representation. The author also meticulously examines how this amendment led to the underrepresentation of northern and western India, including the Hindi belt as well as Maharashtra and Gujarat.

With its empirical depth, incisive analysis, and critical engagement with historical data and policies, *Demography, Representation, Delimitation* becomes a must-read book for researchers and analysts.'

— Vinay Sahasrabuddhe, Former MP, Rajya Sabha

'Ravi K. Mishra's *Demography, Representation, Delimitation* presents a scholarly analysis of India's demographic evolution and political restructuring. This book critically examines the regional demographic variations in India in the broader global context of demographic transition, challenging conventional notions of the north–south divide. It brings a fresh perspective to a debate that has shaped policy and federal dynamics for decades.

Mishra's research intricately explores the historical roots of India's population growth while integrating the influences of economic development, public health advancements and social modernisation. His comparative approach reveals how Europe, North America and East Asia experienced similar transitions over centuries, while India's states have undergone these transitions within drastically different timelines. The north's ongoing transition is akin to later-developing regions of the Global South, and the south's early demographic transformation mirrors the experience of industrialised Western nations.

The book's rigorous historical analysis—drawing from over 150 years of census data—dispels the notion that the north is uniquely responsible for India's population explosion. It has analysed the redistribution of parliamentary seats and the implications of fiscal federalism, and addresses the fundamental questions on the principle of equal representation.

As India approaches the 2026 reassessment, this book serves as an essential reference for policymakers, scholars and informed citizens. Ravi Mishra's work offers a fresh perspective on India's demographic trajectory while providing a crucial framework for navigating future political and economic challenges. I had the opportunity of examining the impact of the Kalinga War in Bihar and Orissa and its relevance to reorganisation of states beyond Orissa and reflect upon it. I have examined in some details its impact on states in India's north-east, which have been reflected in my books on the subject and also particularly when I was working on it in the University of Cambridge where I had the privilege of becoming a Chancellor for a brief period in 1987. My article titled 'North-East India: Demography, Culture and Identity Crisis' was published in *Modern Asian Studies* in 1987.

Ravi Mishra's work not only provides fresh reflections of our understanding of India's demographic past but also gives a much-needed framework for addressing the political and economic challenges of the future.'

— Balmiki Prasad Singh, Former Governor of Sikkim and Former Home Secretary, Government of India

'This book redefines the national debate on demography and delimitation in India. Meticulously researched and eye-opening, it demolishes the long-held myth of the north–south population divide. Ravi Mishra masterfully unveils the false narrative that the north is responsible for India's so-called 'population explosion'. Using historical data, he demonstrates that the south actually experienced a demographic boom between 1881 and 1971, before the north's growth entered the peak phase. With sharp insights, this book reveals how India's seat-freeze policy has led to a shocking imbalance in democratic representation. Ravi Mishra lays bare how India's electoral system has been locked in time, with a political structure still based on the 1971 population figures. His solution? A population-based delimitation and reallocation of seats in parliament. A thought-provoking and data-backed read, *Demography, Representation, Delimitation: The North-South Divide in India* gives a new direction to the current debate on delimitation.'

— Ram Bahadur Rai, President, IGNACA

'Dr Ravi Mishra's work is an important scholarly intervention with wide ramifications in a current political debate. His deep dive into India's demographic history will be invaluable for those seeking to better understand the nuances and also go beyond the current polemics on parliamentary seat redistribution between different states. A timely and thought-provoking book.'

— T.C.A. Raghavan, Former High Commissioner to Singapore and Pakistan

'Public discourse is often shaped by factoids, rather than facts, and it takes empirical data, intelligent insight and a clear conceptual framework to remove the distortion, especially when it is laced with political contestation. Ravi Mishra's painstaking work has demolished the myth that the "cow belt" is responsible for the demographic bulge: rather he has shown that over the *longue durée* (from 1872, when the first census was conducted, to 2024, when the manuscript was given the final shape), the growth rate of the southern and western states was significantly higher than that of the northern belt. He also argues that the family planning policy was driven by the uncritical adoption of the Western fears of the rapidly growing population of the Third World as a destabilising factor in the US-led global order. The book could not have been better timed as India gears up for the next census, which will spur the demand for delimitation based on current demography.'

— Dr Sanjeev Chopra, Historian, Columnist and Festival Director

'Dr Ravi K. Mishra's book titled *Demography, Representation, Delimitation: The North–South Divide in India* is the fruit of deep research over years. It is a valuable addition to the contemporary discourse on the intrinsic relationship between population growth and equitable regional representation in the Indian Parliament. India is today the world's most populous democracy. Its demography and democracy are key attributes that should form the subject of objective analysis, particularly at their intersection. Once the object of Malthusian reproach, India's burgeoning demographic dividend is increasingly considered an important asset in realising the nation's political and economic destiny.

The principle of proportional representation in the Lok Sabha explored by the author, and the delimitation of constituencies based on an updated population census, remain important. As India progresses, its growing infrastructure, connectivity and prosperity are encouraging mobility and forging a stronger national identity. The relevance of older and inert identities, based on parochial geographies, is increasingly questioned.

This book is a clarion call for adjustment to India's political processes, such that its vibrant democracy responds to the aspirations of every Indian in a *Viksit Bharat*.

— Ambassador Sujan R. Chinoy, Director General of the Manohar Parrikar Institute for Defence Studies and Analyses, New Delhi

'This book draws on 150 years of census data and argues that the north–south fault line that is emerging may be a simplistic way of looking at the issue. The book by Ravi K. Mishra could not have been more timely and will add value to the ongoing debate in the country on delimitation and demography.'

— Neerja Chowdhury, Journalist and Political Commentator

'*Demography, Representation, Delimitation: The North-South Divide in India* delves deeply into a neglected yet far-reaching concern of our nation. In this book, Dr Ravi Mishra expertly explores the demographic dynamics of India, and its effect on political representation in the Parliament. Through thorough research and detailed analysis, this work sheds light on the regional variations in India's population which has led to critical issues like over-representation and under-representation in the Parliament. It provides an extensive overview on the demography of India, exploring nuanced topics and critical issues with comparative case studies and policy suggestions. By connecting statistics to compelling narratives, Dr Mishra has masterfully crafted this brilliant work, which will be integral for policymakers and citizens alike as we draw closer to the 2026 Census.'

— Professor C. Raj Kumar, Vice Chancellor,
O.P. Jindal Global University

'The book *Demography, Representation, Delimitation: The North–South Divide in India* can't be better timed than this when the north–south divide is the central point of discussion around the upcoming delimitation exercises. I am sure this book would not only throw light on this issue but would offer some plausible way out. This book is going to be a great treasure for researchers, academicians, journalists and policymakers working on this issue.'

— Sanjay Kumar, Co-Director Lokniti, Professor,
Centre for the Study of Developing Societies (CSDS)

'The basic principle that guides the political representation and delimitation of constituencies in India's parliamentary democracy has been overtly politicised and kept in abeyance for far too long. Ravi Mishra, in his book, painstakingly brings together the long-term evidence on India's regional demographic transition and the debates on population explosion that forced the hand of the policymakers to place an unjust freeze on the delimitation of constituencies in India in 1976 and its extension in 2001. He shows that posing this issue in terms of the north–south divide and blaming the north for its unchecked population growth is not an accurate framing of the demographic and delimitation concerns. All regions in India have experienced a similar demographic transition albeit at different periods in history, irrespective of the attribution often made to the role of population control policies in that regard. This timely and well-researched study presents the necessary evidence for policymakers to revisit the issue of representation and delimitation on a firmer footing, and consider alternatives for instituting correctives to strengthen the vibrancy and depth of India's electoral democracy.'

— Rajeev Malhotra, Academic and Former Economic Adviser
to the Union Finance Minister of India

'In this original and scholarly work, Ravi Mishra unravels, layer by layer, the complex and tangled issues surrounding "delimitation". As the embargo on the expansion of seats ends in 2026, the prospect of restructuring the Lok Sabha and its likely expansion will throw up several challenges for parliamentary democracy and federalism in India. Lok Sabha seats could rise to 728 or even 791, depending on whether the 2011 Census figures or the 2026 demographic projections are used. South Indian states like Tamil Nadu are already critiquing the delimitation plan, expressing concerns over the downsizing of their parliamentary strength and the "imbalance" in the federal system caused by the dominance of the north. *Demography, Representation, Delimitation* takes a deep dive into this subject. Using a wealth of census data dating back to the late nineteenth century, Ravi Mishra convincingly demonstrates how different regional societies in India have experienced demographic transitions over the last 150 years. In doing so, they have followed different historical clocks, experiencing phases of high birth rates which have progressively moderated over successive decades. Mishra dispels the notion that the north is singularly responsible for India's population explosion. Using a comparative approach, he offers a nuanced perspective on the north–south divide, challenging conventional wisdom on this issue.

Ravi Mishra uses the historian's "tool-kit" to deploy a longer temporality as well as a broader spatiality which has enabled him to offer a fresh perspective on the relationship between demography and political representation.

Demography, Representation, Delimitation shall serve as an essential reference work for the policy debates and political contentions that will inevitably take place as parliamentarians, academics and concerned citizens debate the pros and cons of the likely expansion of the parliament of the world's largest democracy.'

— Gyanesh Kudaisya, Associate Professor, South Asian Studies, National University of Singapore

DEMOGRAPHY REPRESENTATION DELIMITATION

THE NORTH–SOUTH DIVIDE IN INDIA

RAVI K. MISHRA

WESTLAND
NON·FICTION

WESTLAND
NON·FICTION

Published by Westland Non-Fiction, an imprint of Westland Books, a division of Nasadiya Technologies Private Limited, in 2025

No. 269/2B, First Floor, 'Irai Arul', Vimalraj Street, Nethaji Nagar, Alapakkam Main Road, Maduravoyal, Chennai 600095

Westand, the Westland logo, Westland Non-Fiction and the Westland Non-Fiction logo are the trademarks of Nasadiya Technologies Private Limited, or its affiliates.

ISBN: 9789360453763

10 9 8 7 6 5 4 3 2 1

The views and opinions expressed in this work are the author's own and the facts are as reported by him, and the publisher is in no way liable for the same.

The maps used in the book are for representational purposes only.

Typeset by Jojy Philip

Printed at Manipal Technologies Limited, Manipal

यद्यदाचरति श्रेष्ठस्तत्तदेवेतरो जनः ।
स यत्प्रमाणं कुरुते लोकस्तदनुवर्तते ॥

Bhagavad Gita

Affectionately dedicated to
the memory of
my parents
Suraj Prasad Mishra and Veena Rani Mishra

Contents

Preface

My interest in the subject of demography, political representation and delimitation goes back about a quarter century, to the turn of the millennium. This was a time when in the wake of the economic reforms introduced by Prime Minister Narasimha Rao in 1991, the social and economic inequalities at the regional level were getting more pronounced than they had ever been since Independence. In the allocation of resources by the Central government to states, the weightage assigned to population had been a significant parameter along with some other indicators of backwardness. The Report of the Eleventh Finance Commission headed by Shri A.M. Khusro seemed to have favoured the northern states, where the population growth had experienced a spurt in the preceding decades relative to the southern states. This led to rumblings and protests from many leaders from the south, resulting in politicisation of the population debate in terms of a north–south divide, including in the popular media.

The issue of demography and delimitation in this debate came to the forefront in 2001 when the embargo on delimitation placed in 1976 was extended for another twenty five years. The Constitution of India requires that every Census should be followed by delimitation and reallocation of seats in the legislative bodies at the national and state levels, a practice that was set aside in 1976. In a way, five delimitations as envisaged in the Constitution have not been carried out. An argument can easily be extended in defence of that line of thinking; however, it is always going to be at the expense of a violation of the fundamental principle of proportionate representation in a democracy, namely 'one person, one vote, one value'.

Being a student of modern history, a natural starting point for me to understand the complexities of this issue was to go back to the earliest decennial Censuses of India, those from 1872 to 1921, and work my way forward. As I started looking at the demographic trends, I realised that there was a disconnect between facts on the ground and the debate on delimitation as it was playing out in the hallowed halls of the Lok Sabha and in the media. This induced me to undertake a detailed study of regional demographic transition in India and the factors that brought about those changes.

Indeed, demographic transition in India has not been studied with a long-term perspective, possibly due to lack of easy access to relevant data. I started by bringing together the available data in consistent and comparable form, given that there were, since 1881, dramatic and multiple reorganisations of administrative units in India that had to be accounted for in undertaking a long-term comparative analysis of demographic changes. I also wanted to take note of the various debates, at the international and national levels, that had a direct implication for political representation and the public policy towards population growth. Most importantly, their consequence for the political narrative on democratic representation in India, which perhaps prevented course correction in policies, including on the institutional and conceptual basis of delimitation.

Different geographical regions and states of India experienced their demographic transition during different periods, a fact that has been overlooked in the political debates on the subject. The consequence has been a misplaced emphasis on some factors and regions with regard to population growth, making the debate unnecessarily shrill and polemical, without a basis in the relevant long-term empirical evidence. The freeze on the expansion and delimitation of parliamentary and legislative assembly constituencies has undermined the Constitutional provisions and the democratic principle of equality in representation. It has also caused urban–rural distortion in public representation within legislative bodies. The unnecessary deferment in resolving an issue which is at the foundation of India's democracy has given rise to a serious imbalance in political representation across states and regions, impacting the representative character of democracy as it functions presently. This book addresses some of these concerns. While the divide in representation is generally thought in terms of north versus south, my study shows that it is more like the south versus the rest.

My journey in undertaking this study and the writing of the book has passed through many milestones. At each stage, I have been fortunate to have the guidance, kindness and support of many persons. It is almost impossible to acknowledge each one of them personally, there is a danger of offending some who I may unintentionally miss listing here. Yet I must acknowledge my gratitude to all those without whom this journey may not have culminated at this destination.

For the past several years I have immensely benefited from the guidance and support of Shri Nripendra Misra, Professor Lokesh Chandra, Dr A. Surya Prakash, Dr Swapan Dasgupta, Dr Vinay Sahasrabuddhe, Shri Prasoon Joshi, Shri M.J. Akbar, Professor Kapil Kapoor, Shri Sanjeev Nandan Sahai and late Shakti Sinha Ji at the Prime Ministers Museum and Library (PMML), Teen Murti Bhavan, New Delhi, in enriching my approach to work and life, in general. I express my sincere gratitude to all of them. The vibrant academic culture of the Institution nurtured under their guidance in terms of lectures, panel discussions, book discussions, conferences and publications, wherein I had the privilege to participate, contribute and learn, have also benefited me immensely.

I would like to acknowledge my debt to the now-retired faculty of the Centre for Historical Studies, Jawaharlal Nehru University, for their dedicated teaching and for creating a symbiotic intellectual environment which helped evolve my thinking as a historian and a social scientist. I would like to mention Professor Bhagwan Josh, who guided my M.Phil. Research, and Professor Yogesh Sharma, who guided my PhD; I feel a deep sense of gratitude to Professor Cornelius Jean Jaenen of the Department of History, University of Ottawa, who co-guided my doctoral thesis on French–Canadian history. The courses offered by Professor Sabyasachi Bhattacharya, Professor Suvira Jaiswal, Professor Harbans Mukhiya, Professor Muzaffar Alam, Professor K.N. Panikkar, Professor Neeladri Bhattacharya and Professor Majid Hayat Siddiqui helped me evolve intellectually. To my teachers, Professor Madhavan K. Palat, Professor Dilbagh Singh and Professor Indivar Kamtekar, I owe a special sense of gratitude, as they not only mentored me over the years, but have also provided very useful comments on the draft of the book at different stages for me to take this work forward.

I am grateful to Professor Rajeev Malhotra, Professor Makkhan Lal, Dr Sanjeev Chopra, Professor Santosh K. Mehrotra, Dr Atul Bharadwaj, Professor Debal K. Singha Roy and Professor Gyanesh Kudaisya, who reviewed substantial parts of the manuscript and helped in sharpening the analysis and the structuring of the book. This work has benefited immensely from their suggestions. I am also grateful to Professor C. Raj Kumar, founder vice chancellor of O.P. Jindal Global University, Sonipat, where I have taught history for many years, who took time off his busy schedule to discuss the content of the book and made very useful suggestions.

Shri Devendra Swaroop, Shri Swaraj Prakash Gupta, Shri T.N. Chaturvedi and Shri Kamlesh Shukla—all of whom are no more—affectionately guided and mentored me over the decades. My special tributes to them.

For most of us, our life and thinking gets influenced by our friends, well-wishers and the institutional context in which we grow up. It has been no different in my case. Apart from Luke Chandekar, a college friend from Kanpur days, I have greatly benefited from the conversations and the time I spent with my friends and seniors at JNU, Pushkar Mishra, Ashok Dogra, Hari Mohan Sharma, Shivraj Singh and K.P. Singh; my batchmates and friends, Ashok Tanwar, Shiv Shakti Bakshi, Vikas Pathak and Dhrub Kumar Singh; and friends who came into my life a little later, Mayur Shekhar Jha, Mohsin Ali, Uma Shankar Pandey, Raman Chadha, Jyotish Joshi, Saurav Jha, Devapriya Roy, Sajjan Kumar, Swadesh Singh, Hari Krishan Sharma, Prateek Kumar, Sushant Chandra and Atulindra Nath Chaturvedi.

This work would not have been possible without the generous research and incidental support of Akhilesh Pathak, my nephew Prateek Shukla and Kritika Duggal; and of Mukesh Kumar, Rishi Kumar, Yogesh Kumar, Geeta Yadav, Neeraj Kumar, D.S. Rawat and P. Kasi Rajan, my colleagues at PMML, Teen Murti Bhavan, New Delhi.

I would also like to express my gratitude towards my elder sister Ms Archana Mishra and my brother-in-law Shri Pradeep Shukla, who have over the years encouraged me and supported me in handling family responsibilities in my hometown Kanpur, which has helped me focus better on my academic pursuits. I also thank my in-laws, Shri Omkar Prasad Vashishtha and Smt. Savita Vashishtha, who have blessed and supported me.

Working on this book as well as the pursuit of my other academic activities and interests has often kept me away from home, and sometimes inaccessible even at home, thus curtailing the time I would have liked to spend with my immediate family. So, last but not least, my sincere thanks to my better-half Ila, and my two adorable children, Ayushman and Arunima, who are eagerly awaiting the publication of my book, without yet understanding what it is all about.

I am thankful to my friend Karthika V.K., publisher at Westland Books, and other members of the Westland team, including Sonia Madan, Saurabh Garge and Amrita Talwar. I also thank all others at Westland Books who would have worked behind the scenes to contribute to the publication of this book.

Prologue

This book narrates the compelling story of demographic growth in modern India, spanning from 1872, when the first modern census of India was compiled, all the way up to 2024. Based on comprehensive demographic data of the last 150 years derived from all decennial censuses as well as population statistics drawn from other sources such as district gazetteers, boundary commission reports, various states reorganisation Acts and relevant surveys, the book reveals that conventional wisdom about the so-called north–south demographic divide, according to which the north is the culprit of 'population explosion' and the south is the poster boy of population control, has gone horribly wrong.

The book shows that demographic transition has occurred in various parts of India during different periods. Over the last century-and-a-half, all the four regions of India—north, south, east and west—have enjoyed phases of peak population growth lasting over at least four to five decades, but the timing of demographic transition in the four regions, and the states within each, has been different. While some states and regions saw their population grow at a relatively high rate in the nineteenth century itself, others started doing so only after 1921 or 1931. It is this unrecognised difference in timing that is mostly responsible for distortions in our understanding of population growth in modern India.

The book throws up some astonishing facts. Contrary to widely held perceptions among policymakers, experts, academics and the public, southern India has had exponential population growth over the last 150 years. Kerala was the first state of India to have doubled its population. From 1881 onwards, the princely states of Travancore and Cochin and the Malabar district of the Madras Presidency, which constitute the bulk of today's Kerala, had a much higher growth than most other states and regions of India.

The result was that Kerala's population doubled by 1931, rising from about 50 lakh in 1881 to nearly a crore. From 1931 to 1971, it doubled again, reaching around 2.13 crore. Such was the cumulative growth of Kerala's population that by the time it started slowing down after 1971, it had already quadrupled. If we take the entire period from 1881 to 2011, Kerala's population had multiplied roughly by seven times. Because of its high growth from 1881 to 1971, Kerala's share in India's population increased from less than 2.5 per cent to about 3.9 per cent. This was among the highest gains in percentage terms of any state in India. It is only after 1971 that its share started reconverging to its nineteenth-century share by dropping to 2.76 per cent in 2011.

Beginning 1881, Madras Presidency, which was after Independence divided mainly between Tamil Nadu and Andhra Pradesh, witnessed rapid population growth, well above the national average. According to the last British Census of India in 1941, it had grown from a little more than 3 crore in 1881 to nearly 5 crore, a rise of approximately 60 per cent in six decades. Even Mysore state, which became the core of Karnataka after Independence, saw its population rise from 42 lakh in 1881 to more than 73 lakh in 1941—a growth of about 80 per cent. As for the state of Hyderabad, nearly 70 per cent of whose population went to Andhra Pradesh and Karnataka after the reorganisation of states, it saw its population of slightly less than 1 crore in 1881 go up to 1.63 crore in 1941—a growth of about 66 per cent.

Even when we look at the figures from 1901, it is evident that the southern states enjoyed high growth at least until 1971. Karnataka's population of about 1.30 crore more than doubled by 1971, reaching 2.92 crore. Having crossed the figure of 6 crore in 2011, it doubled once again. Tamil Nadu's population grew more slowly overall, but still doubled from roughly 1.92 crore in 1901 to about 4.1 crore in 1971. Between 1971 and 2011, it grew further to nearly 7.2 crore. Thus, between 1901 and 2011, Tamil Nadu's population multiplied by almost four times (about 275 per cent).

At an aggregate level too, the demographic growth of the south has been quite high. Thus, from 1881 to 1901, the southern states of today collectively grew by about 25 per cent, which was well above the national average during that period (11.32 per cent). From 1881 to 1921, they grew by 39.12 per cent; from 1881 to 1951, they grew by 104 per cent. Between 1881 and 1971, which was the period when the south had a clear growth lead over the north, its population nearly tripled (193 per cent), reaching 13.53 crore. From 1881 to 2011, the population of the south has grown by nearly five-and-a-half times (444 per cent), from about 4.62 crore to 25.12 crore.

The relatively high cumulative growth rate enjoyed by the south between 1881 and 1971 ensured that the region's share in India's population experienced big changes. In 1881, it was approximately 21.56 per cent of the national population (retrospectively calculated according to the post-Partition boundaries of India); in 1901, it reached 24.23 per cent; in 1921, it increased to 25.56; in 1951, the south reached 26.08 per cent, its highest share in India's population in recorded history. Even in 1971, it remained very close to the peak, at 24.69 per cent. It is only after 1971, when the south's growth started slowing down as it had almost completed the second phase of demographic transition, that its share in the national population started falling. Showing a long-term convergence with its 1881 figure, it has reached 20.75 per cent in 2011.

What has been the demographic story of the north over the last 150 years? The north (defined as all the states in the Hindi belt and the National Capital Territory of Delhi) experienced a population growth far below the south for nearly half of the period, and clearly below the south even for the entire period. Uttar Pradesh, the most populous state of the country by far, hardly grew between 1881 and 1921. The United Provinces of Agra and Oudh, as it was then called, had a population, along with its princely states, of nearly 4.5 crore (4,48,76,499) in 1881. It should be emphasised that this was only slightly less than the population of the whole of the south (4.62 crore). By 1921, including today's Uttarakhand, it had inched up to only 4.66 crore (4,66,72,411), which was a negligible growth over a period of forty years, during which the population of the south reached 6.4 crore (6,42,28,692). In fact, as a whole, the Hindi belt remained virtually stagnant during the forty-year period from 1881 to 1921, with its population hovering around 11 crore. This is among the least-known facets of the demographic history of modern India.

The trend of slower growth as compared to the south continued until about 1961. In fact, in the Census of 1971, Uttar Pradesh's share in India's population stood at the bottom, at only 15.30 per cent. This was in contrast with the state's share of 20.94 per cent in India's population in 1881. This was clearly the biggest percentage fall for any state. It took Uttar Pradesh no less than a century to double its 1881 population of 4.5 crore; in 1971, its population had barely reached about 8.4 crore. It was only in 1981 that it reached 10.50 crore, which is somewhat more than double the 1881 number. Taking the entire period (1881–2011), Uttar Pradesh has grown by less than four-and-a-half times (340 per cent). Even including Uttarakhand, which was earlier part of the United Provinces, the combined population of the two states at around 21 crore (20,98,98,633) shows a growth of only 368 per cent, which is well below the national average and far below the entire south's growth of about five-and-a-half times (444 per cent) during the same period.

Taken as a whole, the north could double its 1881 population of approximately 10.67 crore only by 1971, when it reached 22.9 crore—taking nearly ninety years. By contrast, the south's population had more than doubled from the 1881 figure of about 4.62 crore to 9.4 crore by 1951. Between 1881 and 1971, the south tripled its population while the north could only double it. Even when we include the post-1971 period in our analysis, taking 1881–2011 in one sweep, the north's population growth is slightly more than five times (427 per cent). The south's growth during the same period is closer to five-and-a-half times (444 per cent). While such macro-level calculations may have a slight margin of error, the point remains that the population growth of the north had by no means been extraordinary as compared to that of the south. It has, in fact, been below that of the south during 1881–2011. From 1881 to 1971, of course, it was much below that of the south. In fact, even for 1901–71 it was well below that of the south. The bulk of the growth in the north happened only after 1951, by which time the south had more than doubled its population of 1881.

What may come as a surprise to most is that far from gaining a higher share in the population of India because of its 'population boom', the Hindi-speaking north lost a considerable chunk of it over the last one-and-a-half centuries. In 1881, the north constituted roughly 49.85 per cent of the population of India as calculated after retrospectively adjusting for the post-Partition boundaries of the country; by 1951, it had fallen to 42.61 per cent, both because of its growth being far below the national average and also due to the much higher growth of all the other regions, that is, the east, the west and the south. As a matter of fact, though the north had started its growth spurt after 1951, its growth was still slower than that of the other three regions, so that by 1971 there was a further decline in its population share, which fell to 41.90 per cent—the lowest recorded figure in history.

Since 1971, the peak growth rates of 20 per cent or more, usually seen in the second phase of demographic transition all over India, have ensured that the north has achieved noticeable convergence with the *longue durée* of history in terms of population. Inching back to 46.47 per cent in 2011, the north has gone past its 1901 share of 46.16 per cent. However, it is still well below its 1881 share of 49.85 per cent. With its fertility rates declining and the population growth slowing down, the north is unlikely to converge with the 1881 share in the foreseeable future. That is natural, as both convergence and divergence have played their role in the demographic history of India since the nineteenth century. Figures 1, 2 and 3 present a graphic picture of population growth in the different regions of India from 1881 onwards.

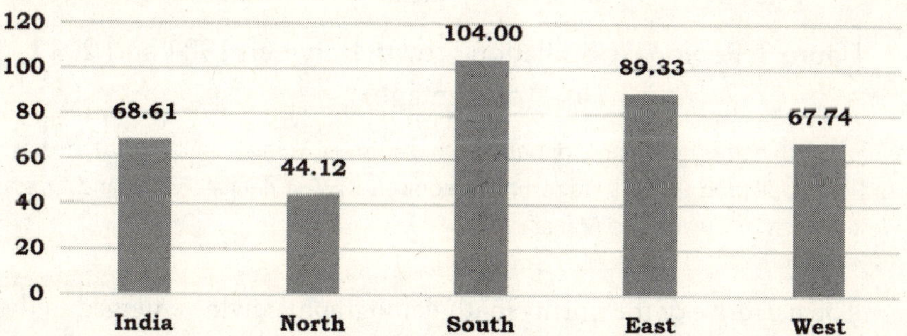

Figure 1: Regional population growth between 1881 and 1951 (percentage)

Note: North comprises the Hindi belt; south consists of Kerala, Tamil Nadu, Karnataka and the undivided Andhra Pradesh; east comprises West Bengal, Assam and Orissa; west consists of Gujarat and Maharashtra.

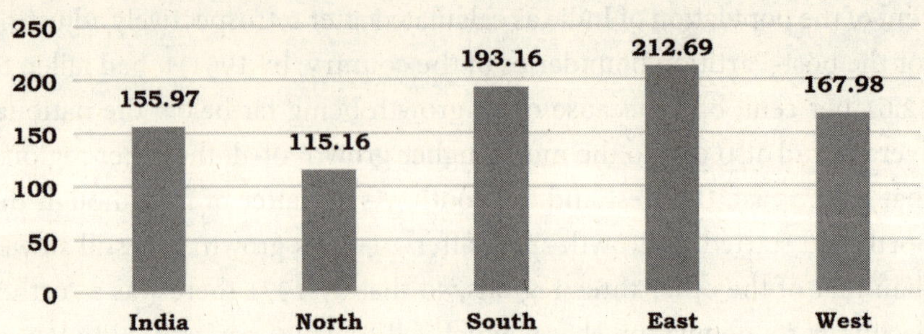

Figure 2: Regional population growth between 1881 and 1971 (percentage)

Note: North comprises the Hindi belt; south consists of Kerala, Tamil Nadu, Karnataka and the undivided Andhra Pradesh; east comprises West Bengal, Assam and Orissa; west consists of Gujarat and Maharashtra.

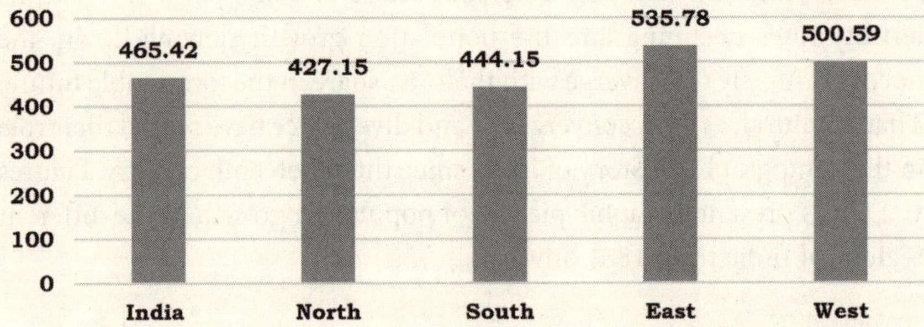

Figure 3: Regional population growth between 1881 and 2011 (percentage)

Note: North comprises the Hindi belt; south consists of Kerala, Tamil Nadu, Karnataka and the undivided Andhra Pradesh; east comprises West Bengal, Assam and Orissa; west consists of Gujarat and Maharashtra.

The narrative of the north–south demographic divide emerged in the 1970s. After the Second World War, there was a sudden spurt in population growth in both Europe and America, known as the baby boom. The period between the two World Wars had been marked by uncertainty, which had contributed to a decline in fertility. The Great Depression of the 1930s had also played a role in limiting population growth. The Second World War was, of course, a big factor in limiting births, just as it led to millions of deaths in Europe and America. The end of the War, along with increased prosperity and improvements in healthcare, created an environment suitable for population growth. This sudden spurt fuelled concerns of 'overpopulation' in the West. In the case of Europe, much of which was already densely populated, there may have been some genuine reasons to believe that the population boom was unsustainable. But for a country as thinly populated as the United States of America, there was no ground whatsoever for the exaggerated concerns expressed about 'overpopulation'.

It was, however, the accelerated pace of demographic transition in the Third World countries of Asia and Africa, many of which had gained independence from the Western empires around the middle of the twentieth century—including two of the largest countries by population, India and China—that gave birth to the alarmist idea of 'population explosion', a term coined around this time by sociologist and demographer Kingsley Davis. Later, in 1968, Stanford biologist Paul Ehrlich wrote his doomsayer's account, *The Population Bomb*.

Apart from Rockefeller and Ford foundations, the various multilateral institutions working under the umbrella of the United Nations became invested in the idea of a rapidly growing 'world population' that needed to be controlled for a sustainable global future. In the emerging geopolitics of the Cold War, the rapid demographic growth of the Third World was seen as a threat to the post-War global order led by the West. The dominant discourse of 'overpopulation' linked demographic growth in the Third World to global food supply and economic development. Especially with regard to India, it was argued that unless it controlled its population growth it would neither be able to feed itself nor be able to ensure social and economic development.

In reality, all that had happened was that the demographic transition which had occurred in developed countries over two or three centuries—and was therefore much less noticeable—was unfolding in these Third World countries within a shorter timeline of a few decades. Owing to slightly increased levels of prosperity, nutrition, public sanitation and healthcare advances mostly borrowed from the West, mortality rates, especially of infants and children, suddenly plunged in many countries, even as birth rates remained high. This brought about a spurt in their population. Ignoring the history of population growth in the world, policymakers were perturbed by the rapid escalation, as it seemed to negate their efforts at development.

In India, policymakers and experts were all the more alarmed for good reason. The anti-imperialist critique of the Indian freedom struggle led by Mahatma Gandhi revolved around the core issues of underdevelopment, poverty, hunger, illiteracy, short life expectancy, and high mortality in famines caused by Britain's exploitation of India. The underlying promise was that once the British were made to leave India, all these problems would soon be resolved. This was, of course, a tall order.

However, the Constitution of India did enshrine this vision of social and economic development, and the newly independent state was expected to deliver on it. Rapid development was the only option for the nation's progress, as also for fulfilling the promises of the Gandhian freedom struggle and of the founding fathers of the Constitution.

While a relatively stable population was seen as desirable from the viewpoint of governments that were called upon to fulfil the widely shared vision of independent India, the reality on the ground was just the opposite. At the national level, population growth had started its peak phase only around the mid-twentieth century and was accelerating. In a newly independent India, this unprecedented growth of population, which seemed to be getting out of control, became a cause of concern for the leaders of the nation, policymakers, experts and even some sections of the educated public. The policymakers felt that their diligent and well-meaning efforts at developing India through poverty alleviation programmes, expansion in literacy, improvement in health, including reduction in mortality, providing urban housing and other amenities, building infrastructure, and providing a better standard of living in general to the expectant public were apparently neutralised by high population growth.

The challenge was felt most acutely in feeding India's growing population. As mentioned, frequent famines during the British Raj, in which an estimated 20–30 million Indians had perished, constituted an important component of the nationalist critique of the empire. The Bengal famine of 1942-43, causing the death of about 3 million people, was still fresh in the memory of decision makers. Food shortages in the 1960s, caused by consecutive droughts and two wars, made India vulnerable and partly dependent on international suppliers of food grains. There was an increased dependence on the US, which had been supplying food grains to India under the Agricultural Trade Development and Assistance Act, commonly known as PL–480 or Food for Peace, signed into law by President Dwight D. Eisenhower in 1954. The shortages convinced the leaders that unless India curbed its population surge, it faced imminent threat of hunger and famine. While the Green Revolution would increase agricultural output by the early 1970s, the alarmist narrative of 'population explosion' continued unabated. The increasing population seemed to fritter away the gains of development.

Unfortunately, just as 'population explosion' was becoming a popular concept in the 1960s, the Hindi belt, which had entered the second phase of demographic transition a couple of decades earlier, started experiencing its peak growth phase of 20 per cent or higher decadal growth. It was the last of the four regions of India to do so. The three other regions—south, east and west—had started their peak growth phase decades earlier and were now in the process of gradually exiting it. The south, because of its early start, was showing signs of slowing down in both fertility rates and population growth after 1971; the north was still going up. It was in this context that the narrative of the north–south demographic divide acquired wide acceptance. Indeed, the narrative sounded so convincing, and such was its hold on the national imagination, that not only the south but also the north was persuaded to believe that it had failed to control its population growth. There was hardly any serious attempt to go deeper into the historical reasons behind the divide. The social and economic backwardness of the north as compared to the south seemed to explain it well enough.

What has also been overlooked in this north–south demographic divide is Gujarat and Maharashtra's very high growth rates for more than a century. These two states have been classified as the west in this book. The west was the third region of India to have experienced the demographic transition, soon after the south and the east. Since 1901, it has enjoyed rapid growth, so that even after apparently completing its second phase of rapid growth its population has continued to swell.

In the nineteenth century, there was a slight decline in the population of the west. Between 1901 and 1971, however, Maharashtra and Gujarat witnessed rapid growth. Their population almost tripled during this period (171 per cent growth). More importantly, they continued to grow rapidly even after 1971—when the south and the east had started slowing down—and reached their combined peak share only in 2001. When we take the period 1901–2011 into account, the west's growth at 506 per cent comes to be the highest of the four regions. For 1881–2011, it is the second-highest at 501 per cent. For both the periods, its population has grown around six times. If we look at the period from 1951 to 2011, its growth at 258 per cent has been only slightly below that of the north at 266 per cent, and it is far above that of the south during the same period (167 per cent). In 1881, the west had a population of only about 2.88 crore; in 2011, it had nearly 17.3 crore. That is well above the growth in both the north and the south and significantly below that in the east.

Not surprisingly, the west's share in the country's population increased from 13.44 per cent in 1901 to peak at 14.34 per cent in 2001. Even in 2011, it remains at 14.27 per cent. All this indicates that the unknown story of demographic growth really lies in western India, and not necessarily in the north.

The east (Assam, West Bengal and Orissa) had started growing substantially in the nineteenth century itself. Between 1881 and 1971, its population of about 2.59 crore had more than tripled to almost 8.08 crore. In fact, during this ninety-year period, the east had the highest population growth (213 per cent), though factoring in the flow of migration first from East Bengal and later Bangladesh, it is quite comparable to the growth of the south (193 per cent) and the west (168 per cent). Even for the entire period of 1881–2011, its growth comes to nearly 536 per cent, which means that its population has increased more than sixfold in 130 years. During the same period, its share in the population of the country has also gone up from 12.08 per cent to 13.58 per cent. It had touched the peak at 14.76 in 1971.

As is evident, all parts of India have witnessed high population growth over the last one-and-a-half centuries. Both the south and the north have grown below the national average, while the east and west have grown above it. The result is that in terms of population share they have gained at the expense of the north and the south.

Ever since the British started counting the population of India in a systematic manner, Kerala was the first state of the country to have doubled its population by 1931. Tamil Nadu doubled its population by 1961. There is nothing unique about Kerala and Tamil Nadu. These states were just following the global phenomenon of demographic transition. Over the last few decades, the population of states like Uttar Pradesh, Rajasthan and Madhya Pradesh has grown at a higher rate than the rest of India, which has led to much ill-informed criticism, sometimes implying that there is something 'culturally wrong' with them. These and most other fast-growing states entered the second phase of transition much later than the rest of India, and their populations are also expected to stabilise in the coming decades.

However, in violation of the Indian constitutional principle of 'one person, one vote, one value', a freeze on the Lok Sabha seats was effected in 1976. This was a time when some states had already undergone the demographic transition, while others were decades behind. With fresh delimitation and reallocation of seats in Parliament, deferred until 2026, the shares of the north and the west will go up, while that of the south as a proportion will go down because in 1971 it was close to its peak in the national demographic pie. The anomaly in representation caused by the freeze needs to be addressed, because it gives higher representation to some states and lower representation to others, thereby violating a basic constitutional premise. After examining the various facets of India's demographic transition and that of its regional constituents, this issue has been analysed and alternative proposals to address this impending national concern are presented in the final chapter. India's demographic scenario as outlined here is in conflict with the political empowerment of the people and a fundamental tenet of Indian democracy.

1

Delimitation and the North–South Divide

An Overview

Demography, representation and delimitation have been at the heart of the so-called north–south divide in India over the last fifty years. The 42nd Amendment to the Constitution of India passed during the Emergency (1975–77) placed an embargo on delimitation and reallocation of Lok Sabha seats to the various states for twenty-five years. It froze the total number of seats in Parliament and their state-wise allocation as per the 1971 Census figures. The freeze was extended for twenty-five years by the 84th Amendment passed in 2001. On both occasions, the embargo on delimitation was justified on the ground of incentivising family planning implementation in the southern states, which apparently had performed better than the northern states on 'population control'. The north–south divide has also expanded to include the allocation of fiscal resources to the states by the Union government and bodies such as the Finance Commission and the erstwhile Planning Commission, to which the use of 1971 population figures was extended on the basis of the same logic.

Forming the core of this book is this narrative of the north–south demographic divide, which has been told and retold for at least half-a-century now, by policymakers and experts alike. In *Demography, Representation, Delimitation*, this divide is revisited and re-examined from a fresh perspective, employing historical data over the last 150 years.

Many pertinent questions arise. When did population in the north start growing faster than that in the south? What is the link, if any, between the family planning programme and population growth in India? Can the decline in fertility rates and population in the south and some other parts of India be attributed to a greater commitment to family planning in those regions? What is the link between demographic transition and socio-economic development? When did the south go past the north in terms of economic performance? This study is an attempt at providing answers to such questions.

Ever since the 1970s, prominent leaders from the south have repeatedly and successfully demanded that seats in Parliament must not be redistributed on the basis of the latest census. The ground for their demand has been that while the south has faithfully implemented the family planning programme and controlled its population growth, the north has failed to do so. Therefore, the south must not be 'penalised' for its supposedly responsible conduct and the north should not be 'rewarded' for its irresponsible conduct with regard to control of population growth. The 1976 embargo on delimitation and redistribution of seats for twenty-five years was demanded and supported by them. In 2001, its extension for twenty-five years through another constitutional amendment was demanded by representatives from the south and was acceded to by the Atal Bihari Vajpayee–led National Democratic Alliance (NDA) government at the Centre.[1]

The southern states have also argued that it is wrong to make current population one of the criteria for resource allocation, since that would supposedly lead to the north—which has witnessed faster population growth in the last fifty years—getting an unduly large share of grants from the Union government. They have claimed it to be a grave injustice to the south, which has supposedly behaved in a more responsible manner than the north with regard to population growth.[2] This chapter focuses on the political and constitutional debate on representation and delimitation over the last fifty years.

I

Population, Representation and Financial Allocation

It is not surprising that both political representation and fiscal allocation from the Centre have emerged as focal points of the debate around the north–south demographic divide in the last few years. The old fears of the south have been reawakened because of the approaching 2026 deadline of the embargo. On 14 February 2024, the Tamil Nadu Assembly passed a unanimous resolution against delimitation and reallocation of seats in Parliament:

> This august House urged the Union Government that the delimitation process to be carried out after 2026 on the basis of the census should not be carried out. Due to unavoidable reasons, if the number of seats on the basis of population were to increase, it shall be maintained at the present ratio of the constituencies between the States in the State Assemblies and both Houses of Parliament fixed, based on the population of 1971.[3]

The passage of the Women's Reservation Act in September 2023 set the immediate context and elicited a strong response from the south. This is because for its implementation the Act requires a delimitation and redistribution of seats after a fresh census. The backlash was immediate and strong. Chief Minister of Tamil Nadu M.K. Stalin said:

> It is unjust that southern states, which have diligently followed the Union government's policies to control population growth, may face punitive measures during the constituency delimitation.[4]

Stalin's statement reiterates the longstanding position about the south's success in controlling population growth through family planning, as against the failure of the north to do so. Thus, the rationale for opposition to delimitation is the same as it was almost fifty years ago. Calling it a 'political conspiracy', Stalin said:

> We will have to defeat the political conspiracy of increasing the number of MPs based on population and reducing the political representation of South India. The attempt to render injustice to a politically aware Tamil Nadu should be nipped in the bud.... I urge the PM to provide assurance that southern states, particularly Tamil Nadu, will not experience a reduction in representation during the impending delimitation process based on population.[5]

Participating in the Women's Reservation Bill debate, Kanimozhi Karunanidhi, Lok Sabha MP from Dravida Munnetra Kazhagam

(DMK), quoted her brother Stalin, asking why the bill was being linked to delimitation:

> India is the only country that has not conducted the decadal census. If delimitation is going to be based on population census, it will deprive and reduce the representation of southern states. It will become like a sword hanging over our heads.[6]

She further said:

> There is a fear in the minds of the people that our voices will be undermined. There should be a clear clarification about this because we don't want our representation to be reduced in any way. As it is, this (current set-up) has to continue so that we get an equal say in what is being discussed.[7]

This is reminiscent of what Kanimozhi N.V.N. Somu, a DMK MP in the Rajya Sabha (not to be confused with the other Kanimozhi), had said in 2022:

> South Indian states, particularly Tamil Nadu, have controlled their population growth to 6 per cent. In the North Indian states, family planning was not implemented with sincerity and due respect. As a result, there is an increase in the population of states like Uttar Pradesh and Bihar. It is absolutely ridiculous and very unfair that states which successfully implemented family planning are penalised and states that are reckless are being incentivised politically.[8]

The claim here, too, was that because of implementation of the family planning programme, the south has controlled its population even as the north could not. Hence, there was no justification for reallocation of seats in Parliament.

Coming back to the passage of the Women's Reservation Act, Communist Party of India (Marxist) (CPI(M)) politburo member M.A. Baby, who had earlier been Minister for Education, Kerala, told *India Today:*

> The delimitation exercise is a false democratic form imposed on the South. It will invariably lead to a north–south divide. By silencing the South and its dissenting voice, the Union government is periling the federal structure of India.[9]

Other leaders from the south have similarly voiced their strong opposition to delimitation and redistribution, also citing the difference between the demographic growth rates of the north and the south over the last fifty years—a difference that is attributed to effective implementation of family planning by the south. For instance, Congress MP from Sivaganga, Karti Chidambaram has the following to say on the matter:

> If you start allocating seats based on population, the Southern representation as a percentage will further go down. The Southern states will be penalised for effectively implementing population control. Southern states contribute more tax per GDP. They contribute per capita more to the GDP. But then you cannot have a lesser representation for us in the Southern states and increase the representation of the North. That will be completely unacceptable.[10]

Writing in *The New Indian Express* in December 2023, former Cabinet Secretary K.M. Chandrasekhar stated that 'all the South Indian states will stand to lose their political influence in comparison with the North'.[11] He went on to conclude:

> The next government would therefore need to tread very carefully when the question of delimitation comes up. It has the potential to blow up into a major conflagration as has happened in the past when another constitutional provision relating to the official language was taken up in the mid-sixties of the last century. Political sagacity and statesmanship of the highest order and wide consultation with states, communities and social formations would be essential.[12]

Congress MP and author Shashi Tharoor is among the most influential voices from the south. He has on many occasions criticised the idea of fresh delimitation. In his latest statement of 2 July 2024, made during the launch of a book *The Republic Relearnt: Renewing Indian Democracy (1947–2024)*, Tharoor has reiterated his stand:

> There are some states in the South that will feel disenfranchised if it becomes possible to amend the Constitution without any reference to them. For example, if it is technically possible to pass an amendment that makes Hindi the national language.... I think that you'll have a serious revolt in Tamil Nadu.[13]

He has also expressed his hope that in the aftermath of general elections delimitation may not be undertaken:

> This (delimitation) is a subject that I hope will benefit from common sense and wisdom of those in power, who can certainly create a huge mess if they think in short term political gains. But now that UP has taught them that there can be pushback from the Hindi belt ... they (the BJP) might not be that enthusiastic about creating a massive majority for the Hindi belt in their own interest.[14]

In the essay, 'For the Sake of the South', written in *Open* magazine in October 2023, Tharoor presented a comprehensive critique of delimitation and state-wise redistribution of Parliament seats. Significantly, the principal ground for his opposition is again the lower population growth of the south in the last fifty years. He asserts that 'the reward for responsible stewardship by a state of demography and human development could not be political disenfranchisement.'[15] He further explains:

> While there is some logic to the argument that a democracy must value all its citizens equally—whether they live in a progressive state or in one that, by failing to empower its women and reduce total fertility, has allowed its population to shoot through the roof—no federal democracy can survive the perception that states would lose political clout if they developed well, while others would gain more seats in Parliament as a reward for failure.[16]

Referring to the constitution of the Fifteenth Finance Commission in 2017, which introduced the use of the 2011 Census figures rather than the 1971 figures for its recommendations for allocation of the revenues collected by the Union government to the states, and had elicited a strong opposition from southern leaders, Tharoor maintains:

> To take just one example, Karnataka meets 72 per cent of its expenses from the state's own taxes, whereas Bihar covers just 23 per cent, getting 77 per cent of its expenses from Central taxes. In other words, unlike most federal systems, India's revenues are going disproportionately to its worst-performing states, those with poor levels of education, high rates of fertility and population growth, while the high-performance states in the south get short shrift.[17]

Tharoor further asserts:

> The states of the 'cow belt'—the Hindi-speaking heartland, once called the BIMARU states—have comprehensively failed to improve their development indicators, notably relating to female literacy and women's empowerment. As a result, their population growth has outstripped that of the southern states.[18]

So, the argument that the south effectively controlled its population through successful implementation of family planning measures, contrasting with the north's record, is reiterated by Tharoor. Comparing the significantly asymmetrical population growth rates of the northern and southern states from 1971 to 2011, he enquires:

> Why should Kerala be punished for its impressive performance by receiving less revenue from the finance commission and also losing seats in Parliament, thereby being forced to dilute its voice in national affairs? Why should Tamil Nadu's reward for extraordinary economic success, sustained growth and population control be lower tax revenues from the Centre?[19]

He concludes his essay by, in effect, calling for a new political covenant:

> The only remedy is to acknowledge that we need a more decentralised democracy, one in which the Central share of tax resources is not so crucial, and the political authority of New Delhi not so overwhelming.[20]

In an article written in December 2022 for *Project Syndicate*, Tharoor had taken the same line. While conceding that as a result of the 1976 freeze 'some southern MPs represent fewer than two million voters, while some from the north represent as many as 2.9 million', he had said that 'ignorance about family planning and the benefits of smaller families in the less-literate north is likely the principal factor behind India's uneven population growth'.[21] He then expressed his political reservations about any possible rectification of asymmetrical political representation:

> Prime Minister Narendra Modi's ruling Bharatiya Janata Party (BJP), which elicits overwhelming support from voters in the northern Hindi-speaking Cow Belt, appears set to end this anomaly and to restore equal representation when the amendment lapses again in 2026. While this

> scenario would make the Indian parliament more representative, it would also give the northern states a two-thirds majority, enabling the BJP to amend the constitution at will without regard to the wishes of the southern states. Modi's cabinet would be able to pursue nationalist policies that the less populous states may find unpalatable or discriminatory, thus threatening India's hard-won national unity.[22]

Other important commentators from the south have also voiced their opposition to fresh delimitation. On 30 May 2024, speaking at a national conference on 'Constitution in a Changing India', former Supreme Court Justice K.M. Joseph expressed his concern about the impending delimitation:

> When that happens, states like Kerala and Tamil Nadu are going to lose the number of constituencies that they have and states like Bihar and Uttar Pradesh, where the population is not controlled, will have more constituencies. What will be the state of federalism in India? What will happen to the concept of Union of India as was contemplated.[23]

Similarly, in an article that appeared in the American journal *Foreign Affairs* in February 2024, Ramachandra Guha says that 'the strains placed on Indian federalism may boil over in 2026, when parliamentary seats are scheduled to be reallocated according to the next census, to be conducted in that year. Then, what is now merely a divergence between north and south might become an actual divide.'[24] He then emphasised how the NDA government led by Atal Bihari Vajpayee had accommodated the wishes of the south in 2001 by extending the embargo on delimitation:

> In 2001, when a reallocation of seats based on population was proposed, the southern states argued that it would discriminate against them for following progressive health and education policies in prior decades that had reduced birth rates and enhanced women's freedom. The BJP-led coalition government then in power recognized the merits of the south's case and, with the consent of the opposition, proposed that the reallocation be delayed for a further 25 years.[25]

Guha expresses his fear that the present government will not put it on hold again:

> But if Modi and the BJP are in power, they will almost certainly mandate the process of reallocation based on population in both the Lok Sabha, the lower house, and the Rajya Sabha, which will then substantially favor the more populous if economically lagging states of the north. The southern states are bound to protest. Indian federalism and unity will struggle to cope with the fallout.[26]

In the article 'The Geography of Power, in North, South & West India', published in *Deccan Chronicle* on 11 December 2023, Sanjay Baru, economist, author and former media advisor to Prime Minister Manmohan Singh, analysed delimitation and reallocation of seats in Parliament in terms of a regional balance of power which he believes has over the years tilted in favour of the north and the west to the detriment of the south. He concluded:

> It is therefore not surprising that many political leaders from southern states have been articulating their concern about the impact of a new delimitation exercise that may increase the parliamentary representation of the Hindi-speaking states and further tilt political power in their favour.[27]

Some other experts have also expressed their reservations about delimitation. Kalaiyarasan A. and Christophe Jafferlot argued in an article published in the *Indian Express* on 3 August 2023:

> The exercise to delimit parliamentary constituencies could deepen the north-south divide. The south has controlled population growth by following central government policies. The continued emphasis on women's education in the south has contributed to a fall in the total fertility rates in the region much before several other states in the country and now is in the zone of less than replacement rate…The exercise of delimitation could reduce the political clout of the southern states.[28]

They concluded, 'while recognizing a person's equal voice in the democratic process is important, recognizing the regional balance of power in a federal structure is also essential.'[29]

—w—

Let us move on to the issue of fiscal devolution from the Centre, which is closely related to the north–south demographic as well as the development divide, since population is an important criterion for fiscal allocation from the Centre to the states. For nearly a quarter of a century, leaders from the south have protested against the north getting a 'disproportionate' share because of its larger population. The latest round of protest has taken a serious turn. Reacting to the interim budget presented by Finance Minister Nirmala Sitharaman on 1 February 2024, D.K. Suresh, a Congress Member of Parliament from Karnataka, crossed the red line to advocate a separate country for south India:

> Today, we are seeing development funds being given to North Indian states. We are seeing a lot of injustice. If we don't condemn it, in the coming days we might be forced to demand a separate country due to the imposition on us by Hindi regions.[30]

He further said:

> From us (Karnataka) more than Rs 4 lakh crore is collected as various taxes. How much are we getting back? If it is not addressed in the 16th Finance Commission, then people of South India have to raise their voices.[31]

Though D.K. Suresh's unprecedented statement has been widely criticised even in the south, it does show the depth of emotions associated with the north–south divide. Earlier, in 2019, some media stories evoking similar sentiments, clubbing the southern states under the label of 'The Republic of South India' had appeared.[32] Prime Minister Modi had to face protest on his visit to Chennai in 2018; he was greeted with slogans of 'Go Back, Modi'.[33]

In February 2024 itself, southern states such as Karnataka and Kerala organised protests in Delhi against the Central government. Karnataka's protest, which took place on 7 February, was led by Chief Minister Siddaramaiah, who stated:

> We are raising the issue of discrimination meted out by the government of India to the state of Karnataka and other southern states.[34]

The next day there was a similar protest led by Kerala Chief Minister Pinarayi Vijayan, who said 'the body blow to India's federal structure is coming from the Union eating into the states' financial resources. It is being alleged that the same people who wax eloquent about cooperative federalism, have tried to undercut the resources to be allocated to the states by the Finance Commission.'[35] An even wider political rift between the north and the south on the subject of population growth might, therefore, be in the making.

There are many other, far more moderate, voices. Thus, the former governor of Reserve Bank of India D. Subba Rao said in an interview with *Business Today* published on 2 May 2024:

> If you take rich states like Maharashtra and Tamil Nadu, every rupee they contribute to the central tax pool, they get back less than a rupee. On the other hand, poor states like Bihar and Jharkhand get more than a rupee for every rupee they contribute to the central tax pool.[36]

Defending this as a 'cross-subsidisation' prevalent in many countries, Subba Rao, however, cautioned:

> Today, South India has a bigger representation in the Parliament than North India on a ballpark estimate. And if the delimitation is done, that will be equalized. That means that South Indian states will lose parliament seats relative to north Indian states ... So what will happen then is a double whammy for the South that even as they lose political clout, they have to continue to subsidise the rest of the country.[37]

His advice was:

> It's (delimitation) got to be phase-wise. And, there have to be some end dates put forth for cross-subsidisation ... India is one country, and we want prosperity to be evenly distributed. But I think this has to come about through some formula-based adjustments both on the fiscal and political dimensions.[38]

Similarly, participating in a panel discussion on 'The Big Bets for Tamil Nadu's Trillion US Dollar Economy' at the two-day Global Investors Meet 2024 organised by the state government, former Chief Economic Advisor to the Government of India, Arvind Subramanian, said:

> If, for example, the political representation is changed which gives more relative power to the Hindi heartland relative to the Southern states that have slower population growth, the disaffection will grow because the

> Southern states will say we contribute much more fiscally (but) we are losing political power.[39]

On fiscal devolution from the Centre to the states, he said:

> The devolution (of central taxes) has a big amount of redistribution, going from the richer southern states to the poorer Hindi heartland states. That is a part of national building, keeping India together. But over time, when other things went bad, southern states are increasingly saying 'Why should we contribute to the redistribution consistently over time.'[40]

Subramanian then gave the following advice:

> Southern states including Tamil Nadu should retain a slightly larger portion of resources that are coming from the Centre. I think that has to be part of the new social contract going forward.[41]

Earlier, the constitution of the Fifteenth Finance Commission in November 2017 had sparked a major controversy. It was the eighth point of the Terms of Reference (ToR) saying 'the Commission shall use the population data of 2011 while making its recommendations' that led to the controversy.[42]

It was alleged that the power given to the Commission by the ToR would have huge implications—economic as well as political—for federalism. The then Finance Minister of Kerala, Thomas Isaac, opposed the move because, in his opinion, it would go against the interests of the states that had already attained the replacement rate of population growth.[43] Similar opposition came from the Chief Minister of Karnataka, Siddaramaiah, who had asserted that Karnataka contributes 10 per cent to the tax revenue of the country, but, owing to this move, might receive only 5 per cent of the total Central funds allocated to the states.[44]

Another stalwart from the south, former Chief Minister of undivided Andhra Pradesh N. Chandrababu Naidu issued a statement on 7 May 2018, objecting to the change in the mandate of the Fifteenth Finance Commission:

> South Indian states are under the threat of losing their eminence because they were successful in population control. It is not right for the Centre to penalise such states.[45]

In another statement, he reiterated his stance:

> It is not right to penalise states that are in the forefront in population control. We will not tolerate this injustice. We will fight till justice is secured.[46]

What Naidu wanted to convey was that it was essential to recognise the commendable commitment of the south Indian states towards family planning. Consequently, penalising them unjustly through the utilisation of the 2011 Census for fiscal allocation by the Fifteenth Finance Commission or by fresh delimitation and redistribution of parliamentary seats was unwarranted. It should be noted here that the population size of the various states of the country is among the important criteria used by various Finance Commissions, the erstwhile Planning Commission and by the Union government in general for the devolution of fiscal resources in the form of tax revenues as well as grants-in-aid. Using fifty-year-old data clearly increases the weightage of states whose population experienced earlier growth spurt.

The seriousness of the issue can be gauged from the use of the word 'penalise' by Chandrababu Naidu, who was equally concerned that south Indian states might lose seats in Parliament, if redistribution is carried out on the basis of the 2011 Census.[47] There was an indignant tone in Naidu's statement, who claimed to speak on behalf of the whole of the south when he declared that they were not prepared to tolerate the 'injustice' meted out to them, and they will put up a fight until 'justice is secured'. Sticking to his twenty-year-old line of argument over dividing the north and the south in terms of population control and fiscal discipline, Naidu asserted: 'There is nothing called Centre's or state's money. It's the taxpayers' money. The southern states contribute maximum tax revenues to the Centre. But they are diverting the money to the development of northern states.'[48]

This echoes a similar debate when the recommendations of the Eleventh Finance Commission headed by A.M. Khusro were announced in 2000. Naidu's statement as Chief Minister of undivided Andhra Pradesh in 2000 while reacting to the recommendations of the Eleventh Finance Commission is strikingly similar in tone to his statement of 2018. In 2000, his Telugu Desam Party (TDP) was an ally of the NDA government, then in power at the Centre. Denouncing the provisions recommended by the Commission, an upset Naidu had said:

> The recommendations are loaded in favour of governments that flouted fiscal discipline and resorted to reckless borrowing while putting a dampener on progressive and pro-development governments like Maharashtra, Gujarat, Haryana, Tamil Nadu, Karnataka and Andhra Pradesh.[49]

Naidu had convened a meeting of the chief ministers of seventeen states on 21 August 2000, apparently to take stock of the situation and address the common grievance shared by other states. In this endeavour, he found support from the then Chief Minister of Maharashtra Vilasrao Deshmukh, who described the aggrieved states as the 'injured' parties.[50] Deshmukh dubbed it as 'injustice to the developed states which should have received incentives and bonus'. He asserted that 'we have been penalised for our work. This is a disincentive for progress'.[51] A dismayed Deshmukh had added:

> We have tapped as many sources as we could and squeezed the maximum out of them. Yet we are giving to the Centre the maximum in collection of duties and taxes. But this way in the not-so-distant future Maharashtra will turn into another Uttar Pradesh or Bihar.[52]

In response to the report, which was seen as reducing the volume of aid and Central tax revenue share rightfully due to the southern states, former Vice-Chairman of the Kerala State Planning Board, I.S. Gulati, had lamented: 'It is not just the shareable Central tax revenues, but also the grants-in-aid where the southern States lose out. Their better economic performance is being considered a liability.'[53] He rhetorically enquired of the Union government: 'Are we being penalised for our achievements?' Gulati further expressed his disapproval of the recommendations: 'It is a particularly serious grievance which the southern States will not take lying down.'[54]

—~—

Considering the salience of the political debate over delimitation in the last fifty years, it is evident that it stirs strong emotions and encompasses multiple dimensions. The strong opposition to delimitation and reallocation of seats in Parliament from prominent southern leaders such as M.K. Stalin, Kanimozhi, Shashi Tharoor and others is merely a reflection of the significance of the north–south divide in contemporary times. The supposed injustice highlighted by Naidu and others both in the course of the discussions revolving around the Eleventh Finance Commission and the Fifteenth Finance Commission reflects the same divide and ignites many other discontents in the southern states.[55] Their opposition is grounded in their sincere belief that the population growth of the south came down since 1970s due to their better implementation of the family planning programme, while the north has failed on this front and has, instead, increased its population disproportionately.

Thus, maintaining the 1976 embargo on delimitation and redistribution of seats in Parliament has been one of the principal concerns of the leaders from the south, though fund allocation has also stirred up emotions from time to time. The issue is also symptomatic of a pronounced divide that has emerged over the last forty years between India's north and south on many counts—social, economic, political, as well as cultural.[56]

From this vantage point, one might ask the following questions: What are the rationale and implications of using the Census of 1971 for population-based allocations such as the number of seats in Parliament? What is the validity of the claim of 'injustice' made by some leaders from the south? Is the mandate to use the latest data for calculations involving population really 'penalising' for the south? *Demography, Representation, Delimitation* strives to provide plausible answers to such questions. It also suggests measures to address the north–south divide. It debunks the myths about the north–south demographic divide that have been nurtured over the last fifty years.

II

The Debate Around Delimitation and the Constitutional Provisions for Representation

Since the 1970s, population growth in India has become inextricably linked with delimitation and redistribution of seats in Parliament. The 1976 embargo on seat distribution in Parliament was scheduled to expire in 2001. A fresh delimitation as well as distribution of seats among states was to be done based on the Census of 2001. However, the Vajpayee government chose to bring a constitutional amendment to extend the embargo for twenty-five years, until 2026. There is nothing in the Amendment itself explaining its rationale, but the Statement of Objects and Reasons of the Act says:

1. Provisos to Articles 82 and 170(3) of the Constitution provide that no fresh readjustment of constituencies can be undertaken until the figures of the first census taken after the year 2000 are published. These provisos were inserted by the Constitution (42nd Amendment) Act, 1976 as a measure to boost family planning norms. Since the first census to be taken after the year 2000 has already begun, the constitutional embargo on undertaking fresh delimitation will lapse as soon as the figures of this census are published.
2. There have been consistent demands both for and against undertaking the exercise of fresh delimitation. Keeping in view the progress of family planning programmes in different parts of the country, the Government, as part of the National Population Policy strategy, recently decided to extend the current freeze on undertaking fresh delimitation up to the year 2026 as a motivational measure to enable the state governments to pursue the agenda for population stabilisation.[57]

What is unequivocally stated in the Statement of Objects and Reasons is that Parliament was looking for a rationale for the passage of the bill (91st Amendment Bill) and being well aware of the differences between the performance of various Indian states on family planning, the NDA government decided to continue with the policy launched in 1976 of incentivising the states with a better record of family planning. The decision to freeze 1971 as the base year for seat allocation until 2026 was clearly based on this logic.

The Parliamentary debate on the bill provides valuable insights into the thought behind the extension of the embargo, as also the critiques of that thinking made by several members. Moving the bill, Law Minister Arun Jaitley said:

> The rationale for which the number of constituencies will be frozen and subsequent increases in population will not be taken into consideration

while determining the seats for election to this House and also to the State Assemblies, essentially has been that there are some States which have implemented the family planning programme very effectively and there are some States where it has not been effectively implemented. The National Population Policy also envisages the year 2026 as the year in which the population of the country would stabilise. Therefore, what was true till 2000 is sought to be frozen till the year 2026, that is, the year in which we anticipate hopefully that the population figure in the country would stabilise. The effect of this amendment would be that the number of constituencies in each State, and therefore totally throughout the country, would remain as they are at present.[58]

The NDA government was, therefore, convinced that family planning could effectively curb population growth in a couple of decades and that certain states, mainly those from the south, had controlled their population by better implementation of family planning, as compared to some other states (read north Indian states) which had not effectively implemented family planning.

This idea is fundamentally flawed and is part of a myth built over the decades, both because it gives too much credit to family planning in the decline of population growth and because it completely ignores the historical aspect of the matter. The statement 'what was true till 2000 is sought to be frozen till 2026' gives an impression that this was just a routine extension of an existing provision about which the government need not give any careful consideration. The assertion that population will stabilise by 2026 also seems to have been belied, as we are now just one year away from 2026 and the population of India is still growing rather well. Jaitley then went on to say that while the number of seats of every state will thus remain frozen, fresh delimitation to even out the vast inequalities in the size of constituencies within states will be allowed by the Amendment.

The most compelling argument against the logic of disincentivising some states with a view to secure greater commitment from them towards population control was articulated by veteran parliamentarian and former Lok Sabha Speaker Shivraj Patil on 21 August 2001 in the Lok Sabha during his participation in the debate on the 91st Amendment Bill.

Responding to the claim made by Arun Jaitley with respect to stabilisation of India's population by 2026, Patil said:

> What was the population in 1975? It was nearly 70 crores. In 2001, we are about 100 crores, and in 2026, we would be nearly 140 crores. The hon. minister says that the population will stabilise in 2026. Sir, I find it very difficult to accept this optimism. In 1976 it was thought that the population may not increase because of this provision. But population has increased and has reached a figure of nearly 100 crore and more. What is the guarantee that population would remain where it is today? I find it very difficult to accept this logic. To think that because the number is frozen, population will not increase is not correct.[59]

The point made by Patil takes us to the heart of the problem: the idea that the freezing of seats would somehow act as a strong enough disincentive for the northern and western states to control their population. It assumes that there is a causal link between the two and that population growth could be effectively curbed by such measures. If population growth continued unabated for a quarter of a century despite the embargo, there was no basis to assume that the extension of the embargo over the next quarter century would make any difference whatsoever. In effect, then, the extension of the embargo only meant continuation of distortion in democratic representation ostensibly on the ground of creating a level playing field for population control. Patil further asserted:

> I do not understand the logic adopted by the Government. Now, in the Statement of the Objects and Reasons of the Bill it has been stated that as part of the National Population Policy Strategy recently decided to extend the current freeze on undertaking fresh delimitation up to the year 2026 as a motivational measure. What kind of a motivational measure? This logic is not acceptable. Whom are we trying to hoodwink? This is not correct. Something else is required. If any law that could be helpful in controlling population is required, then a law like disallowing a person to contest elections if he or she has more than two children will be more useful than a law of this kind. The Government is proposing a law on a logic which is not acceptable and is also not correct. It is not scientific.[60]

Shivraj Patil, therefore, questioned the fundamental logic behind the extension of the embargo. He argued that there was no evidence that the embargo would effectively curb population growth in the states that were perceived as lacking efficient implementation of the family planning programme. What he implied was that people do not base their family choices on political representation with the members of Parliament in mind. Thus, like the previous twenty-five years, there was no realistic chance of the embargo having any effect on the rapid population growth in many states over the next twenty-five years. Highlighting the anomaly of keeping the numbers in the Lok Sabha frozen for fifty years, despite massive growth in population, he said:

> Sir, the number of Members in the Lok Sabha in 1976 was 545. The number of Members in the Lok Sabha in 2001 is 545 and the number of Members in the Lok Sabha in the year 2026 is going to be 545. Each Member of this Lok Sabha today represents more than ten lakh voters. In the year 2026, each Member of Lok Sabha would represent nearly 15 lakh voters.[61]

He also suggested a via media to satisfy all states:

> It can be possible for us to find a formula which can say that on the basis of increase in the population of a State that has implemented family planning programme in a proper manner, increase in the seats in other States should be allowed so that no State is allowed to have an advantage over any State that has implemented the family planning programme in a proper manner. It can be possible. But, I think this issue has not been considered.[62]

However, there were other members like Anadi Sahu from Orissa who put the blame for rapid population growth on five 'delinquent' and 'recalcitrant' states, including Uttar Pradesh, Rajasthan, Madhya Pradesh, Bihar and Orissa.[63] While concluding, he justified the freeze on the ground that the population of India 'has grown five-fold compared to the three-fold population growth of the world'.[64] Sahu's untenable implication was that the population rise in different parts of the world which had such vastly different demographic history as well as social and economic development should have happened at the same rate.[65] This was, in effect, a reiteration of the problematic concept of 'world population'—a notion that had faced strong criticism from the French demographer Alfred

Sauvy in 1949. It highlighted how the narrative of a 'population explosion' had overshadowed and stifled rational thinking on demographic growth.

Another critical intervention in the debate was made by Somnath Chatterjee, a veteran parliamentarian from the Communist Party of India (Marxist) who later became Lok Sabha Speaker. Recalling that he was present in Parliament when the freezing happened in 1976 during the Emergency, he noted that 'hardly there was any discussion on that. Since then, I do not find any real study of the situation'.[66] He emphatically denied the presumed link between the embargo and population growth:

> Let us not try to give an impression that through this Bill we shall be able to control the population. After all, nobody produces children on the basis of who will be representing his son in Parliament. I do not know why it is being repeated here. One could have understood the so-called justification then. In the Statement of Objects and Reasons it is stated that it was done to boost family planning norms. Of course, family planning is essential for this country. Everybody admits that, but no government follows that.[67]

He unequivocally declared, 'I do not know what is the connection between the number of Members and the fertility rate in this country. This is only *ad hocism* and this is only to carry on the present state of affairs.'[68]

Though the Bill was passed with an overwhelming majority, it was quite evident that the principal impetus for the extension of the embargo came from the southern states. The interventions of the MPs from the south make it abundantly clear. Senior TDP leader K. Yerrannaidu said:

> We are the first to represent this case to the Union Government. The hon. Chief Minister of Andhra Pradesh, Shri Chandrababu Naidu represented many times to the effect that status quo should be maintained. In 1976, the then Prime Minister, Shrimati Indira Gandhi amended the Constitution to bring in amendments in the National Family Planning Policy for freezing the constituency number. This Government is also continuing the same thing. Hence, we support this amendment.[69]

Similarly, welcoming the Bill, A. Krishnaswamy of DMK noted that 'due to decline in the rate of growth of the population, earlier there was a proposal to decrease the number of Lok Sabha constituencies in our state.

So, the people of Tamil Nadu were against the policy of the Government'.[70] He proceeded to reiterate the long-standing, yet unverified, assertion that the southern states had managed to reduce their population growth due to improved family planning:

> Our TDP leader, Shri Yerrannaidu, spoke very well. I appreciate his speech. When we decide about the seats, we have to make the policy about family planning compulsory. Tamil Nadu is number one State in following the Government's policy for implementation of family planning. Instead of giving a reward for that, they are trying to punish us by declining the seats. It is an injustice.[71]

T.M. Selvaganapathy of DMK repeated the claim that the 'States in the Southern region are sincerely and wholeheartedly following the population control measures' and '... we will stoutly oppose any move that would reduce our representation in the Lok Sabha.'[72] He then presented the southern perspective on embargo in a forthright manner:

> If this Bill is not passed, we would be placed in a very precarious situation of losing many number of seats in the Lok Sabha as well as in the Assemblies. If this Bill is not passed, the Southern States, that is, Andhra Pradesh, Tamil Nadu, Kerala and Karnataka would be losing a sizeable number of seats in the Lok Sabha. Whereas the States in the Northern region, the BIMARU, that is, Bihar, Madhya Pradesh, Rajasthan and Uttar Pradesh would be gaining more seats. Their seats will go up to 219 from 204, whereas we will be giving up almost about 16 seats, if this present situation continues till 2026 and if this Bill is not passed.[73]

There were, however, other voices of protest too. Questioning the claim made by some of his fellow MPs 'that people have deliberately increased their population to have more Parliament seats', Raghuvansh Prasad Singh of Rashtriya Janata Dal (RJD) pointed out that the bill was a violation of democratic principles:[74]

> The present Constitution Amendment Bill is not based on any principle. It does not have any uniform policy. I am not ready to support it. The democracy is based on the power of votes and the fate of the Governments are decided by the number of votes. So, the number of Parliamentary seats of a State should be based on the population of the State. The

> Constitution Amendment Bill which has been moved in the House is not based on the uniform policy. Since you have majority in the House so you may get this Bill passed by the House but it is not based on the common principle of justice.[75]

Replying to the questions raised by members, Arun Jaitley emphasised the necessity of embargo because of presumably differential implementation of family planning in the states:

> The Family Planning Programme has to be enforced by the States. The Central Government has a responsibility. There are some State Governments which are trying to effectively implement the Family Planning Programme. Now, those States which are effectively trying to implement the Family Planning Programme, if they are faced with the political disincentive that their representation in Parliament will decline because they have effectively implemented the Family Planning Programme, we are then creating a disincentive for those who are effectively trying to implement the Family Planning Programme in this country.[76]

III
History and Pre-history of Delimitation Embargo

A quarter century prior to 2001, the 42nd Amendment Act passed in 1976 during the Emergency without much debate had made the embargo on delimitation a part of the National Population Policy (NPP), which included many other measures for population control. The Act stated the following:

> In Article 81 of the Constitution, to clause (3), the following proviso shall be added, namely:
>
> Provided that the reference in this clause to the last preceding census of which the relevant figures have been published shall, until the relevant figures for the first census taken after the year 2000 have been published, be construed as a reference to the 1971 census.[77]

The rationale behind the amendment is not clear from the Act itself. The Statement of Objects and Reasons made by Law Minister H.R. Gokhale, however, explained:

> A Constitution to be living must be growing. If the impediments to the growth of the Constitution are not removed, the Constitution will suffer a virtual atrophy. The question of amending the Constitution for removing the difficulties which have arisen in achieving the objective of socio-economic revolution, which would end poverty and ignorance and disease and inequality of opportunity, has been engaging the active attention of Government and the public for some years now.[78]

The mention of 'socio-economic revolution' was evidently an ideological stance embedded in the Act. It was one of the motives for fixing the 1971 Census as the baseline for freezing delimitation. Has this socio-economic revolution happened, one wonders? Have poverty and ignorance ended? Has the promise of bringing down inequality been fulfilled? Insofar as inequality is concerned, it can be safely asserted that instead of it being wiped out, there has been a steady and worrisome growth in regional disparity in terms of social and economic development.

There is no clarity on how the decision was arrived at within the government, as records show only an incomplete picture. The note on freezing of delimitation initiated by A.K. Srinivasmurthy, Joint Secretary and Legislative Counsel, Election Commission of India (ECI), does not mention how and when the decision to freeze the seats was made, but it asserts that the 'the Government has taken a decision that representation in Parliament and State Legislatures and in other elective bodies will remain tied to the 1971-Census figures till 2001'.[79] It asserts that the move 'will certainly help to improve the performance of family planning programme by removing the fears of some of the States which have been showing good progress in family planning that their representation in Parliament would be adversely affected.'[80] The legal section of the ECI advised that even the limit of 2001 on the lifting of embargo was not required, as 'this would avoid further amendments of the Constitution in case this freezing is extended beyond 2001 AD'.[81] So, there was clearly an anticipation that the embargo might be extended in 2001. On 18 June 1976, based on the advice of Deputy Election Commissioner P.I. Jacob, Chief Election Commissioner T. Swaminathan noted his preference for freezing of constituencies: 'In order to prevent undue gain in numbers of seats to areas dominated by communities or group of people who are against the practice of family planning, it is our view that the extent of constituencies should also be frozen'.[82]

Earlier, in January 1976, there was an interesting proposal put forward by C.K. Chandrappan, an MP from Kerala, to treat voters, and not population, as the point of reference for seat allocation and to put a cap of 5 lakh voters on each constituency. Chandrappan moved a private member's bill to this effect. In the official records, it was argued that 'this will have the effect of increasing the number of seats in the House of the People to an unlimited number, whenever there is an increase in the number of voters in the country'.[83] The proposed change from the constitutional norm of population-based and not voter-based seat allocation was also pointed out in discussions. The practical problems in the implementation of such a scheme were pointed out. It was further argued that 'the fixing of maximum limit of 5 lakh voters to a constituency will prove extremely difficult, if not physically impossible, to delimit the constituencies'.[84] Moreover, it was noted that 'a similar restriction that the population of a Parliamentary Constituency returning one member shall not exceed 7,50,000 existed in the Constitution and it was removed by suitable amendment to the Constitution in 1953'.[85] The Bill was not passed by the Parliament.

Among the most intriguing aspects of the freeze on delimitation placed in 1976 is that in 1971, DMK MP Murasoli Maran—who later occupied many important portfolios as Union Cabinet Minister—had, on behalf of his party, moved a private member's bill demanding such a freeze based on the Census of 1951. The grounds were also the same, the supposedly differential implementation of family planning in the south versus the north. During the debate on the Bill in the Lok Sabha, Maran had argued 'that no state should be penalised by the loss of its representation in the House of the people for sincerely implementing the family planning programme and no State should be deprived of revenues by way of grants or plan assistance by the Union just because of that reason'.[86] He highlighted the loss of two seats each by Andhra Pradesh and Tamil Nadu in the previous delimitation based on 1961 Census and argued that a freeze was needed to address 'the problem of galloping rise in population'.[87] Maran claimed that because of its sincere implementation of family planning programme formulated by the Union government, Tamil Nadu incurred a loss of two seats.[88]

Maran also claimed that his state was not getting 'enough grants, allowances and assistance normally recommended by the Finance Commission only because that also follows the pattern of Population figures of the previous census'.[89] Tamil Nadu's population share had decreased from 8.3 per cent in 1951 to 7.5 in 1971, and this resulted in the loss of ten crore rupees annually for the state, according to Maran. He proposed that 'the alternative should be that those States which are implementing the family planning programmes should get increased representation in this Parliament'.[90] He preferred 1951 both because, as per his statement, Tamil Nadu had implemented family planning better than other states, but also because 'we began our democratic career with our republican constitution in 1950–51, which should be the benchmark'.[91] Maran dismissed the constitutional provision of 'one person, one vote', one value as tantamount to 'the more the children, the merrier the politicians';[92] 'the larger the population, regardless of unemployment, illiteracy, backward agriculture or oppression by the crime of untouchability against the socially under-privileged, the larger will be the share of their parliamentary representation'. He described this as 'an antisocial policy'.[93] He claimed that Rajamannar Committee on States Autonomy, whose report had just been submitted, had supported the idea that 'the number of seats fixed for each State in 1951 should remain unaltered except where there was population increase subject to a maximum'.[94] Maran demanded either implementation of this formula or a 'bonus of seats in the Parliament' to the states that were supposedly implementing family planning better than others.[95]

There was almost universal opposition to the Bill by members cutting across regions and parties. Thus R.D. Bhandare, Congress MP from Bombay Central (Maharashtra), dismissed the demand on the ground that the Constitution was based on 'the principle of equality of the people.'[96] He asserted that no country was doing anything like this, citing the example of Canada and USSR. He concluded that 'these grievances are not sufficient enough to amend the Constitution and giving up the principle of equality of the people enunciated and incorporated in the Constitution under articles 81 and 82'.[97]

Somnath Chatterjee of the CPI(M) was emphatic in his rejection of the demand:

> We cannot amend the Constitution and make a provision in regard to the representation in the House of the People on the basis of the failure or success of the family planning programme. It requires something more than that.[98]

He argued that freezing seat allocation at the 1951 figures will create an 'unreal situation' that will give 'preference of weightage to particular states'. Importantly, he underlined that 'increase or decrease in population may not be only due to the success or failure of the family planning programme. There may be diverse causes and reasons for it'.[99] In any case, Chatterjee concluded, increase or decrease in population over time had to be taken into consideration as per the latest census figures.[100]

N. Sivappa, MP from Hassan in Karnataka, was equally strong in his criticism: 'After all, we are living in a world of progress and committed to progressive policies and programmes. When that is our commitment, when that is our aspiration, I do not know why we have to go back from 1971 to 1951.'[101] He also countered Maran's facts by pointing out that Tamil Nadu had lost two seats in the previous delimitation mainly because of the transfer of territory to other states as per the States Reorganisation Act, 1956.[102] He dismissed the demand for freezing representation at 1951 and asserted that there was 'no reason why it should be 1951. No case has been made out'.[103] Further, he took 'strong objection to some States developing some disintegrating tendencies, methods and manners'.[104]

Similarly, N.K.P. Salve, MP from Betul in Madhya Pradesh, who would later occupy many important ministerial positions at the Centre, strongly criticised Maran's Bill, describing equality of representation as 'a cardinal and a very basic and fundamental concept' not to be tinkered with.[105] He even asked: 'Would it make any difference if instead of 30, there will be 32 members here?'[106] He dismissed the presumed connection between acceptance of family planning by people and representation in Parliament:

> Sir, rarely have I heard arguments which are more fantastic than this. They have no idea; it makes little difference to people whether there are 30 representatives of Tamil Nadu or 31 or 32, 33 or 35. 35 of them can do as good work as all 520 of us put together … the Mover seems to reduce

> the entire human problem to a simple mathematical formula like the Malthus theory. He worked this out with some geometry and came out with certain Malthusian proposition on population—someone said he propounded this theory without consulting his wife and that is why the human aspect was completely forgotten. But, Sir let us not be guilty of amending the Constitution without proper consultations.[107]

Salve concluded with a damning comment on Maran and his Bill:

> Voluminous statistics have been quoted by my hon. Friend. I was simply overwhelmed by it. I am a student of accounts, but I was overwhelmed by the statistics. I was reminded of the saying that there are three types of lies, namely lies, damned lies and statistics.[108]

It is, therefore, evident that the delinking of latest population figures from representation in Lok Sabha has been discussed in Parliament at least since 1971, even before the embargo on delimitation was placed in 1976, at the behest of the south.

IV
Critiques of the 2001 Freeze on Delimitation

Coming back to the extension of the freeze in 2001, the discussion continued outside of the Parliament as well. There were several media reports on the subject. On 3 August 2001, Jay Raina wrote in the *Hindustan Times*:

> Several states, especially from the south, have been demanding extension of the embargo on increasing the Lok Sabha and state Legislative Assembly seats due to fear of losing out after successfully implementing family planning programmes, at least as compared to Northern States such as Uttar Pradesh, Bihar, Rajasthan, etc. Andhra Pradesh and Tamil Nadu governments have been in the forefront of this demand. The contention of these southern states has been supported by the Union Ministry of Health and Family Welfare. The ministry foresees national level achievement of the replacement level of fertility in around 25 years.[109]

On 22 August 2001, *The Statesman* noted how Jaitley had presented the bill 'as part of the National Population Policy strategy'. It further said, 'the bill ensures continuity in terms of number so that states failing to check population don't benefit by having more seats in the Lok Sabha and states implementing population control measures are not punished by reduced representation in the lower house'.[110]

The Times of India of 24 August 2001 reported:

> The passage of this Bill comes after a fierce national debate, with the BIMARU (Bihar, Madhya Pradesh, Rajasthan and Uttar Pradesh) ranged on one side and the rest—particularly the southern States—ranged on the other. While the BIMARU states were for an increase in the number of seats as the population in these states has grown considerably, the others felt that if the seats were increased, their political clout would shrink as the number of seats would proportionately decrease since they have been more successful in family planning.[111]

So, according to all three newspaper articles, the rationale for extension of the embargo was the so-called north–south divide on population control through family planning.

There were critical comments from some experts on the freezing of seats until 2026. Thus, K.C. Sivaramakrishnan, honorary research professor and chairman of the governing board of Centre for Policy Research (CPR) and former secretary in both the Ministry of Urban Development and the Ministry of Commerce, wrote an article 'North-South Divide and Delimitation Blues' in *Economic & Political Weekly* (*EPW*) in September 2000, questioning the rationale behind it:

> Our political parties and their leaders feel that by continuing the freeze on the inter-state allocation of Lok Sabha seats they are absolved of all need to think about political demography for another 25 years. This is yet another reflection of an uninformed mind-set, tending to avoid difficult questions, as much out ignorance as of apprehension.[112]

He called the freeze of 'questionable value' and asserted that 'the real fear is not about population control but 'political control'.[113] Noting that the north would have gained seats at the expense of the south, Sivaramakrishnan asserted that 'this is the crux of the fear about the so-called 'north-south divide'.[114] He emphasised the need for periodic delimitation because 'parity of constituencies is an essential part of the representative character of all elected bodies', and concluded:[115]

The 42nd Amendment to the Constitution carried out in 1976 put the process in cold storage. As a result, a whole generation of political parties and voters have grown up unaware of the need, usefulness and application of the delimitation process. The underlying principle of periodic delimitation is that the value of any one citizen's vote should be the same as that of another, no more no less.[116]

In April 2001, after the Bill was introduced, in an article published in *EPW*, political scientist Alistair McMillan said:

The connection between the implementation of family planning strategy and the allocation of seats to the national parliament is far too tenuous to be taken other than as a smokescreen for more meaningful political considerations. To deny a person an equal voice in the democratic process because they happen to be living in a state that has had a high population growth rate is clearly undefendable.[117]

Explaining the reasons for the Bill, McMillan surmised:

This seems to be partly driven by the regional ambitions of the BJP and the Congress parties, who are unwilling to alienate support, and are probably right in thinking that the losers are more likely to make an issue of any redistribution of seats than the winners. The issue has been sensitised by the key role played in the National Democratic Alliance by parties from Tamil Nadu, and the fact that assembly elections are due in Kerala and Tamil Nadu in May 2001.[118]

McMillan also mentioned that DMK leader Murasoli Maran had politicised delimitation by making it an issue in Tamil Nadu Assembly elections, accusing the Congress of not supporting the bill for extension of freeze on delimitation.[119]

On 21 August 2001, Yogendra Yadav of the Centre for the Study of Developing Societies (CSDS) wrote an article for *The Indian Express* titled 'Democracy in Deep Freeze'. He argued:

The same specious reasoning is used to justify this freeze today as was used by the Sanjay Gandhi coterie during the Emergency: that it is a population control measure! Allocating Lok Sabha seats according to population, goes the argument, will amount to punishing states that have succeeded in controlling population. I have never understood

> this assumed relationship between political geography and human reproductive behaviour. To my knowledge, no couple produces children with an eye on the calculus of parliamentary seats. Nor is there any instance of a state undermining its population control measures in order to gain more seats in Parliament.[120]

Similarly, Sanjay Kumar, Yadav's colleague at CSDS, wrote an article in *The Hindu* on 17 September 2001, titled 'Delimitation of Constituencies', in which he raised the question, 'Does this not lead to disenfranchisement of a large section of the population, a majority of whom are poor, deprived and backward?' He then went on to make an important point that three delimitations had taken place before the embargo of 1976, and that the north had actually lost some seats in them:

> Merely because of the fear of a possible North–South divide, is it right to impose a freeze on the number of seats till 2026? In the past from the first delimitation in 1952 till the third in 1972, Karnataka and Kerala gained seats—from 26 to 28 and from 18 to 20—while Uttar Pradesh lost. From 86 seats allocated during the first delimitation, its number of seats was reduced to 85 during the second delimitation.[121]

—∞—

It is, therefore, evident that for the last fifty years, Indian policymakers have decided to keep in abeyance the constitutional requirement of fresh delimitation and state-wise redistribution of seats in Parliament every decade based on the success or failure of family planning. There has been little effort to understand why the population growth rates of many Indian states have been higher after 1971. In a critical examination of the purported rationale for such a connection, Alaka Malwade Basu (1997) has described it as 'politicization of fertility',[122] whereby population control is accorded primacy over everything else, potentially even overshadowing the fundamental democratic right of citizens to equal representation. Over the decades, the policy has become so entrenched that the very thought of using a date later than 1971 creates ripples across the Indian political scenario and reignites the old fear among the southern states. These fears are suitably expressed by former Union Law Secretary and Secretary General of the Lok Sabha T.K. Viswanathan:

> The concerns expressed by the States in 1976 which necessitated the freezing of seat allocation on the basis of 1971 population figures would appear to hold good even today and have to be addressed to the satisfaction of all stakeholders.[123]

In 2016, Chandrababu Naidu took the country by surprise when he claimed:

> Hitherto, our focus was on population control. But now we have to promote population. The trend has changed.[124]

In fact, he made his agenda clear in 2019 when in a statement he unambiguously favoured population growth:

> Our government has done away with this clause. Now those having even four children can contest the elections.[125]

The clause Naidu was referring to was an earlier decision by the Andhra Pradesh government to debar those with more than two children from contesting local body elections. Naidu, who is currently the chief minister of what is now Andhra Pradesh, has again stirred up the subject of declining population growth in the south. In a statement made on 19 October 2024, he has talked about 'population management' and said: 'The state government is thinking of bringing a law that would make only those with more than two children eligible to contest local body elections.'[126] Naidu asserts that 'government may provide more benefits to families with more children'. The reversal of his quarter-century-old stand on population growth emanates from a larger concern about ageing, which is a common feature of post-transition societies:

> Though we have a demographic advantage until 2047, signs of ageing problem are starting to appear in south India, including Andhra. Many countries like Japan, China, and some European nations are struggling with this problem, having a larger elderly population. In south India, the problem is compounded by young people migrating to other parts of the country or abroad.[127]

This sets the political and constitutional debate on the link between demography and representation in the right perspective, leading to a series of pertinent questions that need to be addressed. For instance, is it possible that the states that continued to experience rapid population growth in the post-1971 period did so for reasons other than apathy towards family planning? What do the general principles of demographic transition reveal in this regard? Can we separate Indian states on the basis of the sigmoid curve of population growth into states that had already peaked before 1971 and those that would achieve their peak growth rates after 1971? How does the carrying capacity of each state influence the population growth that the state has achieved? And, most importantly, how justified is the use of the 1971 population data for the allocation of seats in Parliament to each state and for fiscal devolution by the Finance Commission, considering that 1971 marks a watershed moment in India's demographic history, dividing the south from other regions of India?

2

The 'Overpopulation' Debate

India and the World

The contemporary debate surrounding the topics of 'overpopulation' and 'population control' in India and other parts of the world emerged in Western countries after the Second World War. The war had led to millions of deaths in Europe. Even in the United States, owing to the turmoil and uncertainty that defined the era, birth rates had significantly declined. From 1945 onwards, birth rates began to rise in the 'baby boom', while increased prosperity and medical advances significantly reduced death rates, leading to rapid population growth. Looking back, we find that in a country with a population density of just nineteen persons per square kilometre in 1955, there were already serious concerns expressed by politicians, scholars and journalists about overpopulation. Leading American magazines and journals hosted fervent debates on this issue.[1]

But it was the rapid population growth in the Third World, especially large countries like India, that became the principal concern in the West. The international debate on India's 'overpopulation' that started during the Second World War intensified during the 1950s. The term 'population explosion' was coined around this time by the American sociologist and demographer Kingsley Davis. A number of American experts, apart from a handful of Indian, started focusing increasingly on the 'uncontrolled' population growth in the newly decolonised countries of Asia and Africa. One of the principal objectives of this emerging discourse was to link demography with Cold War geopolitics. As the most populous country of the 'free world', India was at the heart of the US-led global order's framing of population growth in relation to availability of food as well as economic development. The argument was that unless India could control its population growth in a couple of decades its future was doomed; it would neither be able to feed itself nor succeed in ensuring social and economic development. The leading role in building up the discourse of 'overpopulation' was played by the United Nations' Food and Agriculture Organization (FAO), World Health Organization (WHO), the Ford Foundation, the Rockefeller Foundation and the various population experts associated with them.

The idea of 'world population' was promoted by these international organisations and experts. Moreover, production of food grains in different parts of the world was reconfigured as 'world food supply' in relation to 'world population'. With its emergence as the leader of the so-called free world, the US felt that it was responsible for feeding that world. Therefore, population, food and development became the three coordinates of the emerging geopolitics in the post-Second World War period.

I

Population Experts and 'Overpopulation'

That population had emerged as a critical geopolitical factor in the international arena around the mid-twentieth century is exemplified by the fact that, even as the Second World War was going on, there was a report[2] sponsored by the Office of The Population Research, Princeton University in 1943 titled *The Future Population of Europe and the Soviet Union: Population Projection 1940–70*. The lead author of the report was Frank W. Notestein, the director of Population Research at Princeton University. Co-authors of the report were Irene B. Taeuber, Dudley Kirk, Ansley J. Coale and Louise K. Kiser, all of whom contributed significantly to the discourse of 'overpopulation' in the Third World. Published by the League of Nations, Geneva, Switzerland in 1944, the report made a comprehensive comparative analysis of the fertility and growth trends and future estimates for Europe and the Soviet Union, arguing that 'plans for rebuilding the world after the war necessarily involve judgments about the population trend for the future'.[3] It asserted that future population changes 'will profoundly affect the social, economic and political life of the area and of the world'.[4] Giving primacy to demography, the report said that 'it is scarcely possible to think of an aspect of a society that will not be demonstrably changed within the next decade by demographic forces.'[5] It further asserted that the future demographic changes 'will be of critical importance in the problems of establishing a just and a durable peace in a world whose changing economic and military manpower exerts shifting pressures on the maintenance of fixed political relationships'.[6] The report mentioned the declining fertility in Europe, coming after long-term decline in mortality that had in the past led to rapid population growth. It specifically mentioned the fertility decline in Northwestern Europe, especially in France and England, and contrasted it with the higher fertility trends in Southern and Eastern Europe and the USSR. After the onset of the Cold War in 1945, the population growth of Eastern Europe and USSR would become an explicit geopolitical concern for the West.

Notably, the Population Council set up by the Rockefeller Foundation in 1952 took deep interest in India's population growth from its inception. For the population experts at the Council, India immediately emerged as the prime example of an 'overpopulated' country that needed strong attention and intervention to push it towards 'population control'.[7] It was feared that rapid demographic growth in India would outstrip food supply and defeat the country's efforts at development. India's so-called population problem was also associated by the experts with communist ideology and propaganda that were supposedly against birth control. The projects funded by the Population Council focused on training and research in population control, including the activities of United Nations' Demographic Training and Research Centre (DTRC) established in Bombay in 1956. The centre funded a number of population studies programmes at Indian universities and instituted fellowships for Indian scholars to study demographics at Western universities. The Council also funded the Family Planning Association of India and the Christian Medical Association of India.[8]

Let us now examine in detail the role of experts—many of whom were driven at least partly by geopolitical implications of rapid demographic growth in the non-Western world—in building up the debate. As mentioned, among the most influential experts was the American sociologist and demographer Frank W. Notestein, who coined the term 'demographic transition'. Apart from highlighting the demographic changes in post-War Europe and their implications for international relations, Notestein underscored the interdependence of population changes and technological advancements as essential components of political strength in the international arena. From this viewpoint, Notestein also highlighted rapid population growth in developing nations such as India. He estimated the birth rates of the newly decolonised nations as between 40 and 55 per thousand—nearly double that of US and Europe. He argued that while the dangers of unchecked population growth threatened modernisation and political stability, advances in family planning, public interest in limiting childbearing, and improving contraceptive technologies might help mitigate these. Notestein held up South Korea and Taiwan as examples of successful family planning to be emulated by other countries, including India.[9]

Another American sociologist and demographer Warren S. Thompson—who gave the concept of demographic transition—focused on the demographic changes and population challenges faced by India since 1921, highlighting the principal factors that had influenced population growth, including decline in death rates and famines, and health improvements.[10] Thompson believed that family planning initiatives to control population growth were critical to economic development plans, such as the first and second five-year plans. According to him, 'the most serious problem independent India has had to face has been the shortage of food.'[11] He wondered: 'Can the economy be expanded fast enough to care for a rapidly increasing population and also provide for a slowly rising level of living for the entire population?'[12] Citing the Indian government-sponsored study done by the WHO, he expressed his faith that 'in the agricultural villages, many women were interested in reducing the number of their conceptions'[13]. Thompson's conclusion was, 'If a simple, cheap and effective method of preventing conception were developed—one also well adapted to Indian conditions of life—it might come into use far more rapidly than contraception did in the West during the latter half of the nineteenth century and the first quarter of the twentieth.'[14]

Another influential expert, the American sociologist and demographer Kingsley Davis—who coined the term 'population explosion'—employed Thompson's analysis of the evolving population dynamics of India, highlighting the shift from high mortality rates caused by famine and disease to rapid population growth following Independence.[15] Davis highlighted the implications of this growth for future resource needs and the need for effective family planning, suggesting that the increasing population might hinder development. The critical fact was that 'the poorer countries are now contributing far more than their share to the inflated growth of the world's population.'[16] He saw three implications in this. The Third World suppliers of raw materials were 'becoming glutted with people'; scientific advances 'are being made in those countries which have the least need of it in terms of population expansion';[17] and 'the gap in wealth and power as between the rich and poor nations is becoming wider'.[18] 'Technological advance' of the industrial nations and the 'excessive population growth' of the non-industrial nations was responsible for 'the continuing economic disparity' in the world.[19] According to Kingsley Davis, 'Unimpeded human multiplication is giving the non-industrial countries exactly what most of them do not need—more people. It is hindering their acquisition of what they do need—more capital, more skill and greater productivity.'[20]

American anthropologist David G. Mandelbaum—who in 1970 wrote the book *Society in India: Continuity and Change*—highlighted the struggle between rapid population growth and economic development.[21] In the graphic description of Mandelbaum, India gave 'the impression of a vast sump of humanity, proliferating rapidly, unable to slow its rate of increase until it raises its standard of living, and helpless to raise that standard because of its reckless rate of increase'.[22] However, comparing India with UK and Japan, he acknowledged that India's growth 'has been substantial but not phenomenal'.[23] Mandelbaum recommended comprehensive planning that integrated social measures to encourage smaller families alongside economic reforms in order to address the so-called demographic challenges. Higher levels of education among women, higher household income, urbanisation, availability of contraceptives and family planning services were some of the factors identified by him for arresting population growth. What he failed to realise was that a country that enjoyed all these would in any case become a developed country which might not need such population control in the first place. He argued that 'there could be no sustained rise in the Indian standard of living',[24] unless small family norms became popular. Mandelbaum concluded that 'the pressure of population will handicap nationalist measures for industrialization and improved agriculture, but will not necessarily block such measures completely.'[25]

American economist Stephen Enke, the author of *Economics for Development*[26]—who was the founding member of the Rand Logistics Department of the Rand Corporation and in 1958 joined the Centre for Naval Analysis at the Institute of Defence Analysis—also played an important role in shaping the overpopulation debate and in strengthening the evolving opinion that population growth was inversely related to economic development. He argued that India's population growth threatened economic progress, necessitating population control measures.[27] Enke estimated the value of preventing a birth at Rs 500–600 and argued that resource investment in population control was expected to provide a far greater economic return than conventional development expenditures.[28] He discussed the potential benefits of implementing population control measures in India through financial incentives, such as bonuses for families that limited their births. Enke proposed specific schemes, including sterilisations and non-pregnancy payments, emphasising the high return on investment compared to traditional development strategies.[29] It is believed that Enke's economic argument played a crucial role in President Lyndon Johnson's decision to link food aid to population control.[30]

Irene Taeuber—co-author of the League of Nations' report *The Future Population of Europe and the Soviet Union* cited earlier—explored Japan's demographic transformation and highlighted that its unique historical context and policies could not be directly imitated in other Asian nations.[31] She emphasised that in the post-War scenario 'the basic need is not to find a United States policy for the population problems of other countries but a United States policy for cooperation in population policies that other countries themselves have adopted or wish to adopt.'[32] The implication was that India and other poor countries must be persuaded to believe in population control and be guided to develop a customised policy in line with the international discourse of 'overpopulation'.

Indian sociologist and demographer S.N. Agarwala, trained at Princeton University in the 1950s, highlighted the 'unprecedented' growth rate that had resulted from declining death rates and persistently high birth rates.[33] He outlined the historical context of population trends, evaluated the progress and challenges faced by the family-planning movement in India, and examined the attitudes of the Indian population towards contraception. He believed that education in family planning and contraceptives were effective tools of population control. Citing a number of surveys—mostly sponsored by the international institutions—Agarwala concluded that there was considerable consumer interest in family planning, mainly among older women, but fear and misunderstanding about contraception persisted in rural areas and needed to be removed. Some of the results of such surveys conducted in the 1950s and cited by Agarwala, finding that in the rural areas an 'ideal family is constituted of four children, in the urban areas, three children'[34] appear to be highly questionable. While acknowledging the high population growth of many other countries, Agarwala highlighted that 'the net annual addition to its (India's) population is about 8,000,000.'[35] Moreover, he feared that it would not be possible to improve living standards 'despite efforts at economic planning'[36] because of the 'backlog of underfed and ill-nourished population.'[37] In contrast with most others, he underscored the global applicability of demographic transition while highlighting the very short duration in which it was happening in developing countries: 'In Europe, this period of rapid population expansion, called the "transition period," lasted three centuries and brought about a seven-fold increase in population. Whether the underdeveloped countries of the world will follow the same pattern of demographic evolution as was experienced by countries of the West cannot be said with any certainty'.[38]

American demographer Moye W. Freymann—chief consultant to the Ford Foundation in India on health and population in the 1950s and 1960s and later the founder of the Population Centre at the University of North Carolina—viewed the population control movement in India in the context of the need for maintaining sufficient food supplies and healthcare amidst high birth and declining death rates.[39] He argued that the emergence of a national family planning programme represented a shift towards addressing fertility rates more effectively, aiming to curtail population growth through education and community engagement while acknowledging cultural factors that promoted higher fertility. According to Freymann, family planning was essential for social and economic development.[40]

Hudson Hoagland—influential American neuroscientist and president of the American Academy of Arts and Sciences (1961 to 1964)—in his article 'Mechanisms of Population Control', published in 1964 in *Daedalus,* addressed the biological and social mechanisms involved in controlling population growth.[41] Hoagland examined how both natural processes and human intervention influenced population dynamics, framing his argument within the broader global concerns of 'overpopulation', rapid population growth, particularly in underdeveloped countries, and the societal and ecological challenges arising from it. He highlighted the role of scientific discoveries in public health, such as vaccinations and antibiotics that had reduced death rates, particularly in underdeveloped countries, while birth rates had remained high. This imbalance had led to exponential population growth, which had strained resources, worsened poverty and increased social stress in many parts of the world. Asserting that there were only two fundamental mechanisms for controlling population, increasing death rates or reducing birth rates, Hoagland advocated for the widespread adoption of birth control and family planning as the most rational and ethical approach. Hoagland's discussion was informed by biological analogies, particularly the behaviour of non-human species in managing population growth. He described the population dynamics of microorganisms, insects and mammals, where natural limitations—such as food scarcity, predation and disease—act as checks on population growth. He emphasised that humanity, unlike other species, possesses the ability to deliberately control its population through conscious decision-making and technological innovation.[42]

Leo G. Reeder and Goteti B. Krishnamurty emphasised the complex interplay of education, social norms and economic conditions in shaping attitudes towards family planning practices in rural India.[43] They concluded that despite recognising a population problem, many individuals resisted adopting birth control due to cultural traditions and personal preferences. However, they pointed out that 'the dharma tradition itself allows for social change and, hence, tradition, per se, is not an impediment to long-run change'.[44] They perceptively added that 'India's relatively high death rate, particularly in rural areas and among infants, is still an inhibiting factor' for family planning.[45]

American sociologist Dennis H. Wrong presented a more nuanced view, discussing prevalent misconceptions surrounding global population growth, and emphasising that these myths exist among both optimists and alarmists.[46] He deplored the use of terms like 'population explosion' and 'population bomb'. Wrong argued that population growth was a complex issue not limited to underdeveloped countries, as even developed nations faced significant challenges from increasing numbers, although he argued that 'some sociologists and demographers have also pointed to the fact that the fertility levels prevailing today in the *tiers monde* are higher than was the case at the beginning of modernization in the West'.[47] He emphasised that growth stemmed more from declining death rates, rather than rising birth rates, and that controlling population growth was essential to prevent potential socio-economic crises. Wrong regarded the notion that population size would by itself alter global power dynamics in the nuclear age as misleading, as sheer numbers do not translate to military strength.[48]

Canadian population expert T.J. Samuel explored the historical development of India's population control policy from pre-Independence to the early 1960s.[49] He identified four key phases of indifference, neutrality, experimentation, and the formal initiation of population control measures,[50] underscoring various socio-economic, political and ideological factors that shaped government attitudes towards population management. According to Samuel, India faced significant economic challenges due to rapid population growth.[51]

American sociologist J. Mayone Stycos—who was the founder director of the International Population Centre at Cornell University—examined the complex interplay between politics and population control in Latin America, highlighting the significant shifts in US policy regarding family planning and the varied nationalist responses from Latin American countries.[52] He recorded that while attention to population issues had increased since the 1960s, there remained widespread suspicion and hostility towards North American initiatives, driven by concerns about economic motives and cultural imperialism. According to Stycos,

Marxism and Malthusianism influenced Latin American intellectuals' perspectives on demographic growth and socio-economic reform.[53]

The American sociologist and demographer Donald Bogue argued that the world faced an impending food shortage, if population growth continued outpacing agricultural technology, particularly in developing nations.[54] He underlined that 'no matter how well we reconcile ourselves to eating algae, "hearts of oak" breakfast cereal, and beefsteak synthesized from soybeans, there is always a dooms-day-year-plus-one facing us.'[55] However, he believed that the prevailing demographic pessimism might be unwarranted, as evidence indicated a growing awareness and action towards fertility control among global leaders. Moreover, a significant movement for family planning was taking hold across various cultures. According to Bogue, newly introduced ideas or practices could spread exponentially, hinting at rapid increase in contraceptive use in the coming decades. Unique socio-economic factors were influencing rural populations to embrace family planning, showcasing an unexpected adaptability and responsiveness to these initiatives. Bogue concluded that the adoption of family planning could lead to stabilisation of population growth by 2000, challenging the Malthusian perspective of unavoidable 'overpopulation'.[56]

Liebmann and Hans Lehfeldt discussed India's population control measures during the early 1970s, highlighting the government's family planning policies and the challenges faced in their implementation due to cultural, economic and practical barriers.[57] They highlighted that India, possessing only 2.4 per cent of the world's land but 15 per cent of the population, faces challenges in managing population growth.[58] Despite budget increases for family planning, the effectiveness of contraceptive methods like oral contraception and IUDs had been limited in real-world application. They promoted mobile sterilisation camps to increase access and training for sterility operations in rural populations.

The American biologist Paul Ehrlich's famous and alarmist book *The Population Bomb*, published in 1968,[59] played a pivotal role in creating the fear of 'overpopulation'. In the prologue, he declared: 'The battle to feed all of humanity is over. In the 1970s and 1980s hundreds of millions of people will starve to death in spite of any crash programs embarked upon now.'[60] The book marked the culmination of Western and, subsequently, global concerns about the rapid expansion of the world's population, particularly in developing countries, since the end of the Second World War. Interestingly, Ehrlich's visit to Delhi a few years earlier when he saw crowding in a slum was among the triggers for writing the book:

> I have understood the population explosion intellectually for a long time. I came to understand it emotionally one stinking hot night in Delhi a few years ago. My wife and daughter and I were returning to our hotel in an ancient taxi … As we crawled through the city, we entered a crowded slum area. The streets seemed alive with people. People eating, people washing, people sleeping. People visiting, arguing, and screaming. People thrusting their hands through the taxi window, begging. People defecating and urinating. People clinging to buses. People herding animals. People, people, people, people. As we moved slowly through the mob, hand horn squawking, the dust, noise, heat, and cooling fires gave the scene a hellish aspect.[61]

While Ehrlich's description was, indeed, alarmist, it is not hard to imagine that many other foreigners as well as Indians saw 'population explosion' as a serious threat to India and the world.

Many other experts also contributed to the overpopulation debate. For instance, in 1944 D.B. Blacklock in his article 'India's Population Problem' argued that low agricultural productivity of the country would limit its ability to sustain a growing population and advised rapid industrialisation.[62] Writing in the *Foreign Affairs* in 1961, Jack Zlotnick discussed the economic development challenges arising from the rapid population growth in the Third World countries, caused mainly by sudden decline in mortality.[63]

II
Alfred Sauvy and 'World Population'

The international discourse on 'overpopulation', especially in the newly decolonised countries of Asia and Africa, was built around the idea of 'world population' mainly driven by geopolitical considerations of the Cold War that had just set in. Coinciding with the emergence of international organisations like the United Nations, the World Bank and many other global institutions, the concept of 'world population' gained prominence. Since the world—especially the Third World—was sought to be shaped and governed by these global institutions dominated by the West, the concept of 'world population' became a natural corollary, reflecting their influence and concerns about global demographics. Their primary concern was that given the limited carrying capacity of the planet, it was important to keep an eye on population growth, especially in the Third World. Former US Secretary of Defense and World Bank President Robert S. McNamara's statement is emblematic of the agency's approach to population growth in decolonised countries of Asia and Africa:

> The greatest single obstacle to the economic and social advancement of the majority of peoples in the underdeveloped world is rampant population growth... the threat of unmanageable population pressures is very much like the threat of nuclear war.... Both threats can and will have catastrophic consequences unless they are dealt with rapidly and rationally.[64]

However, as early as 1949, the French demographer, historian and public intellectual Alfred Sauvy, who coined the term '*tiers monde*' or Third World, severely criticised the concept of world population, regarding it as erroneous and meaningless:

> To demonstrate this, let us carry the reasoning to its absurd limit. Let us imagine that we could enumerate human beings, like ourselves, who live on other planets. Considerations relating to the total population of the solar system would then be no less meaningful than those about the population of the globe. Without claiming that the lines of separation within the latter are equally wide, the terrestrial compartmentalizations are sufficiently well established to render any global calculus that ignores them quite pointless.[65]

Sauvy's argument is that the population of the world is not evenly distributed, and that as long as there were strong restrictions on the movement of people from one part of the world to the other, discussing world population served little purpose. He clarifies:

> For the time being, there exists no world government, nor are there institutions that would come close to such a construct. Even if some political conflicts are adjudicated at international tribunals, and even

> if some studies are carried out internationally and some principles are established on that level, such coordination of efforts falls far short of the degree of solidarity that would be needed to make the expression 'world population' acquire real meaning.[66]

The crucial question that arises is why the population of any country should be of concern to any other country or countries. With well-established national boundaries and stringent restrictions on the movement of people in the contemporary world, the population of other countries or 'world population' should not have held much significance. The fact that it did owes a lot to the prevalent discourse of development and peace in the period after the Second World War.

There was an imagined adverse impact of rapid population growth on economic development and international economic inequality, with likely implications for international peace and security.[67] The underlying message was that rapid population growth, particularly in the Third World, could upset the global power balance and pose a threat to the environment amid the unprecedented economic growth.[68] This growth came with a reasonable prospect of peace and security, which the post-Second World War global order, established by the victors, seemed to have achieved, notwithstanding the hostility of the Cold War. As Paul Demeny and Geoffrey McNicoll have put it:

> From the vantage point of the immediate post-World War II years the future appeared fraught with danger. Demography played a major role in that perception. Around 1950, minor exceptions apart, the third world had one conspicuous common trait: high fertility and high demographic growth potential. Seen by many in the West, and with less consistency by many third-world leaders themselves, this put an ominous shadow on the economic prospects of the less developed countries, and, by the same token, lowered the chances for an outcome advantageous for the West in the Cold War competition with the Soviet bloc.[69]

Population growth was perceived as a problem for diverse reasons. Sociologists and urban planners regarded it as an escalating challenge in densely populated urban areas. For economists and policymakers, a large part of economic growth appeared to be absorbed by a growing population, without any improvement in the standards of living. The bigger challenge lay in locating resources such as land, capital and employment opportunities to accommodate millions of additional people. Yet, the most pressing concern lay with scientists and policymakers who saw the imminent threat of food shortages, famines and starvation, especially in the Third World countries of Asia and Africa. All these were genuine concerns in themselves. Food shortages were, indeed, a problem faced by large underdeveloped countries like India and China. However, what the pessimists failed to recognise was that this was by no means the first time in modern history when population growth appeared to outstrip resource growth. Technological innovations had addressed similar challenges in the past, and could do so in future as well.

It is not as if there was no understanding of the demographic transition theory—'a generalisation of the historical pattern of change from a traditional demographic regime characterized by high fertility and high mortality to a modern demographic regime characterized by low fertility and low mortality'.[70] However, the rapid population growth of the decades following the Second World War was alarming because the transition that had taken centuries in the West was happening in less-developed countries within a few decades, giving the impression of a 'population explosion'. The dissemination of medical advancements from the West to less-developed countries, which helped combat many infectious diseases, coupled with improved nutrition and sanitation, contributed significantly to reduced mortality rates in poor countries. The reduced mortality was not accompanied by a compensating decline in fertility rates—a decline that usually occurs with a lag. Hence, the global phenomenon of demographic transition to the second phase of rapid growth occurred in many Third World countries in a sudden wave, but was generally not recognised as such.

Instead, the 1954 conference in Rome and the 1965 conference in Belgrade were convened by the United Nations to address the challenge of 'population explosion'.[71] Thus, concerns about population growth in poor countries assumed importance in the 1950s, but the seeds were sown much earlier:

> In the early 20th century, as mortality rates among the poor declined, the pseudo-scientific 'eugenics' movement emerged. It sought to prevent allegedly inferior people from reproducing. Roughly 70,000 people

were forcibly sterilized in the 20th century under eugenic legislation in the United States alone. Eugenicists and Malthusians often allied in policymaking, as they both believed that childbearing should be limited for people they deemed undeserving.[72]

However, 'by mid-century, tainted by Nazi eugenics, the aim of selective breeding was abandoned and Western eugenics transmuted into advocacy of birth control, better pre-natal care, and provision of better information on genetic diseases'.[73] Before long, surveys sponsored mainly by American foundations concluded that there was an unsatisfied latent demand for contraceptives in countries such as India.[74] Therefore, one of the principal aims of the official development aid should be to make contraceptives available to them at highly subsidised rates, or even free of charge.[75]

What exacerbated the problem was the fact that, until the 1950s, annual gross domestic product (GDP) growth beyond 3–4 per cent had not been experienced anywhere in the world on a sustainable basis. With the post-War population growth rates of 2–3 per cent per annum, it appeared to many that unless population growth could be curbed, economic progress and development would be impossible, especially in developing countries. It was only from the 1960s that Japan and the Association of Southeast Asian Nations (ASEAN) countries began experiencing unprecedented economic growth rates of 8–10 per cent per annum. Many leading economists such as Nobel prize-winning Gunnar Myrdal had a pessimistic view about the prospects of economic-growth in India and other parts of Asia.[76]

III

Critiques of the 'Overpopulation' Debate

In his 2019 book, *Emergency Chronicles,* Princeton historian Gyan Prakash has shown how the post-Independence Indian discourse on 'overpopulation' and 'population control' was shaped by United Nations and its multiple agencies, including the FAO, the WHO and leading American foundations such as Rockefeller Foundation and the Ford Foundation after the Second World War.[77] It was the demographic rise of

Asia and Africa which had triggered this Western response. Gyan Prakash shows how Frank W. Notestein, who founded the Office of Population Research at Princeton University in 1936, took the lead in creating an overarching narrative of demographic growth. Kingsley Davis's book *The Population of India and Pakistan,* published in 1951, was sponsored by the Office of Population Research.[78] Further, a Population Division was established in the United Nations in 1946[79] and Notestein was its first Director. FAO and WHO played a leading role in the evolving population control policy, 'as UN officials saw population policy as a step toward the global governance of population'.[80] In 1952, John D. Rockefeller III founded the Population Council. Gyan Prakash has highlighted how the Ford Foundation in particular deployed large-scale funding and manpower in India to entrench repressive policies of population control in the country. Further, the Minister of Health and other important ministries were persuaded by the head of Ford Foundation in India, Douglas Ensminger, to believe that without population control, hunger and starvation threatened India and that there was little possibility of economic development of the country.[81]

Gyan Prakash has shown how mobile sterilisation camps led by Colonel B.N. Raina of the Army Medical Corps had begun to be organised in the 1960s as part of outreach.[82] It is also shown that Mrs Gandhi's faith in population control had deeper origins, as she had given her ancestral home in Allahabad to house a family planning institute. With her becoming prime minister, the family planning programme got a big boost. The day after she became prime minister, the Ministry of Health was renamed as Ministry of Health and Family Planning. Dr Sushila Nayyar, who was a close associate of Mahatma Gandhi, had been Health Minister from 1952 to 1955 and again since 1962. The advocates of family planning, both international and in the Indian government, were not happy with her approach to birth control and family planning. In 1967, she was replaced by the US-trained demographer Sripati Chandrashekhar, 'who had for long wished to make sterilisation compulsory for every man with more than three children'.[83] Gyan Prakash has also shown that once monetary incentive for sterilisation began to be paid in 1966 at the behest of Population Council, International Planned Parenthood Federation, the Ford Foundation and the World Bank, the programme acquired a new coercive dimension.[84] The food shortages during the Bihar famine of 1966-67 'drove the poor to sterilisation camps'.[85] In other parts of India, too, hunger and food shortages pushed people into getting themselves sterilised for the monetary benefit. Thus, the 'overpopulation' debate in the 1950s and 1960s prepared the ground for increasingly drastic and coercive measures of birth control.

In his 2018 book *The Price of Aid*, David Engerman examines the negative aspects of the development aid provided to the newly decolonised countries of Asia and Africa.[86] He argues that development aid was always politically guided as a tool of the Cold War in which India occupied an important position, and that aid came attached with conditionalities such as population control that fulfilled the geopolitical goals of the superpowers, US and the Soviet Union. The Indian leadership was committed to modernisation and industrialisation of Indian economy, which had hitherto been a colonial economy characterised by underdevelopment. The shortage of capital needed for rapid industrialisation made India critically dependent on the superpowers. According to Engerman: 'In short, officials in the superpowers used development aid as a Cold War weapon, while constituencies in recipient nations used the Cold War as a development weapon'[87]. So, officials from the donor countries and those from India pursued their own geopolitical goals. Moreover, Engerman notes, foreign aid created deep divisions within the Indian state and distorted the Indian political economy. Thus, India in a sense became a laboratory for aid experimentation in the Cold War.

Nick Cullather's 2010 book *Hungry World: America's Cold War Battle Against Poverty in Asia* presents a detailed and enlightening account of how in the post-Second World War period, global politics, especially that of the US, came to be linked with the production and supply of food grains to poor countries like India.[88] This 'modernisation' of agriculture to take care of the 'hungry world' was led by the US government and the Ford and Rockefeller foundations. Foreign aid and technology were employed to make effective interventions in Indian agriculture to 'modernise' it, culminating in the 'Green Revolution', whose motives and results are questioned by Cullather. He argues that the American effort was to turn the subsistence peasants of India into modern 'farmers'. He has a critical approach towards the much-celebrated Norman Borlaug, the American agronomist and Nobel Peace Prize winner who is credited with inventing the high-yield variety of seeds and other technology and methods required for the 'Green Revolution'. Cullather seeks to debunk the prevalent view that but for the Green Revolution—a name given by the USAID in response to unexpectedly large crops in 1968 in India in the areas where high-yield varieties of wheat seeds were sown—India would have continued to face severe food shortages. Importantly, he argues that India was not really facing a famine in the 1960s, but only a food deficit, which originated at least partly in the Indian state's preference since the 1950s for spending more resources on industrialisation rather than on agriculture. The idea of famine stalking in India and elsewhere helped President Lyndon Johnson link American aid with geopolitical objectives, including population control. According to Cullather, the American idea of progress in India was dominated by improvement in agricultural productivity, and not industrialisation, as in the Cold War context, controlling global food supply became an important concern for the US.[89]

Matthew Connelly's 'Population Control in India: Prologue to the Emergency Period' provides a comprehensive analysis of the complex history and international dynamics that shaped India's population policies, which were 'emblematic of everything that can go wrong in a programme premised on population control'.[90] He highlights the influence of eugenic thought on both domestic and international discourse on population control. Connelly's work traces how coercive family planning measures, which became synonymous with the Emergency, were actually rooted in earlier policies and were influenced by international organisations and foreign advisors, as by the 1950s India had become a key focal point for global population control efforts. Connelly uses the archival records of the Population Council to understand why this happened, citing economist Isador Lubin's statement on the second day of the Council's inaugural meeting:

> At luncheon today I raised the question as to why it was that almost everybody who spoke this morning talked about India. What is there about India that makes this situation so acute? And I think unconsciously we are scared, and I think we have a right to be. In other words, that is where the ferment is taking place. That is where the pressure is the greatest.

International agencies like the United Nations, the Ford Foundation, the Population Council founded by John D. Rockefeller III, and the World Bank were all heavily involved in shaping India's approach to population management, often advocating coercive policies and influencing the government to adopt aggressive family planning programmes.[91] This collaboration created a system that treated family planning as a critical national priority, even at the expense of individual rights. Connelly shows how international advisors, often driven by concerns about poverty alleviation and economic development, played a part in normalising these measures as part of the population control discourse where reducing fertility was seen as a solution to economic and social problems. The involvement of international organisations helped legitimise these policies and shielded the Indian government from criticism, as population control was framed as a necessary step towards national development. He highlights the unreliability of the surveys conducted in India and used by experts such as Notestein and Stycos to advocate small families.

Connelly also examines the collaboration between Indian officials and international advisors leading to a gradual escalation of coercive tactics in family planning. For example, India's experiments with sterilisation and IUD insertion were heavily influenced by foreign experts who believed that rapid, widespread fertility control was essential. In the 1960s, a major campaign to insert intrauterine devices in millions of women was launched, supported by international funding and technical advice.[92] Connelly's analysis emphasises that, while the Emergency is often remembered for its extreme abuses, the policies enacted during this period were not a sudden departure from earlier practices. Rather, they represented the culmination of a long process in which population control was prioritised over reproductive rights.

Deepak Lal—Indian economist and the author of the book *The Poverty of Development Economics*—in his article 'India: Population Change and Its Consequences' provides a comprehensive analysis of India's demographic transition and its social, political and economic implications.[93] He delves into the debate about 'overpopulation', questioning long-held views that rapid population growth is detrimental to economic development. Lal critiques Malthusian perspectives which argue that overpopulation leads to resource scarcity, poverty and environmental degradation. He argues that this fear, although intuitive for many, is based on simplistic arithmetic and ignores more nuanced economic analysis. Lal refers to the views of Julian Simon, who famously argued that human ingenuity and economic growth can offset the negative effects of population increases. He points out that historical trends, especially in the West and East Asia, show that population growth often coincides with economic development, once a country passes through the demographic transition—a shift from high birth and death rates to lower ones as a society becomes more industrialised and affluent. He contrasts India's relatively laissez-faire approach to population control with China's one-child policy, arguing that China's coercive measures have created significant social and economic problems, including an ageing population and a distorted sex ratio. By comparison, India's more organic demographic transition allows for a gradual population stabilisation, which, Lal argues, will benefit the country in the long run.

Lal also explores the economic effects of population growth on employment, wages and poverty. He challenges the idea that rapid population growth inevitably leads to unemployment and declining wages, arguing instead that in an open economy, the effects of population expansion depend on global market conditions and the demand for labour-intensive goods. Another key aspect of Lal's analysis is his discussion of the long-term effects of population growth on savings and economic development. He refers to the work of Jeffrey Williamson, who argues that demographic changes can boost economic growth by increasing the proportion of working-age adults in the population. As India's dependency ratio declines (with fewer young dependents), the country stands to benefit from a 'demographic gift' that can fuel further economic growth, provided that the labour force is efficiently utilised. Lal also touches on the potential impact of rising savings rates on future growth, suggesting that as more households move into higher income brackets, aggregate savings will increase, creating a virtuous cycle of growth and investment.

Hungary-born British development economist Peter Bauer forcefully questioned the idea that population growth was responsible for poverty and inadequate economic development in the Third World since the 1960s.[94] He argued that contrary to popular belief, rapid population growth had often coincided with rapid economic growth in both developed and developing countries. Bauer highlighted that 'in the Third World itself, population growth has often gone hand-in-hand with rapid material advance'[95]. He cited the development of the Malaya of 1890s—'a sparsely-populated area of hamlets and fishing villages'—into a 'country with large cities and extensive plantation and mining operations'[96] by the 1930s, along with a fourfold rise in population, from about 1.5 million to about 6 million due to immigration and natural increase. Citing Taiwan, Hong Kong, Kenya, the Ivory Coast, Mexico, Colombia, and Brazil, Bauer underscored that 'other Third World countries have also combined rapid population increase with rapid, even spectacular, economic growth for decades on end.'[97]

According to Bauer, the focus on population control as a solution to poverty overlooked the complexities of economic development and the diverse factors that contributed to prosperity. The idea that limiting population growth will automatically lead to economic progress is simplistic and ignores the importance of other factors such as education, infrastructure and innovation. Moreover, the coercive methods employed in some countries to enforce population control policies raised serious ethical and political concerns. Ultimately, economic development in the Third World depended on a range of factors beyond just population size, and efforts to improve living standards should focus on empowering individuals and communities through economic opportunities and access to resources rather than imposing population control measures. Bauer showed the complicity of international agencies in the birth control campaign during the Emergency:

> The methods and results of this program were encouraged by the West. Thus at the height of the campaign, New Scientist, a magazine generally sympathetic to the Third World, reported: 'The Western aid agencies … either kept quiet or applauded the sterilization program. World Bank President, Robert McNamara, took time off from his busy schedule during his Indian visit to call upon the Indian Health and Family Planning Minister to congratulate him for the Indian government's political will and determination in popularizing family planning.'[98]

According to Bauer, these people believed 'that Third World people do not know about birth control, they procreate heedless of consequences, and the West must persuade or even force them to change their reproductive habits'.[99] He perceptively argued that 'the demand for cheap Western contraceptives is limited not because people in the Third World are ignorant of them but rather because they do not want to restrict their families, or prefer other, more traditional ways of doing so'.[100] He criticised such 'unwarranted condescension or contempt, which in turn soon becomes a justification for coercion'.[101] Bauer acknowledged the association between higher incomes and lower fertility, but doubted that 'higher incomes as such lead to smaller families':

> Both the higher incomes and the smaller families reflect greater ambition for material welfare for oneself and one's family. Both, in other words, reflect a change in motivation. By contrast, when parental incomes are increased as a result of subsidies or windfalls, without a change in attitudes, the parents are likely to have more children, not fewer. This last point is pertinent to the proposals of many Western observers who contradictorily urge both population control and also more aid to the poor with large families.[102]

IV
The 'Overpopulation' Debate in India

Although the 'population problem' in India was discussed among British officials and Indian leaders in the pre-Independence period, especially since 1931, an urgent need to address what was seen as the menace of 'overpopulation' arose around Independence under the shadow of international discourse on rapid population growth in the Third World, especially India. The 1951 Census showed growth of 13.31 per cent during 1941–51 and a total population of more than 36 crore, adding to itself several millions a year. This was a situation that reminded many of the Malthusian trap, triggering concern over avoiding a 'population explosion' that would, apart from neutralising the positive effects of development, threaten the ability of the country to even feed itself. Both food and development struck a chord with Indian leadership, mainly because of the historical legacy of famines and underdevelopment during the British Raj. The sentiment was widely shared and expressed by leaders and policymakers from different parts of India and triggered a debate that has continued till date.

The debate after Independence involved a three-stage process. In the first stage, it followed the general pattern of the global demographic debate on 'overpopulation', whereby rapid population growth was seen as a serious problem that needed to be solved by family planning, education and broader human development. The policymakers rather naively regarded 'family planning' as an effective measure that would bring down the population growth rate within a couple of decades. In the second stage, 'population control' through these methods was vigorously implemented. In the 1960s, the country scaled up its family planning programme, which had been launched in 1952, into an ambitious programme of 'population control'. However, it was soon realised that despite all possible measures the goal of population control remained elusive. Far from coming down, the growth rate was only going up. This realisation ushered in the third stage of the demographic debate in India. From the 1970s, there began a quest for an explanation for why the policy had failed. The 1971 Census with a growth of 24.80 per cent seemed to confirm the failure of family planning. It was around this time that straightforward regional comparisons showing the accelerating population growth of the north, on the one hand, and the stabilising growth of the south, on the other, emerged as an important axis of the demographic debate in India. Over the ensuing decades, the discussion gradually became focused on this aspect. Certain states in the north were largely held responsible for what was increasingly seen as uncontrolled growth leading to wide demographic divergence between the various regions of India. This was seen as an injustice being meted out to the states, mainly in the south, which, it was claimed, had successfully controlled their population growth by implementing the family planning programme. The differential population growth rates of the south and the north emerged as one of the major explanations for underachievement of development goals. The 1976 decision to freeze representation at 1971 Census figures was a corollary to the international and national debate on 'overpopulation' in India.

The Pre-Independence Debate in India

The pre-Independence population debate in India had started in the early twentieth century. P.K. Wattal's 1916 book *The Population Problem in*

India: A Census Study was the first major study of this kind.[103] However, it was only after the 1931 Census, which showed a national growth rate of 10.6 per cent, that the debate intensified. Birth control clinics were started in Mysore state. In Madras, a Neo-Malthusian League was founded. American birth control activist Margaret Sanger visited India to popularise birth control. She had a meeting with Mahatma Gandhi to persuade him to support the use of contraceptives. But the Mahatma remained steadfast in his belief that abstinence was the only morally acceptable way to exercise birth control, when needed. In 1937, the Indian National Congress (INC) appointed a National Planning Committee, chaired by Jawaharlal Nehru. A sub-committee on the subject of birth control was appointed under Radha Kamal Mukerjee, professor of economics and sociology at Lucknow University who had written on India's population problem.[104] The sub-committee endorsed birth control, while the view taken by the National Planning Committee was more nuanced in advocating both birth control and economic development to reduce poverty, which contributed to high birth rates. D. Ghosh in a report titled 'Pressure of Population and Economic Efficiency in India'—sponsored by the Indian Council of World Affairs and published in 1946—examined the impact of India's growing population on its economic efficiency, highlighting the increase in population over preceding decades.[105] Ghosh attributed it to high birth rates and falling mortality. He discussed the socio-economic challenges posed by rapid population growth, such as poverty, inadequate housing, and strain on agricultural and industrial resources. Ghosh advocated for a deeper awareness among Indians about the consequences of unchecked population growth and suggested that better economic policies, aimed at controlling population growth while enhancing productivity, were essential to achieve sustainable development. Gyan Chand wrote a number of books and articles on population both before and after Independence. In 1939, he wrote the book *India's Teeming Millions* in which he expressed concern over the population growth of the previous decades.[106] In *The Problem of Population* published in 1944, he presented a nuanced view on the subject. While advocating population control, he cautioned that 'anyone who suggests restriction of numbers as the panacea for our economic ills betrays an ignorance of the real nature of the problem'.[107] Gyan Chand argued that 'the population problem of the country is essentially a part of the problem of remaking the nation and its solution will have to be undertaken as part of an all-round plan for the country'.[108]

Interestingly, Nehru wrote on the issue of population in his famous book *The Discovery of India,* dedicating to it the chapter titled 'The Problems of Population: Falling Birth Rates and National Decay'.[109] Discussing the population question in a world context, Nehru mentioned falling birth rates in many European countries as well as the loss of millions of lives during the Second World War, especially in China, Russia, Poland and Germany. He noted the fact that the eastward sweep of technology, along with education, sanitation and public health, had led to rapid growth in the Soviet Union, which had geopolitical implications.[110] He noted that these changes would sweep Asia, too, and then asserted that 'some of these countries, like India, far from needing a bigger population, would be better off with fewer people'.[111]

V

The 'Population Control' Debate in India: Policymakers and Experts

One of the most influential voices for population control in the early years after Independence was that of R.A. Gopalaswami, Registrar General and Census Commissioner of the 1951 Census of India. The report on the census submitted by him in a way sums up all that would later go wrong with the family planning programme launched by the Union government.[112] With the conviction of an overzealous birth controller, Gopalaswami compared his report to P.K. Wattal's study called *The Population Problem in India: A Census Study*, published in 1916. He foregrounded his arguments in the Planning Commission's report, which had mentioned that 'the recent increase in the population of India and the pressure exercised on the limited resources of the country have brought to the forefront the urgency of the problem of family planning and population control', and that this could be secured 'only by the realization of the need for family limitation on a wide scale by the people'.[113]

On the basis of rudimentary estimates of the future agricultural output in India—which he thought could increase by only about one-third—

Gopalaswami concluded that 'this would correspond to the need of total population strength of 45 crores' by 1969.[114] So, in his almost unreal assessment, the population could be stabilised by state initiative in a mere fifteen years. He defined the objective of the population policy 'so to limit the number of births that they do not materially exceed the number of deaths and thus achieve a stationary population before our number exceeds 45 crores'.[115] He coined the fancy-sounding term 'improvident maternity', defining it 'as a child birth occurring to a mother who has already given birth to three or more children, of whom at least one is alive'.[116] Gopalaswami then calculated India's 'improvident maternity' at about 40 to 45 per cent. He calculated that out of a crude birth rate of 40 per thousand, 17 births could be prevented. The resultant birth rate of 23 compared to a death rate of 22 would then reduce 'the rate of growth of population from about 13 per cent per decade to about 1 percent per decade'. Gopalaswami then pontificated:

> The task before the nation is first of all to bring about such a change in the climate of public opinion that every married couple will accept it as their duty (to themselves, to the family, and to the larger family the nation) that they should avoid improvident maternity. The occurrence of improvident maternity should evoke social disapproval as any other form of anti-social self-indulgence. This is necessary, but not enough. There should be standing arrangements for ensuring that advice is given to every married couple on the various ways opened to them for discharging its duties and to make available necessary facilities.[117]

One cannot, however, accuse Gopalaswami of discrimination along class, caste, creed or region, as he suggested that this threshold level of 'improvident maternity' must be the same for all. Births over three must not be allowed 'even if the peculiar circumstances of the family or the state of health of the mother are such that further maternity may be allowed to occur and the offspring supported without such difficulty. Whether or not one individual can afford it, the nation cannot—and hence it is improvident maternity all the same'.[118] His pious conclusion was that 'there is in fact no conflict in this matter between the interest of the individual, of the family, and of the nation as a whole'.[119]

Gopalaswami then delineated his utopian population control plan spanning a mere fifteen years. He argued that within five years 'the personnel needed for the work can be got together'. He also supported the Planning Commission's idea of a central research and information unit that would 'recommend a few acceptable, efficient, harmless and economic methods' of population control. The second phase of Gopalaswami's plan would supposedly start after five years, when 'a nationwide campaign should be launched for the elimination of improvident maternity from the life of the people'. He believed that 'once the mind of the people has been won the rest will be easy'.[120]

Gopalaswami suggested an annual review by the Central government and Parliament, the state government and state legislature, municipal councils, district boards and panchayats 'at what rate the incidence of improvident maternity was actually following [falling?] among the people committed to their charge'.[121]

Gopalaswami even worked out the per capita financial support required for his grandiose plan of birth control. He calculated an approximate expense of half-a-rupee per head of people covered. This would have meant the expense of at least 20 crore rupees at that time. Gopalaswami concluded that 'the growth of population cannot be checked unless there are maternity and child welfare services; and we cannot have such services unless we find money for it'.[122] Comparing the costs involved in raising agricultural productivity with that of reduction in 'improvident maternity', Gopalaswami concluded that 'the latter offers a permanent solution of the problem, while the former doesn't. The former opens up a prospect of indefinite duration of hard labour without immediate results. The latter will be rewarded by visible reduction of human suffering and promotion of human happiness while the effort is still proceeding. The choice is clear.'[123]

It should not be imagined that the grandiose plan of Gopalaswami had no takers. As late as the turn of the millennium, another Registrar General and Census Commissioner and former Chief Secretary of Kerala M. Vijayanunni in an article titled 'R.A. Gopalaswami's 1951 Census Report Revisited' lamented its non-implementation.[124] After noting that 'as per the present portents we are expected to fumble and bumble along with inadequate policy interventions and at the same time hurtle forward on the population growth path, leaving the periodically reset population policy objectives and goals unfulfilled' and projecting India's population at 200 crore in 2100,[125] Vijayanunni said:

> One would wish that Gopalaswami's improvident maternity plan had been implemented stabilizing India's population at 45 crores, the right size for the country's carrying capacity and ecological balance. In that case India would now have been one of the prosperous nations of the world ranking, high in per capita income as well as human development indicators.[126]

The Indian demographer Sripati Chandrasekhar, brought in by Prime Minister Indira Gandhi as the Minister for Health and Family Planning in 1967 in the place of the Gandhian Dr Sushila Nayyar, played a key role in the population control movement. Interestingly, in his first article published in 1943, he had questioned the idea that India was overpopulated or that its population growth was too high. However, after pursuing his doctoral studies in the US, during which he also worked in the American Office of Strategic Services, the forerunner of the Central Intelligence Agency (CIA), as an expert on Indian demography, he took a U-turn and started a birth control propaganda in India.[127] He wrote a large number of articles and books on the subject. Author of books such as *Population and Planned Parenthood in India* and *Hungry People and Empty Hands*, Chandrasekhar in fact ran a lifelong campaign for population control in India. He started the Indian Institute of Population Studies and edited the journal *Population Review* for forty years.

So pessimistic was Chandrasekhar about India's ability to feed itself and to develop that even the prospect of a 50-crore population of 1967 rising to 60 crore over the next decade or so frightened him: 'The average citizen is going to face absolute misery. Food supply will dwindle. There will be no living space. We will be reduced to the level of a cabbage patch'.[128] He also feared the rise of communism in India in such a situation. The next year, in 1968, Chandrasekhar became even more alarmist: 'Our house is on fire. We can get the blaze under control' with male sterilisation.[129]

So, for Chandrasekhar, population control was akin to fire control. He was a much-celebrated man in the official media. The *Yojana* magazine described him as someone 'impatient with those who don't match up to his exacting standards' and asserted that he had 'the moral force of a crusader and the ruthless efficiency of a high-power salesman'.[130] Chandrasekhar would later boast that 'it was only after the formation of the new cabinet early in 1967 that a vigorous, new anti-natalist policy was formulated and an all-out campaign begun to halve the nation's birth rate by 1975–76'.[131]

Echoing the American opinion on the link between population and food in a lecture, Chandrasekhar said that 'food production and family planning are simply two sides of the coin of national economic and social development'.[132] He described Mrs Indira Gandhi as 'a dedicated champion of the cause' and added that 'the fact that she is a woman and the mother of two sons gives her support special significance in the Indian cultural milieu'.[133] In 1976, during the Emergency, Chandrasekhar wrote the book *Population and Law in India* in which he defended coercive birth control and presented an elaborate plan to make it legal.[134]

According to Chandrasekhar, there was a clear adversarial relationship between population growth and economic development, although he failed to produce any empirical evidence in support of his claim. He argued that despite obstacles such as cultural resistance and infrastructural issues, India was determined to achieve a birth rate of 25 per thousand by 1975-76, down from 41 in 1961, through a vigorous family-planning campaign, which had begun to take serious shape since 1967.

On the basis of dubious surveys sponsored by international agencies and organisations interested in population control in India, Chandrasekhar asserted that approximately 70 per cent of couples surveyed supported family planning. He underscored that various contraceptive methods were being promoted, including sterilisation, IUDs, condoms and the pill, with community-based initiatives for broader accessibility. Chandrasekhar lamented that cultural attitudes towards family size and economic conditions hinder widespread adoption of family planning in rural areas, but underscored that international aid and support had bolstered India's family-planning initiatives, reinforcing the programme as a matter of public health and economic stability.[135]

Another important expert was Ashish Bose, arguably the most well-known Indian demographer, who played a leading role in building up the perception of a north–south demographic divide within the larger debate on India's 'overpopulation'. He picked up the loose strands of the debate and formulated a coherent framework of the north–south divide. Bose underlined the difference not just in unequal population growth but also in other demographic indicators, such as birth rates, total fertility rates, infant mortality rates, death rates, literacy rates and contraceptive usage, all of which are important to demographic transition and per capita income growth. Finally, in a policy briefing to Prime Minister Rajiv Gandhi in 1985, Bose introduced the condescending term BIMARU as an acronym for Bihar, Madhya Pradesh, Rajasthan and Uttar Pradesh.[136] The insidious insinuation was that these states were sick because their demographic indicators were worse than those of the southern states.

Ashish Bose conceived it as a straightforward battle between a regressive north and a progressive south. What is most astonishing is that the leading demographer of the country made hardly any effort to understand the demographic history of India to find out why the growth rates and other indicators varied significantly across regions and states. The reductive reasoning used by Bose to move from the 'world population' problem to India and then to north India is illustrated in an article he wrote in 1996:

> The world population problem is zeroing in on South Asia and in particular, India, Pakistan and Bangladesh. India has a special responsibility in this regard because it is the second most populous country in the world, and is threatening to be the most populous country by the year 2035 or so. India owes to the world a speedy resolution of the population problem by rapidly curbing the birth and death rates as also the infant mortality rate. The crux of India's population problem lies in the states of Bihar, Madhya Pradesh, Rajasthan and Uttar Pradesh, with a total population of 335 million in 1991, accounting for 40 per cent of India's population. Our acronym for these states is BIMARU (in Hindi *bimaru* means sick).[137]

Based on a completely ahistorical analysis, Bose regarded high-growth states as demographically sick. How could an analytical framework focus solely on the present demographic indicators, ignoring historical trends and reach such sweeping conclusions? Oblivious of these factors, Bose elaborated:

> As a matter of fact, all the southern states, Kerala, Tamil Nadu, Andhra Pradesh and Karnataka are doing well in family planning, whereas the four large states in the North, Uttar Pradesh, Bihar, Madhya Pradesh and Rajasthan, are lagging far behind. As a result, a peculiar situation has arisen in India in terms of what we call 'North–South Demographic Divide'.[138]

So, from the apparently better demographic indicators of the southern states in the post-1971 period, Ashish Bose concluded that they had done well in family planning, while the BIMARU states had lagged. What is most striking is that for Bose the issue of variable population growth of the north versus the south was inextricably linked with the question of political representation. Thus, strongly supporting the 1976 embargo on the reallocation of seats in Parliament, Bose says:

> In 1976, during the Emergency period, a National Population Policy was formulated by the government. This policy stated that for the purpose of deciding the number of seats in Parliament and State Assemblies, the 1971 Census population would decide the position of each state and this would remain so till the year 2001. In other words, the state of Uttar Pradesh will not have more members in Parliament because its population growth rate was higher than that of Tamil Nadu. Now there is every possibility that the whole issue will be reopened in 2001. The Expert Group on Population Policy headed by Dr. M.S. Swaminathan recommended in its 1994 report that this freeze should continue right up to the year 2011.[139]

The Atal Bihari Vajpayee government went beyond 2011 and extended the freeze until 2026. Returning to his favourite theme ten years later, in 2007, Bose cites the Registrar General's statement that 'an increase of 187 million is likely to occur in seven states of Bihar, Chhattisgarh, Jharkhand, Madhya Pradesh, Rajasthan, Uttar Pradesh and Uttarakhand (termed as BIMARU states)'[140] and goes on to assert:

> Incidentally, I had coined the term BIMARU for the states of Bihar, Madhya Pradesh, Rajasthan and Uttar Pradesh to pinpoint India's demographic malady as far back as 1985 when I was asked to brief the then prime minister on India's family planning programme. It is unfortunate that the BIMARU states continue to be BIMARU (the acronym suggests the Hindi word for "sick") even today and what is worse, these states will continue to be BIMARU even after 25 years, as per the registrar general's projections. I must emphasise that my acronym refers only to demographic sickness. I concede that of late, Rajasthan and Madhya Pradesh have made some progress on the economic front but unfortunately, on the demographic front, they continue to be BIMARU.[141]

Incidentally, Bose does compare the population shares of the BIMARU and the southern states, demonstrating how the latter's share is declining. But he does it without any reference to the past, starting from 2001 and projecting it into the future up to 2026. Thus, he uses statistics as if the past did not exist. This study shows that far from helping in an objective understanding of India's demography, the BIMARU approach has obfuscated it by putting forward a political argument under the garb of demographic indicators. This is done with utter neglect of empirical evidence from the recent past.

VI
The Implementation of Population Control

Flowing from the international debate on 'world population', 'overpopulation' and 'population explosion' with its focus on India, the issue of population growth came to the centre-stage shortly after Independence. Rural development, land reforms, poverty reduction and industrialisation were critical components of the nationalist discourse during the freedom struggle. After Independence, the country's leaders were eager to implement these programmes without delay. However, the aspirations of the newly independent nation far surpassed its capacity to bring about such transformative changes within a decade or two, as was the initial expectation.

In the 1951 Census, India recorded a population of approximately 36 crore—a post-Partition number that was much lower than what it would have been if the approximately 7.5 crore people who left had stayed on in the country. The decade of 1941–51 saw comparatively rapid population growth, which was a matter of deep concern for policymakers. With the launch of an official family planning programme in 1951-52, the hope was that the annual birth rates, fertility rates, the average size of families and the rate of population growth would come under control within a decade or two.

Family planning was evidently part of a broader political and technocratic vision of planning promoted under the leadership of the first Prime Minister of India, Pandit Jawaharlal Nehru. This vision held that the newly independent India needed comprehensive planning in every sphere in order to ensure its progress. The dream child of this Nehruvian belief in planning was, of course, the Planning Commission, which came into existence in 1952. It must be mentioned that the 1950s were, even in many developed countries, a period of increased state intervention in the economy and society.

It was in this national and international context that population control (renamed euphemistically to 'family planning') was taken up as a matter of high priority. The Planning Commission's efforts in the fields of agricultural development and industrialisation were mirrored by the family planning programme in the realm of demographics, driven by the belief that improvements in standard of living, health, education and other indicators could be made only if population remained under control. Unfortunately for the planners, India was already in a phase of rapid population growth by the 1950s. In large parts of the country, death rates were falling, but birth and fertility rates remained high, which is a general phenomenon during the second phase of demographic transition. The dream of population control was fast turning into a nightmare.

What exacerbated the problem was that the country's GDP growth rate at about 3 per cent per annum and the population growth rate at around 2 per cent per annum witnessed during 1951–81 remained too close to each other for the country to register any appreciable rise in per capita income or reduction in poverty levels. The surge in India's population unaccompanied by a correspondingly higher degree of industrialisation or economic growth was seen by policymakers and experts as among the biggest hurdles faced by the newly independent nation in the pursuit of development and poverty eradication.

In the 1960s, the term 'population explosion', coined by Kingsley Davis earlier, gained prominence in India and many other parts of the world, especially in the West.[142] Contemporary evidence from the Third World appeared to support the idea. Predictions of an imminent humanitarian disaster resulting from this population growth appeared to be rather convincing to many people.

Even the leaders of Indian industry such as J.R.D. Tata were convinced that India was facing a 'population explosion'. In his speech delivered at the sixtieth Annual General Meeting of the Indian Merchants' Chamber, Bombay on 20 February 1968—a copy of which he sent to Prime

Minister Indira Gandhi—JRD included a section titled 'Population Explosion'. Here, he mentioned the 'fantastic fact' that 'since we achieved Independence, in less than one generation, we have added 200 million people to our population, roughly equivalent to the total population of Western Europe, or of Soviet Russia, or the United States of America'.[143] He asserted that population growth should not be seen only in relation to food, but also to improvement in standards of living. JRD highlighted that much of the growth occurred in rural areas and advocated the use of contraceptives and mobile clinics for population control.[144] His faith in family planning is exemplified by the fact that on his initiative nine family planning centres were opened by Tata Steel in 1984 to encourage sterilisation. Incidentally, the United Nations' Population Award of 1992 was given jointly to J.R.D. Tata and the Population Council of India.

This was the national and international environment in which the demographic debate in India originated and progressed. Policymakers and scholars, especially demographers and economists, bought into the demographic disaster story. They started desperately looking for ways to control population, without any reference to the demographic history of India as a whole or of its various regions. The future alone seemed to matter, and it was seemingly threatened by 'population explosion'. In hindsight, it might seem peculiar, but at that time there was genuine faith in the ability of the Indian state to substantially change the reproductive choices of hundreds of millions of people across a vast, diverse, impoverished and underdeveloped nation in a short span. This faith was reflective of the immense self-confidence of a youthful nation-state coming into existence after a long struggle for freedom that was driven by idealism and expectations for the country after liberation from the British Raj. The leaders sincerely believed that the lives of the common people would be transformed within a couple of decades.

As the 1960s progressed, political leaders and other policymakers began to realise that things were not going according to plan. Population growth was not only failing to decline but, to their great dismay, was actually accelerating. The 1961 Census reported a growth of 21.64 per cent over the previous decade. What exacerbated the problem was the general political and economic situation of the country, which faced two wars in a span of three years as well as a severe drought running for two years and the food shortages resulting from it. In a country such as India—which had suffered more famines during the British Raj than any other country in the history of the modern era, including the devastating Bengal famine of 1943-44 in which at least 3 million people had died—food shortages triggered deep fears and insecurities.

During the 1960s, food shortages were alleviated by the import of food grains, mainly wheat and corn, from the United States of America under the Public Law 480, which allowed surplus food grains to be sent to countries with shortages. PL-480 was as much an instrument of American geopolitics in the Cold War environment as of humanitarian aid to needy countries, especially given the fact that the US was the only country which had surplus food grains in the quantities that India needed. The American food aid played a critical role in providing food to millions in India. But President Lyndon Johnson's policy of permitting PL-480 grains in small shipments in order to keep India on tenterhooks at a time when the American invasion of Vietnam had intensified was a humiliating experience for Indian leaders. They came to regard it as a 'ship-to-mouth' existence. This experience evoked two main responses.

The first was a concerted effort that began during the tenure of Prime Minister Lal Bahadur Shastri and continued under Prime Minister Indira Gandhi—rather ironically with the help of the US—to implement measures for agricultural improvement, later referred to as the Green Revolution. The objective was to make India self-reliant by significantly raising the per-acre productivity of food grains, especially of wheat, for which the required technology had just become available.

The second response was an increased emphasis on 'population control' through what was euphemistically described as 'family planning', launched earlier in 1952. The programme was boosted both in terms of government funding and political prioritisation. The first five-year plan launched in 1952 allocated a sum of Rs 65 lakh; the second plan, 5 crore; the third, 50 crore; the fourth, 315 crore; and the fifth, 516 crore for family planning. Moreover, in 1966, a new department of family planning was created in the Central government, and the Ministry of Health was renamed as Ministry of Health and Family Planning.

It was felt that even with the Green Revolution, it would not be possible to cater to the needs of a population growing in an uncontrolled manner. This response got tremendous impetus from the 1971 Census, which revealed that growth had accelerated in the previous decade, reaching its highest rate to date at 24.80 per cent. The social and political turmoil of the 1970s—high inflation, low economic growth and burgeoning poverty—was perceived to be associated with rapid population growth, which was seen as one of the key challenges before the country. Population control, therefore, emerged as one of the most critical policy objectives, reflected in the 1976 embargo on the reallocation of seats in Parliament according to the latest census, and in the forced vasectomies, both of which were implemented during the Emergency.

Population control emerged as a magic bullet solution for the myriad problems facing the country. The goal was to be achieved as swiftly as possible, disregarding considerations of freedom, justice and democracy, and sidestepping the universal process of demographic transition. Since the 1970s, the demographic debate in India has revolved around the axis of the north–south divide, even if the strong public reaction to forced sterilisations, manifested in INC's unprecedented defeat in the general election of 1977, ensured that at the level of state policy or programme there would be no coercive measures to control population.

Therefore, the global debate on 'overpopulation' and 'population explosion' starting around the end of the Second World War and driven substantially by geopolitical considerations shaped Indian responses to population growth after Independence. Population control, under the euphemistic name of family planning, became one of the prime goals of the country. This emanated from an empirically unproved link between rapid population growth and development. It was believed that without effective 'population control' neither food security nor development would be possible. Over time, moral and ethical considerations involved in family planning would get increasingly diluted. This will be discussed in detail in Chapter 9.

3

Demographic Transition
A Conceptual Review

This chapter provides a conceptual framework of demographic growth to help develop a useful perspective on the so-called north–south divide in India. Population growth in all societies had been slow and halting for most of human history, marked as it was by high mortality rates in general and by frequent reversals caused by famines, epidemics and warfare. Mankind had to face a constant struggle for survival, so population growth was welcomed in all societies. But before the Industrial Revolution, no large group is known to have grown for long at more than 1 per cent per annum anywhere in the world.[1] In fact, long-term growth rates were generally so modest that it took centuries for population to double in any large country or continent.

The slow growth of population in the pre-modern world is exemplified by the fact that it took nearly three centuries for the population of the world to increase from an estimated 438 million in 1500 to 1.04 billion in 1820.[2] In a way, it took mankind the entire period from the beginning of its existence to 1820 to reach the figure of 1 billion. In contrast, human population has multiplied roughly by eight times in the last two centuries, with the 2023 estimate at about 8 billion. The key transformation in population growth occurred during the transition from the pre-modern to the modern era, which has had an enormous impact on the growth as well as distribution of population across the world.

I

Demographic Transition and Malthus

The term 'demographic transition' was coined by the American sociologist and demographer Frank Notestein in 1945,[3] although a model of demographic transition was developed by Warren Thompson in 1929.[4] In modern demographics, almost all populations, separated by culture and geography, generally follow a pattern marked by shifts in birth rates, death rates, fertility rates, etc., that provide a basis for demographic transition characterised by a least three distinct phases. Three major variables—birth rate, mortality rate and fertility rate—determine the dynamics of demographic transition across societies, including its pace and timing. Migration is, of course, an independent variable extrinsic to the above-mentioned variables of natural growth. The Industrial Revolution, which began in the late-eighteenth century in England, had a significant impact on societies worldwide, leading to demographic transition at various points with varying speeds, yet tracing a broadly similar trajectory.

The pre-modern first phase of this transition, which covers virtually all societies until the seventeenth century, is marked by high birth rates and high mortality rates, resulting in very slow population growth. The second phase—which began in some European countries in the eighteenth century—witnesses a decline in mortality rates at a much higher pace than reduction in birth rates, giving an impetus to growth, sometimes leading to a population boom. In the third and final phase, both birth and death rates are low, coupled with declining fertility rate. As a consequence, population begins to age, stagnate, and in the long run, decline.

Ecological limitations on population growth historically influenced the rate at which a particular population could grow, sometimes regarded as the carrying capacity of a land,[5] though the role of modernisation, especially in European society, cannot be ignored. It has been found that the birth rates and the overall fertility rates in France had begun to decline right around the time of Enlightenment in the late-eighteenth century.[6] Some believe that this pattern bore an ideological imprint and was not primarily the outcome of ecological limitations or carrying capacity.

Many other European countries showed a similar pattern of birth rate decline during the second half of the nineteenth century.

Nonetheless, in eighteenth-century Europe there was a social phobia regarding the supposed cataclysmic effect of population growth, exemplified in the pioneering work of the English clergyman Thomas Malthus. In 1798, he propounded the theory that predicted an apocalyptic competition between population growth and food production:

> … the power of population is indefinitely greater than the power in the earth to produce subsistence for man. Population, when unchecked, increases in a geometrical ratio. Subsistence increases only in an arithmetical ratio.[7]

According to him, the relationship between population growth and food supply was at the heart of the well-being of every society:

> The happiness of a country does not depend, absolutely, upon its poverty or its riches, upon its youth or its age, upon its being thinly, or fully inhabited, but upon the rapidity with which it is increasing, upon the degree in which the yearly increase of food approaches to the yearly increase of an unrestricted population.[8]

Malthus argued that given this equation the population of a country would inevitably surpass the means of its subsistence, thus necessitating some depopulation if those alive were to survive for long. He suggested in a way that mass deaths caused by tragic events such as epidemics, famines, droughts and other natural and man-made calamities appear to serve a necessary function. These events quickly chisel off a considerable chunk of population from the existing mass, thereby providing subsistence for the survivors. Malthus explained the interplay of population and calamities, both natural and man-made:

> Famine seems to be the last, the most dreadful resource of nature. The power of population is so superior to the power in the earth to produce subsistence for man, that premature death must in some shape or other visit the human race. The vices of mankind are active and able ministers of depopulation. They are the precursors in the great army of destruction; and often finish the dreadful work themselves. But should they fail in this war of extermination, sickly seasons, epidemics, pestilence, and

> plague, advance in terrific array, and sweep off their thousands and ten thousands. Should success be still incomplete, gigantic inevitable famine stalks in the rear, and with one mighty blow, levels the population with the food of the world.[9]

Though he was not probably aware of it, Malthus's ideas on population growth took shape at a time when England was already in the second phase of demographic transition—sometimes described as 'demographic revolution'[10]—and had experienced a very high population growth for more than a century. England's long-term population boom would multiply the Anglo-Saxon population of just about four million at the beginning of the sixteenth century to at least 200 million today, spread over different countries and continents, including the United States, Canada, Australia, New Zealand, South Africa, apart from the United Kingdom itself.[11] Moreover, this 'demographic revolution' was linked to economic growth.

II
World Demographic Divergence: The Economic Dimension

Over the last several centuries, there is a discernible link between economic development and population growth worldwide, which will be analysed in detail in Chapter 8. Above a threshold, higher levels of development are associated with moderate population growth rates, while lower levels are associated with higher growth rates. This differential has been consistent since relevant data for world population growth have been available. Plotting the growth rates of more developed regions against those of less-developed ones, Figure 3.1 depicts the pattern of world population growth between 1760 and 2010.

It is evident from Figure 3.1 that a growth rate in excess of 2 per cent per annum has only ever been achieved in the less-developed regions of the world. The more developed regions have grown only around 1 per cent per annum even in their fastest-growing period. This is partly because in the developed regions, the second phase of demographic transition marked by rapid growth lasted far longer—effectively two centuries—than in the less-developed regions, where it has lasted just fifty years. Notably,

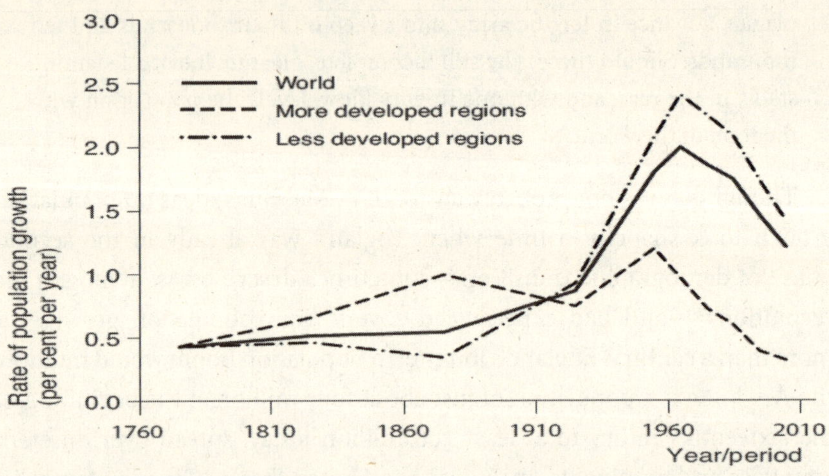

Figure 3.1: Population growth rates of more developed regions of the world vis-à-vis less-developed regions, 1760–2010

Source: Tim Dyson (2010)[12]

although the population growth rate of the developed regions never exceeded 1 per cent per annum, from 1760 to 1910 it was consistently higher than the world growth rate. During this period, the growth rate of the less-developed regions was much lower, since they were still below the threshold level of social and economic development that eventually ushers in the period of rapid demographic growth by reducing mortality. They would consistently surpass the growth rates of the developed regions and of the world only after 1910 and gradually recover their long-term share in the world demographic pie, probably triggered by a rudimentary economic development that some of them started experiencing. This will be discussed in detail in Chapter 8. How relevant is this to India's demographic divergence centred on the north–south divide? Is regional economic disparity related to the demographic characteristics of the respective regions? This will be examined in detail in Chapter 7.

As the increased growth in the more developed regions depicted in Figure 3.1 shows, despite its great popularity when it was propounded, the Malthusian theory was belied within the next couple of generations. Tremendous technological improvements in agriculture in Europe and some other parts of the world ensured an unprecedented rise in agricultural productivity which had not been foreseen by Malthus. This raises a question: Is the Malthusian theory more relevant to the history of the world before the nineteenth century?

An affirmative answer is found in a well-known work on economic history, *A Farewell to Alms*, by Gregory Clark, professor of economics at the University of California, Davis , USA. In this book, Clark demonstrates that almost all societies before 1800 existed under 'Malthusian equilibrium'. The pace of technological advance in all economies was so slow that incomes could not escape the Malthusian equilibrium.[13]

Clark regards famines, epidemics, etc., as a blessing in disguise because the survivors transition from scarcity to survival. This shift not only ensures immediate relief but also contributes to future growth through procreation. In his comprehensive analysis of real wages in medieval Europe, Clark maps the impact of the catastrophic Black Death of the fourteenth century on the European population. He suggests an upward trend as population dwindled after the 1348 bubonic plague that took millions of lives.

This trend continued until the 1450s, after which wages started to decline, implying the applicability of the Malthusian theory.[14] Other sources also corroborate that the ratio of earnings to cost of subsistence—or the subsistence ratio—was high in major European cities in the fifteenth century.[15] Figure 3.2 gives a pictorial representation of the subsistence ratio for labourers in six major cities of the world from 1375 to 1875.

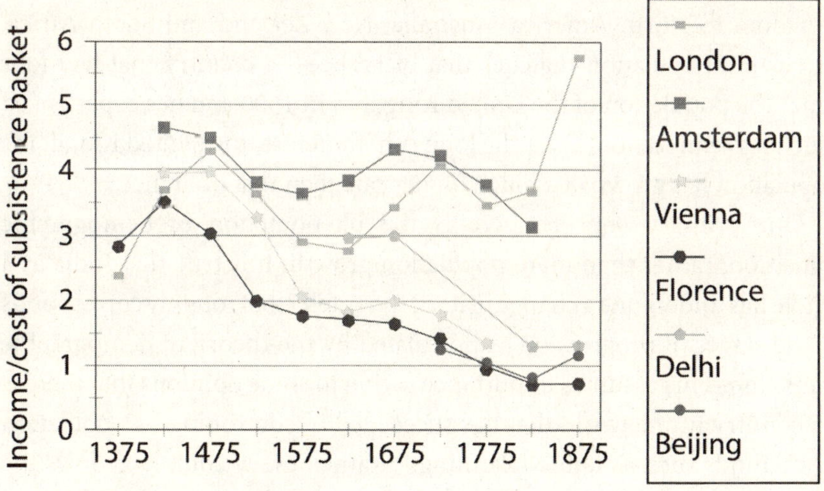

Figure 3.2: Subsistence ratio for labourers, 1375–1875

Source: Robert C. Allen (2008).[16]

The Malthusian trap might have impacted human history prior to the Industrial Revolution in Europe. But, akin to many other forecasts about the distant future, Malthusian clairvoyance proved to be inaccurate over the next two centuries. Instead of the resource crunch he had predicted in 1798, technological advancements and higher economic growth not only sustained the existing population but also led to a spurt in Western Europe. Economic historian Angus Maddison (2001) estimated that per capita income in Western Europe tripled in approximately a century compared to its level in 1820. More surprisingly, it multiplied almost fifteenfold by the end of the twentieth century.[17] Other estimates see the GDP of Western Europe grow forty-two times between 1820 and 1998—a period during which the world GDP multiplied forty-nine-fold.[18] How was this related to demographic transition?

Let us turn to population growth during 1820–1998. In France, population growth lagged the GDP growth rate. Its population was 31.25 million in 1820; by 1998 it had risen to 60.1 million.[19] The United Kingdom experienced more substantial population growth, nearly tripling from 1820 to 1998. Its population increased from 21.24 million to 58.74 million.[20] According to data from 2021, the United Kingdom is still a country of 67.7 million, reflecting a growth of nearly 3.5 times compared to its population in 1820.[21] As of 2022, France's population at 67.97 million is only about double that of 1820.[22] Despite significant emigration from the United Kingdom to North America, Australia, New Zealand and South Africa, its current population matches that of France—a country that had four times the population of the United Kingdom in 1500 and has experienced much less emigration. Over the long run, therefore, the United Kingdom's population has grown at a much higher rate than that of France.

Our primary concern here is the phenomenon of demographic transition, rather than mere population growth. It is true that India as a whole has undergone a change in its demography that roughly corresponds to the stages of progression as postulated by the theory of demographic transition. This assumes importance owing to some opinions that there is no country in the world that has succeeded in controlling its population by methods such as family planning.[23] Rather, every country follows the process of demographic transition before arriving at a point where its population stabilises or declines.

III
The Demographic Transition Theory

Demographic transition theory, which is based on conclusions derived from the demographic history of the world, is doubtless among the great theories of the modern world. Its primary strength lies in its ability to provide the most comprehensive understanding and explanation of the demographic history of mankind as well as current global population dynamics. Over the last two centuries, the shift of much of the world's population from a high birth rate, high death rate and high fertility to a low birth rate, low death rate and low fertility rate is a clear indication that the world has gone through the process of demographic transition. Almost every country has gone through, or will go through, a phase of rapid population growth, though its specific features may differ widely. In Europe's case, there is a debate on whether it was the rise in birth rates or the fall in death rates that caused a spurt in population growth in the nineteenth century. The demographic transition that usually begins with decline in mortality, thus inflating population growth, can be seen in the relative difference between crude birth rates and crude death rates of the world population since 1900 (Figure 3.3).

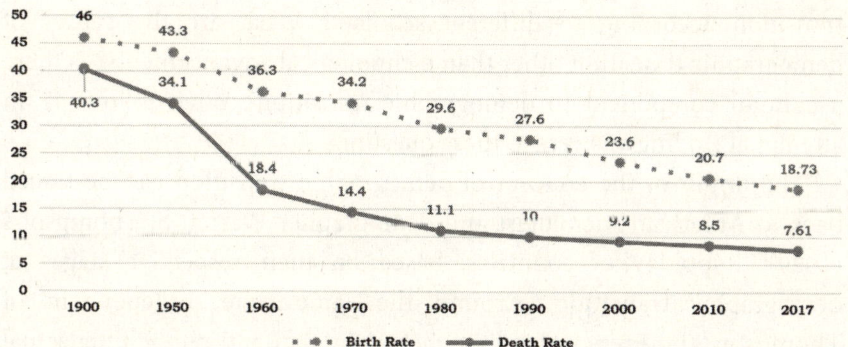

Figure 3.3: A comparison between worldwide birth rates and death rates (per thousand), 1900–2017

Sources: Figures prior to 1950 are derived from Biraben (1979), Hauser (1971) and Grauman (1977). Figures for 1950 and later are from the United Nations (2008, 2009). Figures for 2017 are from the World Bank Open Data[24] (Table 3.1, Appendices).

Between 1900 and 1950, the gap in the rate of decline in birth and death rates of the world population gradually widened. This was followed by a sharp decline in mortality rates, especially during 1950–60, while birth rates continued to be high. Owing mainly to this decline in the death rate, the population of the world, which had been growing annually at the rate of 0.6 per cent between 1800 and 1900, grew at 0.9 per cent between 1900 and 1950. The upward trend persisted as the world's annual population growth rate reached its peak at 2 per cent in the 1960s, marking a rapid expansion during the middle phase of demographic transition. Concomitantly, the Total Fertility Rate (TFR), which represents all births throughout a woman's reproductive cycle, declined from 5.7 in 1900 to 5 in 1950 and to 2.43 in 2017.[25] This unprecedented reduction in fertility was the defining element in the story of demographic transition. It is now accompanied by historically unprecedented rates of urbanisation and the recent phenomenon of population ageing—two processes that will be taken up later in the book.

For now, suffice it to reiterate that world population did undergo demographic transition since 1800; of course, with a difference in the developed and the developing regions.[26] It is against this backdrop that some vital questions arise: How did demographic transition enter the arena of academic discussion? What are the stages of demographic transition according to different scholars? What are the causes of demographic transition other than technological advancements? Is there a cultural component to demographic transition? What follows is an attempt at finding answers to these questions.

The origin of the concept of demographic transition can be traced back to American sociologist and demographer Warren S. Thompson's (1929)[27] typology of countries, based on their respective stages of demographic transition. Around the same time, independent of Thompson, the French demographer, politician and public intellectual Adolphe Landry, who wrote several influential books on demographics and economics, came to similar conclusions about the history and pattern of population growth in parts of the world.[28] In his observations about France, he perceptively noted that the country had transitioned over the centuries from high birth rates and high mortality to low birth rates and low mortality, accompanied by very slow population growth which might in the near future decline further, eventually leading to a shrinking of population.[29]

Thompson presented a three-tiered classification of countries based on the point at which they were then located along the process of demographic transition.[30] The first cluster of countries, designated Group A, represented the countries of Western Europe which had already begun to experience a decline in their population growth. Both birth and death rates had taken a downswing by then, but the growth decline was largely due to a reduction in the fertility rates in this group of countries. The phase of decline being experienced by these countries was thus underpinned by an overall cultural transformation that fuelled the fall in their fertility rates. It was not merely a consequence of the numerically determined population, which is the difference between the birth and death rates.

An interesting facet of the drop in fertility rates across cultures has been underlined by American demographer Dudley Kirk. Based on observations from the European Fertility Project, he argues that once a transition in the fertility rate occurred in a particular linguistic or cultural area, it spread rapidly irrespective of socio-economic forces, thus reinforcing the 'cultural' argument.[31] In the same article, Kirk (1996) asserts:

> All the suggested causes of the transition are, in fact, closely linked, and like the demographic transition itself are an essential part of the process of modernization. No country has been modernized without going through the demographic transition, and this is likely to be the case in the future as well [32]

According to the British physicist, epidemiologist and historian of medicine Thomas McKeown, economic conditions played the dominant role in shaping the course of demographic transition across cultures.[33] After the onset of mortality decline, the onward march of demographic transition follows its own course with minor variations, depending on the specific conditions of a given society or culture. British demographer Tim Dyson (2010) argues that rich and poor countries have experienced similar patterns of demographic transition at some point.[34] He is of the opinion that a rise in per capita income is not a precondition for the onset of demographic transition.[35]

The connection between cultural notions—sometimes even ideology—and demographic change, especially fertility decline, has been expressed well by the Australian demographer J.C. Caldwell: 'New ideologies justify low fertility and even childlessness, and the religions' old attitudes to fertility are forgotten or reinterpreted.'[36] This is an apt comment on the modern demographic transition—a global phenomenon marked by an influx of women into the industrial and service-sector labour force, as against agricultural work, which is closely related to decline in fertility rates.

Therefore, the link between modernisation and demographic transition suggests that achieving a stable population in the long run is related to the cultural change that the wheels of modernisation set rolling in almost every society it influences. This change includes the process of urbanisation which is closely related to modernisation, so much so that American sociologist Brigitte Berger has summed it up as 'urbanisation equals modernisation'.[37] It is, of course, technological advancement and economic development that usher in the processes of modernisation and demographic transition in the first place.

Returning to Thompson's classification, the second group in his analysis comprises those countries where both birth and mortality rates had reached low values. However, the population of these countries continued to grow due to a more rapid decline in death rates preceding a fall in birth rates. This resulted in a net increase in population. Thompson categorised Eastern and Southern European countries as Group B. The last group, labelled Group C, represented countries facing the challenge of 'overpopulation' and, in Thompson's view, exemplified the Malthusian Trap.[38] This group primarily included Japan, India and Russia.

In addition to the above typology that categorises countries based on their features, demographic transition can also be viewed as a process comprising four distinct stages:

Stage 1: Typically seen in less-developed countries where birth rates are high but a large number of people die of preventable causes, leading to a largely stable population.

Stage 2: Death rates fall steeply as deaths from preventable causes are reduced by better food supply and improved public health. But birth rates remain high due to high fertility, poor social development and limited access to health and contraceptive availability. This leads to a spurt in population.

Stage 3: Birth rates fall but population continues to grow because of a prevalence of many people in the reproductive age group due to the high fertility of previous generations.

Stage 4: Countries achieve a stable population once again, with low birth and death rates but at a higher level of social and economic development. Population is stable but higher than in stage one.

IV
Stages of Demographic Transition

Let us start the discussion on the various stages of demographic transition with a depiction of the classical three-stage model:

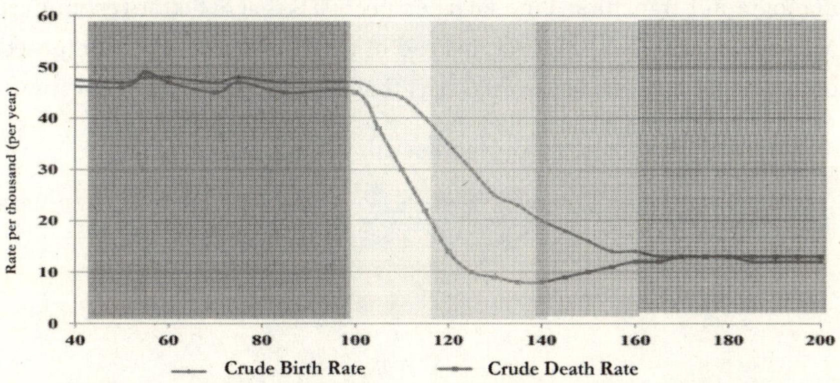

Figure 3.4: The three stages of demographic transition

Purushottam M. Kulkarni of Jawaharlal Nehru University, India views demographic transition as a more complex three-phase process: pre-transitional, transitional with three sub-phases, and post-transitional:[39]

Pre-transitional: High and nearly equal birth and death rates.

Transitional: Declining death rates and, after a lag, also declining birth rates.

- Early transitional: Decline in death rates but high birth rates continue
- Middle transitional: Decline in birth rates and continuing decline in death rates

- Late transitional: Continuing decline in birth rates and slowdown in the fall in death rates

Post-transitional: Low and nearly equal birth and death rates.[40]

We have outlined here the stages through which populations grow while undergoing demographic transition. According to British demographer Tim Dyson (2010), this involves five essential processes[41] in the following order:

1. Mortality decline
2. Population growth
3. Fertility decline
4. Urbanisation
5. Population ageing

There are other perspectives on the stages involved in the process of demographic transition. One such perspective is that of Oxford economist Max Roser, who believes that, instead of three, the process is composed of five stages.[42] Given below is a chart that depicts a five-stage transition:

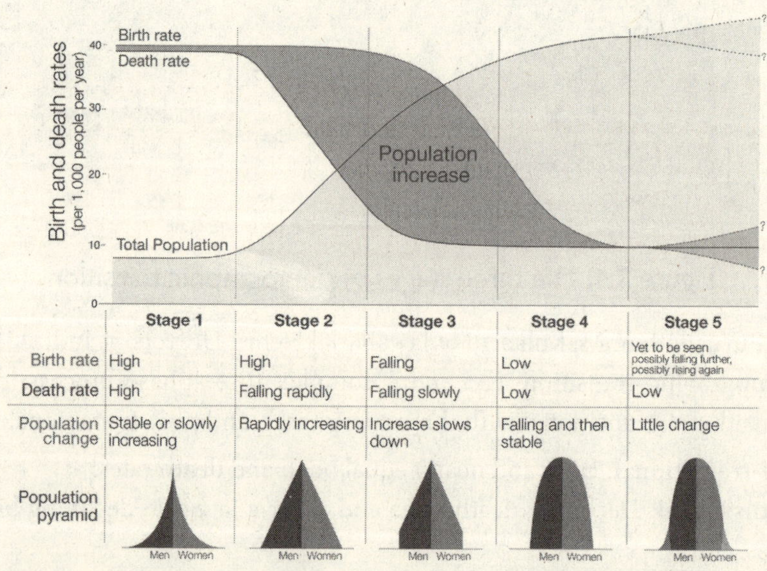

Figure 3.5: The five stages of the demographic transition

Source: ourworldindata.org[43]

It is widely accepted that every society has experienced in its demographic history a phase marked by high birth and death rates, thus limiting the natural growth of population. As mentioned, for most of human history, societies across the world lived in this phase.[44] High infant and child mortality rates, lowering life expectancy as a whole, and the ravages of wars, famines and epidemics ensured high death rates. As a result, growth of population anywhere in the world was very slow compared to the last two centuries.[45] It might, therefore, be seen as a phenomenal feat performed by mankind that the world population has increased eightfold since 1820, the year it first crossed the 1 billion mark.

Though there are numerous factors behind this massive growth in population over the last two centuries, what is indisputably the most important is the steep decline in mortality rates. This decline is largely attributed to better nutrition, sanitation and healthcare.[46] Coupled with birth rates that mostly remain as high as they had been in the course of human history, the mortality decline causes the onset of the phase of rapid population growth. This has been the second phase of the demographic transition universally.

While a decline in mortality rates usually indicates the onset of transition, the issue of 'population explosion' or 'population bomb' that worried Kingsley Davis and Paul Ehrlich in the 1950s and 1960s is an inevitable consequence of sharply falling death rates coupled with continued high birth rates. From the mid-twentieth century to the present, this has been the experience of the majority of less-developed countries, including India. The decline in mortality that was spread over two centuries or more in the West unfolded in India and many other countries within a few decades after the Second World War. With a decline in birth rates and fertility rates occurring only after a lag, rapid population growth was unavoidable. Figure 3.6 depicts the world demographic growth since 1960.

According to Figure 3.6, the fastest growth rate was registered in 1969, with a growth of 2.11 per cent. Oxford economist Max Roser disputes this, arguing that the growth peaked in 1962-63, with 2.20 per cent as the peak. This is demonstrated by Figure 3.7. Although the two sources differ on the exact year when the world population growth peaked and on the

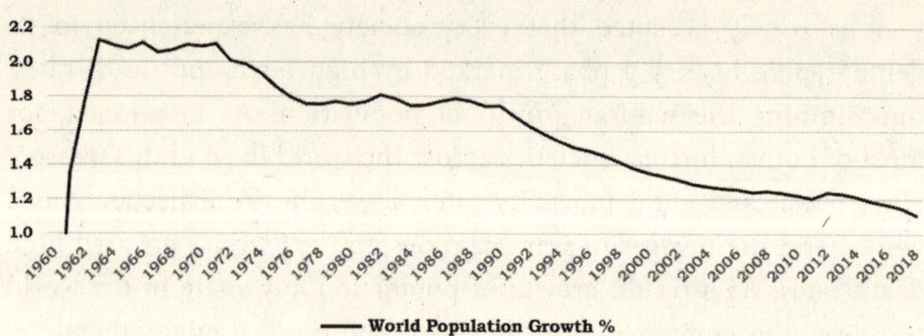

Figure 3.6: Peak rate of population growth at the world level – I

Source: World Bank Open Data[47]

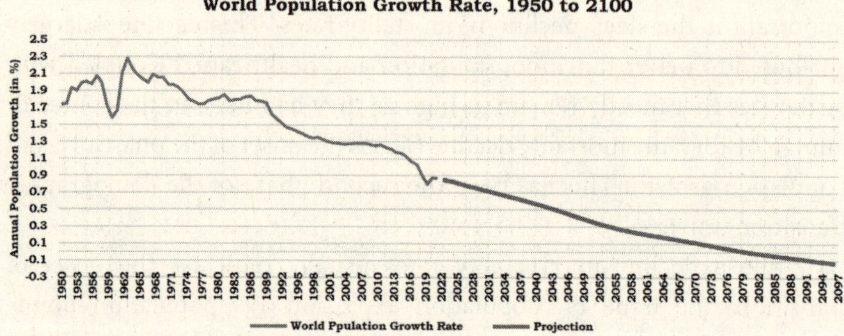

Figure 3.7: Peak rate of population growth at the world level - II

Source: ourworldindata.org[48]

rate of growth, they agree it occurred in the same decade. That is all that matters at this point.

V

Causes of Demographic Transition

While a variety of reasons can be cited for each of these changes along the trajectory of demographic transition, the primary concern at this point is to identify the driving force behind these changes. The enduring debate on the subject oscillates between the role of socio-economic forces versus cultural variables as being the primary agents of demographic transition. Ever since Malthus, the emphasis has largely been on the significance of economic forces in shaping the growth curve of population in any given society. More recently, scholars such as Thomas McKeown have continued to prioritise socio-economic variables in explaining demographic change.

For McKeown, improvement in economic conditions in Europe and some other parts of the world since the 1770s was responsible for the decline in mortality rates. Increased level of nutrition, and not public medicine or better hygiene, accounted for the dip in mortality rates in many countries globally.[49] In his view, other factors such as better medical facilities and access to newly developed vaccines seem to have contributed only marginally to the process of change in population growth witnessed over the last two centuries. Change in socio-economic conditions primarily explains the demographic change that has taken place since the late-eighteenth century:

> The rise of population was due primarily to the decline of mortality and the most important reason for the decline was an improvement in economic and social conditions.[50]

Here an important question arises: Why does McKeown think that medical advancement did not contribute significantly to the demographic transition in the eighteenth and nineteenth centuries, at least in the West? According to McKeown, the downward trend in mortality rates in most societies preceded the introduction of most medical improvement techniques. He was also critical of the approach taken by modern medicine regarding well being. Too much emphasis on curing rather than caring seems to have stemmed from a wrong understanding of the history of medicine.[51] His thesis elicited mild criticism as well as recognition in the 1970s, summed up lucidly in the statement below:

> McKeown's professional and political battle was primarily directed against those who argued for ever greater diversion of the new National Health Service resources into curative technical medicine—invasive surgery and biochemical 'treatments'—at the expense of preventive, humanistic medicine—efforts to understand and modify the health implications

> of the environment in its widest sense.... McKeown's exploration of the historical record was fantastically effective in these professional, political terms, thoroughly puncturing the inflated claims to importance, on the grounds of a supposed long history of life-saving achievements, of the medical 'technocrats'.[52]

Thus, with a blend of vindication and criticism, the debate seems far from settled, with McKeown retaining his significance even now.

VI
Urbanisation and Demographic Transition

It is widely acknowledged that the extraordinary rise in population growth around the world since 1800 has been accompanied by a correspondingly high growth of urban population.[53] Some rather conservative estimates suggest that only 5 per cent of the world's population lived in urban centres in 1800, which rose to 14 per cent by 1900.[54] Urban population growth, however, significantly outpaced the total population growth of the world between 1950 and 2010. During these six decades, the world population grew at an annual rate of 1.7 per cent, while the growth rate of urban population has been 2.6 per cent.[55] Therefore, it is crucial to understand the relationship between the processes of urbanisation and demographic transition.

It has been argued by some that demographic transition is responsible for urbanisation.[56] However, Tim Dyson (2010) cites a number of research works, arguing the other way round: urbanisation affects rates of mortality and fertility, thus causing demographic transition. At this stage, it is immaterial to our analysis as to which of the two is the cause and which is the effect. All that matters is that the two processes bear a close relationship with each other, wherein one typically accompanies the other. The significance of studying the two in tandem is emphatically expressed by Dyson:

> To put the matter differently: any account of the demographic transition that fails to include urbanization as one of its major components is seriously incomplete.[57]

Therefore, urban spaces with small family norms play an important role in demographic transition. Lewis Mumford, an American sociologist and historian known for his contributions to the field of urban studies, has pointed out that urbanisation gives rise to an increased pressure on economic resources, as the cost of services in urban areas often exceeds the cost in rural areas by up to three times[58] Therefore, it is not surprising that a rapid pace of urbanisation can alter cultural norms around family size. Large families may cease to be beneficial both for families and society because of the vastly increased economic burden of raising children in cities. What further exacerbates the situation is the lack of adequate economic compensation by children through their early involvement in productive activities, as observed by Notestein (1953):

> Urban life stripped the family of many functions in production, consumption, recreation, and education.... In factory employment the individual stood on his own accomplishments. The new mobility of young people and the anonymity of city life reduced the pressure toward traditional behaviour exerted by the family and the community. In a period of rapidly developing technology new skills were needed and new opportunities for individual advancement arose. Education and a rational point of view became increasingly important. As a consequence, the cost of child-rearing grew and the possibilities for economic contributions by children declined. Falling death rates at once increased the size of the family to be supported and lowered the inducements to have many births. Women, moreover, found new independence from household obligations and new economic roles less compatible with child-bearing.[59]

Notestein's argument about the vastly increased cost of child-rearing in urban areas being related to a shift to small-size families has been reiterated in recent research that tries to establish that at the microeconomic level, as housing prices in urban areas go up, the cost of raising children escalates, which in turn leads to a decline in fertility rates.[60] Hence, it is not at all surprising that urban fertility rates are most of the time below rural fertility rates worldwide, though caution must be exercised in taking the urban–rural difference in fertility rates as the defining feature of demographic transition. Keeping that in mind, Dutch economic historian Jan de Vries (1990)[61] directs his attention to the urban–rural difference in mortality rates more than the difference in fertility rates. It could be argued that there is a limit to how urban a given population can become and it is this cap that becomes the driving force for population stabilisation, as urbanisation and demographic transition occur simultaneously. The process of demographic transition in rural and urban areas is shown in Figure 3.8.

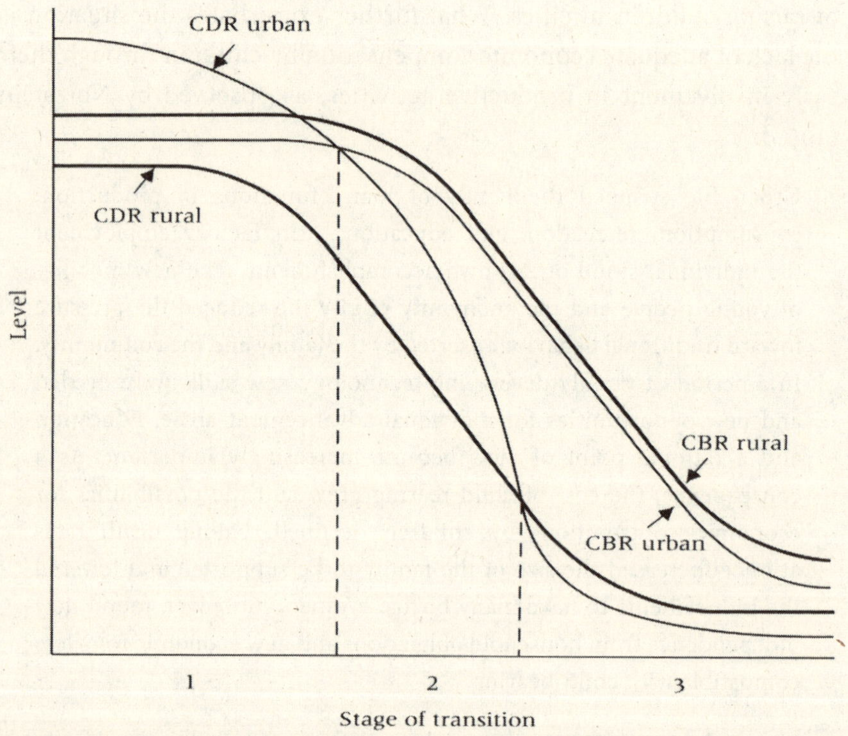

Figure 3.8: A stylised model showing the rural–urban difference in demographic transition[62]

Source: de Vries (1990, p. 58).[63]

So, there is an association between urbanisation and demographic growth globally. Figure 3.9 demonstrates this for fifty-six countries.

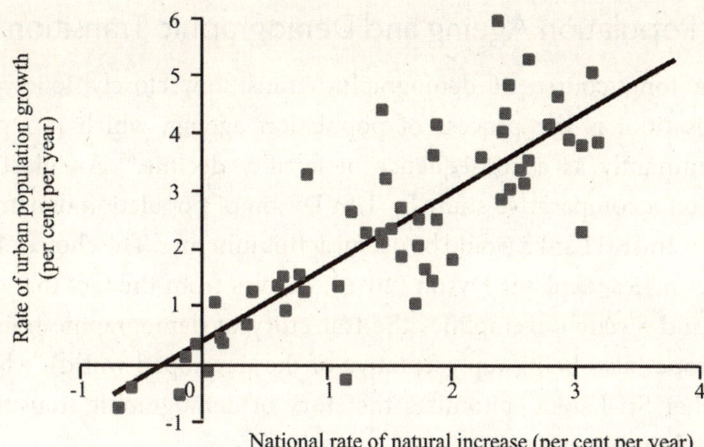

Figure 3.9: The rate of natural population growth vs rate of urban population growth in 56 countries, 1995–2005

Source: Tim Dyson (2015)[64]

In fact, the general growth of the world population and that of the urban population follow similar trajectories, as depicted in Figure 3.10.

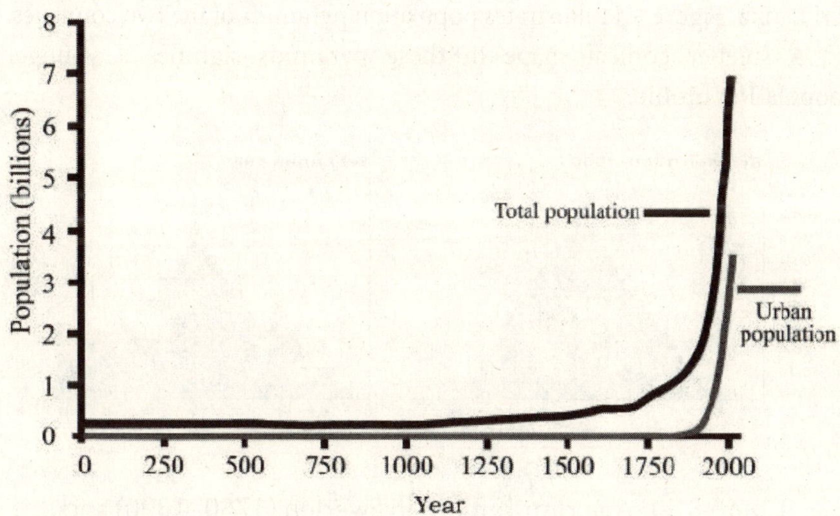

Figure 3.10: Growth of the world population since first century AD

Source: Tim Dyson (2015)[65]

VII
Population Ageing and Demographic Transition

In the long course of demographic transition, closely followed by urbanisation, is the process of population ageing, which is regarded predominantly as a consequence of fertility decline.[66] An illustration based on a comparative study by Tim Dyson of population dynamics in Sweden and Sri Lanka would be useful at this juncture. The choice of these two countries, explains Dyson (2010), derives from the fact that on the one hand Sweden exemplifies the trajectory of demographic transition in Europe (also being representative of the developed world), while on the other Sri Lanka epitomises the story of demographic transition in developing countries.

Compared to Sri Lanka, the process took much longer in Sweden. The first phase—mortality decline—took 130 years, during which the death rate fell from 30 per thousand to 10; whereas an identical decline in death rate in Sri Lanka took just thirty-five years. The key takeaway is that depending on other mediating factors at work in various social, economic and cultural settings, the duration of demographic transition might vary considerably. Let us delve into a comparative analysis of age structures in Sweden and Sri Lanka. Figure 3.11 illustrates population pyramids of the two countries.

A steeper conical shape in these pyramids signifies a younger population profile:

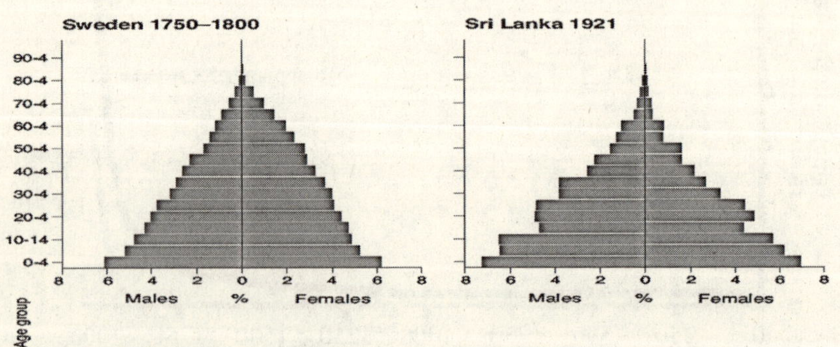

Figure 3.11: Age distributions in Sweden (1750–1800) and Sri Lanka (1921)[67]

Sources: Sweden, 1750–1800 (derived from data in Thomas, 1941)[68] and Sri Lanka, 1921 (data is from Ceylon, 1923)[69]

It is clear from Figure 3.11 that the age structures of population in Sweden between 1750 and 1800 and Sri Lanka in 1921 exhibit similarities, but during vastly different periods. The age distribution of population in Sweden also matched the age distribution of population in Sri Lanka. Thus, though fertility decline took place in both these countries, owing to a difference in the timing and duration of demographic transition, the shapes of the pyramids in 2010 look quite different from each other, as shown in Figure 3.12.

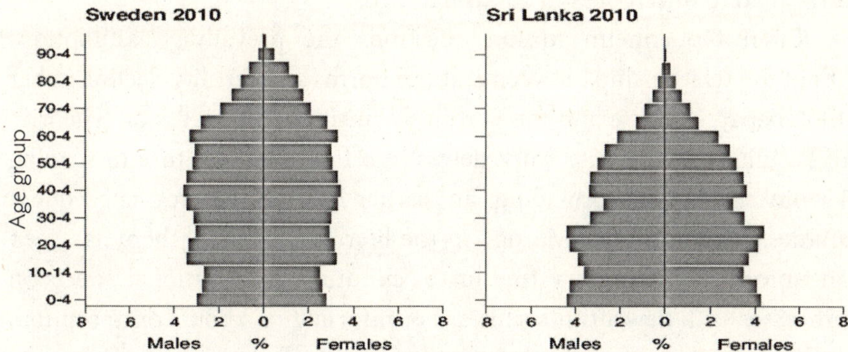

Figure 3.12: Age distributions in Sweden and Sri Lanka in 2010[70]

Source: United Nations, 2009[71]

Having noted the major processes accompanying demographic transition, we turn to the debate on the role of cultural element in shaping the process. This perspective holds some significance in the north–south divide addressed in this study.

VIII
The Role of Cultural Norms in Demographic Transition

Long before modern scholarship began to study the linkages between cultural change and demography, Thomas Malthus (1798) had done early groundwork on the subject. He used the term 'preventive check' to signify a self-imposed cultural restraint of not marrying so as to avoid distress from having to maintain a large family. Malthus considered it unviable in the long run.[72] Subsequently, the correlation between the two parameters has been explored in several studies.

Ron Lesthaeghe's classic study in 1977 highlighted the significance of culture in shaping demography. He argued that even similarly placed contiguous populations differ widely in their fertility rates and other demographic variables depending on their culture.[73] The study found that in Belgium fertility rates varied dramatically between the Flemish, a Dutch-speaking people of Germanic origin, and the Walloons, a French-speaking, Roman-Catholic social group, living just a few kilometres apart from each other. According to Lesthaeghe, this variation could only be attributed to differences in cultural norms.[74]

Karen Oppenheim Mason questions the prevailing assumptions about the relationship between cultural norms and fertility decline in her 1992 paper, 'Culture and the Fertility Transition: Thoughts on Theories of Fertility Decline'. Her work delves into the role of culture in shaping fertility transition, providing an earlier perspective for subsequent studies.[75] According to Mason, 'in the literature to date, there has been an unfortunate tendency to equate "cultural" or "ideational" decision processes with new attitudes toward or information about contraception, and in turn, to equate these new attitudes or information about fertility regulation with the diffusion of innovation.'[76] Mason argues that 'new ideas about the value or valuation of children can diffuse just as rapidly as can new ideas about fertility regulation.'[77] She questions the popular assumption that in human history populations lacked intelligence or were too conformist to control fertility.[78] She argues:

> There seems to be little question that in some historical populations, perhaps even the majority, the average married couple did not go around making self-conscious decisions to limit the number of children according to their perceived self-interests. In this sense, fertility may have been outside the realm of conscious calculation. But this does not mean that what brought it into this realm was the diffusion of the idea that one could practice fertility control. Nor does it mean that fertility was formerly relegated to the realm of unconscious behavior simply because people were ignorant about how to control their fertility or too cowed by traditional religious strictures to dare to think about controlling it.[79]

Akerlof, Yellen and Katz (1996) regard shifting cultural norms as the prime determinant of rising non-marital child-bearing in the

United States in the 1990s.[80] Using this study as the starting point in her article that seeks to analyse the relationship between culture and demography, Christine Bachrach posits that culture significantly shapes demography.[81] However, she acknowledges a certain ambivalence in the relationship.[82] Looking at the issue from a cultural evolutionary perspective, Heidi Colleran (2016) attempts to eliminate ambiguity regarding fertility norms being dependent on culture.[83] She argues that 'global transition to low fertility is one of the most striking cultural convergences in human history'.[84] As we discuss the impact of culture on demographic transition, it must be mentioned that one of the prime determinants of demographic transition across the globe has been the gradual transformation in social mores with respect to family and gender. It has been argued that the greater participation of women in the industrial labour force infused foundational changes in the social norms determining agricultural morality,[85] which accounts for significant changes in fertility norms. It was also established that the 'second demographic transition' in Europe was a consequence of the reduction in the importance of children in the labour force. In fact, it was found that the level of 'progressiveness' among countries, as measured by the attitudes of individuals towards matters such as sexuality, marital relationship, divorce, cohabitation and abortion, is an indicator of fertility rates, and that an inverse relation exists between the two.[86]

What is the relevance of these findings in the Indian context? It has been suggested by some scholars that low-fertility norms in India originated in the coastal south and there has been a slow diffusion of these norms towards northern regions of the country.[87] Notwithstanding the manifest implausibility of such norms spreading across a continent-size country like India, it remains relevant to investigate the role of norms and culture in population growth and fertility reduction. The real problem is to determine whether existing norms and culture such as they are cause a decline in fertility or are the effects of a decline stemming from social and economic development associated with transition. In the context of this study, many questions become pertinent.

Is there a cultural aspect to the 'demographic divergence' among Indian states, especially if they are clubbed into two groups such as the north and the south? Can the decline in fertility and growth rates that the southern states such as Kerala and Tamil Nadu have achieved over several decades be attributed to cultural difference or social and economic development? Did family planning play a critical role in decline in fertility and population growth? Or, is it merely a matter of following the trajectory of demographic transition—driven by social and economic development—wherein fertility rates are bound to take a downturn once the population has reached the stage represented by Group A in Thompson's schema? Is it a demonstrable fact that every Indian state has traced a broadly similar path in its demographic journey, though at different points in time? This study addresses some of these questions.

4

The Demographic History of India (1872–1941)

One of the principal arguments of this study is that unless the demographic history of India is studied from the beginning of the modern Census exercise in 1872, we cannot really make sense of the apparent divergence in fertility and population growth rates of different provinces and regions. There is a major flaw in the prevailing concept of the north–south divide, as it relies only on post-Independence data or, at times, only on post-1971 data for comparing demographic growth across provinces and regions.

This approach leads to misleading conclusions since demographic forces unfold over the long term. Meaningful insights require studying demographic trends over a sufficiently extended span. There may, of course, be occasions when for a specific purpose a micro-period of demographic history needs to be studied within a comparative framework. But the aims and objectives of such studies will have to be very different from those of macro studies, which enable us to develop a historical perspective on population growth.

This chapter incorporates the nineteenth-century censuses in the comparative demographic framework to examine the validity of prevailing notions about which states or regions account for the so-called population explosion of India. It has also incorporated the decennial censuses up to 1941, that is, the last British Census, without adjusting for post-Independence changes in administrative units. In the next chapter, a retrospective view according to current administrative units will be taken up, which permits us to make more precise comparisons from 1901 to 2011.

I

The Nineteenth-Century Demographic Data: 1872 Census

Let us embark on a comparison starting from 1872—the year when the first modern Census of India was compiled. As is well-known, the Census of 1872 was not a synchronous exercise, and the figures were sometimes from earlier censuses or were based on extrapolations. The Memorandum on the Census of British India of 1871-72 published in 1875 admits the limitations of the data:

> In the year 1871-72 the first approach was made to the taking of a general census for the whole of India at a given date. Enumerations of the people had already been made in the North-West Provinces in 1853 and 1865, in Oude 1869, in the Punjab in 1855 and 1868, in the Hyderabad Assigned Districts in 1867, and in the Central Provinces in 1866; while in Madras quinquennial returns have been prepared since 1851-52 by the officers of the Revenue Department, giving with more or less accuracy the numbers of the people in each district, and in British Burma also a tolerably correct census is made each year for the purpose of the capitation rate.[1]

The Memorandum goes on to clarify:

> Unfortunately, the enumeration was not carried out in all the provinces, it being thought undesirable to incur the expense or disturb the people in the Punjab, Oude, and Berar so soon after the last Census taken in those parts of the country. In the following endeavour, therefore, to bring into one view particulars relating to the whole population of British India, it will be necessary to use for those provinces returns which are from three to six years antecedent in date to the general census of 1871–72.[2]

The deficiencies of 1872 Census undermine its usefulness and reliability, especially for aggregate figures and cumulative growth calculations. In fact, the 1901 Census Report would later assert: 'No statistical value attaches to the India total for 1872, which omits several important areas not then enumerated, and includes in certain cases figures for different years, some earlier and some later than 1872.'[3] Notwithstanding these limitations, the Census does help in constructing the broad demographic picture of India around 1870.

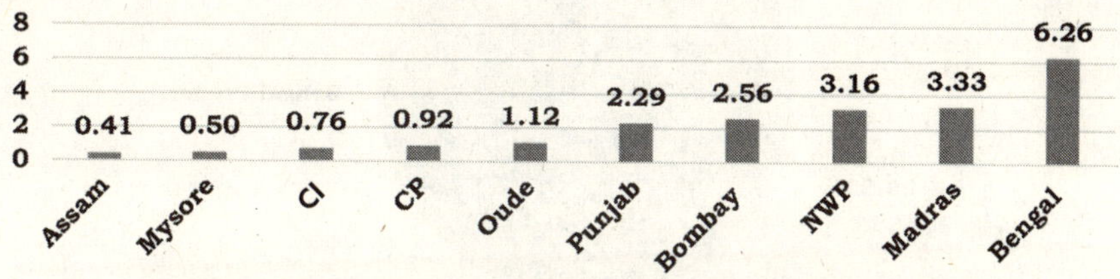

CI: Central India; CP: Central Provinces; NWP: North-West Provinces

Figure 4.1: Population of major administrative units as per 1872 Census (crore)

Source: Memorandum of the Census of British India, 1871-72 (Table 4.1, Appendices)

Figure 4.1 provides a broad demographic distribution of India in 1872. It shows that the largest concentration of population was in the Bengal Presidency, which included Bengal proper, Behar, Chota Nagpore and Orissa. As mentioned in the Census of Bengal 1872 (see Table 4.2 in Appendices), Behar was then divided into two divisions: Patna and Bhagulpore, out of which the first was the larger and the more populous. Their respective populations were 1,31,22,743 and 66,13,358, while the total for Behar was 1,97,36,101. What is striking is that with 465 persons per square mile, Behar had a significantly higher population density than Bengal proper, at 389 persons per square mile. This equation would be reversed in the twentieth century because of the consistently higher growth rate of Bengal over Behar. After 1981, this trend was again reversed. Chota Nagpore had a single division with a population of 38,25,571. Orissa again with one division contained a population of only 43,17,999. Assam had a population of 22,07,453. Bengal proper had a population of 3,67,69,735 spread over six divisions. The pie chart depicted in Figure 4.2 elucidates this.

Punjab had a population of 2,29,10,946, including that of its numerous princely states. Bombay Presidency, which included Sind, returned a population of 2,56,47,818. Minus Sind's population of about 23 lakh, Bombay—which roughly corresponds to today's Maharashtra and

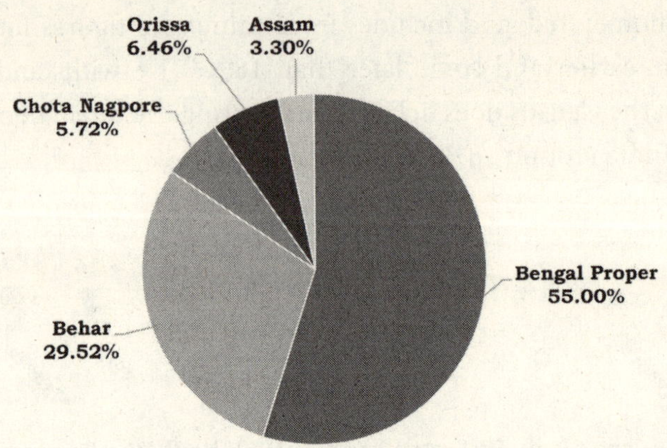

Figure 4.2: Population distribution of Bengal Presidency, 1872 (6,68,56,589)

Source: Census of Bengal, 1872 (Table 4.2, Appendices)

Gujarat (minus Berar and Marathwada which were added later)—had a population of 2,32,47,818, nearly half that of the North-West Provinces and Oude. Of course, the Kannada-speaking districts of the presidency with a population of 28,07,254 will have to be taken out of the reckoning while making regional comparisons.

The North-West Provinces, along with its feudatory states, accounting for much of the later-day United Provinces, had a population of 3,16,88,217. Combined with the smaller but denser region of Oude, with a population of 1,12,20,232, the total population of the United Provinces rose to 4,29,08,449—significantly higher than Bengal proper (3,67,69,735). Decades of higher growth would change this equation drastically in favour of Bengal. Therefore, analysing the trends since the first Census of 1872, one can very well conclude that the 2024 estimate of the combined population of Uttar Pradesh and Uttarakhand (which correspond to North-West Provinces and Oude) at about 25 crore and the combined population of West Bengal and Bangladesh of approximately 27 crore have the same ratio with each other. What has happened is that the equation has been reversed: Whereas in the first census, the population of the North-West Provinces and Oude exceeded that of Bengal by 16.70 per cent, now it is 8 per cent less.

These long-term calculations are, of course, meant to be taken neither in absolutely precise terms nor in isolation. In addition to the inadequacies of the 1872 data mentioned earlier, famines, migration, territorial adjustments and, finally, the Partition of India have all left their imprint on the regional distribution of population across the country. In spite of these factors, a consistent pattern in demographic distribution appears to have been maintained. Over the last century-and-a-half, Bengal's rapid growth rate slowed, and Uttar Pradesh started catching up after 1971.

Let us now turn to the south. In 1872, southern India was divided administratively into the Madras Presidency directly under the British rule and the princely states, the largest of which were Hyderabad, Mysore, Travancore and Cochin. Madras Presidency had a population of 3,33,08,225 and Mysore 50,55,412. Separate figures for Cochin and Travancore are not provided. No census was conducted in Hyderabad, which also had Marathi-speaking areas, accounting for slightly less than one-third of the population of the state. After Independence, these were included in Maharashtra and would need to be distinguished from the Telugu and Kannada areas of the state, which later became part of various southern states.

II

Having discussed the broad demographic statistics for various parts of India, let us take up the aspect of population density, which is vital for studying the historical trends in India's demographic transition. Figure 4.3 gives the density of different parts of India in 1872.

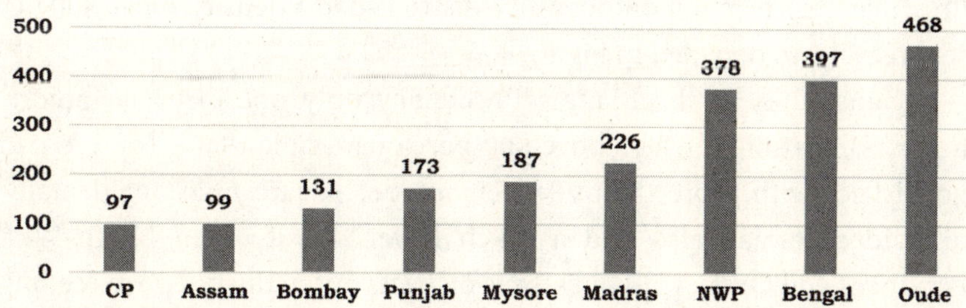

Figure 4.3: Density of population (persons per sq. mile), 1872

CP: Central Provinces; NWP: North-West Provinces

Source: Memorandum of the Census of British India, 1871-72 (Table 4.3, Appendices)

According to the Census of 1872, out of the two regions that combined to form the state of Uttar Pradesh today, Oude, as it was then called, had a population density of 468 persons per square mile, while the North-West Provinces had a density of 378. Bengal, which included Behar and Orissa, had a density of 397. The figures for these regions are much higher than 226 for Madras and 187 for Mysore. This indicates that most of the south had only half the density of what is now Uttar Pradesh. The princely states of Travancore and Cochin were exceptions; they likely had a comparable density, but the Census of 1872 does not provide separate figures for them. What is further striking is that population density as high as 500 persons per square mile was recorded for seven out of twelve districts in the Oude region, as shown in Figure 4.4.

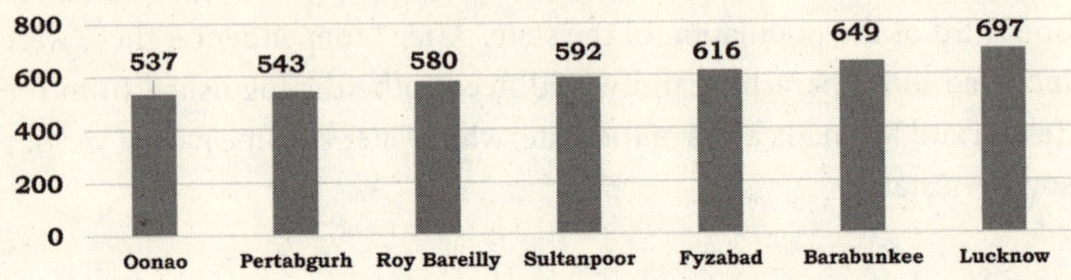

Figure 4.4: High-density districts in Oude (persons per sq. mile), 1872

Source: Memorandum of the Census of British India, 1871-72 (Table 4.4, Appendices)

Similarly, as per Table 4.5 (See Appendices), in the North-West Provinces, thirteen out of thirty-five districts had a density above 500 per square mile, as depicted in Figure 4.5.

Against this, in the Madras Presidency only one district, Tanjore, had a population density above 500 per square mile (540). Mysore had no district with more than 284 persons per square mile. Incidentally, undivided Punjab also had a much lower density than North-West Provinces and Oude, with only three districts out of thirty-two exceeding the figure of 500 persons per square mile: Jalandhar (596), Amritsar (532) and Sialkot (510). What these figures underline is that population density was the highest in the Gangetic plain. In fact, the census report had noted: 'When, however, we quit the valleys watered by the great rivers,

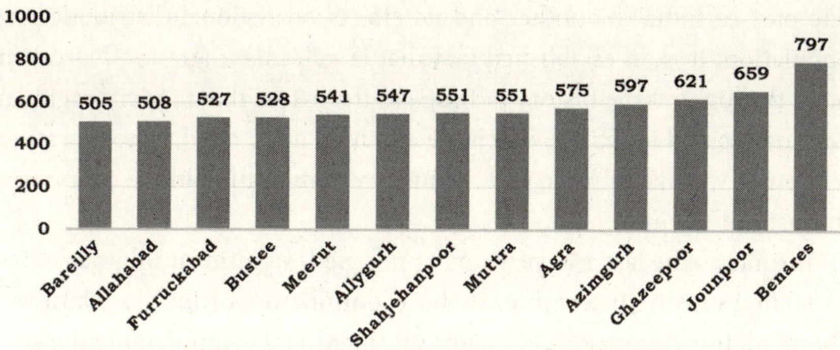

Figure 4.5: High-density districts in North-West Provinces (persons per sq. mile), 1872

Source: Memorandum of the Census of British India, 1871-72 (Table 4.5, Appendices)

the Brahmapootra, Ganges, and Jumna, the Gogra and the Goomtee, we find a much more sparsely populated country.'[4] As the Census of 1891 would later show, this area alone contributed roughly 44 per cent of the population of India, out of which the then North-West Provinces and Oude accounted for about two-fifths.[5]

These historical trends contradict the idea that the north has witnessed an abnormally high population growth in the modern era. For an objective assessment, what is required is a long-term perspective covering the entire period of modern Indian history since the beginning of the decennial census in 1872. While the 1872 data are not entirely reliable and need not be taken as precise, they do indicate that because of favourable geographical and climatic conditions the Gangetic plain had a much higher population density than most of the south, west, north-west and central India, except what is now Kerala, around this time. It was the early growth spurt of population in the south, epitomised by Kerala, that either narrowed this gap or reversed it. The subsequent growth spurt of the northern states after 1971 merely restored the long-term historical trend.

There is no linear direction in which divergence has happened. This is because, as we shall see, in the long run, the regions have shown both divergence and convergence vis-à-vis one another and some sort of movement towards an equilibrium can be faintly visualised. One might, of course, object to this by raising the question of migration from one part of India to another and its effects on regional distribution of population. It is an established fact that large-scale migration has taken place throughout the history of India, to the extent that modern regional boundaries and identities which are assumed to be fixed, become rather tenuous if we take into account the history of migration in the country in the last millennium.

Insofar as the last 150 years are concerned, significant migration has happened mostly in search of better economic opportunities. Until the 1980s, mainly Bombay and Calcutta attracted a large number of migrants from all over the country, but in the last thirty years or so, southern India, with its flourishing economy and fast-growing cities such as Bangalore and Hyderabad, has also attracted large numbers, especially from the north.

Though migration may have contributed to population growth in the west and the south to some extent, considering India's immense population, it does not seem to have occurred on a large-enough scale to make a fundamental difference on its own to the long-term regional distribution of population in the country. However, in the case of Assam, migration from Bengal and later Bangladesh has been a critical factor. Migration as a factor in population growth and in divergence across regions is embedded in this study, in the sense that both push and pull factors—famines, plagues, economic opportunities and urbanisation—behind migration are in most cases phenomena that routinely affect population growth and need to be acknowledged as such; the exception being extreme instances like the Partition of India, which forced around 15 million people to leave their birthplace in a sudden and violent turn of events.

Therefore, provincial and regional population growth rates and shares in both undivided British India and post-Partition India exhibit long-term convergence, even amid substantial fluctuations in Total Fertility Rates (TFR) and decadal growth rates across different periods, along with the effects of migration.

III

The Census of 1881: Original versus Reconstructed as per Post-Partition Boundaries

As mentioned, the Census of 1872 suffered from several drawbacks. The fundamental problem was that it was not a synchronous census all over India; for Punjab, Oude and Berar, the figures collected three to six years earlier were used. Moreover, there was no census in Hyderabad, and extrapolations were used for Rajputana and many other territories. The Report on the Census of British India 1881 elaborates how 1881 Census was very different from that of 1872:

> The Census of the 17th February 1881 was the first synchronous enumeration which has been attempted for all India. Not that no previous count of the people had been effected in the various Provinces and States composing the British Indian Empire. In the majority of these States, and in all the British Provinces, there has been a previous census. But the enumeration in the various Provinces and States has been effected at different times and by independent agencies. There had too been no attempt to secure uniformity in the arrangement of the statistics then obtained. On the present occasion the operation has been effected upon a different principle. The work has been done under one controlling authority, and the Census was taken on one uniform date.[6]

The second most serious issue in the 1872 Census was that the people showed considerable reluctance to share full and correct information about their families with the census authorities. Notwithstanding 'suspicion of forced recruitment for the Afghan War, or the imposition of a general tax', there was much less reluctance on the part of the people to share the required information in 1881. As the Census report noted:

> There have been so many previous enumerations in large tracts of the country, particularly in the older British Provinces, that the people are now fairly accustomed to what originally was looked upon by them as a very suspicious operation, and in general the Census of 1881 was viewed by the population with calmness, if not indifference.[7]

The Census of 1881 indeed provides comprehensive and reliable data that encompass the entire country and its various constituents. Therefore, for long-term calculations of population growth and shares of various regions of India, the Census of 1881 is used in this study. The census tables will, of course, have to be reconstructed according to our analytical requirements.[8] In order to ascertain the share of each administrative unit as it was in 1881, we have to add a column on percentage share. The second and the more difficult task is to calculate the figures for 1881 of India with its post-Partition boundaries. To achieve this, we have to factor out the population of East Bengal, West Punjab, Sind and North-West Frontier Provinces that were partitioned out in 1947. In addition, Burma needs to be removed from the calculations. The reconstructed data would enable us to calculate the approximate shares of states and regions in 1881 and their cumulative growth figures over the next 140 years. This long-term comparative perspective is critical because demographic transition unfolds over the long term. While we have the figures for NWFP, Sind and Burma in 1881, which can simply be deducted from the total population of India, the figures for East Bengal and West Punjab will have to be retrospectively constructed at the level of divisions, districts and, at times, sub-districts (tehsils). Let us start with depicting the distribution of population in Bengal Presidency.

From the Bengal Census of 1881, the pie chart on the population of Bengal proper as per divisions and districts is presented in Figure 4.6.

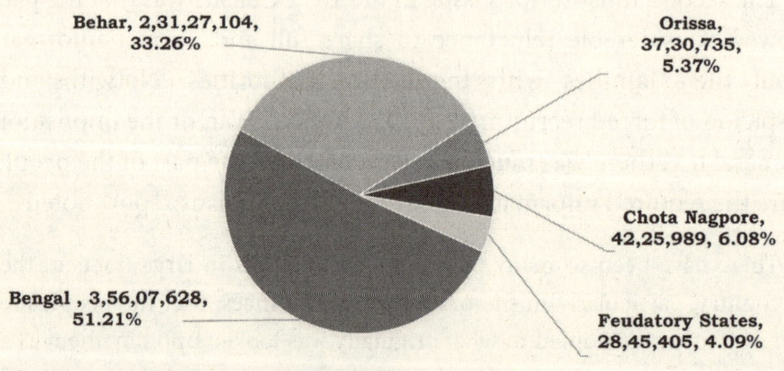

Figure 4.6: Distribution of population in Bengal Presidency, 1881[9]

Source: Census of Bengal, 1881 (Table 4.6, Appendices)

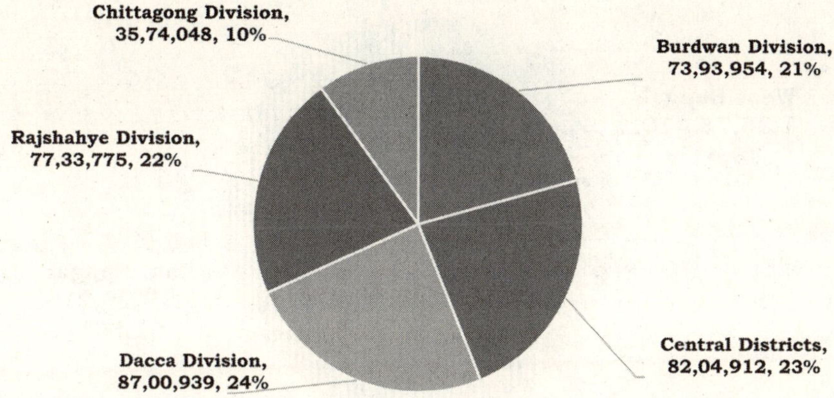

Figure 4.7: Distribution of population among Bengal Divisions, 1881[10]

Source: Census of Bengal, 1881 (Table 4.6, Appendices)

Among the various divisions of Bengal proper, Burdwan would remain with India in its entirety in 1947. Out of the Central districts, Jessore and Khulna would go to East Pakistan. From the Rajshahye division, Dinajepore, Rajshahye, Rungpore, Bogra and Pubna would be partitioned out, while Darjooling and Julpigoree would remain with India. Out of the Dacca division, the districts of Dacca, Fureedpore, Backergunje, and Mymensing would go to today's Bangladesh, as would the entire Chittagong division. The population of these units adds up to 2,19,29,218. Deducting this figure from the total of 3,56,07,628, we get 1,36,78,410 as the population in 1881 of what is now West Bengal. Figure 4.8 is a pie chart depicting the population distribution between East and West Bengal.

In order to compare the data from 1881 to 2011, the population of East Bengal has to be subtracted from the population of India as well. Of course, for our analysis, Bihar's population of 2,31,27,104 (spread over the two divisions of Patna and Bhagulpore), Chota Nagpore's 42,25,989, Orissa's 37,30,735 and the Feudatory States' 28,45,405 (which would remain with India) will have to be segregated from Bengal, so as to ascertain their share in the population of India.

From the Punjab Census, we get a table that provides population figures according to divisions and districts. The table includes the figures for the

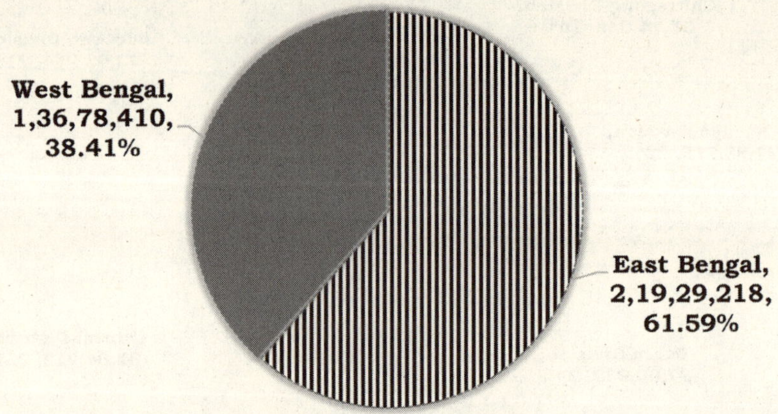

Figure 4.8: Distribution of population for East Bengal and West Bengal, 1881[11]

Source: Census of Bengal, 1881 (Table 4.6, Appendices)

numerous princely states of the province. This table has been simplified to remove unnecessary information and is available in the Appendices (Table 4.7). Figure 4.9 is a pie chart based on the table.

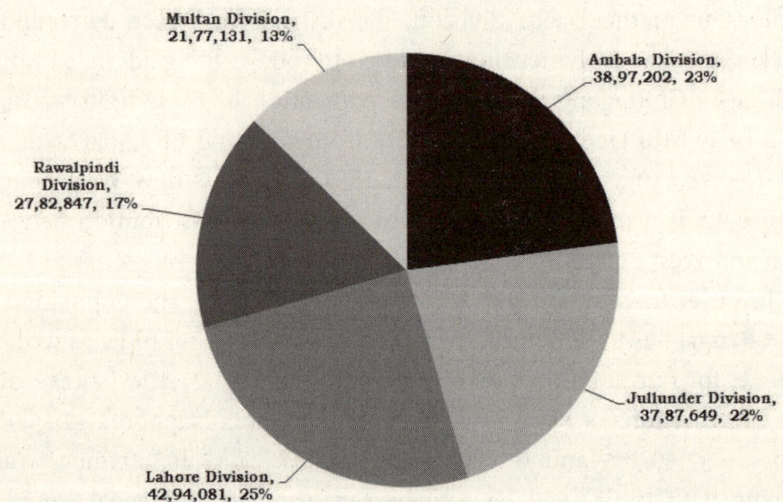

Figure 4.9: Distribution of population in divisions of Punjab, 1881[12]

Source: Census of India, 1921, vol. XV (Table 4.7, Appendices)

Analysing Figure 4.9, one can see that Ambala (38,97,202) and Jullundur (37,87,649) divisions would remain entirely with India in 1947. Out of the Lahore division (42,94,081), four districts—Lahore (7,68,873), Sialkot (9,40,832), Gujranwala (5,79,258), and Sheikhupura (2,88,043)—would go to Pakistan, while Amritsar (8,93,380) and Gurdaspur (8,23,695 minus Shakargarh tehsil's 2,19,511, that is, 6,04,184) would remain with India. Rawalpindi and Multan divisions, with populations of 27,82,847 and 21,77,131 respectively, would go entirely to Pakistan. Coming to the princely states, all but Bahawalpur (5,73,494) would remain with India. Adding it all up, we get the figure of 83,29,989 for West Punjab. Deducting this figure from the total of 2,08,00,593 for Punjab, we get 1,24,70,604. This aggregate represents the population in 1881 of those areas of Punjab which would remain with India after the Partition. Figure 4.10 is a pie chart that depicts the population division between West and East Punjab.

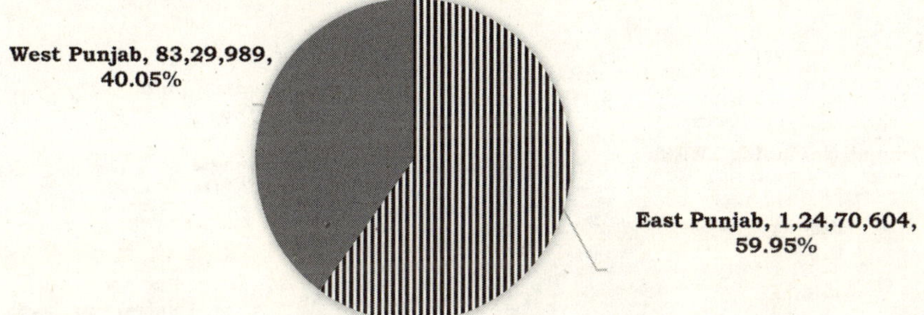

Figure 4.10: Distribution of population for West Punjab and East Punjab, 1881

Source: Census of India, 1921, vol. XV (Table 4.7, Appendices)

The figure of 83,29,989 for West Punjab would have to be deducted from the population of India as well. Sind's population of 24,17,057 and Burma's 37,36,771, too, would have to be removed. North-West Frontier Province's population of 15,75,943 in 1881 would have to be deducted. Sylhet was incorporated into Assam in 1881 and subsequently became a part—minus Karimganj tehsil, 3,43,470—of East Pakistan (now Bangladesh) at the time of the Partition. Its 1881 population of 16,25,539 would also need to be deducted. The case of Baluchistan needs some explanation. Baluchistan (districts and administered territories) and Baluchistan agencies' population was enumerated for the first time only in 1901, and the figures came to 3,08,246 and 5,02,500 respectively. Since we do not have the figures for Baluchistan in 1881, nor did it form a part of the total population of India in 1881, for our purposes it can simply be ignored.

Finally, deducting East Bengal, Sylhet—minus Karimganj—from Assam, West Punjab, Sind, the North-West Frontier Province and Burma from the 1881 total for India (25,38,91,821), we get a net figure of 21,41,51,396 in 1881 for India, roughly with its present territorial boundaries. This is the total from which the shares of provinces and regions have to be calculated to make broader comparisons about India's demography in the first synchronous census. Let us first see the demographic picture of India (excluding Burma) in 1881 without factoring in the change of boundaries that happened in 1947.

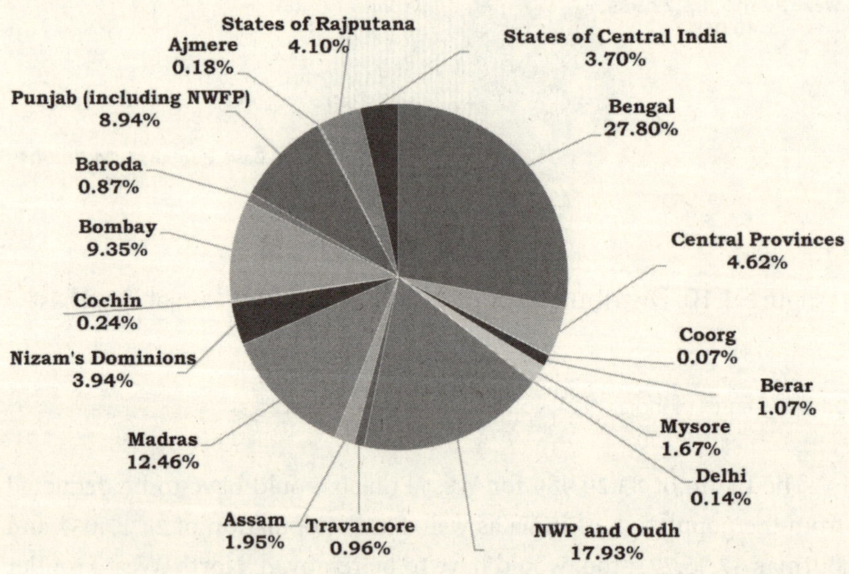

Figure 4.11: Distribution of population, Census of 1881

Source: Census of India, 1881 (Table 4.8)

Figure 4.11 gives the percentage figures for territorial boundaries of India and its administrative units in 1881. Making a comparative analysis, Bengal Presidency (which included Bihar, Chota Nagpore and Orissa) accounted for 27.80 per cent of the national population, though the share of Bengal proper in this was only 14.23 percentage points (51.20 per cent). Coming to the North-West Provinces and Oudh, at 17.93 per cent, its share was much higher than that of Madras at 12.46, Bombay at 9.35, and Punjab (including NWFP) at 8.94 per cent.

Let us now move on to the reconstructed figures for India and its various units and regions according to the post-Partition boundaries. Taking out Burma (37,36,771) and Aden (34,860), from the gross India total (25,38,91,821) we get the net figure of 25,01,55,050. Presented below is the reconstructed census table giving the percentage share of each administrative unit as it was in 1881 as well as retrospectively constructed units by adjusting for later territorial changes effected due to the Partition of the country.

Table 4.8: Abstract (Census of 1881)

British Possessions

Province	*Population*	*Percentage share*	*Adjusted percentage share*
Bengal	**6,95,36,861**	**27.80**	
East Bengal	2,19,29,218	8.77	
West Bengal	1,36,78,421	5.9	6.39
Bihar	2,31,27,104	9.25	10.79
Chota Nagpore	42,25,989	1.48	1.97
Orissa	37,30,735	1.49	1.74
Feudatory States Bengal Chota Nagpore Orissa	28,45,405 6,98,261 6,78,002 14,69,142	1.14	1.33
North-West Provinces and Oudh	4,48,49,619	17.93	20.94

Province	*Population*	*Percentage share*	*Adjusted percentage share*
Madras	3,11,70,631	12.46	14.56
Bombay Presidency	2,33,95,663	9.35	
Sind	24,17,057		
Khairpur State	1,25,919		
Bombay	2,08,52,687		9.74
Punjab (incl. NWFP)	2, 23,61,621	8.94	
Punjab West Punjab 83,29,989 East Punjab 1,24,70,604 (Hindi Punjab 63,29,776 Punjabi Punjab 61,40,828)	2,08,00,593	8.31	5.82
NWFP	15,75,943		
Delhi	3,50,499	0.14	0.16
Central Provinces	1,15,48,511	3.14	5.39
Assam Sylhet (minus Karimganj) 3,43,470) Net Assam	48,81,426 16,25,539 32,55,887	1.95 0.65 1.30	 1.52
Berar	26,72,673	1.07	1.25
Ajmere	4,60,722	0.18	0.22
Coorg	1,78,302	0.07	0.08

Native States

States of Rajputana	1,02,68,392	4.10	4.79
Nizam's dominions	98,45,594	3.94	4.60
States of Central India	92,61,907	3.70	4.32
Mysore	41,86,188	1.67	1.95
Travancore	24,01,158	0.96	1.12
Baroda	21,85,005	0.87	1.02

Province	*Population*	*Percentage share*	*Adjusted percentage share*
Cochin	6,00,278	0.24	0.28
All India (minus)	25,01,55,050		25,01,55,050
East Bengal			-2,19,29,218
Sylhet (minus Karimganj tehsil)			-16,25,539
West Punjab (including Shakargarh tehsil)			-83,29,989
Sind			-24,17,057
Khaipur State			-1,25,919
NWFP			-15,75,943
Adjusted India Total			**21,41,51,396**

More crucial than these provincial comparisons, however, would be regional demographic comparisons over the last one-and-a-half centuries. Regional comparisons overcome the challenge of frequent changes in territorial boundaries of states within each region and would also help in macro-analysis of long-term demographic trends. This allows us to draw meaningful conclusions about population growth in India in modern times.

With a view to make regional comparisons, this study, as mentioned earlier, categorises the country into four zones: north, south, east and west. The north, for our purpose, consists of north as well as central India so as to encompass the Hindi belt; the south includes all the southern states as they were until 2014 (Andhra Pradesh, Karnataka, Tamil Nadu and Kerala); the east includes West Bengal, Assam and Orissa; the west includes Maharashtra and Gujarat. Very small states and union territories have been excluded to keep the analysis simple and manageable. Punjab and Jammu & Kashmir are the only exceptions of states that are not really small in terms of population, but have been left out of these four zones, because they do not fit into this comparative framework. This exclusion does not adversely affect our findings in any manner.

Though located in the north, Punjab is officially not a Hindi-speaking state, even if Hindi is widely spoken there. Additionally, Punjab has been a relatively prosperous state with good social and economic indicators since the success of the Green Revolution in the 1960s. Its demographic indicators such as fertility rates and population growth rates have also been lower than those of the Hindi-speaking states. The most important difference, of course, is that unlike those states there has been no prevalent perception in the country of Punjab being a non-performer in population control. Jammu and Kashmir has not been included in the north for somewhat similar reasons: its linguistic difference and higher levels of social and economic development. Both Punjab and Jammu and Kashmir will be analysed separately.

Let us take up the retrospectively adjusted population percentages (provided in the fourth column of Table 4.8) in order to make the data comparable to post-Partition India. These adjusted percentages are critical to this study as they provide a panoramic view of the demographic history of India in the last one-and-a-half centuries by enabling a direct and continuous comparison according to post-Partition boundaries. It is this comparison that provides a realistic sense of how the forces of convergence versus divergence have worked in the demographic arena.

As expected, the deduction of population figures for East Bengal, Sylhet (minus Karimganj tehsil) West Punjab (including Shakargarh tehsil of Gurdaspur district), Sind, Burma and the North-West Frontier Province giving a lower all-India figure of 21,41,51,396 results in upward revision of the shares of all units, except those that lost population due to the Partition. The revised figure is 6.39 per cent for West Bengal. For Bihar, the figure is 10.79 per cent, for Chota Nagpore 1.97 per cent and for Orissa 1.74 per cent. North-West Provinces and Oudh now occupies the first place with a massive share of 20.94 per cent, which is much higher than its present share. Madras Presidency's share goes up to 14.56 per cent. Bombay Presidency minus Sind comes to 9.74 per cent. The truncated Punjab's share goes down to 5.82 per cent, which would gradually decline further over the next century or so. The Central Provinces (5.39 per cent), Assam (1.52 per cent), Berar (1.25 per cent), Rajputana (4.79 per cent), Hyderabad (4.60 per cent), Central Indian States (4.32 per cent), Mysore (1.95 per cent), Travancore (1.12 per cent), Baroda (1.02 per cent) and

Cochin (0.28 per cent) all see their shares rise or remain stable. Figure 4.12 depicts the changed percentage shares as per the reconstructed fourth column of Table 4.8.

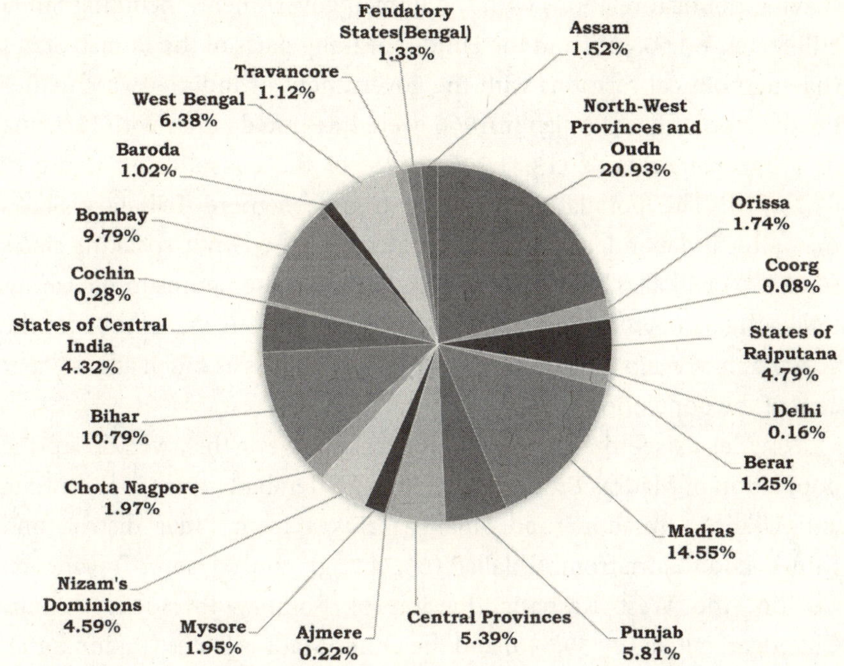

Figure 4.12: Census of 1881, reconstructed chart

Source: Census of British India, 1881 (Table 4.8)

What are the macro trends emerging from these statistics? Evidently, provincial comparisons across time are possible in some cases but not in others. However, regional comparisons provide deep insights into the demographic distribution of India in 1881, that is, almost at the beginning of the modern census exercise in the country. In accordance with the above-mentioned scheme of regional classification, the population of all Hindi states and territories (Bihar, Chota Nagpore—minus Manbhum Sadr, now Purulia—NCT of Delhi, North-West Provinces and Oudh, Central Provinces—minus Nagpur, Chanda, Bhandara and Wardha districts from Nagpur division and Sambalpur and Oriya feudatory states—Ajmere, Rajputana and the States of Central India) adds up to as much as 9,98,70,549. Now, the population of Hindi-speaking parts of the undivided Punjab of 1881 (broadly, present-day Haryana and Himachal Pradesh) will have to be added to it. Adding up the Hindi-speaking Ambala division (38,97,202), Kangra (7,30,845), Punjab States (having political relations with the Punjab government, including Simla Hill States—3,60,423) and the Hindi-speaking parts of the Punjab States (having political relations with the government of India)—which, after the division of East Punjab in 1966, were integrated either with Haryana or Himachal Pradesh (13,41,306)—we get the consolidated figure of 63,29,776. The population of those Chota Nagpore Tributary States that, after Independence, were integrated into the Hindi-speaking states (5,46,007) will also have to be added. Adding these figures to the earlier total of 9,98,70,549, we get the final figure of 10,67,46,332 in 1881 for the area that makes up the Hindi belt of today. That was as much as 49.85 per cent of the population of India.

Now let us see the share of southern India. For this, we add up the population of Madras Presidency, Coorg, Hyderabad minus Marathwada and Udgir, Ahmadpur and Nilanga talukas from Bidar district and Kinwat and Rajura from Adilabad (63,74,727)[13] and Mysore, Travancore, Cochin, the West Karnatic division of Bombay Presidency minus Chandgad taluka (27,59,636) and the Other Madras States (Puddukottai, Banganpalle, Sandur) 3,43,431, and deduct the figure of the Oriya-speaking population of Ganjam and Vizagpatam (15,66,966) which was then a part of the Madras Presidency and would be transferred to Orissa in the 1920s. Adding it all up, we get 4,61,68,966, which means that in 1881 the southern states of today had approximately 21.56 per cent share in the net population of India (21,41,51,396).

Interestingly, the south's share of 21.56 per cent was only marginally above that of North-West Provinces and Oudh at 20.94 per cent. Comparing the figure for the south to the 4,48,49,619 for the North-West Provinces and Oudh (later United Provinces and present-day Uttar Pradesh), along with the princely states, reveals that around the very beginning of the modern census exercise the population of the upper Gangetic plain was no less than 97.14 per cent of the entire south's. This should not cause surprise because through millennia the highest concentration of population in the Indian subcontinent was in the Gangetic plain.

Remarkably, in both the regions, population has grown roughly five times in 130 years, though the south has a clear edge. In 2011, Uttar Pradesh, along with Uttarakhand (which roughly corresponds to the 1881 administrative unit), had a population of 20,98,98,633, while the states now constituting the south had a population of 25,12,29,165. This means that UP and Uttarakhand's combined ratio has fallen to only 83.54 per cent of the population of the south, notwithstanding the rapid growth in Uttar Pradesh over the last fifty years. Given the continued growth differential, however, this combined ratio is likely to increase in the next census. This buttresses the position that different parts of India have followed a similar trajectory over the last 150 years and that the differences between them in terms of Total Fertility Rate (TFR) and decadal growth rates are more apparent than real. The differences are given disproportionate importance in a short-term view that takes into account only the period from the 1960s, when northern India had just entered the peak phase of demographic growth.

What was the share of the east? Adding up the populations of West Bengal (1,48,05,369)—including Manbhum Sadr, now Purulia (5,24,324) transferred from Chota Nagpore division of Bihar in 1956 and Cooch Behar (6,02,624)—Orissa's approximately 81,79,511 (Orissa division and Orissa Tributary States of Bengal Presidency, plus Oriya-speaking parts of Madras Presidency, plus princely states of Chota Nagpore and Central Provinces and Sambalpur district that would later become part of Orissa with its present boundaries) and Assam's 28,82,080 roughly with its present-day boundaries (minus Sylhet, except Karimganj tehsil, which went to Bangladesh and minus the various hill states of the north-east carved out from it over time), we get the figure of 2,58,66,760. That was 12.08 per cent of the population of India in 1881 (21,41,51,396)—much lower than the share with united Bengal.

Moving on to the western zone, the Bombay Presidency roughly corresponds to Maharashtra and Gujarat, minus Sind and the Kannada-speaking division of Western Karnatic, containing four districts of Belgaum, except Chandgad taluka, and Bijapur, Dharwad and Kanara, with a consolidated population of 27,59,636. Marathwada, Berar, and the five talukas of Hyderabad state transferred to then Bombay province in 1956 will have to be added to the adjusted population of Bombay.

The four districts of Nagpur division of Central Provinces transferred to today's Maharashtra by the States Reorganisation Act, 1956 have to be added. Baroda, too, will have to be added. Now taking up Bombay Presidency's population of 2,33,95,663, we deduct Sind's 24,17,057, Khairpur state's 1,25,919, Western Karnatic's 27,59,636; and add up Nagpur, Chanda (minus Telugu-speaking 65,012), Bhandara and Wardha districts of Nagpur division of Central Provinces (24,17,502), from Hyderabad state Marathwada's 31,47,000,[14] and Udgir, Ahmadpur, Nilanga talukas of Bidar district and Kinwat and Rajura from Adilabad (3,23,867), Berar's 26,72,673 and Baroda's 21,850,05. We get the net figure of 2,87,74,086, which is 13.44 per cent of the net adjusted population of India (21,41,51,396). This means that today's Maharashtra and Gujarat, categorised as the west in this book, had the combined share of 13.44 per cent in the national population in 1881. The reconstructed regional divisions are shown in the pie chart depicted in Figure 4.13.

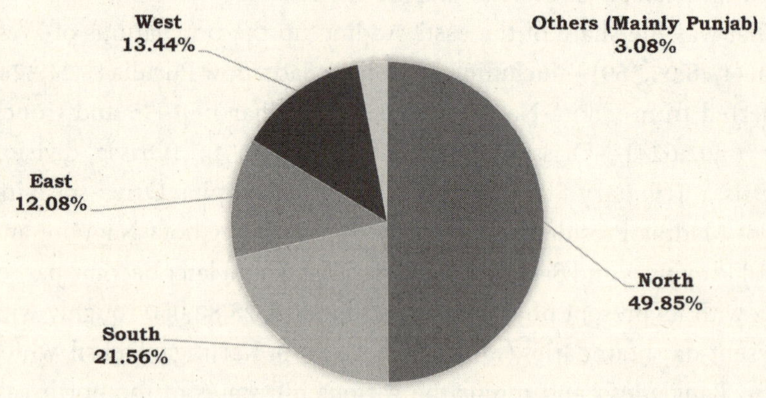

Figure 4.13: Reconstructed population shares in 1881

Source: Census of British India, 1881 (Table 4.8)

While there may be minor discrepancies within the standard statistical margins of error in the 1881 figure for India with its post-Partition boundaries, they would not in any way affect the argument presented in this study. That also applies to the 1881 population figures of the various regions, wherein small discrepancies can have a measurable effect on the cumulative growth rate. The numbers derived from the above analysis provide a critical point of reference in comparative study of the population trends since 1881. As the book progresses, it would become increasingly evident that what is required is a long-term analysis of divergence versus convergence in the backdrop of both the demographic distribution that prevailed in India around the Census of 1881 and the process of demographic transition.

IV

Let us move on to the 1881 statistics for population density. Figure 4.14 compares the density of India with that of several other countries.

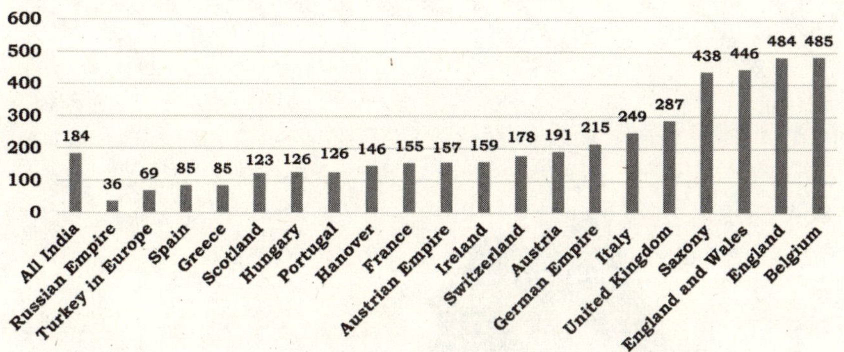

Figure 4.14: Comparison of population densities (persons per sq. mile) of India versus other countries, 1981

Source: Census of British India, 1881 (Table 4.9, Appendices)

Figure 4.14, which depicts the comparative density of India and European countries in 1881, shows that India's population density was by no means abnormally high. While the German Empire, United Kingdom, Italy, England and Belgium all had a higher density (with England at more than two-and-a-half times), most other parts of Europe also had comparable densities.[15] The conspicuous exception was the Russian Empire, which had a much lower density. Let us now examine comparative densities within India.

From Figure 4.15, it is evident that there was wide variation in the population densities of different parts of British India in 1881. The Census report summed up the situation in the following manner: 'Thus it will be observed, looking at the provinces geographically, while in the north and north-east we have this extreme density, and again, in the south, a density high, though by no means so great as that of the north, the central tracts of India are comparatively thinly populated.'[16]

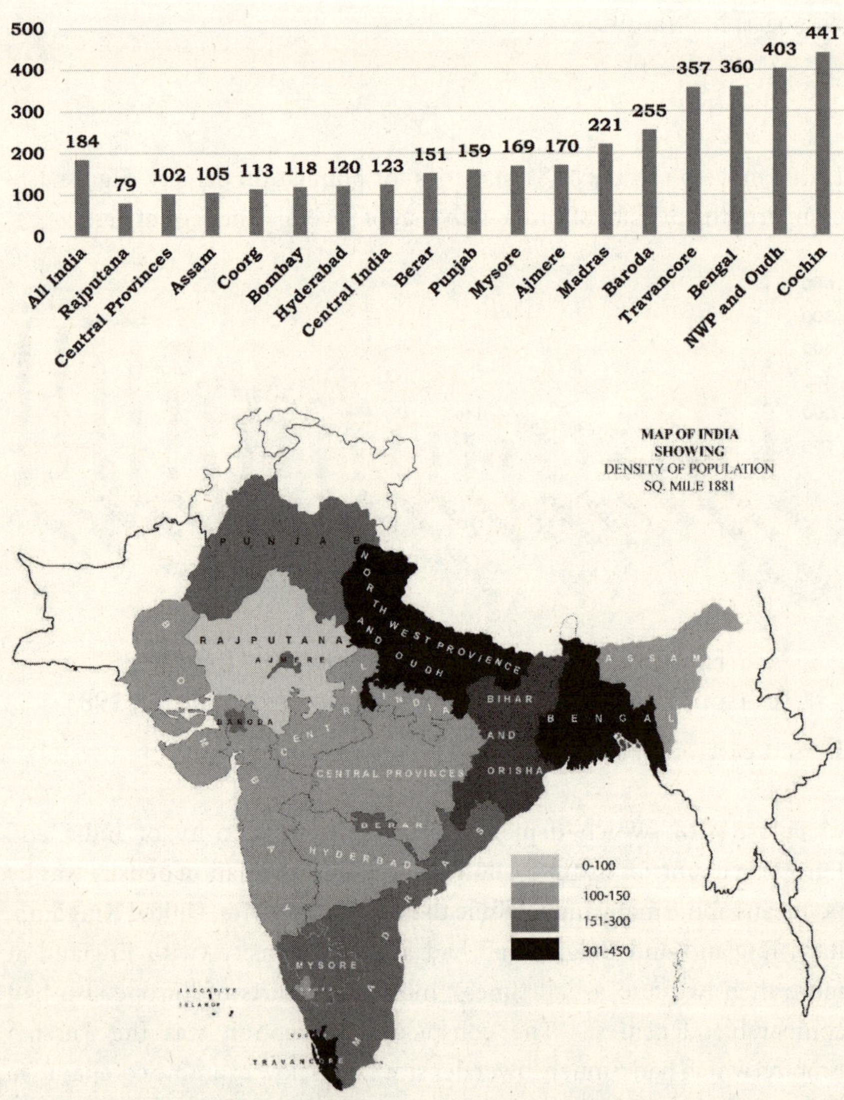

Figure 4.15: Population density (persons per sq. mile) for British India, 1881

Source: Census of British India, 1881 (Table 4.9, Appendices)

At 403 per square mile, the North-West Provinces and Oudh had the highest density of all the provinces directly under British rule, while the Bengal Presidency was close behind at 360. The density was much lower in other parts of the country, with Madras at 221, Punjab at 159, Bombay at 118 and the Central Provinces at only 102. Rajputana was even lower at only 79. The national average of 184 was less than half that of the North-West Provinces and Oudh. This establishes the fact that at the onset of the modern census exercise in India, the Gangetic plain had the highest countrywide population density by a huge margin, even though there were smaller regions in other parts of the country with comparable densities. It is widely acknowledged that the vast Gangetic plain, stretching over the three states of Uttar Pradesh, Bihar and Bengal, apart from Bangladesh, was among the most fertile regions of the world and, throughout recorded history, had the capacity to support a large and dense population, which is reflected in the high density even in the nineteenth century.

Further, it is important to note that this trend of high population density in the Upper Gangetic plain had continued. Many districts in the North-West Provinces and Oudh exceeded the figure of 700 persons per square mile, according to the Census of 1881—a jump which also implies that the Census of 1872, which in any case had compiled figures collected for North-West Provinces in 1865 and Oudh in 1869, might have left out a large number of people. Bengal was the only other region in India that had a comparable population density, with some parts exceeding 700, according to the 1881 Census. Some districts of the Bengal Presidency, which are now part of Bihar, had a density of over 800. Figures 4.16 and 4.17 depict the case in the Bengal Presidency and the North-West Provinces respectively where the density exceeded 700 persons per square mile.

In Bengal Presidency, excluding Howrah, which was an urban area, density measured in persons per square mile was 870 for Sarun, 860 for Mozufferpore, 845 for Patna, 828 for Hooghly, 790 for Darbhanga and so on. Similar high density was also found in at least four districts of the North-West Provinces. The four districts were Benares, with a density of 894, Ballia 808, Jaunpur 778 and Azamgarh 747.

Further, the Census of 1881 observed that India's southern region also had a dense population, but was nowhere near the high density

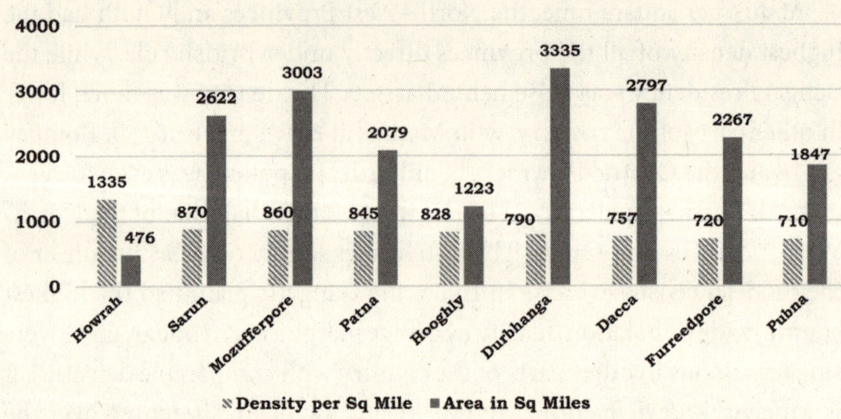

Figure 4.16: Population density of Bengal Presidency, 1881

Source: Census of British India, 1881 (Table 4.10, Appendices)

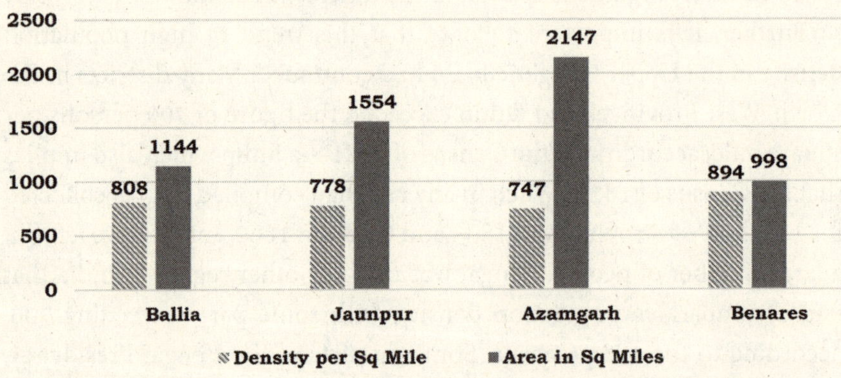

Figure 4.17: Population density of North-West Provinces, 1881

Source: Census of British India, 1881 (Table 4.10, Appendices)

of the northern region. Commenting on these high-density areas and comparing them with other parts of the country, the census report stated: 'These densities, however, are exceptional; and north-west above the Ganges or south of Bengal we do not find any tracts with a population so thick as is found in the Doabs of the North-West and Oudh, or in the north of Bengal and the east of that province.'[17]

However, it should be noted that although most of the south had only about half the population density of the Gangetic plain, the exception was the Kerala coast, where densities in the princely states of Cochin and Travancore were almost equally high. The North-West Provinces and Oudh, corresponding to present-day Uttar Pradesh, had a density of 403 persons per square mile in the Census of 1881. Cochin was reported to have a density of 441, while Travancore had a density of 357 persons per square mile. Cochin and Travancore, along with Malabar district which was a part of the Madras Presidency, combine to form the bulk of today's Kerala.

Thus, the population density of Kerala has been recorded as high since the beginning of the modern census exercise due to significant geographical and historical reasons. The Malabar coast is a climatically favoured zone with high precipitation and fertile soils and was historically a hub for international trade across the Indian Ocean. During British rule, these advantages were accentuated by the presence of relatively well-governed princely states such as Cochin and Travancore, which ensured better social and economic progress of their people in comparison to most other princely states of India.

V
The Census of 1891

The Census of 1891 provides further insights into regional variations in population growth. Table 4.11 and Figure 4.18 present the data for the various parts of British India.

Out of undivided India's net population of 27,95,73,792 (arrived at after deducting Burma's and Aden's figures from the total of 28,72,23,431), the Bengal Presidency accounted for about 7.13 crore or 25.52 per cent. Since the presidency included Bihar and Orissa at this juncture, it would be relevant to find out the breakup of the population among the three regions. Bengal proper contributed roughly 4.04 crore to the total of 7.13 crore, Bihar contributed 2.12 crore and Orissa 40.05 lakh, while the remaining population of about 33 lakh was contributed by the princely states of the presidency. This would give figures of approximately 57 per cent for Bengal proper, 30 per cent for Bihar and 5.5 per cent for Orissa, while the rest went to the princely states located in these areas.

Table 4.11: Census of India, 1891

Province, State, or Agency	*Area in Square Miles*	*Population, 1891*	*Percentage on Total*	
			Area	*Population*
Bengal	151,543	71,346,987	9.71	24.84
Madras	141,189	35,630,440	9.05	12.40
N.W. Provinces	83,286	34,254,254	5.34	11.93
Oudh	24,217	12,650,831	1.55	4.40
Panjab	110,667	20,866,847	7.09	7.26
Bombay	77,275	15,985,270	4.95	5.56
Sindh	47,780	2,871,774	3.06	1.00
Central Provinces	86,501	10,784,294	5.55	3.75
Upper Burma	83,473	2,946,933	5.35	1.03
Lower Burma	87,057	4,658,627	5.64	1.63
Assam	49,004	5,476,833	3.14	1.91
Berar	17,718	2,897,491	1.14	1.01
Ajmer	2,711	542,358	0.17	0.19
Coorg	1,583	173,055	0.10	0.06
Aden	80	44,079	0.01	0.02
Quettah, & c.	—	27,270	—	0.01
Andamans	—	15,609	—	—
Total British Pronvices	**964,993**	**221,172,952**	**61.85**	**77.00**
Haidrabad	82,698	11,537,040	5.30	4.02
Rajputana	130,268	12,016,102	8.35	4.18
Central India	77,808	10,318,812	4.99	3.59
Mysore	27,936	4,943,604	1.79	1.72
Baroda	8,226	2,415,396	0.53	0.84
Kashmir	80,900	2,543,952	5.19	0.89
States connected with				
Bombay	69,045	8,059,298	4.42	2.81
Madras	9,609	3,700,622	0.62	1.29
Central Provinces	29,435	2,160,511	1.89	0.75
Bengal	35,834	3,296,379	2.30	1.15
N.W. Provinces	5,109	792,491	0.32	0.28
Panjab	38,299	4,263,280	2.45	1.48
Fort Steadman, Shan Outposts	—	2,992	—	—
Total, Feudatory States	**595,167**	**66,050,479**	**38.15**	**23.00**
Grand Total, India	**1,560,160**	**287,223,431**	**100.00**	**100.00**

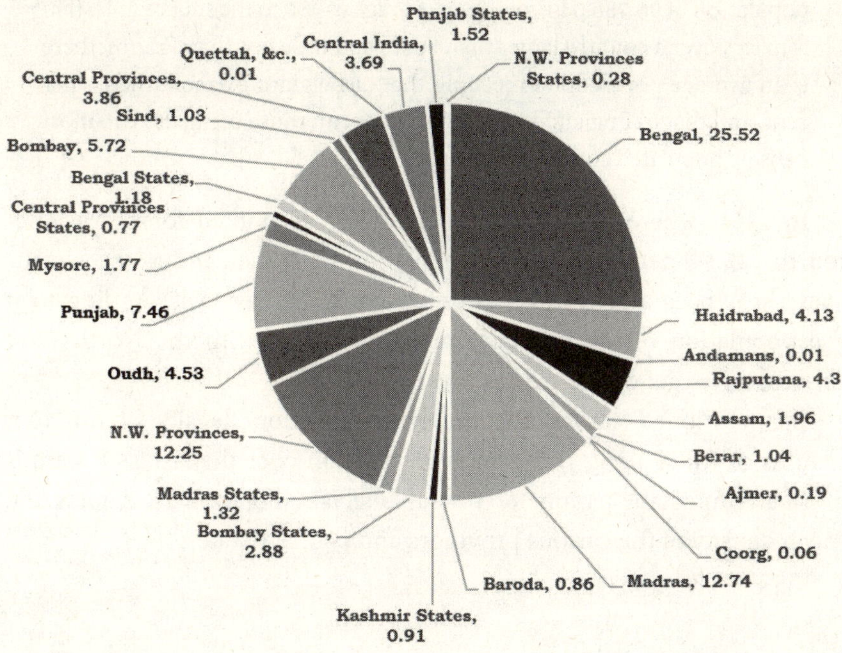

Figure 4.18: Percentage shares of provinces, states and agencies, 1891

Source: Census of India, 1891 (Table 4.11)

What is equally noteworthy is that the population density of Bihar was almost the same as that of Bengal. The Census of 1891 divided Bengal into three regions: northern, western and eastern, with respective densities of 459, 562 and 531 persons per square mile. The two divisions of north Bihar and south Bihar had densities of 667 and 520 respectively. What this highlights is that in the late-nineteenth century the Gangetic plain had an almost uniformly high density from the upper regions to the riverine east Bengal, constituting no less than 44.10 per cent of the population of undivided India.[18] In fact, this was not so different twenty years earlier, as the Census of 1872 had noted with amazement:

> Taking the three provinces of Bengal, Oude, and the North West (with the exception of the outlying districts of the Chittagong Hill Tracts, Cooch Behar and Kumaon, on the north, and the Sunderbuns, Chota Nagpoor, and Jhansi, on the south), we have an area of 201,581 square miles, and a

> population of 96,788,049, giving an average of 480 to the square mile; that is to say, over a country larger than Spain and little less than France, there is an average population exceeding that of Belgium by more than 7 per cent, and that of England by nearly 14 per cent, those being the two most densely populated countries in Europe.[19]

In 1891, whereas the Bengal Presidency accounted for nearly one-fourth (25.52 per cent) of the population of British India, the North-West Provinces and Oudh accounted for 16.78 per cent. Adding to it the population of the princely states associated with the North-West Provinces, we get the figure of 17.06 per cent.

As mentioned earlier, the relative population density of different regions of India along with variations therein over the last 150 years is another important parameter in our analysis. Figure 4.19 depicts the mean density of the various provinces and princely states.

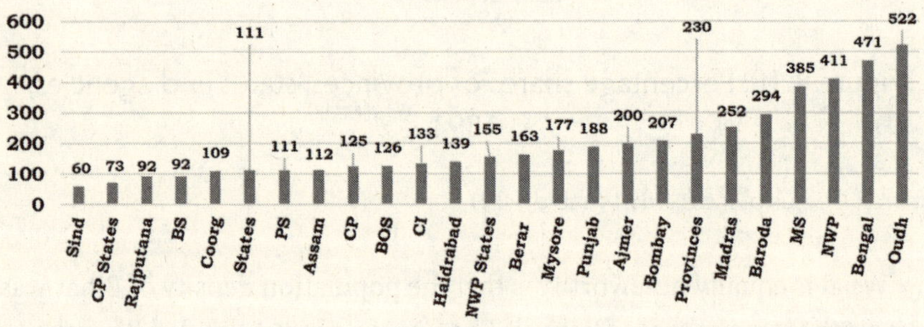

Figure 4.19: Mean density of population (persons per sq. mile), 1891

BS: Bengal States; PS: Punjab States; CP: Central Provinces; BOS: Bombay States; CI: Central India; MS: Madras States; NWP: North-West Provinces

Source: Census of India, 1891 (Table 4.12, Appendices)

As before, the density figures provide insights into regional variations of population. Among the larger areas, the three most thickly populated were Bengal with a density of 471, North-West Provinces with 411 and Oudh with 522. Since the Bengal Presidency at this time included Bihar, it is evident that the Gangetic plain had by far the highest density in India and all the other regions were far behind, with Madras Presidency at 252, Bombay Presidency at 207 and Punjab at 188. Central India at 133,

Central Provinces at 125 and the Rajputana States at 92 had an even lower density. Even the southern princely states generally had a much lower density, with Haidrabad at 139, Mysore at 177, while the comparatively smaller Madras States (Travancore, Cochin, Banganapalle, Pudukottai and Sandur) registered a high density of 385 persons per square mile.

Figures 4.20 and 4.21 depict the highest and lowest densities of population within each province or princely state in India in 1891.

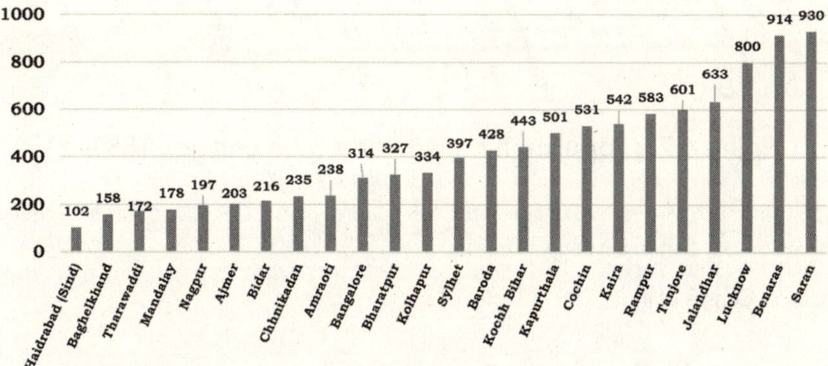

Figure 4.20: Highest density areas (per sq. mile) in provinces and states, 1891

Source: Census of India, 1891 (Table 4.12, Appendices)

One can see from Figure 4.20 that at 930 persons per square mile, Saran from Bihar topped the density chart, closely followed by Benares with 914, and Lucknow at 800. Similar to findings in 1872, only one district, Tanjore, from the Madras Presidency, had a relatively high density of 601. These statistics from the nineteenth century help us construct a more objective picture of modern India's demographic history than the prevalent assessments focusing on the post-Independence era. Over the ensuing decades, southern India's density would rise because of its earlier demographic spurt, before the north started to catch up after the 1960s, partially restoring the long-term pattern.

Having analysed the overall figures and population densities which, as we have seen, differed widely across and within the provinces and states due to geographical and historical reasons,[20] let us shift to a comparative analysis of growth rates as depicted in Figure 4.21.

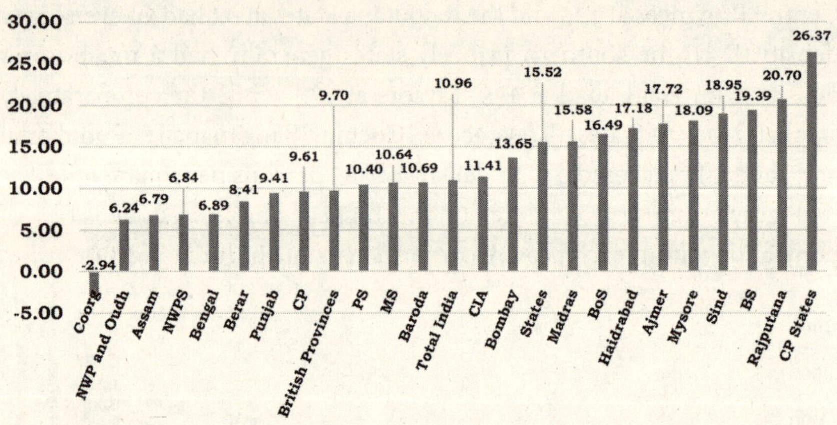

Figure 4.21: Population growth rates (percentage), 1881–91

CP: Central Provinces; PS: Punjab States; MS: Madras States; CIA: Central India Agency; BoS: Bombay States; BS: Bengal States

Source: Census of India, 1891 (Table 4.13, Appendices)

Figure 4.21 shows the wide variations in population growth rates in different parts of India. The high growth of Central Provinces states is partly attributable to territorial adjustments. Out of the four major regions, the south had the fastest growth during 1881–91. Madras Presidency grew at 15.58, Haidrabad at 17.18, Mysore at 18.09 and the Madras States at 10.64. This is in sharp contrast to the much lower growth in the North-West Provinces and Oudh at 6.24 per cent and 6.84 per cent in the princely states associated with this province. Central India grew by 11.41 per cent and Central Provinces by 9.61 per cent. Most other parts of India also lagged the south in population growth. Bombay Presidency witnessed a growth of 13.65 per cent, Bengal Presidency 6.89 per cent and Punjab 9.41 per cent.

VI
The Census of 1901: A Comparative Analysis

The demographic trends shown by earlier censuses are confirmed by the Census of 1901. Figure 4.22 (based on Table 4.14 in which a percentage column based on the Census table has been added) provides growth percentages.

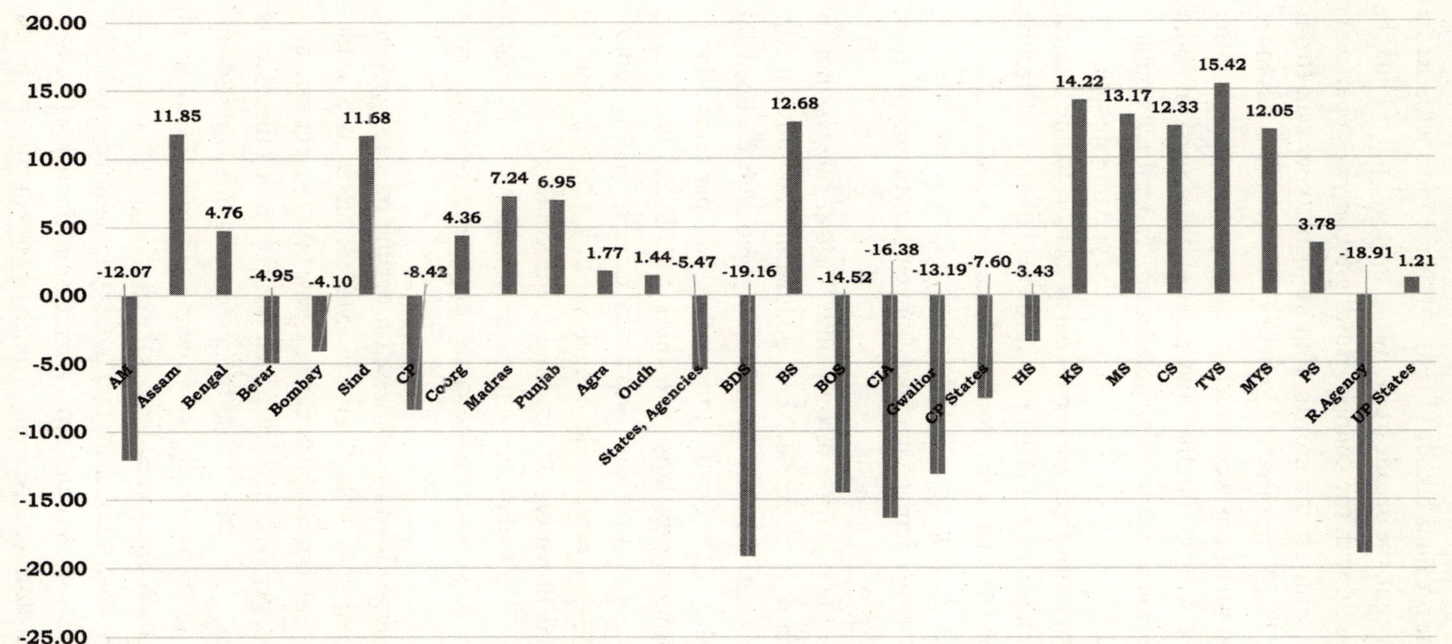

Figure 4.22: Population growth (percentage), 1891–1901

Source: Census of India, 1901 (Table 4.14, Appendices)

AM: Ajmer-Merwara; CP: Central Provinces BDS: Baroda States; BS: Bengal States; BOS: Bombay States; CIA: Central India Agency; CP States: Central Provinces States; HS: Hyderabad State; KS: Kerala State; MS: Madras State; CS: Cochin State; TVS: Travancore State; MYS: Mysore State; PS: Punjab States; R. Agency: Rajputana Agency; UP States: United Provinces States

Compared to the previous decade of 1881–91, when India witnessed a growth of 10.96 per cent, the decade from 1891 to 1901 was not favourable for population growth, with the country growing by only 1.50 per cent. Taking out Burma, which had a growth of more than 20 per cent (from about 76 lakh to 91 lakh), the growth falls below 1 per cent. What is more important, regional variations were much more pronounced than in the previous decades. Owing to famines and plagues, large parts of India experienced a substantial fall in their population. Thus, the Rajputana Agency, which had witnessed high growth over the previous decade, saw its population fall by as much as 18.91 per cent or 22.67 lakh; the Central India Agency, which too had enjoyed rapid growth, experienced decline of 16.38 per cent or 16.90 lakh; the Bombay States saw a decline of 14.52 per cent or nearly 11.73 lakh. Overall, the states and agencies experienced a steep decline of 5.47 per cent, going down from 6.60 crore to 6.24 crore, having suffered a loss of 36.13 lakh.

The scenario in the provinces directly under British rule was not so bleak, although many of them saw their population fall substantially. Among the larger ones, Bombay Presidency's population declined by 1.69 per cent and that of the Central Provinces by 8.42 per cent. What is noteworthy is that among the larger provinces, the Madras Presidency, with its growth rate of 7.24 per cent, was a very close second to Punjab, which grew by 6.95 per cent, while Bengal grew by 4.76 per cent. In contrast, the United Provinces of Agra and Oudh could grow only by 1.68 per cent, signifying a huge gap with Madras's rate. Not only this, if we look at the princely states from the south, the gap in growth becomes wider.

Except for Hyderabad, which witnessed a decline of 3.43 per cent, all other states enjoyed very high growth. Madras States as a whole grew by 13.17 per cent, out of which Cochin grew by 12.32 per cent and Travancore by 15.42 per cent. Mysore, which was not among the Madras States, grew by 12.05 per cent. These figures provide ample testimony that, as compared to the north, the south witnessed an earlier onset of demographic transition going as far back as the late-nineteenth century. It was also reported by the 1901 Census that India's population dwindled by around 4,00,000 between 1891 and 1901, a decrease attributed to famines, plagues and malaria during the period.[21] A much larger reduction in India's population would occur during 1911–21, with the influenza epidemic of 1918 claiming around 1.5 crore lives.[22]

VII
Consolidated Census Analysis, 1881–1901

Having analysed four consecutive censuses, it is time to make a cumulative growth comparison. To the existing census table, a column on percentage growth between 1881 and 1901 has been added for a better comparison (See Appendices, Table 4.14). Depicted in Figure 4.23 is a chart that compares the figures for 1901 with 1881, giving a rough assessment of the nineteenth-century demographic experience of India.

It is evident that during 1881–1901 population growth across India experienced significant variations. Bengal States grew by 34.53 per cent. Among the larger political units, Bengal experienced a growth of 11.98 per cent over these two decades, which should be regarded as a high growth rate for an area whose initial population was upwards of 6 crore. Punjab grew by 17.01 per cent. Moving on to the Madras Presidency, one can see a high growth rate of 23.95 per cent, with its population increasing from 3.08 crore to 3.82 crore in just two decades. High as this is, it is the growth

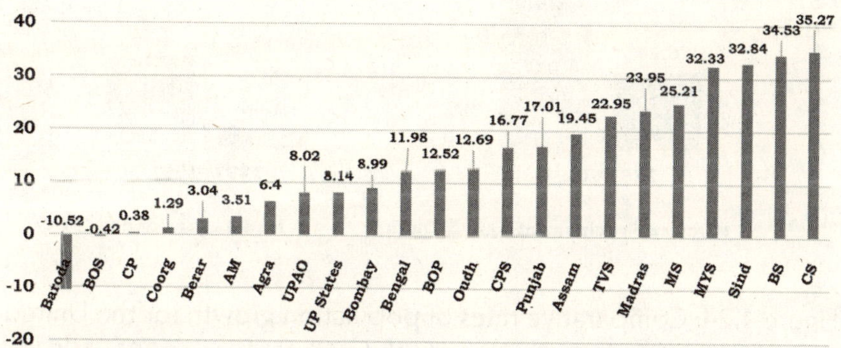

Figure 4.23: Cumulative growth (percentage), 1881–1901

BOS: Bombay States; CP: Central Provinces; AM: Ajmer-Merwara; UPAO: United Provinces of Agra and Oudh; BOP: Bombay Presidency; CPS: Central Provinces States; TVS: Travancore State; MS: Madras States; MYS: Mysore States; BS: Bengal States; CS: Cochin State

Source: Table 4.14, Appendices

rate of many princely states from the south that is astounding. The Madras States as a whole grew by 25.21 per cent, out of which Cochin grew by 35.27 per cent and Travancore by 22.95 per cent. Mysore, which was not a part of Madras States, grew by 32.33 per cent, although on a lower base.

Moving on to the United Provinces of Agra and Oudh, one can see a growth of 8.02 per cent, with the population rising from 4.41 crore in 1881 to 4.77 crore in 1901. This increase was roughly one-third of the growth achieved by Madras Presidency and states. Incidentally, even Bombay Presidency, with a rate of 12.52 per cent, performed better than the United Provinces. This was primarily driven by the exceptionally high growth of 32.84 per cent in Sind, which was part of the Bombay Presidency at the time. The growth rates of the Central Provinces (0.38 per cent) and Berar (3.04 cent) were negligible. Assam's growth of 19.45 per cent was caused partly by migration from the Bengal Presidency. Figure 4.24 provides a graphic comparison of population growth rates between the Madras Presidency and the United Provinces of Agra and Oudh for the period 1881–1901.

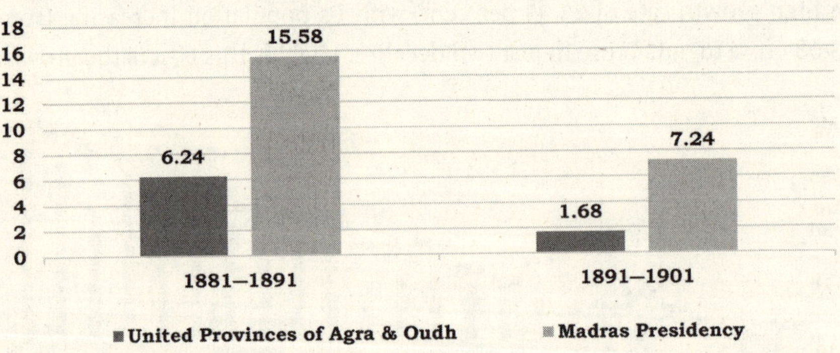

Figure 4.24: Comparative rates of population growth for the United Provinces of Agra & Oudh and Madras Presidency, 1881–1901

Source: Office of the Registrar General of India (Table 4.14, Appendices)

While the Madras Presidency was growing at a decadal rate above 15 per cent during 1881–91, the United Provinces of Agra and Oudh grew at only 6.24 per cent—well below half that of Madras. In the next decade, that is, 1891–1901, when the population of India was virtually stagnant on account of famines and epidemics, the Madras Presidency outgrew the United Provinces by more than four times.

This comparison is only for the British territories. To get a fuller picture, let us look at the growth rates in the relevant states as well, as depicted in Figure 4.25.

Looking at Figures 4.24 and 4.25, it is evident that during the closing decades of the nineteenth century the south grew much faster than the north. The southern princely states occupy the upper portion of Figure 4.25 due to their higher growth rates, while the United Provinces States languish at the bottom. What also needs to be emphasised is that the Madras States (which included Travancore and Cochin, along with others) increased their growth rates during 1891–1901. This was in contrast to the national trend of decline. The United Provinces States showed a growth decline commensurate with the provincial trend.

During 1881–91, while the United Provinces States grew by just 6.84 per cent, Cochin grew at a staggering rate of 20.43 per cent, closely followed by Mysore at 18.09 per cent. Thus, much of the south grew at roughly three times the rate of the north during this period. What is further striking is that the gap widened over the next decade. When the

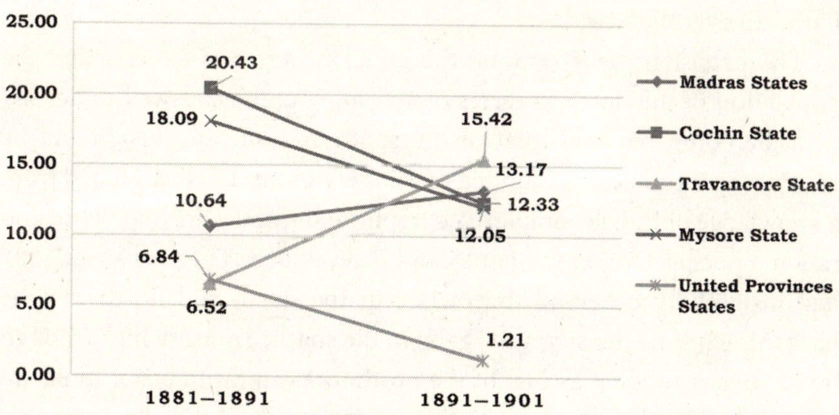

Figure 4.25: Comparative rates of population growth for the princely states of India representing India's north and south, 1881–1901

Source: Office of the Registrar General of India (Table 4.14, Appendices)

national growth rate was below 1 per cent during 1891–1901, all four southern states had double-digit growth rates. The difference continued to be staggering. Between 1891 and 1901, the princely states of the United Provinces registered a growth rate of just 1.21 per cent. In contrast, the southern princely states grew at a rate that was more than ten times higher. However, it is important to note that unlike the southern states, the United Provinces states were demographically marginal to the province.

The statistics cited and analysed in the preceding pages clearly indicate that the south had an early growth spurt which started in the nineteenth century itself when most of the country, especially the north, saw only marginal growth.

The dominant narrative woven around the high growth rates of the north in the recent decades owes more to an entirely ahistorical view of the north–south demographic divide, which is more apparent than real, as the long-term evidence cited in this study establishes. It is just that the timings of the demographic transition in the south and the north have been very different. The south witnessed a spurt in its population growth between 1881 and 1971, while the north lagged for decades only to gain momentum around the mid-twentieth century, when it entered the second phase of transition marked by high birth rates and low death rates. Such variations in the timing of demographic transition can be found all over the world.

The persistent belief among the policymakers and experts that the population of the north in terms of absolute numbers as well as density must be compared with that of the south and any surplus should be regarded as a problem is founded on slippery ground. It is detached from a knowledge of India's complex geography and history, without which no rational perspective on the issue can be developed. The Census of 1881 had insightfully observed that 'while in the north and north-east we have this extreme density, and again, in the south, a density high, though by no means so great as that of the north, the central tracts of India are comparatively thinly populated.'[23] Understanding the demographic histories of the various regions is imperative for a meaningful demographic comparison among them. Neglecting this aspect might lead to fallacious interpretations and misleading conclusions.

VIII
Demographic History of India, 1881–1941: A Comparative Analysis

Exploring nineteenth-century Census data is undoubtedly relevant. However, for a comprehensive comparative framework of the demographic history of modern India, we need to consider all the decennial censuses of the British period from 1881 to 1941 collectively. That would help us better understand how different parts of India grew during those six decades. The political Independence of India in 1947 does not signify any fundamental shift in the demographic trajectory either of the country or its parts, except in terms of the country being partitioned and losing about one-fifth of its population—a fact that does not really affect our analysis. As the 1931 Census was much more comprehensive than that of 1941, whose data collection was restricted because of the budget cuts effected during the Second World War, let us first take up 1881–1931, a period of fifty years. Presented below are two maps in Figures 4.26 and 4.27. The one in Figure 4.26 gives a broad picture of demographic growth during the period.

The map in Figure 4.27, published by the Royal Geographical Society, London, provides district-wise cumulative growth figures for undivided India during 1881–1931. It furnishes strong evidence of much higher demographic growth in the south as compared to the north.

Figures 4.28 and 4.29 depict 1881–1931 growth as per provinces and princely states. It is evident from the map depicted in Figure 4.26 that the south and east enjoyed demographic growth far in excess of north and central India during 1881–1931. Western India also experienced better growth than the north. The north-west—mostly the area that went to Pakistan, including west Punjab, North West Frontier Province and Sind—experienced exceptionally high growth.

The map depicted in Figure 4.27 gives a district/princely state level population growth data for 1881–1931. This enables micro mapping of the geographical distribution of demographic growth in India from a comparative regional perspective. Considering the large number of units involved and the range of growth figures—with the national population

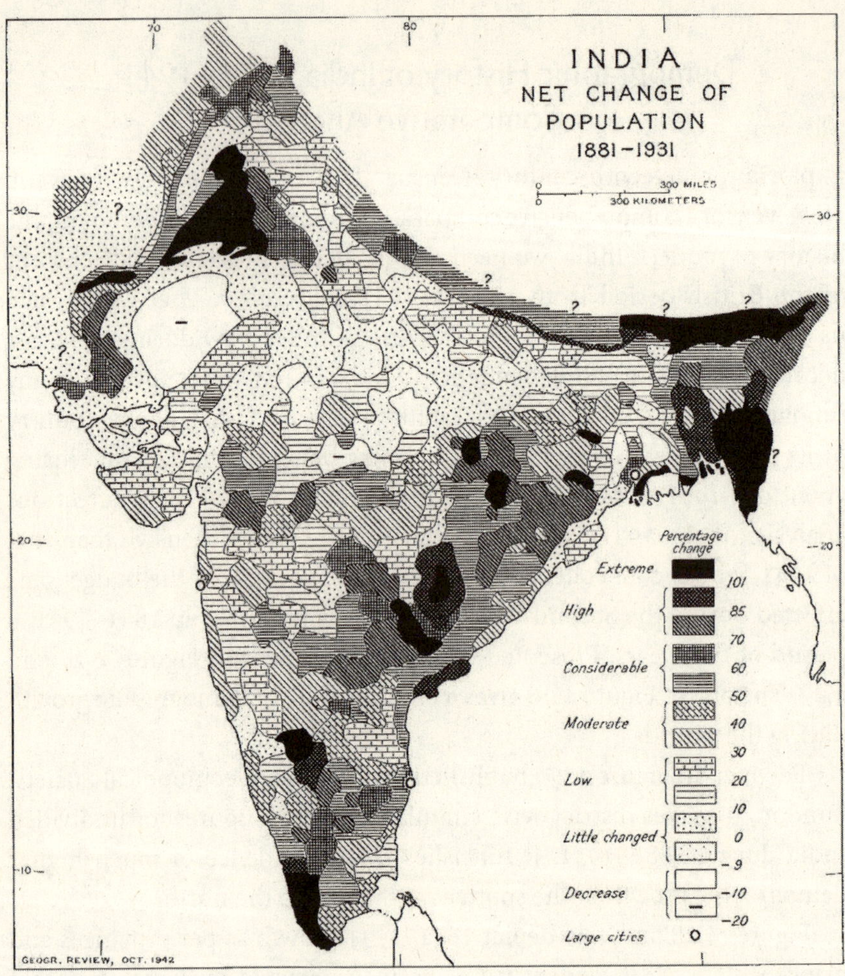

Figure 4.26: Net change in population of India, 1881–1931

growth around 40 per cent—we may classify growth rates under seven categories:

1. Extremely High: 75 per cent and above
2. Very High: 50 per cent to 75 per cent
3. High: 30 per cent to 50 per cent
4. Moderate: 20 per cent to 30 per cent
5. Low: 10 per cent to 20 per cent
6. Negligible 0 per cent to 10 per cent
7. Negative: less than zero per cent

Figure 4.27: Population changes in India, 1881–1931

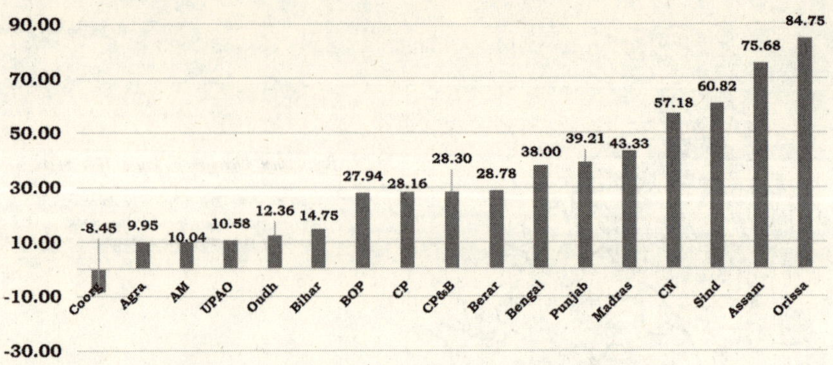

Figure 4.28: Population growth (percentage), 1881–1931

AM: Ajmer-Merwara; UPAO: United Provinces of Agra & Oudh; BOP: Bombay Presidency; CP: Central Provinces; CP&B: Central Provinces and Berar; CN: Chota Nagpur

Source: Table 4.15, Appendices

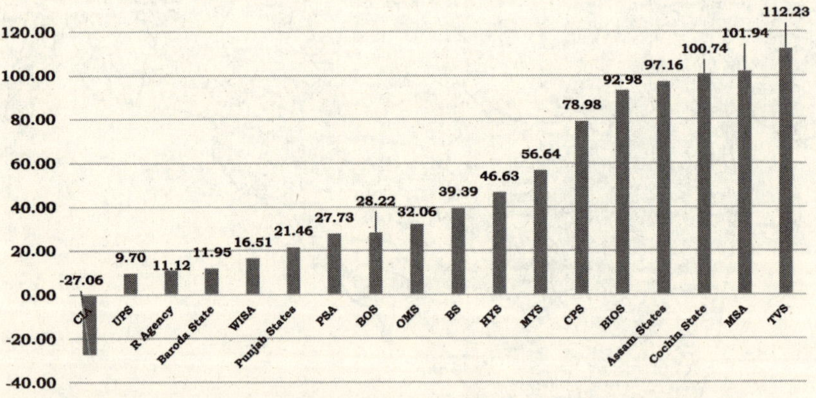

Figure 4.29: Population growth (percentage), 1881–1931

CIA: Central India Agency; UPS: United Provinces States; WISA: Western India State Agency; PSA: Punjab State Agency; BOS: Bombay States; OMS: Other Madras States; BS: Bengal States; HYS: Hyderabad States; MYS: Mysore States; BIOS: Bihar and Orissa States; MSA: Madras State Agency; TVS: Travancore State

Source: Census of India, 1931 (Table 4.15, Appendices)

Let us now analyse demographic change in the various regions of India based on the above ranges. Taking up the south, out of about fifty districts/states, no less than eleven scored growth in the extremely high category. In descending order of growth, these were Warangal (120),

Travancore (112), Cochin (108), Chital (106), Mahbubnagar (99), Tumkur (93), Adilabad (86), Nalgonda (85), Nilgiris (85), Kistna (78) and West Godavari (78). Another ten registered growth in the very high category; these were Bangalore (73), Karimnagar (67), Guntor (67), East Godavari (62), Kolar (59), Medak (58), Aitraf-i-Balda (58), Gulbarga (57), Madura (54) and North Arcot (53). Then, sixteen experienced growth in the high category; these were Salem (49), Coimbatore (48), Chin (47), Mysore (44), Malabar (42), Tinnevelly (42), Nizamabad (39), Hassan (39), Bijapur (38), Raichur (37), South Kanara (37), Vizagapatam (35), South Arcot (32), Trichipoly (32), Ramnad (32), and Kurnool (30). Only five, Anantpur (29), Chittoor (29), Belgaum (25), Nellore (24) and Dhar (23), grew at moderate level. Two, Kadur (19) and Bellary (13), experienced growth in the low category. Only three districts, Cuddapah (9), Tanjavor (9) and Shimoga (2), registered negligible growth. North Kanara was the only district/state of southern India with negative growth (-1 per cent).

Taking up the north next, out of about 126 districts/states only fifteen scored growth in the extremely high category. Almost all of these were princely states. In descending order of growth, these were Udaipur (232), Korea (203), Bastar (169), Jashpur (125), Kanker (120), Raigarh (114), Bhilwada (93), Surguja (86), Nimar (85), Bikaner (84), Sarangarh (82), Delhi (81), Thar & Parkar (80), Khair (79) and Tehri (75). Another seven—Chhindwara (74), Bhilsa (70), Almora (66), Bilaspur (59), Raipur (55), Garhwal (54) and Sirohi (52)—registered growth in the very high category. Then, thirteen of them—Mandla (49), Palamau (48), Dungurpur (48), Ranchi (48), Sagar (38), Gorakhpur (37), Hazaribagh (37), Mandsaur (35), Hissar (34), Bala (34), Betul (33) Santal Parganus (32) and Jind (30)—experienced growth in the high category. Twelve Bahraich (29), Jhalwad (28), Basti (27), Champaran (25), Shajapur (24), Gonda (24), Meerut (23), Bulandshahar (23), Ajmer-Merwara (22), Sitapur (22), Jodhpur (21) and Darbhanga (20)—experienced moderate growth. Further down, the number increased with as many as twenty-three scoring growth in the low category. These were Indore (19), Ujjain (19), Muzaffarnagar (18), Purnea (18), Bijnaur (16), Monghyr (16), Aligarh (15), Rampur (14), Etah (14), Hardoi (14), Muzaffarpur (14), Jubbulpur (13), Kheri (13), Lucknow (13), Bhagalpur (13), Jhansi (12), Gaya (12), Moradabad (11), Budaun (11), Fyzabad (11) Sultanpur (10) and Alwar (10). No less than twenty-eight of them fell in the negligible category. These were Durg (9), Saran (8), Agra (8), Pratapgarh (7), Rewa (7), Rohtak (7), Saharanpur (6), Udaipur or Mewar (5), Patna (5), Jaipur (4), Barielly (4), Barabanki (4), Chandla (3), Shahjanpur (3), Etawa (3), Cawnpore (3), Sheopur (2), Jalaun (2), Fatehpur (2), Raibreily (2), Jaunpur (2), Shahbad (2), Allahabad (1), Buxar (1), Mirjapur (0), Karnal (0), Pilibhit(0), Mathura (0) and Bharatpur (0). What is most striking is that twenty-six districts/states of northern India had negative growth. These were Farrukhabad (-1), Saugor (-2), Gurgaon (-2), Kotah (-3), Garhwal (-3), Tonk (-3), Karauli (-5), Unnao (-5), Hamirpur (-6), Banda (-6), Ballia (-6), Mainpuri (-6), Gwalior (-7), Orchha (-7), Bijapur (-8), Ghazipur (-9), Ambala (-11), Hoshangabad (-12), Panna (-14), Bundi (-15), Datia (-18), Chhattarpur (-18), Nainital (-20), Bharatpur (-25), Jaisalmer (-30) and Bhopal (-30).

In the eastern region, out of about thirty-two districts/states no less than twelve scored growth in the extremely high category. In descending order of growth, these were Singhbhum (105), Keonjhar (95), Kalahandi (93), Patna (93), Sonepur (93), Bonai (93), Bamra (93), Dhenkanal (93), Boudh (93), Gangpur (93) and Mayurbhanj (93). Another three—Manbhum (71), Pargana (66), and Sambalpur (59)—registered growth in the very high category. Five—Malda (48), Khulna (45), Angul (38), Koraput (35) and Ganjam (35)—saw moderate growth. Only four, Cuttack (21), Puri (17), Bankura (12) and Murshidabad (12) were in the low category. And only six—Midnapore (8), Birbhum (8), Balasore (5), Burdwan (5), Nadia (2) and Rajshahi (1)—experienced negligible growth. Jessore was the only district of Eastern India with a negative figure.

Coming to the west, out of about fifty-one districts/states, four—Balwani (85), Baloch and Punch Mahals (80), West Khandesh (80) and Amjhera (77)—scored growth in the extremely high category. Another four—Yeotmal (66), Rawakaniha (61), Alirajpur (54) and Sholapur (50)—registered growth in the very high category. Eight—Banswara (48), East Khandesh (45), Bhandara (36), Nagpur (35), Wardha (33), Ahmad Nagar (32), Thana (31) and Ratnagiri (30)—saw high growth. Twelve districts/states—West Kathiawar (29), Aurangabad (29), Chanda (29), Poona (29), Nasik (28), Ratlam (25), Bhaur (25), Jhabua (25), Pabhari (25), Amrawati (22), Sman (20) and Osman (20)—fell in moderte category. Only ten—Buldana (19), Akola (19), Bidar (19), Kolahpur (19), Ahmadabad (16),

Rajpipla (13), Bhir (13), Palanpur (13), Kolaba (11) and Satara (11)—fell in the low growth category. Only seven—Baroda (8), Nander (5), Junagarh (4), Kadi (2), Broach and Panchmahal (2), Idar (0) and Cutch (0)—experienced negligible growth. Khaira was the only district of Western India with negative growth.

The district-level demographic growth data cited above present a comprehensive micro picture of the massive differential in growth between different regions of India, especially the north and the south, for much of the pre-Independence period. It is evident that almost all the districts/princely states from southern India experienced growth in the four categories of extremely high, very high, high and moderate. This was in contrast with the north, where a vast majority of administrative units experienced low, negligible or negative growth. This exemplifies the earlier onset of demographic transition of the south. The growth patterns in the east and the west also follow roughly the same trend as the south, although the overall growth is less pronounced in the west, as compared to the south.

An interesting aspect of demographic growth that emerges from Figure 4.27 is the extremely high growth in almost all the districts/states which later went to Pakistan, especially in the canal colonies of west Punjab. Thus, Lyallpur registered an unparalleled growth of 2039 per cent, although on a very low base. Montgomery (187 per cent), Multan (115 per cent), Shahpur (114 per cent), Sargodha (99 per cent) and Lahore (80 per cent) also experienced extremely high growth. On the eastern side, in what is now Bangladesh, growth rates were again much higher, with Chittagong Hill Tract 100 per cent, Tipperah 94 per cent, Mymensing 92 per cent, Backerganj 59 per cent, Khulna 45 per cent, Faridpur 42 per cent and Sylhet 38 per cent.

The picture that emerges from the district-level data is corroborated by the data for provinces and princely states depicted in Figure 4.28. The population growth rates of Madras (51.55 per cent), Punjab (39.21 per cent), Bengal (39.97 per cent) are much higher than those of Bihar (14.79 per cent) and United Provinces (10.58 per cent). A similar picture emerges from Figure 4.29, which depicts growth in princely states between 1881 and 1931.

IX

Let us now incorporate data from the 1941 Census—which was the last British census—in the analysis. Though less comprehensive than the 1931 Census, its population figures are reliable. To make such a comparison, a comprehensive table for 1881–1941 has been constructed on the basis of tables provided in various decennial censuses. (See Appendices, Table 4.15). Figures 4.30 and 4.31 are based on the table, though in order to simplify the charts, some small units have been left out.)

The information depicted in Figures 4.30 and 4.31 has some unavoidable gaps in statistics and some territorial, and consequently, demographic adjustments that slightly affect the comparability of the data from 1881 to 1941, though this does not pose any fundamental analytical challenge.

The data presented in Figures 4.30 and 4.31 yield several broad conclusions. To begin with, it can be seen that between 1881 and 1941 the

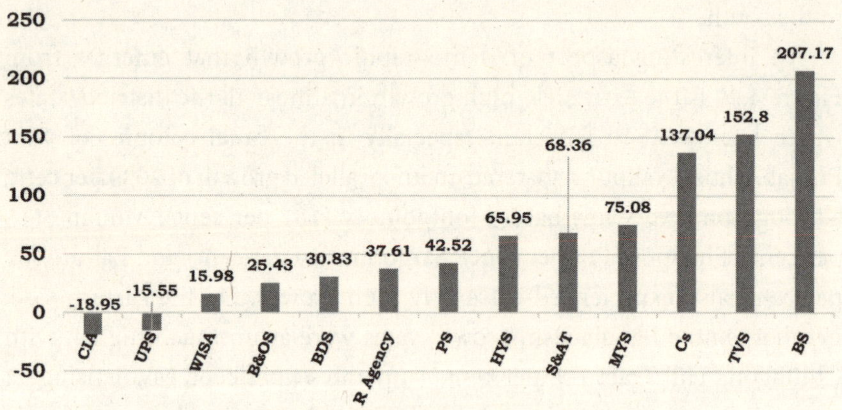

Figure 4.30: Percentage growth in states, 1881–1941

CIA: Central India Agency; UPS: United Province States; WISA: Western India State Agency; B&OS: Bihar and Orissa States; BDS: Baroda States; R Agency: Rajputana Agency; PS: Punjab States; HYS: Hyderabad State; S&AT: States and Agency Total; MYS: Mysore State; Cs: Cochin State; TVS: Travancore State; BS: Bengal States

Notes: (i) The growth rate for Bengal States is artificially inflated because of territorial adjustments.
(ii) The figures for WISA are from 1891–1941.

Source: Table 4.16, Appendices

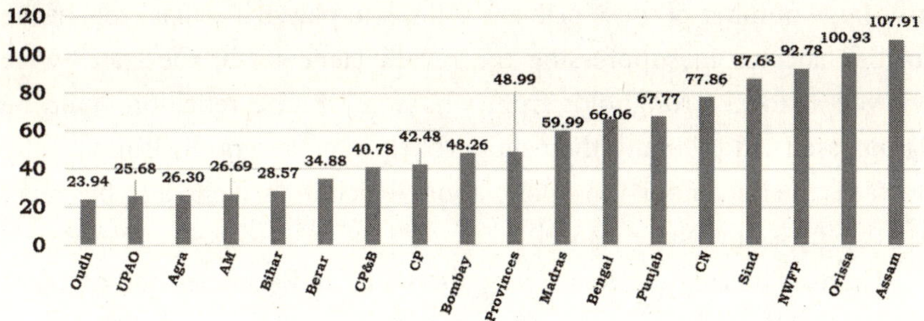

Figure 4.31: Percentage growth in provinces, 1881–1941

UPAO: United Provinces of Agra and Oudh; AM: Ajmer-Merwara; CP&B: Central Provinces and Berar; CP: Central Provinces; CN: Chota Nagpur; NWFP: North West Frontier Provinces

Source: Table 4.16, Appendices

states and agencies witnessed a much higher population growth (68.36 per cent) than the provinces directly under British rule (48.99 per cent). The former covered roughly 40 per cent of the territory of British India, but contained less than one-fourth of its population, which signifies that they had a much lower density than the provinces. The diversity of the political and administrative structure of British India, as reflected here, was primarily a consequence of the very nature of the British conquest of India, which happened over a century and involved big and small victories, interspersed by defeats and setbacks, alliances and counter-alliances, annexations and amalgamations. At the end of it all, the most fertile tracts of the country that could yield the highest amount of land revenue to sustain the empire mostly ended up under British rule. For instance, the entire Gangetic plain, stretching from the foothills of the Himalayas, in what is now Uttar Pradesh, to the Bengal delta was directly under British rule, except for a few very small princely states.

The larger princely states were mostly located in the less fertile and more sparsely populated regions of the subcontinent, though there were exceptions like Travancore, Cochin, Mysore, Baroda and Patiala. As is well known, the British strategy of maintaining hundreds of loyal native states across India had evolved in the First War of Independence in 1857 during which they came very close to being ousted from India. The loyalty of a large number of these princely states had played a crucial role in the British success in suppressing the revolt. Henceforth, the states were viewed as loyal strongholds from which any future rebellion could be suppressed. Additionally, their support helped create goodwill and loyalty towards the Raj among their population, which in turn had a ripple effect on the British provinces as well.

Coming to the question of why the states and agencies had a higher population growth during pre-Independence period than the provinces, two plausible explanations can be given. The first and the more controversial explanation going against the dominant nationalist narrative that emerged during the freedom struggle is that, on the whole, the areas ruled by Indian princes experienced much less economic exploitation of the people than those directly under British rule, thus creating conditions for higher population growth. The point here is not that the princely states had industrialised or modernised more than the provinces or that they granted more political rights to their people. Rather, the appropriation of resources in the form of land revenue and other taxes was probably lower and these areas were less exposed to the exploitative colonial economic structure that fundamentally aimed at transferring wealth from the colony to the metropolis. The second explanation is that these states and agencies had, with some exceptions, a comparatively sparse population accompanied by large tracts of unused cultivable land, which helped in the expansion of agriculture, raising food supply, and thus, population. The two explanations are obviously not mutually exclusive. It is quite likely that less economic exploitation encouraged an extension of agriculture.

Referring to Figure 4.30, the exorbitant growth of the Bengal States (207.17 per cent) is mainly a result of territorial adjustments and is, therefore, not comparable to the growth of other states. Going deeper into the data, it is evident that among the major states the highest growth was achieved by Travancore (152.8 per cent) and Cochin (137.04 per cent), and then Mysore (75.08 per cent), followed by Hyderabad (65.95 per cent). The growth in the Punjab States (42.52 per cent) is substantial but not extraordinarily high. Rajputana's growth (37.61 per cent) is substantial but not high. What may be of some interest is the fact that the United Provinces states, which had a very small population to begin with, experienced a further decline (15.55 per cent). The figures show in no uncertain terms that the southern states had by far the fastest population growth, followed by Punjab and Rajputana Agency. Overall, the northern states experienced low growth from 1881 to 1941.

Coming to the provinces directly under British rule, we notice that the comparative growth rates across regions are not markedly different from those of the states and agencies. Here, Assam's growth (107.91 per cent) is largely a result of migration from Bengal; and Orissa's (100.93 per cent) is partly a result of territorial transfers from adjoining provinces. North-West Frontier Provinces grew by 92.78 per cent. Sind's growth (87.63 per cent) from a low base reflects both the growth of Karachi as a large port city to which people migrated in search of opportunities and the expansion of agriculture in unused cultivable land, which in turn promoted higher population growth. Chota Nagpur registered a growth of 77.86 per cent.

Among the larger provinces, Punjab takes the lead with a growth rate of 67.77 per cent. Close on the heels is Bengal with a growth rate of 66.06 per cent. Considering that Bengal sent out so many people to Assam and already had a high population density, this rate is extraordinarily high. Some of this growth would, of course, be accounted for by the migration to Calcutta from other parts of India. The other factor could be that, as shown in district-level analysis, the growth happened disproportionately in East Bengal, now Bangladesh, where extension of agriculture could happen on a large scale because of the availability of unused cultivable land.

Madras Presidency grew at 57.99 per cent. The next highest growth rates can be seen in Bombay Presidency at 48.26 per cent, and the Central Provinces and Berar at 42.48 per cent. What is striking is that almost the entire north India had a much lower population growth between 1881 and 1941. Bihar (28.57 per cent) grew at half the rate of Madras. The United Provinces of Agra and Oudh, the most populous province by far in north India with 40.57 per cent of the Hindi-belt population, achieved a growth of only 25.68 per cent over a long period of sixty years. This was well below half the rate of Madras Presidency. Even this modest growth occurred mainly between 1921 and 1941. Between 1881 and 1921, Bihar (from about 2.24 crore to 2.33 crore, a growth of just 4.29 per cent) and United Provinces (from about 4.38 crore to 4.54 crore, growth of just 3.65 per cent) remained virtually stagnant. During this time, south, east and west experienced significant growth. The population stagnation of the two largest Hindi-belt states over a period of forty years is a relatively unknown aspect of modern India's demographic history.

The growth figures for 1881–1931 and 1881–1941 help us draw several conclusions. Clearly, the fastest growth rate in the subcontinent was enjoyed by the eastern and north-western extremities—a rate that was more than twice that of the United Provinces and much higher than even the consolidated rate of the entire north India. In Punjab's case, the effect of British policy was significant, as they focused on building up the province as a bastion of loyalty. This was achieved by recruiting more than 50 per cent of their military personnel from Punjab and building the world's largest canal network there, which could irrigate as much as 37 million acres of land—much larger than even in the United States at that time. This extensive canal network enabled the extension of agriculture in large parts of the province that were semi-arid and not fit for farming without reliable irrigation. In addition, the British policy included settling retired soldiers in the canal colonies. This indicates that population growth in British India was at least partly determined by British imperial policies whose fundamental premise was the safety of the empire and the exploitation of India for its own benefit.

As with Bengal and Punjab, the high growth rate of the Madras Presidency reflects an earlier growth spurt compared to north India. Combined with the growth in the southern princely states, the population growth of the south between 1881 and 1941 was 67.71 per cent, which is roughly two-and-a-half times that of the United Provinces at 25.68 and slightly more than three times than that of the United Provinces, Bihar and Rajputana combined. In fact, even when the Hindi-speaking Central Provinces is added to this group, the differential goes down only slightly. Therefore, the conclusion is hard to avoid that for a variety of reasons—many of which have been discussed in the preceding pages—the north was at the bottom of the demographic growth chart during British rule, while Bengal, Punjab and the south were at the top. It is only after Independence, especially after 1961, that the north would enter its peak growth phase.

What may partly explain this lag is that though British rule in India was deeply exploitative as a whole, there were regional variations caused by agricultural settlement patterns with the more exploitative zamindari in the north and east and the less exploitative ryotwari in the west and south. Moreover, the maritime nature of the British Empire ensured more development of the coastal belt. These factors may partly account for the fact that as compared to the south and the west, the northern hinterland witnessed much less growth during 1881–1941, since income, nutrition and health facilities are key factors behind population growth. This would change from the 1960s, by which time north India probably crossed the threshold of social and economic development necessary to support high population growth.

The statistics presented here establish that, over the long term, population growth in different parts of India has tended to converge and that the divergence among regions and provinces is an artefact of a comparative framework based exclusively on trends from the post-Independence period. Demographic transition is primarily contingent on social and economic factors and has little to do with the country attaining Independence, except to the extent that it might affect growth by making a change in social and economic conditions—a factor that is of some relevance in the context of India.

It is, of course, conceivable that in other societies the political system might play a critical role if the state intervenes in the family choices of people in an authoritarian and coercive manner, preventing them from having larger families either by directly and effectively prohibiting them or by raising the cost of exercising one's choice in this matter. The perfect example of this in recent times is China, which since 1980 effectively forced its citizens in urban areas into adopting a one-child norm.

The prevalent comparative framework that confines itself to a few decades after the 1960s places too much emphasis on high growth in the north. The required corrective clearly lies in studying the modern historical demographics of India since 1872 in a comprehensive and objective manner. Once that is done, it becomes self-evident that different regions of India have experienced comparable growth in their population over one-and-a-half centuries, and that there is no reason, therefore, to focus on any one region in isolation regarding population. This study does not, of course, rule out cultural or other factors in population growth. All that it does is to show that as far as the differential growth rates of various regions of India are concerned, there is no need to fall back upon such factors. The long-term demographic data fully explain the phenomenon on their own.

5

India's Demographic Divergence versus Convergence (1901–2011)

This chapter examines the empirical evidence of India's demographic history between 1901 and 2011. Although there is an overlap with the period 1901–41, which was discussed in Chapter 4, in this chapter we have taken up retrospectively reconstructed data according to the current administrative units of India, allowing for a more detailed and precise comparison across provinces and regions. The reconstructed 1881 figures for post-Partition India and its various regions as calculated in Chapter 4 (Table 4.8) are then juxtaposed with the 1901–2011 series in order to arrive at aggregate growth and percentage shares for important junctures in the demographic journey of modern India, such as 1921, 1951, 1971 and 2011. This helps develop a holistic perspective on the process of demographic transition in different parts of India over the entire period of 1881–2011.

I
Divergence versus Convergence: Historical Demography of India

In order to gain a deeper and more comprehensive understanding of the demographic history of modern India, we use a nationwide comparative framework that examines long-term demographic data from all regions of the country. Table 5.1 (See Appendices) gives decade-wise data for states on total population, growth in absolute numbers, growth in percentage and the share of each state in the population of the country. The basic table is from the Census of India, but a few modifications have been made to adapt it to the specific requirements of this study. The column on population share has been added to enable us to precisely track how regional variations in the distribution of population took place over 1901–2011. Further, cumulative growth for each state since 1901 has been added. With a view to compress the large and unwieldy table, small states and union territories that have not been separately analysed in this study have been removed, without making any appreciable difference to this comparative analysis.

The table has been constructed by taking up the administrative units of India as they existed in the last Census of 2011 and then going backwards to 1901 by isolating the population of their present territories from the rest of the administrative units they might have been part of in the past. This approach is very different from the comparative framework employed in the preceding chapter in which statistics from 1872 to 1941 were analysed according to the administrative units at that time. For Punjab and Haryana, the state-level data series do not have break-up for all districts and sub-districts (tehsils) for many censuses from 1881 onward, and this may cause minor discrepancies in aggregate figures. We examine the statistics presented in Table 5.1 in the Appendices with the help of charts and diagrams.

The regional classification of north, south, east and west follows the original scheme, that is, the north consists of the Hindi region, including central India; the south includes all the southern states; the east consists of Bengal, Assam and Orissa; and the west is composed of Maharashtra and Gujarat. Let us first examine the demographic growth of the north.

The small hill state of Himachal Pradesh has experienced a cumulative growth of 257.48 per cent, its population having risen from 19.20 lakh in 1901 to 68.64 lakh in 2011. Between 1901 and 1951, the state achieved moderate growth, which is in line with the trend for other Hindi-speaking states. The state witnessed rapid growth from 1951 to 2001, with its peak decadal growth rate coming up to 23.71 per cent during 1971–81. However, Himachal's share in India's population has gone down from 0.81 per cent in 1901 to 0.57 per cent in 2011—a substantial decline for a small state, which shows that its growth has been considerably below the national average for the period as a whole.

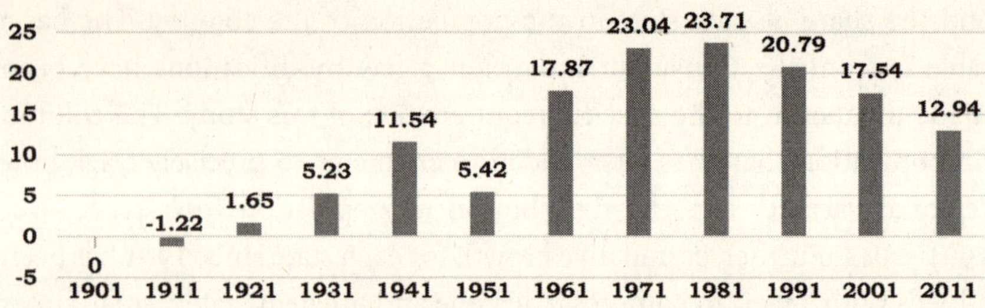

Figure 5.1: Population growth of Himachal Pradesh (percentage)

Source: Table 5.1, Appendices

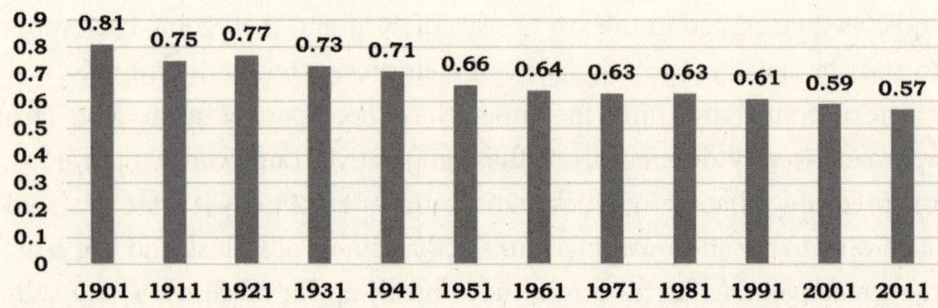

Figure 5.2: Population share of Himachal Pradesh (percentage)

Source: Table 5.1, Appendices

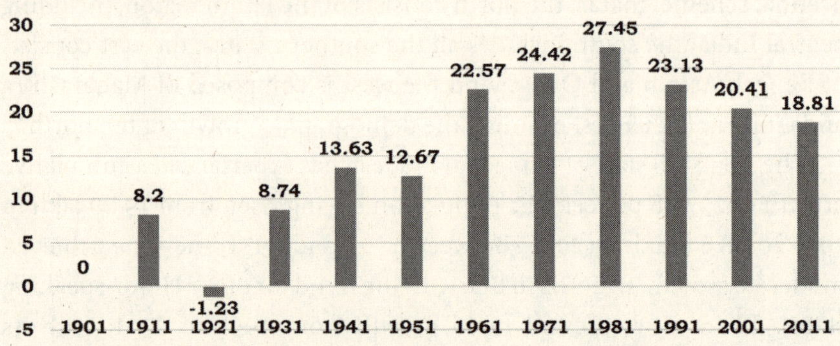

Figure 5.3: Population growth of Uttarakhand (percentage)

Source: Table 5.1, Appendices

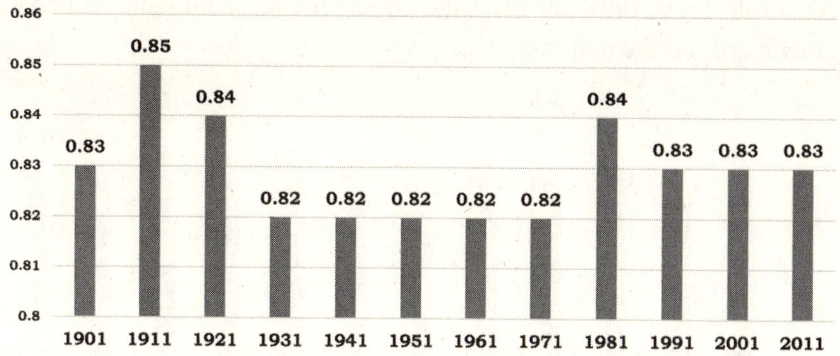

Figure 5.4: Population share of Uttarakhand (percentage)

Source: Table 5.1, Appendices

Uttarakhand, the other small hill state from the north, has seen its population go up from 19.79 lakh in 1901 to about 1 crore in 2011, which is a cumulative growth of 409 per cent. The state again had modest growth until 1951, and a phase of rapid growth between 1951 and 2001, with a peak rate of 27.45 in the decade of 1971–81. Quite interestingly, the state's share in the population of India has fluctuated very little over the century (only within a range of 0.82 to 0.85). In 2011, it was the same (0.83 per

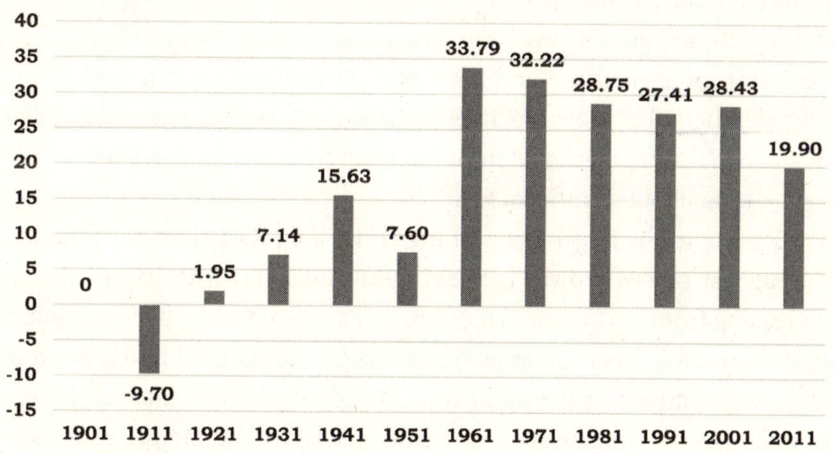

Figure 5.5: Population growth of Haryana (percentage)

Source: Table 5.1, Appendices

cent) as it was in 1901. Clearly, Uttarakhand has just about maintained its growth around the national level.

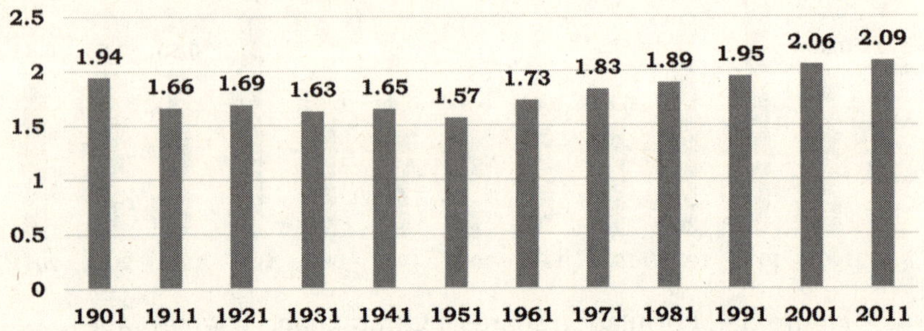

Figure 5.6: Population share of Haryana (percentage)

Source: Table 5.1, Appendices

Haryana, which was carved out of post-Partition east Punjab only in 1966 and officially became a Hindi-speaking state, though with a significant presence of Punjabi speakers, has seen its population grow by 448.37 per cent between 1901 and 2011, from 46.23 lakh in 1901 to 2.53 crore in 2011. Haryana's peak growth phase started in 1951 and continued until 2011. The effects of Partition, which brought 9 million refugees to India, many of whom settled in what is now Haryana, are visible in the significant growth over the two decades after Independence. The extension of agriculture and the Green Revolution contributed to the high demographic growth of the state since 1951, which has ensured that its share in the population of India has risen from 1.94 per cent to 2.09 per cent—a small but significant rise.

Coming to the larger states of the Hindi belt, Rajasthan has achieved the highest rate of growth between 1901 and 2011, with its population increasing from 1.02 crore to 6.85 crore—a rise of 565.90 per cent or just under sevenfold. Its peak growth phase seems to have set into motion in 1951 and continued right up to 2011. It should be noted that the growth rate for 1951–61 includes the increase caused by the merger of Ajmer-Merwara with the state in 1956. The peak growth of 32.97 per cent was achieved between 1971 and 1981. As a result of high growth, Rajasthan's share in India's population has gone up from 4.32 per cent in 1901 to

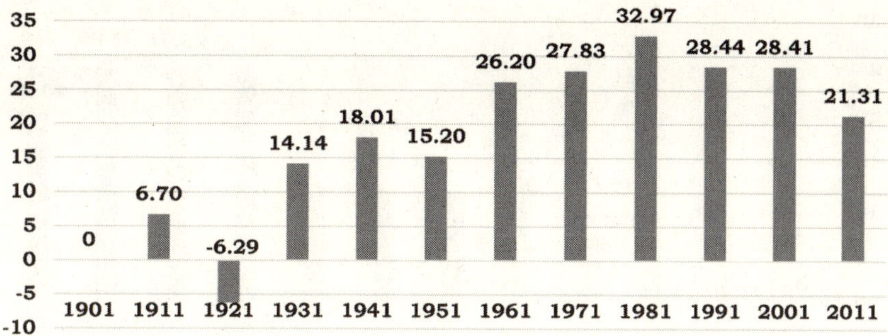

Figure 5.7: Population growth of Rajasthan (percentage)

Source: Table 5.1, Appendices

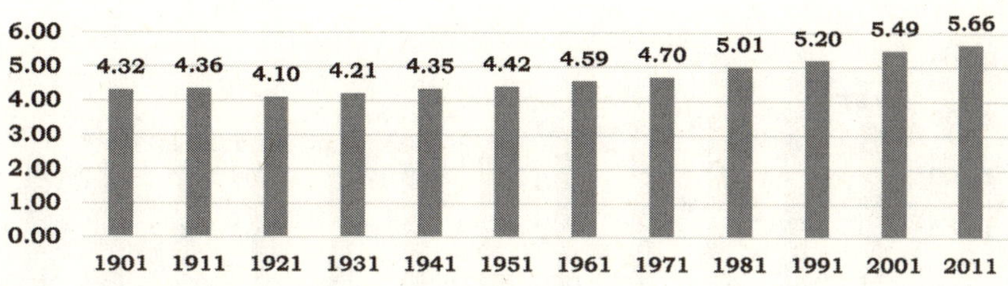

Figure 5.8: Population share of Rajasthan (percentage)

Source: Table 5.1, Appendices

5.66 per cent in 2011, though the bulk of this growth has happened only after 1951. The massive growth achieved by Rajasthan, especially in the last seventy years, fits into the pattern identified earlier, whereby the sparsely populated western and central regions of India with higher scope for agrarian expansion have shown faster growth.

Uttar Pradesh, the largest state in the country by population, has registered a cumulative growth of 328.42 per cent in 110 years, having risen from 4.66 crore to 19.98 crore. Between 1901 and 1921, it suffered a decline of nearly 5 per cent in its population. The state experienced a low or moderate decadal growth between 1921 and 1951; the peak growth phase extended from 1961 to 2011, when the state achieved a growth of 20 per cent or more every decade. The highest growth of 25.85 per cent was achieved in the decade of 1991–2001. Impressive as this growth

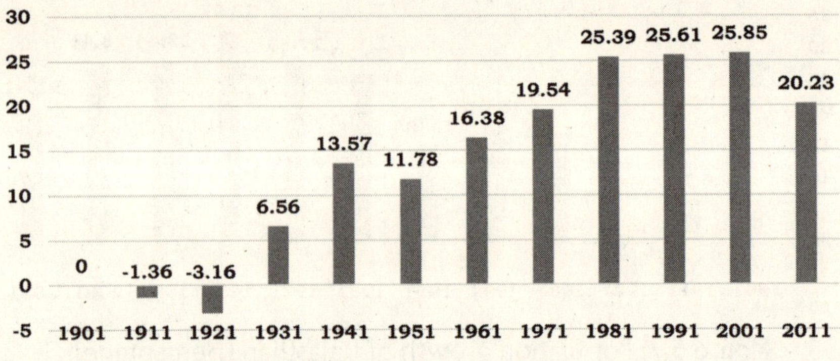

Figure 5.9: Population growth of Uttar Pradesh (percentage)

Source: Table 5.1, Appendices

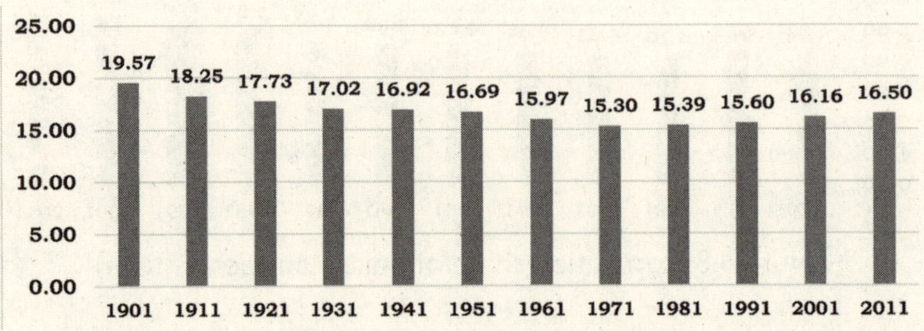

Figure 5.10: Population share of Uttar Pradesh (percentage)

Source: Table 5.1, Appendices

seems, the fact is that Uttar Pradesh's share in the population of India has taken an unparalleled hit, having come down from 19.57 per cent in 1901 to 16.50 in 2011. This is by far the largest percentage decline in share for any state. It underlines the fact that, contrary to prevalent notions, Uttar Pradesh has not witnessed extraordinarily high growth; on the contrary, it has actually lost a massive share of 3 percentage points. That is so because the state entered its peak growth phase only after 1961, while the period from 1921 to 1961 saw just low or moderate growth.

Quite predictably, in terms of share, Uttar Pradesh reached the bottom in 1971, with a figure as low as 15.30 per cent. Between 1901 and 1921 alone, its share in India's population declined from 19.57 per cent to 17.73 per cent. Going back to the calculations made in the previous chapter about the percentage shares of provinces and regions in 1881 after adjusting their populations as well as the population of India for post-Partition boundaries, the decline in Uttar Pradesh's share from 20.93 per cent in 1881 to 16.50 in 2011 is even higher, since the state had seen very little net growth from 1881 to 1921. In contrast, many other parts of India such as Punjab, Bengal and the south had experienced considerable growth. Even with the addition of Uttarakhand's population of 1,00,86,292 in 2011, the share comes to only 17.33 per cent—a loss of 3.6 percentage points in the national population. The obvious conclusion is that the state's demographic growth has been significantly below the national average over the period 1881–2011. Even more significantly, there appears little chance of the state achieving convergence with the high share of the late-nineteenth century.

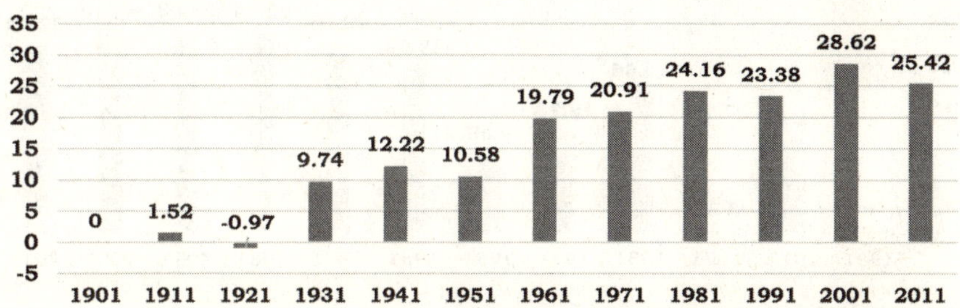

Figure 5.11: Population growth of Bihar (percentage)

Source: Table 5.1, Appendices

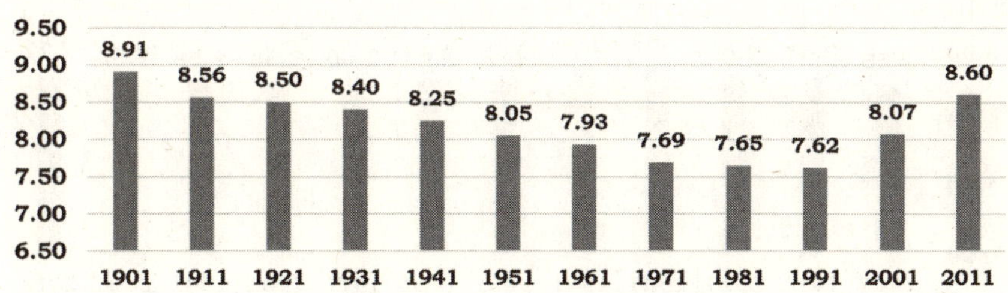

Figure 5.12: Population share of Bihar (percentage)

Source: Table 5.1, Appendices

Moving on to Bihar, the state's population has grown from 2.12 crore in 1901 to 10.41 crore in 2011, which is a rise of 390.03 per cent or a little less than five times. Bihar experienced negligible growth from 1901 to 1921. The state had low or moderate growth from 1921 to 1951. Its growth spurt began in the decade of 1951–61. Bihar entered its high growth phase, with more than 20 per cent a decade in 1961–71, continuing right up to 2011. The peak growth rate of 28.62 per cent was achieved between 1991 and 2001. Insofar as its share in India's population is concerned, Bihar started with a high of 8.91 per cent, experienced divergence to touch the bottom (7.62 per cent) in 1991, before starting to converge with the old position, reaching 8.60 per cent in 2011. Thus, unlike Uttar Pradesh, the state has lost only a little of its share in India's demographic pie and, given its continued growth, is likely to recover it in the foreseeable future.

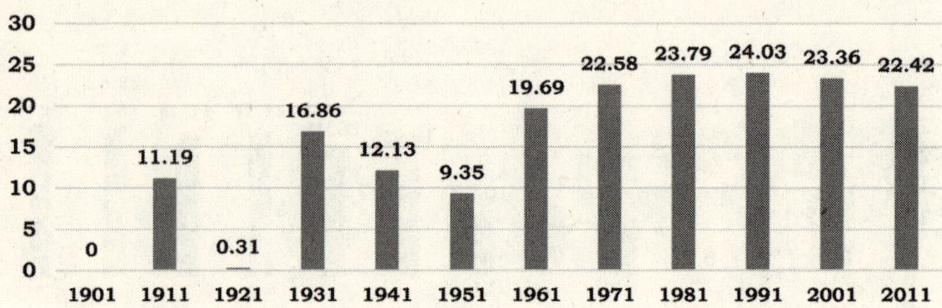

Figure 5.13: Population growth of Jharkhand (percentage)

Source: Table 5.1, Appendices

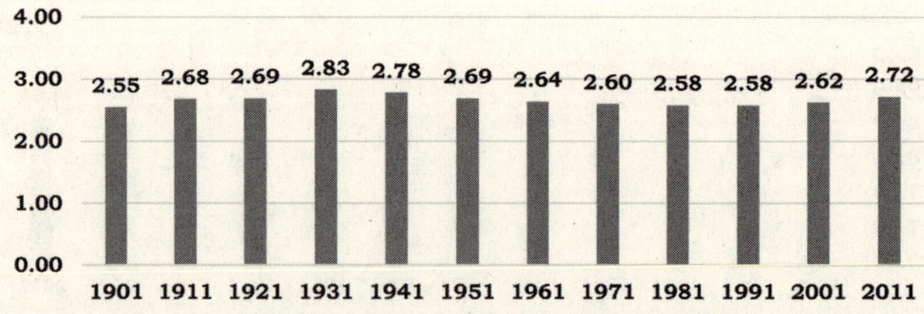

Figure 5.14: Population share of Jharkhand (percentage)

Source: Table 5.1, Appendices

The next state from the Hindi belt for our consideration is Jharkhand, which was part of Bihar until 2000. The state has registered a high cumulative growth of 443.62 per cent, with its population rising from 60.68 lakh in 1901 to approximately 3.30 crore in 2011, or roughly five-and-a-half times. Unlike many other Hindi states, Jharkhand experienced moderate growth between 1901 and 1951, with its population share moving up from 2.55 per cent to 2.69 per cent. The state saw a spurt in the 1950s and entered the peak phase of above 20 per cent growth in the decade of 1961–71. Its highest growth (24.03 per cent) was achieved during 1981–91. Looking at the pattern of population share over the period, there has been considerable fluctuation, but within a narrow range, starting with 2.55 per cent in 1901, reaching a high of 2.83 per cent in 1931, falling to 2.58 per cent by 1991, before rising to 2.72 per cent by the Census of 2011. On the whole, it could be concluded that the demographic growth of the state has been on the higher side.

The next Hindi state, Chhattisgarh, is from central India, and was a part of Madhya Pradesh until 2000. With a demographic growth of 510.90 per cent, from 41.81 lakh in 1901 to 2.55 crore in 2011, the state could be characterised to have had very high growth over the long term, as its population has grown a little over six times. Rather surprisingly, it registered a growth of 24.15 per cent during 1901–11 and then went on to achieve only low or moderate growth over the next forty years, before entering the peak phase in 1961, which has continued—though with a minor deviation—until 2011. The very high growth rate over the long term has ensured a rise in the state's share in the population of India from 1.75 per cent in 1901 to 2.11 per cent in 2011—a significant increase for a small state. The high growth of Chhattisgarh again fits into the pattern observed in the sparsely populated central and western India, which grew at a faster pace primarily due to the availability of unused cultivable land that could be developed for agriculture with the help of surplus labour.

Madhya Pradesh, too, has experienced high demographic growth between 1901 and 2011. Its population of 1.26 crore has increased to 7.26 crore—a rise of 472.80 per cent—signifying that the state's population has grown nearly sixfold in 110 years. As is the case with most other Hindi states, Madhya Pradesh saw only low or moderate growth until

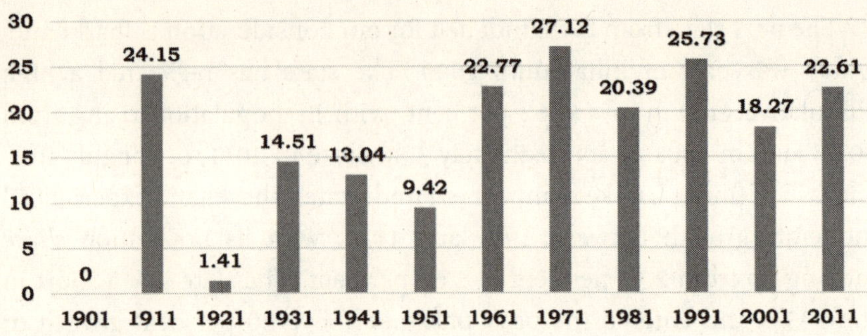

Figure 5.15: Population growth of Chhattisgarh (percentage)

Source: Table 5.1, Appendices

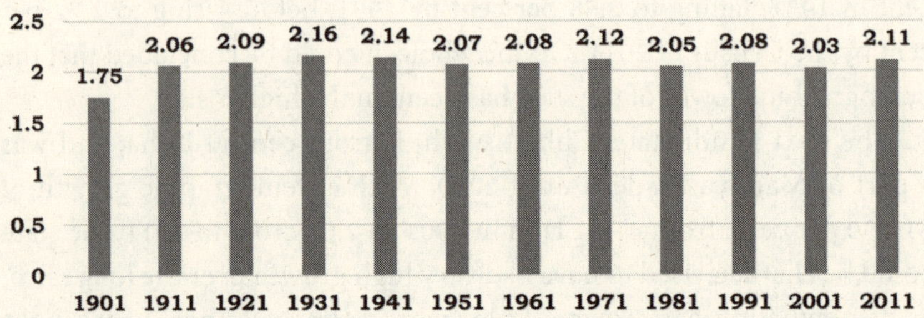

Figure 5.16: Population share of Chhattisgarh (percentage)

Source: Table 5.1, Appendices

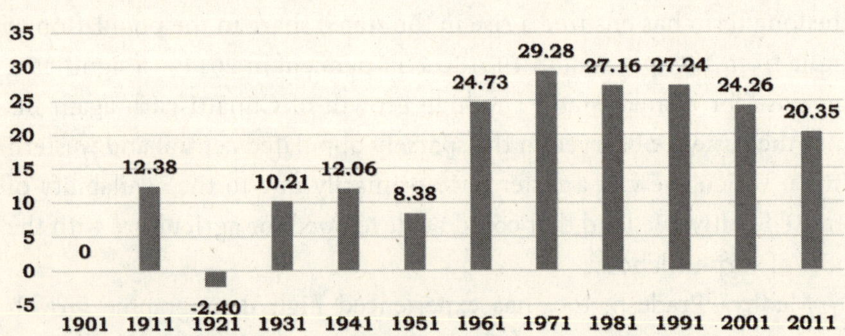

Figure 5.17: Population growth of Madhya Pradesh (percentage)

Source: Table 5.1, Appendices

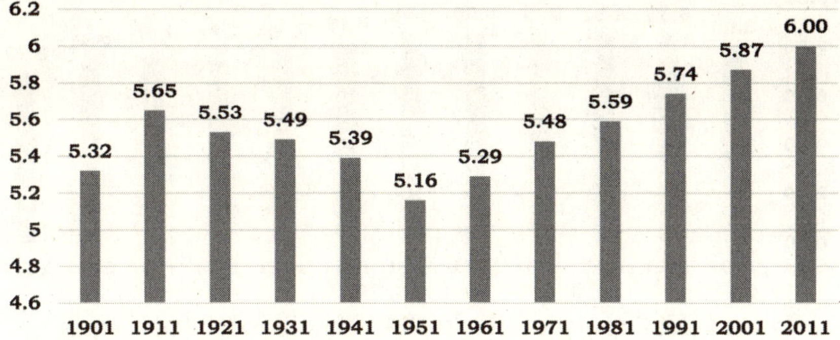

Figure 5.18: Population share of Madhya Pradesh (percentage)

Source: Table 5.1, Appendices

1951 and then entered its peak growth phase of above 20 per cent during 1951–61. The peak phase continued up to 2011, with the fastest growth occurring during 1961–71. In accordance with the high growth over the period of 1951–2011, the state's percentage share of India's population has almost consistently risen in every decennial census. Between 1901 and 2011, it has increased from 5.32 per cent to 6 per cent. The growth of 0.68 percentage points should be regarded as quite significant. The pattern of sparsely populated regions growing at a higher rate has been followed by Madhya Pradesh as well.

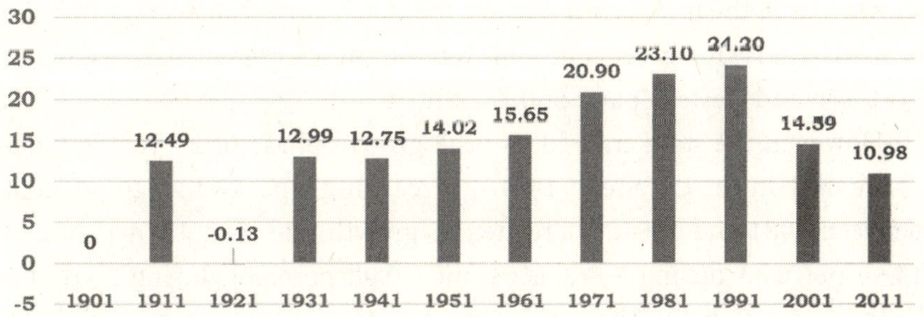

Figure 5.19: Population growth of Andhra Pradesh (percentage)

Source: Table 5.1, Appendices

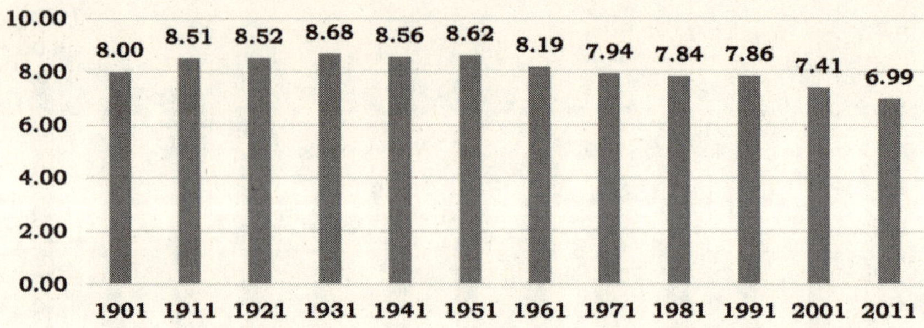

Figure 5.20: Population share of Andhra Pradesh (percentage)

Source: Table 5.1, Appendices

Let us now move on to the statistics for the south, which, until 2014, consisted of four major states: Andhra Pradesh, Tamil Nadu, Karnataka and Kerala. Since Andhra Pradesh was still united in the last Census of 2011, for the purpose of this study, it would be convenient not to separate Telangana from it. Andhra Pradesh's population has increased from 1.90 crore in 1901 to 8.45 crore in 2011—an overall growth of 343.62 per cent or nearly four-and-a-half times. Further, the state enjoyed a moderate growth rate of 12 to 16 per cent between 1901 and 1961, except during 1911–21 when there was a fall in the population of the country due to the influenza epidemic. In fact, combining the growth rates from 1881 to 1901 of the Madras Presidency (23.96 per cent) and Hyderabad (13.16 per cent)—from which Andhra Pradesh was carved out in 1953—shows that in the nineteenth century the state enjoyed an average decadal growth of close to 10 per cent. This rate was much higher than that of the northern and western parts of the country.

However, the state entered its peak growth phase of 20 per cent and above only in the decade of 1961–71, reaching a peak of 24.20 per cent between 1981 and 1991. Thereafter, its growth rate abruptly declined to 14.59 per cent during 1991–2001 and 10.98 per cent during 2001–11. With its growth below the national average since 1991, the state's share in the population of India has come down to 6.99 per cent from 8.0 per cent. Andhra Pradesh's peak population share of 8.68 per cent was achieved in 1931, which indicates early onset of demographic transition.

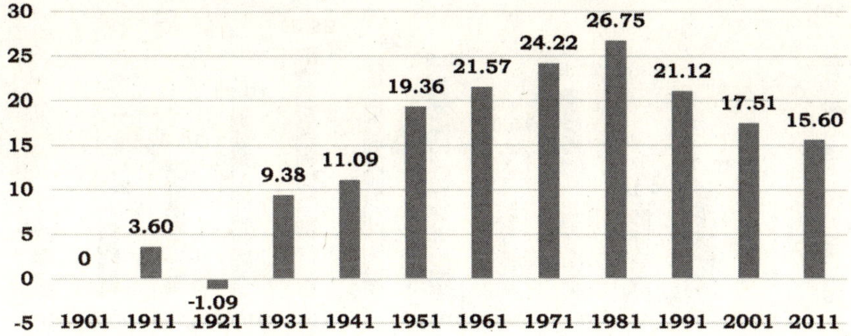

Figure 5.21: Population growth of Karnataka (percentage)

Source: Table 5.1, Appendices

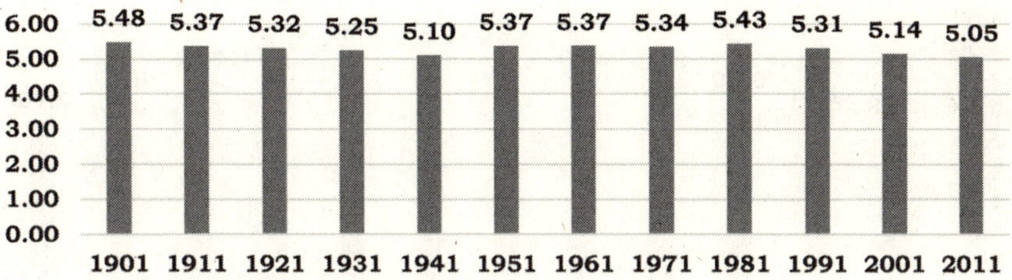

Figure 5.22: Population share of Karnataka (percentage)

Source: Table 5.1, Appendices

The next state from the south taken up for analysis is Karnataka. Its population has risen from 1.30 crore in 1901 to 6.10 crore in 2011—a rise of 367.99 per cent or just under fivefold. In contrast to Andhra Pradesh, Karnataka witnessed its growth spurt from 1941 onwards and maintained its peak growth phase of 20 per cent and above between 1951 and 1991. The fastest growth during these four decades (26.75 per cent) was achieved during 1971–81. Another point to be noted is that, unlike Andhra Pradesh, the fall in growth rate after 1991 is not steep. Thus, even in the 2011 Census, Karnataka registered a relatively high growth rate of 15.60 per cent. It comes as no surprise, therefore, that the state has witnessed only a modest fall in its share of India's population, from the peak of 5.48 per cent to 5.05 per cent.

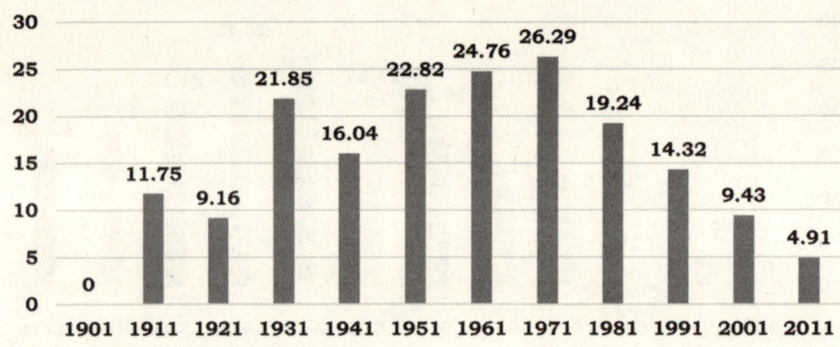

Figure 5.23: Population growth of Kerala (percentage)

Source: Table 5.1, Appendices

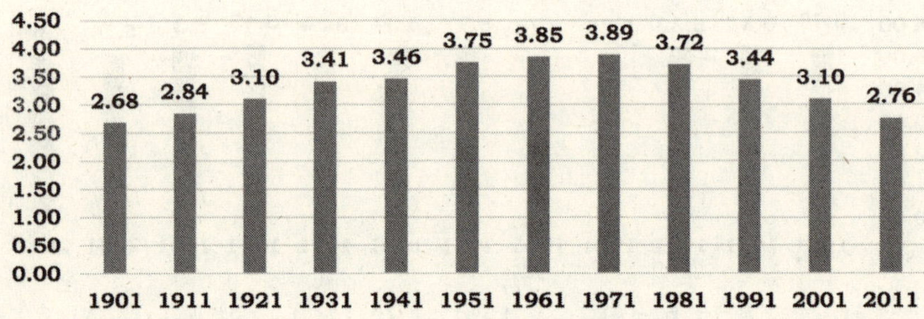

Figure 5.24: Population share of Kerala (percentage)

Source: Table 5.1, Appendices

Kerala, the smallest of the four southern states, stands apart from all the other states of the south, and also from India as a whole. It had started experiencing relatively high growth rates in the nineteenth century itself, at a time when many other parts of the country were barely growing. It continued this trend, entering the peak growth phase (20 per cent and above) in 1921, the earliest in India, and completed it by 1971, again the earliest. Kerala continued to enjoy good growth for another twenty years, that is, 19.24 per cent during 1971–81 and 14.32 per cent during 1981–91. Between 1901 and 2011, Kerala's population grew from 63.96 lakh to 3.34 crore—a cumulative increase of 422.27 per cent or a little higher than five times. As for its share in the population of India, it started with 2.68 per cent and rose steadily, reaching a peak of 3.89 per cent in 1971, gradually declining to 3.44 per cent in 1991, after which there was a steeper decline to 2.76 per cent in 2011.

Tamil Nadu's demographic history presents several peculiarities. Among the larger states of the country, it has registered the second-lowest growth rate (274.74 per cent), after Punjab's 267.72 per cent (from 1.92 crore to 7.21 crore). What is even more important is that, unlike all other states, Tamil Nadu has not experienced a well-defined peak growth phase. Its population grew at a moderate rate for the first six decades of the twentieth century, apparently entering the peak phase in 1961–71, with a growth rate of 22.30 per cent, but this dropped in the very next decade to 17.50 per cent. However, just like Karnataka, growth has not

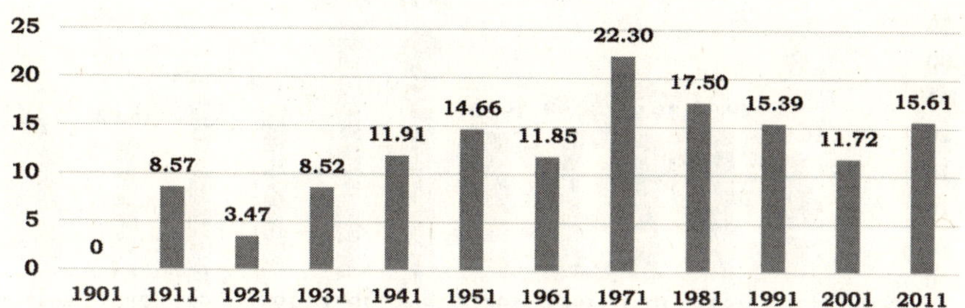

Figure 5.25: Population growth of Tamil Nadu (percentage)

Source: Table 5.1, Appendices

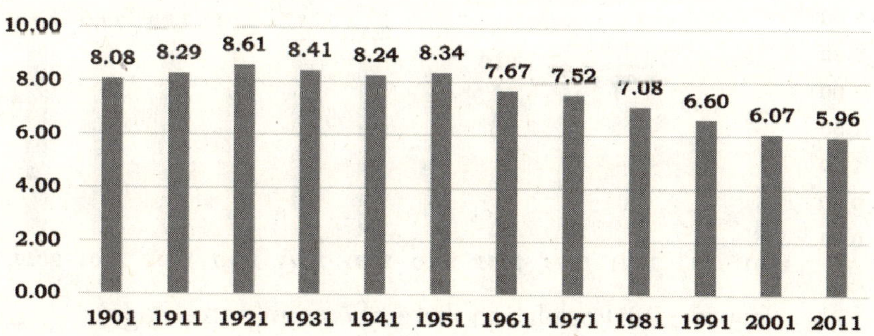

Figure 5.26: Population share of Tamil Nadu (percentage)

Source: Table 5.1, Appendices

fallen consistently, which usually happens after the peak growth phase. Rather, it has followed a trajectory marked by multiple rises and falls. Even in the Census of 2011, Tamil Nadu grew by a good 15.61 per cent. That was the fastest rate for any southern state, although Karnataka was close on its heels, at 15.60 per cent.

The journey of Tamil Nadu in terms of share in the population of India has been equally complex. Beginning with 8.08 per cent in 1901, it reached the peak of 8.61 per cent in 1921, stayed close to it (8.34 per cent) until 1951, and has steadily fallen ever since, reaching 5.96 per cent in 2011. This represents a massive fall in share for the state, comparable to that of Uttar Pradesh which decreased from 19.57 per cent in 1901 to 16.50 in 2011.

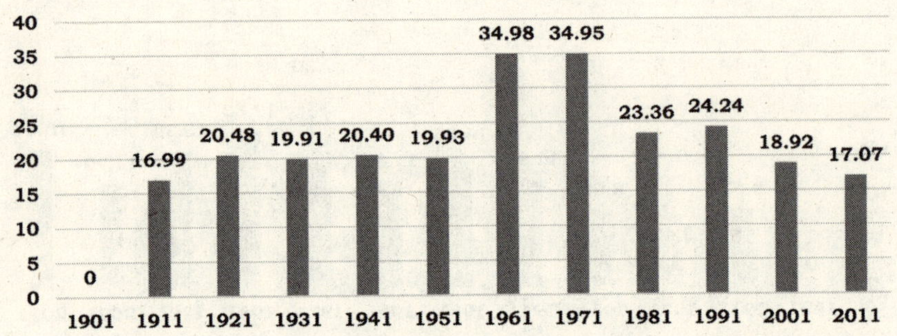

Figure 5.27: Population growth of Assam (percentage)

Source: Table 5.1, Appendices

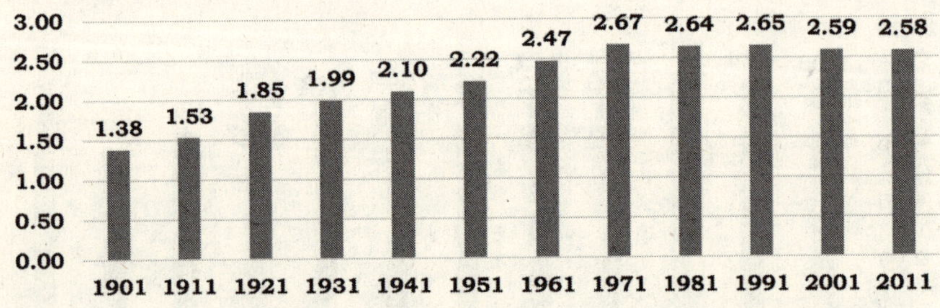

Figure 5.28: Population share of Assam (percentage)

Source: Table 5.1, Appendices

Having analysed the demographic history of the southern states, let us now move on to eastern India, which includes Assam, Bengal and Orissa. Assam's case is *sui generis*. Its small population of 32.89 lakh in 1901 expanded to 3.12 crore in 2011—an exorbitant increase of 848.59 per cent or nine-and-a-half times in 110 years. This is by far the highest growth rate for any large state in the country. As is well known, Assam has experienced large-scale migration of Bengali-speaking people since the nineteenth century. This sustained migration, as much as natural growth, lies behind the extraordinary demographic growth of Assam. Therefore, to measure the true extent of population growth in the east, Assam and Bengal need to be analysed together.

Throughout the twentieth century, Assam was either close to or within the peak growth phase, with its highest rates of 34.98 per cent and 34.95 per cent occurring in the two-and-a-half decades after Independence, when there was a large Bengali influx into the state. Regarding its share in the population of India, Assam started at 1.38 per cent, peaked at 2.67 per cent in 1971 and has stayed close to this figure ever since, falling only slightly to 2.58 per cent in 2011.

Moving on to West Bengal, we find that the state has enjoyed a high growth of 438.82 per cent, or slightly less than five-and-a-half times, between 1901 and 2011. Its population increased from 1.69 crore in 1901 to 9.12 crore in 2011. The state experienced a low growth rate until 1931, before suddenly entering the peak growth phase (20 per cent and above)

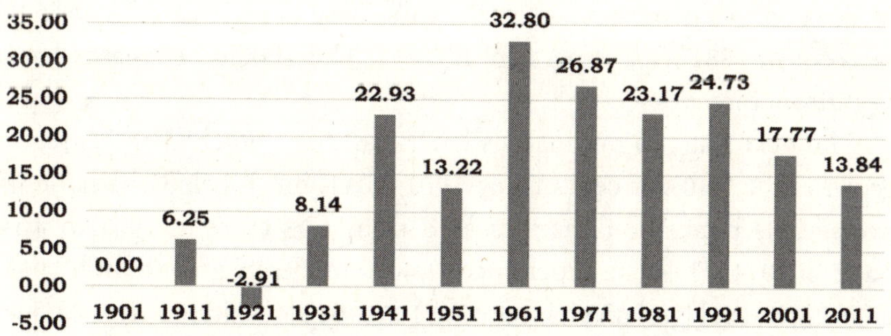

Figure 5.29: Population growth of West Bengal (percentage)

Source: Table 5.1, Appendices

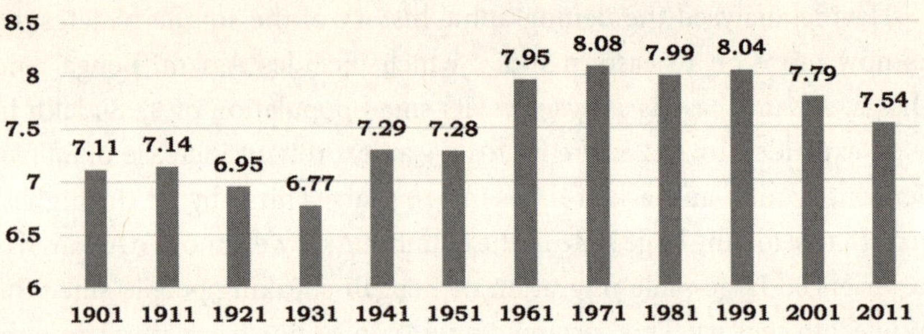

Figure 5.30: Population share of West Bengal (percentage)

Source: Table 5.1, Appendices

during 1931–41. The next decade saw a fall in growth (13.22 per cent), primarily due to the great Bengal famine in which nearly 3 million people (about 5 per cent of undivided Bengal's 1941 population of about six crore) starved to death. But growth resumed its upward trajectory between 1951 and 1961, reaching an exorbitant 32.80 per cent, partly as a result of large-scale migration from what had become East Pakistan, now Bangladesh. Even in the Census of 2001, West Bengal showed a growth of 17.77 per cent. Thus, for seventy years the state has enjoyed a rapid growth phase.

It is not surprising, then, that its share in India's population has increased considerably, starting from 7.11 per cent in 1901, peaking at 8.08 per cent in 1971, and settling at 7.54 per cent in 2011. In fact, if the adjusted population figures for 1881, calculated in Chapter 3, are taken as the point of departure, West Bengal's share has increased from 6.38 per cent in 1881 to 7.54 per cent in 2011. This should be regarded as a significant increase.

The next state up for analysis is Orissa. It has notched an aggregate growth of 307.40 per cent during 1901–2011, much below the national average. Its population has increased from 1.03 crore in 1901 to 4.19 crore in 2011. The state experienced low to moderate growth until 1951, entering its peak growth phase during 1951–61 and exiting it in 1991, just after three decades. But it continues to record a healthy growth rate of 14.05 per cent even up to 2011.

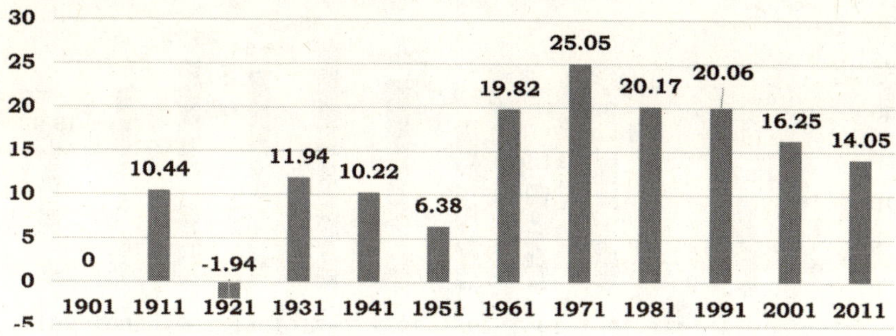

Figure 5.31: Population growth of Orissa (percentage)

Source: Table 5.1, Appendices

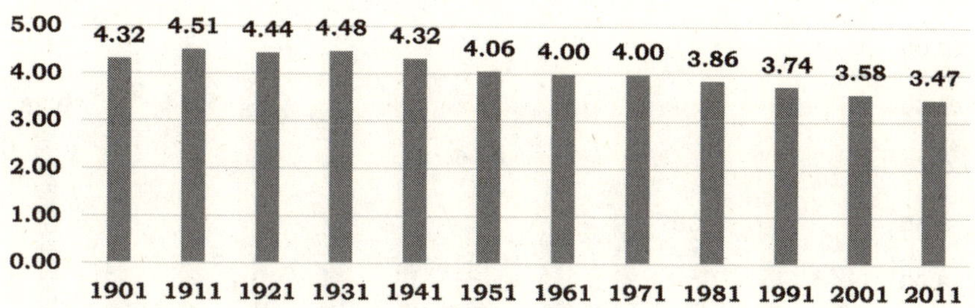

Figure 5.32: Population share of Orissa (percentage)

Source: Table 5.1, Appendices

Orissa's demographic history shows that its growth has been below the national average. Consequently, it has lost out in terms of share in India's population. It started from 4.32 per cent in 1901, touched the peak of 4.48 per cent in 1931, declined to 4 per cent in 1971, and has fallen further to 3.47 per cent in 2011—a decrease that should be regarded as quite significant. Orissa's case is anomalous. Despite poverty and low socio-economic indicators since the nineteenth century, the region has not experienced high population growth.

Let us now turn to western India, which, in our analytical framework, consists of Maharashtra and Gujarat. Maharashtra's demographic history from 1901 to 2011 corroborates the previous chapter's point about sparsely populated western and central India registering high growth during 1881–1941. Maharashtra's population has grown from 1.93 crore

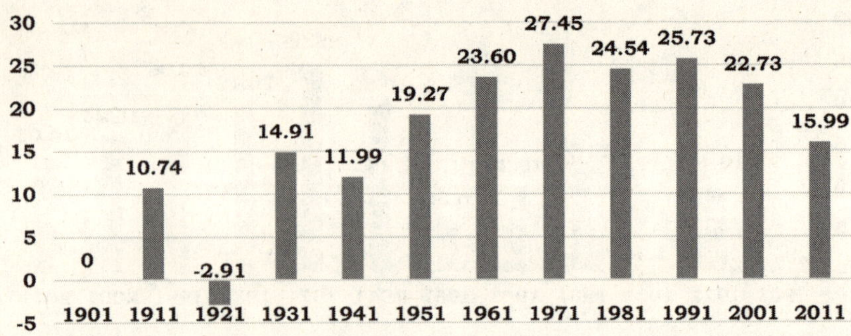

Figure 5.33: Population growth of Maharashtra (percentage)

Source: Table 5.1, Appendices

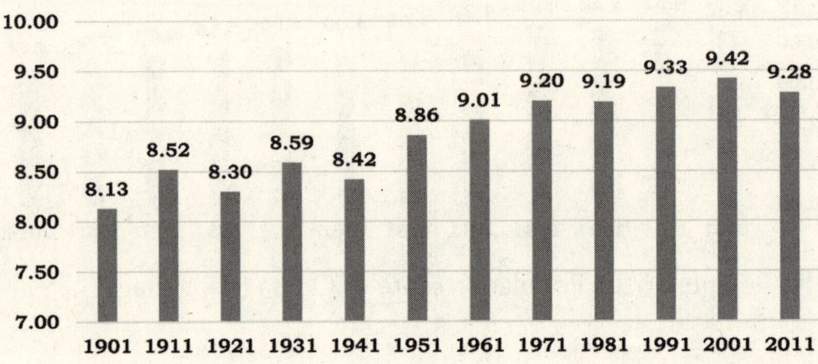

Figure 5.34: Population share of Maharashtra (percentage)

Source: Table 5.1, Appendices

to 11.23 crore—a rise of 479.49 per cent or slightly less than six times, which is remarkable for such a large state. In fact, if we take only the larger states of India, this is the third-highest rate after that of Rajasthan (565.90 per cent) and Gujarat (564.55 per cent).

It is evident that at least a part of this high growth can be attributed to migration to Bombay from other parts of the country throughout the twentieth century and beyond. The state enjoyed moderate growth until 1941, started growing rapidly during 1941–51 (19.27 per cent). It entered the peak growth phase of 20 per cent and above in 1951, and maintained it until 2001. The state sustained a peak growth phase for fifty years, which is in line with other fast-growing states. Even during 2001–11, Maharashtra has grown at a relatively high rate of 15.99 per cent.

With such high growth over nearly a century, the state has naturally increased its share in the country's population, though marked by fluctuations. Starting from 8.13 per cent in 1901, Maharashtra reached the peak in 2001 with 9.42 per cent, before dipping slightly to 9.28 per cent in 2011. The increase of more than one percentage point in the share of the second-largest state by population should be regarded as significant.

Gujarat, the other state in western India, has experienced even more spectacular growth. Starting with just 90.94 lakh in 1901, the state's population has reached an impressive 6.04 crore in 2011—a rise of no less than 564.56 per cent or nearly sevenfold. This growth rate is the second highest among the larger states of the country. Gujarat experienced low or moderate growth until 1931, picked up pace during 1931–41, registering a growth of 19.25 per cent in 1941, and entered the peak growth phase between 1951 and 1961.

The peculiarity of Gujarat is that it has consistently remained within or just below the peak growth phase from 1931 to 2011, which is quite an astonishing growth for such a large state. Similar to Maharashtra, migration has probably been a key factor in Gujarat's growth. As a result of its rapid growth, Gujarat has seen its share in India's population rise from 3.81 per cent in 1901 to a peak of 4.99 per cent in 1981. After

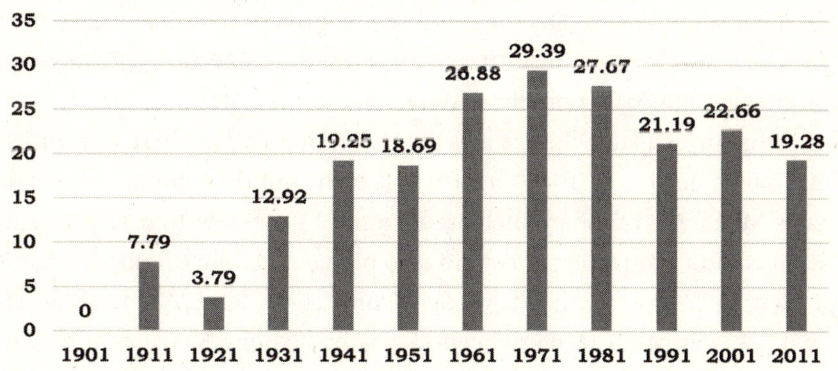

Figure 5.35: Population growth of Gujarat (percentage)

Source: Table 5.1, Appendices

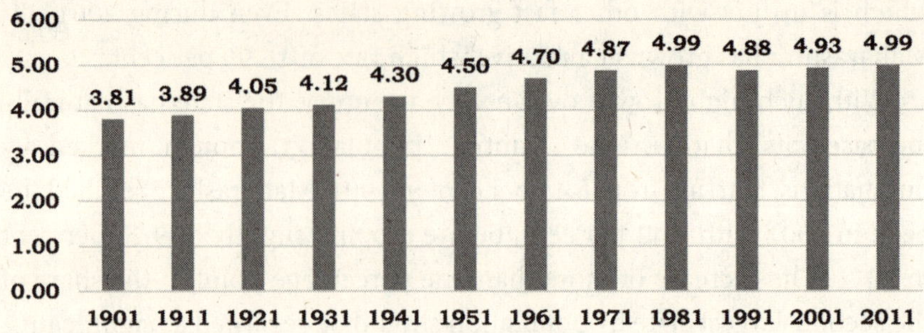

Figure 5.36: Population share of Gujarat (percentage)

Source: Table 5.1, Appendices

witnessing a decline during 1981–91, Gujarat has rebounded to touch 4.99 per cent again in 2011. This increase is clearly among the highest for any large state.

II
Decadal Variations in Population Shares of States

So far, we have analysed the population growth rates and the fluctuations in states' shares in the national population, taking each state separately over the period 1901–2011. Another way of analysing the data would be to take up the decennial censuses one by one and study the fluctuations in the states' shares caused by their differential growth rates. Let us begin by taking up the Censuses of 1901 and 1911. Figures 5.37 and 5.38 illustrate the changes in population distribution among the states over that decade.

Let us investigate which states gained in population share and which ones saw a decline in 1901 and 1911. It turns out that among the major states Maharashtra's share increased from 8.13 per cent to 8.52 per cent; Tamil Nadu's from 8.08 per cent to 8.29 per cent; Andhra Pradesh from 8 per cent to 8.51 per cent; West Bengal from 7.11 to 7.14; Madhya Pradesh from 5.32 per cent to 5.65 per cent; Rajasthan from 4.32 per cent to 4.36 per cent; Kerala from 2.68 per cent to 2.84 per cent; and Gujarat went up from 3.81 per cent to 3.89 per cent. In contrast, Uttar Pradesh's share dropped from 19.57 per cent in 1901 to 18.25 per cent in 1911—a major

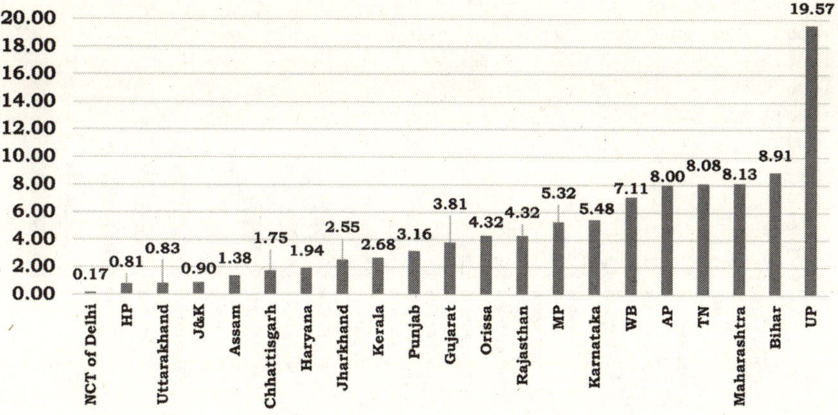

Figure 5.37: Population shares of states, 1901

Source: Table 5.1, Appendices

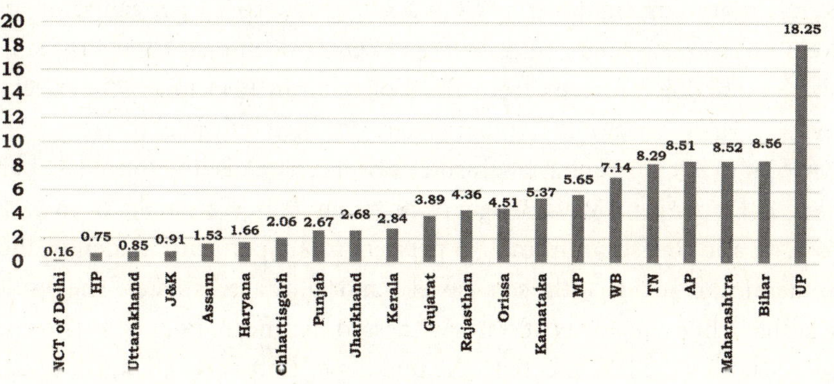

Figure 5.38: Population shares of states, 1911

Source: Table 5.1, Appendices

loss; Bihar's came down from 8.91 per cent to 8.56 per cent. So, the two largest states of the Hindi belt lost in share. What happened in the next decade, 1911–21, which saw the devastating influenza epidemic of 1918? Let us analyse Figure 5.39.

Tamil Nadu's share in India's population increased from 8.29 per cent in 1911 to 8.60 per cent in 1921; Andhra Pradesh from 8.51 per cent to

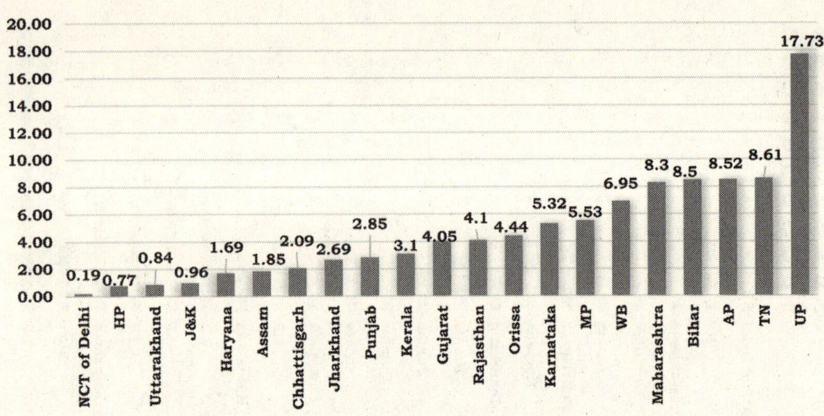

Figure 5.39: Population share of states, 1921

Source: Table 5.1, Appendices

8.52 per cent; Gujarat's share went up from 3.89 per cent to 4.05 per cent; Kerala moved up significantly from 2.84 per cent to 3.1 per cent; Punjab went up from 2.67 per cent to 2.85 per cent. In contrast, Uttar Pradesh's share came down further, from 18.25 per cent in 1911 to 17.73 per cent in 1921, again a major loss; Bihar's share declined only slightly from 8.56 per cent to 8.5 per cent; Maharashtra saw its share decline from 8.52 per cent to 8.3 per cent; West Bengal from 7.14 to 6.95; Karnataka from 5.37 to 5.32; and Rajasthan from 4.36 per cent to 4.1 per cent. Evidently, the epidemic did not cause the same level of mortality across states. The result was that while a majority of states witnessed significant population losses, some states were less affected. The ranking of states also changed. Thus, from 1901–21, Bihar lost the second spot to Tamil Nadu; Maharashtra lost the third spot to Andhra Pradesh; Karnataka lost the seventh spot to Madhya Pradesh; while Punjab lost the twelfth spot to Kerala. Let us now move on to Figure 5.40.

The decade of 1921–31 was the first in which India's population as a whole experienced a significant rise. How did the shares and ranks of the states change? Andhra Pradesh went up from 8.52 per cent to 8.68 per cent; Maharashtra from 8.3 to 8.59 per cent; Gujarat from 4.05 to 4.12; Orissa from 4.44 to 4.48; Kerala from 3.1 to 3.41; and Punjab from 2.85 to 2.87. By contrast, Uttar Pradesh decreased further, from 17.73 per cent to 17.02

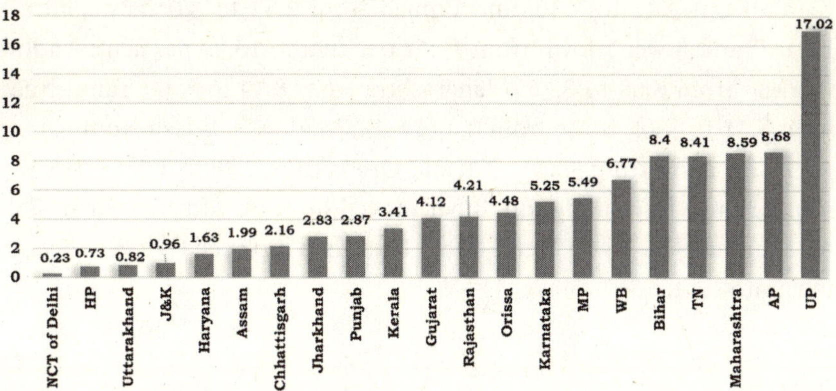

Figure 5.40: Population share of states, 1931

Source: Table 5.1, Appendices

per cent; Tamil Nadu from 8.6 to 8.41; Bihar from 8.5 to 8.4; West Bengal from 6.95 to 6.77; and Karnataka from 5.32 to 5.25. The second rank was now held by Andhra Pradesh, while Tamil Nadu dropped to fourth place; Bihar moved from fourth to fifth; and Maharashtra from fifth to third. Let us now turn to Figure 5.41, which depicts the 1941 Census.

During 1931–41, West Bengal saw a big jump from 6.77 per cent to 7.29 per cent; Gujarat from 4.12 to 4.30; Rajasthan from 4.21 to 4.35;

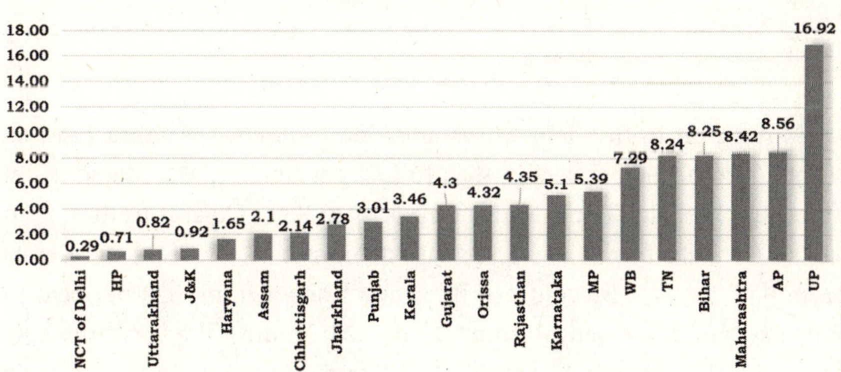

Figure 5.41: Population share of states, 1941

Source: Table 5.1, Appendices

Kerala from 3.41 to 3.46; and Punjab from 2.87 to 3.01. By contrast, Uttar Pradesh went down from 17.02 per cent to 16.92 per cent; Andhra Pradesh from 8.68 to 8.56; Maharashtra from 8.59 to 8.42; Tamil Nadu from 8.41 to 8.24; Bihar from 8.4 to 8.25; Madhya Pradesh from 5.49 to 5.39; Karnataka from 5.25 to 5.1; and Orissa from 4.48 to 4.32. There was some change in ranking too. Bihar moved up from fifth to fourth rank, exchanging places with Tamil Nadu. Rajasthan replaced Orissa to occupy the ninth spot.

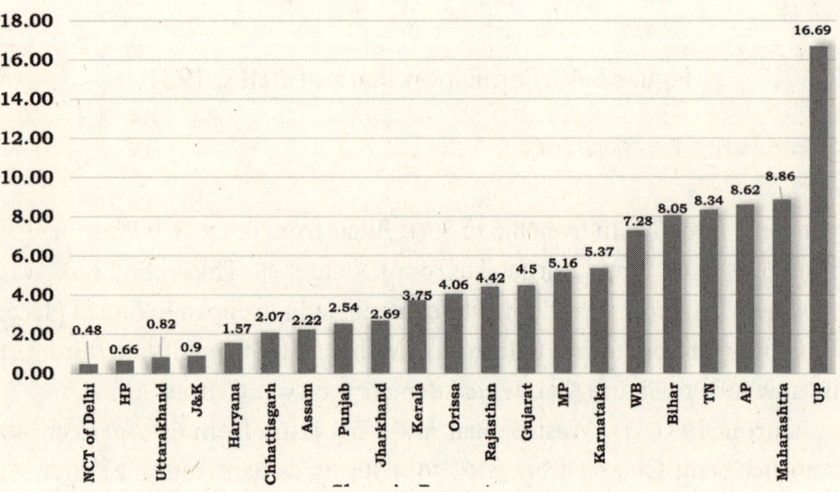

Figure 5.42: Population share of states, 1951

Source: Table 5.1, Appendices

Moving on to the first census after Independence, Andhra Pradesh went up from 8.56 per cent in 1941 to 8.62 per cent in 1951; Maharashtra from 8.42 to 8.86; Tamil Nadu from 8.24 to 8.34; Gujarat from 4.30 to 4.50; Karnataka from 5.1 to 5.37; Rajasthan from 4.35 to 4.42; and Kerala from 3.46 to 3.75. By contrast, Bihar went down from 8.25 per cent to 8.05 per cent; West Bengal from 7.29 to 7.28; Madhya Pradesh from 5.39 to 5.16; Orissa from 4.32 to 4.06; and Punjab from 3.01 to 2.54, mainly because of the migration caused by the Partition of India. There is some change in ranking as well. Maharashtra reached the second spot and Karnataka reached the seventh spot; Andhra Pradesh moved down to third place; Bihar dropped to fifth; Tamil Nadu went up to fourth; Madhya Pradesh went down from seventh to eighth; Punjab from thirteenth to fourteenth place.

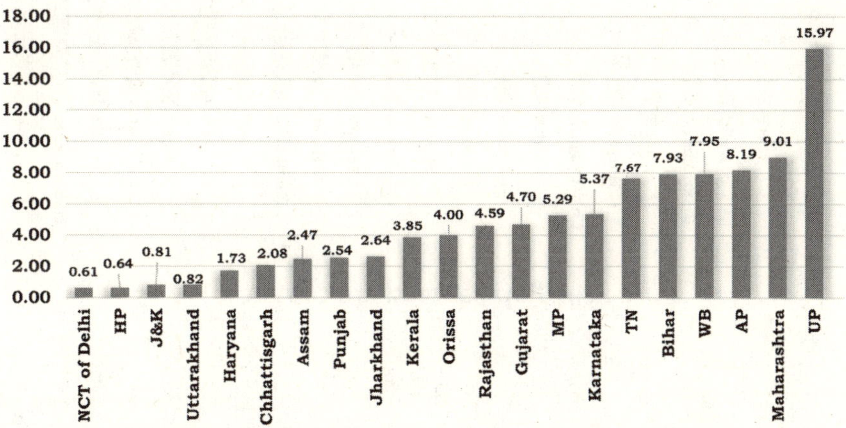

Figure 5.43: Population share of states, 1961

Source: Table 5.1, Appendices

In the Census of 1961, Maharashtra's share went up from 8.86 per cent to 9.01 per cent; West Bengal from 7.28 to 7.95; Gujarat from 4.50 to 4.70; Madhya Pradesh from 5.16 to 5.29; Rajasthan from 4.42 to 4.59; and Kerala from 3.75 to 3.85. Karnataka (5.37 per cent) and Punjab (2.54 per cent) retained their shares. Uttar Pradesh went down from 16.69 per cent to 15.97 per cent; Andhra Pradesh from 8.62 to 8.19; Bihar from 8.05 to 7.93; Tamil Nadu from 8.34 to 7.67; and Orissa from 4.06 to 4.0 per cent. How did the ranks change? Tamil Nadu lost the fourth spot to West Bengal and dropped to the sixth place. All other states among the top twelve retained their respective ranks. Let us now take up the Census of 1971, which represents a turning point in India's demographic history and has provided the *raison d'etre* of the imbalance in political representation among the different regions of India.

Maharashtra raised its share from 9.01 per cent to 9.2 per cent; West Bengal from 7.95 to 8.08; Gujarat from 4.70 to 4.87; Madhya Pradesh from 5.29 to 5.48; Rajasthan from 4.59 to 4.7; Kerala from 3.85 to 3.89;

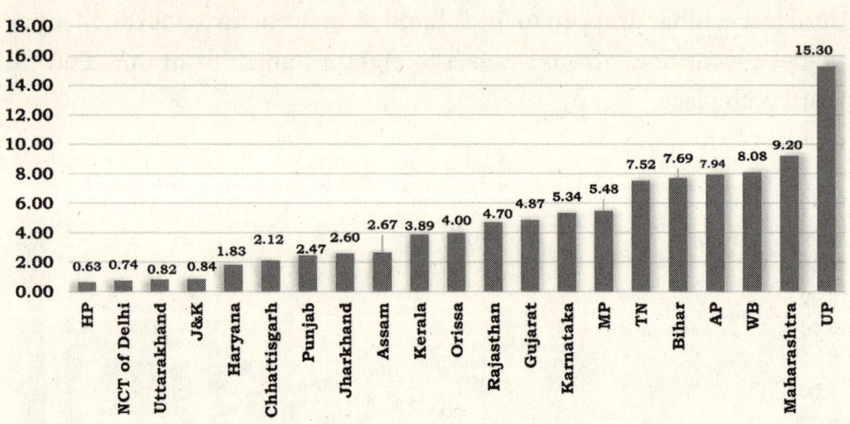

Figure 5.44: Population share of states, 1971

Source: Table 5.1, Appendices

and Assam from 2.47 to 2.67. Conversely, Uttar Pradesh went down from 15.97 per cent to 15.3 per cent; Andhra Pradesh from 8.19 to 7.94; Bihar from 7.93 to 7.69; Tamil Nadu from 7.67 to 7.52; Karnataka from 5.37 to 5.34; and Punjab from 2.54 to 2.47. There are changes in the ranks too. West Bengal moved to the third spot, replacing Andhra Pradesh,

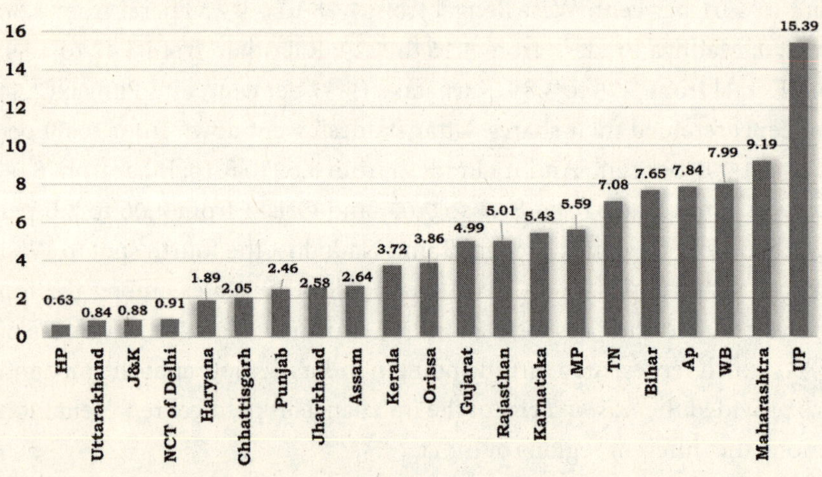

Figure 5.45: Population share of states, 1981

Source: Table 5.1, Appendices

which moved down to the fourth place; Madhya Pradesh moved up to seventh place, Karnataka dropped to the eighth rank; and Punjab to the fifteenth.

In the 1981 Census, there was an important shift. For the first time since 1901, Uttar Pradesh raised its share from 15.3 per cent in 1971 to 15.39 per cent in 1981. Maharashtra remained virtually stagnant; Madhya Pradesh went up from 5.48 to 5.59; Karnataka from 5.34 to 5.43; Rajasthan from 4.7 to 5.01. Conversely, Andhra Pradesh dropped from 7.94 to 7.84; Bihar from 7.69 to 7.65; Tamil Nadu from 7.52 to 7.08; Orissa from 4.0 to 3.86; Assam from 2.67 to 2.64; and Punjab from 2.47 to 2.46. Surprisingly, there is no change in the ranking of the top ten states, except that Rajasthan moved up from tenth to ninth rank, replacing Gujarat which went to the tenth spot.

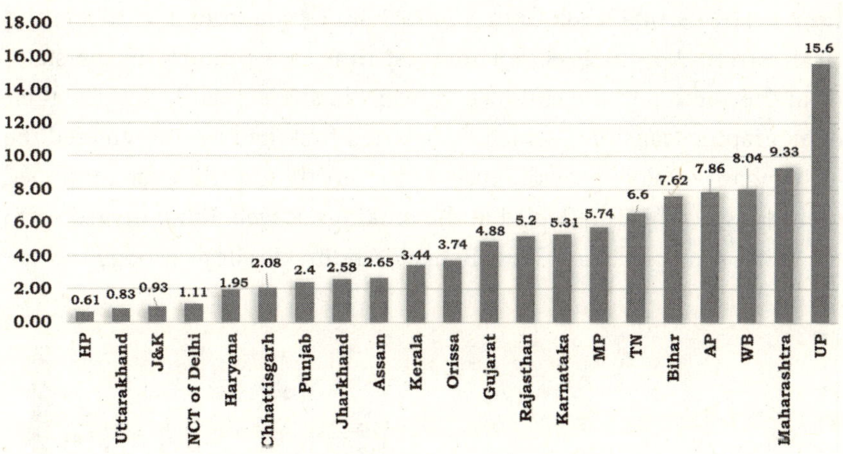

Figure 5.46: Population share of states, 1991

Source: Table 5.1, Appendices

Let us now analyse the variations in the states' shares in the 1991 Census, depicted in Figure 5.46. Uttar Pradesh went up from 15.39 per cent to 15.6 per cent; Maharashtra from 9.19 to 9.33; West Bengal from 7.99 to 8.04; Andhra Pradesh from 7.84 to 7.86; Madhya Pradesh from 5.59 to 5.74; Rajasthan from 5.01 to 5.2; and Assam from 2.64 to 2.65. By contrast, Bihar went down from 7.65 per cent to 7.62; Tamil Nadu from 7.08 to 6.60; Karnataka from 5.43 to 5.31; Gujarat from 4.99 to 4.88; Orissa from 3.86 to 3.74; and Kerala from 3.72 to 3.44. Surprisingly, there is no change in the rankings of any of the twenty-one states. The decade of 1981–91 is the only decade of this kind in 110 years.

The next decade would see further changes, as shown in Figure 5.47. Uttar Pradesh climbed up from 15.6 per cent to 16.16 per cent—the biggest decadal gain until now; Maharashtra went up from 9.33 to 9.42; Bihar saw a significant jump from 7.62 to 8.07; Madhya Pradesh from 5.74 to 5.87; Rajasthan from 5.2 to 5.49; Gujarat from 4.88 to 4.93; and Jharkhand from 2.58 to 2.62. So, for the first time, all the big northern states experienced a simultaneous rise in their shares, as the growth differential between them and many other states widened. The states that went down are West Bengal from 8.04 per cent to 7.79 per cent; Andhra Pradesh from 7.86 to 7.41; Tamil Nadu from 6.60 to 6.07; Karnataka from 5.31 to 5.14; Orissa from 3.74 to 3.58; Kerala from 3.44 to 3.1; and Assam from 2.65 to 2.59. For the first time in a century, all the states from the south and the east lose in terms of share, mainly because their demographic transition, which had started first, had by now entered the third phase of slow growth, even as the north and the west continued their growth. This is reflected in the rankings as well. Bihar moved up to the third spot, replacing West Bengal; Andhra Pradesh dropped to the

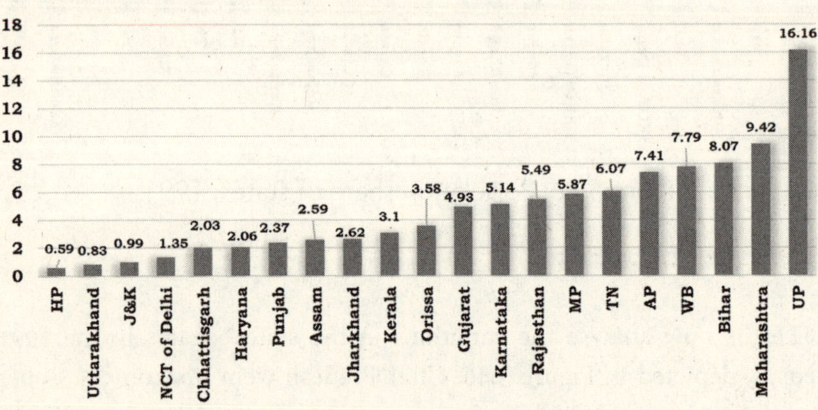

Figure 5.47: Population share of states, 2001

Source: Table 5.1, Appendices

fifth place; Rajasthan moved up to the eighth spot, replacing Karnataka; Jharkhand moved ahead of Assam to occupy the thirteenth place.

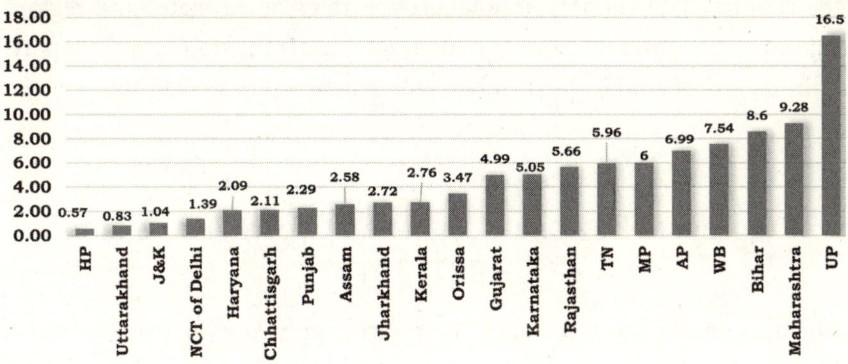

Figure 5.48: Population share of states, 2011

Source: Table 5.1, Appendices

The last decadal Census conducted in 2011 continued the trend of the previous two decades, as shown in Figure 5.48. Uttar Pradesh now climbed up to 16.5 per cent; Bihar from 8.07 to 8.6; Rajasthan from 5.49 to 5.66; Gujarat from 4.93 to 4.99; Jharkhand from 2.62 to 2.72; Chhattisgarh from 2.03 to 2.11; and Haryana from 2.06 to 2.09. Therefore, as the north's growth continued to outpace that of the south and the east, all the major Hindi states saw an increase in their shares. Conversely, all the southern states went down again. So, Andhra Pradesh moved down from 7.41 per cent to 6.99 per cent; Tamil Nadu from 6.07 to 5.96; Karnataka from 5.14 to 5.05; and Kerala from 3.1 to 2.76. The eastern states' population shares also dropped: West Bengal went down from 7.79 to 7.54; Orissa from 3.58 to 3.47; and Assam from 2.59 to 2.58. This is also reflected in the rankings, with Madhya Pradesh ranking sixth and Tamil Nadu going to the seventh spot.

It is observed from the decadal variations depicted in this section that the respective shares of all states have changed every decade, and their rankings in terms of population size have also changed frequently. In fact, Uttar Pradesh is the only state that has consistently retained its position as the largest state of the country. But that is because it is so much bigger than any other state that even when it was growing at a much lower rate than others, and its share was coming down, it retained the first rank. All other states have shown considerable variations in their rankings over the century. The variable decadal growth rates of the states and regions caused by the different timings of demographic transition in various parts of India are, of course, the principal force behind the variations.

III
Aggregate Regional Population Growth and Shares, 1881–2011

The data and analysis presented here throw up many important insights into the demographic history of modern India and its implications for the country. To begin with, it is obvious that within each of the four regions there are considerable variations, even though some important regional patterns emerge. As mentioned before, the north is clubbed with central India to analyse the demographic growth of the Hindi belt, which is commonly perceived as a laggard in population control.

What is the picture emerging from the voluminous data presented in the preceding pages? Out of nine states of north and central India, five—Haryana, Rajasthan, Jharkhand, Chhattisgarh and Madhya Pradesh—have registered long-term growth rates well above the national average of 407.92 per cent. Let us now look at the combined growth rate of the Hindi region. The nine states plus NCT of Delhi had a population of 11,00,43,570 in 1901, which increased to 56,27,10,668 in 2011. This comes to a growth of 411.35 per cent. The combined growth rate of all the Hindi states is, therefore, only marginally above the national average, because the north's largest states, Uttar Pradesh and Bihar, have grown below the national average.

What happens if we calculate the cumulative growth rate from 1881? In that year, the Hindi region had an approximate population of 10,67,46,332. The same region had a population of 56,27,10,668 in 2011, representing a growth of 427.15 per cent. This is less than the consolidated growth in all other regions, including the south.

This trend is also reflected in the percentage share of Hindi-speaking states in the population of India. It was 46.16 per cent in 1901 and 46.47

per cent in 2011, which is just a 0.31 percentage point rise from their combined share in the country's population in 1901. The share has also fluctuated significantly over the past century or more. In the Census of 1941, the last British Census of India, the share was 43.31 per cent; in the 1951 Census, it had fallen to 42.61 per cent; in 1961, it fell to 42.30 per cent; finally, it touched its lowest point at 41.90 per cent in 1971, before it started to rise again, inching up to 46.47 per cent over the next forty years.

In 1881, the north accounted for as much as 49.85 per cent of the population of India. So, if the starting point is 1881 instead of 1901, there is a significant fall in the share of the Hindi region. This is so because, as shown in the previous chapter, compared to the south, east and west the north had a much lower growth between 1881 and 1901. This trend intensified during 1901–21, resulting in negligible overall growth in the north's population during that entire period. Even between 1921 and 1941, its growth rate was distinctly lower than that of the other three regions. From the peak of 49.85 to the lowest point of 41.90 per cent, the Hindi region has experienced the widest range of variation in the last 140 years.

So, two things are evident. The population growth in north and central India, consisting of all the Hindi states, has not been unusually rapid between 1901 and 2011. Additionally, the region's population share in India has just about reached convergence with the figure of 1901, and is quite far from that of 1881. Of course, the argument here is not that long-term demographic convergence must happen; rather, both divergence and convergence have been at work and can best be studied when the entire modern census period from 1881 is covered.

Let us now look at the macro picture emerging from the demographic data of south India. Out of the four southern states—Andhra Pradesh, Karnataka, Kerala and Tamil Nadu—Kerala has clearly grown above the national average; Andhra Pradesh and Karnataka are slightly below the national average; and Tamil Nadu has grown at the slowest pace in this group, much below the national average of 407.92 per cent. Let us check their combined growth rate over 1901–2011. The four states had a population of 5,77,69,567 in 1901, which increased to 25,12,29,165 in 2011. This adds up to a growth of 334.88 per cent—significantly below the national average.

What happens if we add the growth between 1881 and 1901 to this figure? Let us begin by taking the cumulative growth rate of all the units in the south in those two decades. As shown in previous chapters, the southern provinces and the princely states had a higher growth rate in the nineteenth century as compared to many other regions of India. Only the east registered a comparable growth. Between 1881 and 1901, the aggregate population of these units went up from 4,61,68,966 to 5,77,69,567, which adds up to a growth of 25.13 per cent.

Another, and perhaps better, way of calculating the total growth is to take the 1881 and 2011 figures and calculate the cumulative percentage growth for the period. Now the 2011 figure for the whole of the south is 25,12,29,165, as against the 1881 figure of 4,61,68,966. Let us find the cumulative growth rate since 1881. Surprisingly, it amounts to 444.15 per cent, which is somewhat higher than the growth figure of 427.15 per cent for the north, although it is below the national rate (465.42 per cent). This corroborates the point that to develop a holistic understanding of India's demographic history in modern times, the entire period from the beginning of the decennial census exercise in the late-nineteenth century must be analysed as a continuum.

Coming to eastern India, let us examine the macro picture emerging from the historical demographic data. Out of the three eastern states—Bengal, Assam, Orissa—Bengal has grown well above the national average, Orissa is much below it. Assam's case is *sui generis*, as its population has grown at roughly twice the national average (407.92 per cent) mainly because of waves of migration from Bengal, and later Bangladesh. What was the combined growth rate of the three states from 1901 to 2011? They had a population of 3,05,32,685 in 1901, which increased to 16,44,55,909 in 2011. This adds up to a growth of 438.62 per cent—a little above the national average. Now, adding the growth of the nineteenth century to this figure further strengthens the observed trend of high growth in the region since the beginning of the census exercise.

In the eastern region, one has to grapple with the additional problem of the partition of Bengal in 1947, after which only the western one-third of the province remained with India. Calculating the enumerated population in the nineteenth century of what is now West Bengal requires a micro analysis of the census data. According to the district and sub-district level calculations made in Chapter 3, West Bengal had a net population of 1,48,05,369 in 1881. The combined population of the eastern zone (West Bengal, Assam and Orissa) was 2,58,66,760 in 1881. Comparing this to the 1901 figure of 3,05,32,685, we get a percentage growth of 21.63 per cent, which is second only to that of the south, at 18.04 per cent.

Let us now calculate the cumulative growth figure from 1881 to 2011. The population of these three states (minus north-eastern states carved out of Assam) was 16,44,55,909 in 2011. Setting this against the 1881 figure of 2,58,66,760 the growth from 1881 to 2011 works out to be 535.78 per cent. This rate is not only far above the national average of 465.42 per cent during the same period but also much above the growth figures for the south (444.15 per cent) and the north (427.15 per cent).

The macro analysis of the historical demographic data on western India is taken up next. Here, the first point to be noted is that between 1901 and 2011 both Maharashtra and Gujarat have grown at very high rates: 479.49 per cent and 564.56 per cent respectively. This is well above the growth for the three other regions during the same period: north (411.35 per cent), south (334.88 per cent) and east (438.62 per cent). The combined growth rate of Maharashtra and Gujarat provides further insights. Maharashtra (1,93,91,643) and Gujarat (90,94,748) had a combined population of 2,84,86,391 in 1901, which increased to 17,28,14,025 in 2011, marking a growth of 506.65 per cent. Thus, for the period 1901–2011, the western region had the highest growth, followed by the east, the north and the south, in that order.

What happens if we go all the way back to 1881? In this census, the combined west had a population of 2,87,74,086 (Bombay Presidency's population of 2,33,95,663, including that of feudatory states, minus Sind's population of 24,17,057, Western Karnatic's 28,07,254, plus Marathwada's 31,47,000, Berar's 26,72,673 and Baroda's 21,85,005), as against the 2011 population of Maharashtra and Gujarat, which was 17,28,14,025—a growth of 14,40,39,939 or of 500.59 per cent. The national average during 1881–2011 works out to be 465.42 per cent. Depicted in Figures 5.49 and 5.50 are two bar charts showing the demographic growth of the four regions from 1901 to 2011 and from 1881 to 2011.

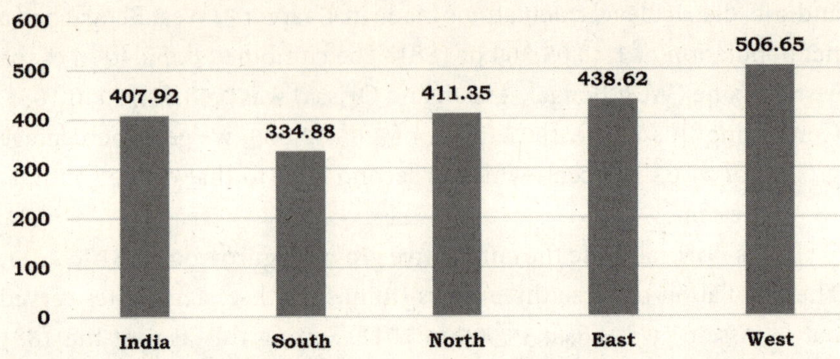

Figure 5.49: Regional population growth (percentage), 1901–2011

Source: Table 5.1, Appendices

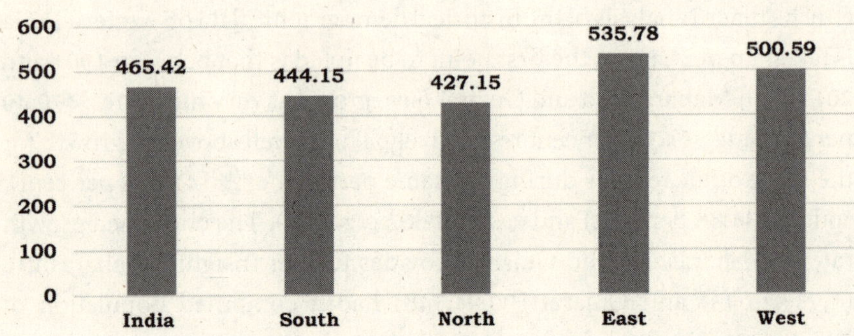

Figure 5.50: Regional population growth (percentage), 1881–2011

Source: Table 4.8 and Table 5.1, Appendices

The comparative bar chart (Figure 5.51) covering growth figures for various regions between 1881 and 1921 is arguably the best illustration of the earlier demographic transition of the south, east and west, in that order, which manifested in rapid growth in these regions while the north was stagnant.

If we take the fifty-year Census period from 1881 to 1931 for which comparative data have been provided by the 1931 Census report, the variations across regions come out very clearly (Figure 5.52).

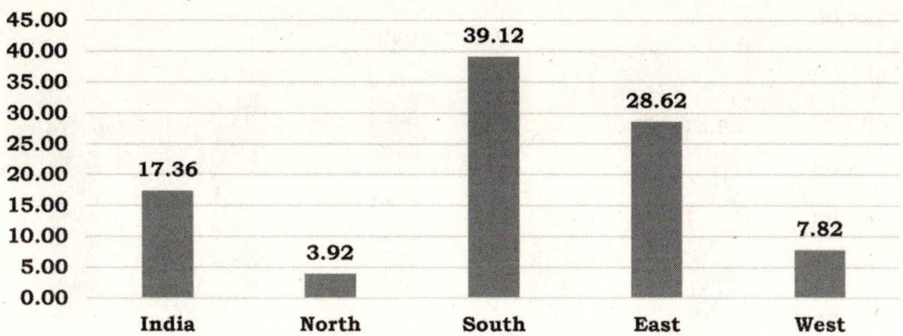

Figure 5.51: Regional population growth (percentage), 1881–1921

Source: Table 5.1, Appendices

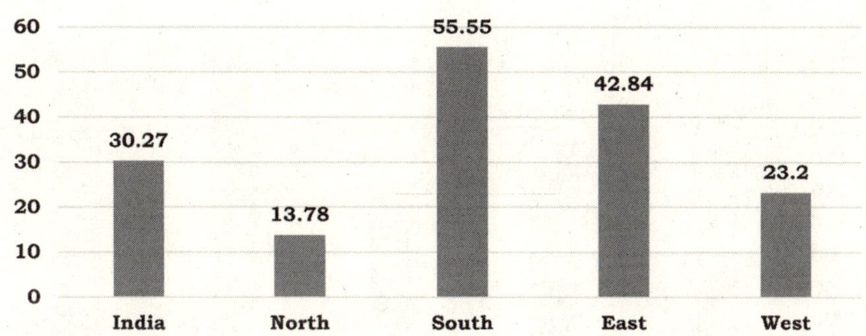

Figure 5.52: Regional population growth (percentage), 1881–1931

Source: Table 5.1, Appendices

The comparison for 1881–1951 provides an important insight into demographic growth for the period before Independence as a whole (Figure 5.53).

A similar comparison for 1901–71 (Figure 5.54) also shows that the Hindi-speaking north had the lowest growth of 108.71 per cent during this period. The south grew by 134.29 per cent; the east by 164.90 per cent; and the west by 170.69 per cent. Therefore, even during 1901–71, the hierarchy of population growth is broadly maintained, that is, west, east, south and north, because the north was the last of the four regions

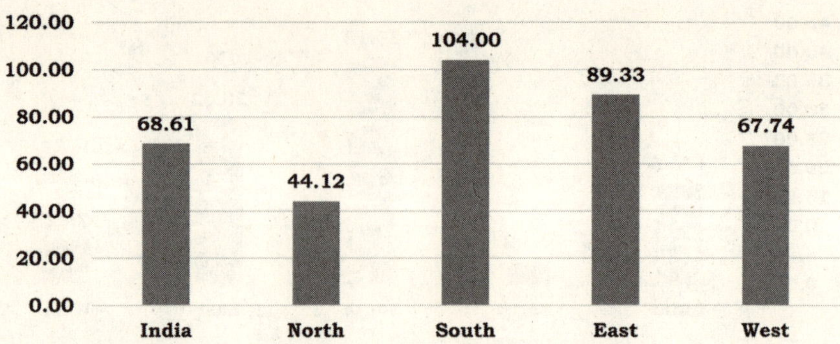

Figure 5.53: Regional population growth (percentage), 1881–1951

Source: Table 5.1, Appendices

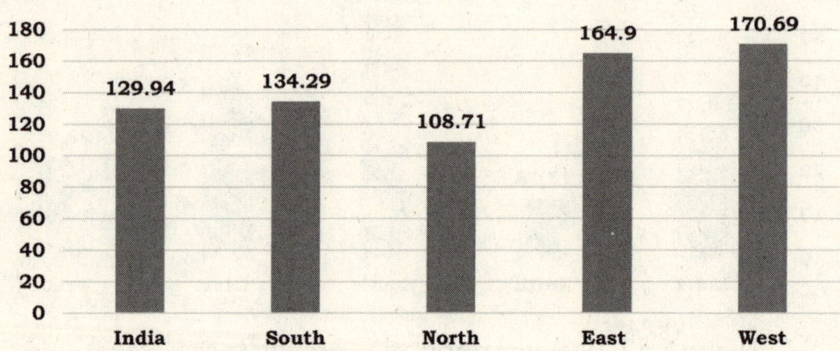

Figure 5.54: Regional population growth (percentage), 1901–71

Source: Table 5.1, Appendices

to embark upon demographic transition. The comparative bar chart for 1901–71 presented in Figure 5.54 illustrates this order of regional growth.

In the comparative analysis of the period 1881–1971, as shown in Figure 5.55, there is again a massive differential between the north and other regions. The east (212.69 per cent), west (168.42 per cent) and south (193.16 per cent) all have much higher growth rates compared to the north, which, at 115.16 per cent, has registered only slightly more than half of the growth of the south and the east during 1881–1971.

Thus, for nearly a century, the north was much below other regions in population growth. Notwithstanding the possibility of statistical margin of error, the regional growth and percentage share variations are large enough to permit us to conclude that out of the four regions of India, the east and the west have experienced the highest demographic growth since the nineteenth century, followed by the south and the north, in that order.

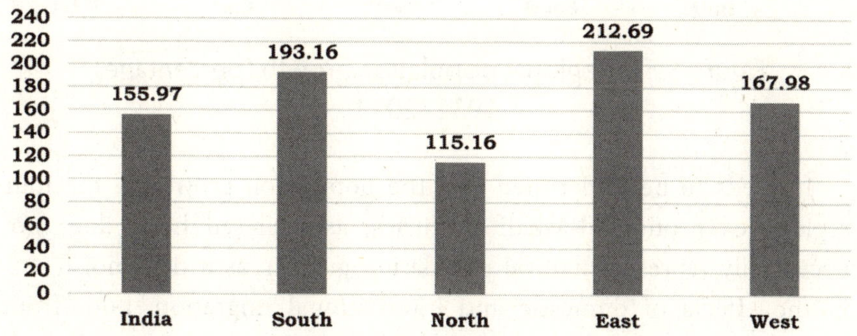

Figure 5.55: Regional population growth (percentage), 1881–1971

Source: Table 4.8 and Table 5.1, Appendices

The 1951 Census was the first one after India gained Independence in 1947. So, it helps provide a perspective on how population growth has occurred since Independence, although it must be reiterated that political independence has no direct relevance to the progress of demographic transition in India. It is during this period from 1951 to 2011 that the north, because of its growth spurt since the 1960s, gains over other regions. While the north grows by 265.76 per cent, the west grows by 258.05 per cent, the east by 235.80 per cent, and the south by 166.74 per cent. So, during 1951–2011, the south's growth is well below that of the other three regions—a fact that accounts for its loss of share in the last fifty years. The comparative growth rates of the various regions from 1951 to 2011 are depicted in Figure 5.56.

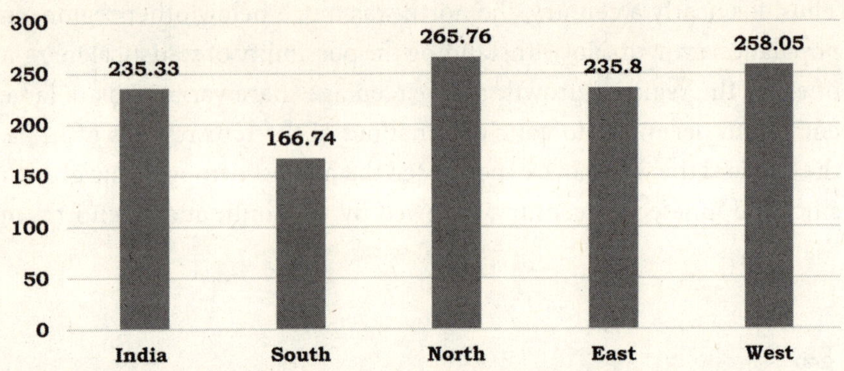

Figure 5.56: Regional population growth (percentage), 1951–2011

It needs to be underlined that the population growth of the four regions over one-and-a-half centuries, as analysed here, does not necessarily represent natural population growth, as it does not factor in the effects of domestic and international migration, both from and to the regions. Though migration has played a role in shaping the demographic statistics of all the regions, it has not been analysed separately as that is not relevant to this study. What matters is the overall population growth, for it is not the origin of people but their current residence in a particular state or region that determines their political representation. However, it should be noted that over the last few decades, the east, west and south have received migrants, while the north has generally sent them out. The case of the east is special, as migration from Bangladesh, both legal and illegal, is an important factor in its high population growth.

IV

These facts demolish several myths and illuminate many grey areas. First, empirical evidence derived from historical demographics establishes beyond doubt that north India—defined as the Hindi belt—has not been the fastest-growing region of the country in the long run; although its demographic growth has been at par with the national average, which is indicative of good but not extraordinary growth. Second, all regions and states of the country have experienced a high-growth phase, though in different periods. The south and the east had an earlier growth spurt as compared to the west and the north. However, what is to be noted is that unlike the south, the east has continued to grow well until recently. The growth spurt of the west, too, has continued until recently. It is evident that most of these variations emanate from the fact that demographic transition started in various regions of India at different points of time.

Third, the regional distribution of the national population has shifted to some extent since the Census of 1881. Comparative variations in population growth over nearly one-and-a-half centuries have caused this shift. Apart from natural growth, migration, industrialisation, urbanisation, economic development and ethnic conflicts have also contributed to these variations.

While it is difficult to arrive at very precise figures for the percentage share of each region in the population of undivided India in the nineteenth century, the reconstructed census tables discussed earlier enable us to understand the regional distribution of population in all its variations between 1901 and 2011. The north had a share of 46.16 per cent in the population of India in 1901, the south 24.23 per cent, the west 11.95 per cent and the east 12.81 per cent. Going back to 1881, the north had a share of 49.85 per cent, the south 21.56 per cent, the east 12.08 per cent and the west 13.44 per cent. There is a sudden spurt in the share of Others, from 3.1 per cent in 1881 to 4.85 per cent in 1901. The shares calculated for 1901–2011 based on the Census of India's tables are not exactly comparable to the 1881 figures, as several small states and union territories (Jammu and Kashmir, Sikkim, Arunachal Pradesh, Goa, Daman and Diu, Dadra and Nagar Haveli, Lakshadweep, Pondicherry, Andaman and Nicobar Islands) that were not a part of British India at that time were not included in the Census of 1881, though they are a part of 1901–2011 data series. Figure 5.57 presents a comprehensive comparison of all regions from 1881 to 2011 in terms of their percentage shares at various points, that is, 1881, 1901, 1921, 1951, 1971 and 2011.

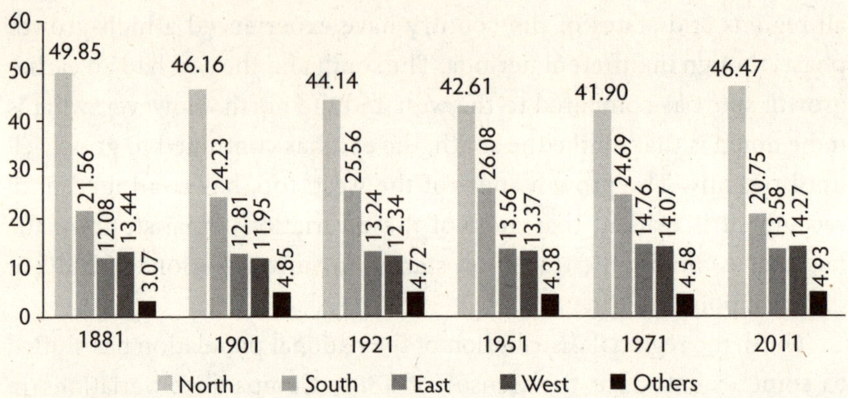

Figure 5.57: Changes in regional population shares, 1881–2011

Source: Table 4.8 and Table 5.1, Appendices

Over the century, these percentage shares fluctuated considerably. The north at first declined almost steadily from 49.85 per cent in 1881 to 46.16 per cent in 1901, then to 44.14 per cent in 1921, 43.54 per cent in 1931, 43.31 per cent in 1941 and 42.61 per cent in 1951. Its lowest point was 41.90 in 1971, which we must remember, was also the census year for the embargo on delimitation and seat redistribution in Parliament.

It is evident that the north's share in India's population began declining steadily from 1881, because the south and east had started growing at a relatively high rate, which was later matched by the west. By contrast, the Hindi belt was almost stagnant between 1881 and 1921. The high growth rate of the north since 1971 has ensured that it has recovered much of the lost share; in the 2011 Census, it came up to 46.47 per cent. The north is, however, well below the 1881 figure of 49.85 per cent share in the national demographic pie.

Let us now examine how the population of the south, as a percentage of India's population, has varied over time. The south started with a 21.56 per cent share in 1881, and because of its early growth spurt, saw this share rise steadily. In 1901, it reached a share of 24.23 per cent because of 25.13 per cent growth during 1881–1901. In 1921, it touched 25.56 per cent, after its population grew further by 11.18 per cent between 1901 and 1921, increasing from 5,77,69,567 to 6,42,28,692. In 1951, the south reached its peak share of 26.08 per cent, before declining to 25.08 per cent in 1961, 24.69 per cent in 1971, and finally, 20.75 per cent in 2011. Thus, over 110 years, the south's share in India's population has experienced a deviation of nearly 5 per cent, which should be regarded as quite high.

The east had a share of 12.08 per cent in 1881, 12.81 per cent in 1901, which grew to 13.18 per cent in 1911, 13.24 per cent in 1921, 13.24 per cent in 1931, 13.71 per cent in 1941, 13.56 per cent in 1951 and 14.41 per cent in 1961. It reached the peak of 14.76 per cent in 1971, before it started falling steadily, to 14.49 per cent in 1981, 14.43 per cent in 1991, 13.96 per cent in 2001, and lastly, 13.58 in 2011. The deviation in the east has been much less as compared to the south and the north. Moreover, its share remains above the 1901 level, although it has declined by more than one percentage point from its peak in 1971. From 1881 to 2011, the east has witnessed the largest rise of 1.50 percentage points among all regions. This also means that the east's representation in Parliament is only slightly above what its 2024 share of the population of India would warrant.

Let us now move on to the west. Its share in the population of India was 13.44 per cent in 1881, 11.95 per cent in 1901, 12.41 per cent in 1911, 12.34 per cent in 1921, 12.71 per cent in 1931, 12.72 per cent in 1941, 13.37 per cent in 1951, 13.70 per cent in 1961, 14.07 per cent in 1971, 14.18 per cent in 1981 and 14.21 per cent in 1991. It touched the peak of 14.34 per cent as late as 2001, and has since come down marginally, to 14.27 per cent in 2011.

Obviously, western India, comprising Maharashtra and Gujarat, has not only recorded a high growth rate comparable to that of the east over 130 years, but has also achieved the second-highest rise of 0.86 percentage points in its share in the population of India. This indicates continued demographic dynamism, at least partly driven by progress in industrialisation, urbanisation and the consequent migration from other parts of India. It could well be said that between 1951 and 2011, the losses suffered by the south have been compensated largely by the west and the east.

It is also evident that most of the rise in the respective shares of the south and the east was achieved between 1881 and 1921. This rise became possible not only because of their own rapid growth but also because of the north's nearly stagnant population during that period. Meanwhile, the growth in the west's share began only in 1901, and with some minor fluctuations, continued until 2001.

—w—

The data presented in *Demography, Representation, Delimitation* amply demonstrate that all regions of the country have enjoyed high growth phases, although the timing and duration of these phases differ widely. The south witnessed it earlier than the other regions. Consequently, its share in the population of India rose steadily from 1881 to 1951, when it reached a peak of 26.08 per cent. Even in 1971, it remained high at 24.69 per cent. The east was the next region to experience a high growth phase, almost simultaneously with the south. Its peak share of 14.76 per cent in the country's population was reached in 1971—twenty years after the south. The west's peak share of 14.34 per cent was reached only in 2001, because its demographic transition started a couple of decades after that of the south and the east. The west has shown continued demographic dynamism, backed by economic progress in the post-1991 period. The north's case is fundamentally different from that of all other regions. It started with a 49.85 per cent share in 1881, declined to 46.16 per cent in 1901 and to 44.14 in 1921. Steadily declining for the next fifty years, it reached its lowest share of 41.90 per cent in 1971. Since 1971, the north has moved towards convergence with its long-term share, reaching a peak of 46.47 per cent in 2011. However, this peak is well below the 1881 figure of 49.85 per cent and is only slightly above the 1901 share of 46.16 per cent. Thus, from 1901 to 1971—and from 1881 as well—the north's demographic growth was well below that of the other regions. After 1971, it has been the highest among the four regions.

All this suggests that over the last 150 years both divergence and convergence have played their role in the demographic history of India. Convergence seems to have a greater role, as there has been no fundamental shift in the demographic distribution of the country. Whatever divergence has happened must be recognised as a natural phenomenon for a large country such as India, which, in 2023, has become the most populous nation on earth.

There is, of course, no underlying assumption in this study that the regions of India should either have equal population growth or maintain a fixed percentage share. Furthermore, the book does not delve into the normative aspects of whether the type of population growth that has happened in India is desirable from a socio-economic perspective. Rather, based on empirical evidence generated from the Census of 1872 onwards, it shows the micro and macro trends of demographic growth across regions to identify both similarities and differences. This exercise makes it abundantly clear that there is no occasion for viewing the population growth of any region or state in isolation.

6

North versus South
The Demographic Divide Re-examined

This chapter adopts a focused north versus south approach. It takes into account birth rates, death rates, fertility rates and population density and growth rates. The comparative framework used here works with reference to both the applicability and implications of the process of demographic transition discussed in Chapter 3. Although the comparison spans the period 1901–2011, the year 1971 serves as an important marker for this analysis.

There is a pointed comparison between Uttar Pradesh from the north and Kerala from the south. Multiple states from the two regions are also compared. This allows us to delve into the intricate details of their demographic histories over more than a century and enables a broader comparison between the north and the south. In short, the chapter closely examines the basis of the 'north–south demographic divide'. Among the primary objectives is to understand both divergence and convergence in the patterns of population growth in the north and the south. The two regions are frequently but erroneously viewed as pole opposites in their demographic behaviour, especially in terms of fertility control through the adoption of family planning. The north is widely regarded as a laggard, and the south as a performer.

I
Demographic Transition and India

Chapter 3 discussed how the world as a whole has been going through demographic transition, especially since the Second World War, with hardly any country left untouched. The close similarity in long-term demographic change in countries as far apart from each other as Sweden and Sri Lanka illustrates that this process is universal. Here, we analyse the process in the Indian context. The Census of India, 2011 provided a concise definition of demographic transition: 'This transition from a stable population with high mortality and high fertility to a stable population with low mortality and low fertility is called demographic transition.'[1]

Based on this definition, India's National Population Policy 2000 aimed at achieving a stable population by 2045.[2] Other estimates saw India's TFR approaching the replacement level of 2.1 by 2025.[3] In reality, it has fallen below that level a few years in advance.[4]

Several questions become relevant. Did India as a whole undergo demographic transition during the past century or so? If yes, what was the dynamic followed by it? Have different parts of India witnessed the same process and at the same pace? How have their individual stories differed in terms of timing of the onset of transition and its duration? Let us first look at India's birth, death and growth rates over the twentieth century and beyond. Figure 6.1 depicts the growth pattern.

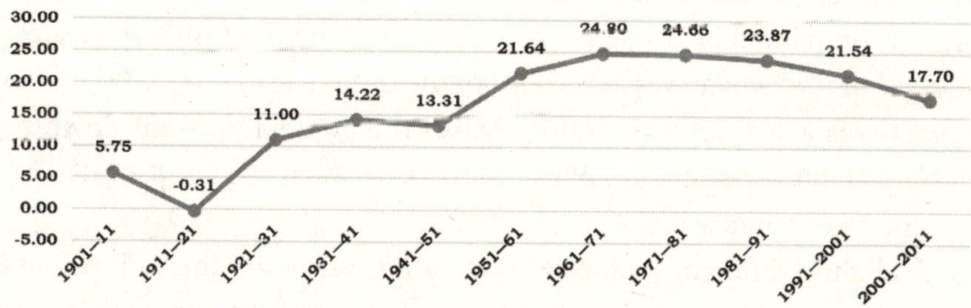

Figure 6.1: Population growth rate of India, 1901–2011 (percentage)

Source: Table 6.1, Appendices

Figure 6.1 shows close parallels between global trends (seen in Chapter 3) and Indian trends in population growth rates over much of the twentieth century, especially the decades following the Second World War. India registered its highest rate of 24.80 per cent during 1961–71, peaking in the same decade as the world. That is so because the post-Second World War period witnessed the entry of India as a whole into the second phase of demographic transition, just as large parts of the world experienced a growth spurt. While demographic transition, which explains the growth of world population in the last two centuries, is clearly applicable to the Indian history, the focus here is on the regional differences that have taken centre stage in the demographic debate. Is India really divided into two camps based on their differing experiences with the long-term demographic processes? In short, what is the truth of India's north–south demographic divergence?

II

North versus South: Birth, Death and Growth Rates

One can try to find answers to these questions by doing a study of birth, death and population growth rates. The critical point is that comparisons should be made over a sufficiently long period; only then can we capture the true nature of demographic transition in the country, especially in the north–south comparative framework. Accordingly, the period 1901–2011 has been taken up for analysis. The slight decline in India's birth rate since the first decade (1901–11) of the last century was accompanied by a rise in the death rate. The net result was a near merger of the two curves at the end of the decade (1911–21). What that meant was a sub-zero natural increase (the population went down by 7,72,177) in the population of the country between 1911 and 1921. This is depicted in Figure 6.2.

A slightly different picture of population variation due to birth and death rates emerges with figures of natural growth (that is growth minus migration) over the same period, that is, 1901–2011 (Figure 6.3). The second dot on the curve nearly touches the horizontal line along the zero mark. For the next two decades, however, there was an upward trend in India's natural growth. The decline in death rate between 1921 and

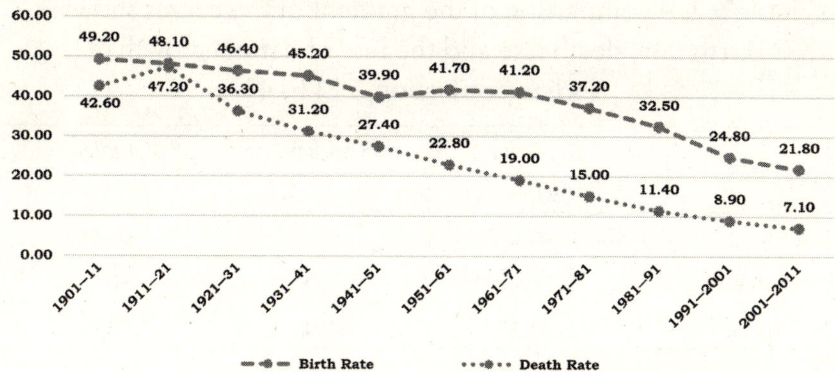

Figure 6.2: Birth and death rate in India (per thousand), 1901–11 to 2001–11

Source: Census of India, 2011 (Table 6.1, Appendices)

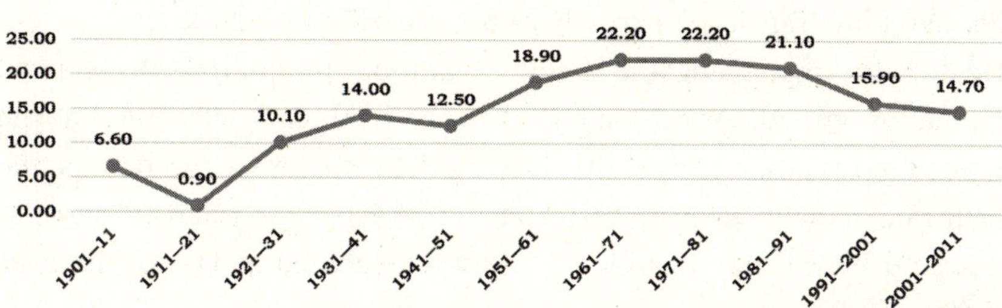

Figure 6.3: Natural growth rate of India's population (percentage), 1901–11 to 2001–11

Source: Census of India, 2011 (Table 6.1, Appendices)

1941 was not matched by a corresponding decline in birth rate. Table 6.2 compares the gradients of the curves of birth and death rates and the consequent natural growth rates.

It is evident that between 1911 and 1921 the death rate climbed up, resulting in a rapid decline in the natural growth rate. Since then, however, birth rates significantly outpaced the death rates. The gradient looks steeper for 1921–31 than for 1931–41. The natural growth for 1921–41 is relatively high at 0.655 per thousand. Moving further, an anomaly is

Table 6.2: A comparison of the gradient of the curves showing birth rate, death rate and the rate of natural growth of India's population, 1911–41

	Gradient (1911–21)	*Gradient (1921–31)*	*Gradient (1921–41)*
Birth Rate	-0.11	-0.17	-0.145
Death Rate	+0.46	-1.09	-0.8
Natural Growth	-0.57	+0.92	+655

noticed in the curve shown in Figure 6.3 which shows a drop in the natural increase between 1941 and 1951. This was a decade marked by famines, epidemics, communal riots and the Partition, resulting in a reduction in India's natural growth rate.

The early decades after Independence are critical to the story of India's demographic transition, partly because as early as 1952 the government decided to implement the family planning programme to control population growth. What happened to the birth and death rates at the national level in the aftermath? Defying policymakers' expectations, the birth rate actually went up; it rose from 39.9 per thousand to 41.7 per thousand between 1951 and 1961; and it remained at 41.2 in the next decade of 1961–71.[5]

Looking at it more statistically, from 1951 to 1961, the birth rate had a positive slope of 0.18 per thousand, against the usual negative gradients observed in all the previous decades since 1901. In the next decade, 1961–71, the curve showed a very minor negative gradient of 0.05. This signifies that India's birth rate was almost the same for the first two decades after Independence. The rate of more than 41 per thousand for 1951–71 was rather high compared to global rates. What is striking is that even though India's population growth peaked around the same period in history as the world's, its birth rates were considerably higher than world birth rates during 1950–70. The birth rates for the world were 36.3 per thousand in 1960 and 34.2 per thousand in 1970—both well below India's approximate birth rate of 41 per thousand. The convergence between India and the world became possible despite India's higher birth rate because its death rate was also correspondingly higher. This is in line with demographic transition worldwide. The national death rate gradually declined during both these decades, leading to rapid growth. It is, of course, a matter of further enquiry as to which Indian states accounted more for the high national birth rate during 1951–71.

III
Demographic Divergence and Fertility Rates

State-wise comparison of population growth will be taken up subsequently. For now, let us compare global and Indian fertility trends. Figure 6.4 shows the variation in the world fertility rate from 1960 to 2017.

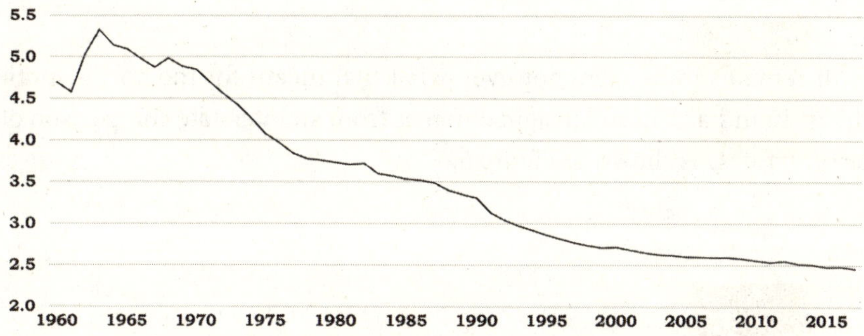

Figure 6.4: World fertility rate, 1960–2017

Source: World Bank Open Data[6]

Evidently, the world fertility rate has been on the decline since 1960. Let us compare this trend with that of India using Figure 6.5.

Figure 6.5 shows that between 1971 and 2011 India's fertility rate has more than halved, dropping from 5.2 to 2.3, and has converged with the world average of 2.4, which had started from the lower point of 4.6. This means that India has made significant progress in lowering fertility rates. Though both curves show a declining trend, in the decade 2001–11, the gradient of India's fertility rate decline (0.07) is five times that of the world fertility rate (0.014). So, India undoubtedly entered a critical phase of fertility decline around the end of the last millennium.

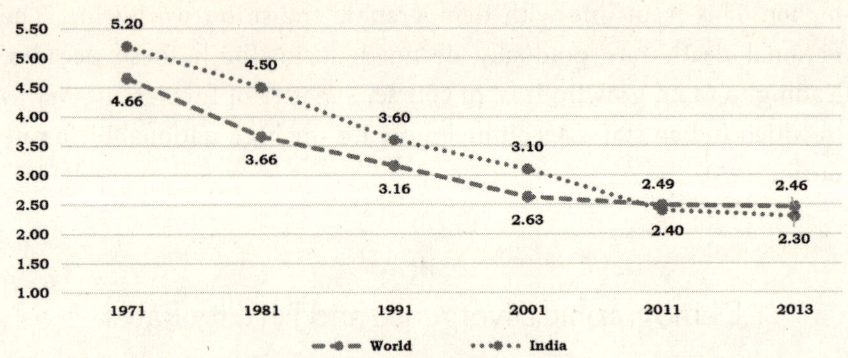

Figure 6.5: Comparison of the fertility rates of India and the world, 1971–2013

Source: Table 6.3, Appendices

It remains to be seen, however, what that means for the north–south divide in India. A useful insight emerges from an interstate comparison of fertility rates, as shown in Figure 6.6.

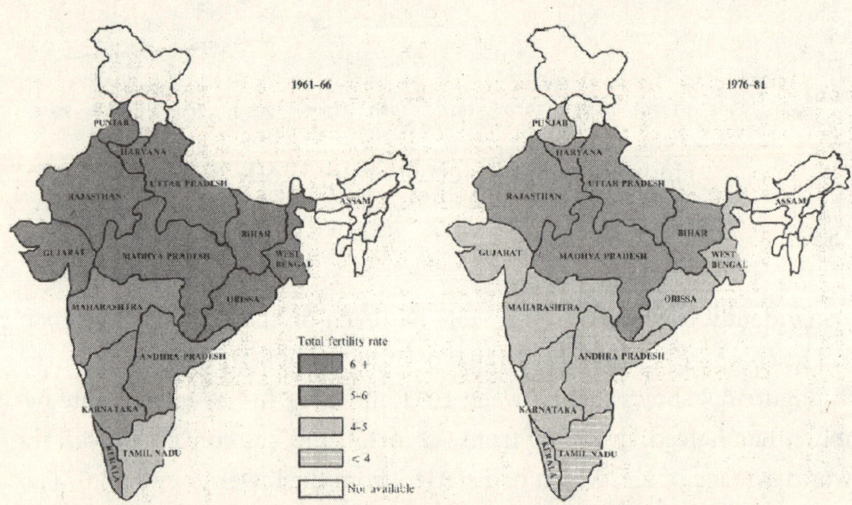

Figure 6.6: Estimates of the Total Fertility Rate for the most populous states of India, 1961–66 and 1976–81

Source: J.R. Rele (1987)[7]

It is evident from Figure 6.6 that in the quinquennial period of 1961–66, there was no pronounced north–south divide in total fertility rates (TFR), with the exception of Tamil Nadu. Fertility, which for most states was in the range of 5–6, showed a rapid drop in the five-year period 1971–76. Now, 1971 was the inflexion point in India's demographic history before which most southern states had attained their peak growth rates and had started showing decline in fertility. However, the north was still in the initial stages of its peak-growth phase. The contrast in fertility rates between the north and the south, as seen in Figure 6.6, simply reflects this fact. Consequently, the present gap in the fertility rates of the two regions—all four southern states have reached below the replacement level of TFR (2.1), while some north Indian states are still slightly above it—can be attributed almost exclusively to the different timelines of their demographic transition. There is no fundamental difference between them in terms of fertility or population growth rates over the century.

IV

Understanding the Reality Behind India's Demographic Divergence: The North–South Comparison

In the story of India's north–south demographic divide, indicators such as birth rate, death rate and fertility rate are important. But ultimately what matters is the population growth rate. Let us, therefore, closely examine how states from India's north and south have fared in terms of decadal growth. What follows is a comparative analysis of the growth rates of select states during the past eleven decades. The analytical framework adopted here has both simplicity and complexity. Since the focus of the book is on the north–south divide, we first analyse the patterns of population growth exhibited by individual states representing the two regions. This is followed by a comprehensive study that simultaneously compares multiple states sampled from either region. Initially, Uttar Pradesh and Bihar from the north, and Kerala and Karnataka from the south are taken up. Let us see how the demographic transition has unfolded in these four states.

We begin with Kerala, which is usually considered a model of demographic maturity. Figure 6.7 depicts how Kerala's growth has varied since 1901.

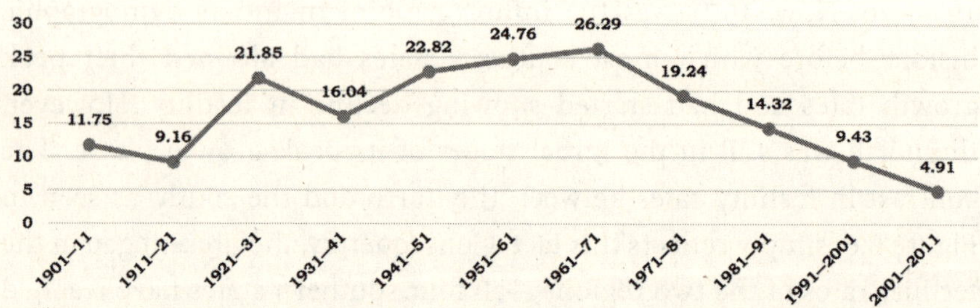

Figure 6.7: Population growth rate of Kerala (percentage), 1901–11 to 2001–11

Source: Census of India, 2011 (Table 6.4, Appendices)

Kerala grew at 11.75 per cent during 1901–11, nearly double the national growth rate of 5.75 per cent. Between 1911 and 1921, despite a net population decline in India of 0.31 per cent (7,72,177 persons) due to the influenza epidemic of 1918, famines and the First World War, Kerala notched up an unmatched growth of 9.16 per cent.

Kerala again registered a rate of 21.85 per cent during 1921–31, while the national rate was less than 11 per cent, roughly half the rate achieved by the state. In fact, it was the only major state to grow at more than 20 per cent during this decade. Assam, with a growth rate of 19.91 per cent, came close. But in Assam's growth, migration from Bengal was an important factor. During 1931–41, Kerala grew at 16.04 per cent, as against India's 14.22 per cent, thus, still maintaining its lead. Its growth during 1941–51 was 22.82 per cent, while the national rate was only 13.31 per cent. So, Kerala's population grew at roughly double the national rate for fifty years preceding Independence. Even after Independence, Kerala's growth of 24.76 per cent during 1951–61 and 26.29 per cent during 1961–71 was significantly higher than India's 21.64 per cent and 24.8 per cent respectively. This is shown in Figure 6.8, which provides a long-term comparative perspective on population growth in Kerala and India over 1901–2011, illuminating an area of darkness in the north–south divide.

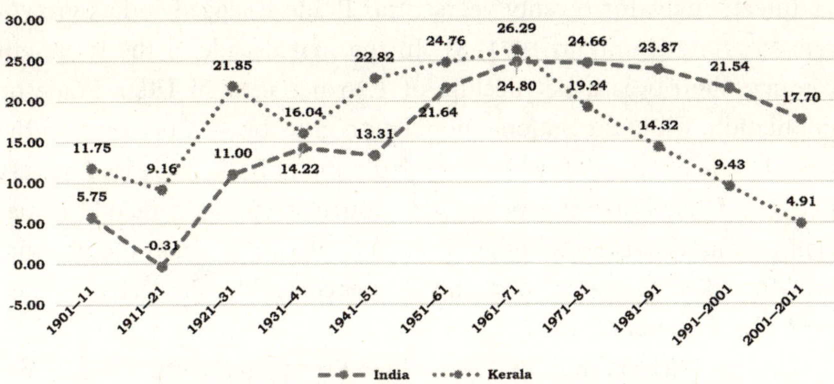

Figure 6.8: Population growth rate of Kerala vis-à-vis the growth rate of India (percentage), 1901–11 to 2001–11

Source: Census of India, 2011 (Table 6.4, Appendices)

Of course, there were other states, too, which grew at a faster pace than the national average during 1901–71. They will be taken up later. Let us first examine how Uttar Pradesh, the most populous state of India, representing the north here, has performed on the demographic front.

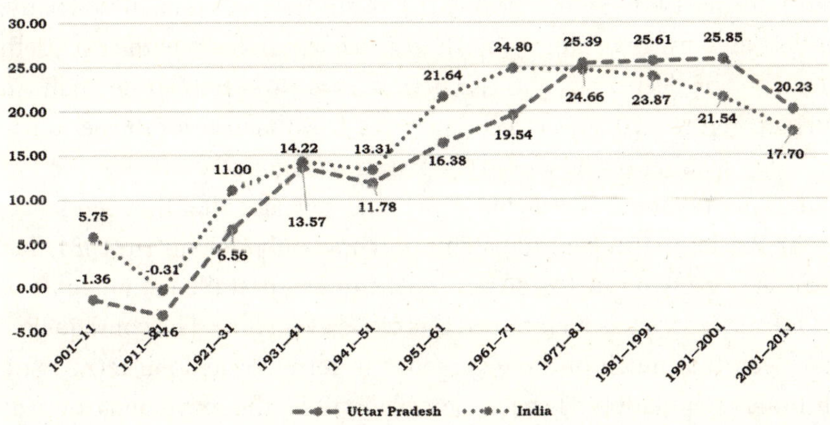

Figure 6.9: Population growth rate of Uttar Pradesh vis-à-vis the growth rate of India, 1901–11 to 2001–11 (percentage)

Source: Census of India, 2011 (Table 6.4, Appendices)

Interestingly, for seventy years Uttar Pradesh lagged India's growth rate, crossing it only in 1971–81. In the first decade of the twentieth century, there was a net decline of 1.36 per cent in Uttar Pradesh's population, while the national population grew by 5.75 per cent. In the next decade of 1911–21, while the population of India decreased by 0.31 per cent, Uttar Pradesh experienced a much steeper decline of 3.16 per cent—around ten times higher. From 1921 to 1931, when the national growth picked up again and reached 11 per cent, Uttar Pradesh remained behind at 6.56 per cent.

During 1931–41 and 1941–51, Uttar Pradesh's growth at 13.57 per cent and 11.78 per cent was still below the national average, at 14.22 per cent and 13.31 per cent respectively. From 1951 to 1961, Uttar Pradesh grew at only 16.38 per cent against the national average of 21.64. This trend continued right up to 1971, with Uttar Pradesh at 19.54 per cent and India at 24.8 per cent. Contrary to popular perception, therefore, the most populous state in the country was not among the fastest-growing for the first seventy years of the twentieth century. It was well below both Kerala and the national growth rate.

Equally interesting is that, except for 1901–11, the gap between the growth rates of Uttar Pradesh and India was the highest (5.26 per cent) during 1951–61 and 1961–71. This underscores that 1971 was the critical juncture in demographic divergence within India in the twentieth century. For deeper insight, the period 1941–81 needs to be analysed further. Figure 6.10 depicts a comparative growth curve for the period.

The meaning of the closed loop seen in Figure 6.10 is that even as India's population was growing at an enhanced pace after Independence, Uttar Pradesh struggled to catch up. It was only during 1971–81 that the state's growth rate (25.39 per cent) climbed past the national rate of 24.66 per cent. It has maintained this trend ever since. The consequence has been that much of the divergence in terms of its long-term share in India's population has been cancelled out by the movement towards convergence in the last fifty years. In order to extend the comparative analysis, another state from the south, Karnataka, can be analysed for its population growth against that of the country. Figure 6.11 offers a graphical representation.

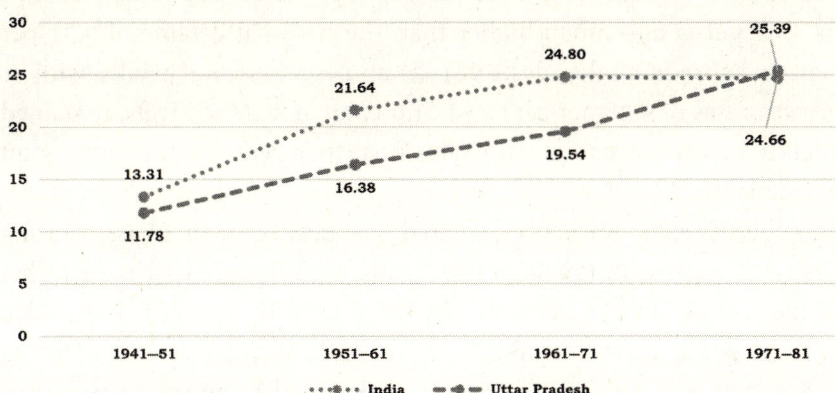

Figure 6.10: Population growth rate of Uttar Pradesh vis-à-vis the growth rate of India (percentage), 1941–81

Source: Census of India, 2011 (Table 6.4, Appendices)

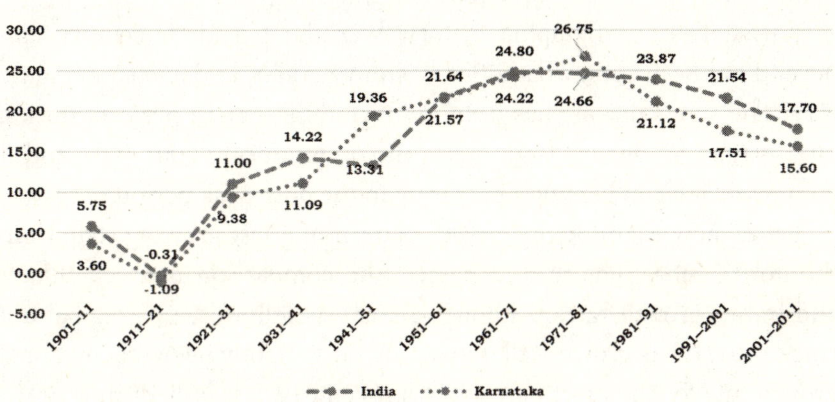

Figure 6.11: Population growth rate of Karnataka vis-à-vis the growth rate of India (percentage), 1901–11 to 2001–11

Source: Census of India, 2011 (Tables 6.4, Appendices)

From 1901 to 1981, Karnataka's population registered almost equal cumulative growth (184.46 per cent) as the national average (186.64 per cent). But there were significant variations. During 1901–11, Karnataka's growth was 3.6 per cent, which was below the national average of 5.75

per cent. The decade of 1911–21 saw the state's population decline by 1.09 per cent—much higher than the national decline of 0.31 per cent. In subsequent decades, 1921–31 and 1931–41, Karnataka, with its growth rates of 9.38 per cent and 11.09 per cent respectively, remained slightly behind India's growth rates of 11 per cent and 14.22 per cent respectively.

Around 1940, Karnataka entered the peak growth phase. During 1941–51, its growth (19.36 per cent) was significantly higher than that of the country (13.31 per cent). In the decade of 1951–61, Karnataka, at 21.57 per cent, was nominally below India at 21.64 per cent. During 1961–71 (the decade of highest national growth), the state again grew marginally below India: 24.22 per cent versus 24.8 per cent. Karnataka's growth peaked in 1971–81, with a rate of 26.75 per cent against the national average of 24.66 per cent. Since then, the state's growth rate has declined in line with the national trend. It has been consistently below the national average, but not by a huge margin.

Karnataka's demographic history over the twentieth century and beyond has been somewhat different from Kerala's, as depicted in Figure 6.11. The state's decline has been quite gradual—21.12 per cent during 1981–91, 17.51 during 1991–2001, and 15.60 during 2001–11—and it has grown at a good enough pace even in the post-peak period.

Let us now examine the growth pattern of a fast-growing state from the north, Bihar. Figure 6.12 depicts the comparison between Bihar's and India's growth rates. Although Bihar has followed a zigzag pattern since 1901, it has grown well, remaining only slightly below the national growth rate for the most part of the last century. It is only during 1991–2001 that Bihar decisively surpassed the national growth rate of 21.54 per cent, peaking at 28.62 per cent. Therefore, Bihar has experienced its peak growth phase mostly after 1971.

Kerala attained its peak decadal growth rate in 1971 and Karnataka in 1981, both having registered decadal growth rates greater than 20 per cent in the previous few decades before hitting their peak rates. In contrast, neither Uttar Pradesh nor Bihar had peaked by 1971, although they were in the process of doing so.

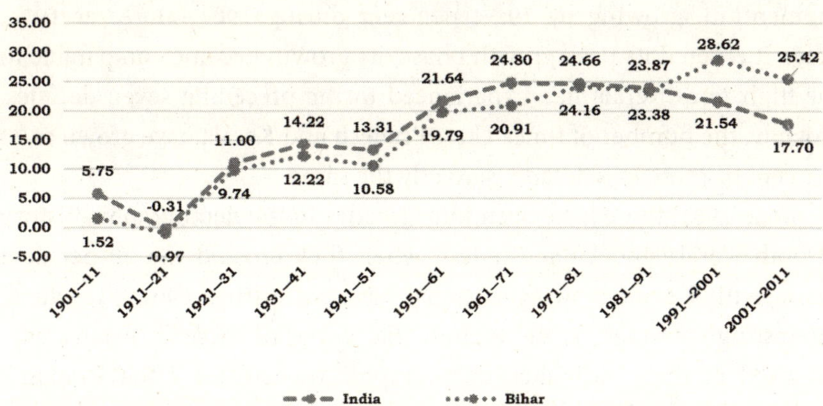

Figure 6.12: Population growth rate of Bihar vis-à-vis the growth rate of India (percentage), 1901–11 to 2001–11

Source: Census of India, 2011 (Table 6.4, Appendices)

The picture that has emerged so far is based only on the analysis of the comparative population growth rates of select states with the national rate. A clearer picture would emerge if states are compared with each other. Figure 6.13 presents a comparison between Kerala, representing the south, and Uttar Pradesh, representing the north.

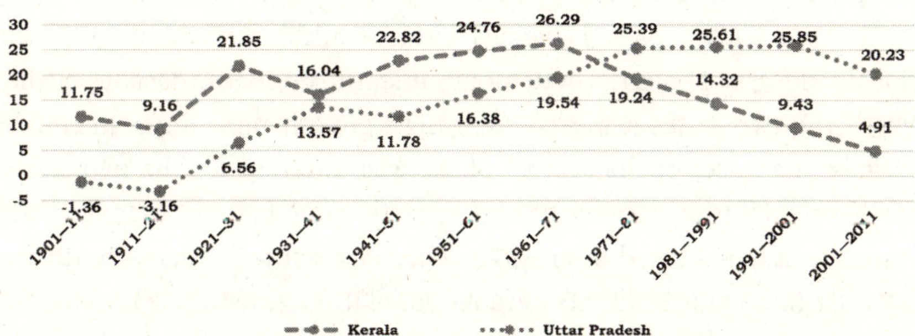

Figure 6.13: A comparison of decadal growth rates of Uttar Pradesh and Kerala (percentage), 1901–11 to 2001–11

Source: Census of India, 2011 (Table 6.4, Appendices)

In Figure 6.13, the first thing that might strike an observer is that until 1971 Kerala consistently registered much higher growth than Uttar Pradesh. It was only after 1961 that Uttar Pradesh gained demographic momentum, growing by 19.54 per cent during 1961–71. After 1971, when it entered its peak growth phasc, its growth became comparable to the high rates Kerala had experienced in the preceding seven decades. Notably, the number of times Uttar Pradesh and Kerala have grown at 20 per cent or more in a decade is exactly the same.

Since 1901, there have been four decades in the demographic history of both Kerala and Uttar Pradesh when they crossed the 20 per cent mark, with Kerala growing at 26.29 per cent during 1961–71, which, interestingly enough, is the highest that either of these two states ever achieved in their individual demographic trajectories. Uttar Pradesh's peak growth rate was 25.85 during 1991–2001.

Kerala's rate of 26.29 per cent is, however, not the highest decadal growth rate among the major states of the country, with Assam (34.95 per cent), Haryana (33.79 per cent), Rajasthan (32.97 per cent), West Bengal (32.80 per cent), Gujarat (29.39 per cent), Madhya Pradesh (29.28 per cent), Bihar (28.62 per cent), Maharashtra (27.45 per cent) and Chhattisgarh (27.12 per cent) all registering a higher growth rate during at least one decade of their demographic journey. It must be noted, however, that in many of these cases large-scale migration caused by events like the Partition of India or the Bangladesh Liberation War of 1971 was as much a factor as natural growth.

Coming back to Kerala versus Uttar Pradesh, consistent with the globally observed patterns of demographic transition, the decades during which the two states achieved such high growth rates differ in timing because the onset of the second phase was different for the two states. For Kerala, all four decades of high growth came before 1971; for Uttar Pradesh, they occurred after 1971. That is because it was only during 1971–81 that Uttar Pradesh's decadal population growth rate crossed the 20 per cent mark for the first time, and it maintained similarly high growth rates for the next three decades, ending 2011. According to estimates, its growth rate is likely to be much lower in the next census. Let us analyse how these two states have expanded during periods of rapid growth. Figure 6.14 presents the high-growth decades of Kerala compared to Uttar Pradesh.

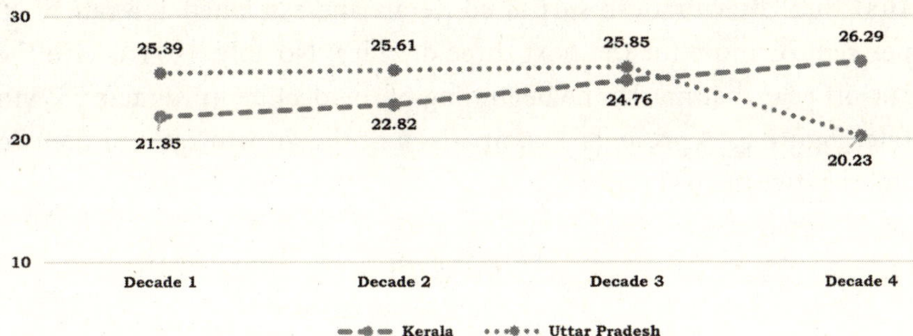

Figure 6.14: Decadal growth rates of Uttar Pradesh versus Kerala (percentage)

Source: Census of India, 2011 (Table 6.5, Appendices)

In the figure, the notation indicating the respective decades varies for the two states. Table 6.5 summarises the mode of analysis adopted:

Table 6.5: Notation for the four decades under consideration in Uttar Pradesh and Kerala

	Kerala	*Uttar Pradesh*
Decade 1	1921–31	1971–81
Decade 2	1941–51	1981–91
Decade 3	1951–61	1991–2001
Decade 4	1961–71	2001–11

Barring 1931–41, all three decades in which Kerala achieved a growth rate exceeding 20 per cent were consecutive. Uttar Pradesh experienced all four decades of high growth as consecutive, beginning from 1971–81 and continuing until 2001–11. This indicates that Kerala and Uttar Pradesh grew at almost the same pace but during different periods in the history of modern India. The second phase of transition marked by rapid growth also occurred in the two states during different time frames. Prior to 1971, at no point did Uttar Pradesh register a growth rate equal to or greater than Kerala—the closest that the two states came before 1971 was during 1931–41. It was only from 1971 to

1981 that Uttar Pradesh surpassed Kerala and remained at a rate of 20 per cent or more for the next three decades. Notably, 1971 is also the cut-off year that marks the beginning of the decline in Kerala's growth rate. Figure 6.15 presents a comparison of the growth rates of the two states between 1931 and 1971.

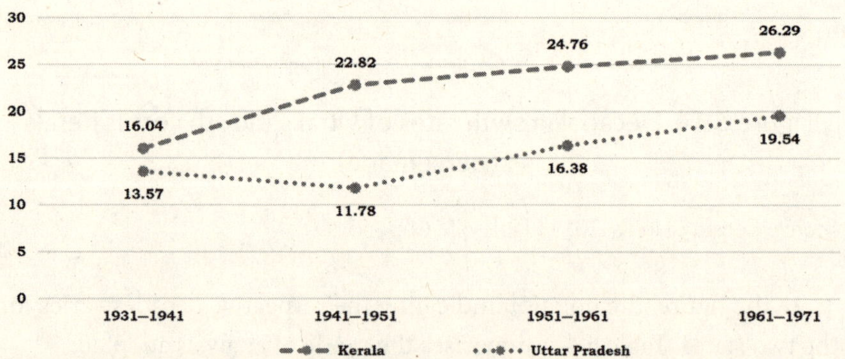

Figure 6.15: Comparison of decadal growth rates of Uttar Pradesh and Kerala (percentage), 1931–41 to 1961–71

Source: Census of India, 2011 (Table 6.4, Appendices)

During the four decades from 1931 to 1971, the population growth rates of Uttar Pradesh were consistently lower than those of Kerala. During 1941–51, when Kerala grew at more than 20 per cent, the growth rate of Uttar Pradesh actually declined. This decline may be partly attributable to the migration of significant number of people from Uttar Pradesh to Pakistan at the time of Partition in 1947. It might be useful to compare the gradients of the two curves. The slope of the curve representing Kerala's growth rate comes out to be 0.327, just a notch higher than Uttar Pradesh's 0.225 gradient. The curves for both states appear to be rising more uniformly after 1941–51. Therefore, let us look at the comparison of the growth rates from 1941 to 1971, with Figure 6.16.

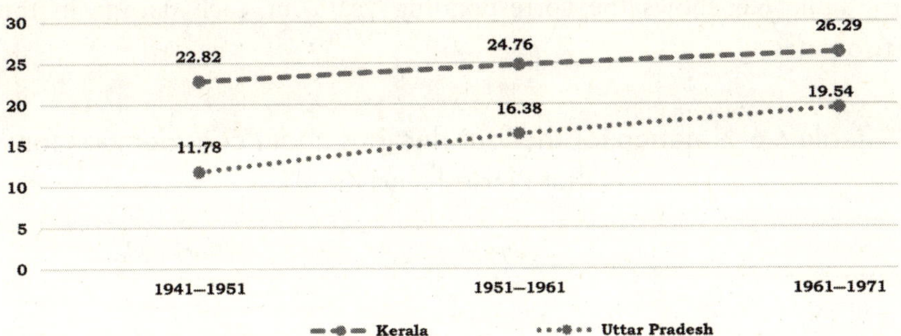

Figure 6.16: Comparison of decadal growth rates of Uttar Pradesh and Kerala (percentage), 1941–51 to 1961–71

Source: Census of India, 2011 (Table 6.4, Appendices)

Having seen that Uttar Pradesh and Kerala experienced demographic transition with striking similarities—although during different periods—it would be interesting to examine the actual pattern of the two states. Presented in Figure 6.17 is a graphical comparison.

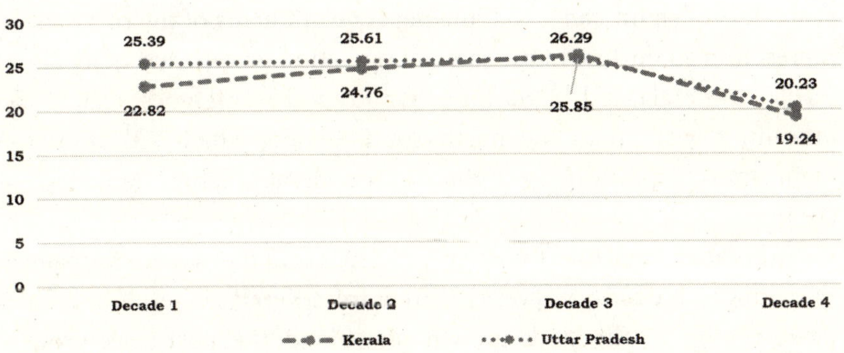

Figure 6.17: Decadal growth rates of Uttar Pradesh versus Kerala (percentage)

Source: Census of India, 2011 (Table 6.6, Appendices)

Table 6.6 shows the corresponding years for each decade in the two states.

Table 6.6: Notation for the four decades under consideration for Uttar Pradesh and Kerala

	Kerala	*Uttar Pradesh*
Decade 1	1941–51	1971–81
Decade 2	1951–61	1981–91
Decade 3	1961–71	1991–2001
Decade 4	1971–81	2001–11

The converging of the two curves in Figure 6.17 is highly illuminating. It confirms that there is no fundamental difference in the pattern of demographic transition in the two states. The pattern followed by the population growth of Kerala between 1941 and 1981 is replicated in Uttar Pradesh between 1971 and 2011. Therefore, the main distinction lies in the timing of their growth phases, which are separated by thirty years. It is of significance that the negative gradients of the two curves, representing a decline in the rate of population growth, are quite close: 0.705 for Kerala and 0.562 for Uttar Pradesh. This goes against the prevailing wisdom in the north–south divide, which attributes the 'population explosion' in India to the demographic transition of the north.

To broaden the scope of comparison, let us shift the focus to Karnataka. Its demographic history is very different from Kerala's in terms of growth rates, timing of the peak growth phase and the post-peak growth. Nevertheless, Karnataka matches up to Uttar Pradesh and Kerala, having grown at more than 20 per cent in a decade on four occasions since 1901. Let us now compare it to Uttar Pradesh with the help of Figure 6.18. Once again, the curves charting the growth in the two states trace almost identical trajectories, but during different periods. This is depicted in Table 6.7.

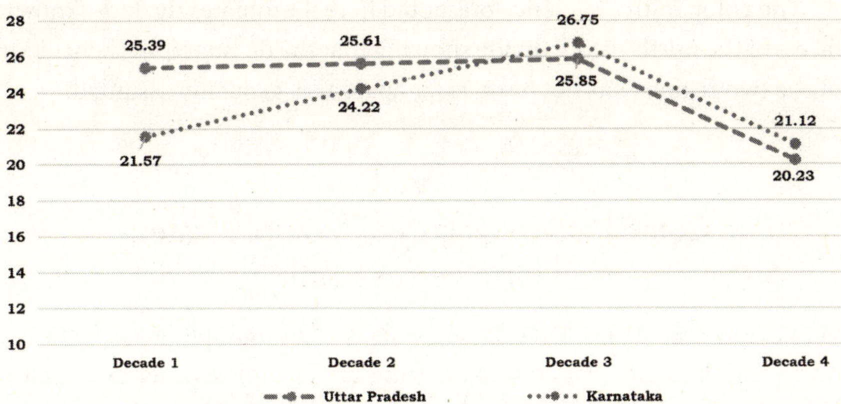

Figure 6.18: Decadal growth rates of Uttar Pradesh versus Karnataka (percentage)

Source: Census of India, 2011 (Table 6.7, Appendices)

Table 6.7: Notation for the four decades under consideration in the case of Uttar Pradesh and Karnataka

	Uttar Pradesh	*Karnataka*
Decade 1	1971–81	1951–61
Decade 2	1981–91	1961–71
Decade 3	1991–2001	1971–81
Decade 4	2001–11	1981–91

It was shown earlier that the rates at which population growth declined in Uttar Pradesh and Kerala were quite similar. It is further interesting to find that the negative slope of the curve for Karnataka in the decade of 1981–91 is 0.563, which is almost identical to 0.562, the negative gradient for Uttar Pradesh during 2001–11. Once again, the difference is simply one of timing. What demographic transition caused in Karnataka in 1981–91 reached Uttar Pradesh two decades later in 2001–11. The peak growth phase spanned forty years, from 1951 to 1991 in Karnataka and from 1971 to 2011 in Uttar Pradesh.

The comparative evidence presented here illuminates the little-known facets of the north–south divide showing that the demographic behaviour of the two regions has not been as far apart as is generally assumed.

V
Comparative Analysis of Multiple States: North versus South

Let us now embark on a comparative analysis of multiple states from the north and the south, with two states from each region selected as samples. Uttar Pradesh and Bihar represent the north; Kerala and Karnataka represent the south. The four states are compared on their population growth rates across the five decades preceding 1971. The choice of the period starting from 1921 stems from the fact that it marks the first signs of demographic transition in India as a whole. Presented in Figure 6.19 is a chart showing the trajectories of the population growth rates of the four states during 1921–71.

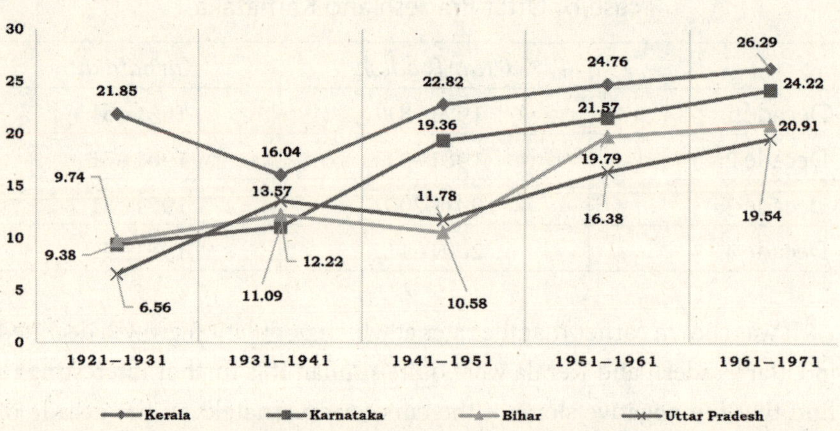

Figure 6.19: Comparison of the population growth rates of India's north and south (percentage), 1921–71

Source: Table 6.4, Appendices

The curve shows a clear demarcation between the north and the south. The two southern states, Karnataka and Kerala, consistently stayed on top of the two northern states, Uttar Pradesh and Bihar. For all five decades prior to 1971, the south grew at a much higher rate than the north. Uttar Pradesh, often claimed to be the worst culprit for India's 'population explosion', never came in the vicinity of the high growth rates that both Kerala and Karnataka experienced during 1921–71—a critical period in the demographic history of modern India. In order to add to analytical rigour, the growth rates for all five decades between 1921 and 1971 for the four states are plotted in the chart depicted in Figure 6.20 with a change of axes.

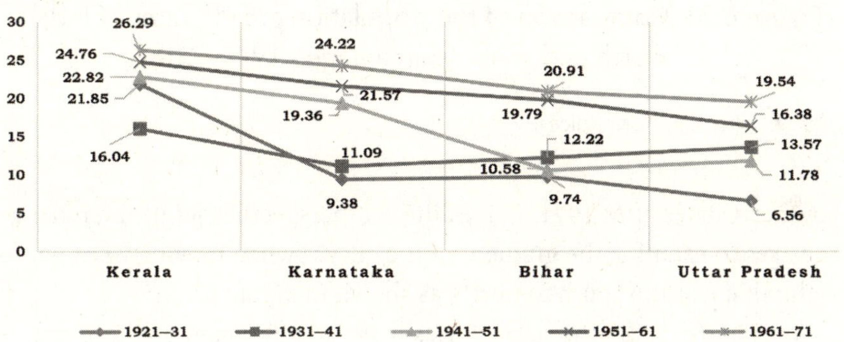

Figure 6.20: Comparison of the population growth rates of India's north and south (percentage), 1921–71, with a change of axes

Source: Table 6.4, Appendices

As we move from left to right in Figure 6.20, we are actually moving from south to north. All five curves representing the five decades have a downward slope, indicating that the south maintained a higher population growth rate during the fifty years before 1971. The south's lead is maintained even when the timeframe is narrowed to the three decades preceding 1971 as Figure 6.21 shows.

It is evident from Figure 6.21 that in population growth Uttar Pradesh was significantly behind Kerala and Karnataka during 1941–71. Bihar, by contrast, came close to Karnataka in 1951–61 but fell behind again. The two states from the north consistently grew at lower rates than the two from the south during 1941–71, although they would outpace the

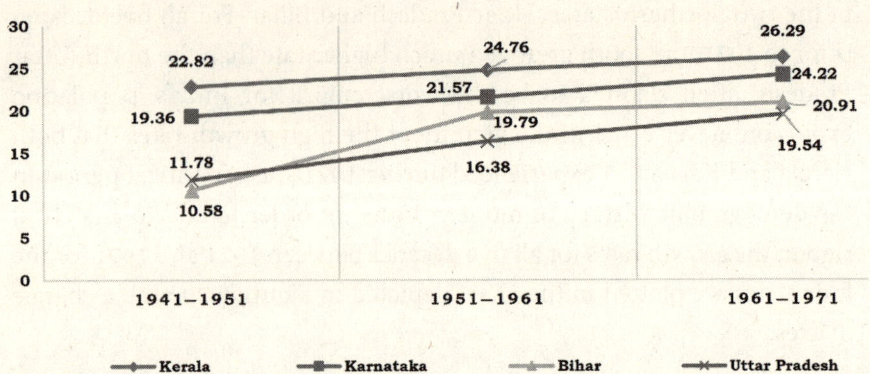

Figure 6.21: Comparison of the population growth rates of India's north and south (percentage), 1941–71

Source: Table 6.4, Appendices

southern states after 1971. For a different perspective, let us interchange the axes to examine the gradient of the curves when moving from left to right, that is, from south to north, as shown in Figure 6.22.

In Figure 6.22, the trajectories consistently maintain a negative gradient from south to north. This is reflective of the fact that between

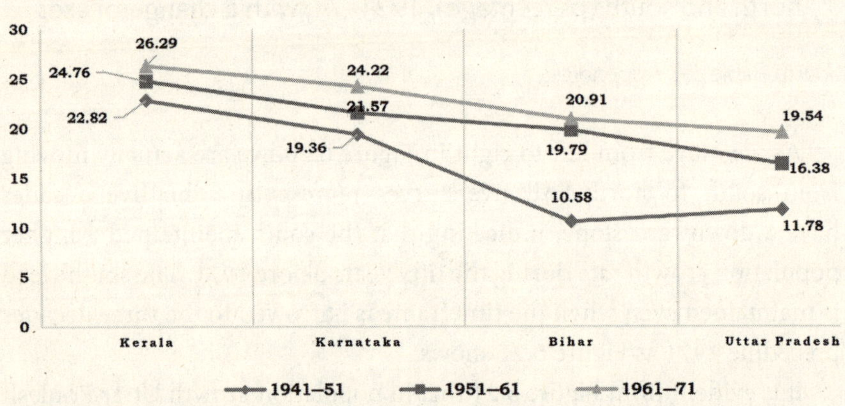

Figure 6.22: Comparison of the population growth rates of India's north and south, 1941–71 (percentage), with a change of axes

Source: Table 6.4, Appendices

1941 and 1971 it was the south that outperformed the north in population growth. Not surprisingly, therefore, the south reached its peak share of India's population (26.08 per cent) in the Census of 1951, before falling slightly to 24.69 per cent in 1971.

Therefore, the conclusion is unavoidable: having experienced high growth rates for five decades, much of the south had already surpassed the stage of rapid population growth in the unfolding story of its demographic transition. Notwithstanding this, Andhra Pradesh and Karnataka continued to enjoy good growth until 1981–91, with the rates of 24.20 per cent and 21.12 per cent respectively. Tamil Nadu and Karnataka also registered rates of 15.61 per cent and 15.60 per cent in the Census of 2011. The declining fertility and population growth that the south collectively displayed after 1971 is in consonance with demographic transition. It implies that the second stage of rapid population growth, irrespective of its duration, is likely to be followed by the third stage of declining fertility, finally leading to the shrinkage of population over the long run. This is being experienced by countries like Japan and Germany.

It follows that the north, which in 1971 had just entered the peak growth phase, could not have avoided growing rapidly for a few more decades. The implementation of family planning programme could not have drastically altered the trajectory, minus of course the adoption of a more stringent measure like China's one-child policy. Government policies, especially those that seek to influence the personal choices of large number of people, can succeed only when the time and conditions are right for them. Otherwise, their impact on shaping a society can only be marginal.

VI

Population Density: Revisiting the North–South Divide

To have a clear perspective on the so-called north-south demographic divergence, we also need to study population density. Historically, population density has been indicative of the potential for growth, determined by the carrying capacity of a particular geographical region. A high fertility rate coupled with high population density denotes something very different from high fertility coupled with low or moderate density. The fact that all four southern states have by now reached below the replacement level of TFR (2.1), while some north Indian states are still above it, should be seen together with population density data for these states.

According to one estimate, at the turn of the millennium the population density of the north was 319 persons per square kilometre, while that of the south was a notch higher at 346.[8] Although it is predicted that by 2025 the population density in the north will reach 496, surpassing the south's 417, for much of modern India's demographic history, the situation has been quite similar to that observed in 2000. Historical statistics comparing Kerala with Uttar Pradesh, as depicted in Figures 6.23 and 6.24, show variations in the two states since 1901.

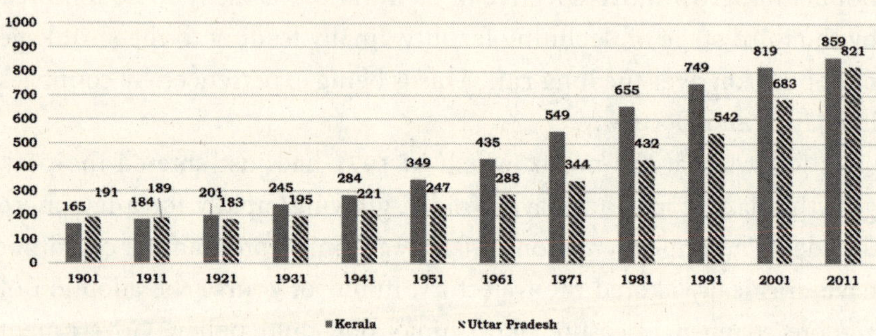

Figure 6.23: Population density in Uttar Pradesh and Kerala (per sq. km), 1901–2011[9]

Source: Census of India, 2011 (Table 6.8, Appendices)

In 1901, Uttar Pradesh (191) still had a higher density than Kerala (165) despite the latter's rapid growth over the preceding two decades. However, the equation was reversed by 1921, with Kerala at 201 and Uttar Pradesh at 183. The gap between the two widened until 1971, when Uttar Pradesh's density as a ratio to Kerala's touched the bottom at 62.66 per cent. After 1971, the gap began to be reversed because of the higher growth of Uttar Pradesh. However, even in 2011, Uttar Pradesh's density at 821 was less than that of Kerala at 859—a fact that might be indicative of the unrealised growth potential of Uttar Pradesh even in 2011, especially with reference to the concept of carrying capacity of a region, which predicts higher densities for the north, as has been the empirical reality historically. A more encompassing comparison of densities across other states from both regions would provide deeper insight on this point. Figure 6.24 depicts the population densities for eight Indian states, four from the north and four from the south.

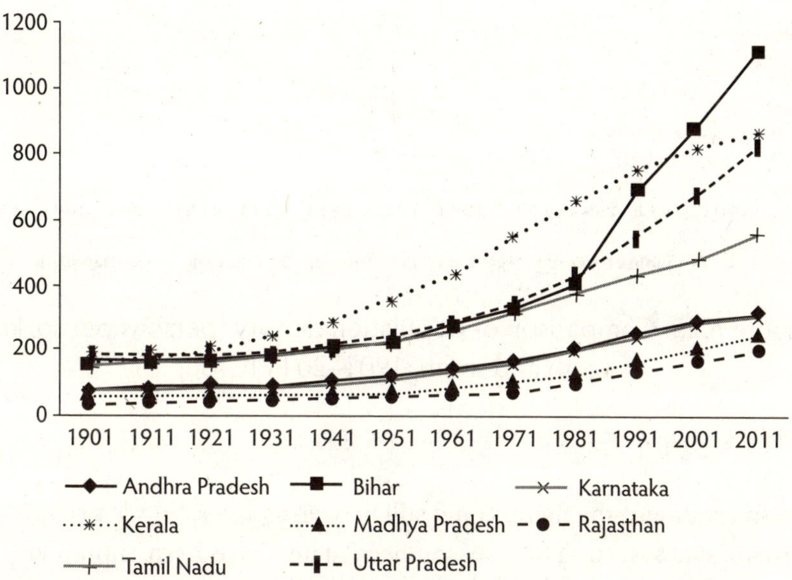

Figure 6.24: Comparison of population density (persons per sq. km) between north and south, 1901–2011

Source: Census of India, 2011 (Table 6.9, Appendices)

Apart from Kerala, none of the other seven states had a density of over 400 persons per square kilometre until 1981. It is also clear from Figure 6.24 that, based on the range of their population density, the eight states can be grouped into two groups of four each. What is even more interesting is that both groups consist of two states from the north and two from the south, thus dealing a blow to the idea of a north–south divide on the basis of India's demographic history in modern times. Let us take a look at the two groups separately. For the sake of simplicity, we refer to the group of four with lower density as Group 1 and the other with higher density as Group 2. Given in Figure 6.25 is a graphical representation of Group 1.

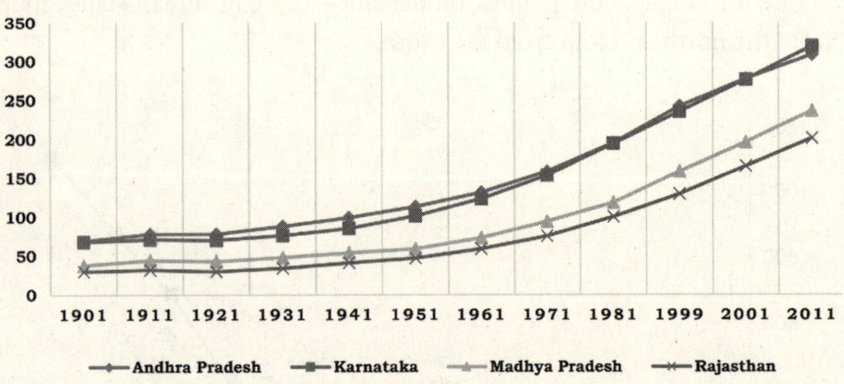

Figure 6.25: Comparison of population density (persons per sq. km) of north and south, 1901–2011 (Group 1)

Source: Census of India, 2011 (Table 6.9, Appendices)

Interestingly, the figure could still be seen as consisting of two groups of two states each. The two southern states have been more densely populated than the two from the north ever since 1901. Rajasthan and Madhya Pradesh experienced more rapid growth than Andhra Pradesh and Karnataka in the decades following Independence, especially after 1971. Nevertheless, this fact needs to be considered alongside long-term trends in population density of the states in modern India's demographic history, as even in the 2011 Census, the two northern states lagged the two southern states, although the gap has narrowed since 1951. Further growth in the population of these states might have little to do with their social or cultural attitudes towards population control or family planning. It may simply be symptomatic of the fact that they have not exhausted their demographic potential. Over the *longue durée* of history, the north could support large populations because of favourable geographical, climatic, agrarian and political conditions. Bearing this in mind, let us examine Figure 6.26, which depicts the trends in population densities of the other group of states, namely, Group 2.

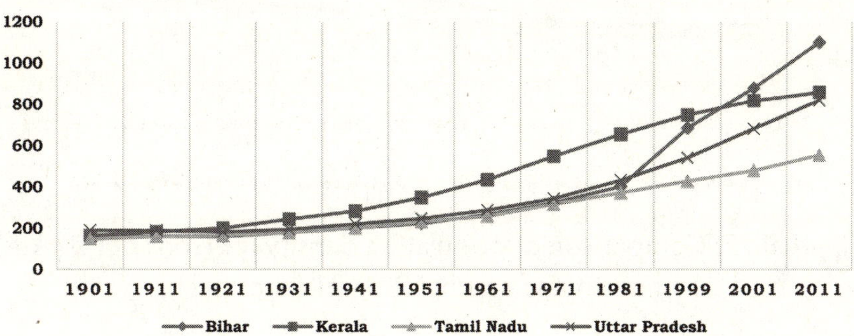

Figure 6.26: Comparison of the population density (persons per sq. km) of north and south, 1901–2011 (Group 2)

Source: Census of India, 2011 (Table 6.9, Appendices)

The most striking feature of the curve seen in Figure 6.26 is its smoothness until 1971, before Bihar and Uttar Pradesh took a decisive upward turn around 1981. It would thus be worthwhile to look at the figure in two parts, with 1971 as the dividing line. The pre-1971 distribution is depicted in Figure 6.27.

In the figure, there is very little difference between the north and south except for Kerala, whose exceptionally high population density even in 1971, as compared to the other three states, stands out. Moreover, the difference in density between Kerala and the others has gradually increased since 1901. In that year, the densities of all four states were nearly equal. Since then, Kerala's density rose steadily to reach almost double that of Uttar Pradesh in 1971. Between 1901 and 1971, the population density of Uttar Pradesh could not even double itself, even as Kerala increased its density by over three times. Figure 6.28 shows a comparison of the two states.

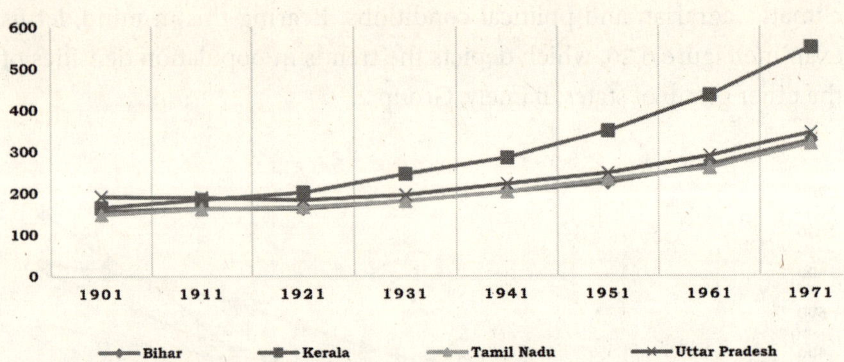

Figure 6.27: Comparison of population density (persons per sq. km) of north and south, 1901–71 (Group 2)

Source: Census of India, 2011 (Table 6.9, Appendices)

Kerala far outshone Uttar Pradesh in density for a good seven decades, from 1901 to 1971 (Figure 6.28), and the gap was widest in 1971. To complete the argument, let us see how the picture has changed since 1971 (Figure 6.29).

The consistent pattern observed for 1901–71 in Figure 6.27 is absent in Figure 6.29. Between 1981 and 2011, Tamil Nadu has shown the

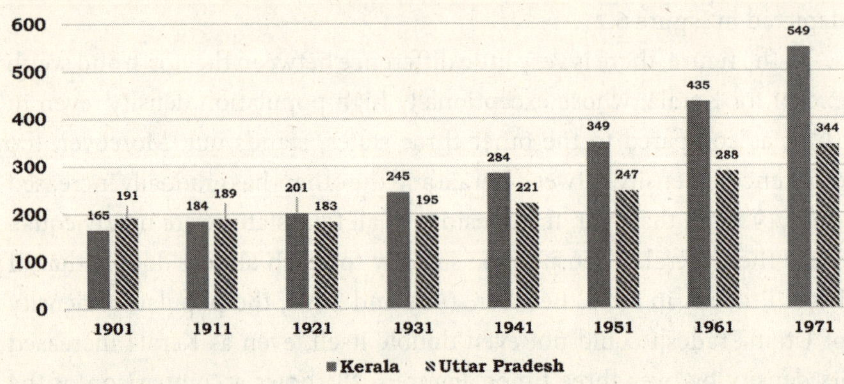

Figure 6.28: Comparison of the population density (persons per sq. km) of Uttar Pradesh and Kerala, 1901–71

Source: Census of India, 2011 (Table 6.9, Appendices)

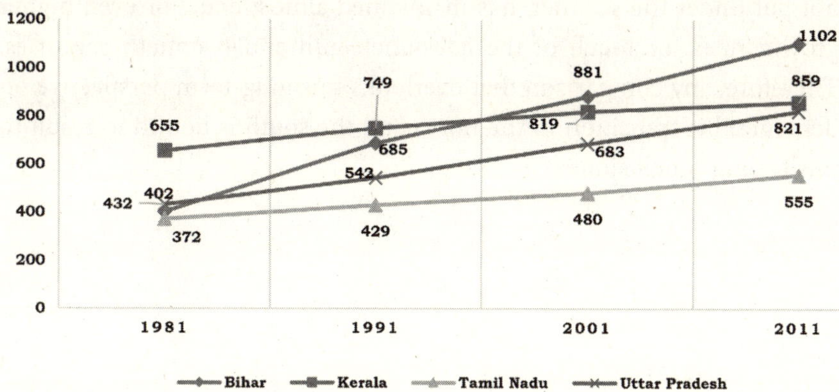

Figure 6.29: Comparison of population density (persons per sq. km) between north and south, 1981–2011 (Group 2)

Source: Census of India, 2011 (Table 6.9, Appendices)[10]

slowest growth in density. What is noteworthy, however, is that it is only as recently as 2001 that Bihar (881) surpassed Kerala (819) in terms of population density. In the 2011 Census, Uttar Pradesh's density stood at 821, still lower than Kerala's 859.

—∾—

Thus, the demographic data drawn from various rounds of census demonstrate that the perceived north–south divide has been blown out of proportion and is part of a larger myth. The focused analysis of the process of demographic transition in the north and south in terms of comparative rates of birth, death, fertility, and population growth and density over 1901–2011 undertaken in this chapter shows that except for differential timings there is no fundamental difference between the two regions.

The analysis corroborates that 1971 is the point of inflexion by which the south was on the verge of exiting the second phase of transition, while the north had just entered it. Therefore, the difference in the fertility and growth rates of the two regions over the last fifty years is part of a natural process that is not significantly affected by government policy and propaganda about family planning. The south, which is usually not put under the scanner, has maintained almost equal or even higher growth rates for much of the late-nineteenth and twentieth centuries. Therefore, any comparison that overlooks this long-term perspective on demographic transition in the north and the south is bound to result in misleading conclusions.

7

Demography, Economic Growth and Urbanisation

The Divide Revisited

In this chapter, we explore the role of some well-known drivers or correlates of demographic transition to assess their significance for India, in particular to explain the apparent north–south divide. The three factors that are examined for their relationship with population growth rate are income growth and level, literacy rate and urbanisation. The relationship was discussed in conceptual terms in Chapter 3, which deals with the concept and process of demographic transition in the global context. The analysis here focuses on India's north–south comparative framework with regard to these important determinants of demographic transition, along with some state-specific analysis. In the first part of the chapter, the relationship between growth in Net State Domestic Product (NSDP) and population is studied. This part includes a review of relevant literature and a focused analysis of select states from the north and the south. In the second part, there is an analysis of female literacy rate and population growth. The third part includes both a general and a focused north–south analysis of a possible relationship between urbanisation and demographic growth. The sections numbered in this chapter cut across the said three parts addressed here.

I

The Economic Perspective: NSDP and Population Growth

The empirical relationship between economic growth, captured through growth in NSDP, and population growth is depicted in Figures 7.1 to 7.5 for different decades. Figure 7.1 indicates that during 1960–70 the relationship between NSDP growth and population growth had a mixed pattern. This was the decade when the demographic growth of India peaked at 24.80 per cent, while the north and the south grew at comparable rates[1]. But there were significant variations in NSDP growth. Uttar Pradesh, Madhya Pradesh and Bihar from the north showed a modest gap between the two rates, while Rajasthan and Haryana had a wide gap because of an elevated NSDP growth. From the south, Tamil Nadu and Andhra Pradesh had an NSDP growth only modestly higher than population growth, while Karnataka and Kerala did much better in NSDP growth. In the west, the two figures had hardly any gap for Maharashtra, but for Gujarat the NSDP figure was much higher.

In general, in most states, growth in NSDP was higher than in population, but there were significant variations. If we leave out Assam and Orissa, which are outliers, the NSDP growth was higher than population growth ranging from less than one percentage point for Madhya Pradesh to nearly 30 percentage points for Rajasthan. On the whole, the NSDP growth was higher in the south than in the north, though the difference was not pronounced. It might be said that while economic

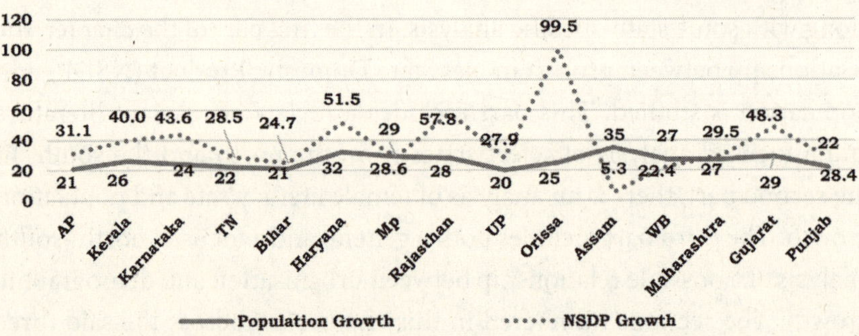

Figure 7.1: NSDP growth versus population growth, 1960–70

Source: Table 7.1, Appendices

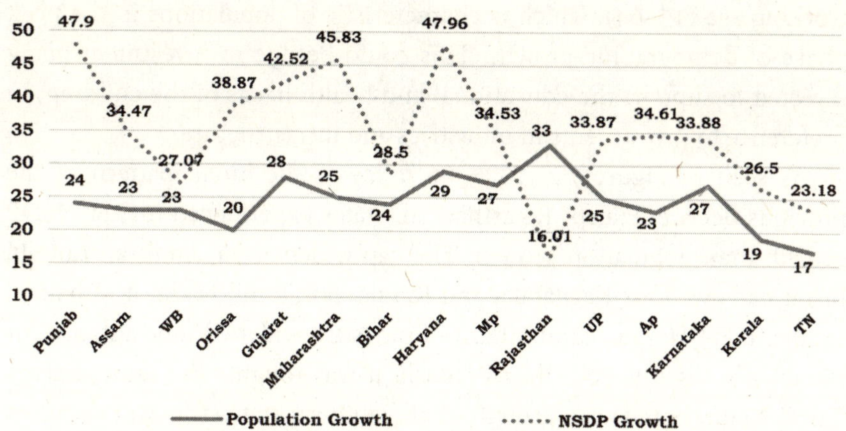

Figure 7.2: NSDP growth versus population growth, 1970–80

Source: Table 7.1, Appendices

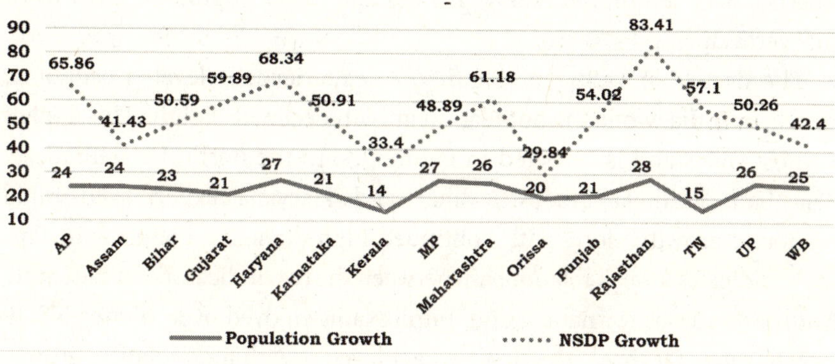

Figure 7.3: NSDP growth versus population growth, 1980–90

Source. Table 7.1, Appendices

growth eventually does contribute to bringing down demographic growth, it usually happens with a lag. As per capita incomes cross a threshold required for higher literacy, education, health, urbanisation, women's education and employment in the (non-farm) formal sector, fertility and population growth rates start declining. In the meantime, however, economic growth is likely to be adversely affected by high youth dependency ratio (percentage of non-working age (0 to 14) population to working age (15–64), which is characteristic of populations in the peak phase of demographic growth. This could be due to investment being directed to support the educational and health needs of the children, in preference to investments in industries and infrastructure.

As seen in Figure 7.2, 1970–80 followed the broad pattern of the previous decade. Except Rajasthan, all states experienced higher NSDP growth than population growth. The gap widened for Andhra Pradesh, but it narrowed for Karnataka and Kerala. For Tamil Nadu, it remained stagnant. For Haryana and Madhya Pradesh, it widened substantially; for Bihar only slightly. For Uttar Pradesh, it was roughly the same. Except Tamil Nadu, population growth of all southern states was still above or only slightly below 20 per cent. It was mainly in five states—Gujarat, Haryana, Maharashtra, Orissa and Punjab—that the gap was substantially wide. In Punjab and Haryana, population growth remained high, even as Green Revolution pushed up the NSDP growth. So, no clear relationship emerges between higher NSDP growth and lower population growth or vice versa during 1970–80.

The decade of 1980–90 (Figure 7.3) experienced elevated economic growth in India, while the population growth declined slightly. This applies to most states and is reflected in Figure 7.3. In the north, Uttar Pradesh, Rajasthan, Madhya Pradesh, Bihar and Haryana experienced rapid economic growth, along with continued high demographic growth. This again indicates a weak relationship between the two indicators. In the south, Andhra Pradesh, Karnataka and Tamil Nadu enjoyed even higher NSDP growth rates. Of these, the first two achieved it with a population growth rate of 20 per cent or above; Tamil Nadu did so with 15 per cent. Kerala's case stands out because decline in population growth was not associated with spurt in economic growth. Conversely, Maharashtra and Gujarat continued to perform well on economic growth, despite high demographic growth[2].

The decade of 1990–2000 represents a watershed in the history of India after Independence because of the liberalisation of economy undertaken by Prime Minister Narasimha Rao. The southern states had by this time a clearly lower population growth rate than the north, with Kerala at only 9 per cent, Tamil Nadu 12 per cent, Andhra Pradesh 15 per cent and Karnataka 18 per cent. Except Andhra Pradesh, the NSDP of southern states grew by roughly 40 per cent. Among other things,

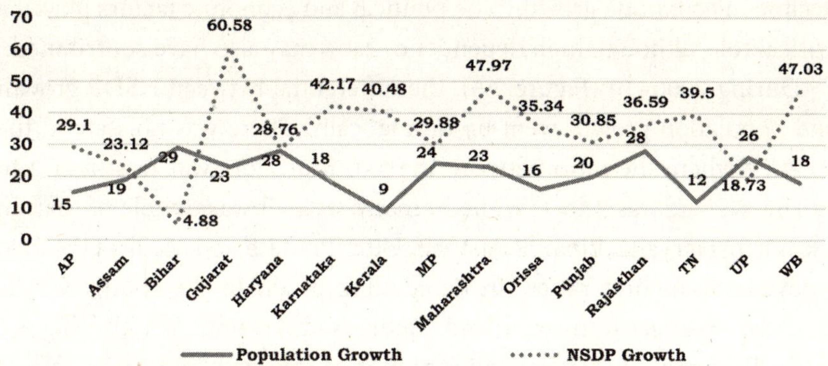

Figure 7.4: NSDP growth versus population growth, 1990–2000

Source: Table 7.1, Appendices

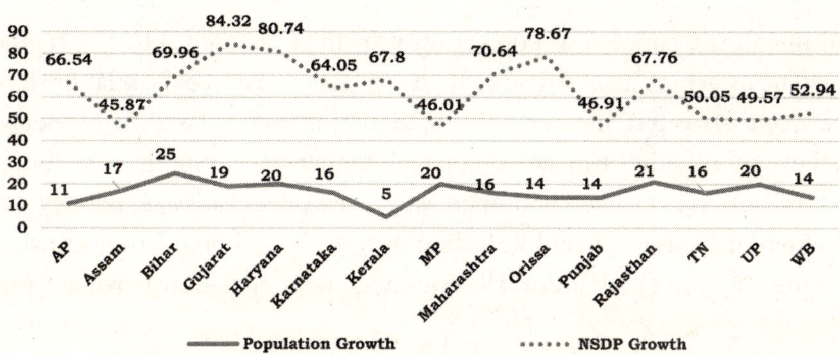

Figure 7.5: NSDP growth versus population growth, 2000–2010

Source: Table 7.1, Appendices

this implies a lower dependency ratio or higher percentage of working age population both with regard to the previous decades and the north, where peak growth phase had started decades after the south. Almost the entire north, including Uttar Pradesh, Rajasthan, Madhya Pradesh and Haryana, saw their NSDP growth decline, while their population growth continued to be high, at close to or above 20 per cent, thus bringing down the differential substantially. However, it should not be assumed that this necessarily represents a relationship between high population growth and decline in economic growth. The political and economic factors played a critical role, although high dependency ratio may also have contributed.

During 2000–10 (Figure 7.5), the differential between NSDP growth and population growth went up dramatically. There was no state in the country where the ratio between the two indicators was less than 2 to 1. The average was 3 to 1, while in many states it was double of that. In the north, Haryana, Bihar, Rajasthan, Uttar Pradesh and Madhya Pradesh enjoyed the highest ratios, in descending order. In the south, Kerala, Andhra Pradesh, Karnataka and Tamil Nadu maintained the highest ratios. Evidently, the general uptick in economic growth in the post-reform period significantly widened the gap, while declining population growth in virtually all states, reflecting lower dependency ratio, also helped.

II

Although the concept of population growth is factored into per capita income or per capita NSDP growth, it is instructive to see the relationship between per capita income and population growth as well. It is widely believed that, other things being equal, higher per capita income above a threshold is associated with increased levels of education, especially for women, urbanisation, and a decline in fertility and population growth. Figure 7.6 shows that almost all states had high population growth in the

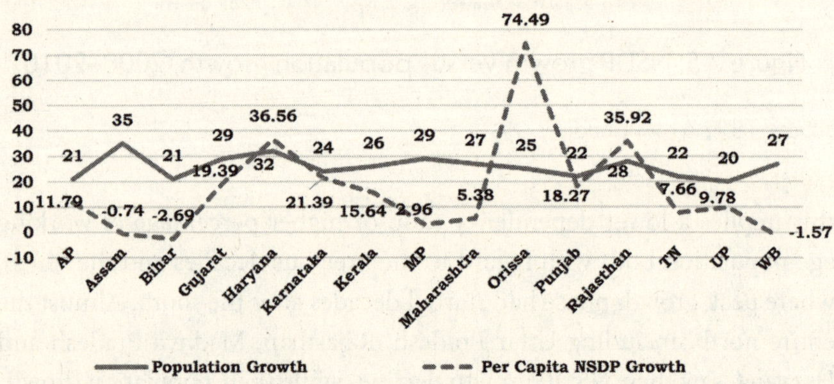

Figure 7.6: Per capita NSDP growth versus population growth, 1960–70

Source: Table 7.1, Appendices

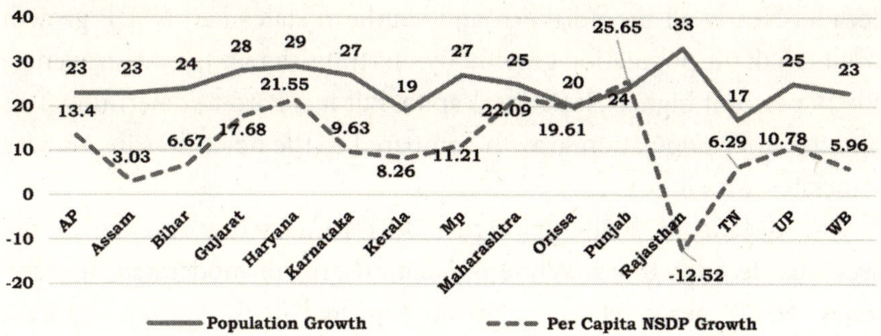

Figure 7.7: Per capita NSDP growth versus population growth, 1970–80

Source: Table 7.1, Appendices

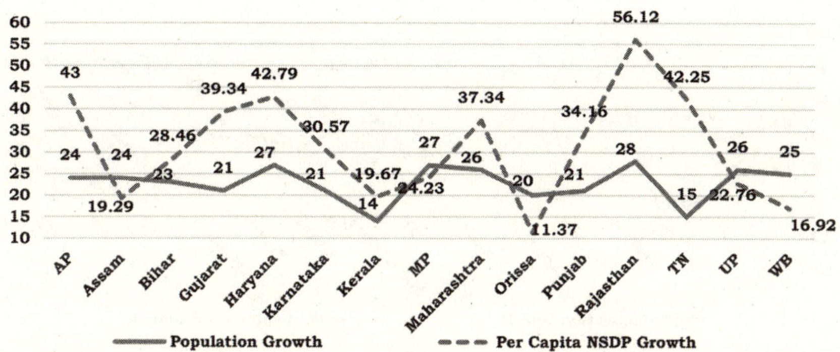

Figure 7.8: Per capita NSDP growth versus population growth, 1980–90

Source: Table 7.1, Appendices

range of 20–32 per cent during 1960–70. However, per capita income growth had wide fluctuations, from about minus 3 per cent to 37 per cent, even if we leave out Orissa's case as anomalous. Some states had higher growth in per capita income than in population, while for others it was the reverse. Perhaps, the income levels across states were at this juncture not divergent enough to be associated with decline in population growth.

The decade of 1970–80 (Figure 7.7), the heyday of the licence-permit-quota raj, experienced a much lower growth in per capita income than in population, although the latter was on average lower than the previous decade. Nearly all the northern and southern states had NSDP growth around half the population growth. By this time, the south had on average 20–25 per cent higher NSDP per capita, but it is hard to determine if its slightly lower population growth compared to the north was in any way associated with it.

The decade of 1980–90 (Figure 7.8) witnessed a reversal of the previous decade's trend. While population growth moderated in many states, NSDP per capita went up on expected lines. Andhra Pradesh, Tamil Nadu and Karnataka enjoyed above-average income growth. The northern states mostly had a narrow gap between the two indicators, implying modest economic growth.

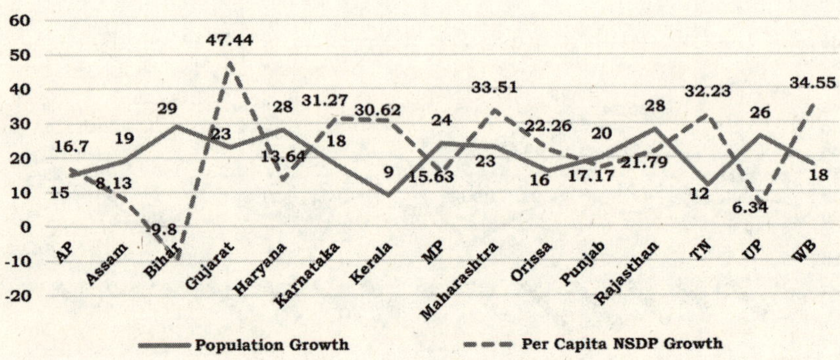

Figure 7.9: Per capita NSDP growth versus population growth, 1990–2000

Source: Table 7.1, Appendices

During 1990–2000 (Figure 7.9), the gap between growth in NSDP per capita and population widened among the southern states. Kerala and Tamil Nadu had a threefold gap, while Karnataka had a much narrower gap. Andhra Pradesh's case is surprising because the two curves almost converge, implying little growth in per capita income. Among the northern states, the performance on per capita growth was so poor that it was either less than population growth or slightly above it. This deceleration is reflective of the political and social turmoil in the north in the 1990s, although high dependency ratio may also have contributed.

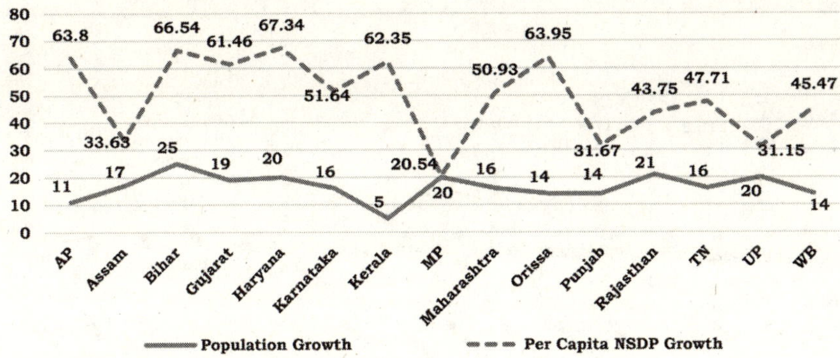

Figure 7.10: Per capita NSDP growth versus population growth, 2000–10

Source: Table 7.1, Appendices

The decade of 2000–11 (Figure 7.10) was obviously the best for India from the viewpoint of per capita income growth. Most states enjoyed growth in the range of 40 to 70 per cent, while population growth in most of them was below 20 per cent. Kerala's and Andhra Pradesh's very high growth of nearly 63 and 64 per cent respectively was accompanied by population growth of 5 and 11 per cent respectively. But it is hard to determine whether high income growth brought down population growth or it was the other way round. Conceptually, the two phenomena are associated with each other.

It is useful to also see the relationship between per capita income growth and population growth of a state relative to the respective growth rates for India as a whole. Using the income data from the study of Sanjiv Sanyal and Aakansha Arora for the Prime Minister's Economic Advisory Council (PMEAC), September 2024, Figures 7.11 and 7.12 present the relationship for the two periods 1960–90 and 1990–2026. The income data in Figure 7.12 is restricted to 2023–24 and the earlier cited population projection for 2026 have been used. It can be seen that during the period 1960–90, Haryana was the only state that exhibited a population growth rate significantly higher than the national rate at 126.1 per cent and a per capita income growth rate 23.9 per cent. Rest of the states that experienced a population growth higher than or close to the national average saw a

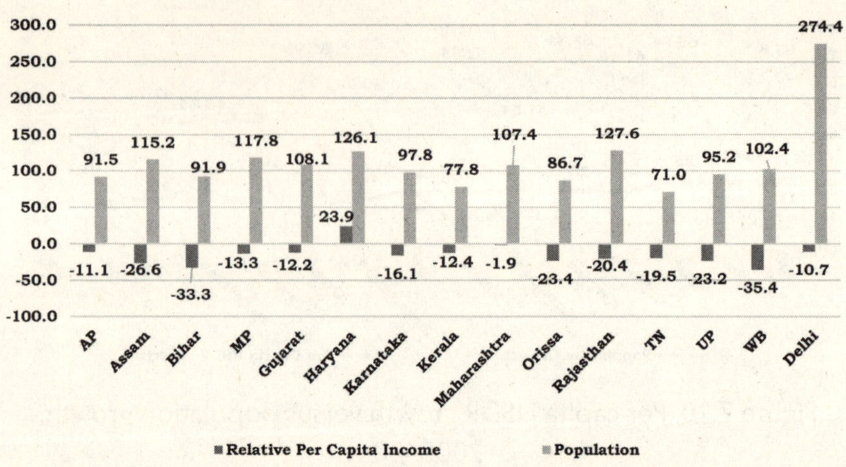

Figure 7.11: Relative per capita income and population growth percentage, 1960–90

Source: Table 7.2, Appendices

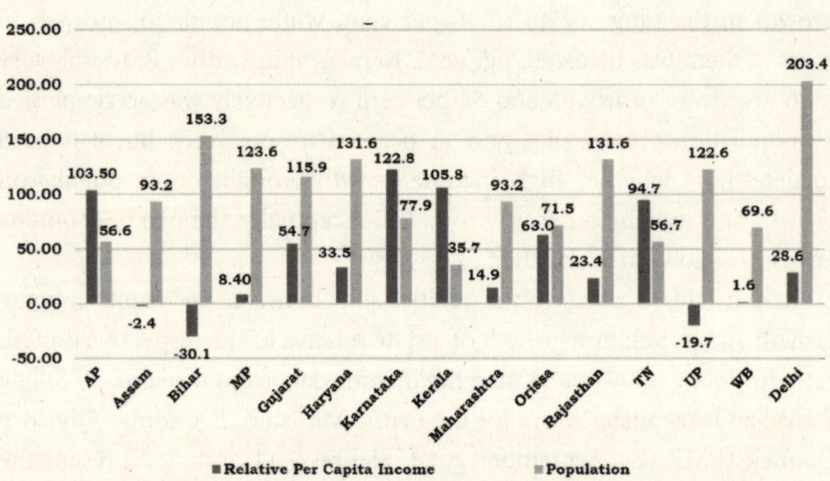

Figure 7.12: Relative per capita income and population growth percentage, 1990–2026

Source: Table 7.2, Appendices

negative growth in per capita income relative to the growth for India as a whole. The picture changes significantly for the period 1990–2026. Here, Gujarat, Haryana Rajasthan and Madhya Pradesh are the only states that experience a higher population growth than national average and also a positive growth in per capita income, although significantly less relative to India. Bihar and Uttar Pradesh had a higher growth in population than the national average, but had a negative growth in relative per capita income. For other states, with population growth rate less than that of India, there is a significantly less growth in per capita income. The exceptions in this case are Andhra Pradesh, Kerala, Karnataka and Tamil Nadu, where the growth in per capita income either exceeds or is close to that of India. In general, as noted earlier, the relationship between per capita income and population growth rate is not straightforward, especially the direction of causality.

III
The Economic Perspective: Literature Review

Having discussed the north–south divide in a wider national context, let us move to a more focused analysis of the economic dimension. From a review of relevant literature, it can be deduced that the economic side of the issue is closely linked to the phenomenon of divergence versus convergence which determines regional disparity. The subject has been of interest to scholars for long.

In a 1971 study undertaken by K.R.G. Nair, it was found that the interstate income differential was constant during 1950–60.[3] Another study done by M.D. Chaudhary in 1974 had similar findings for 1950–70.[4] Dholakia (1994) and Cashin and Sahay (1996) argue for convergence in terms of long-term Gross State Domestic Product (GSDP) growth rates for the periods 1960–90 and 1961–91 respectively.[5] Jha (2000) argues that across Indian states there is conditional convergence in terms of the levels of inequality and poverty measures.[6] Dasgupta, et al. (2000) argue that the states have diverged on GDP, but have shown convergence as far as the share of various sectors in the state GDP is concerned.[7]

However, there are scholars who see a clear divergence among Indian states. For instance, a study from 1984 found that for the period 1962–76, interstate inequalities of income had risen.[8] Other later studies, including that of Kurian (2000), reported divergence among Indian states.[9] Ghosh et al. (1998) also noted a diverging tendency among Indian states since the 1980s.[10] Marjit and Mitra (1996) point out that the states have been diverging in terms of per capita income.[11] A major study conducted by Sachs, Bajpai and Ramiah (2002) on fourteen major states found that between 1980 and 1998 there was a clear divergence among them in per capita income.[12] Moreover, this trend persisted during both pre-reform and post-reform periods.[13]

Apart from the various academic studies, there is a general view on the north–south divide suggesting that since Independence the south has out-performed the north in terms of economic indicators, which in turn impacted demographic indicators. This includes generating a larger GDP and thus contributing a larger share to India's story of development in the recent decades.[14] Taking this into consideration, it would be desirable to further probe the subject of economic performance along the north–south axis.

From an important long-term study of state-wise NSDP size and growth, authored by Sanjiv Sanyal and Aakanksha Arora for PMEAC in September 2024, cited earlier, some interesting observations can be made.[15] During 1960–90 (Figure 7.13) the percentage change in the share of GDP for north was under 1 per cent, but its share in population

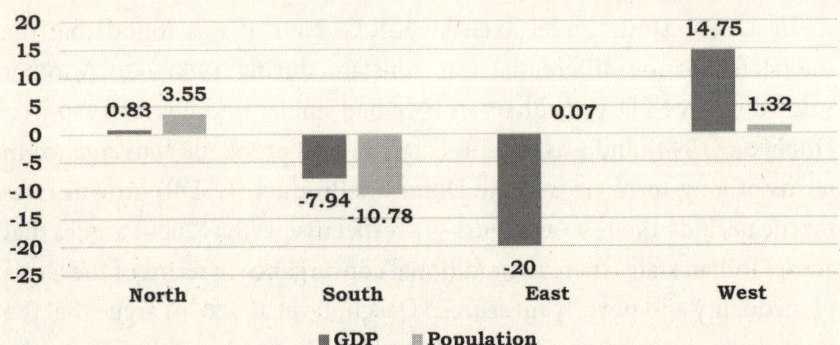

Figure 7.13: Percentage change in GDP and population share, 1960–90

Source: Table 7.3, Appendices

went up by more than 3.5 percentage points. The only other region that registered a positive change both in its GDP and population share was the west. The other two regions, the south and the east, saw a drop in their shares.[16] Figure 7.14 provides the change in GDP and population shares for the four regions analysed in this study for 1990–2026. While east shows a decline in both GDP and population shares, south shows a significant increase in its share of GDP and an equally significant decline in its share of population.[17]

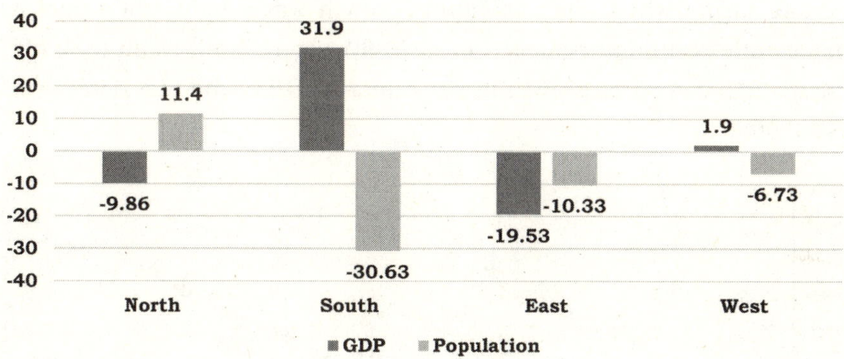

Figure 7.14: Percentage change in GDP and population share, 1990–2026

Source: Table 7.3, Appendices

IV
Per Capita Income and Poverty Levels: Uttar Pradesh versus Tamil Nadu

Let us turn to the relationship between per capita income and poverty incidence in a comparative analysis at state level. The comparison could begin by considering Tamil Nadu and Uttar Pradesh. This is indeed the method used in a study conducted by Paul and Sridhar (2015). They compare the two states on per capita income and poverty over a four-decade period starting in the 1960s. The analysis reveals that as late as 2006-07, Uttar Pradesh (Rs 2,46,998 crore) had a higher NSDP than Tamil Nadu (Rs 1,77,335 crore) at 1999–2000 prices.[18] Since Uttar Pradesh consistently had a much larger population than Tamil Nadu, only a per capita income comparison would provide a real picture of their economic wellbeing. Tamil Nadu's per capita income stood at Rs 5,053 in 1960-61, versus Uttar Pradesh's at Rs 3,338, a significant difference of 51 per cent.[19] The gap narrowed down to 39 per cent in the early 1980s.[20] Around 1987, it began to widen in favour of Tamil Nadu. So, the economic divergence between the two states is a relatively recent phenomenon. Tamil Nadu has had a higher per capita NSDP since 1960-61. However, Uttar Pradesh was only a notch below it for three decades until the late 1980s—a period during which their economic growth was roughly the same. A major inflexion point occurred in 1986-87, when Tamil Nadu took off. Figure 7.15 compares growth in per capita NSDP of the two states over 1960–90.

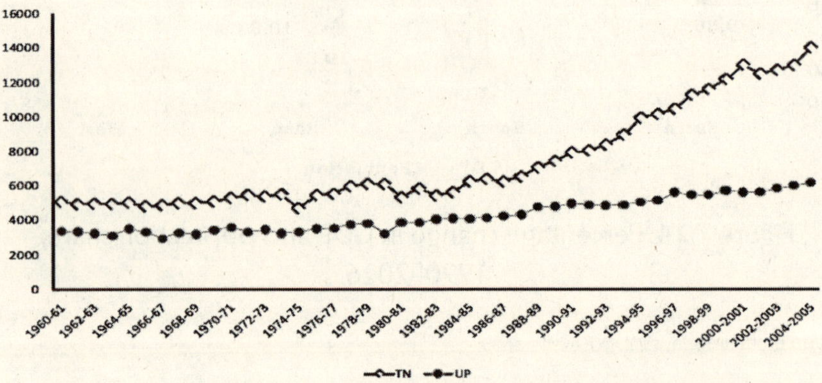

Figure 7.15: Comparison of per capita NSDP of Uttar Pradesh and Tamil Nadu

Source: Paul & Sridhar (2015)[21]

Paul and Sridhar (2015) also compare poverty levels in the two states. The comparison for rural poverty in 1960 seems skewed against Tamil Nadu, with some estimates showing that in 1960 rural poverty in the state was exceptionally high at 70 per cent, while in Uttar Pradesh it was at 48 per cent.[22] As for overall poverty, in 1973 both states had a similar proportion of population living below the poverty line, but Uttar Pradesh's poverty line dropped below that of Tamil Nadu's around 1975, as Figure 7.16 shows.

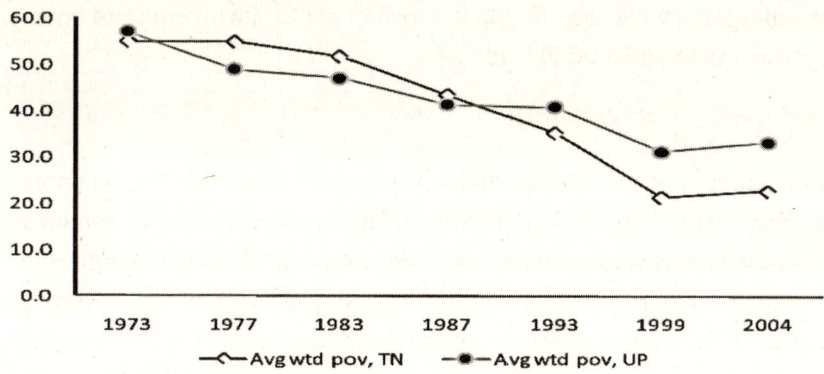

Figure 7.16: Comparison of poverty ratios of Uttar Pradesh and Tamil Nadu

Source: Paul and Sridhar (2015)[23]

Figure 7.16 shows that Uttar Pradesh maintained a lower poverty ratio than Tamil Nadu until 1987. After that year, its poverty ratio has remained consistently above that of Tamil Nadu. This comes as no surprise, given the fact that it is from 1987 that Tamil Nadu's per capita NSDP surged ahead, while Uttar Pradesh continued to grow at the earlier rates until 2004–05, with only a marginal increase. Paul and Sridhar (2015), therefore, question the notion that historically the south has outperformed the north.[24] They argue that until the 1960s there was a large migration of labour from the south to the north in search of greener pastures—a trend that has now been reversed with greater migration from north to south.[25] They also argue that for much of the period after Independence, there was no clear gap in governance between Uttar Pradesh and Tamil Nadu.

This assumes significance because it is the good-governance logic that is often cited by leaders from the south while demanding a larger proportion of the resources allocated by the Finance Commission or continuation of the 1976 embargo on delimitation and reallocation of Parliament seats. This view has also gained popular ground in recent times—an indication of which is discernible from a story in *India Today* published in 2013, which concluded that 'quality of governance and better leadership has led to southern states surging ahead of their northern counterparts, widening the gap in terms of per capita income and poverty between the South and North'.[26]

—~—

The current north–south divide in terms of social and economic development is at times sought to be explained in a geographical framework of coastal areas versus hinterland. Thus, Ramachandra Guha argues that the peninsular region of India had significant geographical advantages vis-à-vis the north, especially its proximity to the sea, which historically provided better access to international trade routes.[27] Guha further argues that having inherited a past that was marked by trade links with foreign countries, the south had an advantage over the landlocked north India, and in independent India, as and when it found the opportunity to grow rapidly, the south was able to capitalise on it. Guha's explanation merely echoes an influential viewpoint in the field of economic history that emphasises the superior economic opportunities enjoyed by coastal areas in most parts of the world as against interior regions.

The fundamental problem with this viewpoint is that most of the evidence on which it is based comes from the last two centuries during which European maritime empires, whose natural focus was on coastal economic development, ruled much of the world. International maritime trade, of course, flourished in India and many other parts of the world for at least two thousand years before the advent of European empires. It may be safely asserted that coastal regions in India and elsewhere must have benefitted from it. That is, however, not the same as arguing that these regions possessed any intrinsic advantage over the agricultural plains located farther from the sea. To establish this comparison, a thorough case-by-case examination of coastal versus inland areas would be necessary—considering the fact that the principal source of wealth revolved around agriculture and trade—along with the corresponding advantages and disadvantages associated with each area.

For the Indian subcontinent, it can be said that while peninsular India may have had some advantage in international trade, it must not be ignored that much of the trade in pre-modern times was land-based, and was conducted across continents through caravan routes, and that the north had a very substantial role to play in Eurasian trade for thousands of years. Moreover, the vast agricultural plains of the north clearly outperformed peninsular India in agricultural productivity as well as output. This assumes importance because in pre-modern history it was agriculture, and not trade, that was the most important source of wealth and income in most parts of the world; the exception being micro-regions that had long specialised in international trade and possessed an inherent advantage that facilitated their long-term success. While peninsular India may have had such micro-regions, there is no convincing evidence to show that the entire region, or even large parts of it, possessed such an advantage. In any case, the focus of this book is on demographic growth and political representation. The economic aspect is touched upon only in relation to the north–south demographic divide.

Kerala versus Uttar Pradesh

Let us now compare Kerala's and Uttar Pradesh's per capita NSDP, as shown in Figure 7.17. It shows that Kerala's NSDP per capita growth moved ahead of Uttar Pradesh only from 1990–91. However, simply comparing the absolute figures might not be sufficient. How Kerala and Uttar Pradesh have fared in terms of percentage changes in their per capita NSDPs is also important. The comparison of the growth rates of per capita NSDP of the two states between 1971 and 2009 is shown in Figure 7.18.

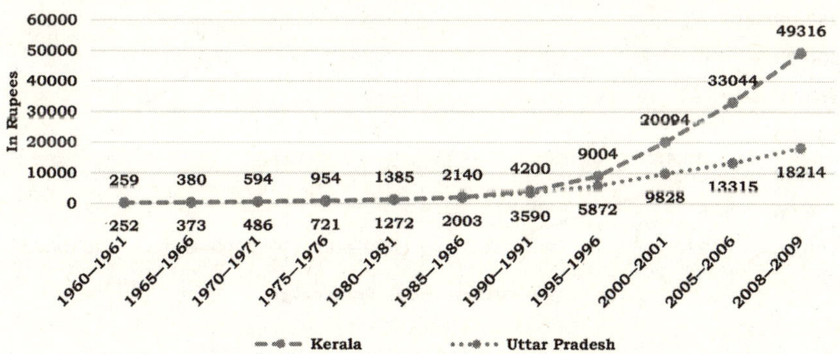

Figure 7.17: Comparison of per capita NSDP for the states of Kerala and Uttar Pradesh, 1960-61 to 2008-09

Source: indiastat.com (Table 7.4, Appendices)

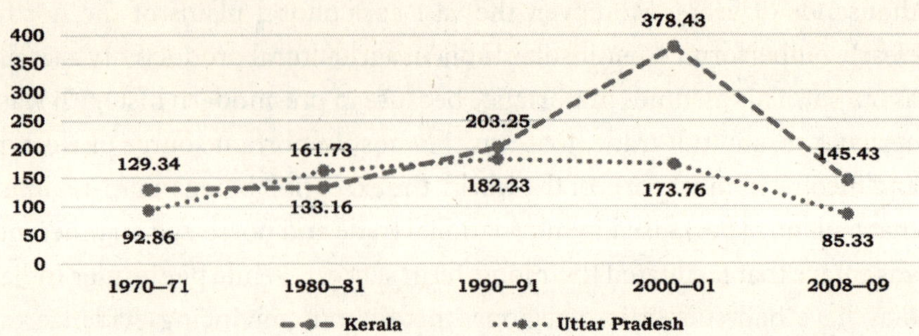

Figure 7.18: Comparison of the growth rate of per capita NSDP for the states of Kerala and Uttar Pradesh, 1970-71 to 2008-09

Source: indiastat.com (Table 7.5, Appendices)

For nearly two decades following 1970–71, the two curves have similar values on the Y-axis which represents the growth rate of per capita NSDP. It is only after 1990–91 that Kerala grew at an exceptionally high rate, while Uttar Pradesh's growth declined slightly, creating a gap that existed until 2008–09. Thus, it is relevant to see how the difference in growth rates of per capita NSDP between the two states has played out during this period, depicted in Figure 7.19.

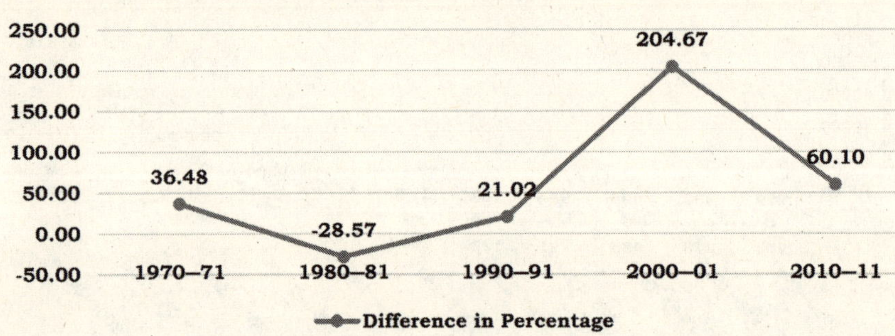

Figure 7.19: Curve showing the difference of the rate of growth of per capita NSDP between the states of Kerala and Uttar Pradesh, 1970-71 to 2010-11

Source: indiastat.com (Table 7.5, Appendices)

It can be seen from Figure 7.19 that until 1990–91 the difference in per capita NSDP growth of the two states was insignificant. In fact, in the decade ending 1980–81, the difference was negative, which would indicate that the per capita NSDP of Uttar Pradesh grew faster than Kerala's. One may, therefore, relate the wide gap since 1991 to the economic reforms initiated by Prime Minister Narasimha Rao. Under the new economic regime, India's GDP growth took an upward turn, although the spurt was not uniform across states because of which economic divergence between the north and south widened considerably over the next two decades. The connection between the north's lower economic growth and its population growth during much of the post-reform period would need further investigation.

Let us also examine the relationship between the growth rates of population and per capita NSDP in Uttar Pradesh and Kerala. Presented in Figures 7.20 and 7.21 are two curves showing the variations in per capita NSDP of the two states with respect to their population growth rates.

Figures 7.20 and 7.21 indicate that there is no visible association between population growth rates and per capita NSDP either for Kerala or for Uttar Pradesh. There has been a gradual decline in Kerala's population growth rate since 1971, but its NSDP growth rate shows a rise only between 1981 and 2001, after which it declines. Uttar Pradesh presents a more interesting case. Its population growth rate has hovered around the 20 per

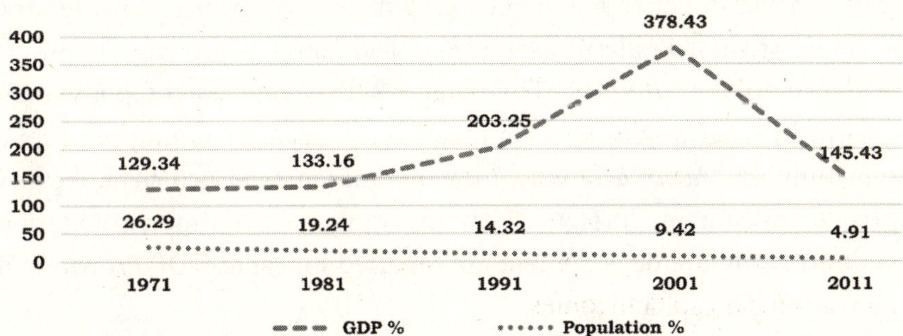

Figure 7.20: Curves showing the variation in the rate of growth of per capita NSDP, and the rate of population growth for the state of Kerala, 1971 to 2011

Source: indiastat.com (Table 7.5, Appendices)

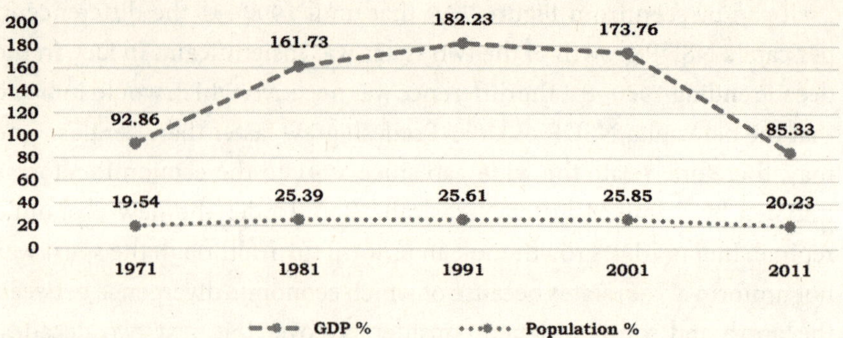

Figure 7.21: Curves showing the variation in the rate of growth of per capita NSDP, and the rate of population growth for the state of Uttar Pradesh, 1971 to 2011

Source: indiastat.com (Table 7.5, Appendices)

cent mark for all five decades, but the per capita NSDP has followed an inverted U-shaped pattern. This implies that changes in per capita NSDP in Uttar Pradesh have been accompanied by a corresponding change in population growth, although the former shows a sharper change. Thus, increase or decrease in population growth is accompanied by an increase or decrease in per capita NSDP growth. This is contrary to the general understanding of the issue.

It is frequently assumed that a fall in population growth rate should lead to a rise in per capita income growth, and vice versa. However, the example of Uttar Pradesh over 1961–71 to 2001–11 provides empirical evidence to the contrary. This suggests that the rate of population growth by itself might not be a major factor in determining per capita growth in the Indian economy. Instead, other factors such as public and private investment, foreign direct investment (FDI), industrialisation and infrastructure development are required for rapid GDP growth and increasing per capita incomes.

It is widely accepted that, other things being equal, an economy has a much higher chance of rapid GDP growth in the initial stages of decline in population growth experienced around the end of the second or the beginning of the third stage of demographic transition. During this period, the youth dependency ratio goes down and participation in labour force goes up. This is because the proportion of dependents, mostly children, to the total population starts going down. A high dependency ratio, especially one marked by a large proportion of children, not only means a reduced proportion of working people, but also forces public and private investment to be channelised in such a way that over the short-to-medium term, it becomes less productive in terms of GDP as well as per capita income growth. Conversely, a fall in the youth dependency ratio brings about a corresponding rise in the proportion of the working-age population, creating a 'demographic dividend' that provides a golden opportunity for rapid growth in GDP and per capita incomes usually for a few decades.[28] However, other enabling factors, such as education, health, infrastructure, investment, employment opportunities and openness to international trade, are required to take full advantage of this demographic dividend. There is no linear relationship between phases of population growth and economic growth either in India or in other countries.

V
Population Growth Rate and Female Literacy

Educated women are known to take informed reproductive and healthcare decisions. These result in stabilisation of population. The India-born British economist Partha Dasgupta in a 1995 paper draws attention to the gendered nature of fertility decisions.[29] He points out that women often bear the greatest costs of high fertility, both in terms of health risks and the burden of childcare, but they have less decision-making power within households. As a result, fertility rates tend to be higher in societies with greater gender inequality. Dasgupta highlights the importance of female education and economic empowerment in reducing fertility rates, as these factors give women more control over reproductive decisions[30]. It should be noted that the link runs mostly through improved female literacy, influencing a decline in fertility rate, better infant care, which is then reflected in lower birth rates and infant mortality rates. The latter further influences the fertility rate over time and thus lowers population growth rate. Figures 7.22 to 7.26 explore the relationship between the two variables at the national and regional levels.

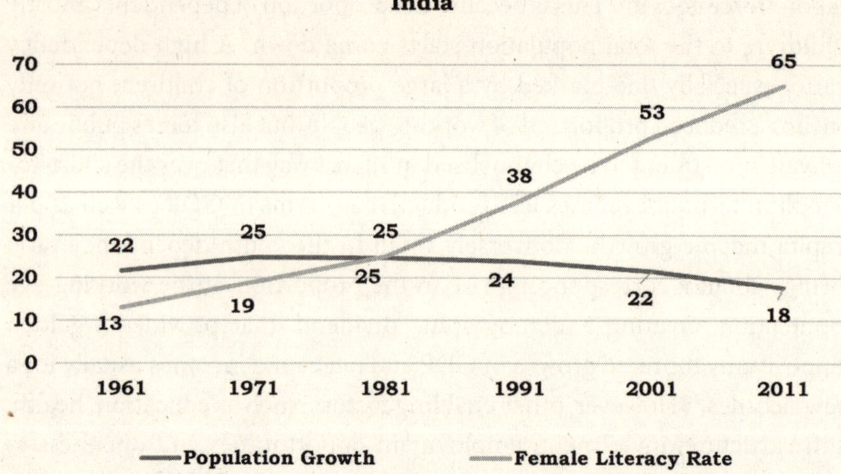

Figure 7.22: Population growth and female literacy rates, 1961–2011

Source: Table 7.6, Appendices

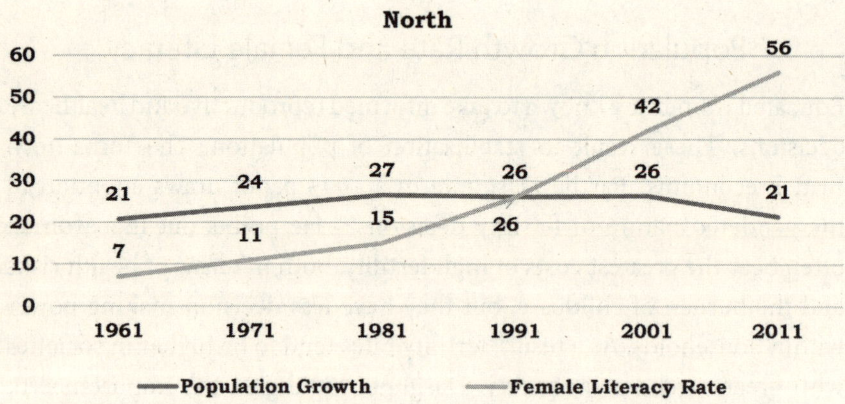

Figure 7.23: Population growth and female literacy rates for north, 1961–2011

Source: Table 7.6, Appendices

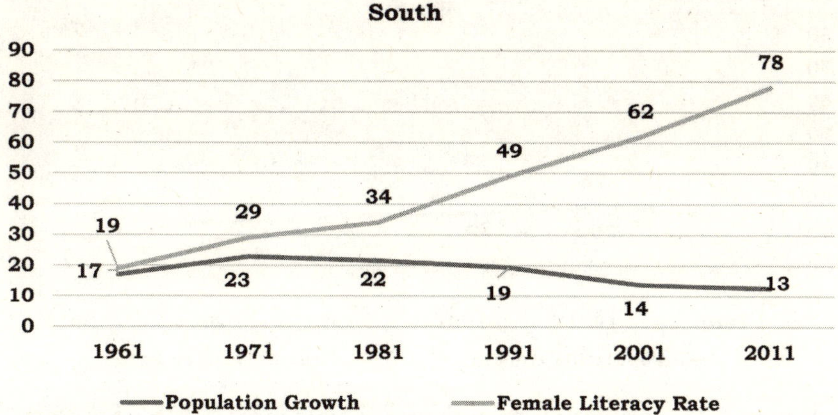

Figure 7.24 :Population growth and female literacy rates for south, 1961–2011

Source: Table 7.6, Appendices

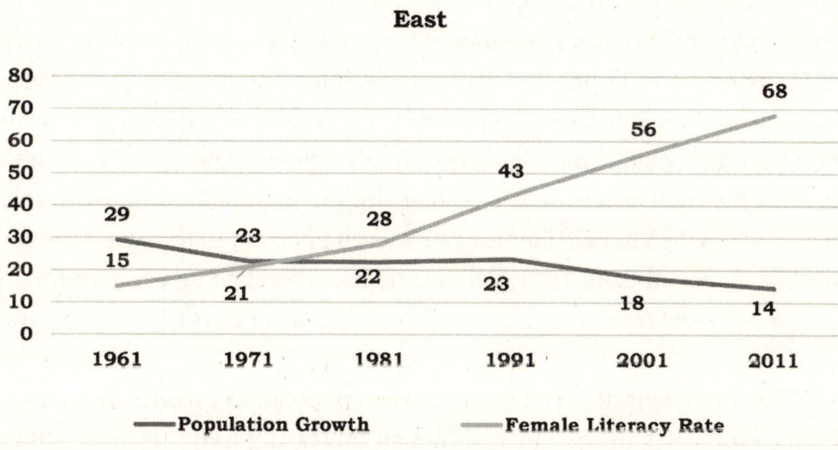

Figure 7.25: Population growth and female literacy rates for east, 1961–2011

Source: Table 7.6, Appendices

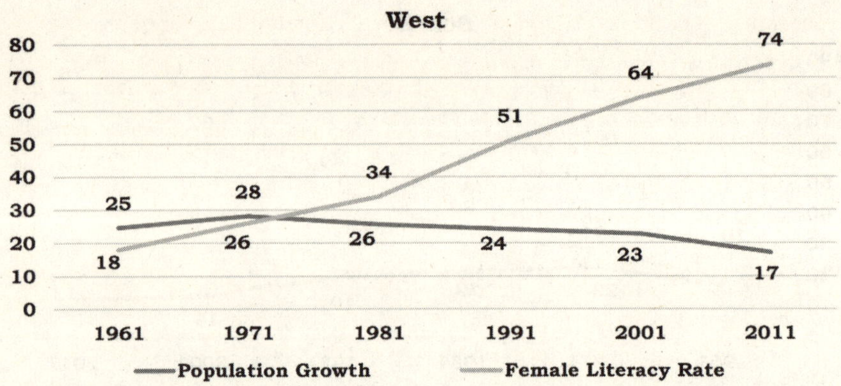

Figure 7.26: Population growth and female literacy rates for west, 1961–2011

Source: Table 7.6, Appendices

Figures 7.23 to 7.26 show the relationship between female literacy rate and population growth rate at the regional level. It can be seen that the female literacy rate was less than half for north (7 per cent) relative to south (19 per cent), in 1961. For east and west, it was comparable to south at 15 per cent and 18 per cent respectively. Interestingly, as soon as female literacy rate touches about 25 per cent the decline in population growth rate becomes visible and significant in all regions. The figure for south is most instructive, showing a secular decline in population growth rate from 1971, when female literacy rate was 29 per cent. In the west also, the decline occurred from 1971, when its female literacy rate was around 26 per cent; in east from 1991; in north, too, this decline is visible from 1991 with a female literacy rate of 26 per cent.

The coefficient of correlation between population growth and female literacy for states in the north shows an increasing trend from -0.258 in 1971 to -0.865 in 2011. For the south, it is 0.841 in 1971 and -0.972 in 2011. The same for all India moves from -0.235 in 1971 to -0.855 in 2011.

VI

Demographic Divergence and Urbanisation in India

Among the major drivers of demographic transition, urbanisation is often thought to be of significance for India as well. States in India have experienced different rates of urbanisation, leading to a difference in the corresponding cultural impact associated with the process. This cultural change is sometimes taken to be the driving force behind the shift in fertility norms. Chinmay Tumbe (2016) contradicts this cultural argument by pointing to mortality and fertility changes as the causal agents of the overall pace of urbanisation in India. Drawing from the demographic divergence between India's north and south, he asserts that in the north demographic transition arrived late, which is also the reason the growth rate of urbanisation in this region has slowed down.[31] Thus, a study of the varying rates of urbanisation versus population growth among Indian states needs to be undertaken in order to appreciate the difference in the timeline of the various phases of demographic transition. Comparing the two trajectories for the period 1901–2011, Figure 7.27 shows a similarity with global trends.

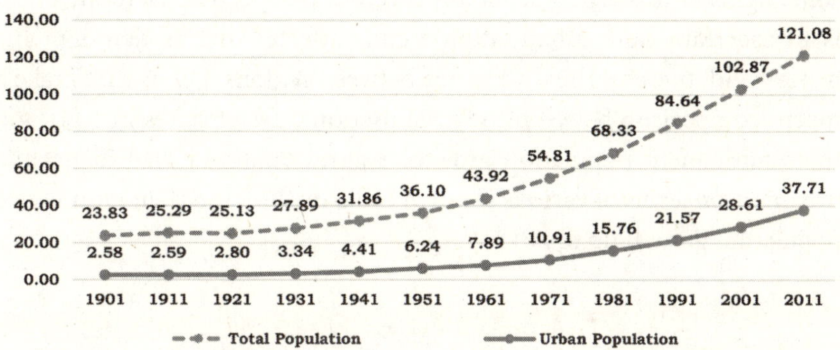

Figure 7.27: Trends in growth of total population and urban population in India (in Rs crore), 1901–2011

Source: Office of Registrar General, Census 2011 (Table 7.7, Appendices)

The two curves depicted in Figure 7.27 show an upswing, although at different rates. This implies a close relationship between the growth of urban population and of the total population in India from 1901 to 2011. It could, thus, be argued that urbanisation is intertwined with demographic transition and should be seen as one of the drivers of the cultural change often referred to as 'modernisation', which, among other things, indicates increased availability of health facilities required for family planning, even if it is ineffective as far as population control is concerned. There is a view that stagnation in agricultural productivity and low rural female literacy levels in large parts of India have resulted in deceleration of the urbanisation process, delaying the later stages of demographic transition.[32] Of course, the limited expansion of the manufacturing sector in urban areas has rendered it into a weak pull factor.

—w—

Let us now examine the relationship between urbanisation and population growth in India. This is done both by comparing urbanisation and population growth rates of various states and regions, and by making a focused comparison between Kerala and Uttar Pradesh. It has been hypothesised by Tim Dyson (2010, 2011) that urbanisation as a process is intertwined with demographic transition.[33] Chapter 3 sheds some light on this aspect from a theoretical perspective. Here the effort is to ascertain how urbanisation trends affected India's demographic history and, thereby, the divergence between regions. Let us first make a macro comparison between the urbanisation rates of states in 1951 and their subsequent population growth. Figures 7.28 and 7.29 depict the urbanisation levels of various states of India in 1951 and their cumulative population growth up to 2011.

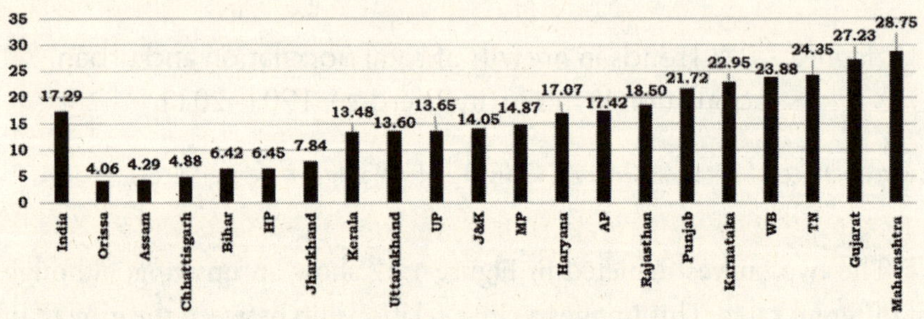

Figure 7.28: Urban population share (percentage), 1951

Source: Table 7.8, Appendices

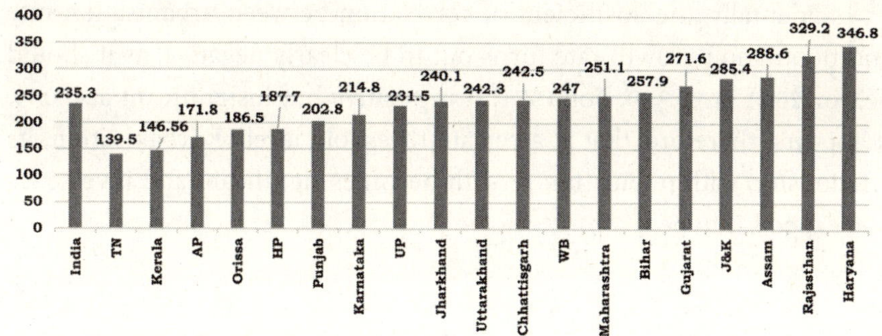

Figure 7.29: Population growth (percentage), 1951–2011

Source: Table 5.1, Appendices

It can be seen from these charts that in 1951 the urbanisation rate of India was 17.29 per cent, and that states such as Maharashtra, Gujarat, Tamil Nadu, West Bengal, Karnataka, Punjab, Rajasthan and Andhra Pradesh were above the national average. Did the higher urbanisation of these states affect their cumulative population growth from 1951 to 2011? No clear pattern emerges if we use India's growth of 235.34 per cent as a benchmark and analyse which states fall below that level and which states are above it. While Tamil Nadu (139.5 per cent), Andhra Pradesh (171.8 per cent), Karnataka (214.8 per cent) and Punjab (202.8 per cent) had lower population growth, the same was true for many states with urbanisation levels below the national average, such as Kerala, Orissa, Himachal Pradesh and Uttar Pradesh. Conversely, among the fast-growing states are those that had higher urbanisation levels in 1951. Thus, Rajasthan (329.2 per cent), Gujarat (271.6 per cent), Maharashtra (251.1 per cent) and West Bengal (247 per cent) had higher cumulative growth. What happens if we take the six states whose urbanisation was above 20 per cent in 1951? Once again, there is no clear relationship, because out of these six states—which were also the six most urbanised states in India—Gujarat, Maharashtra and West Bengal had growth rates above the national average, while Karnataka (214.8 per cent), Punjab (202.8) and Tamil Nadu (139.5 per cent) were below it. Conversely, the states with low urbanisation levels such as Orissa (186.5), Himachal Pradesh (187.7) and Uttar Pradesh (231.5) experienced growth below the national average.

Incidentally, the coefficient of correlation between urbanisation rate and population growth rate turns out to be clearly negative, as it should be, for 2011 at -0.339. For 1971, it is positive but insignificant at 0.059. It appears, therefore, that at a certain threshold level of urbanisation, its relationship with population growth becomes significant and inverse, as one expects it to be.

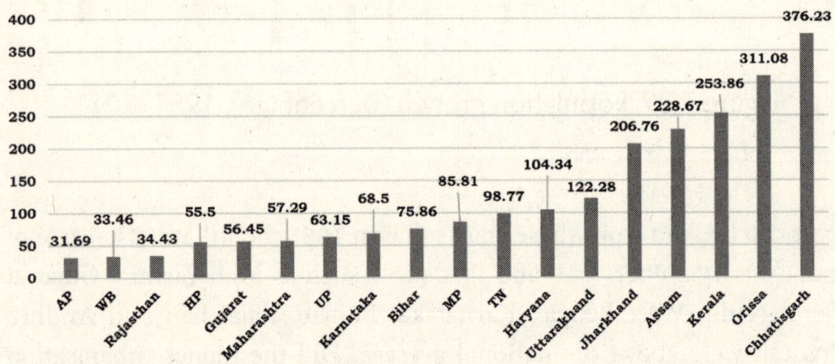

Figure 7.30: Urbanisation growth (percentage), 1951–2011

Source: Table 7.8, Appendices

Another way of analysing the data could be to compare the percentage change in the rate of urbanisation of each state with its cumulative population growth over 1951–2011 (Figure 7.30). Here, the top ten performers turn out to be Chhattisgarh, Orissa, Kerala, Assam, Jharkhand, Uttarakhand, Haryana, Tamil Nadu, Madhya Pradesh and Bihar. Out of these, six (Haryana, Assam, Gujarat, Bihar, Chhattisgarh and Uttarakhand) are also among the top in terms of population growth. Conversely, Andhra Pradesh and Himachal Pradesh, both among the states with lowest population growth, also witnessed smaller increase in urbanisation rate. So, the pattern was mixed. Let us take 1971–2011 for the same comparison, using Figures 7.31 and 7.32.

It is seen from Figure 7.32 that in growth of urbanisation rate Kerala, Chhattisgarh, Orissa, Haryana, Uttarakhand, Uttar Pradesh, Tamil Nadu, Assam, Karnataka and Gujarat were the top ten states. Interestingly, five of them (Haryana, Uttar Pradesh, Gujarat, Uttarakhand and Chhattisgarh) were also among the ten states with the highest cumulative population growth. Conversely, states with lower urbanisation growth, such as Jharkhand, Madhya Pradesh, Maharashtra and Rajasthan experienced high population growth. It should be noted that in this analysis base effect can become very important. On the one hand, states with a very low urbanisation rate in 1951 or 1971 (Chhattisgarh, Orissa and Assam) show disproportionate growth in percentage terms. On the other, states with relatively higher initial rates of urbanisation such as Maharashtra, Gujarat, Rajasthan and Madhya Pradesh show lower growth. While it is generally accepted that higher level and growth of urbanisation is in some way related to lower population growth over the long term, this depends upon many other factors.

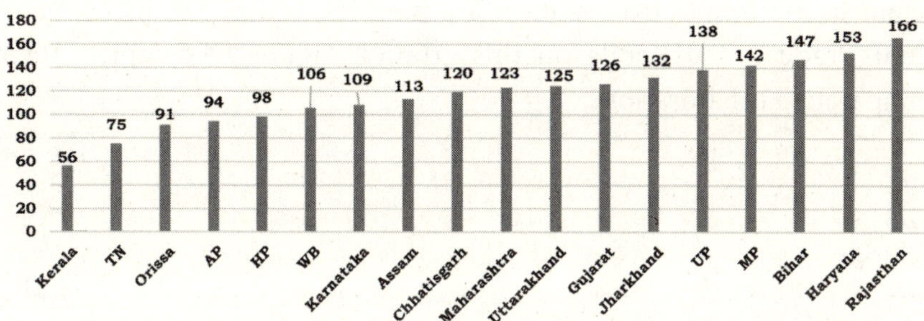

Figure 7.31: Population growth (percentage), 1971–2011

Source: Table 5.1, Appendices

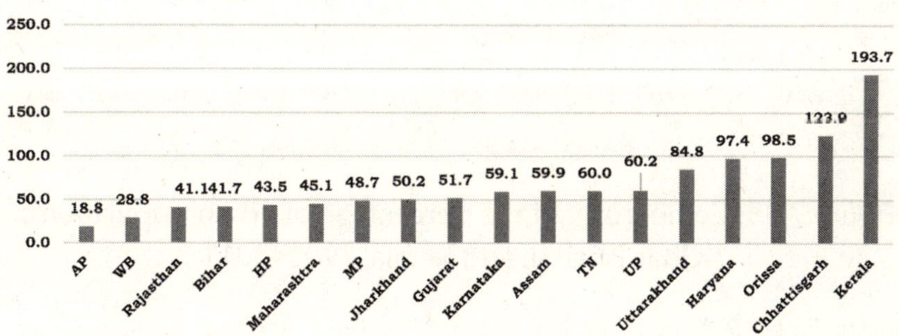

Figure 7.32: Urbanisation growth (percentage), 1971–2011

Source: Table 7.8, Appendices

VII
Urbanisation and Demographic Growth: Revisiting the North–South Divide

Having analysed the link between urbanisation and demographic transition for all major states, let us move to a focused north-south comparison, employing Uttar Pradesh and Kerala. It has been claimed that Kerala had always been a trading hub for merchants from Arab lands, but it gained renewed vigour in the twelfth and thirteenth centuries when Chinese trade on India's southwest coast flourished and revolutionised the cultural milieu of Kerala, giving rise to 'urbanism'.[34] Without delving deeper into the long-term historical advantages that the state had with respect to urbanisation, we need to examine recent urbanisation trends from a comparative perspective. Let us compare Uttar Pradesh and Kerala on this ground. Figure 7.33 depicts their comparative urbanisation:

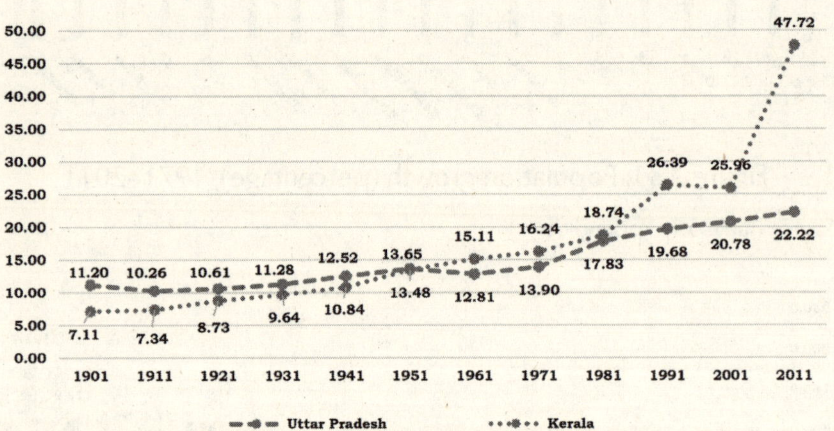

Figure 7.33: Comparison of the percentage of urban population in Uttar Pradesh and Kerala, 1901–2011

Source: Table 7.9, Appendices

It should also be interesting to see how the two states urbanised in relation to the national rate of urbanisation (Figure 7.34).

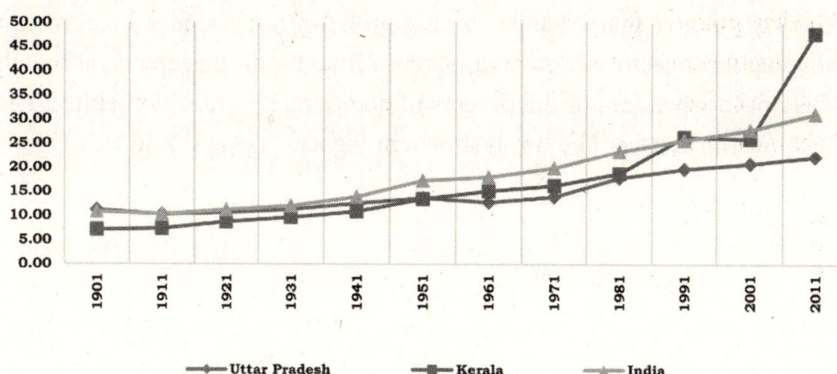

Figure 7.34: Comparison of the percentage of urban population in Uttar Pradesh and Kerala, 1901–2011 vis-à-vis percentage of urban population in India

Source: Table 7.9, Appendices

Figure 7.33 shows that, as late as 1981, Uttar Pradesh and Kerala showed convergence on urbanisation. In the Census of 1951, their urban shares were almost identical, and they showed little divergence over the next three decades. Figure 7.34 shows that both states lagged the national average until 1981. It should also be noted that Kerala's fertility rate had begun to decline after 1971, but its urbanisation rate jumped up only after 2001. So, higher levels of urbanisation did not precede the decline in fertility. Rather, the level of urbanisation in Kerala has risen rapidly during the phase of decline in population growth rate, likely as a result of the economic take-off which Kerala and other coastal states—with the exception of Orissa—experienced in the wake of the 1991 economic reforms of Prime Minister Narasimha Rao. This economic upswing, along with other factors, had the subsidiary effect of widening the development gap of these states with the so-called BIMARU or EAG (Empowered Action Group) states. What is especially relevant for this study is the relationship between the economic take-off and the decline in population growth, both of which are generally associated with increased urbanisation.

Kerala's story of demographic transition stands in contrast to that of Uttar Pradesh, where urbanisation levels kept rising along with rise in the population growth rate. The implication is that while both states have undergone demographic transition, different dynamics have been at play.

The key point is that urbanisation has probably not played a direct role in shaping the trajectory of India's apparent demographic divergence, although it is not independent of the process of demographic transition either. The relationship between the two is shown in Figures 7.35 and 7.36.

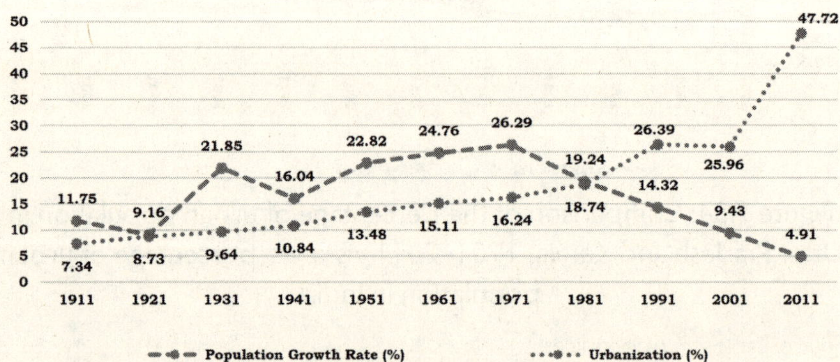

Figure 7.35: Variation of population growth rate with the proportion of urban population in Kerala, 1911–2011

Source: Tables 5.1 and 7.9, Appendices

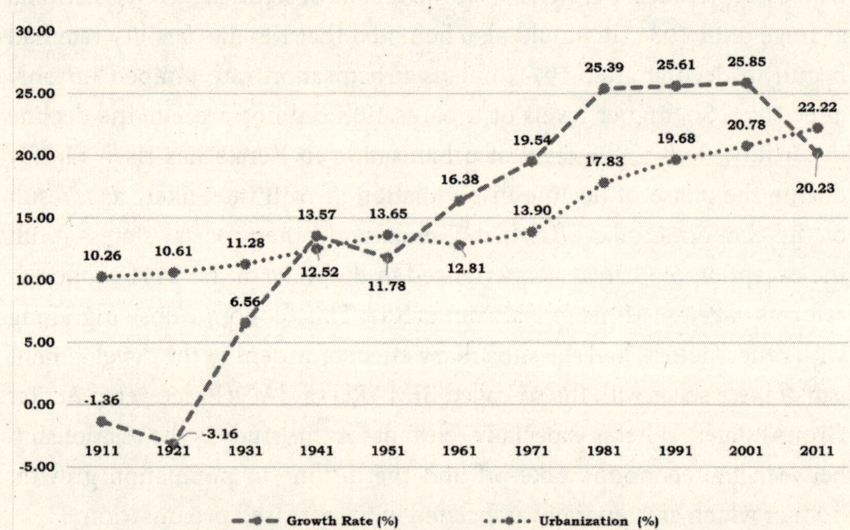

Figure 7.36: Variation of population growth rate with the proportion of urban population in Uttar Pradesh, 1911–2011

Source: Tables 5.1 and 7.9, Appendices

For both states, as urbanisation reaches a threshold, population growth rate is likely to fall, perhaps because of an increased preference for small families. This stems partly from the growing economic pressure that people face in making a living in urban areas.[35]

—~—

The comparative study of Uttar Pradesh and Kerala shows that there is little substantive difference in the relationship between their demographic growth and level of urbanisation. The only difference lies in the timing. Both states exhibit a loop for sixty years, which for Kerala occurred from 1921 to 1981 and for Uttar Pradesh from 1951 to 2011. A similar point of difference between the trajectories of demographic divergence in these two states was noted earlier on comparing the population growth rates alone. It was found that the processes have been broadly similar in the two states, separated only by a gap of three decades.

The rising level of urbanisation has, of course, been a global phenomenon in the twentieth century, India being no exception. Urbanisation is closely related to growth in GDP and per capita incomes, which in turn influence fertility and population growth. The significance of the urbanisation–economic growth link in India has been summed up brilliantly in a paper written by Sachs, Bajpai and Ramiah in 2002:

> A remarkable 82 per cent of the cross-state variation in growth is explained by just the urbanization variable in India, and with no hint of any conditional convergence after controlling for the degree of urbanization. The regression estimate shows that a 10-percentage-point higher rate of urbanization is associated with 1.3 percentage points per year higher annual growth.[36]

While the relationship between economic growth and urbanisation is exemplified in the higher levels of urbanisation achieved by the south and west over the last thirty years of rapid economic growth, the relationship between urbanisation and population growth in India is indeterminate. Population growth, which depends on a multitude of factors, kept rising along with rising urbanisation levels in India, only to start dropping in some states once a certain threshold level of urbanisation had been attained.

It appears, therefore, that the evidence linking urbanisation and population growth in post-Independence India is, at best, tenuous. Perhaps it is not so much the statistical level of urbanisation—which gets skewed in states with one large metropolitan centre, such as with Maharashtra, Tamil Nadu, West Bengal and Gujarat—that influences reduction in fertility and population growth rates. Instead, it might be the diffusion of urban norms and culture caused by a wider geographical distribution of urban areas, as seen in Kerala. This state has long exhibited an urban-rural continuum without having any very large city; and this urban influence has been associated with declines in fertility and growth rates.

The focused analysis of the global drivers or correlates of demographic transition undertaken in this chapter to assess their significance for India, in particular to explain the apparent north–south divide in the country, shows a mixed pattern. The three factors examined for their relationship with population growth rate—income growth and level, literacy rate, and urbanisation—in the two regions show a complex association with demographic growth. Out of the three drivers analysed, the relationship between female literacy and population growth stands out. While per capita income growth and urbanisation levels have played a role in population growth, there is no clear pattern visible.

8

Demography and Development in World Perspective (1500–2024)

The analytical approach followed in this book so far has focused mostly on comparing the population growth rates of states and regions over one-and-a-half centuries. This chapter addresses the supposed demographic divide in India from a tangential perspective. It does this by first situating India's demographic transition within the context of world demographic history over the last half-a-millennium, which gives us a glimpse into how this transition has unfolded in other parts of the world. Secondly, this chapter analyses the relationship between population growth and variable economic and social development in different parts of India by using the Census of India's 2011 classification of the population of the country into Empowered Action Group (EAG) versus non-EAG. This classification is based on variations in the social and economic development of the two groups.

I

India and World Demographic History: *The Longue Durée*

The interplay of the forces of demographic divergence and convergence in India since the nineteenth century needs to be situated in the wider context of world demographic history over the last few centuries. That would provide a suitable frame of reference for interpreting the vast amount of demographic data presented in *Demography, Representation, Delimitation* so far and help develop an appropriate comparative framework. Such an exercise would be helpful in illuminating the less understood aspects of India's historical demographics and would debunk myths about the demographic trajectory that India and its various regions, especially the north and the south, have followed during modern times.

Fortunately, we have comprehensive estimates of historical demographics prepared by two of the leading economic historians of the contemporary era, Paul Bairoch and Angus Maddison. Though the statistics compiled by them are only broad estimates and are not based on historical censuses—which for most of human history were either non-existent or were sporadic exercises undertaken for specific economic or military purposes—they have been accepted by scholars and experts the world over as broadly correct estimates that can be gainfully employed for macro studies in the realms of population and economy. The estimates help reconstruct a reasonably reliable demographic picture of the world before the nineteenth century, during which most of the systematic census efforts began in the West and some other parts of the world.

There are, of course, other estimates, such as those by British polymath, historian, demographer and psychiatrist Colin McEvedy; American sociologist and demographer Ralph Thomlinson; and British-Australian economist and statistician Colin Grant Clark. Estimates of India's historical demography during the Mughal Empire have also been made by Indian historians such as Irfan Habib and Shireen Moosvi.

These historical estimates about the size and growth of population in different parts of the world are extremely helpful for micro and regional studies and are regularly used to understand the role of population in the evolution of human societies. To keep our comparative study simple, however, it is better to take just one comprehensive series of estimates to situate India's demographic history in the world context. Since British economist Angus Maddison's estimates are more comprehensive than those of Swiss economist Paul Bairoch, they can be used for our limited purpose, although without in any way underestimating the equally important contribution made by Bairoch to the field of historical demographics.

Let us see how demographic transition has unfolded and how the world population has changed over the last 500 years, starting from around AD 1500. This was the time when Europeans embarked upon maritime explorations and colonial conquests in the so-called New World as well as Asia, which was the largest and the most important region of the Old World. In 1500, the estimated population of the world, including the New World, the Americas, was 43,84,28,000, of which India had the largest share at 25.1 per cent. Over the next hundred years, it would go up to 55,61,48,000, which adds up to a growth of 26.85 per cent—probably the fastest growth for the world in a century until then. The detailed population movement of various countries, regions and continents in the sixteenth century is presented in Figure 8.1.

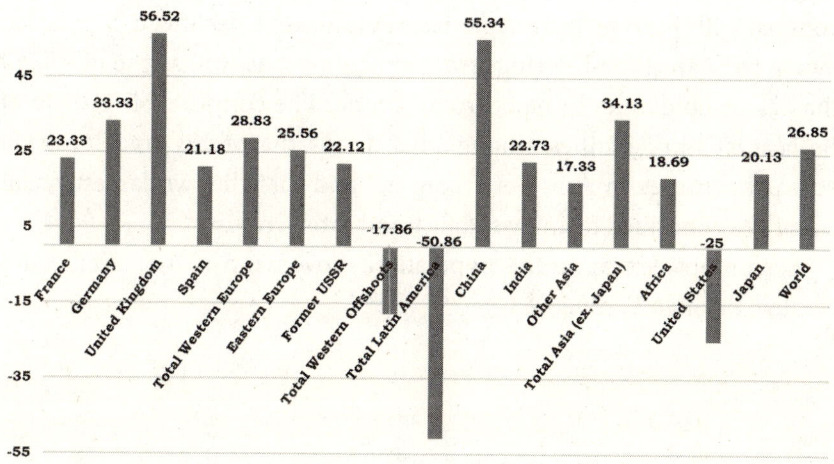

Figure 8.1: Population growth in the world (percentage), 1500–1600

Source: Table 8.1, Appendices

It can be observed that the bulk of the growth during the sixteenth century took place in Western Europe (28.83 per cent), India (22.73 per cent), China (55.34 per cent) and Africa (18.69 per cent), while North America and Latin America lost heavily. Among the countries that experienced rapid growth, the United Kingdom and China were outliers, growing at twice the pace of the world and nearly three times the pace of other countries, which grew close to 20 per cent.

Analysing the trends, it is evident that Western Europe's population grew significantly in the sixteenth century, probably because of hugely increased availability of food and other resources, including gold and silver from the Americas, which vastly added to the prosperity of the region and translated into higher population growth. What should be emphasised here is that in contrast with contemporary times when higher prosperity above a threshold leads to slower population growth or stagnation (even as standards of living improve), for most of pre-modern history increased access to resources and prosperity resulted in higher population growth. With increased prosperity, people preferred to have more children, who, in turn, had better chances of survival into adulthood. Additionally, increased nutrition and access to resources in general improved health standards and lowered mortality rates. In contrast with Europe, Latin America saw a massive decline in population owing to Spanish and Portuguese depredations, as well as the effects of the deadly epidemics brought from Europe. The considerable growth of India and China signifies, among other things, that at this time European colonial ventures in Asia were marginal and that the two largest Asian countries continued to enjoy stability and prosperity.

Let us now examine the population movement in the seventeenth century through Figure 8.2.

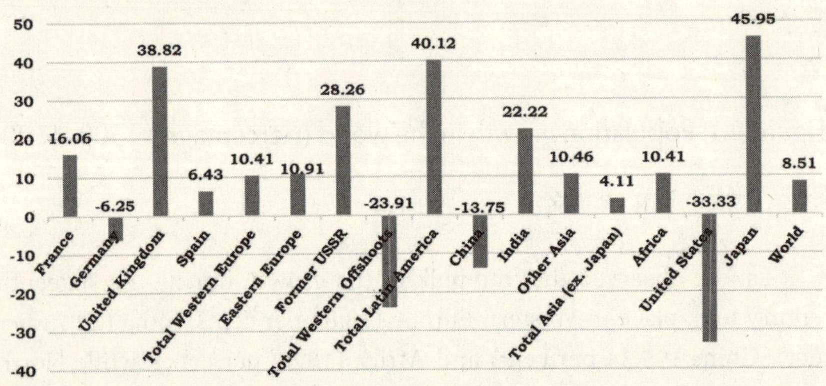

Figure 8.2: Population growth in the world (percentage), 1600–1700

Source: Table 8.1, Appendices

Between 1600 and 1700, the population of the world grew at a much slower pace than in the previous century, rising from 55,61,48,000 to 60,34,90,000—a growth of only 8.51 per cent. During this period, the distribution of the world population growth also changed significantly. At 38.81 per cent, the United Kingdom continued to outpace most other countries, except Japan, which grew at 45.95 per cent. Western Europe grew at 10.41 per cent, just above the world average; India grew at 22.22 per cent, twice the rate of world growth; Africa kept the pace at 10.41 per cent. Latin America rebounded in a big way, growing by more than 40 per cent, indicating that the initial demographic shock of European contact was subsiding, although this growth was on a low base. Among the most striking facts here is that for two centuries the United Kingdom outpaced the world population growth by nearly 100 per cent. This increase would obviously see its share in the world population rise, as will be discussed later.

Let us review the period between 1700 and 1820 through Figure 8.3.

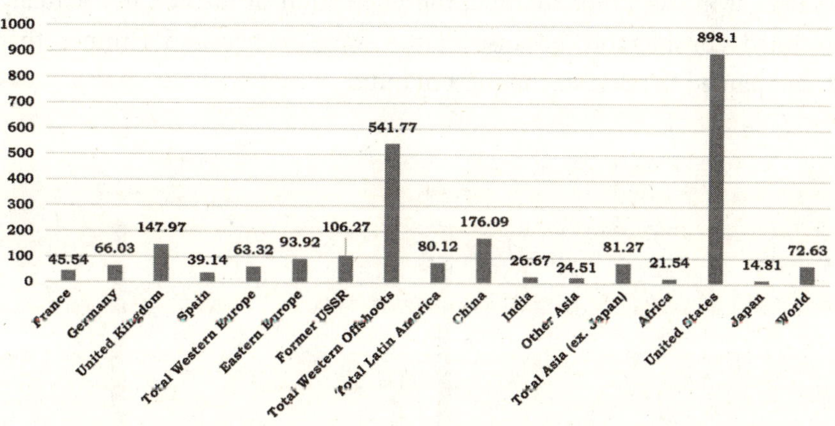

Figure 8.3: Population growth in the world (percentage), 1700–1820

Source: Table 8.1, Appendices

This was a transition period in world history. During the second half of this period, that is, 1750–1820, the West decisively emerged as the dominant power in the world, while large countries like India, China and the Ottoman Empire experienced decline. This is well reflected in the chart. While the world population grew by an unprecedented 72.63 per cent, from 60,34,90,000 to 1,04,18,34,000, the United Kingdom grew by 147.97 per cent; and the United States by 898.1 per cent, mainly because of large-scale migration from Europe, although the growth was on a very low base. China grew at 176.09 per cent and, coupled with a massive fall in India's share of the world population, raised its own share to 36.6 per cent. China could grow well, because it had still not come under the impact of European colonialism and had witnessed economic prosperity and social and political stability under the Manchu rule in the eighteenth century.

During this period, India grew by only 26.67 per cent, roughly one-third of the world growth rate. The rise of Western imperialism in India and other Asian countries was accompanied by the demographic expansion of the coloniser, Britain, and the contraction of India. Further, what these data about India hide is that population growth occurred only during the first half of this 120-year period. From the British occupation of Bengal in the 1760s to 1820, the population of the country actually declined considerably because of the wars, revolts and famines that accompanied the British conquest of India.

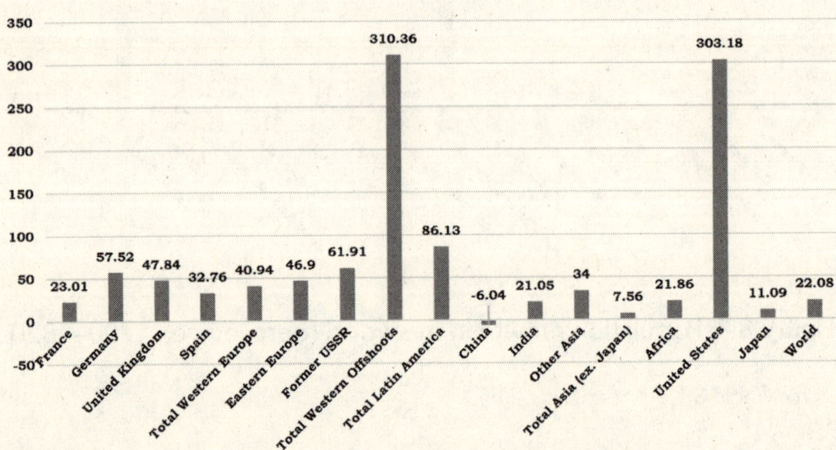

Figure 8.4: Population growth in the world (percentage), 1820–70

Source: Table 8.1, Appendices

Moving on to the period 1820–70, the world population grew from 1,04,18,34,000 to 1,27,19,15,00, as depicted in Figure 8.4. It is seen that the West continued to grow fast. With the exception of France, the major European countries grew much faster than the world average, driven as they were by the success of the Industrial Revolution, increased prosperity, better nutrition and improved health standards. Western Europe grew by 40.94 per cent. The most dramatic expansion was that of the United States, whose population grew by as much as four times in just fifty years (303.18 per cent), mainly because of the large-scale migration from Europe. Almost all Asian countries, such as India (21.05 per cent) and Japan (11.04 per cent), grew at a much slower pace, indeed, below the world average (22.08 per cent), while China experienced a net decline of 6.04 per cent. This indicates that the higher demographic growth of many Western countries was in some way related to the rise and consolidation of their colonial empires, which were in the heyday of their power in the nineteenth century. During the same period, the growth of the colonies suffered, either in absolute or relative terms, perhaps due to impoverishment and worsening social and economic indicators caused by colonial exploitation.

Let us now look at the period from 1870 to 1913 with the help of Figure 8.5.

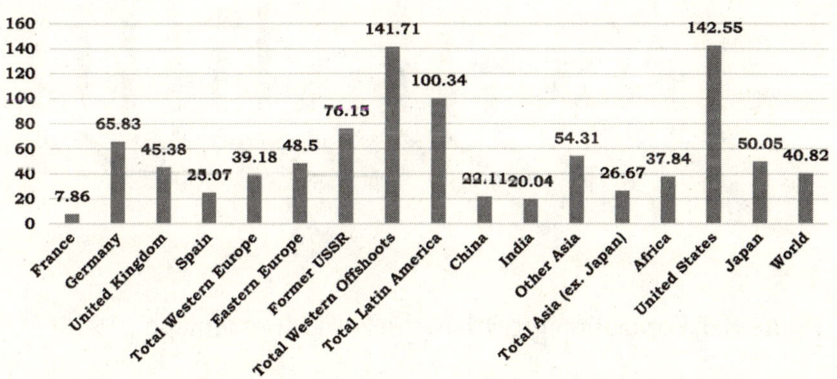

Figure 8.5: Population growth in the world (percentage), 1870–1913

Source: Table 8.1, Appendices

Between 1870 and 1913, there was a major rise in world population growth. Compared to the previous fifty years' growth of just 22.08 per cent, the world registered nearly double the growth at 40.82 per cent (from 1,27,19,15,000 to 1,79,10,91,000), partly due to continued Western expansion and partly because regions like Latin America (100.34 per cent), India (20.04 per cent), China (22.11 per cent), Africa (37.84 per cent) and Japan (50.05 per cent) all grew relatively well. Western Europe (39.18 per cent) grew around the same pace as the world; Germany (65.83 per cent), and United Kingdom (45.38 per cent) secured high growth; the United States (142.55 per cent) again grew much faster because of continued large-scale migration from Europe. Their growth needs to be seen together, as migration to the US was limited to Europeans. Since much of Europe's excess population migrated to the US, the net growth rate of Europe moderated. If we see it as consolidated Western growth, it turns out to be much higher. However, France continued to be the exception in Europe, growing at a negligible rate of 7.86 per cent.

The next period we delve into, with Figure 8.6, is 1913–50, when the population of the world grew from 1,79,10,91,000 to 2,52,43,24,000:

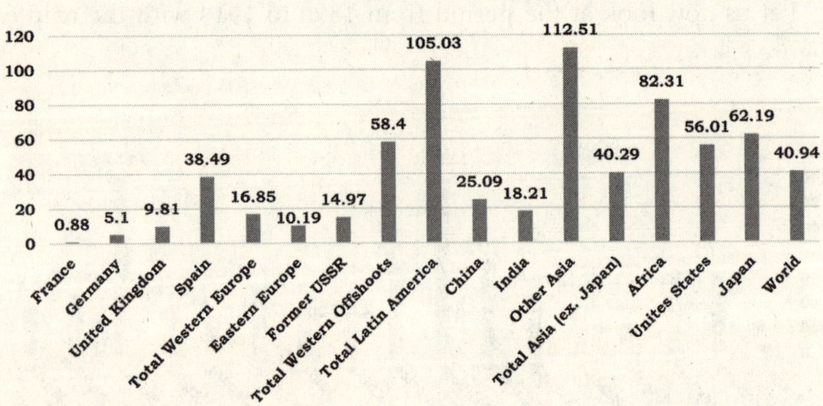

Figure 8.6: Population growth in the world (percentage), 1913–50

Source: Table 8.1, Appendices

A pivotal demographic shift occurred between 1913 and 1950. Western Europe began realigning its share of the world population, marking a significant convergence with the trends observed around 1500. Its growth dropped drastically to just 16.85 per cent. Both Germany (5.1 per cent) and the United Kingdom (9.81 per cent) grew at a much lower rate than in the previous hundred years, and France barely grew (0.88 per cent).

The real story of demographic growth now lay in Latin America (105.03 per cent), which grew two-and-a-half times faster than the world average (40.94 per cent), just as it had done between 1870 and 1913, as it started moving towards reclaiming the demographic share it must have possessed before the European contact. India (18.21 per cent) and China (25.09 per cent) were still well below the world average. Asia, other than India and China, grew much faster than in the past, at 112.51 per cent, as did Africa at 82.31 per cent. So, the growth of a part of the so-called Third World now decisively exceeded that of the West. Japan also witnessed a rapid rise of 62.19 per cent during the period of its imperial expansion in East and Southeast Asia. The growth of the United States came down drastically, from 142.55 per cent during 1870–13 to just 56.01 per cent, mainly due to the end of large-scale European migration, as the western frontier was now closed and there was no free land left to be distributed to immigrants from Europe.

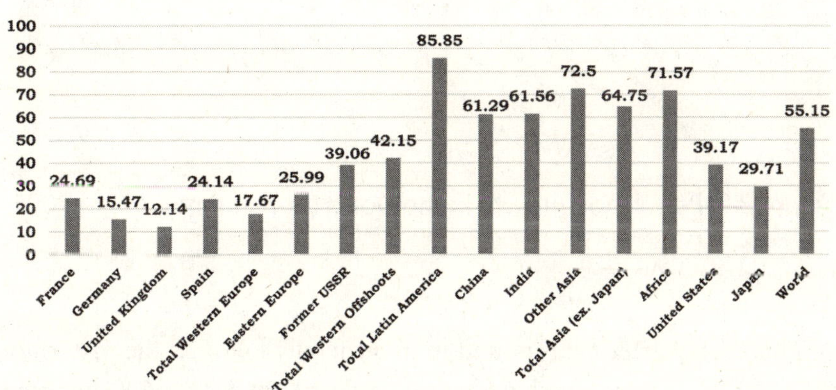

Figure 8.7: Population growth in the world (percentage), 1950–73

Source: Table 8.1, Appendices

The post-Second World War period was marked by the demographic recovery of the colonies, most of which gained their independence within two decades. However, the post-War baby boom ensured continued growth in the West. Figure 8.7 shows how Western Europe grew by 17.67 per cent; United States still secured a relatively high growth of 39.17 per cent; while Japan grew by 29.71 per cent. In contrast, Total Latin America grew by 85.85 per cent; India by 61.56 per cent; China by 61.29 per cent; and Africa by 71.57 per cent. It was not a mere coincidence that the end of the European dominance of India and China triggered an unprecedented demographic expansion in both the countries over 1950–73. As large Asian countries like India and China began to grow rapidly, the world population growth also soared to its highest rate ever. Whereas in the previous two periods of forty-three and thirty-seven years, the world population had grown by 40 per cent each, from 1950 to 1973, it grew by no less than 55.15 per cent in less than a quarter century, from 2,52,43,24,000 to 3,91,64,89,000.

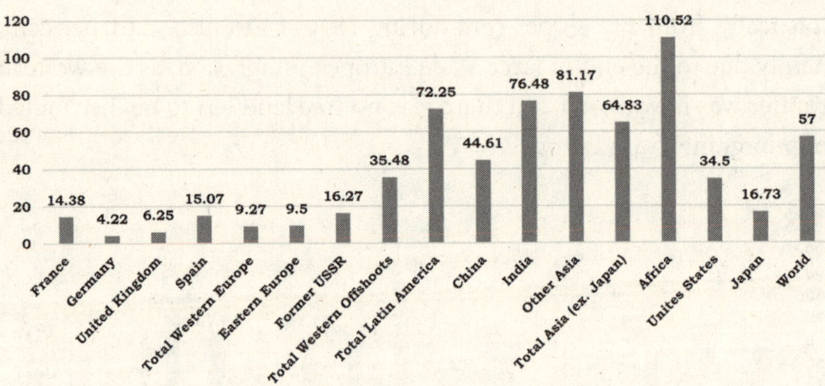

Figure 8.8: Population growth in the world (percentage), 1973–2001

Source: Table 8.1, Appendices

The next quarter-century and more generally followed the pattern of 1950–73, with some notable changes, reflected in Figure 8.8. Between 1973 and 2001, the world population grew from 3,91,64,89,000 to 6,14,90,06,000. Now Western Europe's growth dropped drastically. Compared to the world average of 57 per cent—again the fastest-ever quarter-century growth—it grew at just about 9 per cent, largely due to immigration. Latin America (72.25 per cent) expanded at a higher rate, as did India, which experienced its fastest ever growth, at 76.48 per cent. Other Asia stood at 81.17 per cent, and most remarkably, Africa, which grew at 110.52 per cent, achieved the fastest growth out of all the continents and major countries in the post-Second World War period. China grew at a much slower pace of 44.61 per cent, both because of the improvement in social and demographic indicators during the 1950s and 1960s, despite the disastrous Great Leap Forward and the Cultural Revolution of Mao, and its one-child policy initiated in 1980.

—∞—

The seventeenth century had seen a slower world growth rate than the sixteenth century; the eighteenth century witnessed a much higher growth rate than both those centuries; the nineteenth century—though the data set are not strictly comparable—was somewhat slower than the eighteenth century, until demographic growth took off in the twentieth century, rising to as much as 40.94 per cent between 1913 and 1950, then even faster, at 55.15 per cent between 1950 and 1973, and at 57 per cent between 1973 and 2001. This signifies that the twentieth century proved to be a critical period in modern demographic history. While the previous two centuries had widened the divergence between the West and the rest, the twentieth century started the process of convergence with the *longue durée* pattern of history.

This happened because, on the one hand, after centuries of expansion associated with demographic transition, growth finally started stagnating in the West, especially in Europe; on the other hand, the rest of the world, especially India, China, Latin America and Africa, started growing much faster than in previous centuries, as they gradually entered the second phase of demographic transition. The end of colonial empires in Asia and Africa in the middle of the twentieth century created social, economic and political conditions for demographic convergence for many countries. Their growth had diverged from that of the West for centuries, mainly because of poverty, underdevelopment, slave trade, drain of wealth, deindustrialisation and general economic exploitation at the hands of the West. The world average also rose as these large countries and continents started growing at high rates. The much slower growth of the West, as compared to the rest, resulted in the shrinking of its share in the world demographic pie.

Of course, demographic expansion by itself has no definite meaning. However, in combination with other conditions, it does signify a general improvement in life for non-Western countries, which alone could propel rapid population growth. The normative question of whether this growth was good or bad for development largely misses the point, which is that over the long run forces of divergence and convergence tend to balance each other out, and that depending on social, economic and political conditions and factors, countries and continents pass through different stages of growth in the process of demographic transition. In any case, there is no clear empirical evidence that population growth in Third World countries has by itself acted as an impediment to economic development. Many of these countries, including India, China and ASEAN countries, have developed significantly along with rapid population growth.

World Population Shares of Countries and Regions, 1500–2024

To understand the workings of the forces of divergence versus convergence over the long-term, we also need to examine variations in the population shares of major countries and regions of the world over the last five centuries. Let us begin from AD 1500, as illustrated in the pie chart in Figure 8.9.

As expected, back in 1500, the world demographic distribution looked quite different from the present. Out of an estimated world population of 43,84,28,000, Western Europe accounted for 5,72,68,000 (13.1 per cent), the United States 0.5 per cent, Total Western Offshoots 0.6 per cent, Latin America 1,75,00,000 (4.0 per cent), China 10,30,00,000 (23.5 per cent), India 11,00,00,000 (25.1 per cent), Asia as a whole 61.3 per cent, and Africa 4,66,10,000 (10.5 per cent). Within Western Europe, France was the most populous country (1,50,00,000), with almost four times the population of the United Kingdom (39,42,000). Its population share of 3.40 per cent was roughly equal to that of Japan's 3.50. How did the picture change after a hundred years? The pie chart depicted in Figure 8.10 shows the shift.

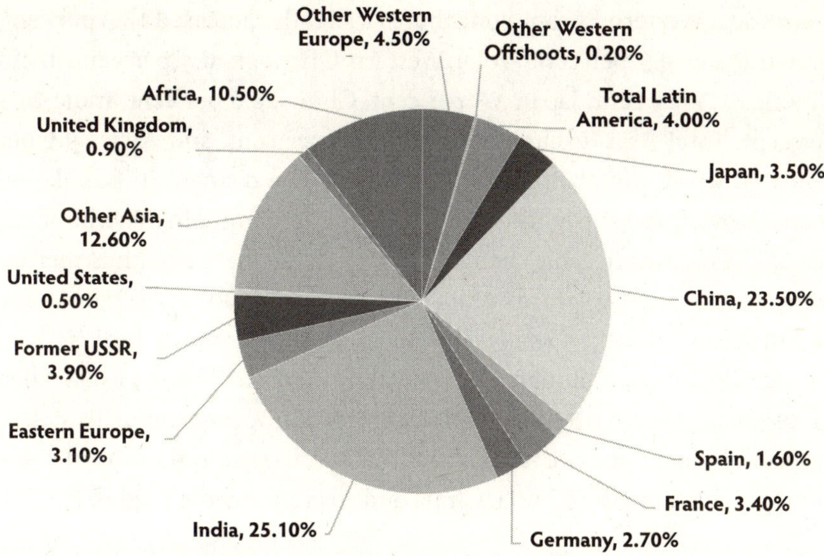

Figure 8.9: World Population Shares, 1500

Note: The figures for India include Pakistan and Bangladesh.

Source: Table 8.2, Appendices

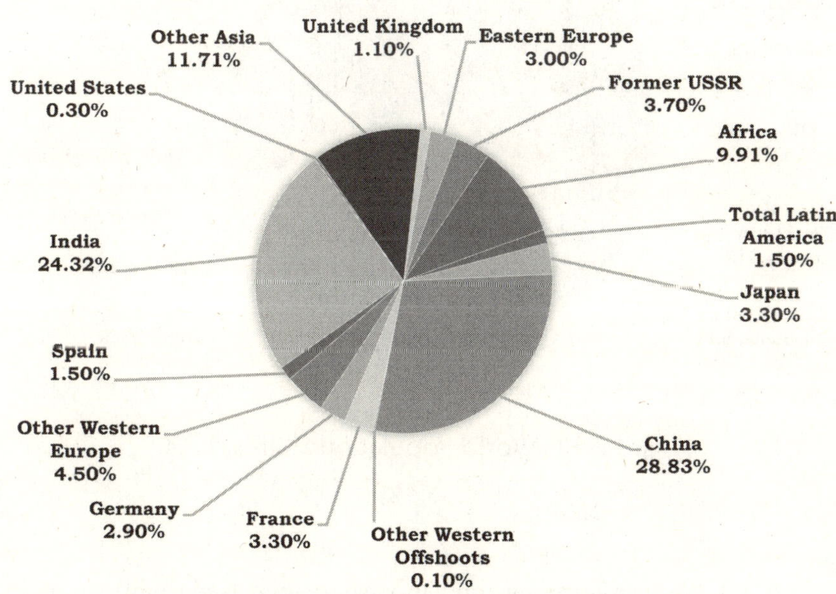

Figure 8.10: World Population Shares, 1600

Source: Table 8.2, Appendices

In 1600, Western Europe contributed a slightly increased 13.3 per cent, United States 0.3 per cent, Total Western Offshoots 0.4 per cent, Latin America 1.5 per cent, Japan 3.3 per cent, China 28.8 per cent, India 24.3 per cent, Total Asia (excluding Japan) 64.7 per cent, and Africa 9.9 per cent to a world population of 55,61,48,000. The changes in population shares provide deep insights into the history of the world in those hundred years. The most noticeable change occurred in the share of Latin America, which lost nearly two-thirds of its population of 1500 (1,75,00,000) due to European contact. Conversely, Asia's share increased; India's share decreased slightly, although its population increased from 11,00,00,000 to 13,50,00,000. In the sixteenth century, European colonialism had only a marginal presence in Asia and this is reflected in the considerable demographic growth of India, China and Asia as a whole (Figure 8.11).

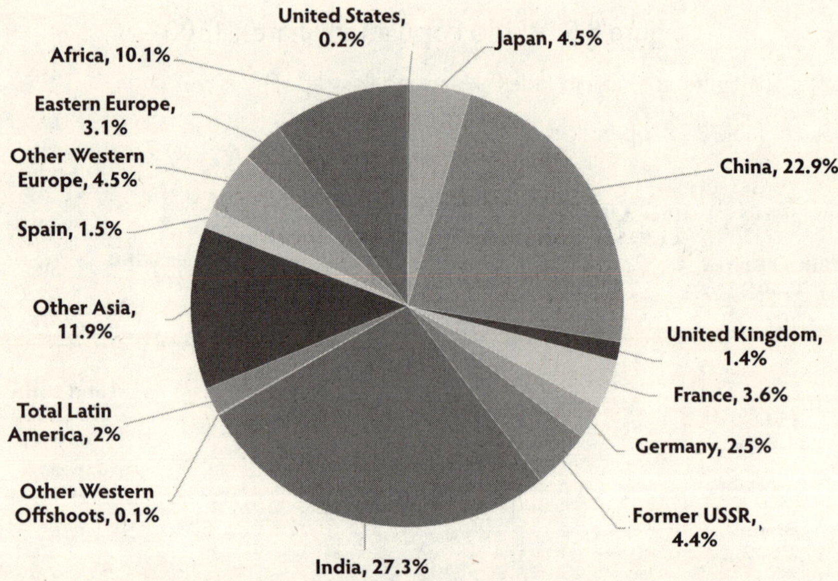

Figure 8.11: World Population Shares, 1700

Source: Table 8.2, Appendices

In 1700, Western Europe's population share increased slightly to reach 13.5 per cent, while the United States saw a decline to 0.2 per cent because of the large number of deaths of Amerindians caused by warfare and Old-

World epidemics such as smallpox, measles, chickenpox, bubonic plague, typhus and malaria to which they had no immunity. Latin America somewhat stabilised after the disastrous sixteenth century. It notched up a higher share of 2.0 per cent as resistance to plagues built up in the native population and there was a significant increase in the number of mixed-race populations involving Amerindians, Europeans and Africans brought in as slaves.

China experienced a major drop of around 6 per cent in its share, falling to 22.9 per cent (from 16,00,00,000 to 13,80,00,000). India saw a massive gain of three percentage points, notching up to 27.3 per cent (from 13,50,00,000 to 16,50,00,000). Because of the major decline in China, Asia's overall share fell by 2.6 percentage points. Africa saw its share increase slightly from 9.9 per cent to 10.1 per cent, as the European slave trade had not yet made a deep demographic impact on the continent—a situation that would change in the following century.

The next series of demographic data covers the period from 1700 to 1820, a period that proved to be critical for the rise of the West over the rest. The population of the world increased from 60,34,90,000 to 1,04,18,34,000. It was only in the second half of this period that Europeans were able to consolidate their hold over North and South America. They began to dominate the maritime trade of Asia and the Indian Ocean and were able to conquer large territories in India, Southeast Asia and Africa to establish their colonies. This is reflected in the population growth and shares of various countries and regions depicted in Figure 8.12:

The country that was most successful in its colonial enterprise in the second half of the eighteenth century was Britain. No wonder its share shot up from just 1.4 per cent in 1700 to 2.0 per cent in 1820. Equally importantly, the United States' share rose from a mere 0.2 per cent to 1.0 per cent—a massive rise of 400 per cent or five times. Latin America remained at 2.1 per cent, while China saw an unprecedented gain of nearly 14 percentage points, partly because India lost more than 7 percentage points to come down to just 20.1 per cent, as it had lost a good deal of its population between 1750 and 1820 in the wars and famines caused by the British conquest and subsequent turmoil in large parts of the country. Equally tragic was the case of Africa, whose share dropped from 10.1 per cent to just 7.1 per cent, mainly due to a massive increase in the

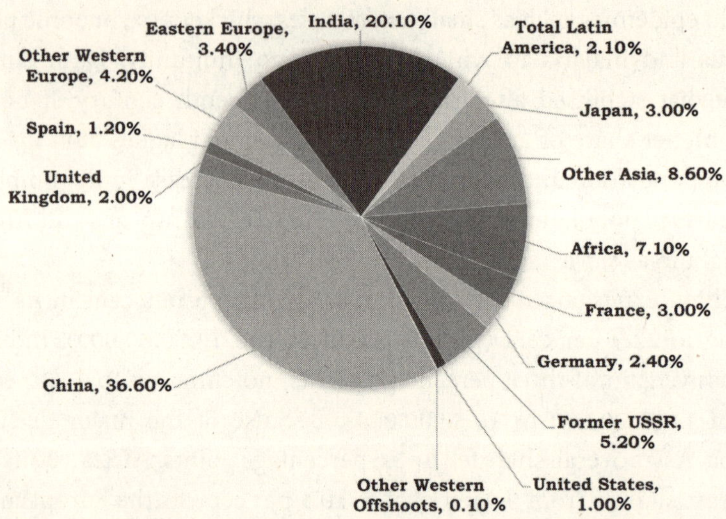

Figure 8.12: World Population Shares, 1820

Source: Table 8.2, Appendices

Atlantic slave trade. This resulted in a shortage of labour for agriculture and other activities in many parts of the continent, particularly in Central and Western Africa, from where people were captured and taken to the Americas as slaves.

The next series, 1820–70, by Angus Maddison, depicted in Figure 8.13, shows somewhat less dramatic changes than the previous one. As expected, the United Kingdom's share rose again, now to 2.5 per cent; Western Europe's share went up to 14.7 per cent—its peak share in history; the United States witnessed a huge rise, going up to 3.2 per cent from a mere 1.0 per cent fifty years ago. These developments are clear indications of the Western domination and conquest of the world, which was more or less completed during this period. It is noteworthy that the combined share of Europe and the United States in 1870 had reached 17.9 per cent, which means that the population of European descent had enormously raised its share from just 13.1 per cent in 1500 to 17.9 per cent. Latin America also saw a considerable rise from 2.1 per cent to 3.2 per cent, as most of the countries had been liberated from Spanish and Portuguese misrule, and improved social and economic conditions led to a higher population growth.

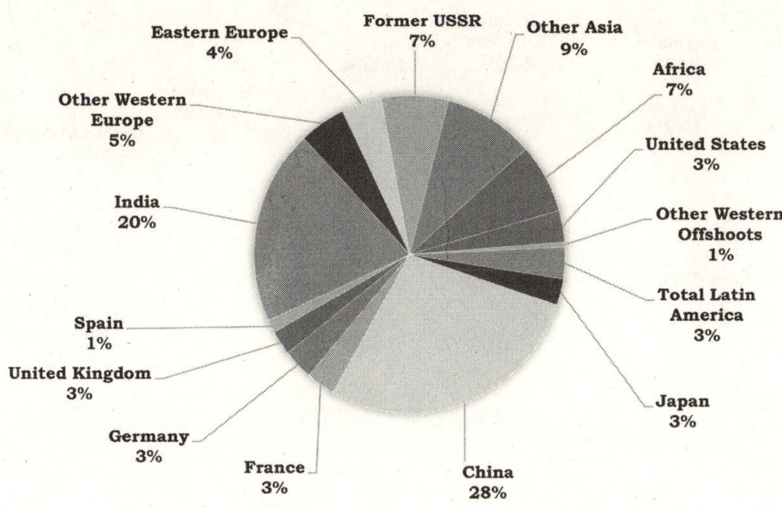

Figure 8.13: World Population Shares, 1870

Source: Table 8.2, Appendices

It is China that witnessed the biggest decline in this period, falling to 28.1 per cent. India (including Pakistan and Bangladesh) went down further to 19.9 per cent, which was its lowest share in history so far, while Asia as a whole also went down drastically to 57.5 per cent, having registered a decline of 7.7 per cent in just fifty years—probably the largest decline in history for such a large population. Let us now turn to Japan. It had started with a 3.5 per cent share in 1500, which fell to 3.3 per cent in 1600 but rose to as much as 4.5 per cent in 1700 in the golden period of the Tokugawa Shogunate, during which international trade based on Japanese silver led to rapid growth in the economy and population. In 1820, it declined to 3.0 per cent; in 1870, it declined further to 2.7 per cent. Asia's case is almost the obverse of the West. As the West's share went up massively, Asia's went down, because with the liberation of Latin America and the end of the Atlantic slave trade, Asia had to bear the brunt of Western colonialism during those fifty years.

The next series, depicted in Figure 8.14, spans from 1870 to 1913. During this period, the United Kingdom retained its share of 2.5 per cent and Western Europe dropped slightly from 14.7 per cent to 14.6 per cent. However, the United States, with a share of 5.4 per cent, and Other

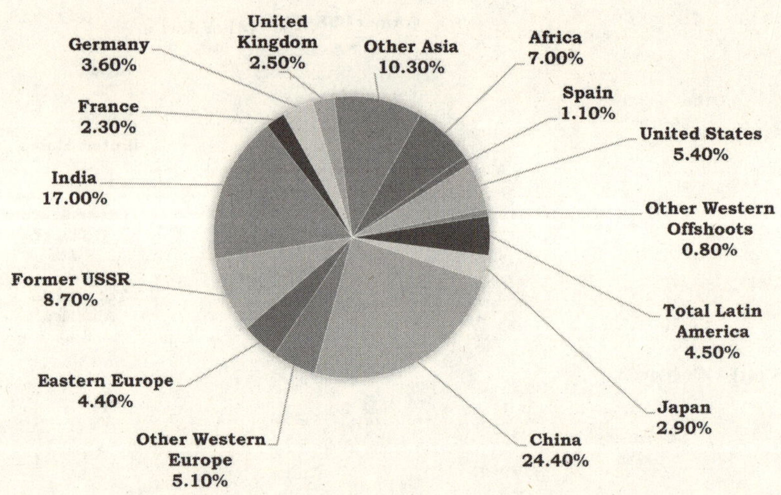

Figure 8.14: World Population Shares, 1913

Source: Table 8.2, Appendices

Western Offshoots like Canada, Australia, etc., with a share of 0.8 per cent, vastly increased their portions. Consequently, in 1913, the West reached its peak share of 20.8 per cent. In contrast, India (including Pakistan and Bangladesh) and Asia reached their lowest shares so far: 17.0 per cent and 51.7 per cent respectively. So, on the eve of the First World War, when the West was at the height of its power and ascendancy, its share of the world population was also at its peak. As mentioned earlier, this indicates a relationship between demography and power in the international arena, even if it cannot be determined precisely.

Coming to Latin America, the period of growth and prosperity seems to have continued, with its share now rising to 4.5 per cent, which is somewhat higher than the 4.0 per cent share it is estimated to have had around the time of the European contact in 1492. In Japan, the Tokugawa Shogunate had been abolished in 1868 with the Meiji Restoration, and the next fifty years witnessed all-round development. This is well-reflected in the rapid population growth, leading to an increase in its share from 2.7 per cent in 1870 to 2.9 per cent in 1913. Meanwhile, Africa witnessed only a nominal decline, from 7.1 to 7 per cent.

The period from 1913 to 1950, depicted in Figure 8.15, represents the last stage of European colonialism, which witnessed two highly destructive world wars, although the emergence of the United States ensured that the Western dominance of the world would continue even after 1950. It is interesting to note that Britain suffered a significant loss in its share, dropping from 2.5 per cent to just 2.0 per cent. This decline coincided with its replacement by the US as the world's predominant power. Western Europe as a whole also saw a major decline, partly because of the world wars and partly because other parts of the world had started growing faster than in the past. In contrast, Japan saw its share increase from 2.9 per cent to 3.3 per cent. Both China and India continued their decline, reaching 21.7 and 14.2 per cent respectively, although in India's case the decline was mainly caused by the Partition and the creation of Pakistan, which accounted for about one-fifth of undivided India's population.

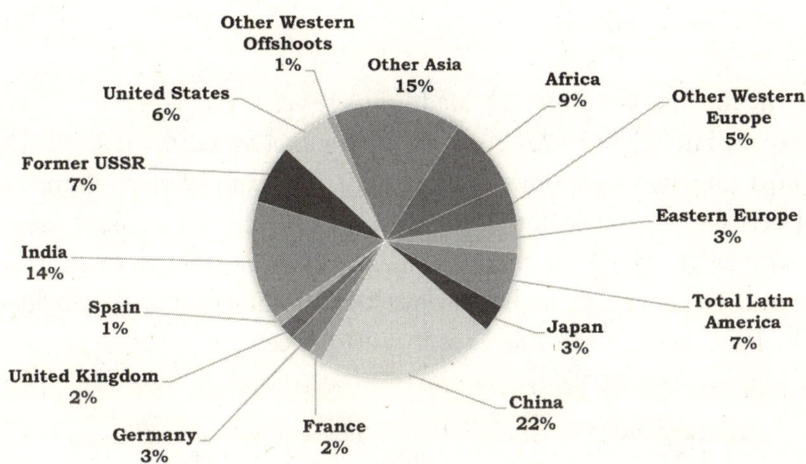

Figure 8.15: World Population Shares, 1950

Source: Table 8.2, Appendices

The next series of data from 1950 to 1973 is depicted in Figure 8.16. In this period, the demographic decline of Western Europe was massive and consistent; by 1973, its share had fallen dramatically to 9.2 per cent, far less than where it had begun in 1500. The United Kingdom came down from 2.0 per cent to 1.4 per cent. In contrast, Latin America rose to 7.9 per cent, China to 22.5 per cent, and India also gained slightly to reach 14.8 per cent. Asia as a whole also started inching its way up, having touched the bottom at 51.4 per cent in 1950.

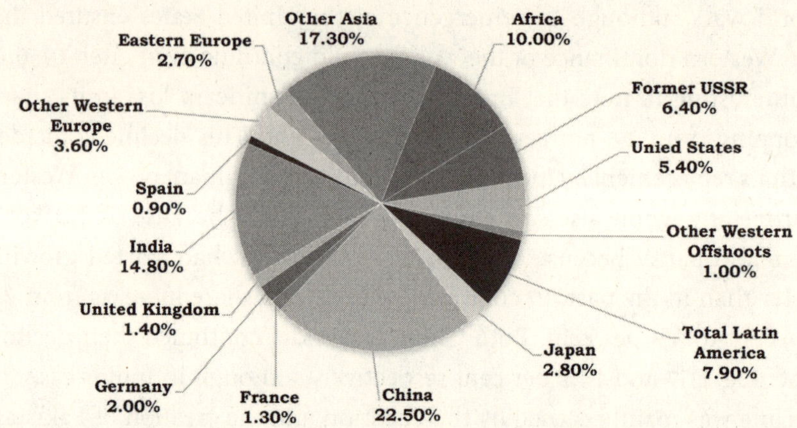

Figure 8.16: World Population Shares, 1973

Source: Table 8.2, Appendices

The final period for which Maddison's series is available, 1973–2001, is depicted in Figure 8.17. This period also witnessed dramatic shifts. The United Kingdom went down to just 1.0 per cent and Western Europe to 6.4 per cent—by far its lowest share in history. The United States saw a modest fall, from 5.4 per cent to 4.6 per cent. Latin America rose further to reach 8.6 per cent from the previous 7.9 per cent; Japan lost a good deal of its share, falling from 2.8 per cent to 2.1 per cent.

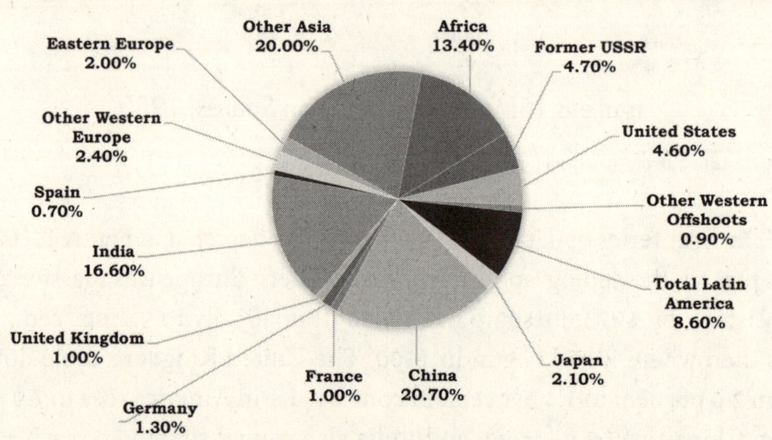

Figure 8.17: World Population Shares, 2001

Source: Table 8.2, Appendices

The critical observation here would be that although the period from 1950 to 2001 continued to be marked by Western hegemony, it was also a period of recovery for non-Western parts of the world. Most of them gained political independence. Many were able to secure steady economic growth over several decades, resulting in much higher standards of nutrition, sanitation and healthcare all of which contributed to rapid demographic growth. While China lost its share mainly because of its forced one-child policy, India gained significantly, from 14.8 per cent to 16.6 per cent. In fact, the entire period of 1950– 2001 was one of recovery for India, both in terms of social and economic progress and demographic expansion.

—ꟿ—

The last two decades since 2001 have witnessed the strengthening of these trends. According to the United Nations estimates, India overtook China in April 2023 to become the most populous nation.[1] The July 2023 estimates of the United Nations put India's population at 1.43 billion, which is around 17.8 per cent of the total population of the world, at approximately 8 billion.[2] China, at 17.6 per cent, is slightly behind India. The combined share of the West, including Western Europe (5.7 per cent), United States (4.23 per cent) Canada (0.48 per cent), Australia (0.33 per cent) and New Zealand (0.06 per cent), has now come down roughly to 10.80 per cent, which is well below Western Europe's share of 13.1 per cent in 1500. However, if we add Eastern Europe to this, we come closer (14.50 per cent) to Europe's (including Eastern Europe) share of 16.2 per cent in 1500. Interestingly, if we add the populations of Pakistan and Bangladesh to that of India, their combined share would amount to about 23 per cent of the population of the world, which is close to undivided India's share of about 25 per cent around 1500.

The overview of world demographic history in the last 500 years shows that, in the long run, the forces of both divergence and convergence play their role in the demographic movements of countries, regions and continents. Migration, wars, famines, plagues, social and economic development have all acted as important factors in shaping population growth in various parts of the world. Coupled with the process of demographic transition, they have ensured that no country, region or continent can enjoy the same growth rate over the long run, let alone hold

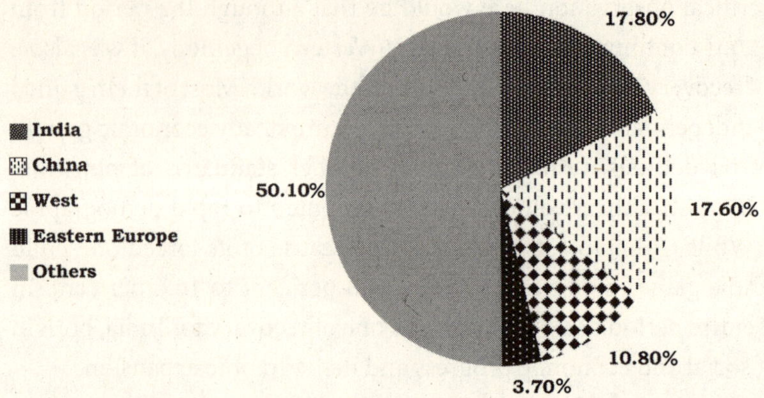

Figure 8.18: Population shares of countries and regions, 2023

a more or less fixed share of the world population. The peak growth phase, whether stretching over a few decades or centuries, does eventually come to an end. Coupled with the fact that other countries or regions may grow faster during this period, the population share of a country can decline, at times drastically.

Even if the analysis is narrowed down to the period from 1870 to the present, making it more comparable to the period of Indian demographic history addressed in this book, the conclusions still hold. From 1870 to 2023, the share of France in the world population has come down from 3 per cent to just 0.80 per cent; Germany from 3.1 per cent to 1.04 per cent; the United Kingdom from 2.5 per cent to 0.84 per cent; Western Europe from 14.8 per cent to just about 5.7 per cent, which is considerably less than half; Japan from 2.7 to 1.53 per cent; China from 28.2 to 17.6 per cent; and India from 19.9 to 17.8 per cent (minus Pakistan and Bangladesh). The share of the United States has gone up from 3.2 to 4.23 per cent; Latin America from 3.2 to 8.28 per cent, and Africa from 7.1 per cent to 17.89 per cent.

Interestingly, at the 1872 population of 42,62,69,90, the erstwhile North-West Provinces and Oudh (which consists of present-day Uttar Pradesh and Uttarakhand) constituted no less than 3.5 per cent of the world population. By 1971, with Uttar Pradesh and Uttarakhand's combined population of 8,83,41,521, the share declined to 2.2 per cent of the world population of 3,91,34,82,000. Since 1971, it has moved towards convergence with the long-term figure, reaching about 3 per cent of the world population in 2024.

It is noteworthy that, with the exception of India, all countries and continents whose share has gone down between 1870 and 2023 had witnessed a significant rise in their shares during the preceding century or so. If we examine the period from 1700 to 1870, this point is clearly illustrated. During that period, the share of Germany increased from 2.5 per cent to 3.1 per cent, the United Kingdom from 1.4 per cent to 2.5 per cent, Western Europe from 13.5 per cent to 14.7 per cent, the United States from 0.2 per cent to 3.2 per cent, and China from 22.9 per cent to 28.1 per cent.

In contrast, India's population share went down from 27.3 per cent to 19.9 per cent. Africa's share dropped from 10.1 per cent to 7.1 per cent. It should be kept in mind here that we are not talking about absolute loss or gain in population, but only relative loss or gain of share in percentage terms in the world. What needs to be emphasised is that a similar process of loss and gain of relative shares would be found at work if we attempt a detailed analysis of the regional distribution of population in any large country, just as in India, which is the subject of this study.

Comparing India's demographic growth to that of the world during 1870–2023 provides an interesting long-term perspective, although it must be reiterated that the concept of world population as formulated in the mid-twentieth century, when the expressions like 'population explosion' and 'population bomb' gained currency, is in some ways problematic, as was pointed out by Alfred Sauvy, who coined the term '*tiers monde*' or 'Third World'.

We do not get from the census reliable aggregate figures for India in 1870. To arrive at approximate figures for post-Partition India in 1870, we can, therefore, use Angus Maddison's estimate for India (including Pakistan and Bangladesh), which is 25,30,00,000. Now, we have already calculated the 1881 figure for India with post-Partition boundaries (21,41,51,396). This works out to 85.61 per cent of undivided India's population in 1881. Assuming the same ratio for 1870, and using Maddison's estimate of 25,30,00,000, we get the figure of 21,65,93,300 for India with its present boundaries in 1870. Let us now calculate the cumulative growth for India from 1870 to 2023. In 2023, India became the most populous country in the world with an approximate population of 1.43 billion. The 1870–2023 cumulative growth comes to 560.22 per cent. Compared to this, the world experienced a growth of 528.97 per cent during 1870–2023.

In terms of share, the reconstructed 1870 figure of 21,65,93,300 for India with its post-Partition boundaries represents 17.03 per cent of the world population of 1,27,19,15,000. This is not much different from India's 2023 share of 17.8 per cent. So, India has not significantly outgrown the world over the last 150 years. Interestingly, if we take the 1870 figure for India derived from Angus Maddison, and assume that the north's share in the country was the same as it was in 1881, that is 49.85 per cent, we get the figure of 10,79,71760 for the north in 1870. This would come to 8.49 per cent of the world population of 1,27,19,15,000 in 1870. Now, if using the Census of India projections for 2026, we add up the population of the nine states plus NCT of Delhi, we get 69,40,19,000, which is 8.68 per cent of the world population of about 8 billion in 2023. So, neither India as a whole nor the north have experienced extraordinarily high demographic growth over the past one-and-a-half centuries, even in comparison with the world demographic history, notwithstanding the objections to the very concept of 'world population' discussed earlier.

The comparative study of 1870–2023 shows that the rapid growth of larger continents, countries, regions and states within countries—such as Asia, Africa, China, India in the world context and the north in the Indian context—not only raises the total growth but also brings about major shifts in relative shares.

While such macro calculations may have a statistical margin of error, the point to be noted is that India's growth over the period has been only slightly above that of the world. This is despite the fact that for 150 years before 1870, India had grown well below the world average and had lost a good deal of share in the world population. Therefore, the idea of 'population explosion' in India is not based on sound evidence. It is based on little more than general impressions.

Population growth depends upon three factors: fertility, mortality and migration. In the absence of migration, whenever the gap between fertility and mortality is narrow, in the sense that fertility rates are not much higher than mortality rates, growth will be slow or population might even become stagnant. This can happen under two conditions:

when fertility and mortality rates are almost equally high, and when they are almost equally low. The critical point is that a society characterised by the second is very different from the one characterised by the first.

These are usually societies which either in the recent or not-so-recent past have gone through a phase wherein, owing to higher fertility and lower mortality, they experienced rapid population growth, whether stretching over decades or centuries. Going deeper, it would be seen that in every large country there are sub-regions that continue to grow even as the rest of it becomes more or less stagnant, simply because they started off on the growth path at a later stage.

Migration, the third variable in population growth, has played as important a role as the other two. Throughout history, migration across villages, cities, counties, districts, regions, countries and continents has been driven by push and pull factors, usually, but not always, from more densely populated areas to less densely populated ones, thus acting as a great stabilising force in the demographic arena.

With the emergence of rigid sub-national or national identities, however, migration has become a highly contentious political issue. Societies with strong demographic pull factors frequently impose all kinds of entry barriers against immigrants, regarding them as outsiders who will undermine the ethnic, linguistic or cultural integrity of the local community. Thus, some might argue that more than high 'world population growth', it is the highly unequal distribution of population across the world that leads to demographic distortion.

II
Insights from Official Reports: The EAG versus Non-EAG in India

As noted earlier, the debate on India's presumed demographic divergence has been well-acknowledged and, indeed, primarily created by the country's policymakers, who have developed some well-established methods of classifying the regions and states of India along the spectrum of social and economic development and population growth. For instance, the 2011 Census explicitly classifies India's states into two groups: Empowered Action Group (EAG) and non-Empowered Action

Group (non-EAG) states/union territories. This classification is based on the differences in the social and economic conditions of the two groups and is linked to their stages in demographic transition.

The Empowered Action Group (EAG) comprises eight states: Rajasthan, Uttar Pradesh, Uttarakhand, Bihar, Jharkhand, Madhya Pradesh, Chhattisgarh and Orissa. It should be noted that all four states belonging to the so-called BIMARU category are included in EAG, while the rest of India automatically gets the nomenclature of non-EAG. There seems to be a consensus in both government and academic circles in India that the EAG states have been historically responsible for India's 'overpopulation'. This consensus is particularly strong for the period after 1971, which marks the year after which the non-EAG states witnessed a drop in their fertility and growth rates.

How close is this view to the historical reality lying hidden in the demographic data of India for the last 150 years? We have seen that the discourse of the north–south divide, holding the north responsible for the supposed overpopulation of India, is fundamentally flawed as it is premised on a comparative analysis of data only from 1971, and not from 1872 when the modern census was first compiled. This study demonstrates that the decline in the population growth rate in southern states was not primarily due to better implementation of the family planning programme, but rather because of their slow entry—after nearly a century of rapid growth—into the third phase of demographic transition—a phase universally characterised by slower growth, eventually leading to stagnation and decline.

Once 1881 is used as the starting point, it becomes clear that all four regions of the country—north, south, east and west— have experienced rapid growth during different periods and have exhibited both divergence and convergence vis-à -vis one another. Growth has followed a declining curve in the order of east, west, south and north. As a result, the east and the west have seen their shares in India's population rise, while the north and the south have seen their shares fall—the first more drastically than the second. Whereas there is a relationship between development and population growth, it is far from simple. For instance, western India has continued to grow rapidly despite good social and economic indicators. The same applies to Haryana. In contrast, Orissa has seen much slower population growth over the twentieth century, although it has been included in the EAG because of its relatively poor social and economic indicators.

A similar but more complex picture with many more departures, variations and ambiguities emerges from a long-term comparative analysis of EAG versus non-EAG states. Figure 8.19 depicts the trend of population growth of EAG vis-à-vis non-EAG states, as shown in the 2011 Census Report:

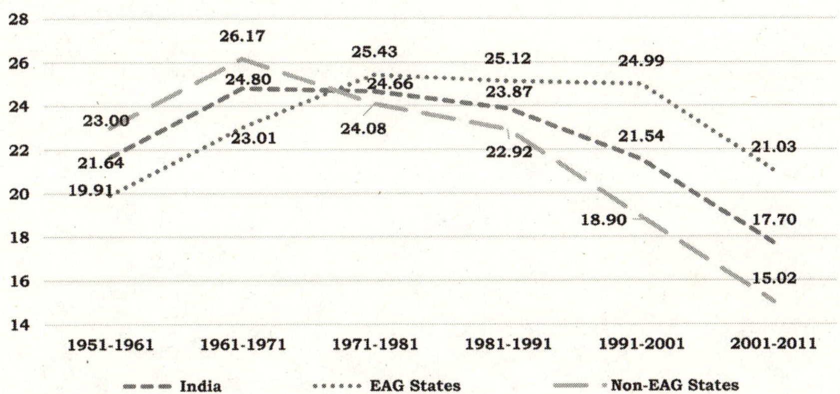

Figure 8.19: Population growth rates of India, EAG states and non-EAG states and UTs, 1951–61 to 2001–11

Source: Census of India, 2011 (Table 8.3, Appendices)[3]

Evidently, between 1951 and 1971 the non-EAG states, including those from the south, had been major contributors to India's population growth—their growth rates being much higher than those of the EAG states. The peak rate at which either of the two groups has grown since 1951 is the non-EAG rate of 26.17 per cent, that too, for the period 1961–71. Moreover, as shown in previous chapters, the states clubbed as non-EAG experienced much higher growth than EAG states since both 1901 and 1881. In fact, even during 1971–81 (24.08 per cent to 25.43 per cent) and 1981–91 (22.92 per cent to 25.12 per cent), non-EAG states' growth rate was only marginally lower (1.35 percentage points to 2.20 percentage points) than that of EAG states. As a result, the overall growth rate of India hovered around the 24 per cent mark until 1991. After 1991, however, there has been a clear decline in the non-EAG fertility and growth rates, while the EAG states maintained their growth rates.

Within the ambit of the supposed divide between the EAG and non-EAG states, it is imperative to take cognizance of the historical pattern that these two groups have followed. In line with the approach followed in this study, let us examine their growth rates since 1901 with the help of Figure 8.20.

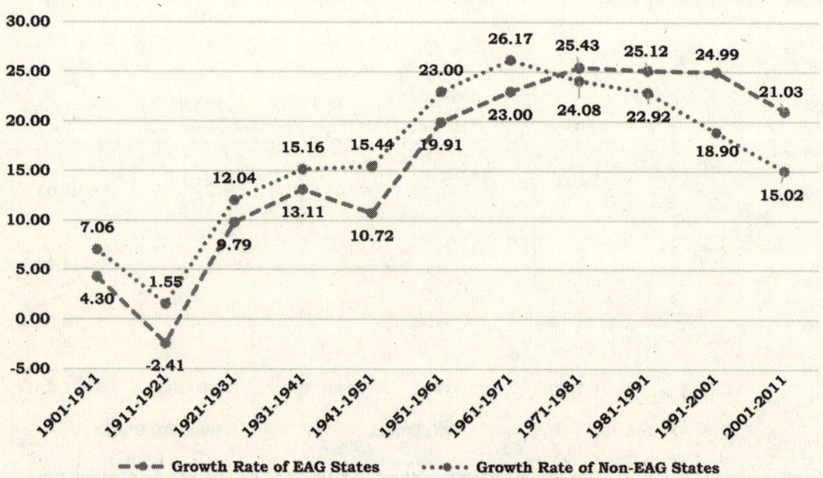

Figure 8.20: Population growth rates of EAG states vis-à-vis Non-EAG states and union territories, 1901–11 to 2001–11

Source: Census of India, 2011 (Table 8.3, Appendices)

What may surprise many is that not only from 1951 to 1971 but also from 1901 to 1951 it is the non-EAG states that consistently grew at a higher rate than the EAG states. It is only at the end of the decade of 1971–81 that the growth curve for the EAG states crossed the curve representing growth for non-EAG states (25.43 per cent versus 24.08 per cent). Thus, 1971 marks the watershed of demographic transition in modern India before which non-EAG states outgrew the states constituting EAG or Empowered Action Group, which includes the economically backward states of the country long held responsible for India's so-called population explosion.

Continuing this line of enquiry, let us now trace the trend of variation in the share contributed to the national population by EAG states since 1901 with the help of Figure 8.21.

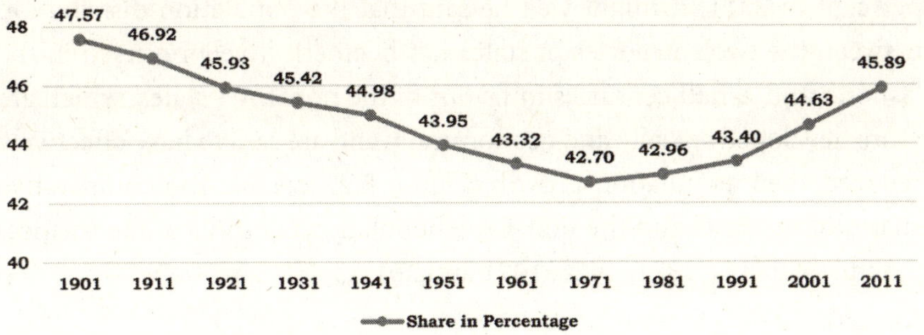

Figure 8.21: Contribution of EAG states to India's population (percentage), 1901–2011

Source: Census of India, 2011 (Table 8.3, Appendices)

Figure 8.21 shows that the share of the EAG states in India's population consistently declined between 1901 and 1971, from 47.57 per cent to 42.70 per cent, until it showed the first signs of an upward swing in 1971. So, for at least seventy years, the non-EAG states far outgrew the EAG, increasing their share in the population of India. During this period, there was a decline of almost five percentage points in the share of the EAG states—a decline that would be regarded as enormous and important by any yardstick.

Equally significant is that even after the EAG states started regaining their share in India's population, the rise was slow. In 2011, at 45.89 per cent, they were still below their 1901 share of 47.57 per cent by 1.68 percentage points. They have begun to show a clear declining trend in their population growth rate, and their Total Fertility Rate (TFR) has also come close to the replacement level. Therefore, the share they contributed to India's population in 1901 is not likely to be surpassed in the next census. It is, of course, even less likely that they would regain the share they had in 1881. Back then, the EAG states of today had a net population of 10,82,45,568 or 50.55 per cent of the population of India with its present boundaries. In 2011, these states had a population of 55,56,80,881, with a share of 45.89 per cent. This is a massive loss of 4.66 percentage points, which is comparable to the loss of 3.38 percentage points in the share of the Hindi belt since 1881. Conversely, the non-EAG states, whose share was approximately 49.45 per cent in 1881, have gained heavily, reaching 54.11

per cent in 2011. It might well be said that the population distribution between the two categories of states has been effectively reversed in the last one-and-a-half centuries in favour of the non-EAG states, which are more developed socially and economically and are said to have effectively reduced their population growth. Figure 8.22 depicts the comparative shares of the EAG and the non-EAG populations of India at four critical junctures, that is, 1881, 1921, 1971 and 2011:

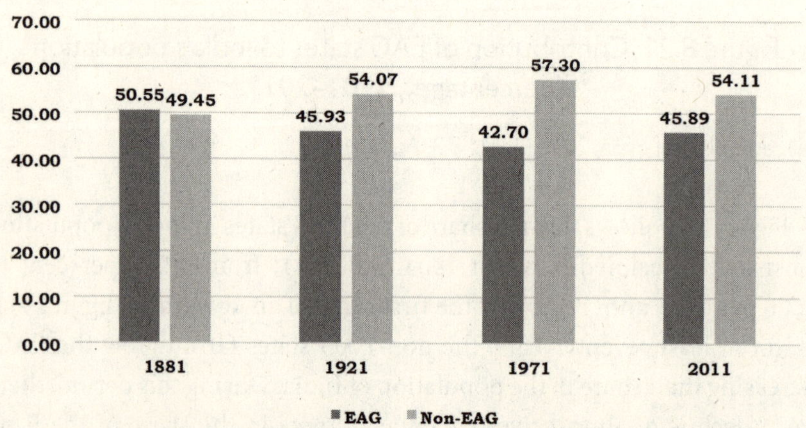

Figure 8.22: Population shares of EAG versus Non-EAG

Source: Table 8.3, Appendices

This book does not argue that individual states or groups such as EAG/non-EAG must enjoy a fixed share of population across time, as that is neither feasible nor desirable. The argument that this book does present is that both divergence and convergence in population growth and shares are observable throughout the country over the last 150 years. States and regions tend to gravitate towards a long-term equilibrium or realignment of their population determined by geographical, physical, climatic, social and economic factors. This includes industrialisation and urbanisation, which lead to migration of labour from one part of the country to another. The higher population share of the western region of India, compared to 150 years ago, can partly be attributed to this internal migration.

What poses a major challenge to an objective understanding of the subject is the enduring yet unfounded belief that the north has inadequately controlled its population, leading to calls for political penalties through embargoes.

The study debunks this belief, showing that the west and the east have grown faster compared to the north and the south, leading to an increase in their share in the population of India. The south has lost its share, but only in relation to the peak it had attained in the 1950s, and not in comparison to its share in 1881. In contrast, the north has lost a significant share, amounting to 3.38 percentage points, over the last 140 years. Figure 8.23 depicts the population shares of the EAG and the various non-EAG regions of India at four different points of time, 1901, 1951, 1971 and 2011:

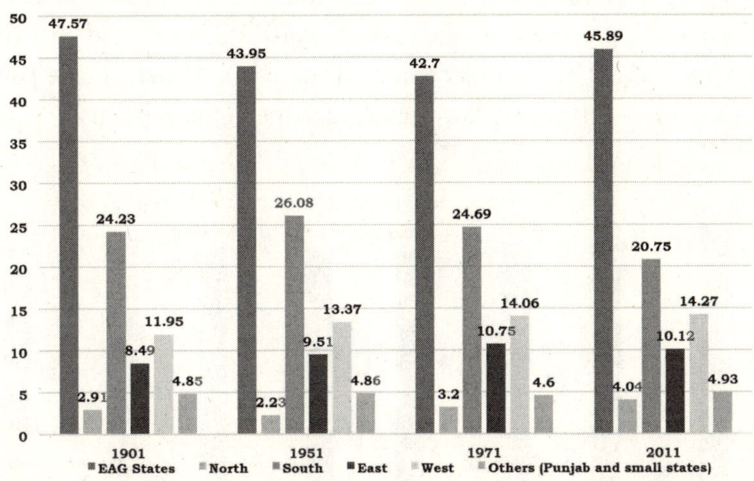

Figure 8.23: Population Shares of EAG versus Other Groups

Source: Table 8.3, Appendices

Figure 8.23 shows that from a high of 47.57 per cent in 1901, the EAG share massively declined to 43.95 per cent in 1951. It declined further, reaching its lowest level of 42.70 in 1971. Therefore, the crucial positioning of 1971 in the divide between the EAG and the non-EAG can hardly be overstated. In order to deepen our analysis, let us now compare EAG states with Maharashtra and Gujarat, non-EAG states which have the social and economic development levels of the south, yet have experienced rapid population growth over the last few decades.

Comparing the population shares of EAG states versus Maharashtra, Gujarat and others (south and much of east), in Figure 8.23, at four different points of time, 1901, 1951, 1971 and 2011, it is evident that the EAG states experienced growth well below both Maharashtra and Gujarat during 1901–71. The result was that the EAG share went down from 47.57 per cent in 1901 to 43.95 per cent in 1951 and dropped further to 42.7 in 1971. This contrasts with a significant rise in the shares of Maharashtra, from 8.13 per cent in 1901 to 9.2 per cent in 1971, and of Gujarat, from 3.81 per cent to 4.87 per cent. Even from 1971 to 2011, when EAG growth was at peak levels and its share has risen to 45.89 per cent, both Maharashtra and Gujarat have increased their respective shares. Over 1901–2011, Maharashtra and Gujarat, which are non-EAG states, have more than compensated for the loss of non-EAG south and east (0.65 percentage points) by gaining combined share of 2.33 percentage points. Even over 1951–2011, they have gained 0.91 percentage points.

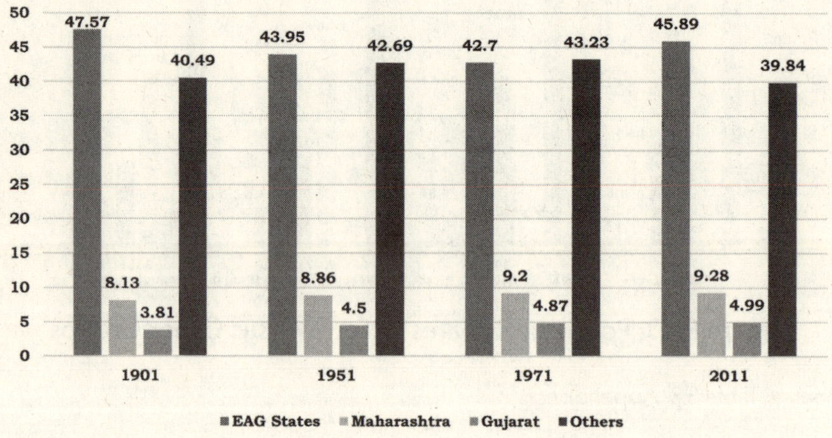

Figure 8.24: Comparison of EAG vs Maharashtra, Gujarat and the rest of Non-EAG India

Source: Table 8.3, Appendices

It is no surprise that the eight EAG states occupying a large area of India have had a large share in the country's population for most of recorded history. Seen in the *longue durée* of history, it is surprising that the region's population share almost consistently declined for at least seven decades out of the last century-and-a-half. Why is it that the region that had a comparatively higher population in the 1881 Census, gradually slipped in terms of its share, hitting the lowest point in 1971? Although finding the answer to this question is not a primary focus of this book, a few surmises may well be made.

—ᵚ—

European colonial empires were predominantly maritime endeavours. Their exploration and expansion beyond Europe led to the carving out of territories across the world. Naval power played a crucial role in shaping the size, longevity and economic profitability of these empires through their ability to extract resources from their colonies. Throughout the colonised world, European powers had entered the colonies via the sea. Their initial bases, including those in India, were usually established in coastal areas, from which they gradually expanded into the hinterland. The metropolises based in Europe were both physically and economically linked to each colony through these coastal belts.

The British Empire in India was a quintessential maritime empire that emerged as dominant by the early-nineteenth century after the downfall of Napoleon in 1815. It focused on international trade and commerce via sea routes, upon which the security of the empire rested. Like other European empires, but with greater efficiency, the economic model of the British Empire was centred on extracting economic resources from the colony for the benefit and development of the metropolis. Whereas for the metropolis, the entire colony functioned as a hinterland, owing to the peculiarities of the nature and orientation of the empire, as well as the model of economic extraction it employed, the colony—India in this case—was itself subdivided into a coastal belt from where the empire mainly operated, and the vast hinterland, upon whose exploitation the empire was based.

Given this colonial model, it should not be surprising that though the British Empire caused damage to India as a whole, the damage was more severe in the vast hinterland of north and central India. This hinterland was exploited for 150 years to extract revenue and agricultural resources to fuel the Industrial Revolution and then London's financial dominance in the world, until almost the beginning of the Second World War. The coastal areas of India, which obviously include parts of the south, received some benefits as a by-product in the form of development of trade, commerce and industrialisation along the coastal belt. This was accentuated by the fact that all three great cities of the empire in India—Calcutta, Bombay and Madras—were situated along the coast to facilitate the functioning of the maritime empire. In relation to the vast hinterland of the Indian subcontinent, these cities operated as colonial metropolitan centres through which resources were funnelled to London, thus incidentally benefitting them to some extent.

The variations in land revenue systems also had an impact on the social and economic wellbeing of the different parts of India during the British rule. It is argued by many that, as compared to the zamindari or mahalwari system applied to much of north and eastern India, the ryotwari system applied by the British in much of peninsular and western India was less exploitative. The agricultural heartland of the subcontinent consisted of the north and the east, owing to the sheer size and fertility of the vast Gangetic plain that stretches from the vicinity of Delhi to the Bay of Bengal.

The earlier social and economic development of the south, east and west as compared to the north likely served as the principal factor for their demographic growth spurt, which occurred a few decades earlier than in the north. The swift decline in mortality rates during the early stages of social and economic development is usually attributed to the substantial reduction in both infant and child mortality rates. Even minor improvements in living standards, notably in nutrition, sanitation and healthcare facilities, play a pivotal role in achieving significant decline in mortality rates. In line with this argument, therefore, it comes as no surprise that in the south, Kerala—primarily consisting of a coastal strip and two relatively well-governed princely states of Cochin and Travancore—had a lead not only over the rest of India, but even over the Madras Presidency, Mysore and Hyderabad, which together constituted the bulk of what is described as south India. Among these, Hyderabad was the least developed. Its backwardness, compared to the coastal Andhra region and most of the south, dragged down the social and economic indicators of united Andhra Pradesh—the last among the southern states to experience the peak demographic growth phase, with its population growing around 20 per cent per decade as late as 1991.

It must be underlined that the slight development lead that the south, the west and even other coastal states—excluding Orissa—might have had over the north before Independence did not stem from any uniform advantage provided by the British rule. In reality, even within these states, it was primarily a narrow coastal belt that directly benefitted from the British maritime empire. The interior regions within each state generally functioned as hinterland to the coast. However, the impetus provided by this incidental social and economic development was probably enough to usher in a population growth spurt in the coastal states a few decades before the north.

9

Family Planning, Emergency and Forced Sterilisation

The Journey of Population Control

This chapter explores the relationship between the family planning programme and population control in India. It shows how the programme that began as a voluntary endeavour in 1952 ended up as an authoritarian measure during 1975–77. It is argued that the coercive implementation of birth control measures during the Emergency, especially the forced sterilisation of 7–8 million men mainly in north India, was a tragic but logical culmination of the discourse of 'overpopulation' and 'population explosion' built up during the preceding decades. The leading role in it was played by the United Nations and its multiple agencies, especially Food and Agriculture Organisation (FAO), American foundations, especially the Rockefeller Foundation, Ford Foundation, think tanks and universities and the Indian policymakers and experts.[1]

The parliamentary debate on National Population Policy (NPP) and on 42nd Amendment to the Constitution is examined at length, both to trace its antecedents in the previous decades and to understand the political psychology of population control in India. The Report of Justice Shah Commission of Enquiry[2]—a judicial commission appointed by the Janata Party government to look into the various transgressions of state power during the Emergency—is a critical source of mapping the excesses, especially in north India, which was completely unprepared for large-scale sterilisations, both because of its late onset of demographic transition and lack of adequate health infrastructure. Media coverage and academic critiques of excesses are also discussed.

I
Family Planning and Population Control

In the light of the evidence presented in this book, it is critical to explore the possible link between the so-called family planning measures taken by the state and the progress of demographic transition in India, especially reduction in population growth. Let us, therefore, examine how and to what extent family planning can be credited for the demographic divergence visible today.

India holds the distinction of being the first country in the developing world to have a comprehensive family planning programme. Launched in 1952, this ambitious programme focused on reducing India's birth rate—which stood at 41 per thousand against the global average of thirty-seven. However, over the next twenty years, India's demographic trajectory did not show any noticeable impact of family planning.[3] In 1971, the birth rate in India was still 41 per thousand. When the family planning programme was launched, the population growth rate in the preceding decade, that is, 1941–51, had been 13.31 per cent. There was a general feeling in policy circles that with the implementation of the programme, population growth would go down rapidly. To the dismay of the policymakers and academics, however, the growth rate kept rising for the next two decades. It was 21.64 per cent in the first decade, 1951–61, followed by a greater surge in 1961–71, to reach 24.80 per cent, which is India's peak decadal growth rate ever. In absolute terms, India added over 18.70 crore people to its population between 1951 and 1971—an increase of 51.80 per cent. In comparison, the previous two decades (1931–51) had witnessed an increase of just 8.2 crore—a rise of 30 per cent. How do we explain such apparently anomalous trends in India's population growth, especially in the first two to three decades after the launch of the ambitious family planning programme?

One of the principal implications of the evidence presented in this book is that family planning, which is largely dependent on human agency, does not have a major causal role in the decline in population growth, though it may coincide with it or be associated with it in some other way. This is in line with McKeown's thesis[4] that it's not much about human agency; rather, population growth is largely dependent on economic forces which, in turn, alter social conditions at the macro level. The state, of course, has a very important role in social and economic development, which in turn contributes to decline in fertility and population growth. Although the success of family planning as a tool to combat population growth may have been limited worldwide, India's experiment with the programme seems to have been an almost complete failure, at least in the first two decades after its launch. Therefore, it is important to enquire into the reasons behind the inefficacy of the programme.[5] The critical question is what explains the regional variations in population growth, the family planning programme, or the progress of demographic transition aided by social and economic development, examined in Chapter 7. Even more important is to examine the emphatic claim made by the southern leaders that it is as a result of better implementation of family planning that the south has been able to register a reduction in fertility and population growth rates since 1971, quite unlike the north.

Mahmud Mamdani's *The Myth of the Population Control* published in 1972 was one of the earliest and most influential critiques of the prevailing discourse of population control through the spread of birth control measures such as contraceptives and sterilisation. Mamdani reviewed the famous Khanna study on birth control in Punjab, which was the first one to have a control as well as test population. Sponsored by Harvard University, the Khanna study began in 1956 and was completed in 1960. There was a follow up study in 1969. Mamdani notes:

> The Follow-up Study showed that the birth control programme had been a failure. Although the crude birth rate of the study population was 40 per 1000 in 1957, at the beginning of the Definitive Study, and 35 per 1000 in 1968, this reduction could not be traced to the birth control programme since it occurred among both the test and control populations.[6]

Mamdani showed that the people in the eight villages that were the subject of study did not really agree with the birth control measures being promoted by the study. But they accepted the contraceptives as a courtesy to the outsiders, without using them. Moreover, people did not speak the truth to the study team about their family size preferences, mainly because they did not want to displease them. Mamdani showed that in any case for most people in these villages having a small family, as promoted by the study, did not make sense, as large families were required for profitable agriculture. In the absence of two or three sons, a farmer had to rely on wage labour, which escalated his input cost without any commensurate gain in output. Of course, there were other reasons also that explained the rationality of large families for the villagers. Mamdani contested the idea that the villagers were ignorant and uneducated and so had large families. Moreover, he questioned one of the fundamental premises behind the family planning programme in India: that population growth was responsible for the lack of economic development. Mamdani argued that 'people are not poor because they have large families. Quite the contrary, they have large families because they are poor'.[7]

American historian Rosanna Ledbetter's appraisal of the family planning programme in its early years shows that it was not as successful as expected in cutting down annual birth rates or the population growth rate.

> For 25 years, the government stressed the importance of family planning primarily as a way to reduce the rate of population growth. In the 1970s, however, government leaders came to realize that spending large sums of money on an elaborate family-planning program had not been effective in reducing the growth rate (still 1.8 per cent to 2.2 per cent as opposed to a world rate of 1.75 per cent).[8]

Ledbetter cited this data in 1984 when the rate of world population growth was considerably higher compared to the rate at which it is growing now. So, at least the first two to three decades of family planning in India lacked efficacy in terms of arresting population growth rate. The south grew at a comparable pace with the north during the period. The annual growth rate of the country's population stood at 2 per cent in 1961, and to the utter dismay of the policymakers, it hovered around that figure even in 1981.[9] Let us now examine the regional variations in this regard. There are persistent arguments supporting the belief that better implementation of family planning in the southern states compared to the northern states has been responsible for their lower population growth rate.

The differential rate of regional growth in India was studied in detail by J.R. Rele (1987).[10] Making a comparative study of the Total Fertility Rates (TFR) of the most populous states of India, Rele drew a line between the northern and the southern India. Citing data separated by a fifteen-year period (the first part of his data includes the period 1961–66 and the second part, 1976–81), he argued that the northern or the so-called BIMARU states have had high TFR in comparison to the southern and western states, at least since 1961.

The fertility estimates for the major states of India show remarkable geographic consistency, with the belt of northern states having higher fertility than southern states in 1961–66, and, with only slight modifications, in 1976–81.[11]

Rele's argument is consistent with the data presented by him. Nevertheless, any analysis of the demographic differential between the north and the south must consider the rate of population growth and not rely too much on fertility rates. This is so for two reasons. Firstly, the difference in TFR between these two groups of states might not have been the same during most of the preceding century. Secondly, population keeps growing for a long time even after the fertility achieves replacement level, although the pace of growth declines.

This is also relevant for demographic comparisons based on other classifications such as the EAG (Empowered Action Group) versus non-EAG states created by the Census of India 2011.[12] As seen in Chapter 8, although the EAG states' share in the national growth has remained high since 1951, their growth was significantly lower than that of the non-EAG states for several decades before Independence.

A.P. Barnabas (1977) compares family planning implementation in Uttar Pradesh and Tamil Nadu and insists that the latter performed much better in terms of actions needed to ensure its success. However, the outcome of at least the first two decades of family planning was not significantly better for Tamil Nadu than for Uttar Pradesh, as far as population growth is concerned.[13] Based on a comparative study of the TFR in Tamil Nadu and Uttar Pradesh between 1971 and 1997, Paul and Sridhar (2015) conclude that owing to better family welfare practices and greater investment in health and education, Tamil Nadu surged ahead of Uttar Pradesh on many social and economic indicators.[14] Nonetheless, what matters most here is the demographic change that took place in these two states, and not development as such. Choosing 1971 as the starting point for comparison might lead one to conclude that the fertility and growth rates of Tamil Nadu have always been below those of Uttar Pradesh. As shown in this study, the population growth rate of Tamil Nadu was much higher than the corresponding rate for Uttar Pradesh in the decades prior to 1971. Moreover, even after the launch of the family planning programme, Tamil Nadu grew by 22.3 per cent during the decade of 1961–71—a period when the population of Uttar Pradesh grew at the rate of 19.54 per cent.[15]

Others have also made similar comparisons, asserting that the TFR of the southern states has always been lower in comparison to the northern states. But most of them fail to use data predating 1971. For example, Carl Haub (2009) of the Population Reference Bureau, United Nations presents a comparison of TFR based on three-year moving averages between Uttar Pradesh and Karnataka from 1971–73 to 2005–07.[16] He presents a familiar picture wherein the south has performed better than the north on population control. However, Haub's analysis leaves out the pre-1971 phase of the south's growth. The population of Karnataka had grown at a much greater rate in at least four decades preceding 1971, reaching its peak in 1981. From 1941–51 to 1971–81, the population of Karnataka grew at a higher rate than that of Uttar Pradesh. It is only during 1981–91 that Uttar Pradesh surged past Karnataka.

Therefore, the choice of 1971 for comparing population growth rates or fertility rate is fundamentally flawed. It pits the south—most of which had already passed through the second phase of demographic transition—against the north, which had just entered it. The prevalent notion is that the southern states have implemented family planning much better than the rest of India. Close examination of the implementation of the programme in various states and regions is not the focus of this study. Nevertheless, let us consider Figure 9.1, which provides a glimpse into the subject.

Interestingly, all four so-called BIMARU states and most of the EAG states feature among top ten performers in this chart. Though the introduction of PPIUCD (Postpartum Intrauterine Contraceptive Device) was a new initiative by the government to ensure family welfare, it was

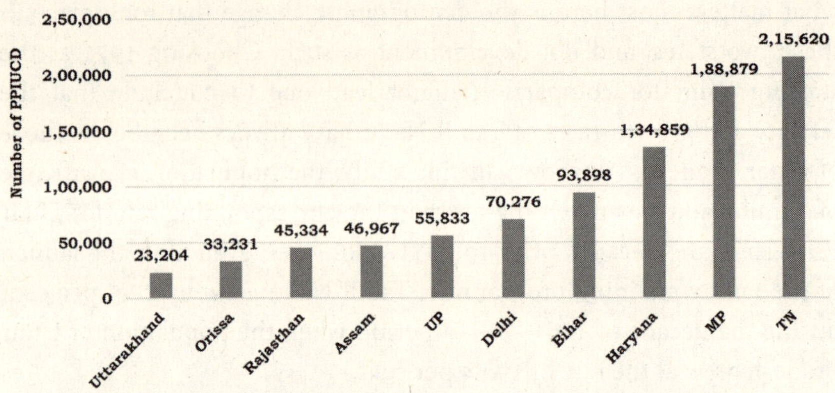

Figure 9.1: Top ten performing states according to total PPIUCD insertions, 2015-16

Source: Ministry of Health and Family Welfare[17]

implemented rather well by the states often criticised for contributing disproportionately to India's population growth. However, the larger issue remains: Has family planning ever been even moderately effective in India, insofar as population control is concerned? It might, of course, have received more success in providing primary healthcare to women and children and in spreading the use of contraceptives. But that is very different from causing reduction in population growth or fertility rates, which is the oft-repeated claim made on behalf of the family planning programme. Several questions arise.

Judged in terms of annual or decadal growth rates, why was its impact negligible in the first two to three decades after its launch? Did a cultural change resulting in responsible behaviour in family matters actually determine the demographic shift that India witnessed later? Or, was it that in order to be effective family planning had to wait until the 1990s when economic reforms led to fairly high economic growth, and that became the actual propeller of a fall in the rate of population growth that we see now? Or, is India's population and that of its various constituent units simply following the course of population growth that demographic transition must follow?

II
The Emergency and the National Population Policy

The political commitment of the preceding decades towards population control took a new avatar with the declaration of the Emergency on 26 June 1975. The coercive measures such as forced vasectomies adopted for population control during the Emergency were arguably a logical, if tragic, culmination of the alarmist environment created both in India and the world about population growth—discussed in detail in Chapter 2—especially in the poor countries of Asia and Africa.[18] The first National Population Policy (NPP) was formulated in 1976 during the Emergency, because as has been argued, 'the government at the centre was getting impatient on the population issue'. The NPP originated in an environment of coercion and authoritarianism, but it was really the culmination of a long-standing debate on 'population explosion' and family planning among policymakers and experts.

The Emergency merely provided the right opportunity for its enunciation and implementation. Freedom and debate were severely curbed both within and outside the Parliament and the media was heavily censored. The few newspapers and media houses that refused to bow to the official dictates had to face the full might of an authoritarian regime. The first newspaper reports about the imminent announcement of the NPP came out in March 1976. It was reported that 'the broad outlines of a national policy on family planning, comprising a package of incentives and disincentives, are believed to have been finalized by the Union cabinet yesterday' and 'the centre itself is not thinking in terms of resorting to compulsion to reduce the birth rate but it might not come in the way of state governments opting for such drastic action'.[19]

The policy formulated by the Union Cabinet and announced on 16 April 1976 by Dr Karan Singh, the Minister for Health and Family Planning, reflects the culmination of official thinking on population control and needs to be closely analysed. The policy statement begins with the observation that 'with 2.4 per cent of the world's land area,[20] India has about 15 per cent of the world's people'.[21] This assumes there is a direct correlation between land area and population, without any reference to geography, climate, history and culture. It is noted that since

Independence '250 millions have been added, equivalent to the entire population of the Soviet Union with six times the land area of India'.[22] Emphasising that 'the increase every year is now equal to the entire population of Australia which is two-and-a-half times the size of our country', the statement goes on to assert that 'indisputably we are facing a population explosion of crisis dimensions which has largely diluted the fruits of the remarkable economic progress that we have made over the last two decades'.[23] As discussed in Chapter 2, parallels with area-population ratios of other countries were frequently drawn in the 'overpopulation' debate for the past several decades.

These comparisons encapsulate the principal reason policymakers were so alarmed about population growth: it seemed to nullify their efforts at development. What they did not realise was that the economic progress since Independence had not been 'remarkable' by any yardstick, although it had been decent enough in the first fifteen years. In any case, even the slightly increased prosperity over the previous decades was bound to bring down mortality rates drastically, without a corresponding decline in birth rates—which worldwide has occurred only with a lag—thereby leading to rapid population growth. The answer was probably more development that focused on labour-intensive industries, export-led growth and entrepreneurial culture—something that India has never been able to do since Independence. Adopting this approach could have catapulted India into the league of ASEAN nations, which had started experiencing the annual economic growth of 8–10 per cent from the 1960s. But India under Prime Minister Indira Gandhi strengthened the licence-permit-quota raj, which was essentially a system of controls of various kinds and of the management of self-produced scarcities. In a policy environment in which the state sought to control the bulk of economic activity in the name of ensuring social justice and equity, population control was a logical step for policymakers. Thus, the failure of the Indian state to ensure rapid economic growth and eradicate poverty was attributed to 'population explosion'.

The critical paragraph in the National Population Policy reads:

> Nonetheless it is clear that simply to wait for education and economic development to bring about a drop in fertility is not a practical solution.

> The very increase in population makes economic development slow and more difficult of achievement. The time factor is so pressing, and the population growth so formidable, that we have to get out of the vicious circle through a direct assault upon this problem as a national commitment. The President in his address to the Joint Session of Parliament this year reiterated the importance of stepping up family planning efforts, and the Prime Minister has on several occasions laid stress upon the crucial role that population control has to play in the movement towards economic independence and social transformation, specially in the light of the 20-Point Economic Programme.[24]

The NPP then fixed a target of bringing the birth rate down from 35 per thousand in 1974 to twenty-five in 1984.[25] In order to achieve this ambitious target, the statement laid down policies and programmes such as raising the age of marriage to eighteen for girls and twenty-one for boys; placing an embargo on the redistribution of seats in Parliament, since the states that were supposedly successful in family planning had demanded it; using the 1971 Census data for allocation of resources by Finance Commissions until 2001; raising female literacy because 'wherever female literacy improves ... fertility drops almost automatically'; inculcating 'population values in the education system' for the younger generation; raising monetary compensation for sterilisation; roping in voluntary organisations, particularly youth and women's organisations; and increasing research in reproductive biology and contraception.[26] Having laid down these measures, the policy statement tackles the delicate question of compulsory sterilisation:

> The question of compulsory sterilization has been the subject of lively public debate over the last few months. It is clear that public opinion is now ready to accept much more stringent measures for family planning than before. However, the administrative and medical infrastructure in many parts of the country is still not adequate to cope with the vast implications of nation-wide compulsory sterilization. We do not, therefore, intend to bring in Central legislation for this purpose, at least for the time being. Some States feel that the facilities available with them are adequate to meet the requirements of compulsory sterilization. We are of the view that where a State legislature, in the exercise of its own powers, decides that the time is ripe and it is necessary to pass legislation for compulsory

> sterilization, it may do so. Our advice to the States in such cases will be to bring in the limitation after three children, and to make it uniformly applicable to all Indian citizens resident in that State without distinction of caste, creed or community.[27]

It was further asserted that 'employees of the Union Government will be expected to adopt the small family norm and necessary changes will be made in their service conduct rules to ensure this'.[28]

The Department of Personnel and Administrative Reforms, Ministry of Home Affairs records show an intense discussion on measures to be adopted for population control in general by devising a scheme of incentives and disincentives for government employees expected to set an example for others and have a 'multiplier effect' on the rest of the society. Financial compensation for sterilisation after two or three children, a graded incentive system based on the number of children and preferential treatment in loans were discussed at various levels. Among the disincentives discussed were denial of maternity leave after the third child, denial of medical benefits for children beyond the third, although both ethical considerations and implementation challenges were also brought up. Family planning was thus sought to be integrated into the Central Civil Services (Conduct) Rules.[29]

III

Parliamentary Debate on Family Planning and National Population Policy

There was considerable debate in Parliament on family planning, extending over sessions from April to November 1976. The vast majority of members expressed their views in favour of the NPP. However, many of them criticised its coercive implementation. Thus, during the debate on 28 April, quoting two other members without naming them, Dr Saradish Roy, CPM, Member of Parliament from Bolpur, West Bengal highlighted the 'compulsory sterilisation of the people of this area (Turkman Gate) during the last few days.'[30] Dr Roy asserted: 'Married or unmarried, old and young are subjected to forcible sterilisation. The people who are resisting are being beaten up mercilessly. Rickshaw pullers, beggars and pavement dwellers became the easy objects for this.'[31]

P. Venkatasubbaiah, Congress MP from Nandyal, Andhra Pradesh welcomed both family planning and the freeze on delimitation, and said: 'The first point is about the freezing of the population at the 1971 level. Of course, some state governments have a grievance that a premium has been placed on those states which did not follow the family planning programmes, whereas they themselves have lost some of their representation in the assemblies and in Parliament.'[32] Interestingly, he also bemoaned the fact that a Telugu film *Thathama Kala*, awarded by state and Central governments, preached against family planning.[33]

Dr V.K.R. Varadaraja Rao, Congress MP from Bellary, Mysore struck a discordant note by asserting that 'reduction in population growth rate will not by itself bring about economic development'.[34] He continued, 'I would go further and say that even having a small family norm, even bringing reduction in birth rate and in the population growth rate itself will be dependent upon what we do by way of development.'[35] Dr Rao, however, supported the idea that 'we are going to freeze for purposes not only of seats in the Lok Sabha but much more important for purposes of Central funds, Plan assistance'.[36]

Welcoming the NPP, Bhargavi Thankappan of the CPI, MP from Adoor, Kerala, said: 'We are on the verge of an explosion and ... if the population rises at this rate, by 2000 AD our people won't get drinking water or fresh air to breathe. They won't get enough space even to move about'.[37]

On the basis of some anecdotal evidence, Mukul Banarjee, Congress MP from Delhi, announced that 'women are really not interested in having more children. Muslim women with *burqa* came and said this'. She added that 'actually it is men who did not care'.[38]

Another Congress MP Sheila Kaul stated that 'the burning problem is not lack of food or accommodation or even pollution but the growth of our population'.[39] Kaul gave an ingenious perspective on birth control maintaining that 'in the *shastras*, the first born one is named *dharmaputra* because he is to do the last rites of the parents when they die; the others who come after him are known as *kamaputras*, children born of the lust of parents'.[40]

Referring to poor people, G. Vishwanathan, DMK MP from Wandiwash, Tamil Nadu, gave his piece of wisdom: 'They have no recreation either. If there is no other recreation, they go in for procreation, that is how the problem of population explosion in this country has come about.'[41] He then welcomed 'freezing the number of seats in assemblies and Parliament based on the 1971 Census'.[42]

P. Ganga Reddy, Congress MP from Adilabad, Andhra Pradesh, opined that without serious efforts at family planning, 'the country will be crushed by the population explosion and that 'It will become a dragon which will swallow the country'.[43] Reddy then added: We should achieve a zero rate of birth rate; that means that the birth rate should not be more than the death rate. It would be very good then if there is no birth next year'.[44]

S.M. Siddayya, Congress MP from Chamarajanagar, Mysore, welcomed the freeze on the parliament seats: 'Similarly, those states which have actually implemented the family planning programme were handicapped in a way that the number of seats in the Lok Sabha was actually reduced last time. But now the Government have realised the mistake and have rectified it by freezing the representation according to the census of 1971. Similarly, central assistance and subsidies given by the government are not based on the present population but based on the population figures of 1971 census. It is good thing.'[45]

During the debate on the 42nd Constitution Amendment Bill on 26 October 1976, C.M. Stephen, Congress MP from Muvattpuzha, Kerala, defended the NPP on the ground that it incorporated the provisions of an earlier rejected private member's Constitution Amendment Bill of DMK leader Murasoli Maran, which had said that 'for purposes of delimitation of constituencies, the population must be frozen at the previous census figure and no further delimitation should take place as a result of expansion in population.'[46] The Bill moved by Murasoli Maran has been discussed in Chapter 2.

Ebrahim Sulaiman Sait of Indian Union Muslim League, Kozhikode, Kerala acknowledged the dangers of 'population explosion but decried compulsion. He highlighted that 'Particularly in UP and Haryana, Bihar and in other places, the coercion is taking place.'[47]

Frank Anthony, nominated Anglo-Indian MP, underlined the need to carry on 'population control' on a war footing since it was 'the most strident challenge the nation faces today'. Referring to an article written by himself, Anthony asserted that 'not only India's progress has been neutralised but the progress has been put into reverse gear'.[48]

Defence Minister Swaran Singh, who also chaired a committee set up by the government to recommend changes in the Constitution leading to the 42nd Amendment, expressed an alarmist view that after twenty years with 100 crore people 'there will be nothing to eat except they will eat each other'. Singh asserted that 'unless this population explosion is stopped and is curbed a very difficult situation would arise'.[49]

P. Venkatasubbaiah welcomed the great impetus given to family planning. Asserting that 'we should pursue this programme in the national interest', he went on to link it to the freeze on delimitation: 'As a matter of fact we have even frozen the delimitation of constituencies till 2001 so as to make family planning a national objective.'[50]

On 3 November, C.K. Chandrappan, CPI, MP from Tellicherry, while welcoming family planning, commented that 'the way it has been done in our country is alarming'.[51] He perceptively cited the example of Puerto Rico, which had probably the highest rate of female sterilisation at 35 per cent, highlighting that 'even after sterilisation to that great extent, that country remains poor and backward'. So, he questioned the supposed link between population control and economic development, which had become the prevailing wisdom.[52]

P.G. Mavalankar, Independent MP from Ahmedabad, Gujarat, acknowledged that population increase 'is a tremendous problem, and we have to face it boldly and squarely' with the help of persuasion and education. Recognising the coercive methods being used, Mavalankar warned 'let not this programme become a matter of terror, something which is creating a fright'.[53]

Krishna Chandra, Congress MP from Uttar Pradesh, acknowledged the 'need for planned parenthood in the country', but expressed his opposition to 'the prevailing atmosphere of threat and force which is being applied to achieve this objective'.[54] He brought up the issue of the Muzaffarnagar conflict on family planning in which 'the police had to open fire and many people were killed'.[55]

Denen Bhattacharya, CPM, Serampore, West Bengal, asserted that 'this type of forcible sterilisation and vasectomy is a criminal offence on the part of the government' and questioned, 'why has force been applied in Delhi, Uttar Pradesh and West Bengal?'[56]

Echoing the prevailing wisdom about the adversarial relationship between population growth and development, Y.S. Mahajan, Congress MP from Buldana, Maharashtra, called population growth 'the root cause of poverty in this country' and highlighted that 'increase in our population is equal to the total population of Russia, which occupies one-sixth of the habitable area of the world', without realising that much of Russia is actually not so habitable.[57]

Vayalar Ravi, Congress MP from Chirayinkil in Kerala, strongly defended the NPP, arguing that there had been earlier discussions on the subject in Parliament and at the 1974 United Nations conference on population in Budapest which had consensus on population control. He then launched a diatribe: 'The family planning programme is being politicised today by the forces of reaction and darkness. We know that. In the last few years, we had been fighting these forces of reaction and darkness politically, defeated them on all fronts. Now they are trying to raise their head again through rumour mongering and opposing family planning, which has a very important content and aspect of the socio-economic transformation of this country.'[58]

There was also a Gandhian flavour to the debate. Citing Gandhi's book *Birth-Control: The Right Way and The Wrong Way* and highlighting his own example of a Gandhian vow of not marrying, Professor S.L. Saxena, Independent MP from Maharajganj, Uttar Pradesh, quoted Gandhi, 'The only method of birth control handed down from ages past is self-control or Brahmacharya'.[59] He further said: 'That is why I have given my cut motion to discuss the anti-national population policy and large-scale forcible sterilisation and tubectomies all over the country and stoppage of monthly salaries and other benefits to Government employees, teachers and others for months ...'[60] Saxena then highlighted the atmosphere of fear in his constituency:

> I see troubles in my constituency. People surround me everywhere and ask me why this coercion is happening. People are terrified. They keep out of their homes to avoid being caught by police. The police get hold of poor people, the rickshaw pullers, and get them sterilised.[61]

M. Satyanarayana Rao, Congress MP from Karimnagar, Andhra Pradesh asserted that 'population explosion is the greatest problem facing this country' and suggested that population control be made into a fundamental duty:

> It should be made a fundamental duty on the part of the citizen that they should not have more than two children. Such a provision is essential to control the increase in population.[62]

Prime Minister Indira Gandhi herself made a decisive intervention in the debate. At the outset, she said: 'We do not approve of compulsion. But we do believe that programmes of sterilisation and the adoption of all other known effective measures for the control of population are important and most urgent.'[63] Then she went on to attack the opposition on their reservations about family planning:

> But, and it is a big 'but', certain parties, groups and individuals have been raising a hue and cry, creating misunderstanding and an atmosphere of fear. As we all know, fear leads to irrational action. Therefore, when a situation of confrontation is deliberately created, there are tragic consequences. Some deaths have taken place due to firing, though the figure given by some hon. Members is greatly exaggerated.[64]

Defending the 42nd Amendment, Prime Minister Indira Gandhi invoked Nehru to criticise those who opposed the amendment:

> Jawaharlal Nehru knew the country had to, and would, change speedily. He himself planted and nurtured the seeds of change. As the House knows, the first amendment to the Constitution came within months of the adoption of the document. Indeed, many will recall that even as the Constituent Assembly was in session so many changes were occurring, for example, the integration of the States, when many clauses were reopened and reorganized. So, revision and adjustment in changing conditions are part and parcel of our Constitution. Those who want to fix it in a rigid and unilateral frame do not know the spirit of our Constitution and are entirely out of tune with the spirit of new India.[65]

She concluded:

> While the Constitution is a very important document, it is but an instrument to serve the people. The Constitution exists for the people. People should certainly respect it, but they cannot be sacrificed for it.[66]

Interestingly, sometime before the declaration of the Emergency, Mrs Gandhi had written an article, 'A World Without Want', published as a special feature in the 1975 edition of the *Britannica Book of the Year*.[67] While 'the essay as a whole casts a critical eye on the closely related issues of poverty and globalisation from the perspective of developing nations', there is also a section titled 'The Overpopulation Question'.[68] Here, she apparently bemoaned the fact that 'underdevelopment, poverty, and hunger are often regarded as consequences of burgeoning population', and perceptively noted:

> Couples do not decide on the size of their family in terms of its effect on the per capita income of the nation or on the world's food problem. What concerns them is the effect on their own standard of living. For educated, well-to-do parents, each new baby makes heavy demands on time and budget. For the really poor, an extra child makes hardly any difference. It may, in fact, be regarded as an earner and a helper.[69]

The irony was that during the Emergency this important insight into population growth was ignored by many functionaries of the state. Mrs Gandhi proudly declared that 'India has the largest officially sponsored family-planning programme of any country',[70] and highlighted that the growth was partly because of a decline in mortality brought about by public health measures. She underlined the variations in family planning across states: 'For the country as a whole, the birth rate has fallen from 41 per thousand population to 37 in the last decade, but it is 30 in Kerala and Tamil Nadu, where education has made great headway, and 33 in Punjab, where the increase in agricultural production has been tangible. Family planning cannot be viewed in isolation. It is part of development.'[71]

IV

Critiques of the National Population Policy

Academic critiques of the National Population Policy, 1976 started appearing in 1977, around the lifting of the Emergency. In an article published in the *Economic & Political Weekly* in March 1977, Kaval Gulhati, associate director of the Centre for Population Activities, Washington DC, noted:

> An examination of the facts about India's population growth and the meagre impact of the family planning programme over almost 25 years will explain, at least partially, the desperate dilemma faced by India's leaders. But the significant change which could possibly explain the *timing* of the move for compulsory sterilization is the new political order which was born on 26 June 1975, when Prime Minister Indira Gandhi declared a state of emergency in India. The Indian body politic of today bears scant resemblance to the one that preceded that declaration ... Prior to the emergency it would have been impossible to endorse compulsory sterilization.[72]

Interestingly, Gulhati then went on to critically refer to R.A. Gopalaswami, the first Census Commissioner of Independent India (discussed in chapter 2), who led the Census of 1951, as a 'prescient advocate of mass sterilization'. Gopalaswami had, according to Gulhati, argued that 'all births after the third were improvident maternity and must be curtailed' and that 'he recommended mass sterilization for achieving this goal'.[73] Gulhati also questioned the idea propagated since the 1950s that there was a 'silent demand for contraceptive usage'. He cited the work (discussed earlier) of Mahmud Mamdani, 'a political scientist who interviewed villagers in the Khanna district of the Punjab', who 'chastised Western researchers in India for failing to appreciate the economic rationality to the rural Indian family of having many children'. Gulhati ended with a grim conclusion:

> Indian policy makers view the use of coercive laws to reduce fertility as a necessary intervention. Maharashtra's leaders seem to regard compulsory sterilization as an easy way to success. But legislative measures in other socioeconomic matters such as the Prohibition of Dowry Act or the Tenancy Act have, in practice, been completely ineffective. Even for a coercion programme to work will require a hugely expanded commitment of administrative and financial resources. The world will be watching closely to see whether and how the Indian state governments will follow up their new policy with bigger budgets and more effective action.[74]

Another powerful and far-sighted critique of the National Population Policy, 1976 was made by Asok Mitra, a former Registrar General and Census Commissioner of India, who authored many important books and articles. In a paper titled 'National Population Policy in Relation to National Planning in India', published in the *Population and Development Review* in September 1977, Mitra noted:

> Ever since 1956, the thrust of the government's family planning program has been on sterilization as the method of choice. Even though never accepted as a panacea, sterilization was widely considered inescapable as a major program. But the country obviously was not prepared for the harshness with which the government sought to implement the April 1976 policy statement. Apart from the terror that attended sterilization, particularly in Northern India, it represented the conversion of the government's administrative resources into an engine of oppression, corruption, and fraud. Sterilization became the symbol of denial of all that one was entitled to expect from one's government.[75]

Mitra insightfully argued that the population growth that had started in India in 1921 was associated with the economic development that started from the First World War onwards and accelerated during the Second World War. These wars provided many opportunities for Indian industry and trade to flourish, even as the British hold on the Indian economy somewhat loosened. Further, 'the two decades between 1920 and 1940 appear, in retrospect, to have been a period of slow but steady improvement in aspirations and economic activity.'[76] Besides, 'this was also an era of acceleration in Indian urbanization with substantial transfers from agricultural to non-agricultural households and impressive expansion of the organized industrial working force and of the organized and informal modern service sector.'[77] According to Mitra, 'the momentum of the economy achieved during and after the two world wars was accelerated considerably after 1950 but declined after 1963'.[78] He added:

> All things considered, the instruments in the hands of the poor to work for their own betterment are fewer today than in the early 1950s. It is in the context of this bleakening economic picture that we must consider the implications of the National Population Policy Statement.[79]

While acknowledging that the 'desirability of a sharp reduction in the birth rate to alleviate the adverse economic conditions is all too evident',[80] Mitra had this to say about the NPP goal of reducing the birth rate from 35 per thousand to 25 per thousand in less than a decade:

> This would require the crude birth rate to fall by one point or more per year over the coming years. Such a rapid decline has occurred elsewhere, in the case of Taiwan and Singapore, for example, and there is definite evidence of a downward fertility trend in India, particularly since 1971. Thus, at first glance, such a course does not seem altogether implausible. However, in no country has such a low level of fertility been reached and sustained without low and stable mortality. In India the death rate is still high—around 17 or 18 for the country as a whole—and has even increased slightly in recent years because of renewed outbreaks of malaria since 1972. The infant mortality rate may be over 125 per thousand live births for the country as a whole.[81]

Brilliantly explaining the low acceptability of the small family norm in India, Mitra asserted:

> The vast majority of households in India still tend to consider large family size an asset. First, a large family is a means of acquiring more earners, each of whom will augment the total income of the family, however marginally. Second, children can share household chores and family enterprise from very young ages, releasing the adults to seek full employment and higher wages. Third, many births are a safeguard against loss of family members through death, which can come suddenly at all ages, particularly at infancy or at young ages. Fourth, children provide sustenance and company in old age. Fifth, they provide emotional satisfaction. Sixth, they are a benefit whose value is great but whose costs by way of maintenance, upbringing, and education are hardly perceived at all, for a child can start contributing to the family enterprise as early as age seven or eight.[82]

In the end, taking the economic argument to its logical culmination, Mitra noted:

> Wherever, as in India, the household remains the basis of economic enterprise and wherever income depends on the contribution made by unpaid family work, children are likely to be regarded as a source of net inflow of wealth to the parents over their lifetime instead of being

an object of net outflow of wealth from the parents to the child. Even the often-significant cost of education borne by the parents may not appear oppressive up to a point, as the investment on education offers the prospect of greater net inflow of wealth to the parents through the educated child's contribution to the family over the parents' lifetime.[83]

V
The Emergency and Forced Sterilisations: The Shah Commission Report

The egregious excesses perpetrated during the Emergency in the name of population control stemmed from the demographic debate of the three preceding decades which had engendered a form of neo-Malthusianism[84] and eugenics.[85] There was arguably a lopsided treatment of the north by the Indian state on this matter. As has been widely reported upon and documented, in the frenzied chasing of low population growth the north had to bear the brunt of excesses during those twenty-one months.

The Justice Shah Commission of Enquiry—appointed in May 1977 by the Morarji Desai Government, and headed by former Chief Justice of India, J.C. Shah—among other things went into the matter of excesses and atrocities committed in the implementation of family planning, including the National Population Policy. The final Report of the Commission has a long chapter titled *Implementation of Family Planning Programme* during the Emergency, which examined the subject in detail. The Commission collected testimonies of various persons and scrutinised documentary evidence from government records on the coercive implementation of family planning during the Emergency. In the section titled 'change in the voluntary nature of the programme during the emergency', Prime Minister Indira Gandhi's address to the Joint Conference of Association of Physicians of India on 22 January 1976 is cited:

> We must now act decisively and bring down the birth rate speedily to prevent the doubling of our population in a mere 28 years. We should not hesitate to take steps which might be described as drastic. Some personal rights have to be kept in abeyance, for the human rights of the nation, the right to live, the right to progress.[86]

What the enquiry Commission wished to imply was that the Emergency excesses originated from the top level in the government.

In his testimony, Secretary, Health and Family Welfare defended the sterilisation campaign saying that the government of India had 'after taking into consideration all factors, set a target of 4.3 million sterilisations for the financial year 1976–77.'[87] He claimed that 'the States, however, decided to give to themselves a higher target', even though 'they were advised from time to time not to indulge in excesses and not to overstrain themselves in this regard'.[88] The Commission, however, found that there was no evidence on record of such advice being given to the states.[89]

The Commission cites a report of the Intelligence Bureau titled *Family Planning Programme–An Assessment* dated 24 September 1976 to corroborate the evidence on inflated targets for sterilisation. After noting that 'certain hostile reactions have come to notice in some states, particularly U.P. and to a lesser extent in Bihar, West Bengal and Maharashtra' the IB report said:

> One of the important reasons which has led to adverse reactions is the fixation of high targets by certain States in vast disproportion to those fixed by Government of India. U.P. has raised the target of sterilisation from 4 lakhs, which was fixed by Government of India to 15 lakhs for the year 1976–77 and West Bengal from 3.25 lakhs to 10 lakhs. The short time available for realising the target and the vast gap between the figures already achieved and to be achieved have led to certain administrative steps resulting in undesirable and in some instances disastrous consequences.[90]

After highlighting the inflation in sterilisation targets attributable to state governments, the IB report tendered the following advice to the Ministry of Home Affairs:

> Government of India may, therefore, consider the advisability of prescribing a certain permissible percentage beyond the fixed target for each category of family planning programme (sterilisation/IUD insertions/other methods) so that the State Governments need not be tempted to aim at unattainable target figures by resorting to unhealthy practices.[91]

Thus, some states went farther than others in the coercive implementation of family planning. The Maharashtra Compulsory Sterilisation Bill, 1976, later changed to Maharashtra Family (Restriction on Size) Bill, 1976, was passed in the Assembly in July 1976. However, the Bill was put on hold by the Central government, although it was initially listed for discussion in Cabinet meeting scheduled for 8 December 1976.[92]

In the section titled 'coercive measures devised by state governments', the Justice Shah Commission noted the sterilisation target escalation by state governments: 'The performance graph touched 2.67 million, sterilisations in 1975–76 and rose to the peak level of 8.1 million in 1976–77. Whereas 10 States and 4 Union Territories had exceeded the targets in 1975–76, 18 States and 5 Union Territories exceeded the targets in 1976–77.'[93] The Report cites a crash wireless message of 7 July 1976 from the Chief Secretary, Uttar Pradesh to all the District Magistrates and the Divisional Commissioners as part of the drive to achieve the inflated target: 'Government attach highest importance to achievement of family planning targets. Presume you have already fixed targets for each district and divisional level officer. Inform everybody that failure to achieve monthly targets will not only result in stoppage of salary but also suspension and severest penalties.'[94]

The Enquiry Commission noted that '548 reports/complaints regarding sterilisation of unmarried persons had been received during the period of emergency'.[95] Out of these, UP (164), Haryana (105); Madhya Pradesh (84), Rajasthan (44), Maharashtra (37), Delhi (32), Bihar (30) accounted for the most.[96]

The Shah Commission cited a note of the Home Department that assessed family planning implementation in Uttar Pradesh. 'The words family planning and sterilisation have almost become synonymous and therefore in the common parlance when people express their views against the family planning, their opposition is actually against sterilisation'.[97] Another letter of the Ministry of Home Affairs also noted the hostility of many government servants who were 'expected to be the active protagonists and motivators'.[98]

The Shah Commission Report has given details of original and revised targets for states both for 1975-76 and 1976-77. The worst culprits in arbitrary upward revision of targets were the northern and western states. For example, Central government's target of 3 lakh sterilisations for Bihar was raised by the state government to 6 lakh.[99] Gujarat exceeded the target of 2 lakh by carrying out more than 3 lakh sterilisations.[100] Haryana was assigned a target of only 52,000, which was initially revised to 1 lakh and later 'the revised target was further raised to two lakhs' by the Chief Minister 'arbitrarily against the advice of the Health Department'.[101] The actual number of sterilisations at 2.2 lakh exceeded even this second revised target. In reply to the Commission's questionnaire on the role of the police in enforcing mass sterilisation, the state government admitted:

> The police was extensively used to coerce the people to undergo sterilisation. Police force was used to surround, round up and coerce people to undergo sterilisation. In fact, such a large number of sterilisations in less than a year would have been impossible without their help … All the instructions regarding the use of coercion in the implementation of the programme, as also the involvement of the police, were issued verbally.[102]

Similarly, in Himachal Pradesh, while the original target was 31,500, there were about 1 lakh sterilisations, which was no less than six times the achievement of the previous year.[103] Rajasthan carried out 3,64,760 sterilisations against the target of 1,75,000 in 1976-77.[104]

The record of Uttar Pradesh was arguably the worst on coercive implementation of family planning. During 1975-76 Uttar Pradesh could not achieve even the target of 1.75 lakh sterilisations, reaching the figure of 1.28 lakh only.[105] The very next year, the state carried out 8.37 lakh sterilisations against the target of 4 lakh only—double the target and almost seven times the actual performance of the previous year. 'Coercive methods such as non-payment of salary to Government servants for failure to fulfil family planning targets were contemplated by the State Government in the beginning of 1976'.[106]

It was decided 'that with the exception of police and staff of Land Records and Collection in Revenue Department, workers of all other departments should be allotted a target of motivating at least one sterilisation case per month'.[107] Further, it was decided that salaries for the months of March and April should be paid only when the Government servant submitted a certificate from the Medical Officer to the drawing and disbursing officer of having motivated a case'.[108]

On 3 July, the state government issued the Uttar Pradesh Essential Articles and Things (Restriction on Grant or Supply to Unplanned Families) Order, 1976, which provided that, subject to certain inter alia exceptions, 'persons having three or more children would be deprived of the following facilities unless 'they or their spouses got themselves sterilised within three months from the date of commencement of the order'.[109] These included the issue of rationed articles for more than four units; allotment of scooters, cars and houses; medical facilities in any hospital or dispensary run by the government or any local authority; concession in education fee or any stipend or reservation of seat in medical college and technical institution; permit for public carrier, mini-bus, auto rickshaw or taxi.[110]

As noted by the Justice Shah Commission, 'there were at least eight instances of firings by the Police to deal with law-and-order situations arising out of resistance to the family planning programme'.[111] These took place in Sultanpur (27 August 1976); Gorakhpur (16 October 1976); Muzaffarnagar (18 October 1976); Rampur (28 October 1976); Bareilly (30 October and 7 December 1976) and Pratapgarh (21 December 1976). The police firing in Gorakhpur, Muzaffarnagar and Pratapgarh are reported to have resulted in the death of 12 persons.[112]

In his statement before the Commission, Dr Karan Singh started with strongly criticising the coercive measures:

> It will remain a matter of grave sorrow and personal regret to me that in the name of family planning Indian citizens, especially those belonging to the weaker sections of society, should have been humiliated in such a barbaric fashion.[113]

Dr Karan Singh testified to the collapse of the normal functioning of the state machinery in the implementation of the family planning programme during the Emergency:

> As I have pointed out, the Ministry of Health and Family Planning over which I presided had never enhanced the sterilisation targets for 1976–77, nor at any stage advocated coercion. It could be asked as to why, despite this, the excesses took place at all. The answer is as clear

as it is tragic. As the Commission is no doubt aware, at that time an extra-constitutional centre of power was operating in the country, and Chief Ministers who owed special allegiance to this centre vied with each other in raising their sterilisation targets in order to gain favour. Once the targets were raised, the whole force of governmental machinery in those States was thrust into use to achieve them, and in the process an atmosphere of fear and coercion became widespread. Once again it was proved that howsoever desirable the ends may be, wrong means can lead to nothing but disaster.'[114]

VI

Media Coverage and Critiques of the Emergency Excesses

According to some experts, around eleven million Indians were sterilised and an additional one million women were fitted with IUDs (Intrauterine Devices). An astonishing 6.2 million Indians were sterilised in 1976 alone, 1.7 million in September.[115] Tales of forced sterilisation under the supervision of Sanjay Gandhi abound in both the reported and unreported events of the period. The five points added at his behest to the government's 20-points programme launched earlier focused on birth control.

Family planning, which had apparently begun as an exercise in persuasion, degenerated into coercion. The target of 4.3 million sterilisations for April 1976–March 1977 is regarded as overambitious by Rosanna Ledbetter (1984), as it exceeded the total number of sterilisations performed in the entire country in the preceding year by more than double.[116] Notwithstanding the coercive nature of the programme, political functionaries and office-bearers, eager to be in the good books of the powers-that-be, set about achieving the goals of forced sterilisation.[117]

Thus, the government of Rajasthan decided to make sterilisation compulsory once a married couple had two or three children.[118] In Punjab and Haryana, the governments threatened their employees with withdrawal of several service benefits if they failed to cooperate in the grand design of nationwide sterilisation.[119] Dire consequences, such as dismissal from service, also awaited government employees in these states if they were unable to pull in volunteers willing to undergo sterilisation.[120] In Bihar, 600 government employees were sacked and another 50,000 had their salaries withheld for three months. Their fault lay in their inability to either bring in volunteers for sterilisation or getting themselves sterilised.[121]

Let us now look into the debate in the media on the National Population Policy. It was reported by *Time* magazine that the government of Uttar Pradesh was happy to raise its target from 4,00,000 to 15,00,000.[122] In its issue of 17 April 1976, *The Hindu* reported on the NPP with the headline 'Lok Sabha Seats for States and Aid Linked to 71 Census'. It then went on to highlight that 'raising the minimum age of marriage by three years, linking representation for States in the Lok Sabha and Plan assistance to States to the level of population in 1971 for the next twenty-five years, increase for monetary compensation for sterilisation and group incentives are among the measures announced by the Central government today to tackle the population explosion'.[123] This coverage makes it evident that freezing of seat allocation in Parliament was seen as a critical component of the policy, which was widely believed to be targeted against a 'population explosion' supposedly caused by the high growth rates in the north.

The *Hindustan Times* highlighted that 'the policy represented the Centre's resolve to grapple with a series of fundamental issues like seats in Parliament and the State Legislatures and the sharing of the Central resources on the population basis'.[124] It then stated that 'according to the new policy the Centre will bring forward necessary constitutional amendment to freeze the representation in the Lok Sabha and the State Legislatures on the basis of the 1971 Census till the year 2001'. Apart from taking note of the freeze on Lok Sabha seats, *The Indian Express* emphasised the fact that there was no central law on sterilisation and that the age of marriage was raised.

Under the impact of censorship, the media at times became a mere instrument for reiterating the government's views on the NPP. *The Times of India* published a story on 28 April 1976 on how 'the national population policy recently announced by the Union Health and Family Planning Minister was generally welcomed by members in the Lok Sabha', although it also noted that members were divided on the question of compulsory sterilisation.

There was a similar story in *The Times of India* on 29 April 1976, headlined 'Big support by MPs to population policy'. The story echoed the official propaganda that it was just a 'massive programme of motivation and education....and that there had not been any attempt at coercion in Delhi or elsewhere'.[125] *The Times of India* of 3 May 1976 ran a story on how the Catholic Union of India had welcomed the NPP in a meeting held in Bangalore.[126] Another *TOI* story of 3 June 1976 headlined 'Minorities increasingly in favour of FP' stated that 'minorities, especially Catholics and Muslims, are increasingly going in for family planning, including sterilisation, a nation-wide survey by Samachar has revealed'.[127]

Writing for *The Times of India* on 23 April 1976, A.S. Abraham welcomed the policy, observing that 'it is clear now as it has never been before, that population limitation is a serious business and must be taken seriously'.[128] Ruing the inadequacies of India's family planning programme in the preceding quarter century, he asserted that 'neither India's endorsement of FP [Family Planning] as an official programme in 1952 nor the creation of a separate department for it 14 years later was, for all practical purposes, more than a token recognition of what was emerging more and more ominously as a major development concern'.[129] He noted that 'it cannot even be said that, on the whole, the campaign to limit the size of families has been fought in any but the most lackadaisical manner'.[130]

According to Abraham, 'the NPP's chief merit is that it puts the issue of population limitation in the wider perspective of national development.'[131] This is again the clincher that sums up how, during this time, opinion-makers of the country started projecting population growth as one of the principal barriers to social and economic development, for which the north was to be blamed explicitly or implicitly.

Some stories of excesses committed by the state appeared in the international media. *Time* magazine reported the death of 56 people in clashes between the public and the police when a community openly revolted against the iron-fisted implementation of forced sterilisations.[132] *The Guardian* informed its readers that in Delhi and Bombay the police sometimes arrested common people and forcibly drove them to sterilisation clinics.[133] To put this into perspective, the figure of 8.26 million sterilisations performed between April 1976 and March 1977 exceeded that of the previous five years in the entire country and was greater than the total number performed in any country until then.

What is striking is that nearly all the forced sterilisations took place in the northern states, although the south was not completely untouched. In 1976, at a mass sterilisation camp organised in Kerala's Ernakulum, 65,000 vasectomies were carried out in a fortnight.[134] Even though until the 1960s, population growth rates had been high in the southern states too, including Kerala, Karnataka and Andhra Pradesh, it was the north that bore the brunt of the forced sterilisation campaign. Vasectomies were hastily performed at railway stations and makeshift camps on a large number of men from Uttar Pradesh and Bihar.[135] The excesses committed in the northern states during the Emergency in the name of population control ultimately owed their origins to the discourse of 'population explosion' propagated from the 1950s.

The National Population Policy of 1976 had both macro and micro components to arrest India's high population growth rate. At the macro level, Central government assistance was linked to state performance in family planning. At the micro level, family size became a parameter for government jobs, promotions, housing and loans.[136]

In his 2019 book, *Emergency Chronicles,* Princeton historian Gyan Prakash discusses population control as a critical and controversial aspect of the Emergency, particularly the role of Sanjay Gandhi, whose population control measures, especially forced sterilisation, were among the most infamous policies during the Emergency. He stresses that there was a pervasive belief that rapid population growth was a primary obstacle to India's economic development and modernisation. The government, influenced by Western ideas of development, emphasised reducing birth rates as a way to achieve socio-economic progress. He also examines how the idea of population control was influenced by global discourse at the time, including Western concerns about 'overpopulation' in developing countries. Indian policy elites adopted these ideas, viewing population growth as an obstacle to modernisation and economic development. Going deep into the intersection of law, politics, and society, Gyan Prakash critiques how this global narrative justified draconian measures in the name of progress. He captures how the Emergency was not just a political crisis but a social one, in which the rights of the poor and the marginalised were trampled upon. Gyan Prakash presents a nuanced critique of how the policy of population control was enforced through authoritarian measures.[137]

Emma Tarlo's *Unsettling Memories: Narratives of Emergency in Delhi* recounts in detail the repression carried out in Delhi during the Emergency in the name of family planning. She argues that the sterilisation campaign divided the local people into two opposite camps, partly because of the monetary reward offered to 'motivators', who brought 'volunteers' to sterilisation camps. The necessity of having a sterilisation certificate for access to basic civic amenities is highlighted by Tarlo.[138]

VII

The role of the United Nations, along with that of other multilateral institutions and American foundations and think tanks, in shaping the discourse of 'overpopulation' has been highlighted in Chapter 2. An interesting aside of the population control movement is that in 1981 the United Nations General Assembly instituted the United Nations Population Award.[139] The first recipients of the award in 1983 were Prime Minister Indira Gandhi and Qian Xinzhong, Minister-in-Charge, State Family Planning Commission, People's Republic of China. In her acceptance speech at the United Nations, Mrs Gandhi said:

> The honour is not to me personally or even to the Government of India, but to the thousands of dedicated family planning workers and the millions of young parents who are willingly planning their families. They will be encouraged that this world body has recognized India's efforts in one of the most difficult areas of social engineering. Even more, it is a reminder of the tremendous responsibility cast on us, because India and China, which is also honoured today, are more than a third of the human race.[140]

She noted the great decline in mortality caused by famines and epidemics, which was responsible for rapid population growth.[141] Surprisingly, in a first, her speech provided a historical comparison of India with the West in the nineteenth century:

> Between 1801 and 1901, the population of Britain increased from 10.5 million to 37 million. And that of Europe from 188 million to 415 million. Thus, the population growth of India is not because of improvidence and dereliction, but a sign that the government is doing its utmost to save lives.[142]

Prime Minister Indira Gandhi perceptively underlined:

> Death rate falls as a result of organised public health services. Birth rate falls with the growth of education and improvement in standards of living. One could say that the death rate is brought down by the community's responsibility to the individual, and the birth rate by the individual's responsibility to the community.[143]

After this insightful observation, however, she went on to reiterate the prevalent belief in a causal relationship between population growth and poverty and underdevelopment. While admitting that 'prosperity is a good contraceptive', she asserted that 'the effects of development are submerged unless we bring about a low birth rate'.[144] 'Family planning is an input for development, an indispensable exercise in human capital formation.'[145] This shows that population growth was still seen in contradistinction to social and economic development. The thinking of the state was fixated on population control, partly because development on the scale required seemed to be elusive.

As delineated in this chapter, what started as a euphemistic 'family planning' programme (a disguised term for birth control) in 1952 mutated into a forced sterilisation campaign. The north was blamed for its apparently poor record on population control and had to bear the brunt of the Emergency excesses. The empirical evidence on demographic transition in India as discussed in preceding chapters makes it clear that most southern states began their peak population growth thirty to forty years earlier than the northern states and had already achieved the apex of their growth rates. They were, therefore, predisposed to register a decline in growth rates with or without the family planning programme. Conversely, the north had just entered its high growth phase in the previous decade and could not have suddenly brought down its fertility and growth rates, as it was imagined in official policy and propaganda. The north had to suffer because of a faulty NPP that was modelled on the demographic conditions prevailing in the south. The Emergency merely created a suitable environment for its formulation and coercive implementation. It was the discourse of 'overpopulation' built up by the international agencies and organisations, with the support of policymakers and experts in India, that was responsible for the widespread belief that population growth was the biggest problem before the country, without addressing which the social and economic development of the nation could not be ensured.[146]

10

Delimitation and Seat Redistribution

History, Implications and Solutions

In this chapter, we map the precise extent of representational imbalance caused by the embargo placed by the 42nd Amendment to the Constitution in 1976 and extended by the 84th Amendment in 2001. This is done both at the level of states and the regions as defined. Apart from a general assessment of the imbalance, there is a focused north versus south analysis. The chapter then goes on to present different scenarios for delimitation and state-wise reallocation of seats for the Lok Sabha. Scenarios for the Rajya Sabha are also presented. The total number of seats for each House and their distribution in accordance with the Census of 2011 as well as the Census of India projections for 2026 are presented.

I

Seat Allocation in the Lok Sabha: 1971 as the Cut-off Year

Before probing the myriad ramifications of fresh delimitation and distribution of seats in Parliament, let us examine the relevant constitutional provisions.[1] Article 81 of the Constitution deals with the allocation of seats in the Lok Sabha (House of the People). Clause 1 of the amended article sets the maximum number of members in the Lok Sabha at 550. Below are the two sub-clauses detailing how those seats are to be filled:

(a) not more than [five hundred and thirty members] chosen by direct election from territorial constituencies in the States, and

(b) not more than [twenty members] to represent the Union Territories, chosen in such a manner as Parliament may by law provide.[2]

It should be noted that the present ceiling of the Lok Sabha was established by the 31st Constitution Amendment Act, 1973, which implemented the delimitation based on the Census of 1971. In accordance with the constitutional provision of a mandatory delimitation after each decennial census, the number of Lok Sabha seats was revised from 525 to 545, and the seats were redistributed. This was the third delimitation since Independence.

II

The Representation Index of India and Its States

Let us now examine the impact that the freeze placed by the 42nd Amendment has had on the country as a whole. In order to capture how represented (or unrepresented) the Indian citizen has been since Independence, we may coin the term 'representation index of India', which is the ratio obtained by dividing the total population of India by the number of seats in the Lok Sabha at a given point of time. Figure 10.1 illustrates a curve that depicts the variations in the representation index since 1951:

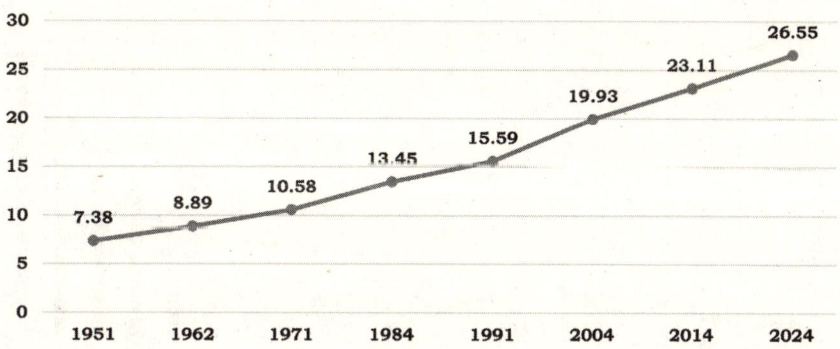

Figure 10.1: Representation index of India (persons per seat, in lakh) since 1951

Note: The population figure for 2024 has been derived from the Census of India projections for 2026.

Source: Table 10.1, Appendices

The upward curve denotes a steadily falling representation, especially since 1971. In the first general election, an Indian citizen was three-and-a-half times better represented than today. A Lok Sabha seat on average represented just 7.38 lakh persons in 1951; 10.58 lakh in 1971; 23.11 lakh persons in 2014; 25 lakh in 2019; and 26.55 lakh in 2024. In practical terms, it means that a Lok Sabha member was expected to represent about 7 lakh people in 1951, while today she is expected to represent nearly 27 lakh. Looking at it from the citizen's perspective, one might say that earlier an Indian citizen was bracketed into a group of 7 lakh individuals, thus rendering one's worth insofar as representation in the Lok Sabha is concerned, one in 7 lakh. By 2024, that worth has deteriorated three-and-a-half times to one in nearly 27 lakh. Therefore, the average Indian citizen stands relatively underrepresented in Parliament today.

National underrepresentation, however, is not the primary concern of this study. Instead, the focus here is on the representational disparity that has emerged among the different states and regions of India over the last fifty years due to the freeze on delimitation and redistribution of seats in Parliament. For a comparative study of how states have fared, the difference between the national representation index and representation index of a state has been calculated. This difference is then plotted in the form of a bar chart. The general pattern for the country in 1951–52 is shown in Figure 10.2.

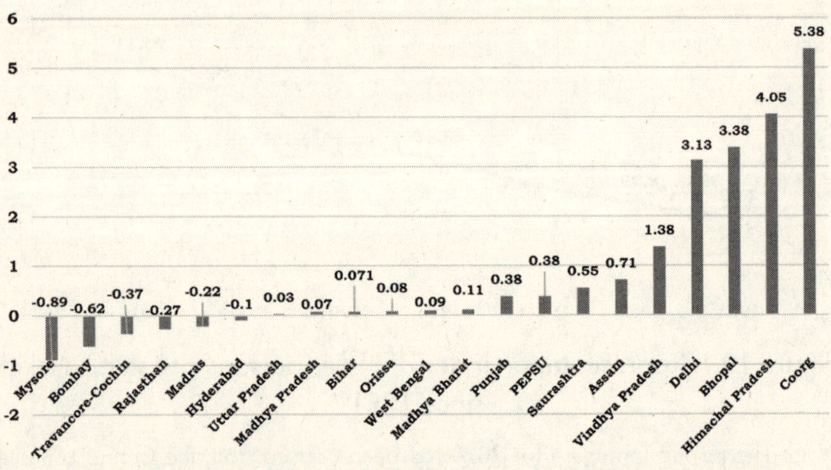

Figure 10.2: Difference in the respective representation indices from the national representation index, 1951 (in lakh)

Source: Table 10.2, Appendices

There is a visible cluster of small states/UTs with abnormally high values compared to the larger states. This pattern, consistent through the decades up to the 2024 general election, exists because the states that do not have enough population to get even one seat in the Lok Sabha have rightly been given representation beyond what the numbers alone would justify. Thus, for the sake of simplicity, what is required is a second level of analysis focusing on the major states, excluding the small states and UTs that have always been overrepresented because of sheer necessity. Let us, therefore, redraw the bar chart as Figure 10.3.

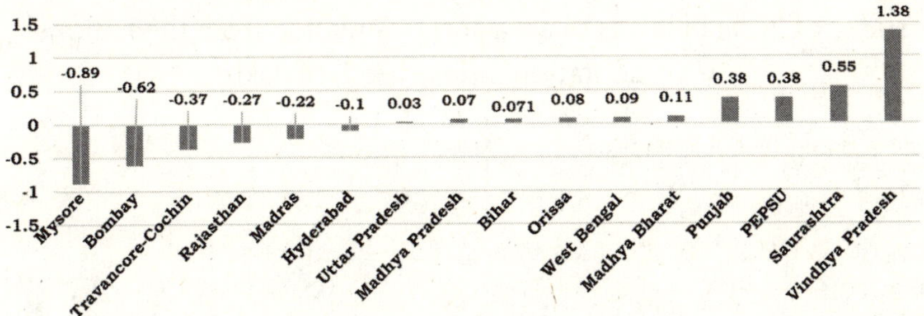

Figure 10.3: Difference in the representation indices of the major states of India in terms of area and population from the national representation index, 1951 (in lakh)

Source: Table 10.2, Appendices

The chart in Figure 10.3 has been prepared after sorting the states in ascending order. The pattern shows the range from the biggest loser to the biggest gainer. In the first general election held in 1951-52, the southern states lagged the north, as they had a smaller representation index, falling on the negative side of the Y-axis in the graph.

The data presented in Figure 10.3 show how representation indices for the major states have evolved at every general election after 1951-52. The patterns for general elections of 1962 and 1971 are depicted in Figures 10.4 and 10.5.

Figure 10.5 shows that in 1971, when population growth in most southern states had peaked, they were slightly behind the northern states such as Madhya Pradesh and Bihar in representation. However, Rajasthan

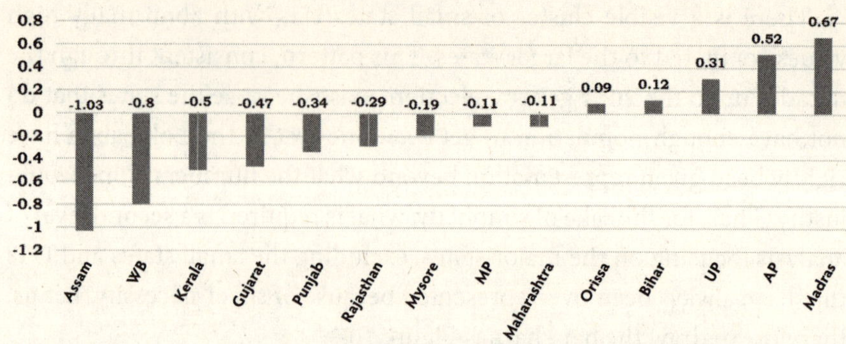

Figure 10.4: Difference of the representation indices of the major states of India in terms of area and population from the national representation index, 1962 (in lakh)

Source: Table 10.3, Appendices

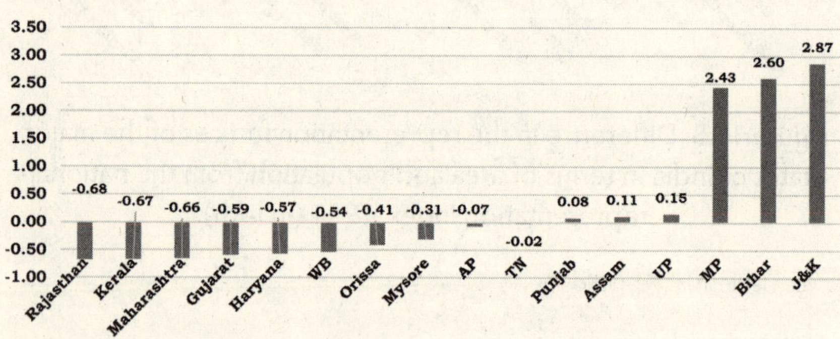

Figure 10.5: Difference of the representation indices of the major states of India in terms of area and population from the national representation index, 1971 (in lakh)

Source: Table 10.4, Appendices

had already become the biggest loser in terms of proportional political representation in the Lok Sabha. Haryana was also among the least represented. Thus, it is hard to establish a clear contrast between the north and the south at this point. Let us examine the changes in the pattern of representation indices since 1971. Figures 10.6, 10.7, 10.8 and 10.9 depict the patterns for 1984, 1991, 2004, and 2014 respectively:

For nearly three decades, Kerala has been among the best-represented states in India. In contrast, Rajasthan has been the top loser. Uttar Pradesh, which remained on the positive side of the chart till 1971, has seen a decline in its representation index in all subsequent general elections. Bihar held on to the positive half of the chart until 1971. Since

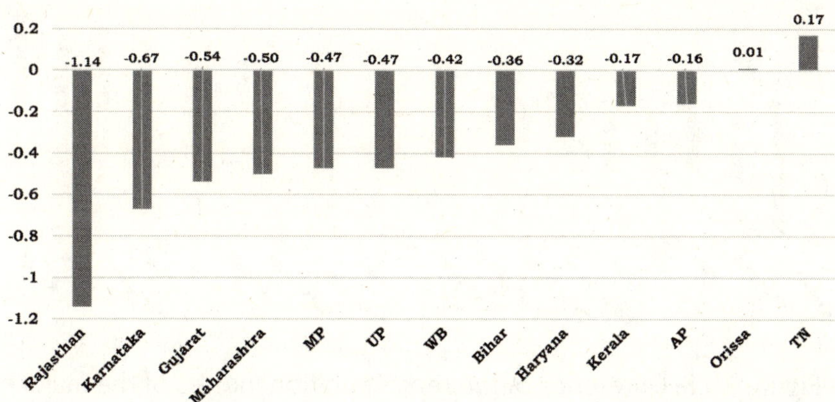

Figure 10.6: Difference of the representation indices of the major states of India in terms of area and population from the national representation index, 1984 (in lakh)

Source: Table 10.5, Appendices

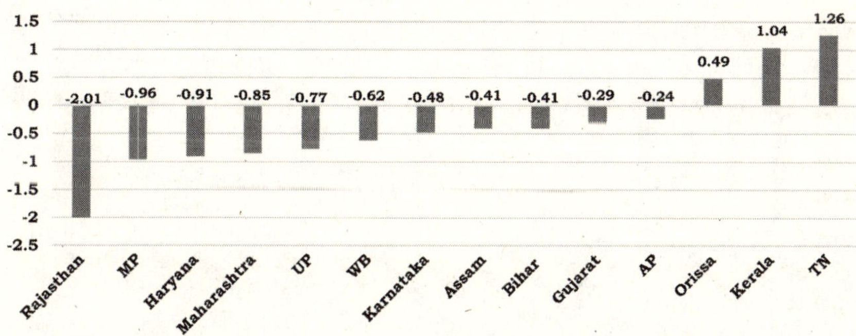

Figure 10.7: Difference of the representation indices of the major states of India in terms of area and population from the national representation index, 1991 (in lakh)

Source: Table 10.6, Appendices

then, however, it has been among the biggest losers. By 2014, Rajasthan, Bihar, Haryana, Madhya Pradesh, NCT of Delhi, Jharkhand, Maharashtra and Gujarat are all among major losers in representation. Let us now look into the representation index for 2024 general election. For this purpose, we may use the Census of India projections for 2026, as the population

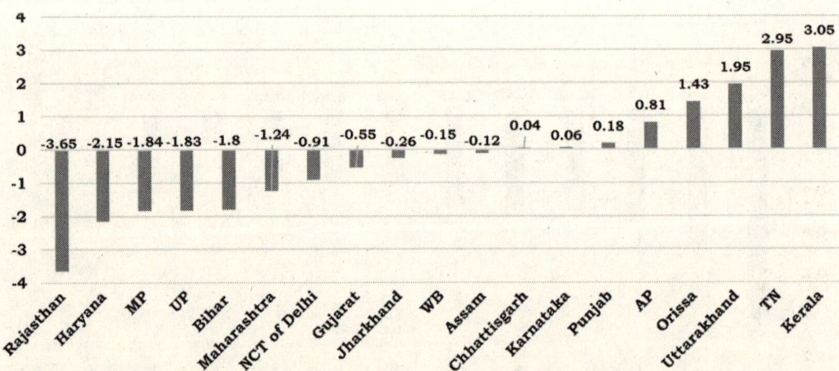

Figure 10.8: Difference of the representation indices of the major states of India in terms of area and population from the national representation index, 2004 (in lakh)

Source: Table 10.7, Appendices

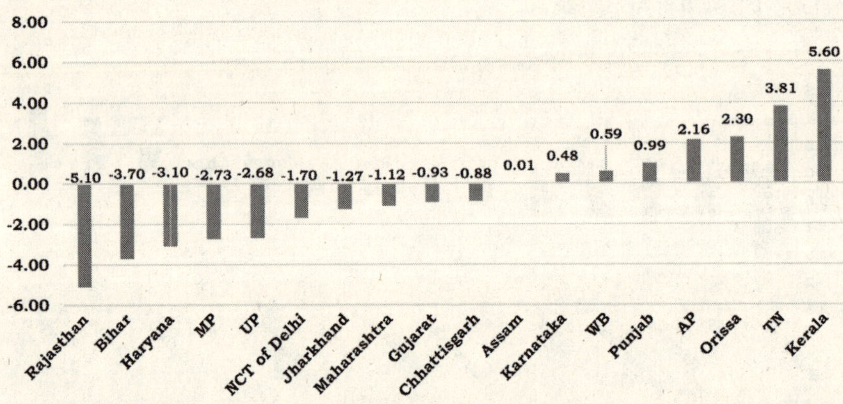

Figure 10.9: Difference of the representation indices of the major states of India in terms of area and population from the national representation index, 2014 (in lakh)

Source: Table 10.8, Appendices

figure provided there appears to have been reached around the time India surpassed China in April 2023 to become the most populous nation on earth with an approximate population of 1.43 billion. Figure 10.10 depicts the current imbalance in political representation.

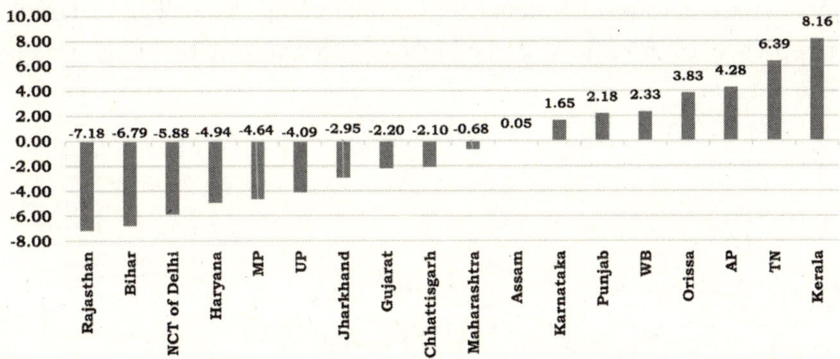

Figure 10.10: Difference of the representation indices of the major states of India in terms of area and population, 2024 (in lakh)[3]

In the 2024 general elections, Kerala, Tamil Nadu, Andhra Pradesh, Orissa, West Bengal, Punjab and Karnataka are among the most overrepresented states, in descending order. In contrast, Rajasthan, Bihar, NCT of Delhi, Haryana, Madhya Pradesh, Uttar Pradesh, Jharkhand, Gujarat, Chhattisgarh and Maharashtra are among the most underrepresented in descending order. Therefore, the representational divide in India is now quite manifest: the south and the east are overrepresented; the north and the west are underrepresented.

III

The North–South Representation Indices Compared

The above analysis indicates that a focused north–south comparative study of representation could throw up more insights. Let us, therefore, look into the ranking patterns of states based on their representation indices by comparing four northern states—Uttar Pradesh, Rajasthan, Bihar and Madhya Pradesh—with four southern states: Kerala, Karnataka, Tamil Nadu and Andhra Pradesh. These eight states are ranked as per their respective representation indices, for which 18 major states are used for calculating rank from 1971 to 1991 and 21 states from 2004 to 2014. We focus on the changes in their ranks since 1971, as that is the point of inflexion in India's demographic history and also because in earlier general elections the political map of India was very different, thus not amenable to proper comparison. The variations in representation indices of northern and southern states are plotted in Figure 10.11.

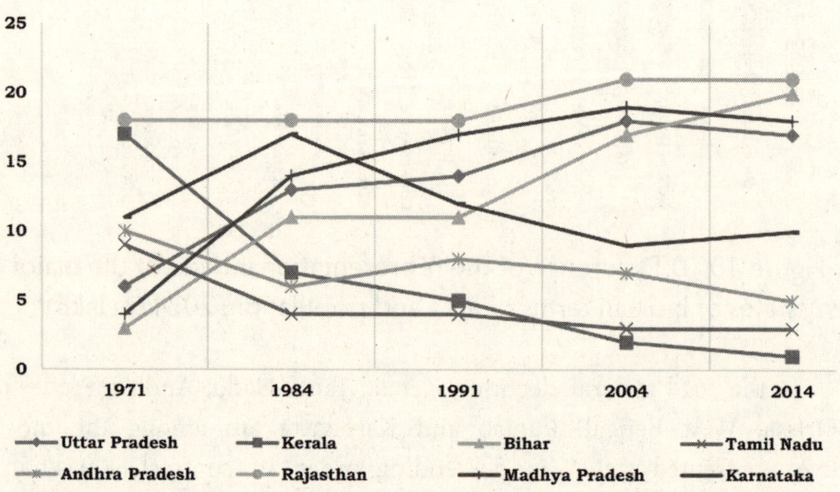

Figure 10.11: Trends in the variation in representation indices of states from the north and south, 1971–2014

Source: Table 10.9, Appendices

The chart displays a clear contrast between the north and the south. The northern states show a steady decline in their rankings, whereas the southern states have risen in the rankings. It is important to note that on this graph an upward trajectory indicates a declining rank—the higher the position on the Y-axis, the lower the rank.

Although the trends have endured for the entire period since 1971, a greater contrast between the northern and southern group of states is discernible since the general election of 1984. Put simply, Figure 10.11 corroborates that the current scheme of seat allocation in the Lok Sabha, which uses 1971 as the baseline year for India's population, disadvantages the northern states. The people of these states are much less represented than those of the southern states. Let us carry out a further analysis of the rankings of the states, taking a smaller sample of one state from the north and one from the south. Figure 10.12 depicts a comparative chart of Uttar Pradesh and Kerala, showing their gains and losses in terms of representation since 1951.

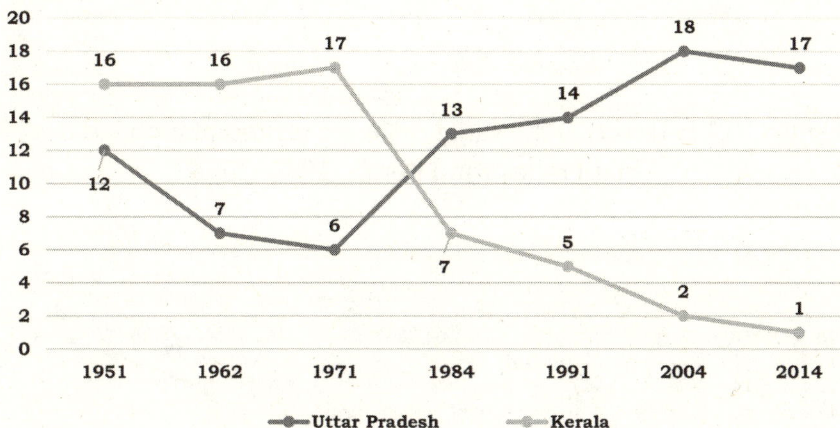

Figure 10.12: Trends in the variation in representation indices of Uttar Pradesh and Kerala, 1951–2014

Source: Table 10.10, Appendices

It is evident that Kerala ranked low in 1951 and improved its ranking slightly in 1962; although the trend saw a reversal, placing it at its lowest rank ever in 1971.[4] Since then, however, there has been no looking back for Kerala. Starting from 2004, Kerala has occupied the pole position among major states in political representation. Uttar Pradesh has traced a reverse trajectory, with a consistent drop in its rankings, touching a new low in each election. The contrast between the two states is highlighted by the graph in Figure 10.13, which traces the patterns since 1971.

Let us make another comparison. Figure 10.14 shows the comparative representation indices of Bihar and Tamil Nadu since the first general election held in 1951-52 (Figure 10.14).

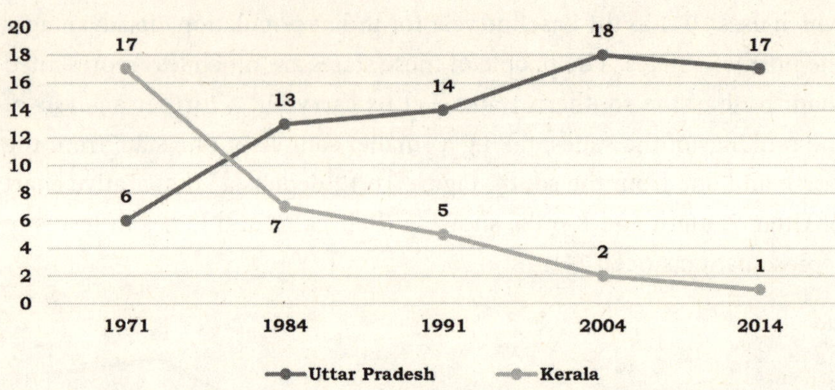

Figure 10.13: Trends in the variation in the representation indices of Uttar Pradesh and Kerala, 1971–2014

Source: Table 10.9, Appendices

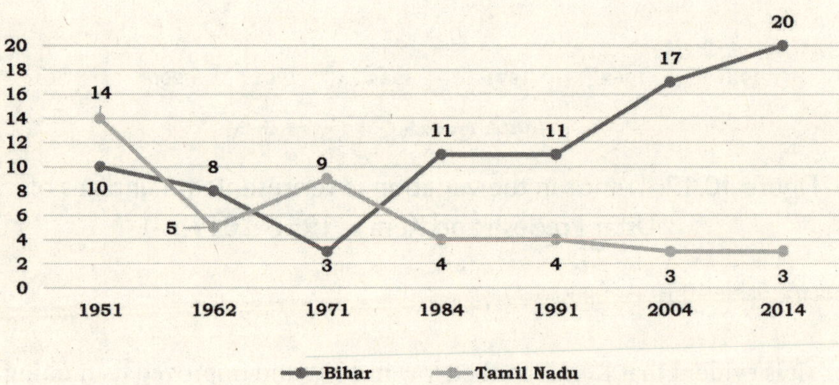

Figure 10.14: Trends in the variation in representation indices of Bihar and Tamil Nadu, 1951–2014

Source: Table 10.10, Appendices

The pattern is similar to that observed in Uttar Pradesh versus Kerala, with Bihar's ranking declining since 1971, and at an accelerated pace after 1991. To get a clearer picture, let us now study the trends from 1971 to 2014, shown in Figure 10.15. Between 1971 and 1984, there was a major decline in Bihar's rank, from 3 to 11. Since 1991, the gap between the two states has increased steadily with every general election, implying that, compared to Tamil Nadu, Bihar has consistently lost on political representation.

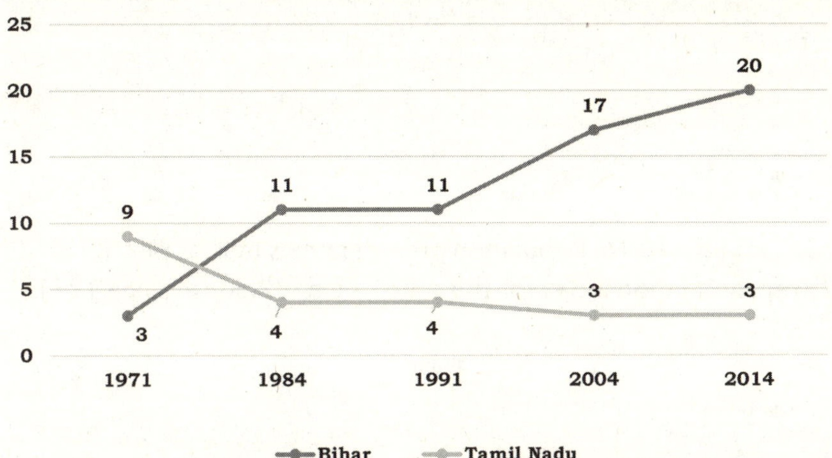

Figure 10.15: Trends in the variation in representation indices of Bihar and Tamil Nadu, 1971–2014

Source: Table 10.10, Appendices

To fully grasp the impact of population growth on political representation in the Lok Sabha, it is crucial to examine the correlation between the growth rates of various political units in India and their representation in the lower house. The aim is to identify the relationship between the rate of population growth and the ranking in representation indices among the states. To accomplish the task, once again the four states—Uttar Pradesh, Bihar, Kerala and Tamil Nadu—can be taken as the sample. A line of best fit is plotted for them to determine the correlation between population growth rate and their rank according to the representation index, which serves as a proxy for political representation in the Lok Sabha. Figures 10.16 to 10.19 display the findings, which have been calculated according to the method explained. Figures 10.20 and 10.21 depict the correlation for Gujarat and Maharashtra.

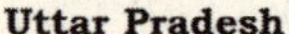

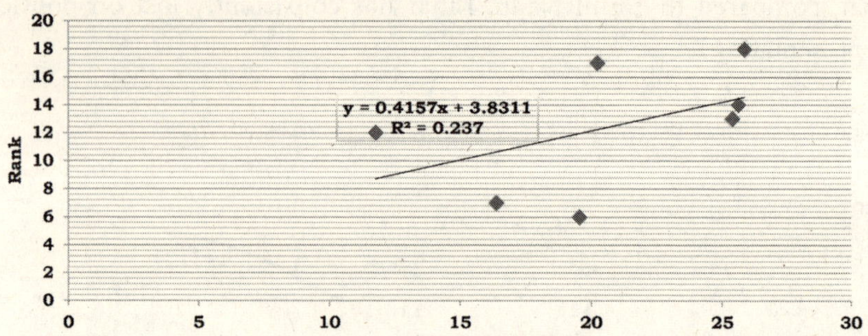

Figure 10.16: Population growth rate vs rank as per the representation index for the state of Uttar Pradesh since 1951

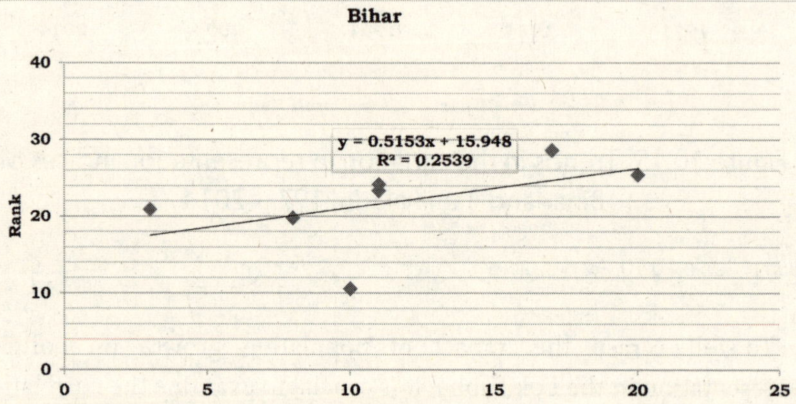

Figure 10.17: Population growth rate vs rank as per the representation index for the state of Bihar since 1951

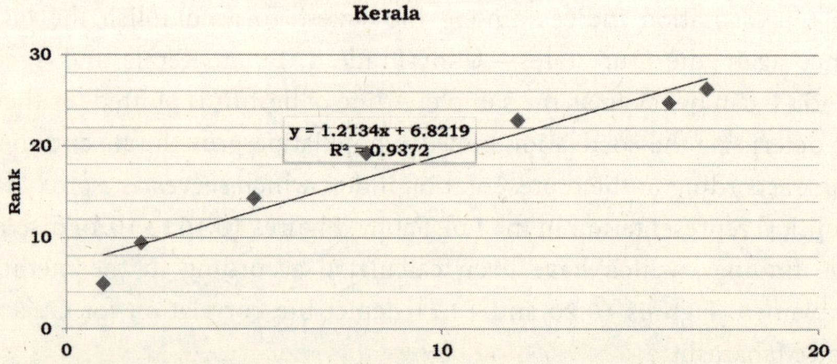

Figure 10.18: Population growth rate vs rank as per the representation index for the state of Kerala since 1951

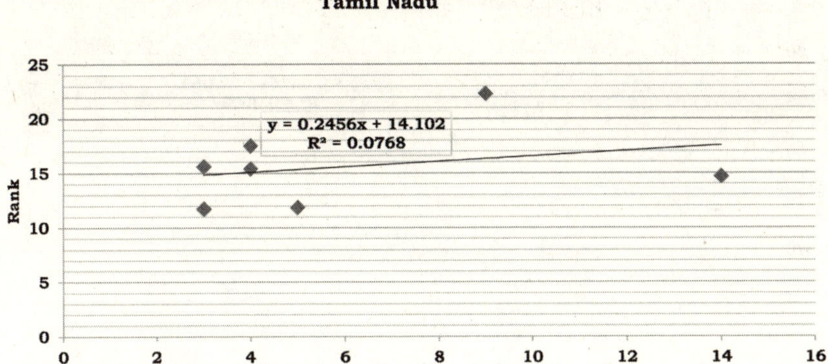

Figure 10.19: Population growth rate vs rank as per the representation index for the state of Tamil Nadu since 1951

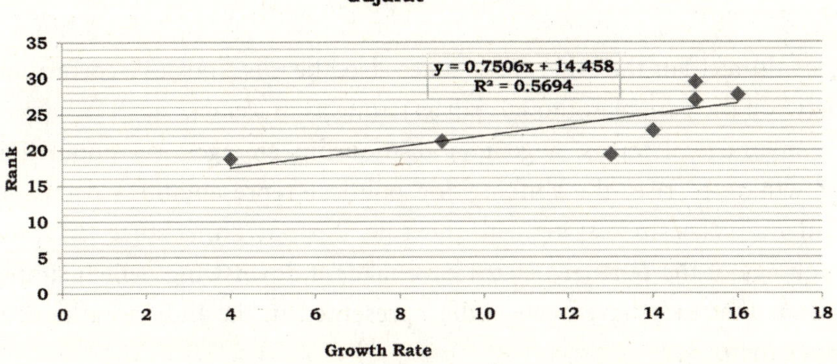

Figure 10.20: Population growth rate vs rank as per the representation index for the state of Gujarat since 1951

To find out correlation between growth rate versus rank, let us use the Pearson correlation coefficient, a measure of the strength of association between two variables which is especially useful for establishing linear relationship between variables. Its value ranges from -1 to +1. While -1 and +1 signify perfect correlation—whether negative or positive—a value of 0 signifies no correlation. Unsurprisingly, the two variables show a fair amount of correlation in all these states. For Kerala it is as high as +0.81, indicating that as the population growth rate of the state declined, its ranking in terms of the representation index improved at par with the

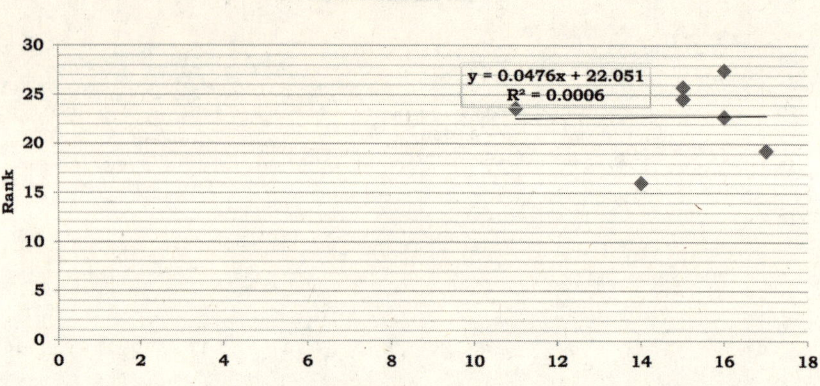

Figure 10.21: Population growth rate vs rank as per the representation index for the state of Maharashtra since 1951

growth rate. For the other three states also, there is a positive correlation between the variables, though not as strong as in Kerala.

In practical terms, a general relationship emerges: As population growth rates rise, the ranking (or political representation) decreases and vice versa. In keeping with this rule, it is noted that since 1971, the rankings of the northern states have taken a downswing, which simply means that they have been underrepresented in the Indian Parliament since then.

IV

Scenarios for Delimitation and Reallocation

Moving on from population and political representation in India, let us now see how the issue has been debated and resolved elsewhere in the world. Expressing concern over the inequality in representation in the Parliament of the United Kingdom, Lord Kenneth Baker argues in favour of slashing the number of seats, which he believes is quite high at 646 (currently, there are 650 seats).[5] Calculating the average based on the size of the electorate, he expresses his discomfort at the fact that there are 14,300 more electors—which is just a fraction of the enormous north–south gap in India—in an English seat in Parliament than a Welsh seat, which means overrepresentation of Wales.[6] The debate over parliamentary representation in Britain strikes a familiar chord. Let us widen the canvas and examine political representation in select countries (Figure 10.22).

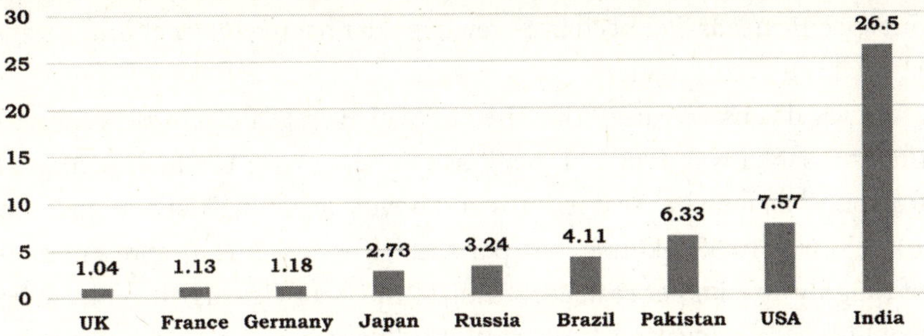

Figure 10.22: Parliamentary representation of some of the major democracies of the world (in lakh)

Source: Table 10.11, Appendices

With 7.57 lakh people per constituency in the House of Representatives, the United States is the worst in political representation, except India. By contrast, the United Kingdom, France and Germany have parliaments with a much higher representation, with a seat for about every 1,00,000 persons. A decline in representation happens in more populous countries like Japan, Russia and Brazil because it is unworkable to increase the size of a parliament beyond a point. Even a comparison with neighbouring Pakistan—which is not a democracy like India—does not look encouraging from the Indian point of view, as every seat in Pakistan's National Assembly represents 6.33 lakh people—just about a fourth of what it is in India.

It is obvious that in an attempt to solve the problem of having constituencies with large populations, India cannot emulate the example of countries with much smaller populations and constituencies of just a few lakh voters. Leave aside Germany, the UK and France, India cannot even consider having constituencies of a similar size as in the US, which has less than one-fourth of India's population; doing so would result in a gargantuan Lok Sabha with nearly 2,300 members, which would be utterly unwieldy and prohibitively expensive, without commensurate gain in strengthening the Indian democracy. What is more important, India need not even try to emulate other democracies because its case both as a nation and as a democracy is *sui generis*. As a nation, we are eminently entitled to have our own modes and practices of people's representation that best suit our specific needs. We need not even consider having international parity of any kind in this matter.

It was discussed earlier that the national average for representation in the Lok Sabha was 7.38 lakh persons per seat in 1951, which increased to around 24 lakh per seat in 2014 and hovers around 27 lakh in 2024. In 1971, it was 10.58 lakh persons per seat.[7] If we assume a representation of roughly 10 lakh per seat, according to the 2011 Census, the Lok Sabha would have a staggering 1,211 seats, and based on the 2026 population projections by the Census of India, it would have around 1,425 seats. That would be an enormous and unworkable increase from the current strength of 543 seats.

In any case, our primary concern here is removing the inequality of political representation across states and regions. So, without losing our way in fruitless speculation, let us limit ourselves to a workable solution to the problem. Figure 10.23 depicts the precise extent of overrepresentation and underrepresentation of each state, as per the 2011 Census.

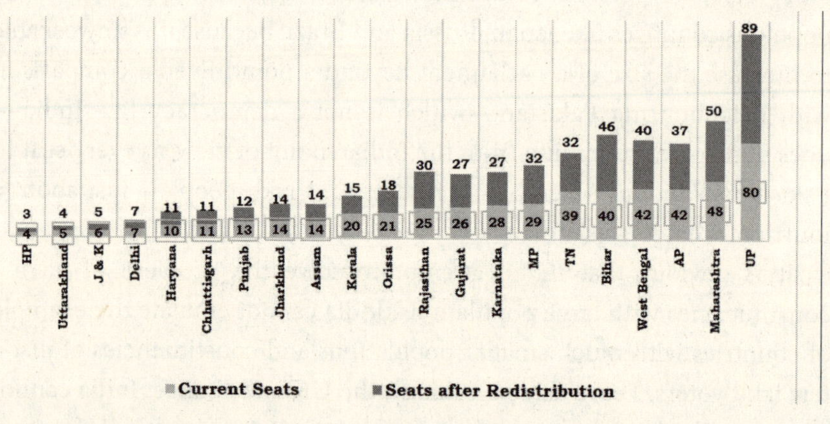

Figure 10.23: Change in number of seats in the Lok Sabha

Source: Table 10.12

Figure 10.23 illustrates the losses and gains of states in absolute terms, that is, the number of seats to be added to or deducted from the current tally of a particular state. It brings the north–south divide on political representation to the centre, as the top four gainers are Uttar Pradesh, Bihar, Rajasthan and Madhya Pradesh—all part of the so-called BIMARU states. Maharashtra and Gujarat also emerge among the major gainers, since western India has shown continued demographic growth mainly because of rapid economic development propelled by industrialisation and urbanisation.

Figure 10.23 also shows that among the top losers in terms of seat allocation would be the three major states from the south, namely, Tamil Nadu, Kerala and Andhra Pradesh. Orissa from the east would be the fourth-largest loser. Let us now find out the percentage change in seat distribution for each state. Figure 10.24 depicts the standings of the states according to percentage gain or loss in the number of seats, if redistribution were to be carried out in the present Lok Sabha of 543 seats.

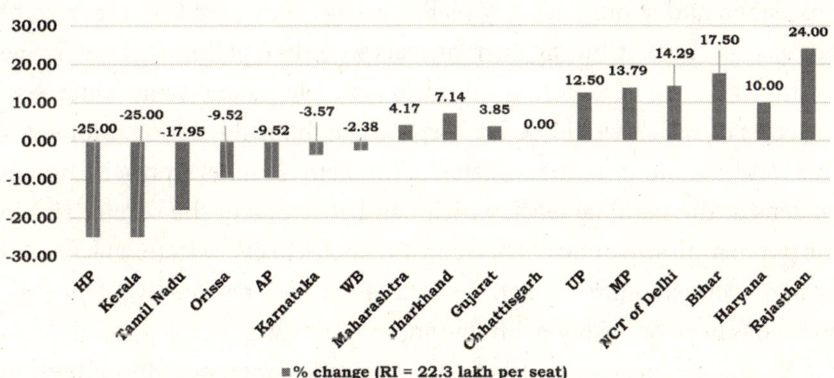

Figure 10.24: Percentage change in number of seats in the Lok Sabha

Source: Table 10.12

Similar to the previous bar chart, there is quite a noticeable gap between the north and the south in Figure 10.24. But there is a difference, too. Uttar Pradesh, which is the topmost gainer in the absolute number of seats, does not retain its position. Although it would still gain substantially

(12.5 per cent), the top five ranks would go to Rajasthan (24 per cent), Haryana (20 per cent), Bihar (17.5 per cent) Delhi (14.29 per cent) and Madhya Pradesh (13.79 per cent). It is also noteworthy that Gujarat and Maharashtra are still among the major gainers, at 7.69 per cent and 6.25 per cent respectively. The three southern states that stand to lose seats—Andhra Pradesh, Kerala and Tamil Nadu—still feature on the negative half of the chart, though not in the same order.

The bar charts presented here provide a graphical view of the major changes required in Parliament. Table 10.12 offers a comprehensive and precise view of those changes across all states and Union Territories, if the number of seats in the Lok Sabha remains 543.

Table 10.12 shows that a large number of states stand to lose their current seats in the Lok Sabha if the seats are redistributed in accordance with the 2011 Census. Once the principle of fresh delimitation and allocation of seats in Parliament is accepted, it would become evident that only two options are available. One is to redistribute the existing 543 seats according to the current population; the other is to enlarge the Lok Sabha and simultaneously reallocate the seats based on the current population. Redistributing current seats would be politically inadvisable as such a course of action is bound to generate passions and bitterness, the costs of which would be unacceptably high for the nation. Moreover, this would do nothing to mitigate the problem of underrepresentation of citizens at the national level, which has arisen due to the secular rise in the population size of Lok Sabha constituencies in every state. The second option is clearly more acceptable from a national perspective. Since the south has been opposing delimitation, let us analyse the two options from the south's perspective. In the first option, the south would lose both in numbers and proportion. In the second, it loses in proportion, but gains in numbers.

It seems, therefore, that the best and the most acceptable solution would be to increase the number of seats in the Lok Sabha in such a manner that all states, except the smallest ones and the UTs—which usually have only a couple of seats anyway and might still be somewhat overrepresented—get proportionate representation based on their current population, without, however, the loss of even a single seat that any state may hold presently. This would maintain the sanctity of the democratic principle of

Table 10.12: Variation of Seats According to the Current Strength of the Lok Sabha

State	*Population (2011)*	*Present seats*	*Population in percentage*	*Seats' (543) distribution on population distribution*	*Round*	*Gain/ Loss*	*Final allocation, with at least 1 seat to each state (543)*
Uttar Pradesh	19,98,12,341	80	16.50%	89.6	90	12.50	89
Maharashtra	11,23,74,333	48	9.28%	50.39	50	4.17	50
Bihar	10,40,99,452	40	8.60%	46.68	47	17.50	46
West Bengal	9,12,76,115	42	7.54%	40.93	41	-2.38	40
Andhra Pradesh	8,45,80,777	42	6.99%	37.93	38	-9.52	38
Madhya Pradesh	7,26,26,809	29	6.00%	32.57	33	13.79	32
Tamil Nadu	7,21,47,030	39	5.96%	32.35	32	-17.95	32
Rajasthan	6,85,48,437	25	5.66%	30.74	31	24.00	30
Karnataka	6,10,95,297	28	5.05%	27.4	27	-3.57	27
Gujarat	6,04,39,692	26	4.99%	27.1	27	3.85	27
Orissa	4,19,74,218	21	3.47%	18.82	19	-9.52	19
Kerala	3,34,06,061	20	2.76%	14.98	15	-25.00	15
Jharkhand	3,29,88,134	14	2.72%	14.79	15	7.14	15
Assam	3,12,05,576	14	2.58%	13.99	14	0.00	14

State	*Population (2011)*	*Present seats*	*Population in percentage*	*Seats' (543) distribution on population distribution*	*Round*	*Gain/ Loss*	*Final allocation, with at least 1 seat to each state (543)*
Punjab	2,77,43,388	13	2.29%	12.44	12	-7.69	12
Chhattisgarh	2,55,45,198	11	2.11%	11.46	11	0.00	11
Haryana	2,53,51,462	10	2.09%	11.37	11	10.00	11
Delhi	1,67,87,941	7	1.39%	7.53	8	14.29	7
Jammu & Kashmir	1,25,41,302	6	1.04%	5.62	6	0.00	6
Uttarakhand	1,00,86,292	5	0.83%	4.52	5	0.00	4
Himachal Pradesh	68,64,602	4	0.57%	3.08	3	-25.00	3
Tripura	36,73,917	2	0.30%	1.65	2	0.00	2
Meghalaya	29,66,889	2	0.25%	1.33	1		1
Manipur	28,55,794	2	0.24%	1.28	1		1
Nagaland	19,78,502	1	0.16%	0.89	1		1
Goa	14,58,545	2	0.12%	0.65	1		1
Arunachal Pradesh	13,83,727	2	0.11%	0.62	1		1
Puducherry	12,47,953	1	0.10%	0.56	1		1

State	*Population (2011)*	*Present seats*	*Population in percentage*	*Seats' (543) distribution on population distribution*	*Round*	*Gain/ Loss*	*Final allocation, with at least 1 seat to each state (543)*
Mizoram	10,97,206	1	0.09%	0.49	0		1
Chandigarh	10,55,450	1	0.09%	0.47	0		1
Sikkim	6,10,577	1	0.05%	0.27	0		1
Andaman & Nicobar	3,80,581	1	0.03%	0.17	0		1
Dadra & Nagar Haveli	3,43,709	1	0.03%	0.15	0		1
Daman and Diu	2,43,247	1	0.02%	0.11	0		1
Lakshadweep	64,473	1	0.01%	0.03	0		1
India	1,21,08,55,027	543	100.00%	543	543	0.00	543

After adjusting the seat allocation based on population distribution, some smaller states are left with zero seats. To adjust this, we allocate one seat to these states and redistribute the remaining seats based on population for the remaining states.

'one person, one vote, one value'. It would also help in reducing the average population size of constituencies in all states, although we need not be too concerned about having large constituencies, as long as general parity in population and political representation across states is maintained.

According to calculations based on the 2011 Census, this magic figure, so to speak, comes out to be 728 for the Lok Sabha—a size that would be acceptable in all respects. It will not make the Lok Sabha unwieldy, while also solving the long-lasting problem of large imbalances in the states' comparative representation in Parliament. This is shown in the Figure 10.25. Figure 10.26 shows the net gains and losses of major states. Table 10.13 provides a more comprehensive view of the changes required

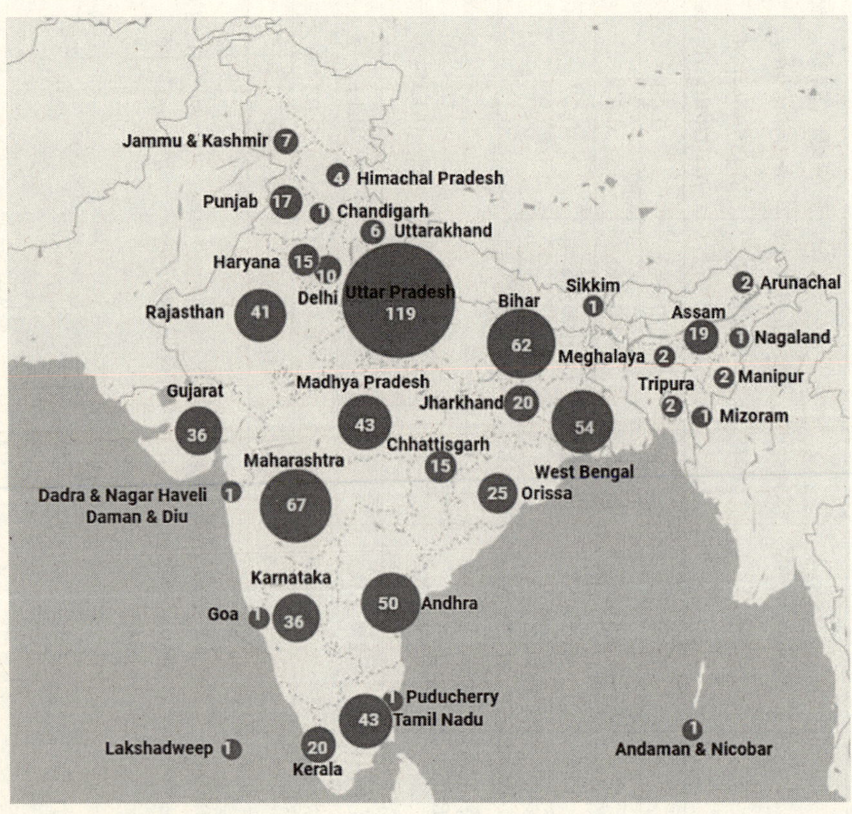

Figure 10.25: Distribution of Lok Sabha seats as per the 2011 Census

Source: Table 10.13

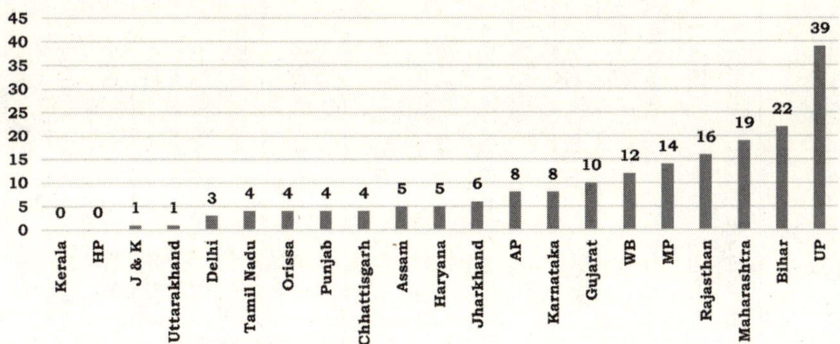

Figure 10.26: Difference of Lok Sabha seats according to the 2011 Census

Source: Table 10.13

in the distribution of seats in the Lok Sabha among states and Union Territories based on the total figure of 728 seats.

In this model, there is a negligible gap between the percentage share of each state in India's population according to the 2011 Census and its share of seats in the Lok Sabha. The minor difference that does exist is primarily due to the necessity of rounding up the number of seats. In this model, there is no change in the number of seats held by very small states and Union Territories, all of which had to be given representation in Parliament even if their population did not merit even one seat. As a result of population growth over the decades and the adjustment model presented here, all such states/UTs (Tripura, Meghalaya, Manipur, Nagaland, Goa, Arunachal Pradesh, Puducherry, Mizoram, Chandigarh, Sikkim, Andaman and Nicobar, Dadra and Nagar Haveli, Daman and Diu, and Lakshadweep) witness no change.

Himachal Pradesh sees no change. Uttarakhand gets an additional seat, taking its number to 6. Jammu & Kashmir gets one more seat, increasing from 6 to 7. Delhi (3), Chhattisgarh (4), Punjab (4), Haryana (5), Assam (5) and Jharkhand (6) will have substantial gains in the number of seats, though, as will be explained later, in terms of percentage this is not uniformly so in this group.

Among the larger states, Kerala's case is unique, as its seats remain at 20. This indicates that at present its overrepresentation is so pronounced that even in a model which increases the number of Lok Sabha seats by

Table 10.13: Proposed Number of Lok Sabha Seats According to the 2011 Census

State	*Population (2011) A*	*Present Seats (543) B*	*Population % (A)/ (Total A)C*	*Seat %(B)/ (Total B) D*	*% OR / UR wrt Population (C-D)/(C)E*	*Final Allocation H*	*Difference in Seats*	*Percentage increase*	*Seat % I*	*% OR / UR wrt Population (C-I)/(I)J*
Uttar Pradesh	19,98,12,341	80	16.50	14.73	10.72	119	39.00	48.75	16.35	0.95
Maharashtra	11,23,74,333	48	9.28	8.84	4.75	67	19.00	39.58	9.20	0.84
Bihar	10,40,99,452	40	8.60	7.37	14.32	62	22.00	55.00	8.52	0.95
West Bengal	9,12,76,115	42	7.54	7.73	-2.61	54	12.00	28.57	7.42	1.63
Andhra Pradesh	8,45,80,777	42	6.99	7.73	-10.73	50	8.00	19.05	6.87	1.70
Madhya Pradesh	7,26,26,809	29	6.00	5.34	10.96	43	14.00	48.28	5.91	1.55
Tamil Nadu	7,21,47,030	39	5.96	7.18	-20.54	43	4.00	10.26	5.91	0.88
Rajasthan	6,85,48,437	25	5.66	4.60	18.67	41	16.00	64.00	5.63	0.52
Karnataka	6,10,95,297	28	5.05	5.16	-2.20	36	8.00	28.57	4.95	2.03
Gujarat	6,04,39,692	26	4.99	4.79	4.07	36	10.00	38.46	4.95	0.94
Orissa	4,19,74,218	21	3.47	3.87	-11.57	25	4.00	19.05	3.43	0.94
Kerala	3,34,06,061	20	2.76	3.68	-33.50	20	0.00	0.00	2.75	0.42

State	*Population (2011) A*	*Present Seats (543) B*	*Population % (A)/ (Total A)C*	*Seat %(B)/ (Total B) D*	*% OR / UR wrt Population (C-D)/(C)E*	*Final Allocation H*	*Difference in Seats*	*Percentage increase*	*Seat % I*	*% OR / UR wrt Population (C-I)/(I)J*
Jharkhand	3,29,88,134	14	2.72	2.58	5.36	20	6.00	42.86	2.75	-0.83
Assam	3,12,05,576	14	2.58	2.58	-0.04	19	5.00	35.71	2.61	-1.25
Punjab	2,77,43,388	13	2.29	2.39	-4.49	17	4.00	30.77	2.34	-1.88
Chhattisgarh	2,55,45,198	11	2.11	2.03	3.98	15	4.00	36.36	2.06	2.39
Haryana	2,53,51,462	10	2.09	1.84	12.04	15	5.00	50.00	2.06	1.61
Delhi	1,67,87,941	7	1.39	1.29	7.02	10	3.00	42.86	1.37	0.93
Jammu & Kashmir	1,25,41,302	6	1.04	1.10	-6.68	7	1.00	16.67	0.96	7.72
Uttarakhand	1,00,86,292	5	0.83	0.92	-10.54	6	1.00	20.00	0.82	1.07
Himachal Pradesh	68,64,602	4	0.57	0.74	-29.94	4	0.00	0.00	0.55	3.18
Tripura*	36,73,917	2	0.30	0.37	-21.39	2	0.00	0.00	0.27	10.44
Meghalaya*	29,66,889	2	0.25	0.37	-50.32	2	0.00	0.00	0.27	-10.81
Manipur*	28,55,794	2	0.24	0.37	-56.17	2	0.00	0.00	0.27	-14.15
Nagaland*	19,78,502	1	0.16	0.18	-12.71	1	0.00	0.00	0.14	18.95
Goa*	14,58,545	2	0.12	0.37	-205.78	2	0.00	0.00	0.27	-56.15

State	*Population (2011) A*	*Present Seats (543) B*	*Population % (A)/ (Total A)C*	*Seat %(B)/ (Total B) D*	*% OR / UR wrt Population (C-D)/(C)E*	*Final Allocation H*	*Difference in Seats*	*Percentage increase*	*Seat % I*	*% OR / UR wrt Population (C-I)/(I)J*
Arunachal Pradesh*	13,83,727	2	0.11	0.37	-222.31	2	0.00	0.00	0.27	-58.40
Puducherry*	12,47,953	1	0.10	0.18	-78.69	1	0.00	0.00	0.14	-24.97
Mizoram*	10,97,206	1	0.09	0.18	-103.24	1	0.00	0.00	0.14	-34.03
Chandigarh*	10,55,450	1	0.09	0.18	-111.28	1	0.00	0.00	0.14	-36.54
Sikkim*	6,10,577	1	0.05	0.18	-265.22	1	0.00	0.00	0.14	-63.29
Andaman & Nicobar*	3,80,581	1	0.03	0.18	-485.93	1	0.00	0.00	0.14	-77.12
Dadra & Nagar Haveli*	3,43,709	1	0.03	0.18	-548.79	1	0.00	0.00	0.14	-79.34
Daman and Diu*	2,43,247	1	0.02	0.18	-816.74	1	0.00	0.00	0.14	-85.38
Lakshadweep*	64,473	1	0.01	0.18	-3358.71	1	0.00	0.00	0.14	-96.12
Total	1,21,08,55,027	543	1	1		728		34.07		

543 Seats – 1,21,08,55,027

1 Seat – 22,29,935.59

- *States with two or less than two seats will be considered small states and will be marked with*.*
- *Kerala has the highest overrepresentation, if we exclude the small states.*
- *Hence, we will correct the bias while keeping Kerala as the base.*

	Population	*Seats*
Kerala	*3,34,06,061*	*20*
	1,21,08,55,027	*724.93*

- *Therefore, we assume 725 seats and reallocate them, keeping in mind that no state ends up with fewer seats than its present allocation.*
- *When we reallocate the seats based on population distribution, seven states lose one seat each.*
- ***We remove these states and their respective seats from the calculation and reallocate the seats based on the population for the remaining states.***

185, Kerala can just about hold on to its current seats. In contrast, all other large states see at least some increase in their seat allocations, even though in unequal proportions. In fact, any effort to raise Kerala's seats by even one will disturb the whole model.

In the Table 10.13, the states above Kerala are the ones that gain the maximum number of seats based on the 2011 Census. Orissa gains 4 additional seats; Gujarat gets a huge addition of 10 seats to its present tally of 26; Karnataka adds 8 seats to its present allocation of 28—the most substantial rise for a southern state. Rajasthan's addition of 16 seats to its present tally of 25 reflects its current gross underrepresentation. Tamil Nadu gains 4 seats. Another heavily underrepresented state, Madhya Pradesh, will see its seats rise from 29 to 43. Andhra Pradesh secures a modest gain of 8 seats. West Bengal gains substantially, going from 42 to 54 seats. The largest increase in sheer numbers occurs in Bihar, Maharashtra and Uttar Pradesh, both because of their large populations and their gross underrepresentation at present. Bihar's seats will increase from 40 to 62; Maharashtra from 48 to 67; and Uttar Pradesh from 80 to 119.

Evidently, the change in the number of seats does not tell the whole story. It is equally important to analyse the change in percentage terms. Since the model of rebalancing the seats in Parliament presented here is designed to expand the number of seats just enough to ensure their allocation in proportion to the current population of each state, it results in many states seeing an increased seat allocation. However, the proportion of a state's seats in the Lok Sabha could still decrease.

Leaving out small states and Union Territories with only one or two seats, the states that gain in numbers but lose out in percentage are Tamil Nadu, West Bengal, Andhra Pradesh, Karnataka, Orissa, Punjab, Jammu and Kashmir, and Uttarakhand. Kerala, of course, gains neither in numbers nor in percentage; its percentage share goes down substantially because of its marked overrepresentation at present. Himachal Pradesh also loses out almost equally in percentage terms because its seats do not increase at all.

Delhi sees a substantial rise. Chhattisgarh and Jharkhand also experience substantial gains in their representation as a percentage of the total number of seats. The biggest gainers here are Rajasthan, Madhya Pradesh, Bihar, Uttar Pradesh, Maharashtra, Gujarat and Haryana.

Moving on to the next stage of analysis, let us examine the percentage gain of each state in relation to its present seats in the Lok Sabha in Table 10.14, and not in relation to the total number of Lok Sabha seats, as was done earlier.

Mapping the current state of underrepresentation versus over-representation in Parliament, the table above provides comprehensive information and crucial insights into the necessary adjustments for rebalancing provincial and regional representation in Parliament after a gap of fifty years. This period has seen a steady growth in imbalance due to divergence in demographic transition. As Table 10.14 shows, Rajasthan is the biggest gainer in terms of percentage over its current number of seats, with a 64 per cent rise. Bihar follows as the second-highest gainer, with a 55 per cent increase; and Haryana sees a 50 per cent increase. Uttar Pradesh (48.75 per cent), Madhya Pradesh (48.28 per cent), Jharkhand (42.86 per cent), Delhi (42.86 per cent), Maharashtra (39.58 per cent) and Gujarat (38.46 per cent) fall in the bracket of high gainers.

Chhattisgarh, with a 36.36 per cent increase, experiences modest gains. Assam (35.71 per cent), Punjab (30.77 per cent), West Bengal (28.57 per cent) and Karnataka (28.57 per cent) are also modest gainers. Uttarakhand (20 per cent), Andhra Pradesh (19.05 per cent) and Orissa (19.05 per cent) are the next lowest gainers. Jammu & Kashmir (16.67 per cent) and Tamil Nadu (10.26 per cent) are the last two states with positive numbers. Kerala remains unchanged at 0.00 per cent; its seats do not increase at all because it is the most overrepresented state at present. Even with a proposed increase of 185 seats in the Lok Sabha, Kerala can just about maintain its present number. After Kerala, the small states and Union Territories see no rise either in numbers or percentage.

The next national population census, which has been due since 2021, is likely to take place in 2026. The Office of the Registrar General of India has given its national and state-wise population projections for 2021 and 2026. The projected figures for 2026 can be used to estimate the total number of Lok Sabha seats and their state-wise allocation based on the formula previously employed. The state-wise allocation of seats is depicted in Figure 10.27:

Table 10.14: Percentage Change in States' Representation

State	*Population (2011)*	*Present seats (543)*	*Population %*	*Final allocation*	*Difference in seats*	*Seat %*	*% OR / UR wrt population*	*Percentage increase*
	A	*B*	*(A)/(Total A)C*	*H*		*I*	*(C-I)/(I)J*	
Rajasthan	6,85,48,437	25	5.66	41	16	5.63	0.52	64
Bihar	10,40,99,452	40	8.60	62	22	8.52	0.95	55
Haryana	2,53,51,462	10	2.09	15	5	2.06	1.61	50
Uttar Pradesh	19,98,12,341	80	16.50	119	39	16.35	0.95	48.75
Madhya Pradesh	7,26,26,809	29	6.00	43	14	5.91	1.55	48.28
Jharkhand	3,29,88,134	14	2.72	20	6	2.75	-0.83	42.86
Delhi	1,67,87,941	7	1.39	10	3	1.37	0.93	42.86
Maharashtra	11,23,74,333	48	9.28	67	19	9.20	0.84	39.58
Gujarat	6,04,39,692	26	4.99	36	10	4.95	0.94	38.46
Chhattisgarh	2,55,45,198	11	2.11	15	4	2.06	2.39	36.36
Assam	3,12,05,576	14	2.58	19	5	2.61	-1.25	35.71
Punjab	2,77,43,388	13	2.29	17	4	2.34	-1.88	30.77
West Bengal	9,12,76,115	42	7.54	54	12	7.42	1.63	28.57
Karnataka	6,10,95,297	28	5.05	36	8	4.95	2.03	28.57

State	Population (2011)	Present seats (543)	Population %	Final allocation	Difference in seats	Seat %	% OR / UR wrt population	Percentage increase
	A	B	(A)/(Total A)C	H		I	(C-I)/(I)J	
Uttarakhand	1,00,86,292	5	0.83	6	1	0.82	1.07	20
Andhra Pradesh	8,45,80,777	42	6.99	50	8	6.87	1.70	19.05
Orissa	4,19,74,218	21	3.47	25	4	3.43	0.94	19.05
Jammu & Kashmir	1,25,41,302	6	1.04	7	1	0.96	7.72	16.67
Tamil Nadu	7,21,47,030	39	5.96	43	4	5.91	0.88	10.26
Kerala	3,34,06,061	20	2.76	20	0	2.75	0.42	0
Himachal Pradesh	68,64,602	4	0.57	4	0	0.55	3.18	0
Tripura *	36,73,917	2	0.30	2	0	0.27	10.44	0
Meghalaya *	29,66,889	2	0.25	2	0	0.27	-10.81	0
Manipur *	28,55,794	2	0.24	2	0	0.27	-14.15	0
Nagaland *	19,78,502	1	0.16	1	0	0.14	18.95	0
Goa *	14,58,545	2	0.12	2	0	0.27	-56.15	0
Arunachal Pradesh *	13,83,727	2	0.11	2	0	0.27	-58.40	0

State	*Population (2011)*	*Present seats (543)*	*Population %*	*Final allocation*	*Difference in seats*	*Seat %*	*% OR / UR wrt population*	*Percentage increase*
	A	B	*(A)/(Total A)C*	*H*		*I*	*(C-I)/(I)J*	
Puducherry *	12,47,953	1	0.10	1	0	0.14	-24.97	0
Mizoram *	10,97,206	1	0.09	1	0	0.14	-34.03	0
Chandigarh *	10,55,450	1	0.09	1	0	0.14	-36.54	0
Sikkim *	6,10,577	1	0.05	1	0	0.14	-63.29	0
Andaman & Nicobar *	3,80,581	1	0.03	1	0	0.14	-77.12	0
Dadra & Nagar Haveli *	3,43,709	1	0.03	1	0	0.14	-79.34	0
Daman and Diu *	2,43,247	1	0.02	1	0	0.14	-85.38	0
Lakshadweep *	64,473	1	0.01	1	0	0.14	-96.12	0
India	1,21,08,55,027	543	1	728				34.07

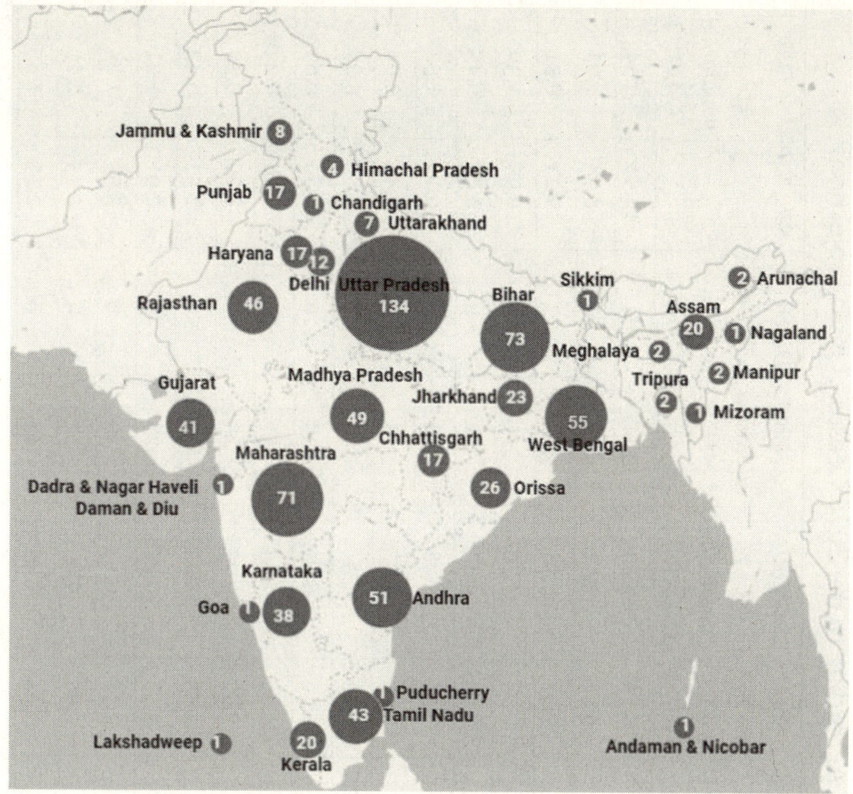

Figure 10.27: Distribution of Lok Sabha seats on the map of India as per the 2026 Census of India projections

Source: Table 10.15

The detailed calculations as per 2026 projections are presented in Table 10.15.

The next delimitation is likely to be based on a fresh census, and not the 2011 Census. According to the Census of India's 2026 population projections—which are unlikely to be too off-the-mark when the next census happens—there will be an even more dramatic shift in the distribution of Lok Sabha seats. As with the earlier model, very small states and UTs have deliberately been left unchanged. With only 4 seats, Himachal Pradesh sees no change, because at present it is overrepresented. Uttarakhand and Jammu & Kashmir will see their seats increase by 2 each, from the present figure of 5 and 6 respectively.

Table 10.15: Proposed Number of Seats According to the 2026 Census of India Projections

State	*Population (2011), 2026 projection*	*Present seats (543) B*	*Population % (A)/ (Total A) C*	*Seat % (B)/ (Total B)D*	*% OR/ UR wrt population (C-D)/(C) E*	*Final allocation H*	*Difference in seats*	*Seat % I*	*% OR/ UR wrt population (C-I)/(I) J*
Uttar Pradesh	24,28,59,000	80	17.03	14.73	13.50	134	54	16.94	0.54
Maharashtra	12,93,08,000	48	9.07	8.84	2.52	71	23	8.98	1.03
Bihar	13,22,65,000	40	9.28	7.37	20.58	73	33	9.23	0.51
West Bengal	10,05,22,000	42	7.05	7.73	-9.72	55	13	6.95	1.39
Andhra Pradesh	9,23,45,000	42	6.48	7.73	-19.43	51	9	6.45	0.45
Madhya Pradesh	8,96,73,000	29	6.29	5.34	15.08	49	20	6.19	1.52
Tamil Nadu	7,75,46,000	39	5.44	7.18	-32.07	43	4	5.44	0.04
Rajasthan	8,36,42,000	25	5.87	4.60	21.51	46	21	5.82	0.87
Karnataka	6,89,62,000	28	4.84	5.16	-6.62	38	10	4.80	0.67
Gujarat	7,40,86,000	26	5.20	4.79	7.84	41	15	5.18	0.24
Orissa	4,71,47,000	21	3.31	3.87	-16.97	26	5	3.29	0.59
Kerala	3,62,07,000	20	2.54	3.68	-45.05	20	0	2.53	0.43
Jharkhand	4,09,58,000	14	2.87	2.58	10.24	23	9	2.91	-1.21
Assam	3,67,17,000	14	2.57	2.58	-0.13	20	6	2.53	1.84
Punjab	3,13,18,000	13	2.20	2.39	-9.00	17	4	2.15	2.20
Chhattisgarh	3,12,11,000	11	2.19	2.03	7.45	17	6	2.15	1.85

State	Population (2011), 2026 projection	Present seats (543) B	Population % (A)/ (Total A) C	Seat % (B)/ (Total B)D	% OR/ UR wrt population (C-D)/(C) E	Final allocation H	Difference in seats	Seat % I	% OR/ UR wrt population (C-I)/(I) J
Haryana	3,12,99,000	10	2.20	1.84	16.10	17	7	2.15	2.13
Delhi	2,25,40,000	7	1.58	1.29	18.45	12	5	1.52	4.20
Jammu & Kashmir	1,42,01,000	6	1.00	1.10	-10.95	8	2	1.01	-1.53
Uttarakhand	1,19,93,000	5	0.84	0.92	-9.48	7	2	0.88	-4.96
Himachal Pradesh	75,79,000	4	0.53	0.74	-38.59	4	0	0.51	5.11
Tripura *	42,60,000	2	0.30	0.37	-23.29	2	0	0.25	18.16
Meghalaya *	34,40,000	2	0.24	0.37	-52.67	2	0	0.25	-4.59
Manipur *	33,11,000	2	0.23	0.37	-58.62	2	0	0.25	-8.16
Nagaland *	22,94,000	1	0.16	0.18	-14.47	1	0	0.13	27.26
Goa *	15,98,000	2	0.11	0.37	-228.66	2	0	0.25	-55.68
Arunachal Pradesh*	16,04,000	2	0.11	0.37	-227.43	2	0	0.25	-55.51
Puducherry *	17,57,000	1	0.12	0.18	-49.46	1	0	0.13	-2.53
Mizoram *	12,72,000	1	0.09	0.18	-106.44	1	0	0.13	-29.44
Chandigarh *	12,67,000	1	0.09	0.18	-107.26	1	0	0.13	-29.72
Sikkim *	7,08,000	1	0.05	0.18	-270.90	1	0	0.13	-60.72

State	*Population (2011), 2026 projection*	*Present seats (543) B*	*Population % (A)/ (Total A) C*	*Seat % (B)/ (Total B)D*	*% OR/ UR wrt population (C-D)/(C) E*	*Final allocation H*	*Difference in seats*	*Seat % I*	*% OR/ UR wrt population (C-I)/(I) J*
Andaman & Nicobar *	4,06,000	1	0.03	0.18	-546.79	1	0	0.13	-77.48
Dadra & Nagar Haveli *	8,36,000	1	0.06	0.18	-214.11	1	0	0.13	-53.62
Daman and Diu*	7,05,000	1	0.05	0.18	-272.48	1	0	0.13	-60.89
Lakshadweep*	70,000	1	0.00	0.18	-3651.40	1	0	0.13	-96.12
	1,42,59,06,000	543				791	248		

543 Seats – 1,42,59,06,000

1 Seat – 26,25,977.90

- *States with two or less than two seats will be considered small states.*
- *Therefore, Kerala has the highest overrepresentation if we exclude the small states.*
- *Hence, we correct the bias while keeping Kerala as the base.*

	Population	*Seats*
Kerala	*3,62,07,000*	*20*
	1,42,59,06,000	*787.64*

- *We assume 788 seats and reallocate them keeping in mind that no state ends up with fewer seats than what it holds now.*
- *When we reallocate the seats based on population distribution, there are seven states which lose one seat.*
- *We exclude these states and their respective seats from the calculation and reallocate the seats based on the population for the remaining states.*

Delhi will experience a substantial gain, with its seats rising from 7 to 12. Haryana and Chhattisgarh also see significant increases, with their seats going up from 10 to 17 and from 11 to 17 respectively. Punjab gets 4 additional seats; Assam gets 6 more. Jharkhand sees a massive gain of 9 seats, rising from 14 to 23.

As in the model previously used for calculations based on the 2011 Census, Kerala's seat allocation remains unchanged at 20, despite the overall increase from 543 to 791—an increase of 248 seats. Among the states placed above Kerala, Orissa sees a modest gain of 5 seats, moving from 21 to 26. Gujarat secures a massive gain of 15 seats, taking it from 26 to 41. Karnataka gets a good addition of 10 seats to its present allocation of 28. Rajasthan, a highly underrepresented state at present, sees it seats go up by a massive difference of 21 (from 25 to 46). Madhya Pradesh sees its seats rise by a massive figure of 20, taking it from 29 to 49. With the addition of 4 seats to its present allocation of 39, Tamil Nadu gets a small gain. Andhra Pradesh secures a modest gain of 9 seats. West Bengal's gain of 13 seats is also modest. The change in seat numbers is most dramatic in Bihar, Maharashtra and Uttar Pradesh, both because of their immense population size and their marked underrepresentation at present. So, Bihar's seats go up by 33 (from 40 to 73); Maharashtra's seats go up by a massive 23 (from 48 to 71); and Uttar Pradesh's seats increase by no less than 54 (from 80 to 134).

The focus of the discussion in this book so far has been on political representation in the Lok Sabha. This is because the Lok Sabha is the house directly elected by the people of India and is, therefore, the primary expression of their will. However, the Rajya Sabha (Council of States) plays a crucial role in our constitutional scheme as a house where the interests of states are better represented, and which acts as a check on any hasty use of legislative power by the Parliament because of its equal role in law-making. The Parliament, of course, consists of both houses. According to Article 80 of the Constitution, 'the representatives of each state in the Council of States shall be elected by the elected members of the Legislative Assembly of the State in accordance with the system of proportional representation by means of a single transferable vote'.

The current maximum strength of the Rajya Sabha is 245. Out of these, 233 are elected by the legislatures of the states and Union Territories. The remaining 12 are nominated by the President from fields such as art, literature and science. The number of Rajya Sabha seats has remained frozen since 1976, except for the addition of one seat the same year on the accession of Sikkim to the Union of India and in 1987, when Goa was conferred statehood and one seat was allocated to it. Similar to the Lok Sabha, each state or Union Territory is assigned a certain number of seats in the Council of States based on its population. The allocation of seats to states is contained in the Fourth Schedule of the Constitution. Of course, here as well, many small states and UTs have been given a minimum representation. Leaving them out, and without reducing the current seats of any state, the required strength for the Rajya Sabha will have to be calculated. Maintaining the present ratio of seats between the Lok Sabha and the Rajya Sabha to the extent possible, the total number of seats in the Rajya Sabha would be around 326 as per 2011 Census. Their distribution is depicted in Figure 10.28.

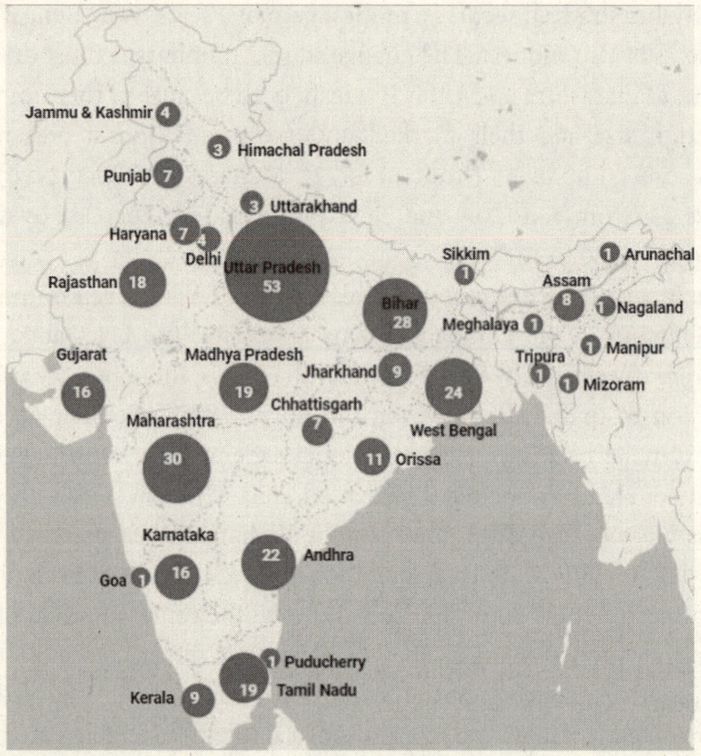

Figure 10.28: Distribution of Rajya Sabha seats (as per 2011 Census) on the map of India.

Source: Table 10.16

The difference of each state from its present allocation is shown in the bar chart in Figure 10.29.

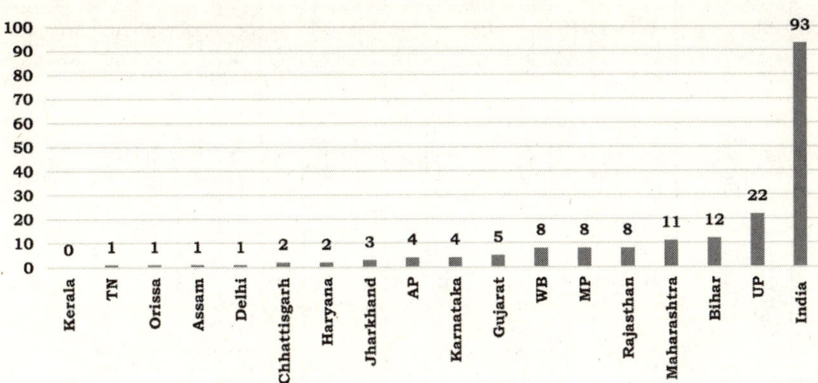

Figure 10.29: Difference in Rajya Sabha seats as per the 2011 Census

Source: Table 10.16

Table 10.16 below provides detailed calculations of the state-wise changes proposed for the Rajya Sabha:

It is evident that the imbalance or distortion in democratic representation is even more pronounced in the Rajya Sabha than in the Lok Sabha. If seats were allocated based on the Census of 2011, with its seats going up from 10 to 18, Rajasthan will be the biggest gainer in percentage terms, at 80 per cent. Bihar will be the second-biggest gainer, with its seats going up from 16 to 28—a rise of 75 per cent. Madhya Pradesh will see its seats increase from 11 to 19— a rise of 72.73 per cent. Just as with the Lok Sabha, Uttar Pradesh will experience the largest increase in the number of seats, from 31 to 53. However, its percentage rise of 70.97 is below that of Rajasthan, Bihar and Madhya Pradesh. These figures highlight the gross underrepresentation of all these states in the Rajya Sabha at present.

Maharashtra will see its seats increase from 19 to 30, a huge increase of 57.89 per cent. West Bengal's seats will rise from 16 to 24, a substantial rise of 50 per cent, matching the increase seen in Jharkhand, whose seats will go up from 6 to 9. Gujarat will experience a 45.45 per cent increase, with its seats rising from 11 to 16. Next in sequence, Chhattisgarh's

Table 10.16: Proposed Number of Rajya Sabha Seats According to the 2011 Census

State	*Population (2011)A*	*Current seats (233)*	*Population %*	*Seat %*	*%UR/OR*	*Final allocation (326)*	*Difference in seats*	*% Increase*	*Seat %*	*%UR/OR*
Uttar Pradesh	19,98,12,341	31	16.50	13.30%	19.37	53	22	70.97	16.26	1.48
Maharashtra	11,23,74,333	19	9.28	8.15%	12.13	30	11	57.89	9.20	0.84
Bihar	10,40,99,452	16	8.60	6.87%	20.13	28	12	75.00	8.59	0.10
West Bengal	9,12,76,115	16	7.54	6.87%	8.90	24	8	50.00	7.36	2.34
Andhra Pradesh	8,45,80,777	18	6.99	7.73%	-10.60	22	4	22.22	6.75	3.39
Madhya Pradesh	7,26,26,809	11	6.00	4.72%	21.29	19	8	72.73	5.83	2.83
Tamil Nadu	7,21,47,030	18	5.96	7.73%	-29.66	19	1	5.56	5.83	2.18
Rajasthan	6,85,48,437	10	5.66	4.29%	24.19	18	8	80.00	5.52	2.47
Karnataka	6,10,95,297	12	5.05	5.15%	-2.07	16	4	33.33	4.91	2.73
Gujarat	6,04,39,692	11	4.99	4.72%	5.42	16	5	45.45	4.91	1.67
Orissa	4,19,74,218	10	3.47	4.29%	-23.81	11	1	10.00	3.37	2.66
Kerala	3,34,06,061	9	2.76	3.86	-40.01	9	-	0.00	2.76	-0.07
Jharkhand	3,29,88,134	6	2.72	2.58	5.48	9	3	50.00	2.76	-1.33
Assam	3,12,05,576	7	2.58	3.00	-16.57	8	1	14.29	2.45	4.78
Punjab	2,77,43,388	7	2.29	3.00	-31.12	7	-	0.00	2.15	6.28
Chhattisgarh	2,55,45,198	5	2.11	2.15	-1.72	7	2	40.00	2.15	-1.78

State	*Population (2011)A*	*Current seats (233)*	*Population %*	*Seat %*	*%UR/OR*	*Final allocation (326)*	*Difference in seats*	*% Increase*	*Seat %*	*%UR/OR*
Haryana	2,53,51,462	5	2.09	2.15	-2.50	7	2	40.00	2.15	-2.56
Delhi	1,67,87,941	3	1.39	1.29	7.13	4	1	33.33	1.23	11.50
Jammu & Kashmir	1,25,41,302	4	1.04	1.72	-65.75	4	-	0.00	1.23	-18.47
Uttarakhand	1,00,86,292	3	0.83	1.29	-54.57	3	-	0.00	0.92	-10.48
Himachal Pradesh	68,64,602	3	0.57	1.29	-127.11	3	-	0.00	0.92	-62.32
Tripura *	36,73,917	1	0.30	0.43	-41.45	1	-	0.00	0.31	-1.10
Meghalaya *	29,66,389	1	0.25	0.43	-75.1%	1	-	0.00	0.31	-25.19
Manipur *	28,55,794	1	0.24	0.43	-81.97	1	-	0.00	0.31	-30.06
Nagaland *	19,78,502	1	0.16	0.43	-162.66	1	-	0.00	0.31	-87.73
Goa *	14,58,545	1	0.12	0.43	-256.30	1	-	0.00	0.31	-154.66
Arunachal Pradesh *	13,83,727	1	0.11	0.43	-275.57	1	-	0.00	0.31	-168.43
Puducherry *	12,47,953	1	0.10	0.43	-316.43	1	-	0.00	0.31	-197.63
Mizoram *	10,97,206	1	0.09	0.43	-373.64	1	-	0.00	0.31	-238.52
Chandigarh *	10,55,450	-	0.09	0.00	100.00	0	-	0.00	0.00	100.00
Sikkim *	6,10,577	1	0.05	0.43	-751.13	1	-	0.00	0.31	-508.32

State	*Population (2011)A*	*Current seats (233)*	*Population %*	*Seat %*	*%UR/OR*	*Final allocation (326)*	*Difference in seats*	*% Increase*	*Seat %*	*%UR/OR*
Andaman & Nicobar *	3,80,581	-	0.03	0.00	100.00	0	-	0.00	0.00	100.00
Dadra & Nagar Haveli *	3,43,709	-	0.03	0.00	100.00	0	-	0.00	0.00	100.00
Daman and Diu *	2,43,247	-	0.02	0.00	100.00	0	-	0.00	0.00	100.00
Lakshadweep *	64,473	-	0.01	0.00	100.00	0	-	0.00	0.00	100.00
India	1,21,08,55,027	233	100.00	100.00	0.00	326	93	39.91	100.00	0.00

- *We will maintain the current ratio between the Rajya Sabha and Lok Sabha seats.*

	Rajya Sabha	*Lok Sabha*
Present	*233*	*543*
2.330472103		
Suggested (2011)	*326*	*728*
2.233128834		

seats will go up from 5 to 7—a 40 per cent rise. Similarly, Haryana, with its seats rising from 5 to 7, also secures a 40 per cent gain. Delhi's seats will increase from 3 to 4, a rise of 33.33 per cent. Andhra Pradesh will see its seats go up from 18 to 22—a rise of 22.22 per cent. Assam's seats will rise from 7 to 8, an increase of only 14.29 per cent. Orissa, whose seats go up from 10 to 11, secures a gain of 10 per cent. Tamil Nadu's seats will rise from 18 to 19—a small gain of 5.56 per cent. As in the case of the Lok Sabha, Kerala will see no rise in seats, remaining at 9. All the states listed below Kerala in the table will also see no change in seat allocation.

Although the broad pattern of imbalance seen in the Lok Sabha is repeated in the Rajya Sabha, there are notable differences. West Bengal and Karnataka, which had each gained only 28.57 per cent in the Lok Sabha, will see a more substantial rise here of 50 per cent and 33.33 per cent respectively. Haryana will see a more modest rise of 40 per cent in comparison with 50 per cent in the Lok Sabha. While Tamil Nadu had gained by 10.26 per cent in the Lok Sabha, in the Rajya Sabha the gain is only 5.56 per cent. Punjab's case is notable because its current Rajya Sabha seats (7) remain unchanged, even though the state had secured a modest gain of 30.77 per cent in the Lok Sabha.

Compared to the Lok Sabha, in the Rajya Sabha there is a smaller increase for Delhi (42.86 per cent versus 33.33 per cent), Assam (35.71 per cent versus 14.29 per cent), Orissa (19.05 per cent versus 10 per cent), Jammu & Kashmir (16.67 per cent versus 0.00 per cent) and Uttarakhand (20 per cent versus 0.00 per cent).

These states secure higher gains in the Rajya Sabha than in the Lok Sabha: Uttar Pradesh (48.75 per cent versus 70.97 per cent), Maharashtra (39.58 per cent versus 57.89 per cent), Bihar (55 per cent versus 75 per cent), Madhya Pradesh (48.28 per cent versus 72.73 per cent), Rajasthan (64 per cent versus 80 per cent) and Gujarat (38.46 per cent versus 45.45 per cent). In many ways, then, the Rajya Sabha is even less representative of the current demographic distribution of the country and would require massive change to align it with constitutional provisions. This distortion becomes even more pronounced when we calculate the total and state-wise numbers as per the Registrar of India's population projections for 2026.

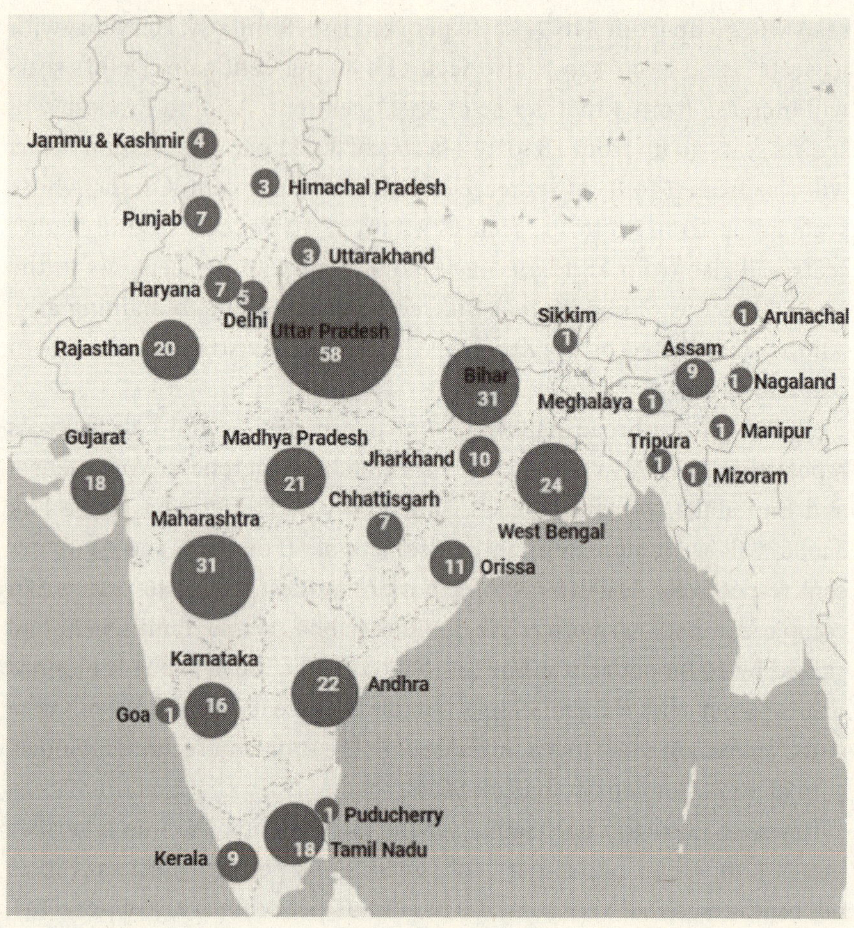

Figure 10.30: Distribution of Rajya Sabha seats as per the Census of India projections for 2026

Source: Table 10.17

The bar chart in Figure 10.31 shows the difference in allocations for major states compared to their present allocations.

Maintaining roughly the same ratio between the Lok Sabha and the Rajya Sabha while distributing seats according to population, the figure for the Rajya Sabha comes out to 343. In terms of number of additional seats, these states are the biggest gainers: Uttar Pradesh (27), Bihar (15), Maharashtra (12), Madhya Pradesh (10), Rajasthan (10), West Bengal (8) and Gujarat (7).

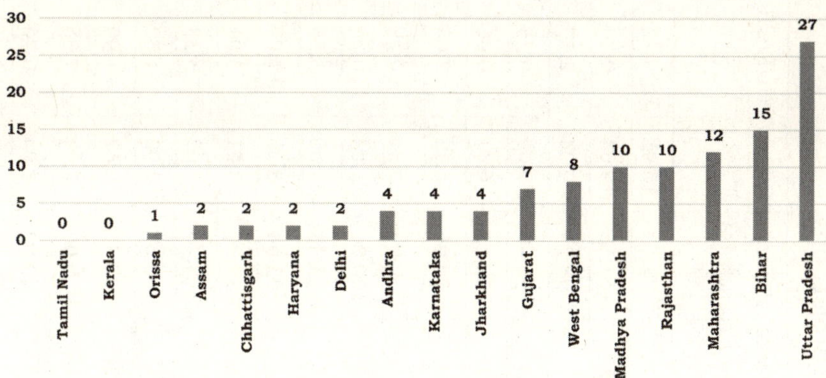

Figure 10.31: Difference in Rajya Sabha seats as per the 2026 Census projections

Source: Table 10.17

In terms of percentage, Rajasthan is the biggest gainer, with its seats going up from 10 to 20—an increase of 100 per cent. After Rajasthan, the states with the highest gain in order are Bihar (93.75 per cent), Madhya Pradesh (90.91 per cent), Jharkhand (66.67 per cent), Delhi (66.67 per cent), Gujarat (63.64), Maharashtra (63.16 per cent) and West Bengal (50 per cent).

Since this study has analysed demographic transition and population growth across both states and regions (north, south, east and west), it would be insightful to examine how Parliament seats are distributed by region. The charts in Figures 10.32 and 10.33 present a panoramic view of the present regional distribution of Lok Sabha and Rajya Sabha seats, the proposed allocation based on the 2011 Census and the proposed allocation according to the 2026 population projections by the Census of India.

Table 10.17: Changes required in the Rajya Sabha as per the 2026 projections

State	*Population (2026) A*	*Current seats (233)*	*Population*	*Seat %*	*%UR/OR*	*Final allocation (343)*	*Difference in seats*	*Per cent increase*	*Seat %*	*%UR/OR*
Uttar Pradesh	24,28,59,000	31	17.03	13.30	21.88	58	27	87.10	16.91	0.72
Maharashtra	12,93,08,000	19	9.07	8.15	10.08	31	12	63.16	9.04	0.34
Bihar	13,22,65,000	16	9.28	6.87	25.97	31	15	93.75	9.04	2.57
West Bengal	10,05,22,000	16	7.05	6.87	2.59	24	8	50.00	7.00	0.75
Andhra Pradesh	9,23,45,000	18	6.48	7.73	-19.29	22	4	22.22	6.41	0.96
Madhya Pradesh	8,96,73,000	11	6.29	4.72	24.93	21	10	90.91	6.12	2.65
Tamil Nadu	7,75,46,000	18	5.44	7.73	-42.05	18	-	0.00	5.25	3.50
Rajasthan	8,36,42,000	10	5.87	4.29	26.83	20	10	100.00	5.83	0.60
Karnataka	6,89,62,000	12	4.84	5.15	-6.49	16	4	33.33	4.66	3.55
Gujarat	7,40,86,000	11	5.20	4.72	9.14	18	7	63.64	5.25	-1.00
Orissa	4,71,47,000	10	3.31	4.29	-29.80	11	1	10.00	3.21	3.01
Kerala	3,62,07,000	9	2.54	3.86	-52.12	9	-	0.00	2.62	-3.33
Jharkhand	4,09,58,000	6	2.87	2.58	10.35	10	4	66.67	2.92	-1.50
Assam	3,67,17,000	7	2.57	3.00	-16.67	9	2	28.57	2.62	-1.90
Punjab	3,13,18,000	7	2.20	3.00	-36.79	7	-	0.00	2.04	7.08
Chhattisgarh	3,12,11,000	5	2.19	2.15	1.96	7	2	40.00	2.04	6.76

State	Population (2026) A	Current seats (233)	Population	Seat %	%UR/OR	Final allocation (343)	Difference in seats	Per cent increase	Seat %	%UR/OR
Haryana	3,12,99,000	5	2.20	2.15	2.24	7	2	40.00	2.04	7.03
Delhi	2,25,40,000	3	1.58	1.29	18.55	5	2	66.67	1.46	7.78
Jammu & Kashmir	1,42,01,000	4	1.00	1.72	-72.38	4	-	0.00	1.17	-17.09
Uttarakhand	1,19,93,000	3	0.84	1.29	-53.08	3	-	0.00	0.87	-3.99
Himachal Pradesh	75,79,000	3	0.53	1.29	-142.24	3	-	0.00	0.87	-64.55
Tripura *	42,60,000	1	0.30	0.43	-43.66	1	-	0.00	0.29	2.41
Meghalaya *	34,40,000	1	0.24	0.43	-77.90	1	-	0.00	0.29	-20.85
Manipur *	33,11,000	1	0.23	0.43	-84.83	1	-	0.00	0.29	-25.56
Nagaland *	22,94,000	1	0.16	0.43	-166.77	1	-	0.00	0.29	-81.22
Goa *	15,98,000	1	0.11	0.43	-282.96	1	-	0.00	0.29	-160.15
Arunachal Pradesh *	16,04,000	1	0.11	0.43	-281.53	1	-	0.00	0.29	-159.17
Puducherry *	17,57,000	1	0.12	0.43	-248.31	1	-	0.00	0.29	-136.61
Mizoram *	12,72,000	1	0.09	0.43	-381.11	1	-	0.00	0.29	-226.82
Chandigarh *	12,67,000	-	0.09	0.00	100.00	0	-		0.00	100.00
Sikkim *	7,08,000	1	0.05	0.43	-764.37	1	-	0.00	0.29	-487.17

State	Population (2026) A	Current seats (233)	Population	Seat %	%UR/OR	Final allocation (343)	Difference in seats	Per cent increase	Seat %	%UR/OR
Andaman & Nicobar *	4,06,000	-	0.03	0.00	100.00	0	-		0.00	100.00
Dadra & Nagar Haveli *	8,36,000	-	0.06	0.00	100.00	0	-		0.00	100.00
Daman and Diu *	7,05,000	-	0.5	0.00	100.00	0	-		0.00	100.00
Lakshadweep *	70,000	-	0.00	0.00	100.00	0	-		0.00	100.00
	1,42,59,06,000	233	100.00	100.00		343	110	47.21	100.00	0.00

- *We will maintain the ratio between the Rajya Sabha and Lok Sabha seats which is present today.*

	Rajya Sabha	*Lok Sabha*
Present	*233*	*543*
2.330472103		
Suggested (2011)	*326*	*728*
2.233128834		
Suggested (2026)	*339*	*791*

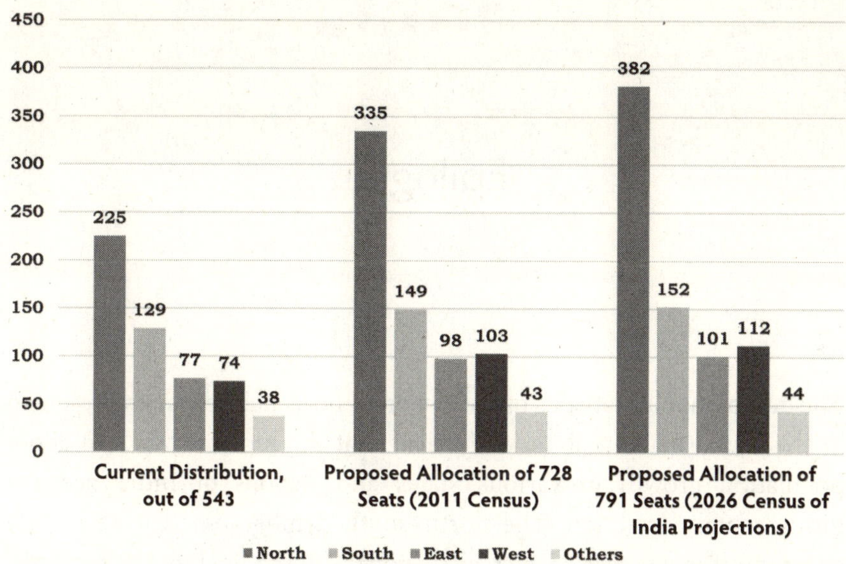

Figure 10.32: Regional distribution of Lok Sabha seats

Source: Tables 10.12, 10.13 and 10.14

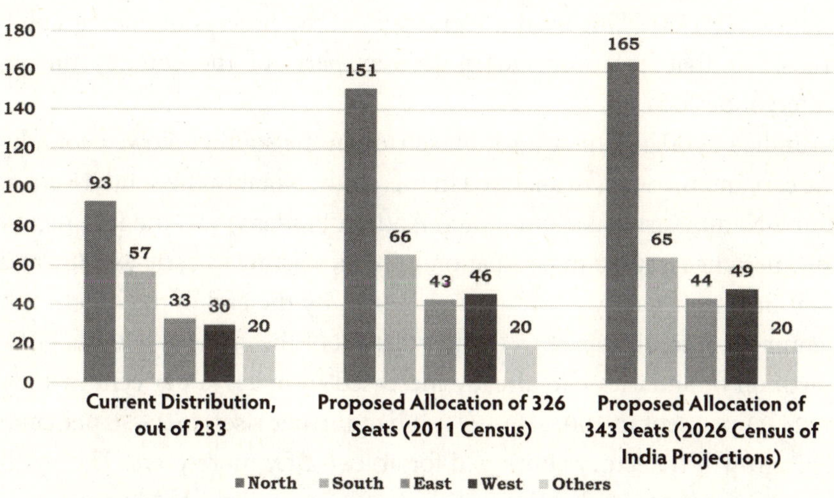

Figure 10.33: Regional distribution of Rajya Sabha seats

Source: Table 10.15 and 10.16

Epilogue

The demographic statistics of the last one-and-a-half centuries presented in this study make it abundantly clear that the received wisdom about population growth in various states and regions of India needs a fundamental correction. The north–south demographic divide is only apparent; it is not real. In fact, all regions of India, including the north, south, east and west, have enjoyed phases of high population growth lasting four to five decades on an average. Their variable growth rates in comparison with the growth rates of other regions have caused considerable fluctuations in their respective shares in the population of India since 1881. This is an integral part of the process of demographic transition that has occurred in various parts of the country during different periods.

India's demographic transition started in the south, followed soon by the east and the west, as analysed in this study. Notably, the south (Kerala, Tamil Nadu, Karnataka and united Andhra Pradesh) was the first region to experience a surge in population growth, starting as early as 1881 and continuing for nearly a century until 1971. By the end of the nineteenth century, the south's share in the population of the country with its post-Partition boundaries had already increased from 21.56 per cent in 1881 to 24.23 per cent in 1901. By 1921, it had further risen to 25.56 per cent. This growth trajectory continued for at least fifty more years. The result was that in 1951, its share of India's population peaked at 26.08 per cent and declined to 24.69 per cent in 1971. That year's census population data has been used for delimitation and allocation of seats in Parliament for the past five decades.

The east (Assam, West Bengal and Orissa) was the second region to witness rapid population growth comparable to that of the south in the nineteenth century itself. From 1881 to 1901, its share in the national population increased from 12.08 per cent to 12.81 per cent. Consequently, at the turn of the twentieth century these two regions had already experienced comparatively high growth. They further enjoyed high growth between 1901 and 1921, during which time the population of the north hardly grew. With relatively high growth over 1881–1971, the east's share in the country's population peaked at 14.76 per cent in 1971.

Soon after the south and the east, the west (Maharashtra and Gujarat) emerged as the third region of India to embark upon demographic transition and to experience rapid growth. While its share in national population fell significantly from 13.44 per cent to 11.95 per cent during the nineteenth century, after 1911 it witnessed rapid growth. Its share increased to 13.37 per cent in 1951, and hit the peak of 14.34 per cent in 2001. Unlike the south and the east, however, the west has shown continued demographic dynamism even after 2001. As a result, its share has decreased only marginally to 14.27 per cent in 2011.

The demographic story of the northern states, consisting of the Hindi belt (Himachal Pradesh, Uttarakhand, Haryana, Rajasthan, Uttar Pradesh, Madhya Pradesh, Chhattisgarh, Jharkhand and the NCT of Delhi) is different from that of the other three regions. From 1881 to 1901, its population growth was nearly stagnant. Its share in the national population came down from 49.85 per cent to 46.16 per cent only. For an additional twenty-year period, extending until 1921, the north's growth was either negative or minimal, at a time when the south and the east were growing rapidly. The result was that in 1921 its share declined to 44.14 per cent. Taken as a whole, between 1881 and 1921, there was very little growth in the north's population. In 1881, it was 10,67,46,332 and in 1921 it was 11,09,36,034. This is a change of only 3.92 per cent over forty years. During the same period, the south (39.12 per cent) and the east (28.62) grew quite rapidly. The population stagnation of the Hindi belt from 1881 to 1921 is one of the unknown aspects of India's modern demographic history.

The Hindi-speaking north was the last of the four regions to go through demographic transition. Its growth started inching up only after

1921 and picked up pace only around mid-twentieth century. Its peak rates were reached after 1971, by which time its share in the country's population had plummeted to a low of 41.90 per cent. Owing to its high growth between 1971 and 2011, the north has shown convergence with its 1901 share by reaching 46.47 per cent, which is still well behind its 1881 share of 49.85 per cent.

The widely held perception that the north has been the culprit behind India's so-called population explosion, while the south has been disciplined in reducing its population growth through family planning and other methods is akin to an optical illusion. This illusion has largely been created by the failure of policymakers and experts to take a sufficiently long-term view of population growth in India. It is not as if there was a deliberate attempt at distortion. As this study has mapped in detail, it was an unfortunate coincidence that just as the north's population growth had started peaking in the post-Independence period, the ideas of 'overpopulation' and 'population explosion' emerged in the western world.

What was mistakenly described as 'population explosion' was nothing more than peak population growth associated with the second phase of demographic transition in many Third World countries after the Second World War. While demographic transition occurred in the developed world over two to three centuries and did not cause the same level of alarm, it occurred in the Third World countries within four to five decades. This happened mainly due to the sudden fall in mortality resulting from technological advancements in medicine and sanitation, as well as the significantly increased availability of food in those countries after their liberation from colonial rule. In fact, even in the developed world, the period was marked by comparatively high population growth for similar reasons, though elevated birth rates for a couple of decades played a more important role there.

Given the overwhelming demographic size of the Hindi-speaking north—roughly equal to all other regions combined—the north's peak growth phase led to a faster overall increase, causing the country's population to rise much more rapidly than in the past. Owing to the south's relatively smaller share of India's population, its high growth rates in the preceding decades did not lead to as much of a spike in the national growth rate, as would happen with similar growth in the north. Moreover, the bulk of demographic expansion in the south happened before 1951. It was barely noticed, as the idea of 'population explosion' was still taking shape at the time.

By the time a demographic surge occurred in the north, the international discourse of 'overpopulation' and 'population explosion'—created and promoted by international organisations like the Rockefeller Foundation, Ford Foundation, and United Nations agencies like FAO and WHO mainly for geopolitical reasons—had gained currency. As the second-most populous country in the world, and the most populous in the so-called free world, India became critical to this discourse; its rapid demographic growth was perceived as a serious threat to global food security and economic development. Unfortunately, these ideas were borrowed by Indian decision-makers without much enquiry. For policymakers, population growth became arguably the biggest threat to food security and the economic development of the newly independent nation.

Importantly, policymakers and experts came to the wrong conclusion that the north's high Total Fertility Rate (TFR) and population growth rates resulted from inadequate implementation of the family planning programme—a euphemism for birth control coined in the 1940s. Since the decline in TFR and growth rates in the south coincided with the scaling up of family planning initiatives from the 1960s, they erroneously concluded that vigorous implementation of family planning in that region was the principal force behind population control. Consequently, the north's perceived failure to emulate the apparent success of the south became the main explanation for its high growth rates. Indeed, the claim that the decline in the south's fertility and population growth rate was attributable to a vigorous family planning implementation since its launch is questionable also because, until 1966, the programme did not have the requisite scale or budgetary support to have the intended impact. In fact, during 1951–71, the decline in the population growth rate of south was not visible at all, although in fertility rate there was appreciable decline in Kerala and Tamil Nadu.

Moreover, as discussed in Chapter 9, it is crucial to analyse the impact of family planning methods on reducing population growth rates in the southern states through empirical evidence rather than general impressions. This study has explored the causal relationship between family planning (a euphemism for birth control) and decline in population growth. The evidence presented makes it clear that there was hardly any causal link between the two. Family planning was not a significant factor in the reduction in fertility and growth. The south had already completed much of its demographic transition by 1971. With or without family planning, its fertility and population growth were predisposed to decline. (However, family planning was arguably more successful in providing much-needed healthcare to mothers and children all over the country, perhaps more in the south than in the north.) Therefore, much more than the family planning programme, it is the inexorable march of demographic transition that shaped the complex pattern of population growth observed across Indian states. Consequently, it is unwarranted to penalise the north, or any region of the country, for merely having undergone demographic transition at the wrong time.

There is, of course, some connection between state policy and demographic transition. By pursuing policies that promote rapid social and economic development, the state can influence the process of transition. It might be argued that this is potentially the most effective possible intervention to slow down population growth. However, given the fact that rapid development itself requires the presence of multiple positive pre-conditions, this was an effective but not an easy path from the viewpoint of policymakers. Birth control, under the euphemistic name of family planning, appeared to be far easier than economic development. Indeed, the natural sequence of socio-economic development eventually leading to decline in fertility and population growth was sought to be reversed by the assumption that the decline in population growth was a necessary pre-condition for economic development, without sufficient empirical evidence of such a linkage either from India or from other countries. Related to this was the assumption that population control was possible through a family planning programme, irrespective of the pace of economic development. Some might argue that this was a case of putting the cart before the horse.

As shown in this study, both divergence and convergence have played their respective roles in India as well as the world over the last one-and-a-half centuries. In India, there has been some increase in the population shares of the east and the west, while both the south and the north have lost—the north slightly more than the south. This shift is a normal process that has occurred in most parts of the world over the long term and should be regarded as such.

The continued use of the 1971 Census for seat allocation in Parliament or for fiscal devolution, as demanded by many leaders from the south, lacks empirical, political and democratic justification. The south's share in the country's population was near its peak in 1971, as was the case with the east. The west's share reached its peak of 14.34 per cent only in 2001, although at 14.07 per cent in 1971 it was not much below its peak. The west remained close to its peak even in 2011 because of its continued demographic dynamism. The east's share has dropped only slightly since 1971. It is the north that had the lowest share in 1971 and has over the next half-century shown significant convergence with the region's long-term demographic trends.

As discussed in Chapter 8, even using the Census of India's alternative classification of EAG versus non-EAG, based on social and economic development, and not just regional comparison, for comparative analysis of demographic growth, there is little empirical justification for continuing the freeze on delimitation. Non-EAG states—which include the whole of the south—have contributed a major chunk to India's population growth until 1991, and their growth peaked in 1971 when the growth rates of EAG states—including most of the north and Orissa—had just picked up. Since the EAG share in India's population started growing only from 1971, keeping 1971 as the baseline year means that the point from which the EAG share started increasing is ignored for delimitation.

Therefore, the distortion in the present scheme of political representation in India is quite pronounced. Leaving aside the small states and Union Territories, the south is highly overrepresented in Parliament; the east is marginally overrepresented; the west is considerably underrepresented; and the north is highly underrepresented. Thus, the divide in representation is not really north versus south; rather, it is south versus the rest. It might be said that in a way all those born after 1971 in the Hindi-speaking north as well as the west have been left out of representation because of the fixation with 1971 as the cut-off year.

The embargo on the delimitation of Lok Sabha seats has serious consequences for the nation. Democracy is based on the concept of 'one person, one vote, one value' as its core principle. The denial of that principle is a denial of democracy itself. Freezing the allocation of seats in the Lok Sabha based on the 1971 Census, on the ground of 'population control' and not 'punishing' states whose population growth and share in the national population have gone down has created a huge democratic imbalance in the country. It causes a serious distortion in people's representation across the country and deprives them of their constitutionally mandated right of equal representation. The policy has been in operation for fifty years. The longer this policy is maintained, the greater the distortion in representation will become, because much of the population growth in the underrepresented regions has occurred after the 1970s.

This growth has not been accounted for because of the continued use of the 1971 Census data. Since the allocation of seats in the under-represented north and west has not been increased, the representational value of their people has gone down drastically, compared to the south. Currently, each Lok Sabha MP from Kerala represents approximately half the people that a Lok Sabha MP from Uttar Pradesh does. An MP from the south generally represents only about two-thirds as many people as an MP from the north does. This imbalance continues because the constitutional requirement for allocating seats to each state based on population remains in limbo.

The disparity in the population size of constituencies between the north and the south creates asymmetry in the elected representatives' ability to service their constituencies. For example, the Member of Parliament Local Area Development Scheme (MPLADS) provides the same level of financial support to each MP, irrespective of the population of their constituency. This adversely affects the development schemes in large constituencies, putting the states and regions where they are concentrated at a disadvantage. The disparity in the size of constituencies also has an impact on campaign finance. Larger constituencies usually require more expenditure, in the process distorting the selection process of peoples' representatives, as those with a greater ability to secure financial support have a significantly higher chance of being elected, compared to others.

Such ability may sometimes be associated with corruption and nepotism, which brings down the quality of political representation.

When the embargo on delimitation and reallocation of Lok Sabha seats was imposed in 1976 by the 42nd Amendment during the Emergency, population control through better implementation of the family planning programme was cited as the principal justification. The southern states had demanded it on the ground that they had actively and successfully reduced their fertility and population growth rates through effective implementation of family planning, whereas the north had failed to do so. It was argued that not freezing the seats would be akin to 'punishing' the south for its better performance and unjustly 'rewarding' the north for its bad performance. In fact, as early as 1971, Tamil Nadu had raised the demand for using the 1951 Census as the benchmark by moving a Private Member's Bill in Parliament. The DMK first came to power in the state in 1967 and in 1971 raised this demand through the Private Member's Bill moved by DMK MP Murasoli Maran. However, the Bill had faced strong criticism cutting across parties and regions and was rejected by Parliament.

Nevertheless, the policymakers bought into this argument in 1976. They concluded that freezing seats in Parliament as per the 1971 Census would act as an incentive for the south to continue to reduce its fertility and growth rates. At the same time, the embargo was meant to be a disincentive for the Hindi-speaking north, which they erroneously concluded, had failed to control its population growth by effectively implementing the family planning programme. Through the 42nd Amendment, the number of seats in the Lok Sabha and state legislatures was frozen until 2001, based on the 1971 Census data. This was done mainly on the ground of safeguarding the representative influence of the southern states. Thus, the choice of 1971 as the base year for allocating seats in the Lok Sabha for the next fifty years simply ignored the representational interests of the north and the west.

In 2001, when the embargo on delimitation and reallocation was further extended for twenty-five years, the southern states gave the same argument about not losing out on their political representation because of better implementation of family planning. The implementation of family planning since the 1960s emerged as the primary dividing factor between the north and the south. The south had effectively implemented family planning measures; the north had failed to do so. Hence, the argument continued, the performer should not be punished, and the non-performer should not be rewarded. This argument is being reiterated more vehemently to oppose delimitation based on the fresh census scheduled for 2025-26.

It is evident that the fall in representation of the northern states is due to the fact that, owing to delayed onset of demographic transition, the major spurt in their population growth occurred only after 1971. Hypothetically, if the first general election of 1951-52 had been held on the basis of the 1881 Census when the north had a share of almost 50 per cent and the south less than 22 per cent, the south would have lost heavily on representation, because much of its demographic growth, triggered by an early transition, occurred during 1881–1951. Leaving out that growth would have seriously undermined the south's representation. In the real-world scenario, however, it is the north and west that have suffered in terms of political representation; the north because most of this growth occurred after 1951 and the west because it has continued to grow well at least until 2011.

As this study establishes on the basis of historical demographic data, the south had already experienced the bulk of its potential population growth by 1971. Its fertility and population growth rates were bound to drop after nearly a century of high growth. Policy measures were only incidental to the decline of these indicators witnessed by the south after 1971, and more clearly after 1981. The reduced mortality rates, caused perhaps by better social and economic conditions, led most of the south to either complete or approach the second phase of demographic transition, marked by reduced mortality and high fertility. Thus, the south was, by this time, predisposed to lower fertility and growth rates in the near future. Irrespective of government policy and propaganda regarding population control, its growth would have declined anyway.

The north, on the contrary, had just entered the peak phase of population growth. Government policy and propaganda regarding population control apparently failed in the north because it was far behind other regions in the process of demographic transition, making it unprepared for a sudden and drastic fall in fertility and population growth. Nowhere in the world do people decide their family size based primarily on government policy or preferences. Instead, they follow their own rationality in choosing their family size. If conditions favour larger families, government emphasis on smaller family norms can at best get a marginal response.

Of course, in an authoritarian country like China, willing to adopt harsh coercive measures, the state did succeed in imposing a one-child norm, at least on urban couples, from around 1980. But that is not possible in a democratic nation, as the Congress learnt to its dismay in the 1977 general election. Partly due to the use of coercive population control methods, such as forced vasectomies practised on men in north India on a massive scale during the Emergency, the party was routed in the region. In the Lok Sabha, its tally was reduced to 154. Interestingly, the Indian National Congress fared very well in the south, winning 92 out of the 129 seats in the region. The south voted differently mainly because it had been left virtually untouched by such coercive measures.

It was partly the hubris of policymakers that made them think that population growth could be artificially arrested by the will of the state. The reality on the ground was different. Government policies affecting the personal choices of large numbers of people can succeed only when conditions on the ground are conducive for them. Voluntary initiatives alone could not have changed the normal course of demographic transition; coercive efforts proved unsustainable in the long run. Thus, the Indian state's population control measures were doomed to 'fail'. It is important to note that the very idea of 'population explosion', which needed to be urgently controlled, was founded on slippery ground.

An interesting thought experiment on the history and politics of family planning in India would be to consider the fact that the supporters of population control, including international organisations and the Indian experts and policymakers, ardently believed that the India of 1951 with a population of just above 36 crore was 'overpopulated', while the India of 2024 has a population of about 144 crore. So, the country has accommodated nearly 1.1 billion additional people in less than seventy-five years without facing doomsday. Does it then mean that, contrary to the view taken by doomsayers, the India of 1951 was seriously underpopulated? For how else could it have four times the population now, along with food security, considerable economic development and improvement in standards of living? The answer is self-evident. The bugbear of 'overpopulation' and 'population explosion' was raised from the 1950s without a proper understanding of the various aspects of demography related to climate, geography, history, science and technology, social and economic development and, above all, the social psychology of large families and of population growth mainly under the influence of post-Second World War geopolitics. Although conceived in general terms, such ideas were applied especially to the newly decolonised countries with rapid population growth, driven mainly by the geopolitical considerations of the Cold War.

For most of human history, India has been the most populous nation on earth. North India has also been the demographic core of the subcontinent for millennia. Convergence with this long-term trend was a natural, though not ordained, phenomenon which should have been viewed as such. Unfortunately, the bugbear of 'population explosion' created an environment in which much of the blame for the Indian state's failure to eradicate poverty and ensure rapid social and economic development, as promised by the founding fathers at the time of Independence, was laid at the door of the high population growth of the north.

The demographic behaviour of the north over the last fifty years is far from being an outlier. In the course of human history, mortality rates across the world had generally been just below birth rates, so that population growth was nearly always very slow and uncertain. Growth was generally regarded as desirable because otherwise a population might face extinction over time. Traditionally, nearly all religions and cultures of the world laid emphasis on marriage and procreation. Large family size was the norm across countries, continents, religions, regions, classes and castes. It is only in the modern world that the small family gradually emerged as the norm among many societies. These societies have become more prosperous over centuries or decades, accompanied by high levels of social and economic development. Factors such as education and healthcare, along with relatively high levels of urbanisation and women's education and employment in the formal sector, have contributed to a cultural transformation that is frequently, though not always, described as 'modernisation'.

It needs to be emphasised that people everywhere make rational choices about their family size, and their reproductive behaviour is primarily guided by their social and economic environment, apart from individual choices. A population that had not yet gone through the peak growth phase of demographic transition could not have been persuaded to suddenly adopt the small-family norm through government policy.

The demographic statistics of India over the last one-and-a-half centuries leave no doubt that there are no heroes or villains in the population growth story of India. Empirical evidence cited here demolishes the prevalent notion that the south has controlled its population, while the north has not. It might, of course, be argued by some that population control measures adopted by the south contributed to the decline in fertility and growth rates to the extent that without these measures the decline might have been slower. There may well be some truth to this. However, the same point can be made in reverse for the north as well. Thus, it can be said that if the north had not adopted family planning at all, its population growth after 1971 might have been higher than what it actually was. There is no way to quantify such effects anyway. The counterfactual is generally difficult to determine in history, since historical focus is on what did happen, rather than on what did not.

It is important to distinguish between the implications of population growth rate and fluctuation of shares. The south's population has in fact continued to grow at a substantial rate as late as 2001-11. However, its share in India's population has declined because of the comparatively higher growth of the north and the west. Therefore, despite having a below replacement level TFR, the south cannot be truly categorised as a post-transition society, since in such societies the growth rate is either close to zero or there is a net decline in population (minus, of course, the effects of migration). Apart from Germany and Japan, there are many examples, such as Greece, Hungary, Poland and Italy, of countries that have a below replacement level TFR. Therefore, irrespective of whether the growth rates in different regions of India are high or low, so long as there are differential growth rates—which would almost always be the case—population shares will continue to fluctuate. This is so because the rise or decline in shares depends upon relative—and not absolute—growth rates. In fact, even in a post-demographic transition scenario in which the population starts shrinking, the rate of decline cannot possibly be the same across regions and states. There is, thus, hardly any possible scenario in which the population share of the south can either go back to the 1971 level or remain stable even at the 2011 level. What this implies is that since the Parliament seats have to be allocated as per the share of various states in the national population, short of abandoning the fundamental principle of democracy of 'one person, one vote, one value', it is virtually impossible to conceive of a way to maintain, in the future, the south's share of representation in the Lok Sabha at its current level.

The freeze on delimitation has also created another kind of distortion in representation, although that is not the focus of this study. Over the decades, a huge but largely unnoticed imbalance in rural versus urban representation has developed. Across India, villages are far better represented than towns and cities. The Census of India has traditionally used a rather restrictive definition of urban areas. Partly because of unplanned urban growth across the country, there is a significant gap between the population within municipal boundaries and the actual urban population, which spills over the periphery not covered by the municipality. However, even by this restrictive classification, the urban population was about 31.1 per cent of the total in the 2011 Census. Variations in the rates of urbanisation of states and regions are depicted in Figures 1 and 2.

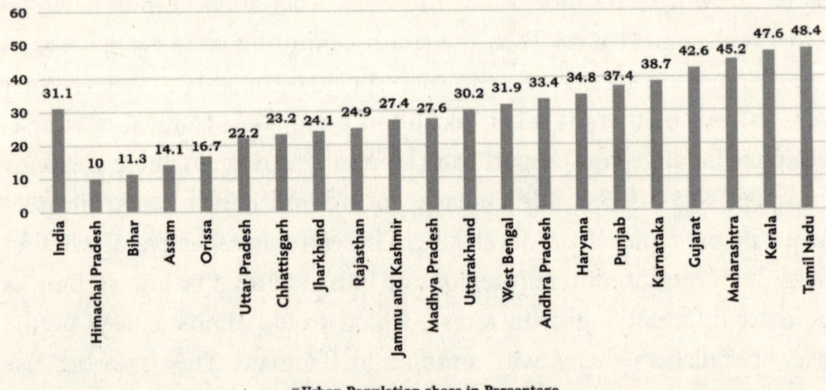

Figure 1: Urban population shares of states (percentage), 2011

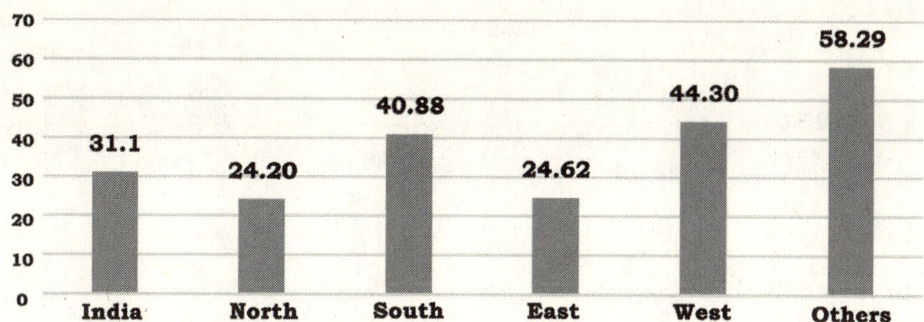

Figure 2: Regional urban population shares (percentage), 2011

According to projections from the Census of India, the urbanisation rate is likely to be around 36 per cent in the upcoming census. Figures 3 and 4 depict the urban population percentage of the various states and regions in 2026.

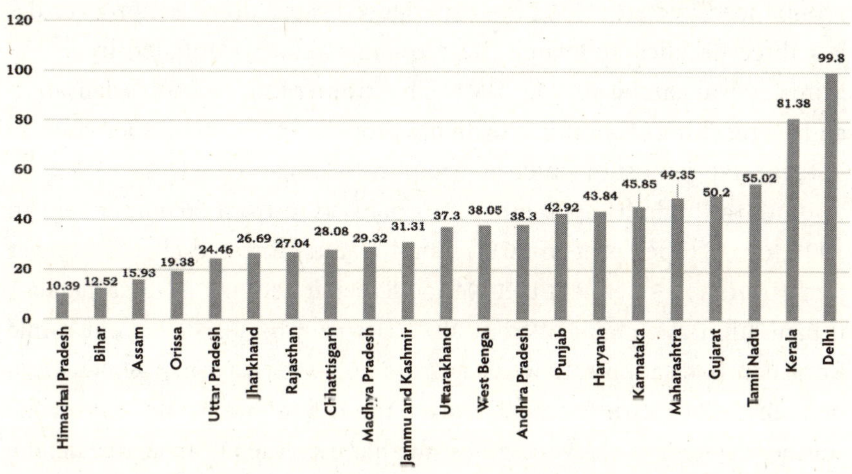

Figure 3: Urban population share (percentage), 2026
(COI estimates)

Presently, urban areas account for only 91 out of the 543 Lok Sabha constituencies, amounting to just 16.76 per cent. While in urban areas a constituency often has nearly 50 lakh people, in rural areas the figure can drop to less than 10 lakh. The average population per urban constituency, according to the 2011 Census, is 41.44 lakh; the rural average is just 18.42

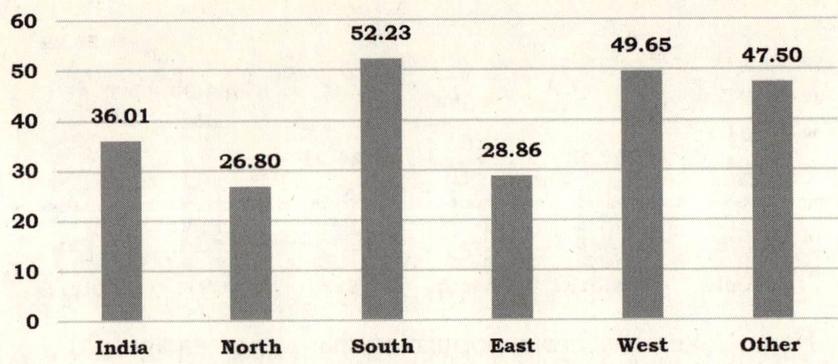

Figure 4: Regional urban population shares (percentage), 2026 (COI estimates)

lakh. This gap widens when we look at the 2026 numbers. The average urban constituency is estimated to have a population of 56.40 lakh; the average rural constituency only 20.19 lakh. The problem is more pronounced in states that have experienced rapid urbanisation over the last three decades, following the economic reforms initiated by Prime Minister Narasimha Rao in 1991. The momentum in industrialisation and the resulting economic growth has propelled the urbanisation process in these states, most of which are from the south and the west.

Andhra Pradesh saw a jump in urbanisation from 26.89 per cent in 1991 to 33.36 per cent in 2011. Tamil Nadu witnessed an even bigger jump from 34.15 per cent in 1991 to 48.40 per cent in 2011. Karnataka's urbanisation rate changed from 30.92 per cent to 38.67 per cent, while Kerala's urbanisation rate went up from 26.39 per cent in 1991 to 47.70 per cent in 2011. In the next census, the urbanisation rates for all the southern states are likely to witness further increase. As an aggregate, the south as a whole is likely to surpass the 50 per cent mark in urbanisation. So, the rural versus urban distortion is more pronounced in the south due to its better performance on urbanisation driven by rapid economic growth over the last several decades.

The distortion is also very significant in the west. Maharashtra's urbanisation rate has increased from 38.69 in 1991 to 45.22 per cent in 2011 and Gujarat's urbanisation rate has gone up from 34.49 in 1991 to 42.60 per cent in 2011. In the next census, these percentages are likely to rise significantly. Thus, the west also suffers acutely from the rural versus urban distortion in representation. The north and the east suffer much less from this distortion because of the slower progress of urbanisation in these regions.

For decades, cities and towns have, therefore, remained grossly underrepresented compared to villages. They currently have got only about 50 per cent of the representation that they should have. If seats were assigned proportionately, urban areas would have around 169 Lok Sabha seats out of 543. In the enlarged Lok Sabha with 728 members, based on the 2011 Census, the number rises to 227. However, it is in the expanded Lok Sabha using the data from the next census that the surge in urban representation will be the most pronounced. This is because, according to the projections from the Census of India (which may well be underestimates), the national urbanisation rate is expected to be around 36 per cent. Going by this estimate, in a proposed Lok Sabha of 791 seats, urban areas would have around 285 seats. The distribution of urban seats across states and regions is depicted in Figures 5 and 6.

Correcting the distortion in rural versus urban representation can arguably be among the most consequential changes in our political system after Independence. It might, of course, be argued that expansion of Parliament seats or their reallocation is not required for this correction, as the objective can be achieved by simply adjusting the

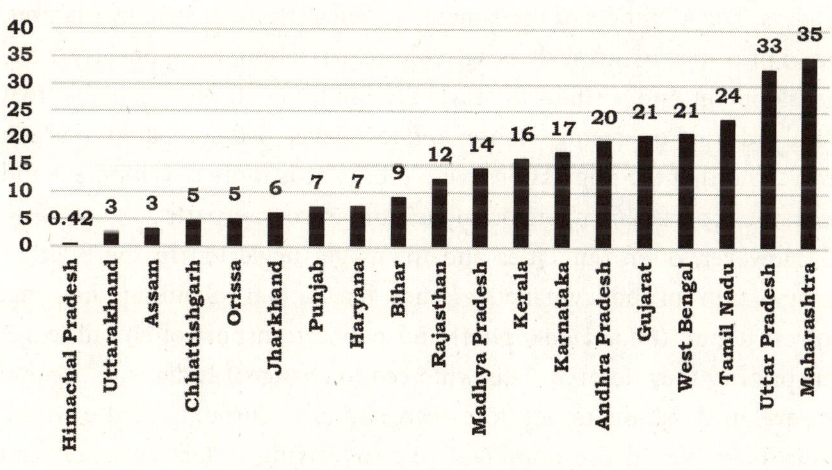

Figure 5: Urban seats in States (2026 estimates, COI)

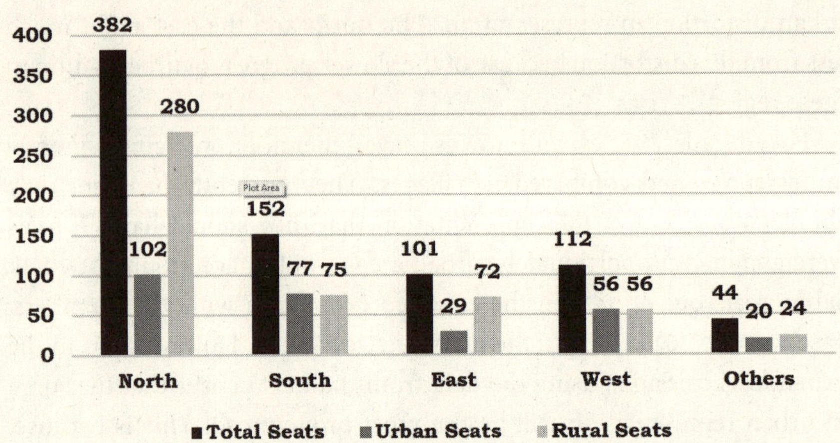

Figure 6: Regional distribution of urban seats (2026 estimates, COI)

boundaries of constituencies within each state in a limited delimitation exercise. However, it is only as part of a solution to the larger problem of representational disparity that this distortion can best be addressed.

The urban–rural imbalance causes a marked rural bias in legislatures and leads to distortions in Indian political debates and policy choices. Since the rural areas are heavily overrepresented, issues concerning the rural population get disproportionate attention from political parties and their leaders. The Members of Parliament, as well as those in state legislatures, often prioritise issues such as agriculture, irrigation, rural poverty, rural development and welfare for rural communities. It is undeniable that rural areas are on average poorer and less developed compared to urban areas, and that the population living there needs more development and welfare support in comparison to their urban counterparts.

However, often our cities and towns get neglected in the political imagination of policymakers. Issues like urban planning, housing, infrastructure (*bijli, sadak, pani*) and public transport often fail to get the priority they deserve. This will need to change if India is to become a developed nation in the foreseeable future. Throughout the world, cities have played the dominant role in driving industrialisation and economic growth, contributing significantly to the transformation of underdeveloped countries into developed ones. The structural change from pre-modern agriculture-based economies to modern industrialised economies, where manufacturing and services take the lead is critical to this transformation. Agriculture now accounts for only 15 per cent of India's GDP, yet it continues to employ nearly 45 per cent of our population. Productivity of agriculture and its growth potential are limited. For further economic development of the nation, the percentage of those who are dependent on agriculture for their livelihood will have to come down drastically, and the role of industry and services in providing employment and driving growth will need to be enhanced.

The south will arguably be the biggest gainer if the distortion in urban versus rural representation is rectified. With its high levels of urbanisation, the south will see the biggest proportional rise in urban seats. Based on the 2026 urbanisation projections of the Census of India, the south alone will have 76 urban seats, out of a total of 152, in the expanded Lok Sabha of 791 seats. Currently, there are 91 urban seats for the entire country. With such a large number and proportion of urban seats, the south will be in a much better position to be the engine of the nation's industrial and economic growth.

This is the case because, as mentioned earlier, the rural bias in our legislatures often results in low priority being given to urban issues. Some might argue that one of the reasons behind India's limited success in becoming an industrialised nation after Independence is the fact that our representatives in Parliament and state assemblies are overwhelmingly elected by rural citizens and, therefore, articulate their interests and concerns, to the detriment of cities and industrial development. However, further research is needed to confirm this assertion.

The policy distortion caused inadvertently has probably had a moderately regressive impact on the economic development of the nation. While this argument may seemingly go against our national commitment to promote rural development and welfare, in the medium to long run, rural areas also stand to benefit from increased industrial and economic growth. After all, the flow of fiscal resources in a modern economy is from urban to rural areas, and not the other way round. In pre-modern economies primarily based on agriculture, towns and cities across the world usually derived most of their income by extracting surplus output from villages in the form of land revenues and rents. In India, too, this was generally the case, as the majority population of cities in both Mughal and British empires derived the bulk of their income from the landed estates they owned in the villages or from agricultural revenues and rents imposed on rural areas. The colonial state in India was, of course, critically dependent on land revenues from villages.

These historical trends were effectively reversed after India's Independence, as removing rural poverty, hunger and underdevelopment was one of the primary goals of the Gandhian freedom struggle. Land revenue was either abolished or made nominal, and agricultural income was left out of the purview of income tax. Simultaneously, there was a multifold increase in public investment in rural areas to relieve their distress and ensure development. The country has largely followed this pattern for the last seventy-seven years. It might, therefore, be argued that the greater the capacity of cities to generate surplus revenues, the larger the potential outflow to the villages to meet their development needs.

—w—

The embargo on delimitation and reallocation of seats in Parliament has led to another critical imbalance in representation in our state legislatures. The total number of assembly constituencies in each state has remained frozen for fifty years. In the meantime, the average size of constituencies has increased significantly in most parts of India, although the effect is more pronounced in the north and the west. Article 170 (1) of the Constitution of India states, 'Subject to the provisions of article 333, the Legislative Assembly of each State shall consist of not more than five hundred, and not less than sixty, members chosen by direct election from territorial constituencies in the State.' Exceptions to these lower and upper limits can be granted by an act of Parliament. Currently, the states of Goa, Sikkim and Mizoram and the Union Territory of Puducherry have assemblies of less than 60 members. It is understandable that small states will inevitably have very small constituencies, since the total size of an assembly cannot be reduced below a minimum level.

However, even if we leave aside small states, which may be defined as those with a population of less than one crore, there are enormous disparities in the ratio between the population of states and the size of their assemblies. Let us first consider the data as per the 2011 Census. In the south, Andhra Pradesh, with an approximate population of

8.45 crore, had an assembly of 294 members. Following the creation of Telangana in 2014, 119 members were allocated to the new state. Karnataka, with a population of 6.10 crore, has an assembly of 224; Tamil Nadu, with a population of approximately 7.21 crore, has 234; and Kerala, with a population of 3.34 crore, has 140 members. Turning to the east, West Bengal, with a population of 9.12 crore, has an assembly of 294; Assam, with a population of 3.12 crore, has an assembly of 126 members; Orissa, with a population of 4.2 crore, has an assembly of 147. In the west, Maharashtra, the second-most populous state of India after Uttar Pradesh, with a population of around 11.23 crore, has an assembly of 288 members. Gujarat, with a population at 6.04 crore, has an assembly of 182.

Let us now come to the north. Himachal Pradesh, which is considered a small state with a population of 68.6 lakh as of 2011, has a 68-member assembly. Uttarakhand, another small state with a population of approximately one crore, has an assembly of 70 members. Haryana, with a population of 2.53 crore, has an assembly of 90 members; the National Capital Territory of Delhi has an assembly with 70 members for a population of 1.67 crore. It is in the large north Indian states that the representational distortion is most pronounced. Rajasthan, with a population of 6.85 crore, has a 200-member assembly; Bihar, with 10.4 crore population, has an assembly of 243 members; Jharkhand has a population of 3.29 crore and an assembly of only 81 members; Chhattisgarh has a population of 2.55 crore with an assembly of 90; Madhya Pradesh, with a population of 7.26 crore, has an assembly of 230 members. Uttar Pradesh, with a population of roughly 20 crore, has a legislative assembly of only 403 members. Figures 7 and 8 illustrate the variations across states of the population represented by each member of their respective legislative assemblies, as per the 2011 Census and 2026 estimates.

As previously discussed, given India's status as the most populous democratic nation, it is not feasible to have Lok Sabha constituencies with just a few lakh people because that would result in an excessively large house. Fortunately, this constraint is not applicable to state assemblies to the same extent. Figure 7 shows that, except for small hill states like Himachal Pradesh and Uttarakhand, for whom the large area of constituency and the hilly terrain are additional factors in determining the size of assembly, the people of Punjab have the best representation at

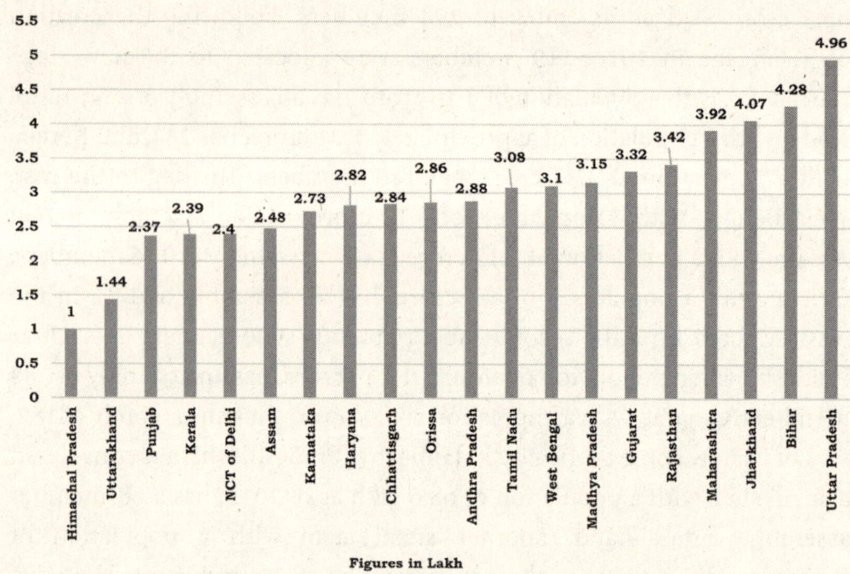

Figure 7: Persons per Assembly seat (in lakh, 2011 Census)

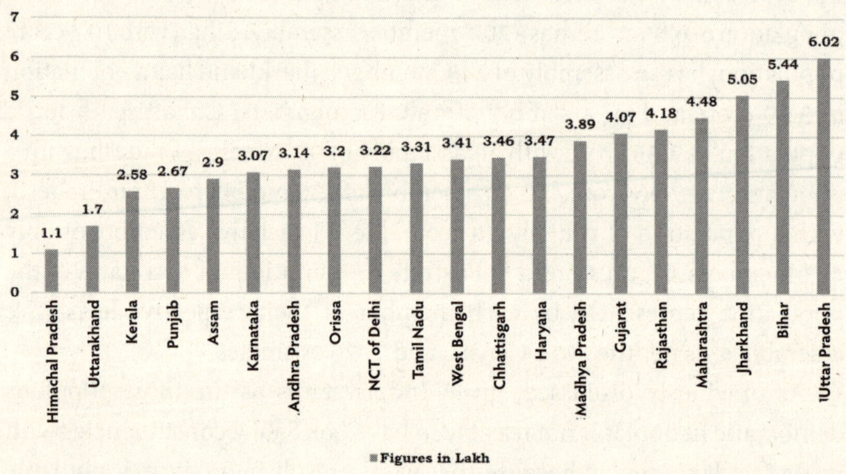

Figure 8: Persons per Assembly seat (in lakh, 2026 COI estimates)

the state level, as each member there represents only 2.37 lakh persons. Kerala is close behind with a figure of 2.39 lakh persons.

It is evident that the maximum size of a state assembly cannot be more than that of the enlarged Lok Sabha. Keeping this in mind, it might be best to revise the upper limit to 700 members. This will not create a complete uniformity in representation, but will allow us to come close to it. In any case, compared to the Lok Sabha, maintaining the same population–seat ratio in state assemblies is not so critical to democratic functioning across the states, though maintaining broad parity in the size of assembly constituencies within each state should be a critical objective.

As in the case of the Lok Sabha, reducing the assembly numbers of any state would not be advisable. However, if we take Punjab, Kerala or the National Capital Territory of Delhi as the benchmark, the size of the Uttar Pradesh legislative assembly will go beyond 800. If we assign a maximum size of 700 members to UP, we get a seat–population ratio of approximately 2.85 lakh. Currently, Orissa has the same ratio of 2.85 lakh persons per assembly constituency. Following closely behind are Chhattisgarh, Haryana, Karnataka, Assam, Kerala and Punjab. We may leave the assemblies of all these states unchanged. The assemblies of states above Orissa, which include Andhra Pradesh, Tamil Nadu, West Bengal, Madhya Pradesh, Gujarat, Rajasthan, Maharashtra, Jharkhand and Bihar, can be revised upwards using the number obtained for Uttar Pradesh as the benchmark. This would mean a substantial but manageable addition of seats for all these states.

The figures given here are based on the 2011 Census. In practice, however, this revision will have to be undertaken with the population figures of the next census. According to the Census of India projection for 2026, Uttar Pradesh's population is likely to be around 24.28 crore. Using this number as the benchmark, and assuming the upper limit of an assembly at 700, we arrive at an approximate population of 3.47 lakh per seat. Again (Figure 8), the states at par or below that number (Haryana, Chhattisgarh, West Bengal, Tamil Nadu, NCT of Delhi, Orissa, Andhra Pradesh, Karnataka, Assam, Punjab and Kerala) may be left untouched; those states above it (Madhya Pradesh, Gujarat, Rajasthan, Maharashtra, Jharkhand and Bihar) may get expanded assemblies based on their actual population in the next census. This would ensure that, as far as possible, there will be parity in people's representation at the state level. Of course, in the delimitation exercise, parity within each state will also have to be achieved to the greatest extent possible.

—w—

Moving on to the normative argument made by prominent leaders from the south opposing the delimitation and reallocation of Lok Sabha seats as per the latest population of various states of India—and not based on the 1971 Census—one can see how it is fundamentally flawed. Democracy is based on the concept of 'one person, one vote, one value'. A denial of that principle is a denial of democracy itself. The Constitution of India clearly lays down that seats in both houses of Parliament will be allocated to each state on the basis of the latest census numbers. Freezing the allocation of seats in Parliament at the 1971 Census, therefore, causes a huge democratic imbalance in the country. This policy has already been in operation for fifty years, and the longer it is continued, the greater will be the distortion in democratic representation of the south versus northern, western and central India.

Delimitation and reallocation of seats in Parliament should not be opposed simply because it would reduce the percentage share of the south and increase that of the north and the west. The failure to reallocate seats on the ground that the north is poor and backward and has failed to control its population as compared to the south, which is affluent and developed, goes against the fundamental principles of democracy both enshrined in our Constitution and practised in India since Independence. Benefits and support are given to those who are poor, weak and disadvantaged, not to those who are rich, strong and advantaged.

The Indian Constitution and democracy are inherently progressive. The Preamble of the Constitution, often described as its soul, enshrines the principles of equality and justice, among others. The Fundamental Rights and the Directive Principles of State Policy also enjoin upon the state to take special care of those who are poorer, weaker, backward and disadvantaged. The principle of reservation in political representation and in jobs for the Scheduled Castes and the Scheduled Tribes enshrined in the Constitution is the most important example of the progressive orientation of Indian democracy. The extension of reservations to Other

Backward Classes (OBC) was also guided by the same principle. The inclusion of Economically Weaker Sections in reservation for jobs and the passing of the Women's Reservation Act in September 2023 are recent examples of the forward-progressive and egalitarian nature of India both as a nation and as a democratic republic.

Not only this, fiscal devolution from the Union to the states has generally followed the same progressive principles. Thus, states that are small, remote, backward, underdeveloped and, therefore, incapable of meeting their development needs out of their own revenues, have always received proportionately more fiscal support from the central government, both in the form of loans and grants-in-aid. In fact, reducing regional disparity in development has been one of the main policy objectives of India since Independence. Based on the same principle, India follows the policy of progressive taxation. Those who have higher incomes are taxed more than those who have lower incomes. Similarly, cities are taxed far more than the villages. The revenue mopped up by such progressive taxation policies is channelised to the welfare and development of the poorer and disadvantaged sections and regions of the country. Hence, denying the north a higher seat allocation in accordance with its current share in India's population on the ground that the north is poorer, less developed and more backward than the south does not stand to reason and goes against the fundamental political philosophy of the country.

It is widely acknowledged that the south has surged ahead of the north, though not ahead of the west, which also stands to gain substantially from reallocation. This gap is evident in per capita income, industrialisation, urbanisation, health, literacy rate and most other indicators of social and economic development. However, questioning notions of the north–south divide in social development, Pratham's ASER Report 2024 shows Uttar Pradesh and Bihar outperforming most southern states in reading and arithmetic skills in rural government schools. In Telangana, just 6.8 per cent standard-3 children in rural government schools could read a standard-2 book in 2024. In Tamil Nadu, the count was 13.2 per cent, in Andhra Pradesh 14.7 per cent and in Karnataka 15.4 per cent. Only Kerala had a 44.4 per cent score. But Punjab, Haryana, Uttar Pradesh and Bihar were ahead of four of the five southern states in grade-3 kids' ability to read grade-2 textbooks. In Uttar Pradesh, 27.9 per cent rural government school children of standard-3 were able to read a standard-2 textbook—12-percentage points above four southern states but 17-percentage points lower than Kerala. Bihar, too, was above four of the five southern states, with a figure of 20.1 per cent. Haryana was the best in the north, with 32.1 per cent; Punjab close behind at 29.7 per cent.

On the class-5 reading indicator in ASER 2024, Tamil Nadu scoring 37 per cent was behind all aforementioned northern states. In Telangana, 29.3 per cent children made the cut. At 58.2 per cent, Kerala, the south's topper, was between Punjab and Haryana. Karnataka (32.8 per cent) and Andhra Pradesh (37.5 per cent) were well behind.

In grade-3 rural government school math, Uttar Pradesh in 2024 beat all southern states except Andhra Pradesh. In 2018, however, southern states were 12-33 percentage points ahead of Uttar Pradesh. Notably, Kerala has shed its 33 percentage point lead over Uttar Pradesh within six years, ceding it a 4-5 percentage point lead. While Tamil Nadu, Kerala, Telangana and Karnataka showed between 23 and 29 per cent grade-3 students possessing the basic arithmetic skills, Punjab and Haryana fared better at 43.9 per cent and 33.1 per cent, respectively. At 12.4 per cent, Kerala registered since 2018 a 21-percentage point decline in the ability of grade-5 children to do division, leaving the state 19-20 percentage points behind Uttar Pradesh and Bihar, and 34-percentage points behind Punjab.

Barring Andhra Pradesh, Bihar and Uttar Pradesh are ahead of all southern states in this class-5 math indicator. Bihar in the last six years jumped from 24.1 per cent to 32.5 per cent, and Uttar Pradesh from 17 per cent to 31.8 per cent, on this count. Uttar Pradesh had tailed all southern states on this indicator in 2018, but is behind just Andhra Pradesh now.

Nevertheless, the overall progress made by the south is creditable. Moreover, the south's lead in development is both the cause and effect of its slower population growth over the past fifty years. It must be pointed out, however, that in most large continental countries of the world, this has been the pattern of development. The coastal areas take the lead. The interior regions mostly develop after the coastal regions. Historically, this was true of Europe and the United States, and in recent times, this has been true of China, where the development deficit between the southern coastal provinces and the interior northern and eastern provinces has been a matter of great concern for policymakers.

There is, therefore, hope for the north in emulating the virtuous example of the south in social and economic development, which would also help stabilise the population of the north and the country in the near future, with some further realignments aimed at long-term convergence and divergence. This means that the current population shares of each of the four regions of India are unlikely to change drastically in the foreseeable future.

Apart from the fact that the population growth of the Hindi-speaking north has not surpassed that of the south, nor exceeded that of the east and west over the last one-and-a-half centuries (which is the appropriate time period for comparative analysis, rather than the period after 1951 or 1971), there is a bigger objection to freezing parliamentary representation by using fifty-year-old population data. That is so because it is not just the population shares of the north or the west that have increased over time; this merely reflects regional variation in population growth. Since Independence, numerous other variations have occurred based on caste, religion and even class.

In 1951, Scheduled Castes (SCs) constituted 14.39 per cent and Scheduled Tribes (STs) 5.36 per cent of India's population. In the 2011 Census, those figures rose to 16.6 per cent and 8.6 per cent respectively, which shows a cumulative gain of 2.21 percentage points for SCs and 3.34 percentage points for STs. Their combined population share was 19.75 per cent in 1951. It increased to 25.2 per cent of the country's population in 2011, and is likely to rise further in the next census. While a tiny part of this increase might be attributable to the inclusion of some small groups in the two categories, the overwhelming contributor is higher population growth. Similarly, Muslims constituted less than 10 per cent of the national population in 1951 (9.8 per cent); in the 2011 Census, their share rose to 14.20 per cent. In the next census, it is likely to be even higher. There might be a link between the significantly higher presence of these three groups in the north (approximately 40 per cent) as compared to the south (approximately 33 per cent) and the higher demographic growth of the north over the last many decades.

Surely no one would argue that the voting rights of any such group should be frozen at the population levels of 1951 or 1971, because their population has increased disproportionately compared to the rest.

Representation in Parliament has to be based on current population figures because that is the fundamental principle of the Constitution and of democracy. It would not necessarily make those whose representation has increased more powerful or influential than others whose percentage representation may come down. That is because political representation is just one among many forms of power and influence for states, regions and communities. There are other markers, like development, income, wealth, education, health and solidarity, that also translate into similar power and influence. The south's manifest superiority across all these markers is likely to ensure that its role in the nation will remain as important as it has always been.

As mapped out in this study, some southern states and leaders have taken a rather strident position on the issue of delimitation and reallocation of parliamentary seats on the ostensible ground that it violates the rights of the states versus the Centre, and is against federal principles. It might be argued by many that in a legal and constitutional sense this position does not hold much ground. India is a Union, and not a federation, of states, even though it has a federal structure. Unlike the United States, which is generally regarded as the ideal federation, there were no pre-existing states in India that came together in 1947 to form the federation by ceding a part of their existing rights and powers to the federal government, while keeping residuary powers with themselves.

The states of the Indian Union as they are today have been brought into existence by the Union, because the Constitution of India has given it the right to divide the states, merge them with others and change their borders, names, etc., even without the states' consent. Indeed, administrative reorganisation of the country over the past seventy-five years has been so drastic that there is not even a single state whose boundaries have remained the same. The result is that today we have 28 states and eight Union Territories, which is much larger than the number that existed prior to the States' Reorganisation Act, 1956. Notably, the state of Telangana was created in 2014 despite large-scale opposition by supporters of a united Andhra Pradesh, and without the consent of the state assembly. This would not have been possible if the Constitution of India had enshrined the principle of treating the area or boundaries of each state as sacrosanct.

The constitutional framework for the delegation of powers, as delineated in the Union List, State List and Concurrent List, also makes it clear that the centre has fiscal, revenue, legislative and executive powers which are typically not provided for in a federation created by pre-existing states. The Union List itself is comprehensive. But more importantly, in the Concurrent List, both the Union and states have legislative powers, and in the event of a conflict between two laws, it is the Union legislation that would prevail. Moreover, while in a true federation, residuary powers remain with the states, in India they rest with the Union. This leaves little doubt that the states in India do not enjoy the same political and legal status vis-à-vis the Union as states in federations like the United States do, even though among themselves they have legal and constitutional equality of status. Moreover, unlike in the US, the states in India are not allowed to have their own flags, supreme courts, constitutions and citizenship. There are historical and political reasons behind it.

The states of India, as we know them today, did not exist before the Constitution of India coming into force, and, therefore, do not enjoy these privileges. These privileges are reminiscent of the original independent status of states in a federation, such as the United States, which came into existence because the states came together to form it. The most important distinction in this regard is that in India, even the Rajya Sabha—which is the Council of States—has neither fixed nor equal representation of states. Rather, states' representation is based on their population. This changes over time and the smaller states—above the threshold of 60 lakh—have less representation, while the larger states have more representation. This is so different from the American Senate, the upper house of the legislature, where each state has two members irrespective of population size, and this number cannot be changed by the federal government. Moreover, the American Constitution bestows upon the Senate a far more important role compared to what the Indian Constitution has accorded the Rajya Sabha.

It is, therefore, evident that in constitutional terms, the states in India do not possess the same status in relation to the Union as seen in a typical federation. They cannot claim parity of representation nor assert the right to claim any fixed number or proportion of representation either in the Lok Sabha or the Rajya Sabha. Both are liable to change if there is any shift in the distribution of population across states and regions. So, there is hardly any constitutional basis to the argument given by some leaders from the southern states that they should continue to enjoy representation according to their population shares of 1971.

This is as far as the constitutional scheme of things is concerned. In practice, of course, India's federal evolution and reorganisation of states since the 1950s have ensured that since Independence at least some of the states have acquired their own political identities and sense of belonging either on linguistic or ethnic basis. This applies to all the southern states to varying degrees, though none of them had ever existed in history as political entities with their current boundaries, which, as mentioned, are post-Independence creations. Overall, in modern times at least, the south has developed a consciousness of being one block within the Indian nation. There are strong sentiments involved on the issue of delimitation and reallocation of parliamentary seats in the south.

Once it is accepted that delimitation is to be carried out based on the latest population data, either the existing 543 seats in the Lok Sabha can be reallocated or seats can be increased and then allocated according to the latest population figures. Seats had, indeed, been expanded and reallocated in the second and third delimitation exercises that took place in 1963 and 1973. In the second delimitation, seats were expanded from 489 to 522; in the third, they were expanded from 522 to 543. Uttar Pradesh's Lok Sabha seats were brought down from 86 to 85; Kerala's seats were increased from 18 to 20; and Karnataka's were increased from 26 to 28. So, out of the two options mentioned above, the second was exercised without creating any controversy. The scenario, however, changed with the embargo of 1976, as the south began claiming that delimitation according to the latest population figures would penalise it for controlling its population through family planning. Accordingly, in 2001 the delimitation commission was tasked with adjusting the internal boundaries of constituencies without any change in the number of seats allocated to each state. Fresh delimitation to be done after the next census scheduled for 2025-26 will mean either a loss of absolute numbers or proportion for the south. The second option would probably be more acceptable from the south's perspective. However, this would depend on political negotiations on the matter, which may lead to some compromises. In any case, the redistribution of seats in a new delimitation is likely to involve only about 5 per cent of the total number of seats, as the fluctuations in regional population shares since 1971 are within this range.

As suggested earlier, it would be ideal to lift the fifty-year-old embargo and reallocate seats in the Lok Sabha—and then the Rajya Sabha—in such a way that proportionate representation is given to each state according to the latest population data without taking away even a single seat held by any state at present. Estimates of what these numbers might possibly be for both the houses have also been provided in Chapter 10 of this book. The suggested expansion of seats will also yield the additional benefit of somewhat reducing the average population size of constituencies across the country, although as the most populous country on earth and as a *sui generis* nation and democracy, India need not emulate the example of smaller countries with smaller population sizes of constituencies.

Going by the 2011 Census, the increased number for the Lok Sabha comes to approximately 728 seats. Maintaining the existing ratio of seats between the two houses, the approximate number for the Rajya Sabha is 326. Based on the Census of India's population projection for 2026, the number for the reconstituted Lok Sabha comes to around 791; for the Rajya Sabha, the number is around 343. The current regional allocation of seats and the proposed change are depicted in Figures 9 and 10.

However, given the strong passions this issue ignites in the south, a compromise of some sort may well be desirable. One such formula could be that only the Lok Sabha seats should be reallocated according to the latest population data. The Rajya Sabha should be left untouched until 2047—the centenary year of India's Independence. This would ensure that at least in the house of the people, that is, the Lok Sabha, people from all parts of India get equal representation. Simultaneously, the fears expressed by many southern leaders about the Hindi-speaking north imposing its will through its increased representation will be addressed adequately. The Rajya Sabha, the council of states, is based on indirect elections and has less than half the numbers of the Lok Sabha. Its powers in normal decision-making, especially those regarding money bills, are less than those of the Lok Sabha. However, as far as constitutional amendments are concerned, the Rajya Sabha enjoys equal powers with

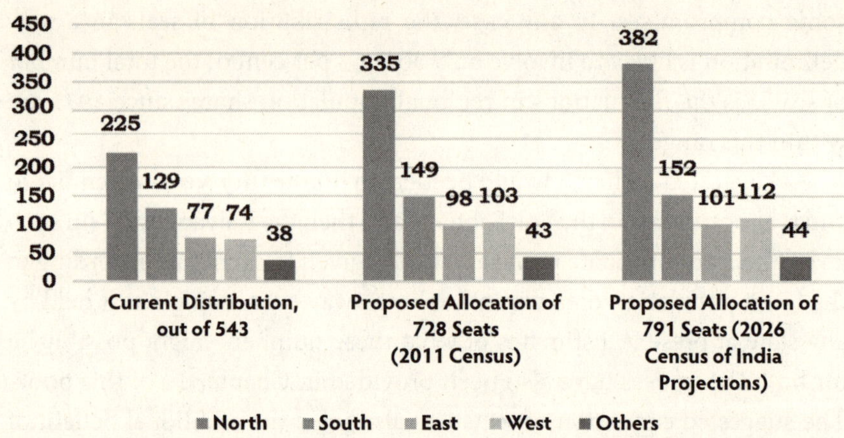

Figure 9: Regional distribution of Lok Sabha seats

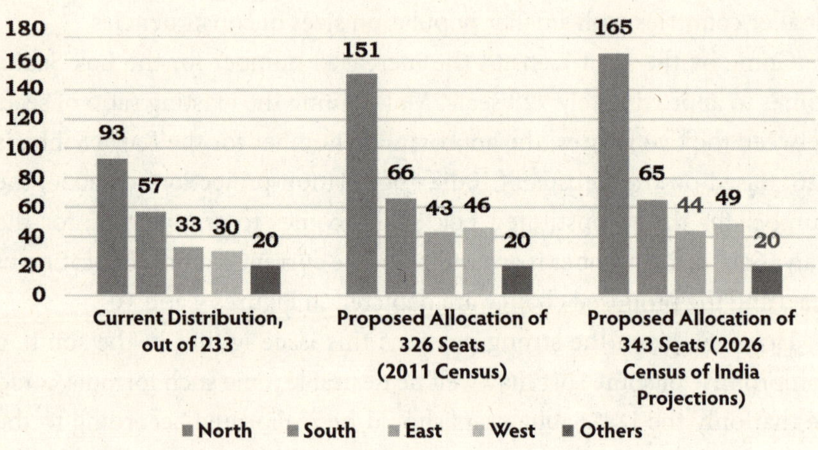

Figure 10: Regional distribution of Rajya Sabha seats

the Lok Sabha: without its approval, no constitutional amendment can be passed.

Crucially, unlike in the case of regular decision-making in the Indian Parliament, in the case of a deadlock between the Lok Sabha and the Rajya Sabha concerning the passage of a constitutional amendment, the Constitution does not provide the option of a joint sitting of Parliament, in which the Lok Sabha would normally prevail because of its much larger numbers. Freezing the states' allocation in the Rajya Sabha at their current levels until 2047 will ensure that the north and the west would not be able to ride roughshod over the federal interests of the south, and would prevent them from using the increased Lok Sabha numbers to amend the Constitution.

Appendices

Table 3.1: Birth and death rates of world population, 1900–2017

Year	*Birth rate*	*Death rate*
1900	46	40.3
1950	43.3	34.1
1960	36.3	18.4
1970	34.2	14.4
1980	29.6	11.1
1990	27.6	10.0
2000	23.6	9.2
2010	20.7	8.5
2017	18.73	7.61

Table 4.1: Memorandum on the Census of British India 1871–72

Provinces	*Under British Administration*		*Feudatory States*		*Total*	
	Area in square miles	*Population*	*Area in square miles*	*Population*	*Area in square miles*	*Population*
Government of India						
Ajmere	2,661	3,16,032	–	–	2,661	3,16,032
Berar	17,334	22,31,565	–	–	17,334	22,31,565
Coorg	2,000	1,68,312	–	–	2,000	168,312
Mysore	27,077	50,55,412	–	–	27,077	50,55,412
Central India and Bundelkund	–	–	81,140	76,99,502	81,140	76,99,502
Hyderabad	–	–	78,008	10,666,080	78,003	1,06,66,080
Munnipoor	–	–	7,584	126,000	7,584	1,26,000
Rajpootana	–	–	1,18,947	89,81,588	1,18,947	89,81,588
Bengal	1,57,598	6,04,67,724	39,321	22,12,909	1,96,919	6,26,80,638
Assam	53,856*	41,32,019	–	–	53,856	41,32,019
North-West Provinces	81,403	3,07,81,204	5,445	9,07,013	86,848	3,16,88,217
Oude	23,992	1,12,20,232	–	–	23,992	1,12,20,232
Punjab	1,01,829	1,76,11,498	1,14,358	52,99,448	2,16,187	2,29,10,946

Provinces	*Under British Administration*		*Feudatory States*		*Total*	
	Area in square miles	*Population*	*Area in square miles*	*Population*	*Area in square miles*	*Population*
Central Provinces	84,963	82,01,519	28,834	10,49,710	1,13,797	92,51,229
British Burma	88,556	27,47,148	–	–	88,556	27,47,148
Madras	1,38,318	3,12,81,177	9,810	20,27,048	1,48,128	3,33,08,225
Bombay	1,24,462	1,63,49,206	63,253	92,98,612	1,87,715	2,56,47,818
Total	**9,04,049**	**19,05,68,048**	**5,46,695**	**4,82,67,910**	**14,50,744**	**23,88,30,958**

* Excluding the Cachar and Luckimpur Hills, of which the population was not counted, the area of Assam is 41,798 square miles

Table 4.2: Report on the Census of Bengal, 1872

Area and population of the several provinces of Bengal

Provinces	*Area of square miles*	*Total population*	*Average number of portions to the square miles*	*Proportion per cent of the area of the several provinces*	*Proportion per cent of the population in the several provinces*
The entire Territory under the Lieutenant-Governor of Bengal	2,48,231	6,68,56,859	269	100	100
Bengal	94,539	3,67,69,735	389	38.08	55.00
Behar	42,417	1,97,36,101	465	17.09	29.52
Orissa	23,901	43,17,999	181	9.63	6.46
Chota Nagpore	43,901	38,25,571	87	17.69	5.72
Assam	43,473	22,07,453	51	17.51	3.30

Area and population of the several commissioners' divisions in Bengal

Provinces	*Area of square miles*	*Total population*	*Average number of portions to the square miles*	*Proportion per cent of the area of the several provinces*	*Proportion per cent of the population in the several provinces*
The entire Territory under the Lieutenant-Governor of Bengal	2,48,231	6,68,56,859	269	100	100
Burdwan	12,719	72,86,957	573	5.12	10.90
Presidency	15,216	65,45,464	430	6.13	9.79
Rajahahya	17,694	88,93,738	503	7.13	13.30

Provinces	*Area of square miles*	*Total population*	*Average number of portions to the square miles*	*Proportion per cent of the area of the several provinces*	*Proportion per cent of the population in the several provinces*
Cooch Behar	13,270	15,70,703	118	5.35	2.35
Dacoa	26,004	93,17,498	366	10.48	14.24
Chittagong	17,459	34,80,136	199	7.03	5.21
Patna	23,732	1,31,22,743	553	9.52	19.63
Bhaugulpora	18,685	66,13,358	354	7.56	9.89
Orissa	23,901	43,17,999	181	9.63	6.45
Chota Nagpore	43,901	38,25,571	87	17.69	5.72
Assam	35,650	16,82,692	47	14.36	2.52

Note: In order to reconcile the areas gives in the two previous tables with the sum of those shown in the district tables, it must be explained that the areas in the former tables include 17,399 square miles of waste or uninhabited country which are omitted from the latter. Of these 17,399 square miles, 8,343 represent the hilly portion of Lackimpore in which no count was taken, 6,361 the Sundarbans, and 8,715 Cauhar hills.

The areas of large rivers have generally been excluded throughout the tables.

Table 4.3: Density of population (Persons per square mile)[1]

Oude	468
Bengal	397
North-West Province	378
Madras	226
Mysore	187
Punjab	173
Bombay	131
Berar	129
Ajmere	119
Assam (excluding uncensused hill country)	99
Central Provinces	97
Coorg	84
British Burma	31

Table 4.4: High density districts in Oude[2]

	Square miles	*Average population*
Lucknow	1,392	697
Barabunkee	1,348	649
Fyzabad	2,332	616
Sultanpur	1,570	592
Roy Bareilly	1,350	580
Pertabgurh	1,724	543
Oonao	1,349	537

Table 4.5: High density districts in North-West Provinces[3]

	Square miles	*Average population*
Benares	996	797
Jounpoor	1,555	659
Ghazeepoor	2,168	621
Azimgurh	2,565	597
Agra	1,908	575
Shahjehanpoor	1,723	551
Muttra	1,612	551
Allygurh	1,964	547
Meerut	2,360	541
Bustee	2,789	528
Furruckabad	1,745	527
Allahabad	2,747	508
Bareilly	2,982	505

Table 4.6: Report on the Census of Bengal 1881, Vol. I

Table showing the Area, Total Population, and Density of Population

FOR EACH DISTRICT, DIVISION AND PROVINCE

	Division and district	*Area in square miles*	*Population*	*Number of persons per square mile*		*Division and district*	*Area in square miles*	*Population*	*Number of persons per square mile*
	BENGAL					BEHAR			
Burdwan	Burdwan	2,007	13,91,823	516.06	Patna	Patna	2,079	17,56,836	845.05
Burdwan	Bankoorali	2,621	10,41,702	397.46	Patna	Gya	4,712	21,24,082	450.91
Burdwan	Boerbhoom	1,756	7,94,428	452.40	Patna	Shahabad	4,365	19,64,969	450.15
Burdwan	Midnapur	5,082	25,17,802	495.44	Patna	Mozufferpore	3,003	25,82,000	859.83
Burdwan	Hooghly	1,223	1,012,768	828.10	Patna	Durbhunga	3,335	26,33,447	789.04
Burdwan	Howrah	476	6,35,381	1,334.83	Patna	Sarun	2,022	22,80,382	869.71
Burdwan	Total	13,855	73,93,954	533.67	Patna	Chumparun	3,531	17,21,608	487.57
					Patna	Total	23,647	1,50,63,944	637.03
Presidency	24-Pergunnahs	2,097	16,18,420	771.78	Bhagulpore	Monghyr	3,921	19,69,774	502.37
Presidency	Suburbs	23	2,52,439	10,932.18	Bhagulpore	Bhaugulpore	4,268	19,66,158	460.67
Presidency	Calcutta	8	4,33,219	54,152.37	Bhagulpore	Purnesh	4,956	18,48,057	373.68
Presidency	Nudden	3,404	20,17,847	592.79	Bhagulpore	Maldah	1,891	7,10,449	375.70
Presidency	Jessore	2,276	15,77,249	692.99	Bhagulpore	Senthal Pergunnahs	5,456	15,68,093	287.41
Presidency	Khulna	2,077	10,79,948	519.96	Bhagulpore	Total	20,492	80,63,160	393.48
Presidency	Moorshedabad	2,144	12,26,790	572.20		Total for Behar	44,139	2,31,27,104	523.96
Presidency	Total	12,029	82,04,912	682.09					

Division	District			
Rajshahye	Dinagepore	4,118	15,14,346	367.74
	Rajshahye	2,361	13,38,638	568.98
	Rungpore	3,486	20,97,964	601.83
	Bogra	1,408	7,34,358	490.23
	Pubne	1,847	13,11,728	710.19
	Darjeeling	1,234	1,55,179	125.75
	Julpigoree	2,884	5,81,562	201.65
	Total	**17,428**	**77,33,775**	**443.76**
Dacca	Dacca	2,797	21,16,350	756.65
	Furreedpore	2,267	16,31,734	719.78
	Backergunge	3,649	19,00,889	520.93
	Mymensingh	6,287	30,51,966	485.44
	Total	**15,000**	**87,00,939**	**580.06**
Chittagong	Chittagong	2,567	11,32,341	441.11
	Naokholly	1,641	8,20,772	500.17
	Tipperah	2,491	15,19,338	609.93
	Chittagong Hill Tracts	5,419	1,01,597	18.75
	Total	**12,118**	**35,74,048**	**294.94**
	Total for Bengal Proper	**70,430**	**3,56,07,628**	**505.57**

Division	District			
	ORISSA			
Orissa	Cuttack	3,517	17,38,165	494.23
	Pooreo	2,473	8,88,487	359.27
	Balasore	2,066	9,45,280	457.54
	Angul	881	1,01,003	115.67
	Banki	116	56,900	490.52
	Total for Orissa	**9,053**	**37,30,735**	**412.1**
	CHOTA NAGPORE			
Chota Nagpore	Ilazaribagh	7,021	11,04,742	157.35
	Purnesh	12,045	16,09,244	133.00
	Maldah	3,753	4,53,775	120.91
	Senthal Pergunnahs	4,147	10,58,228	255.18
	Total for Chota Nagpore	**26,966**	**42,25,989**	**156.72**
	Grand Total for the Province	**1,50,588**		
	FEUDATORY STATES			
Feudatory States	Cooch Behar	1,307	6,02,024	461.07
	Hill Tipperah	4,086	95,637	23.41
	Tributary States, Orissa	15,187	14,69,142	96.74
	Ditto, Chota Nagpore	16,054	6,78,003	42.23
	Total for Feudatory States	**36,634**	**28,45,405**	**77.67**
	Grand Total, including Feudatory States	**1,87,222**	**6,95,36,861**	**371.41**

Note: From the above table the areas of large rivers and the area of the Sundarbans have been omitted. The latter is estimated to be 5,976 square miles.

Table 4.7: Census of India 1921 Vol. XV, Delhi and Punjab

TABLE II.—VARIATI

District or State.	Persons.					Males.			
	1921.	1911.	1901.	1891.	1881.	1921.	1911.	1901.	189
1	2	3	4	5	6	7	8	9	10
PUNJAB ..	**25,101,060**	**23,791,367**	**24,366,625**	**22,915,482**	**20,800,593**	**13,732,048**	**13,093,840**	**13,144,082**	**12,380**
BRITISH TERRITORY.	**20,685,024**	**19,578,573**	**19,942,227**	**18,652,202**	**16,938,910**	**11,306,265**	**10,770,732**	**10,734,273**	**10,056**
Ambala Division.	**3,826,615**	**3,779,853**	**4,199,040**	**4,078,954**	**3,897,202**	**2,088,640**	**2,070,683**	**2,261,991**	**2,197**
1. Hissar ..	*816,810*	804,889	781,589	775,896	672,512	435,562	438,458	418,089	414
2. Rohtak ..	*772,272*	714,834	834,010	779,875	740,444	417,379	385,401	443,650	416
3. Gurgaon ..	*682,003*	729,827	842,550	759,907	761,686	367,800	380,545	442,771	399
4. Karnal ..	*828,726*	801,013	884,616	862,455	855,874	453,637	438,396	479,713	468
5. Ambala ..	*681,477*	690,854	816,808	864,719	831,450	383,802	394,690	452,129	476
6. Simla ..	*45,327*	38,436	39,467	36,102	35,235	30,460	24,193	25,639	22
Jullundur Division.	**4,181,898**	**3,967,724**	**4,305,724**	**4,216,386**	**3,787,649**	**2,276,132**	**2,184,423**	**2,314,631**	**2,26**
7. Kangra ..	*766,065*	770,386	768,124	763,030	730,845	393,615	401,109	399,106	397
8. Hoshiarpur ..	*927,419*	918,569	989,738	1,011,465	901,044	498,662	501,510	525,831	539
9. Jullundur ..	*822,544*	801,920	917,587	907,583	789,555	455,174	449,876	496,690	49
10. Ludhiana ..	*567,622*	517,192	673,097	648,722	618,835	318,845	293,531	369,165	35
11. Ferozepore ..	*1,098,248*	959,657	957,178	885,586	747,370	609,836	538,397	523,839	48
Lahore Division.	**4,997,441**	**4,691,648**	**5,134,874**	**4,859,593**	**4,294,081**	**2,788,355**	**2,640,643**	**2,786,940**	**2,64**
12. Lahore ..	*1,131,336*	1,000,855	1,005,205	900,012	768,873	646,171	575,793	555,099	49
13. Amritsar ..	*929,374*	880,796	1,023,985	992,850	893,380	519,146	496,618	559,933	54
14. Gurdaspur ..	*852,192*	836,771	940,334	943,922	823,695	470,465	469,243	509,951	51
15. Sialkot ..	*937,823*	931,181	996,940	1,027,275	940,832	510,415	515,139	524,723	54
16. Gujranwala ..	*623,581*	605,582	739,546	661,223	579,258	348,695	337,538	398,121	36
17. Sheikhupura ..	*523,135*	436,463	428,864	334,311	288,043	293,463	240,312	239,113	18
Rawalpindi Division.	**3,460,710**	**3,353,052**	**3,106,771**	**3,067,947**	**2,782,847**	**1,838,598**	**1,795,555**	**1,619,005**	**1,62**
18. Gujrat ..	*824,046*	787,999	792,159	806,382	727,044	438,550	425,117	413,445	42
19. Shahpur ..	*719,918*	645,001	488,149	478,289	383,052	392,080	352,365	252,342	24
20. Jhelum ..	*477,068*	511,575	501,424	514,090	494,499	241,380	268,621	253,058	26
21. Rawalpindi ..	*569,224*	547,827	558,699	533,740	471,079	311,636	296,518	299,893	29
22. Attock ..	*512,249*	519,273	464,430	448,420	444,307	264,919	273,037	242,398	23
23. Mianwali ..	*358,205*	341,377	301,910	287,026	262,206	190,021	179,897	157,809	15
Multan Division.	**4,218,360**	**3,786,296**	**3,195,818**	**2,429,322**	**2,177,131**	**2,314,540**	**2,079,428**	**1,751,706**	**1,320**
24. Montgomery ..	*713,786*	501,510	446,987	433,417	362,392	393,372	274,552	241,427	23
25. Lyallpur ..	*979,463*	847,862	589,009	30,136	40,579	546,461	481,210	332,648	1
26. Jhang ..	*570,559*	524,803	426,225	402,341	390,630	305,483	282,397	226,207	21
27. Multan ..	*890,264*	814,213	710,043	635,205	556,100	488,091	444,338	388,249	34
28. Muzaffargarh ..	*568,478*	569,461	527,681	493,914	441,217	308,605	308,350	285,976	267
29 { Dera Ghazi Khan.	*469,052*	499,860	471,786	428,375	386,213	257,386	272,409	256,740	23
29 { Biloch Trans-Frontier Tract.	*26,758*	28,587	24,087	5,934	..	15,142	10,172	13,459	3

TABLE II.—VARIATION

LATION SINCE 1881.

Females.					Variation, Increase (+), Decrease (—).				Net Variation in the Period
921.	1911.	1901.	1891.	1881.	1911 to 1921.	1901 to 1911.	1891 to 1901.	1881 to 1891.	1881 to 1921.
12	13	14	15	16	17	18	19	20	21
369,012	**10,697,727**	**11,222,543**	**10,534,916**	**9,521,320**	**+1,309,693**	**—575,258**	**+1,451,143**	**+2,114,889**	**+4,300,467**
378,759	**8,807,841**	**9,207,954**	**8,595,727**	**7,771,940**	**+1,106,451**	**—363,654**	**+1,290,025**	**+1,713,292**	**+3,746,114**
737,975	**1,709,170**	**1,937,049**	**1,880,973**	**1,784,849**	**+ 46,762**	**—419,187**	**+ 120,086**	**+ 181,752**	**— 70,587**
381,248	366,431	363,500	361,055	308,400	+ 11,921	+ 23,300	+ 5,693	+ 103,383	+ 144,297
354,893	329,433	390,360	363,569	342,744	+ 57,438	—119,176	+ 54,135	+ 39,431	+ 31,828
314,203	340,287	399,779	360,250	357,664	— 47,824	—112,723	+ 82,643	— 1,779	— 79,683
375,089	362,617	404,903	394,026	393,002	+ 27,713	— 83,603	+ 22,161	+ 6,581	— 27,148
297,075	296,164	364,679	388,298	370,329	— 9,377	—125,954	— 47,911	+ 33,269	— 149,973
14,867	14,243	13,828	13,775	12,710	+ 6,891	— 1,031	+ 3,365	+ 867	+ 10,092
905,766	**1,783,301**	**1,991,093**	**1,947,043**	**1,743,832**	**+ 214,174**	**—338,000**	**+ 89,338**	**+ 428,737**	**+ 394,249**
372,450	369,277	369,018	365,969	349,978	— 4,321	+ 2,262	+ 5,094	+ 32,185	+ 35,220
428,757	417,059	463,907	471,513	419,700	+ 8,850	— 71,169	— 21,727	+ 110,421	+ 26,375
367,370	352,044	420,897	414,706	358,120	+ 20,624	—115,667	+ 10,004	+ 118,028	+ 32,989
248,777	223,661	303,932	294,313	279,237	+ 50,430	—155,905	+ 24,375	+ 29,887	— 51,213
488,412	421,260	433,339	400,542	336,797	+ 138,591	+ 2,479	+ 71,592	+ 138,216	+ 350,878
209,086	**2,051,005**	**2,347,934**	**2,213,195**	**1,960,993**	**+ 305,793**	**—443,226**	**+ 275,281**	**+ 565,512**	**+ 703,360**
485,165	425,062	450,106	403,182	343,477	+ 130,481	— 4,350	+ 105,193	+ 131,139	+ 362,463
410,228	384,178	464,052	449,689	402,629	+ 48,578	—143,189	+ 31,135	+ 99,470	+ 35,994
381,727	367,528	430,383	430,493	377,897	+ 15,421	—103,563	— 3,588	+ 120,227	+ 28,497
427,408	416,042	472,217	480,582	441,034	+ 6,642	— 65,759	— 30,335	+ 86,443	— 3,009
274,886	268,044	341,425	299,658	266,883	+ 17,999	—133,964	+ 78,323	+ 81,965	+ 44,323
229,672	190,151	189,751	149,591	129,073	+ 86,672	+ 7,599	+ 94,553	+ 46,268	+ 235,092
622,112	**1,557,497**	**1,487,766**	**1,445,333**	**1,297,179**	**+ 107,653**	**+ 246,281**	**+ 38,824**	**+ 285,100**	**+ 677,863**
385,496	362,882	378,714	379,615	343,000	+ 36,047	— 4,160	— 14,223	+ 79,338	+ 97,002
327,832	292,636	235,807	229,782	183,813	+ 74,917	+ 156,852	+ 9,860	+ 94,637	+ 336,266
235,682	242,954	248,366	245,184	230,767	— 34,507	+ 10,151	— 12,666	+ 19,591	— 17,431
257,588	251,309	258,806	241,083	212,120	+ 21,397	— 10,872	+ 24,959	+ 62,661	+ 98,145
247,330	246,236	222,032	213,945	204,257	— 7,024	+ 54,843	+ 16,010	+ 4,113	+ 67,942
168,184	161,480	144,041	135,724	123,210	+ 16,828	+ 39,467	+ 14,884	+ 24,760	+ 95,939
903,820	**1,706,868**	**1,444,112**	**1,109,183**	**985,067**	**+ 432,064**	**+ 590,478**	**+ 766,496**	**+ 252,191**	**+2,041,229**
320,414	226,958	205,560	199,379	164,188	+ 212,276	+ 54,523	+ 13,570	+ 71,025	+ 351,394
433,002	366,652	249,361	13,861	18,586	+ 131,601	+ 258,853	+ 558,873	— 10,443	+ 938,884
265,076	242,406	200,018	187,685	178,775	+ 45,756	+ 98,578	+ 23,884	+ 11,711	+ 179,929
402,173	369,875	321,794	286,014	249,346	+ 76,051	+ 104,170	+ 74,838	+ 79,105	+ 334,164
259,873	261,111	241,705	226,340	201,037	— 983	+ 41,780	+ 33,767	+ 52,697	+ 127,261
211,666	227,451	215,046	193,707	173,155	— 30,808	+ 28,074	+ 43,411	+ 42,162	+ 82,839
11,616	12,415	10,628	2,197	..	— 1,829	+ 4,500	+ 18,153	..	..

PUNJAB STATES	4,416,036	4,212,794	4,424,398	4,263,280	3,861,683	2,425,783	2,322,908	2,409,809	2,3
A.—HAVING POLITICAL RELATIONS WITH THE PUNJAB GOVT.	408,019	412,173	411,764	392,525	360,423	215,633	216,853	217,794	2
1. Dujana ..	*25,833*	25,485	24,174	26,450	23,416	13,538	13,388	12,481	
2. Pataudi ..	*18,097*	19,543	21,933	19,002	17,847	9,560	10,150	11,511	
3. Kalsia ..	*57,371*	55,909	67,181	68,633	67,708	32,573	31,297	36,980	
4. Simla Hill States—	*306,718*	311,236	298,476	278,440	251,452	159,982	162,018	156,822	1
Bashahr ..	*90,366*	93,203	84,636	75,727	64,345	44,688	43,208	42,066	
Nalagarh ..	*46,868*	49,230	52,551	54,032	53,373	24,665	26,458	28,425	
Keonthal ..	*47,455*	46,224	42,192	37,320	31,154	26,054	24,314	22,575	
Baghal ..	*25,099*	26,008	25,720	24,545	20,633	12,742	13,429	13,772	
Jubbal ..	*25,752*	24,620	22,242	21,412	20,118	14,090	13,126	11,853	
Baghat ..	*9,505*	8,797	9,490	8,668	8,339	5,662	5,072	5,671	
Kumharsain ..	*12,227*	12,219	11,735	10,416	9,515	6,220	6,105	5,949	
Bhajji ..	*14,263*	14,972	13,309	12,205	12,106	7,369	8,296	6,884	
Mahlog ..	*8,296*	8,663	8,968	9,329	9,169	4,394	4,614	4,700	
Balsan ..	*6,137*	6,225	6,704	5,496	5,190	3,280	3,345	3,556	
Dhami ..	*4,786*	4,484	4,505	3,985	3,322	2,377	2,279	2,435	
Kuthar ..	*3,841*	4,016	4,195	3,947	3,648	2,061	2,146	2,258	
Kunihar ..	*1,945*	2,208	2,168	1,957	1,923	950	1,166	1,123	
Mangal ..	*1,193*	1,267	1,227	1,091	1,060	645	697	659	
Bija ..	*943*	1,064	1,131	1,171	1,158	522	508	628	
Darkoti ..	*610*	521	518	595	590	327	246	253	
Tharoch ..	*4,219*	4,493	4,411	3,938	3,216	2,271	2,406	2,470	
Sangri ..	*3,213*	3,022	2,774	2,606	2,593	1,645	1,543	1,479	
B.—HAVING POLITICAL RELATIONS WITH THE GOVT. OF INDIA.	4,008,017	3,800,621	4,012,634	3,870,755	3,501,260	2,210,150	2,106,055	2,192,015	2,
5. Loharu ..	*20,621*	18,597	15,229	20,139	13,754	10,955	9,980	8,160	
6. Nahan ..	*140,448*	138,520	135,687	124,134	112,371	77,003	76,044	75,461	
7. Bilaspur ..	*98,000*	93,107	90,873	91,760	86,546	52,306	50,009	49,384	
8. Mandi ..	*185,048*	181,110	174,045	166,923	147,017	95,191	93,678	90,896	
9. Suket ..	*54,328*	54,928	54,676	52,403	52,484	28,642	29,014	28,964	
10. Kapurthala ..	*284,275*	268,133	314,351	299,690	252,617	156,530	150,220	169,797	
11. Malerkotla ..	*80,322*	71,144	77,506	75,755	71,051	46,950	40,602	41,915	
12. Faridkot ..	*150,661*	130,294	124,912	115,040	97,034	84,206	73,836	69,321	
13. Chamba ..	*141,867*	135,873	127,834	124,032	115,773	74,230	70,612	66,474	
14. Patiala ..	*1,499,739*	1,407,659	1,596,692	1,583,521	1,467,433	837,479	792,540	877,197	
15. Jind ..	*308,183*	271,728	282,003	284,560	249,862	169,658	149,947	153,376	
16. Nabha ..	*263,334*	248,887	297,949	282,756	261,824	146,910	139,319	165,386	
17. Bahawalpur ..	*781,191*	780,641	720,877	650,042	573,494	430,090	430,254	395,684	
DELHI ..	488,188	413,447	405,409	372,766	350,499	281,633	230,653	217,709	

IN POPULATION SINCE 1881.

2	1,990,253	1,889,886	2,014,589	1,939,189	1,749,380	+ 203,242	— 211,604	+ 161,118	+ 401,597	+ 554,353
7	192,386	195,320	193,970	183,401	165,826	— 4,154	+ 409	+ 19,239	+ 32,102	+ 47,596
5	12,296	12,097	11,693	12,679	10,891	+ 348	+ 1,311	— 2,276	+ 3,034	+ 2,417
0	8,537	9,393	10,422	9,049	8,337	— 1,446	— 2,390	+ 2,931	+ 1,155	+ 250
6	24,798	24,612	30,201	31,013	30,812	+ 1,462	— 11,272	— 1,452	+ 925	— 10,337
6	146,756	149,218	141,654	130,660	115,786	— 4,518	+ 12,760	+ 20,036	+ 26,988	+ 53,266
9	45,678	46,995	42,570	36,623	31,326	— 2,837	+ 8,567	+ 8,909	+ 11,382	+ 26,021
2	22,203	22,772	24,126	24,847	24,291	— 2,362	— 3,321	— 1,481	+ 659	— 6,505
9	21,401	21,910	19,617	17,517	13,825	+ 1,231	+ 4,032	+ 4,872	+ 6,166	+ 16,301
6	12,357	12,579	11,948	11,585	9,597	— 909	+ 288	+ 1,175	+ 3,912	+ 4,466
9	11,662	11,494	10,380	9,671	8,989	+ 1,132	+ 2,378	+ 830	+ 1,204	+ 5,634
7	3,843	3,725	3,819	3,627	3,382	+ 708	— 693	+ 822	+ 329	+ 1,166
0	6,007	6,114	5,786	5,145	4,595	+ 8	+ 484	+ 1,319	+ 901	+ 2,712
0	6,894	6,676	6,425	5,868	5,380	— 709	+ 1,063	+ 1,104	+ 99	+ 2,157
6	3,902	4,049	4,202	4,356	4,203	— 367	— 305	— 361	+ 160	— 873
8	2,857	2,880	3,148	2,508	2,312	— 88	— 479	+ 1,208	+ 306	+ 947
0	2,409	2,205	2,070	1,860	1,546	+ 302	— 21	+ 520	+ 663	+ 1,464
0	1,780	1,870	1,937	1,855	1,628	— 175	— 179	+ 248	+ 299	+ 193
7	995	1,042	1,045	943	906	— 263	+ 40	+ 211	+ 34	+ 22
3	548	570	568	487	477	— 74	+ 40	+ 136	+ 31	+ 133
9	421	496	503	535	509	— 121	— 67	+ 40	+ 13	— 215
5	283	275	265	310	295	+ 89	+ 3	— 77	+ 5	+ 20
0	1,948	2,087	1,941	1,706	1,366	— 274	+ 82	+ 473	+ 722	+ 1,003
0	1,568	1,479	1,295	1,217	1,153	+ 191	+ 248	+ 108	+ 13	+ 620
6	1,797,867	1,694,566	1,820,619	1,755,788	1,583,554	+ 207,396	— 212,013	+ 141,879	+ 369,495	+ 506,757
9	9,666	8,617	7,069	9,129	6,215	+ 2,024	+ 3,368	— 4,910	+ 6,385	+ 6,867
5	63,445	62,476	60,226	54,866	49,066	+ 1,928	+ 2,833	+ 11,553	+ 11,763	+ 28,077
3	45,694	43,098	41,489	42,165	39,413	+ 4,893	+ 2,234	— 887	+ 5,214	+ 11,454
8	89,857	87,432	83,149	80,579	71,429	+ 3,938	+ 7,065	+ 7,122	+ 19,906	+ 38,031
0	25,686	25,914	25,712	24,635	23,204	— 600	+ 252	+ 2,273	— 81	+ 1,844
8	127,745	117,913	144,554	136,317	113,979	+ 16,142	— 46,218	+ 14,061	+ 47,073	+ 31,658
0	33,372	30,542	35,591	35,009	32,501	+ 9,178	— 6,362	+ 1,751	+ 4,704	+ 9,271
8	66,455	56,458	55,691	51,131	43,186	+ 20,367	+ 5,382	+ 9,872	+ 18,006	+ 53,627
2	67,637	65,261	61,366	59,471	55,391	+ 5,994	+ 8,039	+ 3,802	+ 8,259	+ 26,094
4	662,260	615,119	719,495	712,054	660,449	+ 92,080	— 189,033	+ 13,171	+ 116,088	+ 32,306
9	138,525	121,781	128,627	128,612	112,953	+ 36,455	— 10,275	— 2,557	+ 34,698	+ 58,321
5	116,424	109,568	132,563	120,931	116,660	+ 14,447	— 49,062	+ 15,193	+ 20,932	+ 1,510
5	351,101	350,387	325,193	294,889	259,099	+ 550	+ 59,764	+ 70,835	+ 76,548	+ 207,697
0	206,555	182,794	187,700	172,445	165,679	+ 74,741	+ 8,038	+ 32,643	+ 22,267	+ 137,689

Table 4.9: Report of the Census of British India 1881, Vol. I Abstract III

	Area in square miles	*Density*	*Population*
Bombay	1,97,875	118	2,33,95,663
Bengal	1,93,198	360	6,95,36,861
Punjab	1,42,449	159	2,27,12,120
Madras	1,41,001	221	3,11,70,631
Rajputana	1,29,750	79	1,02,68,392
Central Provinces	1,13,279	102	1,15,48,511
North–West and Oudh	1,11,236	403	4,48,49,619
Burmah	87,220	43	37,36,771
Hyderabad (Nizam's dominions)	81,807	120	98,45,594
Central India	75,079	123	92,61,907
Assam	46,341	105	48,81,426
Mysore	24,723	169	41,86,188
Berar	17,711	151	26,72,673
Baroda	8,570	255	21,85,005
Travancore	6,730	357	24,01,158
Ajmere	2,711	170	460,722
Coorg	1,583	113	178,302
Cochin	1,361	441	600,278
All India	13,82,624	184	25,38,91,821
Russian Empire	20,88,274	36	7,41,45,223
Austrian Empire	2,40,338	157	3,77,86,346
German Empire	2,10,193	215	4,52,34,061
France	2,04,031	155	3,76,72,048
Spain	1,95,716	85	1,66,25,860
Turkey in Europe	1,36,627	69	94,00,000
Hungary	1,24,431	126	1,56,42,102
United Kingdom	1,21,305	287	3,48,84,848
Austria	1,15,907	191	2,21,44,244
Italy	1,14,325	249	2,84,59,451
England and Wales	58,186	446	2,59,74,439
England	50,823	484	2,46,13,926
Portugal	34,507	126	43,48,551
Ireland	32,524	159	51,74,836
Scotland	30,362	123	37,35,573
Greece	19,342	85	16,53,767

	Area in square miles	*Density*	*Population*
Switzerland	15,977	178	28,46,102
Hanover	14,548	146	21,20,165
Belgium	11,379	485	55,19,844
Saxony	6,777	438	29,72,805

25. The table from which the figures hitherto dealt with have been taken is No. 1 of the series comprised in the second volume of the Indian Census returns. That volume was prepared in India, as the provincial returns, whether in manuscript or proof, came in. Since their receipt slight alterations in the provincial returns have in two instances been effected, and these alterations have necessitated certain corrections in the Indian Table 1. I have therefore reprinted that table, and it is appended.*

* A second copy of Table 1, as reprinted, has been forwarded for incorporation with Volume II, already distributed, and should be substituted for the Table I, as originally compiled, which finds a place in Volume II.

Table 4.10: Population Density Bengal Presidency, 1881

	Density	*Area in square miles*	*Population*
Bengal:			
Howrah	1,335	476	6,35,381
Sarun	870	2,622	22,80,380
Mozufferpore	860	3,003	25,82,050
Patna	845	2,079	17,56,850
Hooghly	828	1,223	10,12,764
Durbhunga	790	3,335	26,33,447
Dacca	757	2,797	21,16,350
Furreedpore	720	2,267	16,31,734
Pubna	710	1,847	13,11,728
Total	**812**	**19,619**	**1,59,00,706**
North–West Provinces			
Ballia	808	1,144	9,24,763
Jhunpur	778	1,554	12,09,663
Azamgarh	747	2,147	16,01,654
Benares	894	908	8,92,684
Total	**793**	**5,813**	**46,31,764**
Grand total	**808**	**25,492**	**2,05,92,470**

* A division is a group of districts ranging from 3 to 7 in number, and forms the charge of a Commissioner of Revenue under whom the District Officers directly act.

Table 4.12:: Specific Population of Provinces and States, 1881

Province or State, & c.	*Mean density per square mile*	*Extreme density*			
		Highest		*Lowest*	
		Name	*Density*	*Name*	*Density*
Ajmer	200 68.45	Ajmer	203	Merwara	187
Assam	112 43.99	Silhet	397	Kachar Hills	11
Bengal	471 25.80	Saran	930*	Chittagong Hills	20
Berar	163 35.71	Amraoti	238	Elichpur	120
Bombay	207 48.33	Kaira	542	Kanara	114
Sindh	60 117.14	Haidrabad	102	Thar and Parkar	23
Upper Burma	35 92.15	Mandalay	178	Upper Khyadwin	4
Lower Burma	53 29.60	Tharawaddi	172	Salwin	7
Central Provinces	125	Nagpur	197	Chanda	65
Coorg	109 49.01	—	—	—	—
Madras	252 42.09	Tanjore	601	Godavari Agency	42
N.W. Provinces	411 21.68	Benares	914	Garhwal	72
Oudh	522 79.78	Lucknow	800	Kheri	305
Punjab	188 55.65	Jalandhar	633	Dehra Ismail Khan	51
Total, British	**230**	**Saran**	**930***	**Upper Khyndwin**	**4**
Haidrabad	139	Bidar	216	Sirpur Trandur	46
Baroda	294	Baroda	428	Amreli	151
Mysore	177	Bangalore	814	Chitaldurg	104
Kashmir	31	Ranbir Singhpura	—	Ladakh	—
Rajputana	92	Bharatpur	327	Jesalmer	7
Central India	133	Baghelkhand[#]	158	Bundelkhand	72
Bombay States	126	Kolhapur	334	Surgana	34
Khairpur *Sindh(	22	—	—	—	—
Madras States	385	Cochin	531	Sandur	71
Central Province States	73	Chhuikadan	235	Bastar	24
Bengal States	92	Kochh Bihar	443	Hill Tippera	33
N.W. Province States	155	Rampur	583	Tehri-Garhwal	58
Punjab States	111 60.81	Kapurthala	501	Bashhr	23
Total, States	111	—	—	—	—

* Excluding the suburban district of Howrah.

[#] The Central India return is approximate only.

Table 4.13: Variation in Population, 1881–91

Province	*1891*	*1881*	*Difference*	*Growth %*
1.	2.	3.	4.	5
Ajmer-Merwara	5,42,358	4,60,722	81,636	17.72
Assam	54,33,199	48,81,426	5,51,773	11.30
Bengal	7,13,46,987	6,67,50,520	45,96,467	6.89
Berar	28,97,491	26,72,673	2,24,818	8.41
Bombay (Presidency)	1,89,01,123	1,65,05,967	23,95,156	14.51
Bombay	1,59,85,270	1,40,57,284	19,27,986	13.72
(B) Sindh	28,71,774	24,13,823	4,57,951	18.97
(C) Aden	44,079	34,860	9,219	26.45
(B) Lower Burmah	46,58,627	37,36,771	9,21,856	24.67
Central Provinces	1,07,84,294	98,38,791	9,45,503	9.61
Coorg	1,73,055	1,78,302	-5,247	-2.94
Madras	3,56,30,440	3,08,27,113	48,03,327	15.58
North-West Provinces	4,69,05,085	4,41,50,507	27,54,578	6.24
(A) North-West Provinces	3,42,54,254	3,27,62,766	14,91,488	4.55
(B) Oudh	1,26,50,881	1,13,87,741	12,63,140	11.09
Punjab	2,08,66,847	1,88,43,186	20,23,661	10.74
Andamans	15,609	14,628	981	6.71
Nett Variation Since 1881	**21,81,55,115**	**19,88,60,606**	**1,92,94,509**	**9.70**
State or Agency				
Hyderabad	1,15,37,040	98,45,594	16,91,446	17.18
Baroda	24,15,396	21,85,005	2,30,391	10.54
Mysore	49,43,604	41,86,188	7,57,416	18.09
Rajputana	1,19,72,386	99,59,012	20,13,374	20.22
Central India	1,03,18,812	93,87,119	9,31,693	9.93
Bombay States	80,59,298	69,26,464	11,32,834	16.36
Madras States	37,00,622	33,44,849	3,55,773	10.64
Central Province States	21,60,511	17,09,720	4,50,791	26.37
Bengal States	32,96,379	27,86,446	5,09,933	18.30
North-Western Province States	7,92,491	7,41,750	50,741	6.84
Punjab States	42,68,280	38,60,761	4,07,519	10.56
Nett Variation Since 1881	**6,34,59,819**	**5,49,32,908**	**85,26,911**	**15.52**
Kashmer	25,43,952	-		
Shan States (Outposts Only)	2,992	-		
Nett	**28,16,14,934**	**25,37,93,514**	**2,78,21,420**	**10.96**

Table 4.14: Variation in Population, 1872–1901

Province, State or Agency	*Persons*				*Variations: Increase (+) or Decrease (-)*			*Growth %*	*Growth %*	*Growth %*
	1901	*1891*	*1881*	*1872*	*1891–1901*	*1881–91*	*1872–91*	*1881–91*	*1881–1901*	*1891–1901*
1	*2*	*3*	*4*	*5*	*6*	*7*	*8*			
INDIA	29,43,61,056	28,73,14,671	25,38,96,330	20,61,62,360	70,46,385	3,34,18,341	4,77,33,970	13.16	15.94	2.45
PROVINCE	23,18,99,507	22,12,39,515	19,91,03,821	18,51,63,353	1,06,59,992	2,21,35,694	1,39,40,468	11.12	16.47	4.82
Ajmer-Merwara	4,76,912	5,42,358	4,60,722	3,96,331	-65,446	81,636	64,391	17.72	3.51	-12.07
Andaman and Nicobar	24,649	15,609	14,628		9,040	981		6.71	68.51	57.92
Assam	61,26,343	54,77,302	51,28,862	41,50,769	6,49,041	3,48,440	9,78,093	6.79	19.45	11.85
Bengal	7,47,44,866	7,13,46,961	6,67,50,494	6,01,65,084	33,97,905	45,96,467	65,85,410	6.89	11.98	4.76
Berar	27,54,016	28,97,491	26,72,673	22,27,654	-1,43,475	+2,24.818	+4,45.019	8.41	3.04	-4.95
Bombay (Presidency)	1,85,59,561	1,88,78,314	1,64,94,416	1,63,01,280	-3,18,753	23,83,898	1,93,136	14.45	12.52	-1.69
Bombay	1,53,04,677	1,59,59,135	1,40,42,499	1,40,75,426	-6,54,438	19,16,636	-32,927	13.65	8.99	-4.10
Sind	32,10,910	28,75,100	24,17,057	22,06,565	3,35,810	4,58,043	2,10,492	18.95	32.84	11.68
Aden	43,974	44,079	34,860	19,289	-105	9,219	15,571	26.45	26.14	-0.24
Burma	1,04,90,624	77,22,053	37,36,771	27,47,148	27,68,571	39,85,282	9,89,623	106.65	180.74	35.85
Central Province	98,76,646	1,07,84,294	98,38,791	81,73,824	-9,07,648	9,45,503	16,64,967	9.61	0.38	-8.42

Province, State or Agency	*Persons*				*Variations: Increase (+) or Decrease (-)*			*Growth %*	*Growth %*	*Growth %*
	1901	*1891*	*1881*	*1872*	*1891–1901*	*1881–91*	*1872–91*	*1881–91*	*1881–1901*	*1891–1901*
1	*2*	*3*	*4*	*5*	*6*	*7*	*8*			
Coorg	1,80,607	1,73,055	1,78,302	1,68,312	7,552	-5,247	9,990	-2.94	1.29	4.36
Madras	3,82,09,436	3,56,30,440	3,08,27,218	3,12,20,973	25,78,996	48,03,222	-3,93,755	15.58	23.95	7.24
NWFP	21,25,480	18,57,504	15,75,943	1,76,09,518	2,67,976	2,81,561	12,40,919	17.87	34.87	14.43
Punjab	2,03,30,339	1,90,09,343	1,73,74,494		13,20,996	+17,34.849		9.41	17.01	6.95
United Province of Agra and Oudh	4,76,91,782	4,69,04,791	4,41,50,507	4,20,02,460	7,86,991	27,54,284	21,48,047	6.24	8.02	1.68
Agra	3,48,58,705	3,42,53,960	3,27,62,766	3,07,81,310	6,04,745	14,91,194	19,81,356	4.55	6.40	1.77
Oudh	1,28,33,077	1,26,50,831	1,13,87,741	1,12,20,950	1,82,246	12,63,090	1,66,791	11.09	12.69	1.44
STATES AND AGENCIES	6,24,61,549	6,60,75,156	5,47,92,509	2,09,99,007	-36,13,607	1,12,82,647	3,37,93,502	20.59	14.00	-5.47
Baluchistan Agencies	5,02,500									
Baroda State	19,52,692	24,15,396	21,82,158	19,97,598	-4,62,704	2,33,238	1,84,560	10.69	-10.52	-19.16
Bengal States	37,48,544	33,26,837	27,86,446	21,70,133	4,21,707	5,40,391	6,16,313	19.39	34.53	12.68
Bombay State	69,08,648	80,82,107	69,38,015	67,98,052	-11,73,459	11,44,092	1,39,963	16.49	-0.42	-14.52

Province, State or Agency	*Persons*				*Variations: Increase (+) or Decrease (-)*			*Growth %*	*Growth %*	*Growth %*
	1901	*1891*	*1881*	*1872*	*1891–1901*	*1881–91*	*1872–91*	*1881–91*	*1881–1901*	*1891–1901*
1	*2*	*3*	*4*	*5*	*6*	*7*	*8*			
Central India Agency	86,28,781	1,03,18,812	92,61,907		-16,90,031	10,56,905		11.41	-6.84	-16.38
Gwalior State	29,33,001	33,78,774	29,93,652		-4,45,773	3,85,122		12.86	-2.03	-13.19
Central Province States	19,96,383	21,60,511	17,09,720	10,49,710	-1,64,128	4,50,791	6,60,010	26.37	16.77	-7.60
Hyderabad State	1,11,41,142	1,15,37,040	98,45,594		-3,95,898	16,91,446		17.18	13.16	-3.43
Kashmir State	29,05,578	25,43,952			3,61,626					14.22
Madras State	41,88,086	37,00,622	33,44,849	32,89,392	4,87,464	3,55,773	55,457	10.64	25.21	13.17
Cochin State	8,12,025	7,22,906	6,00,278	6,01,114	89,119	1,22,628	–836	20.43	35.27	12.33
Travancore State	29,52,157	25,57,736	24,01,158	23,11,379	3,94,421	1,56,578	89,779	6.52	22.95	15.42
Mysore State	55,39,399	49,43,604	41,86,188	50,55,402	5,95,795	7,57,416	-8,69.214	18.09	32.33	12.05
Punjab State	44,24,398	42,63,280	38,61,683		1,61,118	4,01,597		10.40	14.57	3.78
Rajputana State	97,23,301	1,19,90,504	99,34,199		-22,67,203	20,56,305		20.70	-2.12	-18.91
United Province States	8,02,097	7,92,491	7,41,750	6,38,720	9,606	50,741	1,03,030	6.84	8.14	1.21

Table 4.15: Variation in Population, 1881–1931

Province, State or Agency	*1931*	*1921*	*1911*	*1901*	*1891*	*1881*	*Net growth*	*Percentage growth*
INDIA	35,28,37,778	31,89,42,480	31,51,56,396	29,43,61,056	28,73,14,671	25,88,96,330	9,39,41,448	36.29
PROVINCES	27,15,26,933	24,68,56,191	24,37,97,647	23,11,42,489	22,07,65,285	19,84,48,631	7,30,78,302	36.82
Ajmer-Merwara	5,60,292	4,95,271	5,01,395	4,76,912	5,42,358	4,60,722	99,570	21.61
Assam	86,22,251	74,59,128	65,78,768	57,25,871	53,63,777	48,11,572	38,,10,679	79.2
Bengal	5,01,14,002	4,67,02,307	4,54,89,697	4,21,47,895	3,90,95,855	3,63,22,302	1,37,91,700	37.97
Bihar	2,57,27,500	2,33,73,517	2,37,45,337	2,33,53,474	2,35,74,943	2,24,12,662	33,14,838	14.79
Orissa	53,06,142	49,68,873	51,31,753	49,82,142	46,66,227	43,43,964	9,62,178	22.15
Chota Nagpur	66,43,934	56,53,028	56,05,362	49,00,429	46,28,792	42,25,989	24,17,945	57.22
Bombay Presidency	1,79,92,053	1,60,12,342	1,61,36,666	1,53,19,405	1,59,85,427	1,40,63,006	39,29,047	27.94
Sind	38,87,070	32,79,377	35,13,435	32,10,910	28,75,100	24,17,057	14,70,013	60.82
Central Provinces and Berar	1,55,07,723	1,39,12,760	1,39,16,158	1,19,71,328	1,30,48,845	1,19,43,251	35,64,472	29.85
Central Provinces	1,20,65,885	1,08,37,444	1,08,58,996	92,17,312	1,01,51,354	92,70,578	27,95,307	30.15
Berar	34,41,838	30,75,316	30,57,162	27,54,016	28,97,491	26,72,673	7,69,165	28.78
Coorg	1,63,327	1,63,838	1,74,976	1,80,607	1,73,055	1,78,302	-14,975	-8.4
Madras	4,67,40,107	4,23,18,985	4,14,05,404	3,82,29,654	3,56,44,428	3,08,41,154	1,58,98,953	51.55
Punjab	2,35,80,852	2,06,85,478	1,95,79,047	1,99,42,715	1,86,52,614	1,69,39,312	66,41,540	39.21

Province, State or Agency	*1931*	*1921*	*1911*	*1901*	*1891*	*1881*	*Net growth*	*Percentage growth*
United Provinces of Agra and Oudh	4,84,08,763	4,53,75,069	4,68,06,612	4,73,12,441	4,65,01,468	4,37,76,288	46,32,475	10.58
Agra	3,56,13,784	3,32,08,427	3,42,48,608	3,44,79,273	3,38,50,544	3,23,88,456	32,25,328	9.96
Oudh	1,27,94,979	1,21,66,642	1,25,58,004	1,28,33,168	1,26,50,924	1,13,87,832	14,07,147	12.36
STATES AND AGENCIES	8,18,10,845	7,20,86,289	7,13,58,749	6,32,18,567	6,65,49,386	5,54,47,699	2,63,63,146	47.55
Assam States	6,26,606	5,31,118	4,81,753	4,01,074	114,103*	3,17,819	3,08,787	97.16
Baroda State	24,43,007	21,26,522	20,32,798	19,52,692	24,15,396	21,82,158	2,60,849	11.95
Bengal States	9,73,336	8,96,926	8,22,565	7,40,299	7,16,310	6,98,261	2,75,075	39.39
Bihar and Orissa States	46,52,007	39,59,669	39,45,209	33,14,474	30,28,018	24,10,611	22,41,396	92.98
Bombay States	44,68,396	38,67,819	38,63,473	36,09,431	40,99,470	34,85,047	9,83,349	28.22
Central India Agency	66,32,790	60,02,551	61,33,764	54,35,038	1,01,54,521	90,94,057	-24,61,267	-27.06
Central Provinces States	24,83,214	20,66,900	21,17,152	16,31,264	17,12,689	13,87,406	10,95,808	78.98
Gwalior State	35,23,070	31,93,176	32,35,303	30,73,651				
Hyderabad State	1,44,36,148	1,24,71,770	1,33,74,676	1,11,41,142	1,15,37,040	98,45,594	45,90,554	46.63

Province, State or Agency	*1931*	*1921*	*1911*	*1901*	*1891*	*1881*	*Net growth*	*Percentage growth*
Madras States Agency	67,54,484	54,60,312	48,11,841	41,88,086	37,00,622	33,44,849	34,09,635	101.94
Cochin State	12,05,016	9,79,080	9,18,110	8,12,025	7,22,906	6,00,278	6,04,738	100.74
Travancore State	50,95,973	40,06,062	34,28,975	29,52,157	25,57,736	24,01,158	26,94,815	112.23
Other Madras States	4,53,495	4,75,170	4,64,756	4,23,904	4,19,980	3,43,413	1,10,082	32.06
Mysore State	65,57,302	59,78,892	58,06,193	55,39,399	49,43,604	41,86,188	23,71,114	56.64
Punjab States	4,37,787	4,08,019	4,12,173	4,11,764	3,92,525	3,60,423	77,364	21.46
Punjab States Agency	44,72,218	40,08,017	38,00,621	40,12,634	38,70,755	35,01,260	9,70,958	27.73
Rajputana Agency	1,12,25,712	98,31,755	1,05,18,345	98,42,482	1,21,53,631	1,01,02,105	11,23,607	11.12
United Provinces States	12,06,070	11,34,881	11,89,874	11,63,454	11,79,947	10,99,460	1,06,610	9.7
Western India States Agency	39,99,250	35,41,610	35,24,578	32,84,489	39,56,345	34,32,461	5,66,789	16.51

Table 4.16: Variation in Population Province, State or Agency, 1881–1941

	1941	*1931*	*1921*	*1911*	*1901*	*1891*	*1881*	*Growth% 1881–1941*
1	*2*	*3*	*4*	*5*	*6*	*7*	*8*	
INDIA	38,89,97,955	33,81,19,154	31,89,42,480	31,51,56,396	29,43,61,056	28,73,14,671	25,38,96,330	53.21
PROVINCES	29,58,08,722	25,67,57,818	24,70,03,293	24,39,33,178	23,12,59,098	22,08,79,388	19,85,45,380	48.99
Ajmer-Merwara	5,83,693	5,06,964	4,95,271	5,01,395	4,76,912	5,42,358	4,60,722	26.69
Andaman and Nicobar	21,316	19,233	27,086	26,459	24,649	15,609	14,628	45.72
Assam	1,02,04,733	86,22,791	76,06,230	67,14,299	58,42,480	54,77,880	49,08,321	107.91
Baluchistan	5,01,631	4,63,508	4,20,648	4,14,412	3,82,106	....	.....	
Bengal	6,03,06,525	5,01,15,548	4,66,95,536	4,54,82,605	4,21,41,060	3,90,89,217	3,63,16,360	66.06
Bihar and Orissa			3,40,02,189	3,44,89,544	3,32,42,880	3,28,76,600	3,09,88,557	
Bihar	2,88,23,802	2,57,25,683	2,33,80,288	2,37,52,429	2,33,60,309	2,35,81,581	2,24,18,604	28.57
Orissa	87,28,544	80,25,671	49,68,873	51,31,753	49,82,142	46,66,227	43,43,964	100.93
Chota Nagpur	75,16,349	66,42,226	56,53,028	56,05,362	49,00,429	46,28,792	42,25,989	77.86
Bombay (Presi)			1,93,48,219	1,96,96,266	1,85,74,289	1,89,04,606	1,65,14,923	-100
Bombay	2,08,49,840	1,79,92,053	1,60,12,342	1,61,36,666	1,53,19,405	1,59,85,427	1,40,63,006	48.26
Sind	45,35,008	38,87,070	32,79,377	35,13,435	32,10,910	28,75,100	24,17,057	87.63

	1941	*1931*	*1921*	*1911*	*1901*	*1891*	*1881*	*Growth% 1881–1941*
1	*2*	*3*	*4*	*5*	*6*	*7*	*8*	
Aden			56,500	46,165	43,974	44,079	34,860	-100
Burma			1,32,12,192	1,21,15,217	1,04,90,624	77,22,053	37,36,771	-100
CP and Berar	1,68,13,584	1,53,23,058	1,39,12,760	1,39,16,158	1,19,71,328	1,30,48,845	1,19,43,251	40.78
Central Provinces	1,32,08,718	1,18,81,220	1,08,37,444	1,08,58,996	92,17,312	1,01,51,354	92,70,578	42.48
Berar	36,04,866	34,41,838	30,75,316	30,57,162	27,54,016	28,97,491	26,72,673	34.88
Coorg	1,68,726	1,63,227	1,63,838	1,74,976	1,80,607	1,73,055	1,78,302	-5.37
Delhi	9,17,939	6,36,246	4,88,188	4,13,447	4,05,409	3,72,766	3,50,499	161.89
Madras	4,93,41,810	4,42,05,243	4,23,18,985	4,14,05,404	3,82,29,654	3,56,44,428	3,08,41,154	59.99
NWFP	30,38,067	24,25,076	22,51,340	21,96,933	20,41,534	18,57,519	15,75,943	92.78
Punjab	2,84,18,819	2,35,80,864	2,06,85,024	1,95,78,573	1,99,42,227	1,86,52,202	1,69,38,910	67.77
UP of Agra and Oudh	5,50,20,617	4,84,08,482	4,53,75,787	4,68,07,490	4,73,13,339	4,65,02,250	4,37,77,039	25.68
Agra	4,09,06,147	3,56,13,503	3,32,09,145	3,42,49,486	3,44,80,171	3,38,51,326	3,23,89,207	26.3
Oudh	1,41,14,470	1,27,94,979	1,21,66,642	1,25,58,004	1,28,33,168	1,26,50,924	1,13,87,832	23.94
STATES AND AGENCIES	9,31,89,233	3,13,61,336	7,19,39,187	7,12,23,218	6,31,01,958	6,64,35,283	5,53,50,950	68.36

	1941	*1931*	*1921*	*1911*	*1901*	*1891*	*1881*	*Growth% 1881–1941*
1	2	3	4	5	6	7	8	
Assam State (Manipur)	7,25,655	6,25,606	3,84,016	3,46,222	2,84,465	.....	2,21,070	228.25
Baluchistan States	3,56,204	4,05,109	3,78,977	4,20,291	4,28,640	.....	.....	
Baroda State	28,55,010	24,48,283	21,26,522	20,32,798	19,52,692	24,15,396	21,82,158	30.83
Bengal State	21,44,829	18,62,939	8,96,926	8,22,565	7,40,299	7,16,310	6,98,261	207.17
Bihar and Orissa States	30,23,731	26,83,472	39,59,669	39,45,209	33,14,474	30,28,018	24,10,611	25.43
Bombay States			74,09,429	73,88,051	68,93,920	80,55,815	69,17,508	-100
Deccan and Kolhapur	27,85,428	24,57,971	21,55,062	22,12,793	22,55,327	22,88,043		
Gujarat	14,58,702	12,65,078	1,265, 078	1,014,,261	7,93,246	11,02,428		
Western India (States Agency)	49,04,156	42,20,595	37,23,170	36,80,053	33,90,619	42,28,468		15.98*
Central India (Agency)	75,06,427	66,43,761	59,97,023	61,29,019	54,31,767	1,01,36,403	92,61,907	-18.95
Gwalior State	40,06,159	35,23,070	31,86,075	32,27,961	30,66,038	.....	.....	
Central Provinces States			20,66,900	21,17,152	16,31,264	17,12,689	13,87,406	-100

	1941	*1931*	*1921*	*1911*	*1901*	*1891*	*1881*	*Growth% 1881–1941*
1	*2*	*3*	*4*	*5*	*6*	*7*	*8*	
Hyderabad State	1,63,38,534	1,44,36.148	1,24,71,770	1,33,74,676	1,11,41,142	1,15,37,040	98,45,594	65.95
Kashmir State	40,21,616	36,46.243	33,20,518	31,58,126	29,05,578	25,43,952	.....	
Madras States	4,98,754	4,53.495	54,60,312	48,11,841	41,88,086	37,00,622	33,44,849	-85.09
Cochin State	14,22,875	12,05,016	9,79,080	9,18,110	8,12,025	7,22,906	6,00,278	137.04
Travancore State	60,70,018	50,95,973	40,06,062	34,28,975	29,52,157	25,57,736	24,01,158	152.8
Other Madras States			4,75,170	4,64,756	4,23,904	4,19,980	3,43,413	-100
Mysore State	73,29,140	65,57,302	59,78,892	58,06,193	55,39,399	49,43,604	41,86,188	75.08
NWFP (Agencies)	23,77,599	22,59,288	28,25,136	16,22,094	83,962	.....	.....	
Punjab States	55,03,554	44,96,928	44,16,036	42,12,794	44,24,398	42,63,280	38,61,683	42.52
Rajputana Agency	1,36,70,208	1,25,16,029	98,44,384	1,05,30,432	9, 853,366	1,21,71,749	99,34,255	37.61
Sikkim State	1,21,520	1,09,808	81,720	87,920	59,104	30,458		
UP States	9,28,470	8,56,497	11,31,881	1,19,874	1,163, 454	1,179, 947	10,99,460	-15.55

Table 5.1: Variation in Population Since 1901, a 2-Decadal Variation in Population Since 1901

State code	*India/State/Union Territory*	*Census year*	*Persons*	*Variation since the preceding Census absolute*	*Growth per cent*	*% Share in Indian population*
1	2	3	4	5	6	7
00	INDIA	1901	23,83,96,327	---		
		1911	25,20,93,390	+ 1,36,97,063	5.75	
		1921	25,13,21,213	- 7,72,177	-0.31	
		1931	27,89,77,238	+2,76,56,025	11.00	
		1941	31,86,60,580	+3,96,83,342	14.22	
		1951	36,10,88,090	+4,24,20,485	13.31	
		1961	43,92,34,771	+7,76,82,873	21.64	
		1971	54,81,59,652	+10,89,24,881	24.80	
		1981	68,33,29,097	+13,51,69,445	24.66	
		1991	84,64,21,039	+16,30,91,942	23.87	
		2001	1,02,87,37,436	+18,23,16,397	21.54	
		2011	1,21,08,54,977	+18,21,17,541	17.70	
01	Jammu & Kashmir	1901	21,39,362			0.90
		1911	22,92,535	+1,53,173	7.16	0.91
		1921	24,24,359	+1,31,824	5.75	0.96
		1931	26,70,208	+2,45,849	10.14	0.96
		1941	29,46,728	+2,76,520	10.36	0.92

State code	India/State/Union Territory	Census year	Persons	Variation since the preceding Census absolute	Growth per cent	% Share in Indian population
1	2	3	4	5	6	7
		1951	32,53,852	+3,07,124	10.42	0.90
		1961	35,60,976	+3,07,124	9.44	0.81
		1971	46,16,632	+10,55,656	29.65	0.84
		1981	59,87,389	+13,70,757	29.69	0.88
		1991 +	78,37,051	+18,49,662	30.89	0.93
		2001	1,01,43,700	+23,06,649	29.43	0.99
		2011	1,25,41,302	+23,97,602	23.64	1.04
02	Himachal Pradesh	1901	19,20,294			0.81
		1911	18,96,944	- 23,350	-1.22	0.75
		1921	19,28,206	+31,262	1.65	0.77
		1931	20,29,113	+1,00,907	5.23	0.73
		1941	22,63,245	+2,34,132	11.54	0.71
		1951	23,85,981	+1,22,736	5.42	0.66
		1961	28,12,463	+4,26,482	17.87	0.64
		1971	34,60,434	+6,47,971	23.04	0.63
		1981	42,80,818	+8,20,384	23.71	0.63
		1991	51,70,877	+8,90,059	20.79	0.61

State code	*India/State/Union Territory*	*Census year*	*Persons*	*Variation since the preceding Census absolute*	*Growth per cent*	*% Share in Indian population*
1	2	3	4	5	6	7
		2001	60,77,900	+9,07,023	17.54	0.59
		2011	68,64,602	+7,86,702	12.94	0.57
03	Punjab	1901	75,44,790	---		3.16
		1911	67,31,510	- 8,13,280	-10.78	2.67
		1921	71,52,811	+ 4,21,301	6.26	2.85
		1931	80,12,325	+ 8,59,514	12.02	2.87
		1941	96,00,236	+15,87,911	19.82	3.01
		1951	91,60,500	- 4,39,736	-4.58	2.54
		1961	1,11,35,069	+19,74,569	21.56	2.54
		1971	1,35,51,060	+ 24,15,991	21.70	2.47
		1981	1,67,88,915	+ 32,37,855	23.89	2.46
		1991	2,02,81,969	+ 34,93,054	20.81	2.40
		2001	2,43,58,999	+ 40,77,030	20.10	2.37
		2011	2,77,43,338	+33,84,339	13.89	2.29
04	Chandigarh	1901	21,967	---		0.01
		1911	18,437	-3,530	-16.07	0.01
		1921	18,133	-304	-1.65	0.01

State code	India/State/Union Territory	Census year	Persons	Variation since the preceding Census absolute	Growth per cent	% Share in Indian population
1	2	3	4	5	6	7
		1931	19,783	+1,650	9.10	0.01
		1941	22,574	+2,791	14.11	0.01
		1951	24,261	+1,687	7.47	0.01
		1961	1,19,881	+95,620	394.13	0.03
		1971	2,57,251	+1,37,370	114.59	0.05
		1981	4,51,610	+1,94,359	75.55	0.07
		1991	6,42,015	+190,405	42.16	0.08
		2001	9,00,635	+2,58,620	40.28	0.09
		2011	10,55,450	+1,54,815	17.19	0.09
05	Uttarakhand	1901	19,79,866	---		0.83
		1911	21,42,258	+1,62,392	8.20	0.85
		1921	21,15,984	-26,274	-1.23	0.84
		1931	23,01,019	+1,85,035	8.74	0.82
		1941	26,14,540	+3,13,521	13.63	0.82
		1951	29,45,929	+3,31,389	12.67	0.82
		1961	36,10,938	+6,65,009	22.57	0.82
		1971	44,92,724	+8,81,786	24.42	0.82

State code	*India/State/Union Territory*	*Census year*	*Persons*	*Variation since the preceding Census absolute*	*Growth per cent*	*% Share in Indian population*
1	2	3	4	5	6	7
		1981	57,25,972	+12,33,248	27.45	0.84
		1991	70,50,634	+13,24,662	23.13	0.83
		2001	84,89,349	+14,38,715	20.41	0.83
		2011	1,00,86,292	+15,96,943	18.81	0.83
06	Haryana	1901	46,23,064	---		1.94
		1911	41,74,677	-4,48,387	-9.70	1.66
		1921	42,55,892	+81,215	1.95	1.69
		1931	45,59,917	+3,04,025	7.14	1.63
		1941	52,72,829	+7,12,912	15.63	1.65
		1951	56,73,597	+4,00,768	7.60	1.57
		1961	75,90,524	+19,16,927	33.79	1.73
		1971	1,00,36,431	+24,45,907	32.22	1.83
		1981	1,29,22,119	+28,85,688	28.75	1.89
		1991	1,64,63,648	+35,41,529	27.41	1.95
		2001	2,11,44,564	+46,80,916	28.43	2.06
		2011	2,53,51,462	+42,06,898	19.90	2.09

State code	India/State/Union Territory	Census year	Persons	Variation since the preceding Census absolute	Growth per cent	% Share in Indian population
1	2	3	4	5	6	7
07	NCT of Delhi	1901	4,05,819	---		0.17
		1911	4,13,851	+8,032	1.98	0.16
		1921	4,88,452	+74,601	18.03	0.19
		1931	6,36,246	+1,47,794	30.26	0.23
		1941	9,17,939	+2,81,693	44.27	0.29
		1951	17,44,072	+8,26,133	90.00	0.48
		1961	26,58,612	+9,14,540	52.44	0.61
		1971	40,65,698	+14,07,086	52.93	0.74
		1981	62,20,406	+21,54,708	53.00	0.91
		1991	94,20,644	+32,00,238	51.45	1.11
		2001	1,38,50,507	+44,29,863	47.02	1.35
		2011	1,67,87,941	+29,37,434	21.21	1.39
08	Rajasthan	1901	1,02,94,090	---		4.32
		1911	1,09,83,509	+6,89,419	6.70	4.36
		1921	1,02,92,648	-6,90,861	-6.29	4.10
		1931	1,17,47,974	+14,55,326	14.14	4.21
		1941	1,38,63,859	+21,15,885	18.01	4.35

State code	*India/State/Union Territory*	*Census year*	*Persons*	*Variation since the preceding Census absolute*	*Growth per cent*	*% Share in Indian population*
1	2	3	4	5	6	7
		1951	1,59,70,774	+21,06,915	15.20	4.42
		1961	2,01,55,602	+41,84,828	26.20	4.59
		1971	2,57,65,806	+56,10,204	27.83	4.70
		1981	3,42,61,862	+84,96,056	32.97	5.01
		1991	4,40,05,990	+97,44,128	28.44	5.20
		2001	5,65,07,188	+1,25,01,198	28.41	5.49
		2011	6,85,48,437	+1,20,41,249	21.31	5.66
09	Uttar Pradesh	1901	4,66,47,804	---		19.57
		1911	4,60,12,663	-6,35,141	-1.36	18.25
		1921	4,45,56,427	-14,56,236	-3.16	17.73
		1931	4,74,78,533	+29,22,106	6.56	17.02
		1941	5,39,20,630	+64,42,097	13.57	16.92
		1951	6,02,73,743	+63,53,113	11.78	16.69
		1961	7,01,43,635	+98,69,892	16.38	15.97
		1971	8,38,48,797	+1,37,05,162	19.54	15.30
		1981	10,51,36,540	+2,12,87,743	25.39	15.39
		1991	13,20,61,653	+2,69,25,113	25.61	15.60

State code	India/State/Union Territory	Census year	Persons	Variation since the preceding Census absolute	Growth per cent	% Share in Indian population
1	2	3	4	5	6	7
		2001	16,61,97,921	+3,41,36,268	25.85	16.16
		2011	19,98,12,341	+3,36,14,420	20.23	16.50
10	Bihar	1901	2,12,43,632	---		8.91
		1911	2,15,67,159	+3,23,527	1.52	8.56
		1921	2,13,58,905	-2,08,254	-0.97	8.50
		1931	2,34,38,371	+20,79,466	9.74	8.40
		1941	2,63,02,771	+28,64,400	12.22	8.25
		1951	2,90,85,017	+27,82,246	10.58	8.05
		1961	3,48,40,968	+57,55,951	19.79	7.93
		1971	4,21,26,236	+72,85,268	20.91	7.69
		1981	5,23,02,665	+1,01,76,429	24.16	7.65
		1991	6,45,30,554	+1,22,27,889	23.38	7.62
		2001	8,29,98,509	+1,84,67,955	28.62	8.07
		2011	10,40,99,452	+2,11,00,943	25.42	8.60
11	Assam	1901	32,89,680	---		1.38
		1911	38,48,617	+5,58,937	16.99	1.53
		1921	46,36,980	+7,88,363	20.48	1.85

State code	*India/State/Union Territory*	*Census year*	*Persons*	*Variation since the preceding Census absolute*	*Growth per cent*	*% Share in Indian population*
1	2	3	4	5	6	7
		1931	55,60,371	+9,23,391	19.91	1.99
		1941	66,94,790	+11,34,419	20.40	2.10
		1951	80,28,856	+13,34,066	19.93	2.22
		1961	1,08,37,329	+28,08,473	34.98	2.47
		1971	1,46,25,152	+37,87,823	34.95	2.67
		1981	1,80,41,248	+34,16,096	23.36	2.64
		1991	2,24,14,322	+43,73,074	24.24	2.65
		2001	2,66,55,528	+42,41,206	18.92	2.59
		2011	3,12,05,576	+45,50,048	17.07	2.58
12	West Bengal	1901	1,69,40,088	---		7.11
		1911	1,79,98,769	+10,58,681	6.25	7.14
		1921	1,74,74,348	-5,24,421	-2.91	6.95
		1931	1,88,97,036	+14,22,688	8.14	6.77
		1941	2,32,29,552	+43,32,516	22.93	7.29
		1951	2,62,99,980	+30,70,428	13.22	7.28
		1961	3,49,26,279	+86,26,299	32.80	7.95
		1971	4,43,12,011	+93,85,732	26.87	8.08

State code	India/State/Union Territory	Census year	Persons	Variation since the preceding Census absolute	Growth per cent	% Share in Indian population
1	2	3	4	5	6	7
		1981	5,45,80,647	+1,02,68,636	23.17	7.99
		1991	6,80,77,965	+1,34,97,318	24.73	8.04
		2001	8,01,76,197	+1,20,98,232	17.77	7.79
		2011	9,12,76,115	+1,10,99,918	13.84	7.54
13	Jharkhand	1901	60,68,233	---		2.55
		1911	67,47,122	+6,78,889	11.19	2.68
		1921	67,67,770	+20,648	0.31	2.69
		1931	79,08,737	+11,40,967	16.86	2.83
		1941	88,68,069	+9,59,332	12.13	2.78
		1951	96,97,254	+8,29,185	9.35	2.69
		1961	1,16,06,489	+19,09,235	19.69	2.64
		1971	1,42,27,133	+26,20,644	22.58	2.60
		1981	1,76,12,069	+33,84,936	23.79	2.58
		1991	2,18,43,911	+42,31,842	24.03	2.58
		2001	2,69,45,829	+51,01,918	23.36	2.62
		2011	3,29,88,134	+60,42,305	22.42	2.72

State code	*India/State/Union Territory*	*Census year*	*Persons*	*Variation since the preceding Census absolute*	*Growth per cent*	*% Share in Indian population*
1	2	3	4	5	6	7
14	Orissa	1901	1,03,02,917	---		4.32
		1911	1,13,78,875	+10,75,958	10.44	4.51
		1921	1,11,58,586	-2,20,289	-1.94	4.44
		1931	1,24,91,056	+13,32,470	11.94	4.48
		1941	1,37,67,988	+12,76,932	10.22	4.32
		1951	1,46,45,946	+8,77,958	6.38	4.06
		1961	1,75,48,846	+29,02,900	19.82	4.00
		1971	2,19,44,615	+43,95,769	25.05	4.00
		1981	2,63,70,271	+44,25,656	20.17	3.86
		1991	3,16,59,736	+52,89,465	20.06	3.74
		2001	3,68,04,660	+51,44,924	16.25	3.58
		2011	4,19,74,218	+51,69,558	14.05	3.47
15	Chhattisgarh	1901	41,81,554	---		1.75
		1911	51,91,583	+10,10,029	24.15	2.06
		1921	52,64,976	+73,393	1.41	2.09
		1931	60,28,778	+7,63,802	14.51	2.16
		1941	68,14,886	+7,86,108	13.04	2.14
		1951	74,56,706	+6,41,820	9.42	2.07

State code	India/State/Union Territory	Census year	Persons	Variation since the preceding Census absolute	Growth per cent	% Share in Indian population
1	2	3	4	5	6	7
		1961	91,54,498	+16,97,792	22.77	2.08
		1971	1,16,37,494	+24,82,996	27.12	2.12
		1981	1,40,10,337	+23,72,843	20.39	2.05
		1991	1,76,14,928	+36,04,591	25.73	2.08
		2001	2,08,33,803	+32,18,875	18.27	2.03
		2011	2,55,45,198	+47,11,395	22.61	2.11
16	Madhya Pradesh	1901	1,26,79,214	---		5.32
		1911	1,42,49,382	+15,70,168	12.38	5.65
		1921	1,39,06,774	-3,42,608	-2.40	5.53
		1931	1,53,26,879	+14,20,105	10.21	5.49
		1941	1,71,75,722	+18,48,843	12.06	5.39
		1951	1,86,14,931	+14,39,209	8.38	5.16
		1961	2,32,17,910	+46,02,979	24.73	5.29
		1971	3,00,16,625	+67,98,715	29.28	5.48
		1981	3,81,68,507	+81,51,882	27.16	5.59
		1991	4,85,66,242	+1,03,97,735	27.24	5.74
		2001	6,03,48,023	+1,17,81,781	24.26	5.87
		2011	7,26,26,809	+1,22,78,786	20.35	6.00

State code	*India/State/Union Territory*	*Census year*	*Persons*	*Variation since the preceding Census absolute*	*Growth per cent*	*% Share in Indian population*
1	2	3	4	5	6	7
17	Gujarat	1901	90,94,748	---		3.81
		1911	98,03,587	+7,08,839	7.79	3.89
		1921	1,01,74,989	+3,71,402	3.79	4.05
		1931	1,14,89,828	+13,14,839	12.92	4.12
		1941	1,37,01,551	+22,11,723	19.25	4.30
		1951	1,62,62,657	+25,61,106	18.69	4.50
		1961	2,06,33,350	+43,70,693	26.88	4.70
		1971	2,66,97,475	+60,64,125	29.39	4.87
		1981	3,40,85,799	+73,88,324	27.67	4.99
		1991	4,13,09,582	+72,23,783	21.19	4.88
		2001	5,06,71,017	+93,61,435	22.66	4.93
		2011	6,04,39,692	+97,68,675	19.28	4.99
18	Maharashtra	1901	1,93,91,643	---		8.13
		1911	2,14,74,523	+20,82,880	10.74	8.52
		1921	2,08,49,666	-6,24,857	-2.91	8.30
		1931	2,39,59,300	+31,09,634	14.91	8.59
		1941	2,68,32,758	+28,73,458	11.99	8.42
		1951	3,20,02,564	+51,69,806	19.27	8.86

State code	India/State/Union Territory	Census year	Persons	Variation since the preceding Census absolute	Growth per cent	% Share in Indian population
1	2	3	4	5	6	7
		1961	3,95,53,718	+75,51,154	23.60	9.01
		1971	5,04,12,235	+1,08,58,517	27.45	9.20
		1981	6,27,82,818	+1,23,70,583	24.54	9.19
		1991	7,89,37,187	+1,61,54,369	25.73	9.33
		2001	9,68,78,627	+1,79,41,440	22.73	9.42
		2011	11,23,74,333	+1,54,95,706	15.99	9.28
19	Andhra Pradesh	1901	1,90,65,921	---		8.00
		1911	2,14,47,412	+23,81,491	12.49	8.51
		1921	2,14,20,448	-26,964	-0.13	8.52
		1931	2,42,03,573	+27,83,125	12.99	8.68
		1941	2,72,89,340	+30,85,767	12.75	8.56
		1951	3,11,15,259	+38,25,919	14.02	8.62
		1961	3,59,83,447	+48,68,188	15.65	8.19
		1971	4,35,02,708	+75,19,261	20.90	7.94
		1981	5,35,51,026	+1,00,48,318	23.10	7.84
		1991	6,65,08,008	+1,29,56,982	24.20	7.86
		2001	7,62,10,007	+97,01,999	14.59	7.41
		2011	8,45,80,777	+83,70,770	10.98	6.99

State code	*India/State/Union Territory*	*Census year*	*Persons*	*Variation since the preceding Census absolute*	*Growth per cent*	*% Share in Indian population*
1	2	3	4	5	6	7
20	Karnataka	1901	1,30,54,754	---		5.48
		1911	1,35,25,251	+4,70,497	3.60	5.37
		1921	1,33,77,599	-1,47,652	-1.09	5.32
		1931	1,46,32,992	+12,55,393	9.38	5.25
		1941	1,62,55,368	+16,22,376	11.09	5.10
		1951	1,94,01,956	+31,46,588	19.36	5.37
		1961	2,35,86,772	+41,84,816	21.57	5.37
		1971	2,92,99,014	+57,12,242	24.22	5.34
		1981	3,71,35,714	+78,36,700	26.75	5.43
		1991	4,49,77,201	+78,41,487	21.12	5.31
		2001	5,28,50,562	+78,73,361	17.51	5.14
		2011	6,10,95,297	+82,44,735	15.60	5.05
21	Kerala	1901	63,96,262	---		2.68
		1911	71,47,673	+7,51,411	11.75	2.84
		1921	78,02,127	+6,54,454	9.16	3.10
		1931	95,07,050	+17,04,923	21.85	3.41
		1941	1,10,31,541	+15,24,491	16.04	3.46
		1951	1,35,49,118	+25,17,577	22.82	3.75

State code	India/State/Union Territory	Census year	Persons	Variation since the preceding Census absolute	Growth per cent	% Share in Indian population
1	2	3	4	5	6	7
		1951	1,69,03,715	+33,54,597	24.76	3.85
		1971	2,13,47,375	+44,43,660	26.29	3.89
		1981	2,54,53,680	+41,06,305	19.24	3.72
		1991	2,90,98,518	+36,44,838	14.32	3.44
		2001	3,18,41,374	+27,42,856	9.43	3.10
		2011	3,34,06,061	+15,64,687	4.91	2.76
22	Tamil Nadu	1901	1,92,52,630	---		8.08
		1911	2,09,02,616	+16,49,986	8.57	8.29
		1921	2,16,28,518	+7,25,902	3.47	8.61
		1931	2,34,72,099	+18,43,581	8.52	8.41
		1941	2,62,67,507	+27,95,408	11.91	8.24
		1951	3,01,19,047	+38,51,540	14.66	8.34
		1961	3,36,86,953	+35,67,906	11.85	7.67
		1971	4,11,99,168	+75,12,215	22.30	7.52
		1981	4,84,08,077	+72,08,909	17.50	7.08
		1991	5,58,58,946	+74,50,869	15.39	6.60
		2001	6,24,05,679	+65,46,733	11.72	6.07
		2011	7,21,47,030	+97,41,351	15.61	5.96

Table 6.1: Birth and death rate in India, 1901–2011

Year	*Population (in million)*	*Percentage decadal variation*	*Average annual exponential growth rate (per cent)*	*Crude birth rate*	*Crude death rate*	*Sex Ratio (females per 1,000 males)*	*Natural growth*
1901	238.4	NA	NA	45.80	44.40	972	1.40
1911	252.1	5.75	0.56	49.20	42.60	964	6.60
1921	251.3	-0.31	-0.03	48.10	47.20	955	0.90
1931	279	11	1.04	46.40	36.30	950	10.10
1941	318.7	14.22	1.33	45.20	31.20	945	14.00
1951	361.1	13.31	1.25	39.90	27.40	946	12.50
1961	439.2	21.64	1.96	41.70	22.80	941	18.90
1971	548.2	24.8	2.2	41.20	19.00	930	22.20
1981	683.3	24.66	2.22	37.20	15.00	934	22.20
1991	846.4	23.87	2.16	32.50	11.40	927	21.10
2001	1028.7	21.54	1.97	24.80	8.90	933	15.90
2011	1210.6	17.7	1.63	21.80	7.10	943	14.70

Table 6.3: Comparison of fertility rates of India and the World, 1971-2013

Year	*World*	*India*
1971	4.660058	5.2
1981	3.663666	4.5
1991	3.166691	3.6
2001	2.638866	3.1
2011	2.490856	2.4
2013	2.467228	2.3

Table 6.4: Percentage decadal growth rates of population of some major states from north and south of India, 1901–11 to 2001–11

Decade	*India*	*Kerala*	*Tamil Nadu*	*Karnataka*	*Andhra Pradesh*	*Madhya Pradesh*	*Bihar*	*Uttar Pradesh*	*Rajasthan*
1901-11	5.75	11.75	8.57	3.6	12.49	12.38	1.52	-1.36	6.7
1911-21	-0.31	9.16	3.47	-1.09	-0.13	-2.4	-0.97	-3.16	-6.29
1921-31	11	21.85	8.52	9.38	12.99	10.21	9.74	6.56	14.14
1931-41	14.22	16.04	11.91	11.09	12.75	12.06	12.22	13.57	18.01
1941-51	13.31	22.82	14.66	19.36	14.02	8.38	10.58	11.78	15.2
1951-61	21.64	24.76	11.85	21.57	15.65	24.73	19.79	16.38	26.2
1961-71	24.8	26.29	22.3	24.22	20.9	29.28	20.91	19.54	27.83
1971-81	24.66	19.24	17.5	26.75	23.1	27.16	24.16	25.39	32.97
1981-91	23.87	14.32	15.39	21.12	24.2	27.24	23.38	25.61	28.44
1991-2001	21.54	9.43	11.72	17.51	14.59	24.26	28.62	25.85	28.41
2001-11	17.7	4.91	15.61	15.6	10.98	20.35	25.42	20.23	21.31

Table 6.8: State-wise population density in India, 1901–2011[4]

States/UTs	*1901*	*1911*	*1921*	*1931*	*1941*	*1951*	*1961*	*1971*	*1981*	*1991*	*2001*	*2011(P)*
Andhra Pradesh	69	78	78	88	99	113	131	158	195	242	277	308
Andaman & Nicobar Islands	3	3	3	4	4	4	8	14	23	34	43	46
Arunachal Pradesh	-	-	-	-	-	-	4	6	8	10	13	17
Assam	42	49	59	71	85	102	138	186	230@	286	340	397
Bihar	157	163	162	180	202	223	267	324	402	685	881	1102
Chandigarh	193	162	159	174	198	213	1052	2257	3961	5632	7900	9252
Chhattisgarh	-	-	-	-	-	-	-	-	-	130	154	189
Dadra & Nagar Haveli	49	59	63	78	82	85	118	151	211	282	449	698
Daman & Diu	286	290	280	325	382	434	327	559	705	907	1413	2169
Delhi	274	279	329	429	619	1176	1793	2742	4194	6352	9340	11297
Goa	128	131	127	136	146	148	159	215	272	316	364	394
Gujarat	46	50	52	59	70	83	105	136	174	211	258	308
Haryana	105	94	96	103	119	128	172	227	292	372	478	573
Himachal Pradesh	35	34	35	37	41	43	51	62	77	93	109	123
Jammu & Kashmir	NA	NA	NA	NA	NA	NA	NA	NA	59+	77	100	124

States/UTs	*1901*	*1911*	*1921*	*1931*	*1941*	*1951*	*1961*	*1971*	*1981*	*1991*	*2001*	*2011(P)*
Jharkhand	-	-	-	-	-	-	-	-	-	274	338	414
Karnataka	68	71	70	76	85	101	123	153	194	235	276	319
Kerala	165	184	201	245	284	349	435	549	655	749	819	859
Lakshadweep	434	455	426	501	574	657	753	994	1258	1616	1895	2013
Madhya Pradesh	38	44	43	48	54	59	73	94	118	158	196	236
Maharashtra	63	70	68	78	87	104	129	164	204	257	315	365
Manipur	13	16	17	20	23	26	35	48	64	82	103	122
Meghalaya	15	18	19	21	25	27	34	45	60	79	103	132
Mizoram	4	4	5	6	7	9	13	16	23	33	42	52
Nagaland	6	9	10	11	11	13	22	31	47	73	120	119
Orissa	66	73	72	80	88	94	113	141	169	203	236	269
Pondicherry	501	523	496	526	579	645	750	959	1229	1683	2034	2598
Punjab	150	134	142	159	191	182	221	269	333	403	484	550
Rajasthan	30	32	30	34	41	47	59	75	100	129	165	201
Sikkim	8	12	12	15	17	19	23	30	45	57	76	86
Tamil Nadu	148	161	166	180	202	232	259	317	372	429	480	555
Tripura	17	22	29	36	49	61	109	148	196	263	305	350
Uttar Pradesh**	191	189	183	195	221	247	288	344	432	542	683	821

States/UTs	*1901*	*1911*	*1921*	*1931*	*1941*	*1951*	*1961*	*1971*	*1981*	*1991*	*2001*	*2011(P)*
Uttaranchal	37	40	39	43	48	55	67	84	107	133	159	189
West Bengal	191	203	197	213	262	296	394	499	615	767	903	1029
India	77	82	81	90	103	117	142	177[£]	216+[@]	267+*	325	382

Abbr. : P : Provisional.

NA : Not Available.

Note: **£**: While working out the density of India, Jammu & Kashmir has been excluded comparable figures of area and population are not available for that state.

+: For working out density of India, Jammu & Kashmir, the entire area and population of those portions of Jammu & Kashmir which are under illegal occupation of Pakistan and China have not been taken into account.

@: The 1981 Census could not be held in Assam. For calculating density for India and Assam, the population figures for 1981 for Assam as worked out by interpolation have been taken.

*: The 1991 Census was not held in Jammu & Kashmir. For calculating density of India and Jammu & Kashmir, the population figures for 1991for Jammu & Kashmir as projected by Standing Committee of Experts in Population Projections (October, 1989) have been taken.

** Values recalculated based on the population and area of the state for 1901-2011.

N. B.: Unit of population density in the table is persons per square kilometre.

Source: Office of the Registrar General and Census Commissioner, India.

Table 6.9: Variation in population density in some major states from India's north and south, 1901–2011

State	*1901*	*1911*	*1921*	*1931*	*1941*	*1951*	*1961*	*1971*	*1981*	*1991*	*2001*	*2011*[5]
Andhra Pradesh	69	78	78	88	99	113	131	158	195	242	277	308
Bihar	157	163	162	180	202	223	267	324	402	685	881	1102
Karnataka	68	71	70	76	85	101	123	153	194	235	276	319
Kerala	165	184	201	245	284	349	435	549	655	749	819	859
Madhya Pradesh	38	44	43	48	54	59	73	94	118	158	196	236
Rajasthan	30	32	30	34	41	47	59	75	100	129	165	201
Tamil Nadu	148	161	166	180	202	232	259	317	372	429	480	555
Uttar Pradesh	191	189	183	195	221	247	288	344	432	542	683	821

Table 7.1: NSDP and population growth

	1960–70			1970–80			1980–90			1990–2000			2000–10		
No. State/Union Territory	*Population growth*	*NSDP*	*Per capita NSDP*	*Population growth*	*NSDP*	*Per capita NSDP*	*Population growth*	*NSDP*	*Per capita NSDP*	*Population growth*	*NSDP*	*Per capita NSDP*	*Population growth*	*NSDP*	*Per capita NSDP*
Andhra Pradesh	21	31.11	11.79	23	34.61	13.40	24	65.86	43.00	15	29.10	16.70	11	66.54	63.80
Assam	35	5.25	-0.74	23	34.47	3.03	24	41.43	19.29	19	23.12	8.13	17	45.87	33.63
Bihar	21	24.67	-2.69	24	28.50	6.67	23	50.59	28.46	29	4.88	-9.80	25	69.96	66.54
Gujarat	29	48.30	19.39	28	42.52	17.68	21	59.89	39.34	23	60.58	47.44	19	84.32	61.46
Haryana	32	51.46	36.56	29	47.96	21.55	27	68.34	42.79	28	28.76	13.64	20	80.74	67.34
Karnataka	24	43.62	21.39	27	33.88	9.63	21	50.91	30.57	18	42.17	31.27	16	64.05	51.64
Kerala	26	39.97	15.64	19	26.50	8.26	14	33.40	19.67	9	40.48	30.62	5	67.80	62.35
Madhya Pradesh	29	28.58	2.96	27	34.53	11.21	27	48.89	24.23	24	29.88	15.63	20	46.01	20.54
Maharashtra	27	29.53	5.38	25	45.83	22.09	26	61.18	37.34	23	47.97	33.51	16	70.64	50.93
Orissa	25	99.50	74.49	20	38.87	19.61	20	29.84	11.37	16	35.34	22.26	14	78.67	63.95
Punjab	22	28.37	18.27	24	47.90	25.65	21	54.02	34.16	20	30.85	17.17	14	46.91	31.67
Rajasthan	28	57.82	35.92	33	16.01	-12.52	28	83.41	56.12	28	36.59	21.79	21	67.76	43.75
Tamil Nadu	22	28.47	7.66	17	23.18	6.29	15	57.10	42.25	12	39.50	32.23	16	50.05	47.71
Uttar Pradesh	20	27.93	9.78	25	33.87	10.78	26	50.26	22.76	26	18.73	6.34	20	49.57	31.15

	1960–70			1970–80			1980–90			1990–2000			2000–10		
No. State/Union Territory	*Population growth*	*NSDP*	*Per capita NSDP*	*Population growth*	*NSDP*	*Per capita NSDP*	*Population growth*	*NSDP*	*Per capita NSDP*	*Population growth*	*NSDP*	*Per capita NSDP*	*Population growth*	*NSDP*	*Per capita NSDP*
West Bengal	27	22.40	-1.57	23	27.07	5.96	25	42.40	16.92	18	47.03	34.55	14	52.94	45.47
Jharkhand	23			24			24			23			22	65.26	37.69
Chhattisgarh	27			20			26			18			23	90.77	65.42
Uttarakhand	24			27			23			20			19	75.54	70.42

Table 7.2 : Decadal variation in population and economic performance of Indian states since 1960-61

State/UT	1960-61		1990-91		2023–24 to 2026		1960 to 1990			1990 to 2026		
	Relative per capita income	Population	Relative per capita income	Population	Relative per capita income	Population	Relative per capita income	Population growth	Relative population growth	Relative per capita	Population growth	Relative population growth
Andhra Pradesh	89.9	3,59,83,447	79.9	6,65,08,008	162.6	9,22,83,509	-11.1	84.83	91.5	103.5	38.76	56.6
Assam	102.9	1,08,37,329	75.5	2,24,14,322	73.7	3,67,16,444	-26.6	106.83	115.2	-2.4	63.81	93.2
Bihar	70.3	3,48,40,968	46.9	6,45,30,554	32.8	13,22,65,622	-33.3	85.21	91.9	-30.1	104.97	153.3
Chhattisgarh	.	91,54,498	.	1,76,14,928	80	3,12,11,293		92.42	99.7		77.19	112.8
Delhi	218.3	26,58,612	195	94,20,644	250.8	2,25,39,864	-10.7	254.34	274.4	28.6	139.26	203.4
Gujarat	118.3	2,06,33,350	103.9	4,13,09,582	160.7	7,40,85,717	-12.2	100.21	108.1	54.7	79.34	115.9
Haryana	106.9	75,90,524	132.4	1,64,63,648	176.8	3,12,99,538	23.9	116.90	126.1	33.5	90.11	131.6
Himachal Pradesh	.	28,12,463	86.6	51,70,877	127.7	75,78,317		83.86	90.5	47.5	46.56	68.0
Jharkhand	-	1,16,06,489	-	2,18,43,911	57.2	4,09,58,112		88.20	95.2		87.50	127.8
Karnataka	96.7	2,35,86,772	81.1	4,49,77,201	180.7	6,89,62,476	-16.1	90.69	97.8	122.8	53.33	77.9
Kerala	84.6	1,69,03,715	74.1	2,90,98,518	152.5	3,62,06,930	-12.4	72.14	77.8	105.8	24.43	35.7
Maharashtra	133.7	3,95,53,718	131.2	7,89,37,187	150.7	12,93,08,436	-1.9	99.57	107.4	14.9	63.81	93.2
MP	82.4	2,32,17,910	71.4	4,85,66,242	77.4	8,96,72,807	-13.3	109.18	117.8	8.4	84.64	123.6
Orissa	70.9	1,75,48,846	54.3	3,16,59,736	88.5	4,71,47,414	-23.4	80.41	86.7	63.0	48.92	71.5
Rajasthan	92.8	2,01,55,602	73.9	4,40,05,990	91.2	8,36,42,572	-20.4	118.33	127.6	23.4	90.07	131.6

State/UT	1960-61		1990-91		2023–24 to 2026		1960 to 1990			1990 to 2026		
	Relative per capita income	*Population*	*Relative per capita income*	*Population*	*Relative per capita income*	*Population*	*Relative per capita income*	*Population growth*	*Relative population growth*	*Relative per capita*	*Population growth*	*Relative population growth*
Tamil Nadu	109.2	3,36,86,953	87.9	5,58,58,946	171.1	7,75,46,099	-19.5	65.82	71.0	94.7	38.82	56.7
Uttarakhand		36,10,938		70,50,634	141.3	1,19,93,473		95.26	102.8		70.10	102.4
Uttar Pradesh	82.4	7,01,43,635	63.3	13,20,61,653	50.8	24,28,59,394	-23.2	88.27	95.2	-19.7	83.90	122.6
West Bengal	127.5	3,49,26,279	82.4	6,80,77,965	83.7	10,05,21,733	-35.4	94.92	102.4	1.6	47.66	69.6

Source: Sanjeev Sanyal and Aakanksha Arora, 'Relative economic performance of Indian States: 1960-61 to 2023-24', Economic Advisory Council to the PM, EAC-PM/WP/31/2024, September 2024' and 'A - 2 Decadal Variation in Population since 1901, Census of India 2011'.

Table 7.3: GDP

State/UT	*1960–61*		*1970–71*		*1980–81*		*1990–91*	
	GDP share	*Pop. share*	*GDP share*	*Pop. share*	*GDP share*	*Pop. share*	*GDP share*	*Pop. share*
North								
Bihar	7.8	7.9	6.9	7.69	6.3	7.7	6	7.6
Delhi	1.4	0.6	1.5	0.74	2.3	0.9	2.6	1.1
Jharkhand	.	2.6	.	2.6	.	2.6	.	2.6
Madhya Pradesh	6.3	5.3	6.1	5.48	6.6	5.6	6.9	5.7
Chhattisgarh	.	2.1	.	2.12	.	2.1	.	2.1
Haryana	1.9	1.7	2.7	1.83	2.9	1.9	3.1	2
Rajasthan	4.4	4.6	5.1	4.7	3.9	5	4.7	5.2
Uttar Pradesh	14.4	16	13	15.3	13.2	15	12.6	16
Uttarakhand	.	0.8	.	0.82	.	0.8	.	0.8
Himachal Pradesh	.	0.6	0.7	0.63	0.7	0.6	0.6	0.6
North Total	**36.2**	**42.2**	**36**	**41.91**	**35.9**	**42.2**	**36.5**	**43.7**
South								
Andhra Pradesh	7.7	8.2	7.7	7.94	7	7.8	7.6	7.9
Karnataka	5.4	5.4	5.7	5.34	5.3	5.4	5.3	5.3
Kerala	3.4	3.9	3.8	3.89	3.6	3.7	3.2	3.4
Tamil Nadu	8.7	9.4	7.3	8.83	6.9	8.2	7.1	7.4
South Total	**25.2**	**26.9**	**24.5**	**26**	**22.8**	**25.1**	**23.2**	**24**
East								
Assam	2.6	2.47	2.4	2.67	2.1	2.64	2.4	2.65
Orissa	2.9	4	3.2	4	3.2	3.86	2.5	3.74
West Bengal	10.5	7.95	9.7	8.08	8.8	7.99	7.9	8.04
East Total	**16**	**14.42**	**15.3**	**14.75**	**14.1**	**14.49**	**12.8**	**14.43**
West								
Gujarat	5.8	6.1	6.7	6.22	6.3	6.1	6.4	6
Maharashtra	12.50	9.00	11.90	9.20	14.20	9.20	14.60	9.30
West Total	**18.30**	**15.10**	**18.60**	**15.42**	**20.50**	**15.30**	**21.00**	**15.30**

…lation Share

	2010–11		2020–21		2023–24 to 2026		Change seen from 1960 to 1990		Change seen from 1990 to 2026	
…. …re	GDP share	Pop. share	GDP share	Pop. share	GDP share	Pop. share	GDP share	Pop. share	GDP share	Pop. share
1	2.9	8.6	2.8	9.03	2.8	9.28				
4	3.7	1.4	3.7	1.5	3.6	1.58				
6	1.8	2.7	1.5	2.82	1.5	2.87				
9	3.8	6	4.7	6.2	4.5	6.29				
2	1.7	2.1	1.7	2.16	1.7	2.19				
1	3.8	2.1	3.6	2.16	3.6	2.2				
5	4.9	5.7	5.1	5.82	5	5.87				
6	8.7	17	8.2	16.9	8.4	17.03				
8	1.2	0.8	1.1	0.84	1.1	0.84				
6	0.8	0.6	0.8	0.54	0.7	0.53				
5	**33.3**	**47**	**33.2**	**47.97**	**32.9**	**48.68**	**0.83**	**3.55**	**-9.86**	**11.34**
4	8.4	7	9.5	6.64	9.7	6.47				
1	5.9	5.1	8.1	4.9	8.2	2.2				
1	3.8	2.8	3.8	2.6	3.8	2.54				
7	8.4	6	8.9	5.61	8.9	5.44				
6	**26.5**	**20.9**	**30.3**	**19.75**	**30.6**	**16.65**	**-7.94**	**-10.78**	**31.90**	**-30.63**
9	1.6	2.58	1.7	2.57	1.9	2.58				
8	2.9	3.47	2.7	3.35	2.8	3.31				
9	6.7	7.54	5.7	7.2	5.6	7.05				
6	**11.2**	**13.59**	**10.1**	**13.12**	**10.3**	**12.94**	**-20.00**	**0.07**	**-19.53**	**-10.33**
9	7.5	5	8	5.12	8.1	5.2				
0	15.20	9.30	13.00	4.75	13.30	9.07				
0	**22.70**	**14.30**	**21.00**	**9.87**	**21.40**	**14.27**	**14.75**	**1.32**	**1.90**	**-6.73**

Table 7.4: Quinquennial variation in per capita NSDP of UP and Kerala, 1960–61 to 2008-09[6]

State	*1960–61*	*1965-66*	*1970–71*	*1975–76*	*1980–81*	*1985–86*	*1990–91*	*1995–96*	*2000–01*	*2005–06*	*2008–09*
Kerala	259	380	594	954	1,385	2,140	4,200	9,004	20,094	33,044	49,316
Uttar Pradesh	252	373	486	721	1,272	2,003	3,590	5,872	9,828	13,315	18,214

Table 7.5: Comparison of UP and Kerala on the basis of population and growth rates of per capita NSDP, 1971-2011

	1971	*1981*	*1991*	*2001*	*2011*
Kerala Population growth rate (%)	26.29	19.24	14.32	9.43	4.91
Kerala per capita NSDP growth rate (%)	129.34	133.16	203.25	378.43	145.43
UP Population growth rate (%)	19.54	25.39	25.61	25.85	20.239
UP per capita NSDP growth rate (%)	92.86	161.73	182.23	173.76	85.33
Difference in NSDP	36.48	-28.57	21.02	204.67	60.1

Table 7.6: Female literacy versus population growth

Regional literacy	North		South		East		West		India	
	Literacy %	Population growth %	Literacy %	Population growth %	Literacy %	Population growth %	Literacy %	Population growth %	Literacy %	Population growth %
1961	7	21	19	17	15	29	18	25	13	22
1971	11	24	29	23	21	23	26	28	19	25
1981	15	27	34	22	28	22	34	26	25	25
1991	26	26	49	19	43	23	51	24	38	24
2001	42	26	62	14	56	18	64	23	53	22
2011	56	21	78	13	68	14	74	17	65	18

Table 7.7: Trends of Urbanisation in India, 1901–2011

Year	*Total population*	*Urban population*	*% Urban*
1901	23,83,96,327	2,58,54,967	10.85
1911	25,29,09,390	2,59,48,431	10.29
1921	25,13,21,213	2,80,91,299	11.18
1931	27,89,77,238	3,34,62,539	11.99
1941	31,86,60,580	44,162,191	13.86
1951	36,10,88,090	6,24,43,709	17.29
1961	43,92,34,771	7,89,36,603	17.97
1971	54,81,59,652	10,91,13,977	19.91
1981	68,33,29,097	15,76,80,171	23.34
1991	84,64,21,039	21,57,71,612	25.71
2001	1,02,87,37,436	28,61,19,689	27.82
2011	1,21,08,54,977	37,71,06,125	31.15

Table 7.8: Urban share of the states in 1901–2011

	Year	*Urban population*	*Urban share*	*Decadal growth*	*1901–2011*	*1901–51*	*1951–2011*	*1971–2011*
INDIA	1901[$]	2,58,54,967	10.85		186.96	59.35	80.08	56.38
	1951[@]	6,24,43,709	17.29	24.78				
	1971	10,91,13,977	19.91	10.76				
	2011	37,70,00,000	31.1	56.38				
Jammu & Kashmir	1901	1,58,748	7.42		251.89	89.35	85.84	40.45
	1951	4,57,213	14.05	7.11				
	1971	8,58,221	18.59	11.57				
	2011	32,02,812	26.11	2.94				
Himachal Pradesh	1901	77,332	4.03		148.88	60.05	55.50	43.49
	1951	1,53,827	6.45	69.47				
	1971	2,41,890	6.99	10.28				
	2011	6,88,552	10.03	2.36				
Punjab	1901	9,34,766	12.39		202.50	75.30	72.56	57.94
	1951	19,89,267	21.72	25.78				
	1971	32,16,179	23.73	2.94				
	2011	1,03,99,146	37.48	10.51				
Uttarakhand	1901	1,52,958	7.73		291.07	75.94	122.28	84.78
	1951	4,00,631	13.6	31.48				

	Year	*Urban population*	*Urban share*	*Decadal growth*	*1901–2011*	*1901–51*	*1951–2011*	*1971–2011*
	1971	7,34,856	16.36	19.08				
	2011	30,49,338	30.23	17.78				
Haryana	1901	5,74,074	12.42		180.84	37.44	104.34	97.40
	1951	9,68,494	17.07	27.5				
	1971	17,72,959	17.67	2.54				
	2011	88,42,103	34.88	20.6				
NCT of Delhi	1901	2,14,115	52.76		84.80	56.18	18.33	8.70
	1951	14,37,134	82.4	8.72				
	1971	36,47,023	89.7	1.07				
	2011	1,63,68,899	97.5	4.64				
Rajasthan	1901	15,50,656	15.06		65.14	22.84	34.43	41.07
	1951	29,55,275	18.5	21.15				
	1971	45,43,761	17.63	8.29				
	2011	1,70,48,085	24.87	6.33				
Uttar Pradesh	1901	52,37,653	11.23		98.31	21.55	63.15	60.22
	1951	82,25,068	13.65	9.11				
	1971	1,16,53,740	13.9	8.51				
	2011	4,44,95,063	22.27	7.17				

	Year	Urban population	Urban share	Decadal growth	1901–2011	1901–51	1951–2011	1971–2011
Bihar	1901	9,79,010	4.61		144.90	39.26	75.86	41.66
	1951	18,65,911	6.42	21.13				
	1971	33,56,334	7.97	7.56				
	2011	1,17,58,016	11.29	7.93				
Assam	1901	77,074	2.34		502.56	83.33	228.67	59.86
	1951	3,44,831	4.29	37.94				
	1971	12,89,222	8.82	22.33				
	2011	43,98,542	14.1	9.3				
West Bengal	1901	20,66,550	12.2		161.23	95.74	33.46	28.77
	1951	62,81,642	23.88	17				
	1971	1,09,67,033	24.75	1.23				
	2011	2,90,93,002	31.87	13.94				
Jharkhand	1901	1,17,975	1.94		1139.69	304.12	206.76	50.22
	1951	7,60,350	7.84	36.82				
	1971	22,77,632	16.01	39.34				
	2011	79,33,061	24.05	8.14				
Orissa	1901	2,54,684	2.47		575.71	64.37	311.08	98.45
	1951	5,94,070	4.06	35.33				

	Year	*Urban population*	*Urban share*	*Decadal growth*	*1901–2011*	*1901–51*	*1951–2011*	*1971–2011*
	1971	18,45,395	8.41	33.07				
	2011	70,03,656	16.69	11.34				
Chhattisgarh	1901	1,28,600	3.08		654.55	58.44	376.23	123.89
	1951	3,64,024	4.88	12.96				
	1971	12,07,892	10.38	24.61				
	2011	59,37,237	23.24	15.68				
Madhya Pradesh	1901	13,29,445	10.49		163.39	41.75	85.81	48.71
	1951	27,68,913	14.87	24.12				
	1971	55,76,875	18.58	11.66				
	2011	2,00,69,405	27.63	4.42				
Gujarat	1901	20,30,738	22.33		90.77	21.94	56.45	51.71
	1951	44,27,896	27.23	14.46				
	1971	74,96,500	28.08	8.96				
	2011	2,57,45,083	42.6	14.03				
Maharashtra	1901	32,17,202	16.59		172.57	73.30	57.29	45.08
	1951	2,01,013	28.75	36.19				
	1971	1,57,11,211	31.17	10.45				
	2011	5,08,18,259	45.22	6.58				

	Year	*Urban population*	*Urban share*	*Decadal growth*	*1901–2011*	*1901–51*	*1951–2011*	*1971–2011*
Andhra Pradesh	1901	18,39,750	9.65		137.72	80.52	31.69	18.80
	1951	4,20,325	17.42	29.71				
	1971	84,02,527	19.31	10.72				
	2011	1,46,10,410	22.94	-15.97				
Karnataka	1901	16,42,994	12.59		207.15	82.29	68.50	59.07
	1951	44,53,480	22.95	35				
	1971	71,22,093	24.31	8.87				
	2011	2,36,25,962	38.67	13.77				
Kerala	1901	4,54,499	7.11		570.89	89.59	253.86	193.72
	1951	18,25,832	13.48	24.35				
	1971	34,66,449	16.24	7.48				
	2011	1,59,34,926	47.7	83.74				
Tamil Nadu	1901	27,24,781	14.15		242.05	72.08	98.77	59.95
	1951	73,33,525	24.35	23.6				
	1971	1,24,64,834	30.26	13.38				
	2011	3,49,17,440	48.4	9.9				

Table 7.9: Comparison between urbanisation rates in Uttar Pradesh and Kerala vis-à-vis corresponding rate of urbanisation at the all-India level, 1901–2011

Year	*Uttar Pradesh*	*Kerala*	*India*
1901	11.20	7.11	10.85
1911	10.26	7.34	10.29
1921	10.61	8.73	11.18
1931	11.28	9.64	11.99
1941	12.52	10.84	13.86
1951	13.65	13.48	17.29
1961	12.81	15.11	17.97
1971	13.90	16.24	19.91
1981	17.83	18.74	23.34
1991	19.68	26.39	25.71
2001	20.78	25.96	27.82
2011	22.22	47.72	31.15

Table 8.1: World population, 20 countries and regional totals, 1–2001 AD

	1	*1000*	*1500*	*1600*	*1700*	*1820*	*1870*	*1913*	*1950*	*1973*	*2001*
Austria	500	700	2 000	2 500	2 500	3 369	4 520	6 767	6 935	7 586	8 151
Belgium	300	400	1 400	1 600	2 000	3 434	5 096	7 666	8 639	9 738	10 259
Denmark	180	360	600	650	700	1 155	1 888	2 983	4 271	5 022	5 353
Finland	20	40	300	400	400	1 169	1 754	3 027	4 009	4 666	5 176
France	5 000	6 500	15 000	18 500	21 471	31 250	38 440	41 463	41 829	52 157	59 658
Germany	3 000	3 500	12 000	16 000	15 000	24 905	39 231	65 058	68 375	78 950	82 281
Italy	7 000	5 000	10 500	13 100	13 300	20 176	27 888	37 248	47 105	54 797	57 845
Netherlands	200	300	950	1 500	1 900	2 333	3 610	6 164	10 114	13 438	15 981
Norway	100	200	300	400	500	970	1 735	2 447	3 265	3 961	4 503
Sweden	200	400	550	760	1 260	2 585	4 169	5 621	7 014	8 137	8 875
Switzerland	300	300	650	1 000	1 200	1 986	2 655	3 864	4 694	6 441	7 283
United Kingdom	800	2 000	3 942	6 170	8 565	21 239	31 400	45 649	50 127	56 210	59 723
12 Country Total	**17 600**	**19 700**	**48 192**	**62 580**	**68 796**	**114 571**	**162 386**	**227 957**	**256 377**	**301 103**	**325 088**
Portugal	500	600	1 000	1 100	2 000	3 297	4 327	5 972	8 443	8 976	10 066
Spain	4 500	4 000	6 800	8 240	8 770	12 203	16 201	20 263	28 063	34 837	40 087
Other	2 100	1 113	1 276	1 858	1 894	2 969	4 590	6 783	12 058	13 909	16 860
Total Western Europe	**24 700**	**25 413**	**57 268**	**73 778**	**81 460**	**133 040**	**187 504**	**260 975**	**304 941**	**358 825**	**392 101**
Eastern Europe	**4 750**	**6 500**	**13 500**	**16 950**	**18 800**	**36 457**	**53 557**	**79 530**	**87 637**	**110 418**	**120 912**
Former USSR	**3 900**	**7 100**	**16 950**	**20 700**	**26 550**	**54 765**	**88 672**	**156 192**	**179 571**	**249 712**	**290 349**
United States	680	1 300	2 000	1 500	1 000	9 981	40 241	97 606	152 271	211 909	285 024
Other Western Offshoots	490	660	800	800	750	1 250	5 847	13 795	24 186	38 932	54 815
Total Western Offshoots	**1 170**	**1 960**	**2 800**	**2 300**	**1 750**	**11 231**	**46 088**	**111 401**	**176 457**	**250 841**	**339 839**
Mexico	2 200	4 500	7 500	2 500	4 500	6 587	9 219	14 970	28 485	57 643	101 879
Other Latin America	3 400	6 900	10 000	6 100	7 550	15 118	31 180	65 965	137 453	250 756	429 334
Total Latin America	**5 600**	**11 400**	**17 500**	**8 600**	**12 050**	**21 705**	**40 399**	**80 935**	**165 938**	**308 399**	**531 213**
Japan	**3 000**	**7 500**	**15 400**	**18 500**	**27 000**	**31 000**	**34 437**	**51 672**	**83 805**	**108 707**	**126 892**
China	59 600	59 000	103 000	160 000	138 000	381 000	358 000	437 140	546 815	881 940	1 275 392
India	75 000	75 000	110 000	135 000	165 000	209 000	253 000	303 700	359 000	580 000	1 023 590
Other Asia	36 600	41 400	55 400	65 000	71 800	89 400	119 792	184 849	392 827	677 613	1 227 630
Total Asia (excluding Japan)	**171 200**	**175 400**	**268 400**	**360 000**	**374 800**	**679 400**	**730 792**	**925 689**	**1 298 642**	**2 139 553**	**3 526 612**
Africa	**16 500**	**32 300**	**46 610**	**55 320**	**61 080**	**74 236**	**90 466**	**124 697**	**227 333**	**390 034**	**821 088**
World	**230 820**	**267 573**	**438 428**	**556 148**	**603 490**	**1 041 834**	**1 271 915**	**1 791 091**	**2 524 324**	**3 916 489**	**6 149 006**

Table 8.2: Share of world population, 20 countries and regional totals, 1–2001 AD

	1	*1000*	*1500*	*1600*	*1700*	*1820*	*1870*	*1913*	*1950*	*1973*	*2001*
Austria	0.2	0.3	0.5	0.4	0.4	0.3	0.4	0.4	0.3	0.2	0.1
Belgium	0.1	0.1	0.3	0.3	0.3	0.3	0.4	0.4	0.3	0.2	0.2
Denmark	0.1	0.1	0.1	0.1	0.1	0.1	0.1	0.2	0.2	0.1	0.1
Finland	0.0	0.0	0.1	0.1	0.1	0.1	0.1	0.2	0.2	0.1	0.1
France	2.2	2.4	3.4	3.3	3.6	3.0	3.0	2.3	1.7	1.3	1.0
Germany	1.3	1.3	2.7	2.9	2.5	2.4	3.1	3.6	2.7	2.0	1.3
Italy	3.0	1.9	2.4	2.4	2.2	1.9	2.2	2.1	1.9	1.4	0.9
Netherlands	0.1	0.1	0.2	0.3	0.3	0.2	0.3	0.3	0.4	0.3	0.3
Norway	0.0	0.1	0.1	0.1	0.1	0.1	0.1	0.1	0.1	0.1	0.1
Sweden	0.1	0.1	0.1	0.1	0.2	0.2	0.3	0.3	0.3	0.2	0.1
Switzerland	0.1	0.1	0.1	0.2	0.2	0.2	0.2	0.2	0.2	0.2	0.1
United Kingdom	0.3	0.7	0.9	1.1	1.4	2.0	2.5	2.5	2.0	1.4	1.0
12 Country total	**7.6**	**7.4**	**11.0**	**11.3**	**11.4**	**11.0**	**12.8**	**12.7**	**10.2**	**7.7**	**5.3**
Portugal	0.2	0.2	0.2	0.2	0.3	0.3	0.3	0.3	0.3	0.2	0.2
Spain	1.9	1.5	1.6	1.5	1.5	1.2	1.3	1.1	1.1	0.9	0.7
Other	0.9	0.4	0.3	0.3	0.3	0.3	0.4	0.4	0.5	0.4	0.3
Total Western Europe	**10.7**	**9.5**	**13.1**	**13.3**	**13.5**	**12.8**	**14.7**	**14.6**	**12.1**	**9.2**	**6.4**
Eastern Europe	**2.1**	**2.4**	**3.1**	**3.0**	**3.1**	**3.5**	**4.2**	**4.4**	**3.5**	**2.8**	**2.0**
Former USSR	**1.7**	**2.7**	**3.9**	**3.7**	**4.4**	**5.3**	**7.0**	**8.7**	**7.1**	**6.4**	**4.7**
United States	0.3	0.5	0.5	0.3	0.2	1.0	3.2	5.4	6.0	5.4	4.6
Other Western Offshoots	0.2	0.2	0.2	0.1	0.1	0.1	0.5	0.8	1.0	1.0	0.9
Total Western Offshoots	**0.5**	**0.7**	**0.6**	**0.4**	**0.3**	**1.1**	**3.6**	**6.2**	**7.0**	**6.4**	**5.5**
Mexico			1.7	0.4	0.7	0.6	0.7	0.8	1.1	1.5	1.7
Other Latin America			2.3	1.1	1.3	1.5	2.5	3.7	5.4	6.4	7.0
Total Latin America	**2.4**	**4.3**	**4.0**	**1.5**	**2.0**	**2.1**	**3.2**	**4.5**	**6.6**	**7.9**	**8.6**
Japan	**1.3**	**2.8**	**3.5**	**3.3**	**4.5**	**3.0**	**2.7**	**2.9**	**3.3**	**2.8**	**2.1**
China	25.8	22.1	23.5	28.8	22.9	36.6	28.1	24.4	21.7	22.5	20.7
India	32.5	28.0	25.1	24.3	27.3	20.1	19.9	17.0	14.2	14.8	16.6
Other Asia	15.9	15.5	12.6	11.7	11.9	8.6	9.4	10.3	15.6	17.3	20.0
Total Asia (excl. Japan)	**74.2**	**65.6**	**61.2**	**64.7**	**62.1**	**65.2**	**57.5**	**51.7**	**51.4**	**54.6**	**57.4**
Africa	**7.1**	**12.1**	**10.6**	**9.9**	**10.1**	**7.1**	**7.1**	**7.0**	**9.0**	**10.0**	**13.4**
World	**100.0**	**100.0**	**100.0**	**100.0**	**100.0**	**100.0**	**100.0**	**100.0**	**100.0**	**100.0**	**100.0**

Table 8.3: Population, its growth rate and percentage share of EAG and non-EAG states/UTs in India's total population, 1901–2011

State	*1901*	*1911*	*1921*	*1931*	*1941*	*1951*	*1961*	*1971*	*1981*	*1991*	*2001*	*2011*
INDIA	238396327	252093390	251321213	278977238	318660580	361088090	439234771	548159652	683329097	846421039	1028737436	1210854977
Rajasthan	10294090	10983509	10292648	11747974	13863859	15970774	20155602	25765806	34261862	44005990	56507188	68548437
UP	46647804	46012663	44556427	47478533	53920630	60273743	70143635	83848797	105136540	132061653	166197921	199812341
Bihar	21243632	21567159	21358905	23438371	26302771	29085017	34840968	42126236	52302665	64530554	82998509	104099452
Orissa	10302917	11378875	11158586	12491056	13767988	14645946	17548846	21944615	26370271	31659736	36804660	41974218
Chhattisgarh	4181554	5191583	5264976	6028778	6814886	7456706	9154798	11637494	14010337	17614928	20833803	25545198
MP	12679214	14249382	13906774	15326879	17175722	18614931	23217910	30016625	38168507	48566242	60348023	72626809
Jharkhand	6068233	6747122	6767770	7908737	8868069	9697254	11606489	14227133	17612069	21843911	26945829	32988134
Uttarakhand	1979866	2142258	2115984	2301019	2614540	2945929	3610938	4492724	5725972	7050634	8489349	10086292
EAG Total	113397310	118272551	115422070	126721347	143328465	158690300	190279186	234059430	293588223	367333648	459125282	555680881
non-EAG Total	124999017	133820839	135899143	152255891	175332115	202397790	248955585	314100222	389740874	479087391	569612154	655174096
% share of EAG	47.57	46.92	45.93	45.42	44.98	43.95	43.32	42.7	42.96	43.4	44.63	45.89
Growth rate of EAG states		4.3	-2.41	9.79	13.11	10.72	19.91	23	25.43	25.12	24.99	21.03
Growth rate of non-EAG states		7.06	1.55	12.04	15.16	15.44	23	26.17	24.08	22.92	18.9	15.02

Table 10.1: Variation in Representation Index (Persons/Seat) at the all-India level, 1951–2014

Year	*Persons per seat (in lakh)*
1951	7.38
1962	8.89
1971	10.58
1984	13.45
1991	15.59
2004	19.93
2014	23.11
2024	26.55

Table 10.2: Representation Index and the difference from national representation Index for all states and UTs, 1951

S. No.	*State*	*Seats*	*Population (in lakhs)*	*Representation index*	*Difference*
1	Mysore	11	91	8.27	-0.89
2	Bombay	45	360	8	-0.62
3	Travancore-Cochin	12	93	7.75	-0.37
4	Rajasthan	20	153	7.65	-0.27
5	Madras	75	570	7.6	-0.22
6	Hyderabad	25	187	7.48	-0.1
7	Uttar Pradesh	86	632	7.35	0.03
8	Madhya Pradesh	29	212	7.31	0.07
9	Bihar	55	402	7.309	0.071
10	Orissa	20	146	7.3	0.08
11	West Bengal	34	248	7.29	0.09
12	Madhya Bharat	11	80	7.27	0.11
13	Punjab	18	126	7	0.38
14	PEPSU	5	35	7	0.38
15	Saurashtra	6	41	6.83	0.55
16	Vindhya Pradesh	6	36	6	1.38

S. No.	State	Seats	Population (in lakhs)	Representation index	Difference
17	Delhi	4	17	4.25	3.13
18	Bhopal	2	8	4	3.38
19	Ajmer	2	7	3.5	3.88
20	Himachal Pradesh	3	10	3.33	4.05
21	Kutch	2	6	3	4.38
22	Manipur	2	6	3	4.38
23	Tripura	2	6	3	4.38
24	Coorg	1	2	2	5.38
25	Bilaspur	1	1	1	6.38
26	Assam	12			
	India	**489**		7.38	

Table 10.3: Representation Index and the difference from national representation Index for all states and UTs, 1962

S. No.	State	Seats	Population (in lakhs)	Representation index	Difference
1	Tripura	2	8	4.00	4.89
2	Manipur	2	8	4.00	4.89
3	Delhi	5	27	5.40	3.49
4	Himachal Pradesh	4	28	7.00	1.89
5	Madras	41	337	8.22	0.67
6	Andhra Pradesh	43	360	8.37	0.52
7	Uttar Pradesh	86	738	8.58	0.31
8	Bihar	53	465	8.77	0.12
9	Orissa	20	176	8.80	0.09
10	Madhya Pradesh	36	324	9.00	-0.11
11	Maharashtra	44	396	9.00	-0.11
12	Mysore	26	236	9.08	-0.19
13	Rajasthan	22	202	9.18	-0.29
14	Punjab	22	203	9.23	-0.34
15	Gujarat	22	206	9.36	-0.47

S. No.	State	Seats	Population (in lakhs)	Representation index	Difference
16	Kerala	18	169	9.39	-0.50
17	West Bengal	36	349	9.69	-0.80
18	Assam	12	119	9.92	-1.03
	India	**494**		**8.89**	

Table 10.4: Representation index and the difference from national representation index for all major states and UTs, 1971

S. No.	State	Seats	Population (in lakh)	Representation index	Difference
1	Delhi	7	41	5.86	4.68
2	Jammu & Kashmir	6	46	7.67	2.87
3	Bihar	53	421	7.94	2.60
4	Madhya Pradesh	37	300	8.11	2.43
5	Himachal Pradesh	4	35	8.75	1.79
6	Uttar Pradesh	85	883	10.39	0.15
7	Assam	14	146	10.43	0.11
8	Punjab	13	136	10.46	0.08
9	Tamil Nadu	39	412	10.56	-0.02
10	Andhra Pradesh	41	435	10.61	-0.07
11	Mysore	27	293	10.85	-0.31
12	Orissa	20	219	10.95	-0.41
13	West Bengal	40	443	11.08	-0.54
14	Haryana	9	100	11.11	-0.57
15	Gujarat	24	267	11.13	-0.59
16	Maharashtra	45	504	11.20	-0.66
17	Kerala	19	213	11.21	-0.67
18	Rajasthan	23	258	11.22	-0.68
	India	**520**		**10.54**	

Table 10.5: Representation index and the difference from national representation index for all major states and UTs, 1984

S. No.	State	Seats	Population (in lakhs)	Representation Index	Difference
1	NCT of Delhi	7	62	8.86	3.72
2	Jammu & Kashmir	6	60	10.00	2.58
3	Himachal Pradesh	4	43	10.75	1.83
4	Tamil Nadu	39	484	12.41	0.17
5	Orissa	21	264	12.57	0.01
6	Andhra Pradesh	42	535	12.74	-0.16
7	Kerala	20	255	12.75	-0.17
8	Assam	14	180	12.86	-0.28
9	Haryana	10	129	12.90	-0.32
10	Punjab	13	168	12.92	-0.34
11	Bihar	54	699	12.94	-0.36
12	West Bengal	42	546	13.00	-0.42
13	Uttar Pradesh	85	1109	13.05	-0.47
14	Madhya Pradesh	40	522	13.05	-0.47
15	Maharashtra	48	628	13.08	-0.50
16	Gujarat	26	341	13.12	-0.54
17	Karnataka	28	371	13.25	-0.67
18	Rajasthan	25	343	13.72	-1.14
	India	**543**		**12.58**	

Table 10.6: Representation index and the difference from national representation index for all major states and UTs, 1991

S. No.	State	Seats	Population (in lakhs)	Representation Index	Difference
1	Himachal Pradesh	4	52	13.00	2.59
2	Jammu & Kashmir	6	78	13.00	2.59
3	NCT of Delhi	7	94	13.43	2.16
4	Tamil Nadu	39	559	14.33	1.26
5	Kerala	20	291	14.55	1.04

S. No.	State	Seats	Population (in lakhs)	Representation Index	Difference
6	Orissa	21	317	15.10	0.49
7	Punjab	13	203	15.62	-0.03
8	Andhra Pradesh	42	665	15.83	-0.24
9	Gujarat	26	413	15.88	-0.29
10	Assam	14	224	16.00	-0.41
11	Bihar	54	864	16.00	-0.41
12	Karnataka	28	450	16.07	-0.48
13	West Bengal	42	681	16.21	-0.62
14	Uttar Pradesh	85	1391	16.36	-0.77
15	Maharashtra	48	789	16.44	-0.85
16	Haryana	10	165	16.50	-0.91
17	Madhya Pradesh	40	662	16.55	-0.96
18	Rajasthan	25	440	17.60	-2.01
		543		15.59	

Table 10.7: Representation index and the difference from national representation index for all major states and UTs, 2004

S. No.	State	Seats	Population (in lakhs)	Representation Index	Difference
1	Himachal Pradesh	4	61	15.25	3.70
2	Kerala	20	318	15.90	3.05
3	Tamil Nadu	39	624	16.00	2.95
4	Jammu & Kashmir	6	101	16.83	2.12
5	Uttaranchal	5	85	17.00	1.95
6	Orissa	21	368	17.52	1.43
7	Andhra Pradesh	42	762	18.14	0.81
8	Punjab	13	244	18.77	0.18
9	Karnataka	28	529	18.89	0.06
10	Chhattisgarh	11	208	18.91	0.04
11	Assam	14	267	19.07	-0.12
12	West Bengal	42	802	19.10	-0.15

S. No.	State	Seats	Population (in lakhs)	Representation Index	Difference
13	Jharkhand	14	269	19.21	-0.26
14	Gujarat	26	507	19.50	-0.55
15	NCT of Delhi	7	139	19.86	-0.91
16	Maharashtra	48	969	20.19	-1.24
17	Bihar	40	830	20.75	-1.80
18	Uttar Pradesh	80	1662	20.78	-1.83
19	Madhya Pradesh	29	603	20.79	-1.84
20	Haryana	10	211	21.10	-2.15
21	Rajasthan	25	565	22.60	-3.65
		543		**18.95**	

Table 10.8: Representation index and the difference from national representation index for all major states and UTs, 2014

S. No.	State	Seats	Population (in lakhs)	Representation Index	Difference
1	Kerala	20	334	16.70	5.60
2	Himachal Pradesh	4	69	17.25	5.05
3	Tamil Nadu	39	721	18.49	3.81
4	Orissa	21	420	20.00	2.30
5	Andhra Pradesh	42	846	20.14	2.16
6	Uttaranchal	5	101	20.20	2.10
7	Jammu & Kashmir	6	125	20.83	1.47
8	Punjab	13	277	21.31	0.99
9	West Bengal	42	912	21.71	0.59
10	Karnataka	28	611	21.82	0.48
11	Assam	14	312	22.29	0.01
12	Chhattisgarh	11	255	23.18	-0.88
13	Gujarat	26	604	23.23	-0.93
14	Maharashtra	48	1124	23.42	-1.12
15	Jharkhand	14	330	23.57	-1.27
16	NCT of Delhi	7	168	24.00	-1.70

S. No.	State	Seats	Population (in lakhs)	Representation Index	Difference
17	Uttar Pradesh	80	1998	24.98	-2.68
18	Madhya Pradesh	29	726	25.03	-2.73
19	Haryana	10	254	25.40	-3.10
20	Bihar	40	1040	26.00	-3.70
21	Rajasthan	25	685	27.40	-5.10
		543		**22.3**	

Table 10.9: Rankings of some major states from north and south India on the basis of their Representation Indices (Persons/Seat) at the all-India level, 1971–2014

Year	Uttar Pradesh	Kerala	Bihar	Tamil Nadu	Andhra Pradesh	Rajasthan	Madhya Pradesh	Karnataka
1971	6	17	3	9	10	18	4	11
1984	13	7	11	4	6	18	14	17
1991	14	5	11	4	8	18	17	12
2004	18	2	17	3	7	21	19	9
2014	17	1	20	3	5	21	18	10

Table 10.10: Rankings of some major states from north and south India on the basis of their Representation Indices (Persons/Seat) at the all-India level, 1951–2014

Year	Uttar Pradesh	Kerala	Bihar	Tamil Nadu
1951	12	16	10	14
1962	7	16	8	5
1971	6	17	3	9
1984	13	7	11	4
1991	14	5	11	4
2004	18	2	17	3
2014	17	1	20	3

Table 10.11: Ratio of population represented per seat in national parliaments of some major countries of the world

Country	*Population (in lakhs)*	*Number of seats*	*Ratio (Population/no. of seats)*
USA	3,291	435	7.57
Brazil	2,110	513	4.11
Russia	1,459	450	3.24
Japan	1,269	465	2.73
Germany	835	709	1.18
UK	675	650	1.04
France	651	577	1.13
Pakistan	2,166	342	6.33

Notes

1. DELIMITATION AND THE NORTH–SOUTH DIVIDE: AN OVERVIEW

1. TNN, 'Freeze on LS Seats till 2026', *The Times of India*, 24 August 2001, http://timesofindia.indiatimes.com/articleshow/1712525869.cms?utm_source=contentofinterest&utm_medium=text&utm_campaign=cpps.
2. ET Now, 'Devolution of taxes: It's north vs. south', *The Economic Times*, 27 March 2018, https://economictimes.indiatimes.com/markets/stocks/news/devolution-of-taxes-its-north-vs-south/articleshow/63478023.cms?from=mdr.
3. The Hindu Bureau, 'T.N. House passes resolutions against delimitation and "One Nation, One Election" proposal', *The Hindu*, 14 February 2024, https://www.thehindu.com/news/national/tamil-nadu/tn-cm-stalin-moves-resolutions-against-proposed-delimitation-process-and-one-nation-one-election-policy/article67845057.ece.
4. Divya Chandrababu, 'Stalin: Delimitation a Damocles sword hanging over head of TN, southern states', *Hindustan Times*, 20 September 2023, https://www.hindustantimes.com/india-news/stalin-delimitation-a-damocles-sword-hanging-over-head-of-tn-southern-states-101695217578540.html.
5. Ibid.
6. Vijaita Singh, 'Women's reservation Bill will be implemented only after 2029: Amit Shah', *The Hindu*, 20 September 2023, https://www.thehindu.com/news/national/womens-reservation-bill-will-be-implemented-only-after-2029-amit-shah/article67327038.ece.
7. Shilpa Nair, '"Sword hanging over the South": Tamil Nadu leaders raise alarm over delimitation', *India Today*, 21 September 2023, https://www.indiatoday.in/india/story/womens-reservation-bill-tamil-nadu-leaders-on-delimitation-sword-hanging-over-south-2438832-2023-09-21.

8. Express News Service, 'Delimitation on population basis unfair to southern states: DMK MP', *The Indian Express*, 20 December 2022, https://indianexpress.com/article/india/delimitation-population-basis-unfair-southern-states-dmk-mp-8333315/.
9. Jeemon Jacob, 'Why delimitation has intensified the debate on North–South divide', *India Today*, 25 September 2023, https://www.indiatoday.in/india-today-insight/story/why-delimitation-has-intensified-the-debate-on-north-south-divide-2440387-2023-09-25.
10. Shilpa Nair, '"Sword hanging over the South": Tamil Nadu leaders raise alarm over delimitation', *India Today*, 21 September 2023, https://www.indiatoday.in/india/story/womens-reservation-bill-tamil-nadu-leaders-on-delimitation-sword-hanging-over-south-2438832-2023-09-21.
11. K.M. Chandrasekhar, 'Delimitation will require ample sagacity', *The New Indian Express*, 23 December 2023, https://www.newindianexpress.com/opinions/2023/Dec/22/delimitation-will-require-ample-sagacity-2644067.html.
12. Ibid.
13. PTI, 'BJP may not create massive majority for Hindi belt: Tharoor on delimitation', *Deccan Herald*, 2 July 2024' Also see, https://www.deccanherald.com/india/bjp-may-not-create-massive-majority-for-hindi-belt-tharoor-on-delimitation-3089738.
14. Ibid.
15. Shashi Tharoor, 'For the sake of the south: Time to stop geographic discrimination', *Open*, 20 October 2023, https://openthemagazine.com/essays/for-the-sake-of-the-south/.
16. Ibid.
17. Ibid.
18. Ibid.
19. Ibid.
20. Ibid.
21. Shashi Tharoor, 'India's looming demographic divide', Project Syndicate, 16 December 2022, https://www.project-syndicate.org/commentary/india-demographic-divide-north-south-population-growth-by-shashi-tharoor-2022-12.
22. Ibid.
23. Gvani Khanna, 'Justice KM Joseph expresses concerns about "One Nation One Election" proposal, impending delimitation', *Live Law*, 31 May 2024. Also see, https://www.livelaw.in/top-stories/justice-km-joseph-expresses-

concerns-about-one-nation-one-election-proposal-impending-delimitation-259366.

24. Ramchandra Guha, 'India's feet of clay: How Modi's supremacy will hinder his country's rise', *Foreign Affairs*, 20 February 2024, https://www.foreignaffairs.com/india/indias-feet-clay-modi.
25. Ibid.
26. Ibid.
27. Sanjaya Baru, 'The geography of power, in north, south & west India', *Deccan Herald*, 11 December 2023. Also see, https://www.deccanchronicle.com/opinion/columnists/101223/sanjaya-baru-the-geography-of-power-in-north-south-west-india.html.
28 Christophe Jaffrelot and Kalaiyarasan A., 'Why delimitation could deepen India's north-south fault line', *India Express*, 3 August 2023.
29. Ibid.
30. T.A. Johnson, 'D K Suresh's "separate country" remark an echo of Cong's pro-Kannada pitch to counter BJP's Hindutva', *The Indian Express*, 4 February 2024, https://indianexpress.com/article/political-pulse/dk-suresh-separate-country-remark-congress-pro-kannada-pitch-bjp-hindutva-9142599/.
31. Ibid.
32. Tina Edwin, 'The republic of south India', *The Hindu Business Line*, 23 April 2019, https://www.thehindubusinessline.com/specials/india-file/the-republic-of-south-india/article26914315.ece.
33. Mihir S. Sharma, 'North and south India are growing apart and it could be a problem', *Business Standard*, 24 April 2018, https://www.business-standard.com/article/current-affairs/north-and-south-india-are-growing-apart-and-it-could-be-a-problem-118042400129_1.html.
34. HT Correspondent, 'Siddaramaiah leads protest in Delhi against "injustice" to southern states', *Hindustan Times*, 7 February 2024, https://www.hindustantimes.com/india-news/siddaramaiah-leads-protest-in-delhi-against-injustice-to-southern-states-101707299480056.html.
35. Express Web Desk, '"Rights of states being trampled upon, Centre eating into our financial resources": Pinarayi Vijayan at Jantar Mantar', *The Indian Express*, 8 February 2024, https://indianexpress.com/article/india/pinarayi-vijayan-janta-mantra-protest-against-centre-speech-9150474/.
36. Business Today Desk, '"Delimitation cannot be done abruptly": Ex-RBI governor D Subbarao's two-point solution for north-south divide', *Business Today*, 2 May 2024. Also see, https://www.businesstoday.in/india/story/

delimitation-cannot-be-done-abruptly-ex-rbi-governor-d-subbaraos-two-point-solution-to-north-south-divide-428049-2024-05-02.

37. Ibid.
38. Ibid.
39. ETB Sivapriyan, 'Southern states should get "slightly larger portion" of funds from Centre: Arvind Subramanian', *Deccan Herald*, 7 January 2024, https://www.deccanherald.com/india/tamil-nadu/southern-states-should-get-slightly-larger-portion-of-funds-from-centre-arvind-subramanian-2839000.
40. DTNEXT Bureau, '2026 delimitation will increase disaffection between "rich" south & poor Hindi heartland states: Arvind Subramanian', *DT NEXT*, 7 January 2024, https://www.dtnext.in/news/tamilnadu/2026-delimitation-will-increase-disaffection-between-rich-south-poor-hindi-heartland-states-arvind-subramanian-759608.
41. ETB Sivapriyan, 'Southern states should get "slightly larger portion" of funds from Centre: Arvind Subramanian', *Deccan Herald*, 7 January 2024, https://www.deccanherald.com/india/tamil-nadu/southern-states-should-get-slightly-larger-portion-of-funds-from-centre-arvind-subramanian-2839000.
42. Terms of Reference of the 15th Finance Commission, Volume-II Annexes, October 2020, p. 15.
43. Asit Ranjan Mishra and Remya Nair, 'Kerala opposes plan to use 2011 Census data for funds allocation', *Mint*, 18 January 2018, https://www.livemint.com/Politics/k3JXVCawZgbCDoX2gwFfQJ/Kerala-opposes-plan-to-use-2011-Census-data-for-funds-alloca.html.
44. ET Now, 'Devolution of taxes: It's north vs south', *The Economic Times*, 27 March 2018, https://economictimes.indiatimes.com/markets/stocks/news/devolution-of-taxes-its-north-vs-south/articleshow/63478023.cms?from=mdr. Also see, 'Federalism and fairness', *The Hindu*, 3 April 2018, https://www.thehindu.com/opinion/op-ed/federalism-and-fairness/article62111783.ece.
45. PTI, '15th Finance Commission: Progressive states will lose heavily, says Naidu', *The Economic Times*, 7 May 2018, https://economictimes.indiatimes.com/news/politics-and-nation/15th-finance-commission-progressive-states-will-lose-heavily-says-naidu/articleshow/64061986.cms?from=mdr.
46. Ibid.
47. Ibid.

48. Ahona Sengupta, 'Chandrababu Naidu plays sub-nationalism card, says Modi govt diverting taxes collected from south to northern States', *CNN-News18*, 13 March 2018, https://www.news18.com/news/politics/andhra-cm-chandrababu-naidu-alleges-centre-diverting-tax-revenues-from-south-for-development-of-northern-states-1687683.html.
49. See 'Rob X to pay Y', *Outlook*, 28 August 28, updated on 5 February 2022, https://www.outlookindia.com/national/rob-x-to-pay-y-news-209954.
50. Ibid.
51. Ibid.
52. Ibid.
53. See 'Finance Commission recommendation—southern states stand to lose Rs 12,204 cr in revenue share', *Business Line*, 30 July 2000.
54. Ibid.
55. HT Correspondent, 'India cannot afford a north–south divide', *Hindustan Times*, 2 April 2018, https://www.hindustantimes.com/editorials/india-cannot-afford-a-north-south-divide/story-mEgQwOJzuu04pGsEfKzXHM.html.
56. Outlook Web Desk, 'The great divide', *Outlook*, 6 February 2022, https://www.outlookindia.com/society/the-great-divide-news-201412.
57. https://www.india.gov.in/my-government/constitution-india/amendments/constitution-india-eighty-fourth-amendment-act-2001.
58. *Lok Sabha Debates*, Vol. XIX, Nos. 21–29, 21 August 2001, p. 238.
59. Ibid, pp. 240–41.
60. Ibid, p. 241.
61. Ibid.
62. Ibid, p. 242.
63. Ibid, p. 247.
64. Ibid, p. 249.
65. Ibid.
66. Ibid, p. 250.
67. Ibid.
68. Ibid, pp. 251–52.
69. Ibid, p. 253.
70. Ibid.
71. Ibid, p. 255–56
72. Ibid, p. 257–58.
73. Ibid, p. 257.
74. Ibid, p. 264.
75. Ibid, p. 266.

76. Ibid, pp. 285–86.
77. https://www.india.gov.in/my-government/constitution-india/amendments/constitution-india-forty-second-amendment-act-1976.
78. Ibid.
79. National Archives of India, Election Commission of India, Legal I, File No. 5-3-1976, 'Freezing the representation of the states in Parliament and in the State Legislatures on the basis of 1971 Census', p. 1.
80. Ibid.
81. Ibid, p. 8.
82. Ibid, p. 25.
83. National Archives of India, Election Commission of India, Delimitation, File No. 282 – Del–Const–Amendment–76, 'Delimitation of constituencies on the basis of voters–Constitution Amendment Bill by Shri C.K. Chandrappan, M.P', p. 2.
84. Ibid, p. 3.
85. Ibid.
86. *Lok Sabha Debates*, Vol. II, No. 5, 28 May 1971, p. 311.
87. Ibid, p. 312.
88. Ibid.
89. Ibid, p. 317.
90. Ibid, p. 322.
91. Ibid.
92. Ibid. p. 323.
93. Ibid.
94. Ibid.
95. Ibid.
96. Ibid, pp. 323–24.
97. Ibid, p. 327.
98. Ibid.
99. Ibid, p. 332.
100. Ibid.
101. Ibid, p. 336.
102. Ibid.
103. Ibid, p. 337.
104. Ibid, p. 338.
105. Ibid, pp. 343–44.
106. Ibid, p. 345.
107. Ibid, pp. 345–46.
108. Ibid, p. 346.

109. Jay Raina, 'Finally, the delimitation exercise may take off', *Hindustan Times*, 3 August 2001.
110. Statesman News Service, 'Legislature seats frozen till 2026', *Statesman*, 22 August 2001.
111. Times News Network, 'Freeze on number of LS seats extended', *The Times of India*, 24 August 2001.
112. K.C. Sivaramakrishna, 'North-South divide and delimitation blues', *Economic & Political Weekly*, Vol. 35, No. 35/36 (26 Aug.–8 Sep. 2000), p. 3093. Also see, K.C. Sivaramakrishna, *People's Participation in Urban Governance* (New Delhi: Institute of Social Science, 2006).
113. Ibid.
114. Ibid.
115. Ibid, p. 3097.
116. Ibid, p. 3093.
117. Alistair McMillan, 'Constitution 91st Amendment Bill: A constitutional fraud?', *Economic & Political Weekly*, Vol. 36, No. 14/15 (14–20 Apr. 2001), p. 1171.
118. Ibid, p. 1172.
119. Ibid, p. 1174.
120. The Indian Express, 'If accepted, the Bill will reaffirm a 25-yr-old folly and extended it for 25 more yrs', *The Indian Express*, 21 August 2001.
121. Sanjay Kumar, 'Delimitation of constituencies', *The Hindu*, 17 September 2001.
122. Alaka Malwade Basu, 'The "politicization" of fertility to achieve non-demographic objectives', *Population Studies*, Vol. 51, No. 1 (March 1997), pp. 5–18, https://www.jstor.org/stable/pdf/2175069.pdf?refreqid=fastly-default%3A7ef8a360f5d7558c68717e6217951c94&ab_segments=&origin=&initiator=&acceptTC=1.
123. T.K. Viswanathan, 'The dilemmas of delimitation', *The Hindu*, 1 August 2017, https://www.thehindu.com/opinion/op-ed/the-dilemmas-of-delimitation/article19397838.ece.
124. PTI, 'Need to "promote population": N. Chandrababu Naidu', *Financial Express*, 20 April 2016, https://www.financialexpress.com/india-news/need-to-promote-population-n-chandrababu-naidu/240321/.
125. Akash Kolluru, 'Chandrababu Naidu gets facts wrong about number of births registered in Andhra Pradesh', *India Today*, 26 January 2019, https://www.indiatoday.in/india/story/chandrababu-naidu-births-andhra-pradesh-population-1439955-2019-01-26.

126. Srikanth Aluri, 'Chandrababu Naidu's "more kids" mantra for aging southern states', *The Times of India*, 20 October 2024. Also see, https://timesofindia.indiatimes.com/india/chandrababu-naidus-more-kids-mantra-for-aging-southern-states/articleshow/114382808.cms.
127. Ibid.

2. THE 'OVERPOPULATION' DEBATE: INDIA AND THE WORLD

1. For example, see *The Antioch Review, Foreign Affairs, Law and Contemporary Problems, The Review of Economics and Statistics, The Journal of Marriage and Family, Social Problems, Commentary, The Milbank Quarterly, The Public Opinion Quarterly, World Politics, Journal of Farm Economics, Population and Development Review*, etc. during the 1950s.
2. Frank W. Notestein, Irene B. Taeuber, Dudley Kirk, Ansley J. Coale and Louise K. Kiser, *The Future Population and the Soviet Union Population: Projections 1940–1970* (Geneva: League of Nations, 1944).
3. Ibid, p. 15.
4. Ibid.
5. Ibid.
6. Ibid.
7. Rebecca Williams, 'The Rockefeller Foundation, the Population Council, and Indian population control' University of Warwick, UK, 2010, pp. 1–15.
8. Ibid.
9. Ibid, p. 3.
10. Warren S. Thompson, 'The population problem of India', *The Antioch Review*, Vol. 17, No. 1 (Spring, 1957). Also see, Warren Simpson Thompson and David T. Lewis, *Population Problems* (India: Tata McGraw-Hill Publishing Co. Ltd, 1965).
11. Ibid, p. 22.
12. Ibid, p. 25.
13. Ibid, p. 26.
14. Ibid.
15. Kingsley Davis, 'The political impact of new population trends', *Foreign Affairs* (January 1958).
16. Ibid, p. 2.
17. Ibid.
18. Ibid.
19. Ibid.
20. Ibid.

21. David G. Mandelbaum, 'Population problem in India and Pakistan', *Far Eastern Survey*, Vol. 18, No. 24 (30 Nov. 1949). Also see, David G. Mandelbaum, *Society in India: Continuity and Change* (India: University of California Press, 1970). Also see, David G. Mandelbaum, *Human Fertility in India: Social Components and Policy Perspectives* (London: University of California Press, 1974).
22. Ibid, p. 283.
23. Ibid.
24. Ibid, p. 287.
25. Ibid, p. 286.
26. Stephen Enke, *Economics for Development* (Taiwan: Prentice-Hall, 1963).
27. Stephen Enke, 'The gains to India from population control: Some money measures and incentive schemes', *The Review of Economics and Statistics*, Vol. 42, No. 2 (May 1960).
28. Ibid, p. 175.
29. Ibid.
30. Ibid.
31. Irene B. Taeuber, 'Japan's population: Miracle, model or case study?', *Foreign Affairs* (July 1962).
32. Ibid, p. 6.
33. S.N. Agarwala, 'Population control in India: Progress and prospects', *Law and Contemporary Problems*, Vol. 25, No. 3 (Summer, 1960). Also see, S.N. Agarwala, *India's Population Problems* (New Delhi: Tata McGraw-Hill Publishing Co. Ltd, 1972).
34. Ibid, p. 584.
35. Ibid, p. 578.
36. Ibid.
37. Ibid.
38. Ibid, p. 579.
39. Moye W. Freymann, 'Population control in India', *Marriage and Family Living*, Vol. 25, No. 1 (Feb. 1963).
40. Ibid, p. 1.
41. Hudson Hoagland, 'Mechanisms of population control', *Daedalus*, Vol. 93, No. 3, *Population, Prediction, Conflict, Existentialism* (Summer, 1964), pp. 812–29, https://www.jstor.org/stable/pdf/20026860.pdf.
42. Ibid.
43. Leo G. Reeder and Goteti B. Krishnamurty, 'Family planning in rural India: A problem in social change', *Social Problems*, Vol. 12, No. 2 (Autumn, 1964).

44. Ibid, p. 223.
45. Ibid.
46. Dennis H. Wrong, 'Population myths', *Commentary* (November 1964).
47. Ibid, p. 63.
48. Ibid, p. 62
49. T.J. Samuel, 'The development of India's policy of population control', *The Milbank Memorial Fund Quarterly*, Vol. 44, No. 1, Part 1 (Jan. 1966).
50. Ibid, p. 49.
51. Ibid.
52. J. Mayone Stycos, 'Politics and population control in Latin America', *World Politics*, Vol. 20, No. 1 (Oct. 1967). Also see, J. Mayone Stycos, *Demography as an Interdiscipline* (Canada: Transaction Publishers, 1989).
53. Ibid, p. 70.
54. Donald J. Bogue, 'Prospects for population control', *Journal of Farm Economics*, Vol. 49, No. 5 (Oxford University Press, Dec. 1967.)
55. Ibid, p. 1094.
56. Ibid, p. 1097.
57. H. George Liebmann and Hans Lehfeldt, 'Population control in India', *The Journal of Sex Research*, Vol. 8, No. 3 (Aug. 1972), pp. 189–93.
58. Ibid, p. 189.
59. Paul R. Ehrlich, *The Population Bombo* (United States: Buccaneer Books, 1971).
60. Ibid, p. xi.
61. Ibid, p. 1.
62. D.B. Blacklock, 'The population problem of India', *The British Medical Journal*, Vol. 2, No. 4329 (25 Dec. 1943), pp. 805–7.
63. Jack Zlotnick, 'Population pressure and political indecision', *Foreign Affairs*, Vol. 39, No. 4 (Jul. 1961), pp. 683–94.
64. Robert S. McNamara, 'Address to the University of Notre Dame', *World Bank*, 1 May 1969.
65. Alfred Sauvy, 'Le "faux problème" de la population mondiale', *Population*, Vol. 4, No. 3 (1949), pp. 447–62. Also see, Alfred Sauvy, 'Alfred Sauvy on the world population problem: A view in 1949', *Population and Development Review*, Vol. 16, No. 4 (Dec. 1990), p. 760, https://www.jstor.org/stable/1972967.
66. Ibid.
67. Paul Demeny and Geoffrey McNicoll, 'World population 1950–2000: Perception and response', *Population and Development Review*, Vol. 32 (2006), p. 5.

68. Ibid, p. 31.
69. Ibid, p. 7, https://www.jstor.org/stable/pdf/20058943.pdf?refreqid=fastly-default%3A95d4c2fd3321b88c6f909d0a61efebfa&ab_segments=&origin=&initiator=&acceptTC=1.
70. Dudley Kirk, 'Demographic transition theory', *Population Studies*, Vol. 50, No. 3 (Nov. 1996), pp. 361–87, https://doi.org/10.1080/0032472031000149536. Also see, Dudley Kirk, *Europe's Population in the Interwar Years* (United Kingdom: Gordon & Breach, 1969).
71. The World Population Conference, held in Belgrade, Yugoslavia, from 30 August to 10 September 1965, in accordance with the provisions of Economic and Social Council resolutions 820 C (XXI) and 933 B (XXXV) and General Assembly resolution 1838 (XVII), was the second scientific Conference on the problems of population to be convened under the auspices of the United Nations, the first one having been held in Rome in 1954.
72. Chelsea Follett, 'Neo-Malthusianism and coercive population control in China and India: Overpopulation concerns often result in coercion', Cato Institute, 21 July 2020, https://www.cato.org/policy-analysis/neo-malthusianism-coercive-population-control-china-india-overpopulation-concerns#history-neo-malthusianism.
73. Paul Demeny, Geoffrey McNicoll, 'World population 1950–2000: Perception and response', *Population and Development Review*, Vol. 32 (2006), pp. 12–13, https://www.jstor.org/stable/pdf/20058943.pdf?refreqid=fastly-default%3A95d4c2fd3321b88c6f909d0a61efebfa&ab_segments=&origin=&initiator=&acceptTC=1.
74. Some of the important surveys were: S.N. Agarwala, Beliefs and Practices Relating to Family Planning: A Study of Three Delhi Villages (I959), S. Chandrasekhar, Family Planning in an Indian Village: Motivations and Methods (1959), Guha, Research on Contraceptives Used by Abhor Hill Tribes, in Director General of Health Services, Family Planning in India (1959), India-Harvard-Ludhiana Population Study at Khanna, Punjab, K.K. Mathen, A Survey on the Attitude of Men and Women of Calcutta on Certain Aspects of the Population Problems (1954), Indian Institute of Public Opinion, Measurement of Knowledge of Family Planning Amongst Indian Women: A Study in the City of Calcutta, Monthly Public Opinion Surveys (Dec. I958), N.V. Sovani and Kunmudini Dandekar, Fertility Survey of Nasik, Kolaba and Satara (North) Districts (1955), and WHO, Final Report on Pilot Studies in Family Planning (1954), etc.

75. Paul Demeny and Geoffrey McNicoll, 'World population 1950–2000: Perception and response', *Population and Development Review*, Vol. 32 (2006), p. 17, https://www.jstor.org/stable/pdf/20058943.pdf?refreqid=fastly-default%3A95d4c2fd3321b88c6f909d0a61efebfa&ab_segments=&origin=&initiator=&acceptTC=1.
76. Gunnar Myrdal, *Asian Drama: An Inquiry into the Poverty of Nations* (New Delhi: Kalyani Publishers, 1982). Also see, Pierre Jalee, *The Third World in World Economy* (New York: Monthly Review Press, 1969).
77. Gyan Prakash, *Emergency Chronicles: Indira Gandhi and Democracy's Turning Point* (Princeton University Press: 2019).
78. Ibid, p. 262.
79. Ibid.
80. Ibid.
81. Ibid, p. 23.
82. Ibid, p. 265.
83. Ibid, p. 269.
84. Ibid.
85. Ibid.
86. David C. Engerman, *The Price of Aid: The Economic Cold War in India* (Harvard University Press, 2018).
87. Ibid.
88. Nick Cullather, *The Hungry World: America's Cold War Battle against Poverty in Asia* (Harvard University Press, 2010).
89. Ibid.
90. Matthew Connelly, 'Population control in India: Prologue to the Emergency period', *Population and Development Review*, Vol. 32, No. 4 (Dec. 2006), pp. 629–67.
91. Ibid, p. 651.
92. Ibid, p. 631.
93. Deepak Lal, *The Poverty of 'Development Economics'* (United Kingdom: MIT Press, 2000). Also see, Deepak Lal, 'India: Population change and its consequences', *Population and Development Review*, Vol. 32, *The Political Economy of Global Population Change, 1950–2050* (2006), pp. 145–82.
94. Peter Bauer, 'Population scares', *Commentary*, Law, Government & Society, November 1987, https://www.commentary.org/articles/peter-bauer/population-scares/ Also see, Peter T. Bauer, *Equality, the Third World, and Economic Delusion* (United Kingdom: Harvard University Press, 1981).
95. Ibid.
96. Ibid.

97. Ibid.
98. Ibid.
99. Ibid.
100. Ibid.
101. Ibid.
102. Ibid.
103. Pyare Kishan Wattal, *The Population Problem in India: A Census Study* (India: Bennett, Coleman & Company Limited, 1916).
104. Radhakamal Mukerjee, *Population Problems in India* (India: Madras Law Journal, 1938).
105. Dwarkanath Ghosh, *Pressure of Population and Economic Efficiency in India* (India: Indian Council of World Affairs, 1946).
106. Gyan Chand, *India's Teeming Millions: A Contribution to the Study of the Indian Population Problem* (United Kingdom: G. Allen & Unwin Limited, 1939).
107. Gyan Chand, *The Problem of Population* (India: H. Milford, Oxford University Press, 1945), p. 6.
108. Ibid.
109. Jawaharlal Nehru, *The Discovery of India* (Calcutta: Signet Press, 1946), pp. 557–61.
110. Ibid.
111. Ibid.
112. R.A. Gopalaswami, *Census of India 1951*, Vol. 1, Part I-A-Report (New Delhi: Government of India Press, 1953).
113. Ibid, p. 213.
114. Ibid, p. 216.
115. Ibid.
116. Ibid, p. 217.
117. Ibid, p. 218.
118. Ibid.
119. Ibid.
120. Ibid, p. 224.
121. Ibid.
122. Ibid, p. 225.
123. Ibid, p. 226.
124. M. Vijayanunni, 'R.A. Gopalaswami's 1951 census report revisited', *Demography India*, Vol. 29, No. 2 (2000), pp. 131–34.
125. Ibid, p. 134.
126. Ibid.

127. Please see, Sripati Chandrasekhar, *Population and Law in India* (India: Blackie & Son, 1976).
128. Douglas Martin, 'Sripati Chandrasekhar, Indian demographer, dies at 83', *The New York Times*, 23 June 2001, https://www.nytimes.com/2001/06/23/world/sripati-chandrasekhar-indian-demographer-dies-at-83.html. Also see, https://populationreview.com/in-memoriam/.
129. Ibid.
130. Ibid.
131. S. Chandrasekhar, 'How India is tackling her population problem', *Demography*, Vol. 5, No. 2, Progress and Problems of Fertility Control around the World (1968), p. 643.
132. Ibid, p. 5.
133. Ibid.
134. Sripati Chandrasekhar, *Population and Law in India* (India: Blackie & Son, 1976).
135. S. Chandrasekhar, 'How India is tackling her population problem', *Demography*, Vol. 5, No. 2, Progress and Problems of Fertility Control around the World (1968).
136. Please visit: https://indianexpress.com/article/business/business-others/ashish-bose-who-coined-bimaru-dies-at-84/.
137. Ashish Bose, 'Demographic transition and demographic imbalance in India', *Health Transition Review,* Vol. 6, Supplement, The shaping of fertility and mortality declines: the contemporary demographic transition (1996), p. 89.
138. Ibid.
139. Ibid, p. 94.
140. Ashish Bose, 'Beyond population projections: Growing north–south disparity', *Economic & Political Weekly*, Vol. 42, No. 15 (14–20 Apr. 2007), p. 1328, https://www.jstor.org/stable/4419463.
141. Kingsley Davis, *The Population of India and Pakistan* (New Jersey: Princeton University Press, 1951). Also see, Kingsley Davis, 'Population policy: Will current programs succeed?' *Science*, Vol. 158, No. 3802 (10 Nov. 1967), pp. 730–39, doi: 10.1126/science.158.3802.730.
142. National Archives of India, Prime Minister's Office, Establishment, File No. 38/87/68 PMS, Correspondence with JRD Tata.
143. Ibid.

3. DEMOGRAPHIC TRANSITION: A CONCEPTUAL REVIEW

1. David Lam, 'How the world survived the population bomb: Lessons from 50 years of extraordinary demographic history', *Demography*, Vol. 48, No. 4 (Nov. 2011), p. 1234.
2. Angus Maddison, *The World Economy: Historical Statistics* (Paris: Development Centre of the Organisation for Economic Co-operation and Development, 2003), p. 256.
3. Frank W. Notestein, 'Population: The long view' in Theodore W. Schultz (ed.), *Food for the World* (Chicago: University of Chicago Press, 1945).
4. Please visit https://link.springer.com/referenceworkentry/10.1007/978-0-387-33754-8_123, accessed on 27 September 2024.
5. The concept of 'carrying capacity' is an important parameter in the logistic growth equation of population derived and published by Pierre François Verhuls in 1838. It points to the limiting role that environment plays in the context of sustaining a given size of human population. Nonetheless, it must be borne in mind that Verhulst did not coin the term carrying capacity.
6. Please visit https://worksinprogress.co/issue/frances-baby-bust/.
7. Thomas Malthus, *An Essay on the Principle of Population* (London: J. Johnson, 1798), p. 10. Also see, https://oll-resources.s3.us-east-2.amazonaws.com/oll3/store/titles/311/Malthus_0195_EBk_v6.0.pdf.
8. Ibid, p. 42.
9. Ibid, pp. 42–3.
10. Adolphe Landry, 'Adolphe Landry on the demographic revolution', *Population and Development Review*, Vol. 13, No. 4 (Dec. 1987), pp. 731–40, https://doi.org/10.2307/1973031. Also see, Adolphe Landry, *La revolution démographique* (Paris: Sirey, 1934).
11. Angus Maddison, *The World Economy: Historical Statistics* (Paris: Development Centre of the Organisation for Economic Co-operation and Development, 2001).
12. Tim Dyson, *Population and Development: The Demographic Transition* (London: Zed Books, 2010), p. 56.
13. G. Clark, *A Farewell to Alms: A Brief Economic History of the World* (Princeton: Princeton University Press, 2007), p. 30.
14. Ibid, p. 144.
15. Robert C. Allen et al., 'Wages, prices, and living standards in China, Japan, and Europe, 1738-1925', *Economics Series Working Papers* 316, University of Oxford, Department of Economics (2007).

16. R.C. Allen, 'A review of Gregory Clark's *A Farewell to Alms: A Brief Economic History of the World*', *Journal of Economic Literature*, Vol. 46, No. 4 (2008), p. 949.
17. Angus Maddison, *The World Economy: A Millennial Perspective* (Paris: Development Centre of the Organisation for Economic Co-operation and Development, 2001).
18. J.C. Caldwell, *Demographic Transition Theory* (Dordrecht, The Netherlands: Springer, 2006), p. 304.
19. See the Maddison Project Database, 2018, https://www.rug.nl/ggdc/historicaldevelopment/maddison/releases/maddison-project-database-2018.
20. Ibid.
21. Please visit: https://www.ons.gov.uk/peoplepopulationandcommunity/populationandmigration/populationestimates/bulletins/annualmidyearpopulationestimates/mid2021#the-uk-population-at-mid-2021.
22. Please visit: https://data.worldbank.org/indicator/SP.POP.TOTL?locations=FR.
23. Paul R. Ehrlich, *The Population Bomb* (New York: Ballantine Books, 1988), p. 83.
24. Please visit: https://data.worldbank.org/.
25. See https://data.worldbank.org/indicator/sp.dyn.tfrt.in.
26. Tim Dyson, *Population and Development: The Demographic Transition* (London: Zed Books, 2010), p. 56.
27. Warren S. Thompson, 'Population', *American Journal of Sociology*, Vol. 34, No. 6 (May 1929), pp. 959–75.
28. Adolphe Landry, *La revolution démographique* (Paris: Sirey, 1934).
29. 'Challenges of Modernity', Joachim von Puttkamer, Stanislav Holubec and Włodzimierz Borodziej (eds), *The Routledge History Handbook of Central and Eastern Europe in the Twentieth Century*, Volume 1 (Taylor & Francis, 2020).
30. Warren S. Thompson, 'Population', *American Journal of Sociology*, Vol. 34, No. 6 (May 1929), pp. 959–75.
31. Dudley Kirk, 'Demographic transition theory', *Population Studies*, Vol. 50, No. 3 (Nov. 1996), p. 379.
32. Ibid.
33. Thomas McKeown, 'The McKeown thesis: A historical controversy and its enduring influence', *American Journal of Public Health*, Vol. 92, No. 5 (Jun. 2002), pp. 25–29, https://www.ncbi.nlm.nih.gov/pmc/articles/PMC1447153/. Thomas McKeown and R.G. Record, 'Reasons for the

decline of mortality in England and Wales during the nineteenth century', *Population Studies,* Vol. 16, No. 2 (Nov. 1962).

34. Tim Dyson, *Population and Development: The Demographic Transition* (London: Zed Books, 2010).
35. Ibid, p. 5.
36. J.C. Caldwell, *Demographic Transition Theory* (Dordrecht, The Netherlands: Springer, 2006).
37. Brigitte Berger, *Societies in Change: An Introduction to Comparative Sociology* (New York: Basic Books, 1971), p. 174.
38. Thomas Malthus explained this concept in his seminal work, *An Essay on Population*, published in 1798.
39. P.M. Kulkarni, 'Demographic transition in India', CSRD, SSS, Jawaharlal Nehru University (4 December 2014), p. 3. Also see, P.M. Kulkarni, *Shaping India's Population Policy and Programme: Internal Factors and External Influences* (India: Gokhale Institute of Politics and Economics, 2008).
40. Ibid, p. 4.
41. Tim Dyson, *Population and Development: The Demographic Transition* (London: Zed Books, 2010), p. 3.
42. For more, please visit the section on 'Demographic transition' at https://ourworldindata.org/world-population-growth.
43. https://ourworldindata.org/demographic-transition.
44. Also see, Paul Bairoch, *Cities and Economic Development: From the Dawn of History to the Present* (United Kingdom: University of Chicago Press, 1988).
45. Also see, Angus Maddison, *The World Economy: A Millennial Perspective* (Paris: Development Centre of the Organisation for Economic Co-operation and Development, 2001).
46. Also see, Robert William Fogel, *The Escape from Hunger and Premature Death, 1700–2100* (New York: Cambridge University Press, 2004).
47. https://data.worldbank.org/indicator/SP.POP.GROW.
48. https://ourworldindata.org/world-population-growth.
49. Thomas McKeown and R.G. Record, 'Reasons for the decline of mortality in England and Wales during the nineteenth century', *Population Studies,* Vol. 16, No. 2 (Nov. 1962), pp. 94–122. Also see, Thomas McKeown, *The Modern Rise of Population* (Kiribati: Academic Press, 1976).
50. Ibid, p. 121.
51. The summary of his thoughts on this topic can be found in his book, *The Role of Medicine: Dream, Mirage, or Nemesis?* (London: The Nuffield Provincial Hospitals Trust, 1976).

52. Simon Szreter, 'The importance of social intervention in Britain's mortality decline 1850–1914: A reinterpretation of the role of public health', *Society for the Social History of Medicine* journal (1988), p. 33. Among other critiques of McKeown's thesis, at least two stand out: E.A. Wrigley and R.S. Schofield, *The Population History of England 1541–1871: A Reconstruction* (Cambridge, England: Cambridge University Press, 1981) and S. Ryan Johansson, 'Food for thought: Rhetoric and reality in modern mortality history', *Historical Methods*, Vol 27, No. 3 (1994), pp. 101–26.
53. Paul Bairoch, *Cities and Economic Development: From the Dawn of History to the Present* (United Kingdom: University of Chicago Press, 1988).
54. J.V. Grauman, 'Orders of magnitude of the world's urban population in history', *Population Bulletin of the United Nations*, Vol. 8 (1976), pp. 16–33.
55. Tim Dyson, *Population and Development: The Demographic Transition* (London: Zed Books, 2010), p. 53.
56. A.K. Sharma, 'Demographic transition: A determinant of urbanization', *Social Change*, Vol. 13, No. 7 (Sep. 1979), https://pubmed.ncbi.nlm.nih.gov/12338541/.
57. Tim Dyson, 'The role of the demographic transition in the process of urbanization', *Population and Development Review*, Vol. 37 (2011), pp. 34–54.
58. Patricia L. McGrath, Bruce Stokes and Lester R. Brown, 'Twenty-two dimensions of the population problem', *Worldwatch Paper* 5 (1976).
59. Frank W. Notestein, 'Economic problems of population change', Proceedings of the Eighth International Conference of Agricultural Economists, New York, 1953, pp. 13–31, https://u.demog.berkeley.edu/~jrw/Biblio/Eprints/%20M-O/Notestein.EconomicProbsPopChange.pdf.
60. Yuri Yegorov, 'Urbanization and demographic transition' (2003), https://www.researchgate.net/publication/280574724_Urbanization_and_Demographic_Transition.
61. 'Problems in the measurement, description, and analysis of historical urbanization', in A. van der Woude, Akira Hayami and Jan de Vries (eds), *Urbanization in History: A Process of Dynamic Interactions (International Studies in Demography)* (Oxford University Press, 1990).
62. Tim Dyson, 'The role of the demographic transition in the process of urbanization', *Population and Development Review*, Vol. 37 (2011), p. 39, https://www.jstor.org/stable/41762398.
63. 'Problems in the measurement, description, and analysis of historical urbanization', in A. van der Woude, Akira Hayami and Jan de Vries (eds),

Urbanization in History: A Process of Dynamic Interactions (International Studies in Demography) (Oxford University Press, 1990), p. 58.

64. Tim Dyson, 'Population and development: The demographic transition', Keynote address to the 48th session of the United Nations Commission on Population and Development, New York, 13 April 2015, p. 20. Also see, https://www.un.org/development/desa/pd/sites/www.un.org.development.desa.pd/files/undp-cpd48_201504_keynoteaddress_timdyson.pdf.
65. Ibid, p. 6.
66. Tim Dyson, 'The role of the demographic transition in the process of urbanization', *Population and Development Review*, Vol. 37 (2011), pp. 34–54.
67. Tim Dyson, *Population and Development: The Demographic Transition* (London: Zed Books, 2013), p. 22.
68. Dorothy Swaine Thomas, *Social and Economic Aspects of Swedish Population Movements, 1750–1933* (New York: Macmillan, 1941).
69. See Ceylon (1923) *Report on the Census of Ceylon, General Tables, Volume IV*, Department of Census and Statistics (Colombo: Government printer).
70. Ibid, p. 22.
71. *World Population Prospects: The 2008 Revision* (New York: United Nations, 2009).
72. Thomas Malthus, *An Essay on the Principle of Population* (London: J. Johnson, 1798), p. 20.
73. Ron J. Lesthaeghe, *The Decline of Belgian Fertility 1800–1970* (Princeton University Press, 1977).
74. Ibid.
75. Karen Oppenheim Mason, 'Culture and the fertility transition: Thoughts on theories of fertility decline', *Genus*, Vol. 48, No. 3/4 (Luglio-Dicembre 1992), pp. 1–14, https://www.jstor.org/stable/29789099.
76. Ibid, p. 1.
77. Ibid, p. 11.
78. Ibid.
79. Ibid., p. 10.
80. George A. Akerlof, Janet L. Yellen and Michael L. Katz, 'An analysis of out-of-wedlock childbearing in the United States', *The Quarterly Journal of Economics*, Vol. CXI, No. 2 (May 1996), pp. 277–317, https://www.jstor.org/stable/2946680.

81. Christine A. Bachrach, 'Culture and demography: From reluctant bedfellows to committed partners', *Demography*, Vol. 51, No. 1 (Feb. 2014), pp. 3–25, https://www.jstor.org/stable/42919986.
82. Ibid.
83. Heidi Colleran, 'The cultural evolution of fertility decline', *Philosophical Transactions B*, Vol. 371, No. 1692 19 April 2016, https://doi.org/10.1098/rstb.2015.0152.
84. Ibid.
85. The term has been used by John Caldwell. See J.C. Caldwell, *Demographic Transition Theory* (Dordrecht, The Netherlands: Springer, 2006), p. 306.
86. Dirk J. van de Kaa, 'Europe's second demographic transition', *Population Bulletin*, Vol. 42, No. 1 (1 Mar. 1987), pp. 1–57.
87. Christophe Z. Guilmoto and S. Irudaya Rajann, 'Spatial patterns of fertility transition in Indian districts', *Population and Development Review*, Vol. 27, No. 4 (Dec. 2001), pp. 713–38, https://www.jstor.org/stable/2695184.

4. THE DEMOGRAPHIC HISTORY OF INDIA (1872–1941)

1. *Memorandum on The Census of British India of 1871–72* (London: George Edward Eyre and William Spottiswoode, 1875), p. 5.
2. Ibid.
3. *Census of India, 1901*, Volume IA, Part II, Tables, p. 5.
4. See *Census of British India of 1871–72*, p. 8.
5. *General Report on the Census of India, 1891* (London: George Edward Eyre and William Spottiswoode, 1893), p. 11.
6. *Report on the Census of British India taken on the 17th February 1881*, Vol. I (London: Eyre and Spottiswoode, 1883), p. 1.
7. Ibid, p. 2.
8. Ibid, p. 197.
9. Based on the Census of Bengal.
10. Ibid.
11. Ibid.
12. *Census of India, 1921*, Volume XV, Punjab and Delhi, Part II, p. 2.
13. W. Chichele Plowden, *Report on the Census of British India taken on 17 February 1881* (London: Eyre and Spottiswoode, 1883).
14. Ibid.
15. For a discussion on whether India was too densely populated or 'overpopulated' in comparison with other countries, please see, Alva

Myrdal, 'Population trends in densely populated areas', *Proceedings of the American Philosophical Society*, Vol. 95, No. 1 (13 Feb. 1951), pp. 1–7.

16. Ibid, p. 8.
17. Ibid.
18. *General Report on the Census of India, 1891* (London: George Edward Eyre and William Spottiswoode, 1893), p. 11.
19. *Memorandum on the Census of British India of 1871-72* (London: George Edward Eyre and William Spottiswoode, 1875), p. 7, http://piketty.pse.ens.fr/files/ideologie/data/CensusIndia/CensusIndia1871/CensusBritishIndia1871.pdf.
20. Also see, N.V. Sovani, *The Population Problem in India: A Regional Approach* (Poona: Gokhale Institute of Politics and Economics, 1942).
21. See 1901 Census Report.
22. Some estimates of mortality go up to 2 crore. See, for example, D.V. Glass and D.E.C. Eversley (eds), *Population in History: Essays in Historical Demography* (London: Edward Arnold Publishers Ltd, 1965), p. 15.
23. See *Census of British India 1881*, p. 9.

6. NORTH VERSUS SOUTH: THE DEMOGRAPHIC DIVIDE RE-EXAMINED

1. Please visit https://new.census.gov.in/nada/index.php/catalog/42611/download/46274/Census%20of%20India%202011-Provisional%20Population%20Totals.pdf.
2. Ibid, pp. 58–59.
3. P.N. Mari Bhat, 'Indian demographic scenario, 2025', Population Research Centre, Institute of Economic Growth, Delhi (June 2001), p. 4.
4. https://data.worldbank.org/indicator/SP.DYN.TFRT.IN?end=2022&locations=IN&start=1960&view=chart.
5. Please visit: https://cbhidghs.mohfw.gov.in/index4.php?lang=1&level=0&linkid=806&lid=817.
6. Please visit https://data.worldbank.org/indicator/SP.DYN.TFRT.IN.
7. J.R. Rele, 'Fertility levels and trends in India, 1951–81', *Population and Development Review,* Vol. 13, No. 3 (1987), p. 523. Also see, J.R. Rele, *Fertility Levels and Trends in India, 1951–81: Data and Perspectives* (United States: East-West Population Institute, East-West Center, 1988).
8. P.N. Mari Bhat, 'Indian demographic scenario, 2025', Population Research Centre, Institute of Economic Growth, Delhi (June 2021), pp. 7–8. This paper was prepared at the request of Centre for Policy Research, New Delhi, in connection with the project, India 2025.

9. All data related to population density has been extracted from www.indiastat.com.
10. https://cbhidghs.mohfw.gov.in/WriteReadData/l892s/File1131.pdf.

7. DEMOGRAPHY, ECONOMIC GROWTH AND URBANISATION: THE DIVIDE REVISITED

1. See Table 5.1, Appendices.
2. For relationship between population growth and economic development, see, Deepak Lal, 'India: Population change and its consequences', *Population and Development Review*, Vol. 32, *The Political Economy of Global Population Change, 1950-2050* (2006), pp. 145–82.
3. K.R.G. Nair, 'A note on inter-state income differentials in India 1950–51 to 1960–61', *Journal of Development Studies*, Vol. 7, No. 1 (1971), pp. 441–47.
4. M.D. Chaudhry, 'Behaviour of spatial income inequality in a developing economy: India, 1950–70'. This paper was presented at the Conference of the Indian Association for Research in National Income and Wealth, 1974.
5. Ravindra H. Dholakia, 'Spatial dimension of acceleration of economic growth in India', *Economic & Political Weekly*, Vol. 24, No. 35 (27 Aug. 1994). Also see, Paul Cashin and Ratna Sahay, 'Internal migration, Center–State grants and economic growth in the states of India', *IMF Staff Papers*, Vol. 43, No. 1 (1995), pp. 123–71.
6. Raghbendra Jha, 'Growth, inequality and poverty in India: spatial and temporal characteristics', *Economic & Political Weekly*, Vol. 35, No. 11 (11–17 Mar. 2000), pp. 921–28, https://www.jstor.org/stable/4409023.
7. Dipankar Dasgupta, Pradip Maiti, Robin Mukherjee, Subrata Sarkar and Subhendu Chakrabarti, 'Growth and interstate disparities in India', *Economic & Political Weekly,* Vol. 35, No. 27 (1–7 Jul. 2000), pp. 2413–22, https://www.jstor.org/stable/pdf/4409475.pdf?refreqid=fastly-default%3A50c45ed0d1f5dee5159bd7cde15395b0&ab_segments=&origin=&initiator=&acceptTC=1.
8. Grace Majumdar and J.L. Kapoor, 'Behavior of interstate income inequalities in India' (1980). Paper presented at the twelfth conference of the Indian Association for Research in National Income and Wealth.
9. N.J. Kurian, 'Widening regional disparities in India: Some indicators', *Economic & Political Weekly*, Vol. 35, No. 7 (12–18 Feb. 2000), pp. 538–50, https://www.jstor.org/stable/4408933.
10. Buddhadeb Ghosh, Sugata Marjit and Chiranjib Neogi, 'Economic growth and regional divergence in India, 1960–95', *Economic & Political Weekly,*

Vol. 33, No. 26 (1998), pp. 1623–30, https://www.jstor.org/stable/4406929. 514 Demography, Representation, Delimitation.

11. Sugata Marjit and Sandip Mitra, 'Convergence in regional growth rates: Indian research agenda', *Economic & Political Weekly,* Vol. 31, No. 33 (1996), pp. 2239–42, https://www.jstor.org/stable/4404523.
12. Jeffrey D. Sachs, Nirupam Bajpai and Ananthi Ramiah, 'Understanding regional economic growth in India', *Asian Economic Papers,* Vol. 1, Issue 3 (2002), pp. 32–62. Prepared at The Earth Institute at Columbia University and the Massachusetts Institute of Technology, this paper was presented to the Prime Minister of India on 25 December 2001 in New Delhi. https://www.earth.columbia.edu/sitefiles/file/about/director/documents/AEP2002withBajpaiandRamiah-UnderstandingRegionalEconomicGrowthinIndia.pdf.
13. Ibid.
14. PTI, 'North India vs. South India: Who is doing better? Report says South India', *India Today*, 7 May 2013, https://www.indiatoday.in/india/north/story/north-india-vs-south-india-who-is-doing-better-report-says-south-india-162101-2013-05-06.
15. Sanjeev Sanyal and Aakanksha Arora, 'Relative economic performance of Indian states: 1960-61 to 2023-24', *Economic Advisory Council to the PM*, EAC-PM/WP/31/2024, September 2024. News reports required: March 1976 News report – the broad outlines of a national policy on family planning, comprising a package of incentives and disincentives, are believed to have been finalized by the Union cabinet yesterday' and 'the centre itself is not thinking in terms of resorting to compulsion to reduce the birth rate but it might not come in the way of state governments opting for such drastic action'.
16. Ibid, p. 1.
17. Ibid, p. 8.
18. S. Paul and K.S. Sridhar, *The Paradox of India's North–South Divide: Lessons from the States and Regions* (New Delhi: Sage Publication, 2015).
19. Ibid, p. 26.
20. Ibid.
21. Gaurav Datt and Martin Ravallion, 'Why have some Indian states done better than others at reducing rural poverty?', *Economics*, Vol. 65, No. 257 (Feb. 1998), pp. 17–38.
22. S. Paul and K.S. Sridhar, *The Paradox of India's North–South Divide: Lessons from the States and Regions* (New Delhi: Sage Publication, 2015), p. 26.

23. Ibid, p. 27.
24. Ibid.
25. Ibid, p. 2.
26. PTI, 'North India vs South India: Who is doing better? Report says South India', *India Today*, 7 May 2013, https://www.indiatoday.in/india/north/story/north-india-vs-south-india-who-is-doing-better-report-says-south-india-162101-2013-05-06.
27. Ramachandra Guha, 'Southern exceptionalism', *Outlook*, n.d. as cited by Paul and Sridhar (2015).
28. See Deepak Lal, 'India: Population change and its consequences', *Population and Development Review*, Vol. 32, *The Political Economy of Global Population Change, 1950-2050* (2006), pp. 145–82.
29. Partha S. Dasgupta, 'Population, poverty and the local environment', *Scientific American*, Vol. 272, No. 2 (Feb. 1995), pp. 40–45.
30. Ibid. Also see, Elizabeth Spahn, 'Feeling grounded: A gendered view of population control', *Environmental Law*, Vol. 27, No. 4 (Winter, 1997), pp. 1295–1321.
31. Chinmay Tumbe, 'Urbanisation, demographic transition, and the growth of cities in India, 1870–2020', International Growth Centre, London School of Economics (September 2016), https://www.theigc.org/sites/default/files/2016/11/Tumbe-2016-Working-paper.pdf.
32. Ibid.
33. Tim Dyson, *Population and Development: The Demographic Transition* (London: Zed Books, 2010). Also see, Tim Dyson, 'The role of the demographic transition in the process of urbanization', *Population and Development Review,* Vol. 37 (2011), pp. 34–54, https://www.jstor.org/stable/41762398.
34. Kesavan Veluthat, *Notes of Dissent: Essays on Indian History* (Delhi: Primus Books, 2018), p. 83.
35. Frank W. Notestein, 'Economic problems of population change', Proceedings of the Eighth International Conference of Agricultural Economics, London (1953), pp. 13–31, https://u.demog.berkeley.edu/~jrw/Biblio/Eprints/%20M-O/Notestein.EconomicProbsPopChange.pdf.
36. Jeffrey D. Sachs, Nirupam Bajpai and Ananthi Ramiah, 'Understanding regional economic growth in India', *CID Faculty Working Paper No. 88*, March 2002, https://www.hks.harvard.edu/centers/cid/publications/faculty-working-papers/understanding-regional-growth-india.

8. DEMOGRAPHY AND DEVELOPMENT IN WORLD PERSPECTIVE (1500–2024)

1. https://www.un.org/development/desa/dpad/publication/un-desa-policy-brief-no-153-india-overtakes-china-as-the-worlds-most-populous-country/.
2. Ibid.
3. Please visit: https://www.educationforallinindia.com/Final%20PPT%20 2011_chapter3-size-growth-rate-and-distribution-of-population-census-2011.pdf.

9. FAMILY PLANNING, EMERGENCY AND FORCED STERILISATION: THE JOURNEY OF POPULATION CONTROL

1. Matthew Connelly, 'Seeing beyond the State: The population control movement and the problem of sovereignty', *Past & Present*, No. 193 (Nov. 2006), pp. 197–233. Also see, 'Population control in India: Prologue to the Emergency period', *Population and Development Review*, Vol. 32, No. 4 (Dec. 2006), pp. 629–67. Also see, Matthew Connelly, *Fatal Misconception: The Struggle to Control World Population* (N.p.: Harvard University Press, 2010), p. 14. Also see, Robert William Fogel, *The Escape from Hunger and Premature Death, 1700–2100* (New York: Cambridge University Press, 2004). Also see, Rebecca Williams, 'The Rockefeller Foundation, the Population Council, and Indian population control', University of Warwick, UK, 2010, pp. 1–15.
2. Shah Commission of Inquiry, *Third and Final Report*, 6 August 1978, Delhi.
3. For the impact of family planning in India, also see, Elizabeth Spahn, 'Feeling grounded: A gendered view of population control', *Environmental Law*, Vol. 27, No. 4 (Winter, 1997), pp. 1295–1321.
4. Thomas McKeown and R.G. Record, 'Reasons for the decline of mortality in England and Wales during the nineteenth century', *Population Studies*, Vol. 16, No. 2 (Nov. 1962), pp. 94–122, https://www.jstor.org/stable/2173119.
5. Please see Corinna R. Unger, 'The making of the small family norm in post-1947 India', *Contemporanea*, Vol. 18, No. 3, Food Security in the Contemporary World (luglio-settembre 2015), pp. 483–88. Also see, V.A. Pai Panandiker and P.K. Umashankar, 'Fertility control and politics in India', *Population and Development Review*, Vol. 20, Supplement: The New Politics of Population: Conflict and Consensus in Family Planning (1994), pp. 89–104.

6. Mahmood Mamdani, *The Myth of Population Control: Family, Caste and Class in an Indian Village* (New York, Monthly Review Press, 1972).
7. Ibid.
8. Rosanna Ledbetter, 'Thirty years of family planning in India', *Asian Survey*, Vol. 24, No. 7 (Jul. 1984), p. 736, https://doi.org/10.2307/ 2644186. https://www.jstor.org/stable/pdf/2644186.pdf?refreqid=fastly-default%3A8a6b645b73530317024ac4c5cea88ab1&ab_segments=&origin=&initiator=&acceptTC=1. Also see, Rosanna Ledbetter, *A History of the Malthusian League, 1877–1927* (United States: Ohio State University, 1976).
9. Ibid, p. 750. Also see, Rosanna Ledbetter, 'India, An economic survey', *The Economist*, 28 March 1981, p. 48. Also see, *Demographic Estimates for Countries with a Population of 10 Million or More: 1981* (Washington, DC: U.S. Department of Commerce, Bureau of the Census, 1981), p. 63.
10. J.R. Rele, 'Fertility levels and trends in India, 1951–81', *Population and Development Review*, Vol. 13, No. 3 (1987), pp. 513–30, https://www.jstor.org/stable/pdf/1973137.pdf?refreqid=fastly-default%3A82c583005e875541597a73d29cef7d9d&ab_segments=&origin=&initiator=&acceptTC=1.
11. Ibid, p. 527.
12. 'Census 2011: Provisional population totals–India', Office of the Registrar General & Census Commissioner, India, 2011, p. 19, https://censusindia.gov.in/nada/index.php/catalog/42611.
13. A.P. Barnabas, *Population Control in India: Policy-Administration-Spread* (New Delhi: Indian Institute of Public Administration, 1977).
14. S. Paul and K.S. Sridhar, *The Paradox of India's North–South Divide: Lessons from the States and Regions* (New Delhi: Sage Publication, 2015), p. 31.
15. See Census 2011 on state wise decadal variation, https://censusindia.gov.in/nada/index.php/catalog/43333.
16. Carl Haub, *Fertility in India: Trends and Prospects* (Population Reference Bureau, 2009), https://www.un.org/development/desa/pd/sites/www.un.org.development.desa.pd/files/200912_unpd_egm_haub.pdf.
17. Annual Report, 2015–16, Ministry of Health and Family Welfare, Chapter 6, p. 91.
18. Gyan Prakash, *Emergency Chronicles: Indira Gandhi and Democracy's Turning Point* (Princeton University Press: 2019).
19. Times Correspondent, 'Population policy finalised', *The Times of India*, 26 March 1976, p. 11.

20. In 1948, American geographer Lawrance A. Hofman had noted this high ratio between India's land area and its share in world population. However, he pointed out that the population density of India as a whole was only moderate as compared to parts of Europe and East Asia, and that only the northern plains and coastal regions were densely populated.
21. Dr Karan Singh, 'National Population Policy: A statement of the Government of India', *Population and Development Review*, Vol. 2, No. 2 (Jun. 1976), pp. 309–12, https://www.jstor.org/stable/1972074.
22. Ibid.
23. Ibid.
24. Ibid.
25. Ibid.
26. Ibid.
27. Ibid.
28. Ibid.
29. National Archives of India, Ministry of Home Affairs, Department of Personnel and Administrative Reforms, F.No.-12016276-ESTT-A, 'National population policy – Changes in services conduct rules to motivate the Central government servants to adopt the small family norm'.
30. *Lok Sabha Debates*, Vol. LX, Nos 21–30, 28 April 1976, p. 157.
31. Ibid.
32. Ibid, pp. 177–78.
33. *Lok Sabha Debates*, Vol. LX, Nos. 21–30, 28 April 1976, pp. 177–78.
34. Ibid, pp. 181–88.
35. Ibid.
36. Ibid.
37. Ibid, pp. 191–92.
38. *Lok Sabha Debates*, Vol. LX, Nos 21–30, 28 April 1976, pp. 195–97. For the impact of birth control on women, please see, Elizabeth Spahn, 'Feeling grounded: A gendered view of population control', *Environmental Law*, Vol. 27, No. 4 (Winter, 1997), pp. 1295–1321.
39. Ibid, pp. 205–6.
40. Ibid.
41. Ibid, p. 210.
42. Ibid.
43. Ibid, pp. 248–9.
44. Ibid.
45. Ibid.
46. *Lok Sabha Debates*, Vol. LXV, Nos 1–9, 26 October 1976, p. 71.

47. Ibid, p. 159.
48. Ibid, p. 13.
49. Ibid, p. 57.
50. *Lok Sabha Debates*, Vol. LXV, Nos 1–9, 3 November 1976, pp. 168–69.
51. Ibid.
52. Ibid, p. 167.
53. Ibid, p. 174.
54. Ibid, p. 190.
55. Ibid.
56. Ibid, p. 128.
57. Ibid, pp. 143–44.
58. Ibid, pp. 151–52.
59. Ibid, p. 157.
60. Ibid.
61. Ibid.
62. *Lok Sabha Debates*, Vol. LXV, No 3, 27 October 1976, p. 235.
63. Ibid, p. 139.
64. Ibid.
65. Ibid, p. 140.
66. Ibid.
67. Indira Gandhi, 'A world without want: A problem of hunger and food supplies in the less developed nations of the world examined by Indira Gandhi', *Britannica Book of the Year* (Encyclopaedia Britannica, 1975).
68. Ibid.
69. Ibid.
70. Ibid.
71. Ibid.
72. Kaval Gulhati, 'Compulsory sterilization: The change in India's population policy', *Science*, New Series, Vol. 195, No. 4284 (25 Mar. 1977), pp. 1300–5, https://www.jstor.org/stable/1743751.
73. Ibid.
74. Ibid.
75. Asok Mitra, 'National Population Policy in relation to national planning in India', *Population and Development Review*, Vol. 3, No. 3 (Sept. 1977), p. 298, https://www.jstor.org/stable/1971892. Also see, Asok Mitra, *India's Population: Aspects of Quality and Control* (India: Abhinav Publications, 2003).
76. Ibid, pp. 299–300.
77. Ibid, p. 300.

78. Ibid.
79. Ibid, p. 301.
80. Ibid.
81. Ibid.
82. Ibid, p. 302.
83. Ibid. For the economic utility of large families in poor countries, see Partha Dasgupta, 'The population problem: Theory and evidence', *Journal of Economic Literature*, Vol. 33, No. 4 (Dec. 1995), pp. 1879–1902.
84. Chelsea Follett, 'Neo-Malthusianism and coercive population control in China and India', Cato Institute, Policy Analysis, No. 897 (2000). For a critical perspective on Malthusian approach to population in the Indian context, please see, Deepak Lal, 'India: Population change and its consequences', *Population and Development Review*, Vol. 32, The Political Economy of Global Population Change, 1950–2050 (2006), pp. 145–82.
85. For a contemporary controversial eugenic perspective of the effect of high population growth on desirable human attributes such as intelligence, please see, Richard Lynn, *Dysgenics: Genetic Deterioration in Modern Populations* (London: Praeger, 1996). Also see, R. Lynn, 'Sex differences in intelligence and brain size: A paradox resolved', *Personality and Individual Differences* (1994); 'Racial and ethnic differences in psychopathic personality', *Personality & Individual Differences* (2002). Also see, https://doi.org/10.1016/j.paid.2011.03.013.
86. Shah Commission of Inquiry, *Third and Final Report*, 6 August 1978, Delhi, p. 154.
87. Ibid, p. 155.
88. Ibid.
89. Ibid.
90. Ibid, pp. 156–57.
91. Ibid, p. 157.
92. Ibid, p. 162.
93. Ibid, p. 167.
94. Ibid, p. 165.
95. Ibid, p. 167.
96. Ibid.
97. Ibid, pp. 195–96
98. Ibid, p. 169.
99. Ibid, p. 155.
100. Ibid, p. 175.
101. Ibid, p. 176.

102. Ibid, p. 178.
103. Ibid.
104. Ibid, p. 191.
105. Ibid, p. 193.
106. Ibid, p. 194.
107. Ibid.
108. Ibid.
109. Ibid, p. 195.
110. Ibid.
111. Ibid.
112. Ibid.
113. Ibid, p. 206.
114. Ibid.
115. Harris Green, 'The legacy of India's quest to sterilise millions of men'; and Davidson R. Gwatkin, 'Political will and family planning: The implications of India's Emergency experience', *Population and Development Review*, Vol. 5, No. 1 (Mar. 1979), pp. 29–59, https://www.cato.org/policy-analysis/neo-malthusianism-coercive-population-control-china-india-overpopulation-concerns.
116. Rosanna Ledbetter, 'Thirty years of family planning in India', *Asian Survey*, Vol. 24, No. 7 (Jul. 1984), p. 748, https://www.jstor.org/stable/2644186.
117. Dilip Hiro, *Inside India Today* (New York: Monthly Review Press, 1976), p. 290.
118. Sumanta Banerjee, *Family Planning Communication* (New Delhi: Radiant, 1979), p. 173.
119. Ibid, p. 32.
120. Rosanna Ledbetter, 'Thirty years of family planning in India', *Asian Survey*, Vol. 24, No. 7 (Jul. 1984), p. 748.
121. Dilip Hiro, *Inside India Today* (New York: Monthly Review Press, 1976), p. 291. Citing the *Statesman*, 11 March 1977.
122. 'The Issue that inflamed India', *Time*, 4 April 1977, p. 39.
123. Special Correspondent, 'Lok Sabha seats for states and aid linked to 71 Census', *The Hindu*, 17 April 1976, p. 1.
124. *Hindustan Times*, April 1976.
125. Times Correspondent, 'Big support by MPs to population policy', *The Times of India*, 29 April 1976.
126. Times Correspondent, 'Catholics back F.P. policy', *The Times of India*, 3 May 1976.

127. Times Correspondent, 'Minorities increasingly in favour of FP', *The Times of India*, 3 June 1976.
128. A.S. Abraham, 'The fight against poverty: Family planning an essential weapon', *The Times of India*, 23 April 1976.
129. Ibid.
130. Ibid.
131. Ibid.
132. 'The Issue that inflamed India', *Time*, 4 April 1977, p. 39.
133. Dilip Hiro, *Inside India Today* (New York: Monthly Review Press, 1976), p. 291. Citing *The Guardian*, 10 November 1976.
134. Arup Maharatna, 'India's family planning programme: An unpleasant essay', *Economic & Political Weekly*, Vol. 37, No. 10 (9–15 Mar. 2002), p. 972, https://www.jstor.org/stable/4411847.
135. Ibid, p. 973.
136. Ibid.
137. Gyan Prakash, *Emergency Chronicles: Indira Gandhi and Democracy's Turning Point* (Princeton University Press, 2019).
138. Emma Tarlo, *Unsettling Memories: Narratives of the Emergency in Delhi* (United Kingdom: C. Hurst, 2003).
139. For the role of international agencies and the West in shaping coercive birth control policies in Third World countries, please see, Chelsea Follett, 'Neo-Malthusianism and coercive population control in China and India: Overpopulation concerns often result in coercion', Cato Institute, 21 July 2020, https://www.cato.org/policy-analysis/neo-malthusianism-coercive-population-control-china-india-overpopulation-concerns#history-neo-malthusianism.
140. Indira Gandhi, 'United Nations Population Award to Indira Gandhi and Qian Xinzhong', *Population and Development Review*, Vol. 9, No. 4 (Dec. 1983), p. 747, https://www.jstor.org/stable/1973563.
141. Ibid.
142. Ibid, p. 748.
143. Ibid.
144. Ibid.
145. Ibid, pp. 748–49.
146. For the link between population growth and development, see Deepak Lal, 'India: Population change and its consequences' *Population and Development Review*, Vol. 32, The Political Economy of Global Population Change, 1950–2050 (2006), pp. 145–82. Also see, K. Srinivasan, Sumati

Kulkarni and S. Parasuraman, 'Impact of population on selected social and economic sectors', *Economic & Political Weekly*, 10 September 1988, pp. 1913–17.

10. DELIMITATION AND SEAT REDISTRIBUTION: HISTORY, IMPLICATIONS AND SOLUTIONS

1. All references to the Constitution of India are from the document available at the website: https://www.india.gov.in/sites/upload_files/npi/files/coi_part_full.pdf.
2. See Article 81 (1) of the Constitution of India.
3. https://main.mohfw.gov.in/sites/default/files/Population%20Projection%20Report%202011-2036%20-%20upload_compressed_0.pdf.
4. In absence of exact data for the number of seats for the state of Kerala, the number of seats assigned to Travancore-Cochin has been assumed to represent Kerala in 1951.
5. Kenneth Baker, 'Do we really need 646 Members of Parliament?', *The Telegraph*, 11 April 2009, https://www.telegraph.co.uk/comment/5140846/Do-we-really-need-646-Members-of-Parliament.html.
6. Ibid.
7. Please see Figure 10.1.

APPENDICES

1. Memorandum on the Census of British India 1871-72.
2. Ibid.
3. Ibid.
4. The data has been extracted from www.indiastat.com.
5. The figures for 2011 Census are provisional. The data presented here has been compiled and stored at www.indiastat.com.
6. All data presented here has been compiled and uploaded at www.indiastat.com.

Index